STORIES
FROM THE
BOXCAR

A Spiritual Journey

STORIES
FROM THE
BOXCAR

A Spiritual Journey

Michael Frank Varro, Jr.

CITI OF
BOOKS

CITIOFBOOKS, INC.
3736 Eubank NE Suite A1
Albuquerque, NM 87111-3579
www.citiofbooks.com
Hotline: 1 (877) 389-2759
Fax: 1 (505) 930-7244

Ordering Information:
Quantity sales. Special discounts are available on quantity purchases by corporations, associations, and others. For details, contact the publisher at the address above.

Printed in the United States of America.
ISBN-13:   Softcover   978-1-959682-75-2
              eBook   978-1-959682-76-9
              Hardcover   978-1-959682-77-6

Library of Congress Control Number: 2023901385

Stories from the Boxcar

Michael Franklin Varro, Jr.

(Varro, Mihaly Ferenc)

Regi Tehervagon
The Old Boxcar
(A likeness of the old boxcar)

The 'stories of our lives'… are the 'stories in our hearts'
— it is where we live —

CONTENTS

BOOK I

Stories from the Boxcar
The Journey from the Old World

BOOK II

Wheelbarrows & Firecrackers
The Journey from the New World to Cathay

BOOK III

The Long Way Home
The Journey with many Detours

BOOK IV

Boys, Men, and Dreams
The Journey with Many Hurdles

BOOK V

Kicking the Slats Out of the Cradle
The Journey, then Shipwreck, then Victory!

INTRODUCTION

I became a Licensed Professional Counselor in 2001, after completing Internship, Residence, and Advanced Residence programs at the Krist Samaritan Center for Counseling and Education, in Houston, Texas. Included in this training were courses in Child Psychology, one of which was an Art Therapy class that had to do with the child drawing pictures, which, when properly interpreted, can assist in knowing where the child is 'emotionally.' In this exercise, the project includes drawing a picture of a house. Several other items drawn can indicate persons and things which hold various priorities for the child. The main focus, however, is the significance of the "house." It is the child's own life and feelings about his or her self, and where other things and persons fit in.

As I thought about my own story, my interest in my heritage and genealogy, and most of all, my own spiritual journey, it occurred to me that all of this fits into the great oral tradition with which my family of origin had provided me. I began to draw my own 'house.' This house was *my life*. It began in its focus with some of the earliest stories of my dad… how poor they were in Canada, even to the point of having to live in an *'old abandoned boxcar'* alongside the tracks of an old Canadian Pacific rail line. It seemed to be the perfect picture of me, my heritage…and my journey.

I was overwhelmed with the wealth of human interest in both my father's life stories, as well as my mother's great family history of missionary and musical endeavors. I would listen for hours to each of them share with me the stories of my father's birth in Hungary, growing up in Canada, and his call to ministry and missionary life, to which he had dedicated himself. My mother's stories of her heritage–her father's medical training, her growing up in China, and her musical training–they fascinated me completely. My growing up in China, Hong Kong, and Taiwan, also provided me with my own interesting worldwide experiences, stories, even my world view. My life, with my wife Margo, and our three children, then grandchildren, capped a life full of variety, fun, struggle, and then unequaled joy and gratitude. While it is a novel, it is based on true stories, actual history, and oral tradition. Many names and places were changed, or added. Many parts of the story, if unknown, were either added or changed for dramatic purposes. [This summer, June of 2022, Margo and I had the fabulous, and rare, opportunity to personally visit Budapest, and Karcag in Hungary, home to much of the Kuman and Magyar settings of my story, and Bodo (my father's birthplace now in Romania)]. So, enjoy reading what I enjoyed experiencing…with God always by my side… building *our **Boxcar*** together.

Acknowledgements

Stories from the Boxcar is a work that draws on the memoirs of my late father and mother, The Rev. Michael Franklin Varro, Sr., and Elizabeth Finnette Fitz Varro, and my father's two late brothers, Stevan (Istvan) Varro, of Calgary, Alberta, and Louis (Lajos) Varro, of Cape Girardeau, Missouri; other brothers, sisters, and stepmother, from the 'second family,' after their own mother's untimely death, added to the story. It includes stories from my Fitz (maternal) side, and the many stories my mother, aunts, uncles, and cousins told me. It also draws in part on the oral tradition of the Varro family, my own genealogical research, and lastly: it is fiction, but is based on a great deal of genealogical research, history, and oral tradition. In this, there are admittedly various other versions of the facts, according to siblings, children, and many friends, in my story.* I am indebted to my cousin Carlene (Solts-Cogdill-Hansen) for the artwork; my friend, and fellow 'MK' ('missionary kid') Carol McClain Bassett, for editing, Ivan Krowl, for technical support, and my wife Margo, for many hours of proofreading, tears, and patience; and most of all my 'heavenly Father,' who is patient, loving, kind, sustains me, and never leaves me. Most of all, it is my own spiritual journey, and what I learned along the way. My personal relationship with Jesus Christ was my primary focus in this story.

I am…my Boxcar.

*Editorial Note – no attempt was made to show the correct Hungarian inflections and accents (e.g. Mihaly instead of the correct Magyar accent: Mihály, or Varró)

In my Father's house are many [boxcars],

I go there to prepare a [mansion] *for you.*

— John 14:2 (adapted)

PROLOGUE

MIHALY HAD HIDDEN QUIETLY IN THE BUSHES ALONGSIDE THE DANUBE, his leg throbbing from the fall he had sustained during their escape from their unit in the Banat. The 'man with the white hat,' who had met them at the river, had said to stay there until sundown…that he would be back to escort them across the river into Serbia after dark. There was no reason to trust this stranger, but without any other options, cold and wet, they only knew one thing: they had no other choice. Famished and tired to the bone, Mihaly told his two friends that he was in such pain he was not sure he could make it. Istvan went to see if he could find anything to eat and maybe a cloth bandage to wrap Mihaly's leg. Lajos, afraid of being caught there without Istvan, unless his cousin went with him. It was raining, and Mihaly tried to sleep, but fear gripped him every time someone came by on the road. What if the man in the white hat was just an informant, and would collect the reward for deserters? Or maybe he was with the Imperial Hungarian Army, looking to stop the steady flow of military conscripts, who, sensing something big was about to happen, had forsaken all, including family, home, livelihood…to become mere refugees. Mihaly clutched the only blanket the three men had amongst themselves, and tried to wrap part of it around his leg to put pressure on his throbbing wound. He found himself drifting off… into a deep sleep.

* * * * *

Winding down a long road, deeper and deeper into the past, Mihaly felt himself slipping into another time, into a kind of trance…what would

V

happen to him...where did he come from? Who were his people...from whence did his family originate? Many times, he had asked these questions of his father, Sandor, in their home in Piros. It weighed so heavily on his mind, even when Mihaly was only eight years old. With no satisfactory answer, he had gone to his mother, Juliana Barta, and to others on her side of the family. She knew a little, and tried to connect him with his aunts and uncles on the Varro side as well. He finally talked to his Grandmother Julia Sabo, who seemed to know even more about the Varro's than the Sabo's. She couldn't—or wouldn't, tell him, she claimed, but because of his persistence, she finally suggested he go see Grandfather Istvan, who was now nearly 90 years old. "He knows the story," she said, "but he may, or may not, be willing to share what he knows..."

BOOK I

Stories from the Boxcar

The Journey from the Old World

Chapter One

Sythians, Xiungnu, Romans, and Huns

Ancient home of many migrating tribes

Sythians and Xiungnu

Grandfather began the story by telling Mihaly about a fierce and mighty people called the Sythians. He explained that they were ancestors of the people that eventually became the Varro family. Mihaly had never heard much of the Sythians. His father Sandor had once sung him a Scottish (Celtic) folk song, and then followed it with a Hungarian song, illustrating the similarity between the Scottish Snap and the Hungarian Phrase-accent, and then had told him 'we came from an ancient people called the Sythians.' But what was Grandfather telling him? The Celtic people and the Magyars had come from common ancestors – the Sythians? He had only heard of them as a blood-thirsty group of horsemen and bow-and-arrow warriors. He was astounded. So interesting…come to think of it, his neighbor in Timisoara was part Scot.

Grandfather droned on and on…"Nimrod, son of Kush, grandson of Ham, a son of Noah, was a mighty hunter, and an evil king of Akkad, in Mesopotamia, whose people formed the Kingdom of Akkadia, the seat of the Sumerian culture of Babylon, between two great rivers, the Tigris and the Euphrates. These people had built the Tower of Babel. At first, Nimrod was an idol worshipper, and tried to burn Abram at the stake for refusing to worship his idols. Abram was the eighth great grandson of Noah, and he had been warning his uncle Nimrod about the evil of idol worship. Abram escaped to Haran with his father Terah and his family…"Grandfather's voice trailed off, and he fell asleep for a while. Mihaly waited until later to continue the conversation, after Grandfather had rested, and had eaten some of the food Grandmother Juliana brought them. Over the next few days, Grandfather continued the story, with Mihaly sitting in rapt attention, taking notes on the almost unbelievable unfolding of his family's origins.

[Nimrod had had two sons, Hunor and Magor, and, according to the Hungarian legend—as found in **The White Stag**, they became the forefathers of the Hunnic and Magyar groups of people. The document tells the story of the migration of these people to the steppes of Asia where they intermarried with Turkic, Iranian, and further north, the Mongol, and Sibur people, all of which became mighty warriors on horseback, plundering the regions of China and Mongolia, living together, and forming trading alliances within the territories they had left behind. The legend outlined how, generation after generation, they looked for new land to graze their horses and livestock, and were led further and further east, across the great desert of the steppes of Asia. Despite intermarrying with other Hunnic and Turkic people, they still maintained their distinct culture. They also brought the agglutinative characteristics of the Ural-Altaic languages from their Sumerian roots. This, and other Finnic and Uralic groups, they adopted as their own linguistic system. These nomads wandered far and wide and became great herdsmen, introducing saddles, becoming skilled horsemen, and fierce warriors. Eventually, Grandfather said, they became

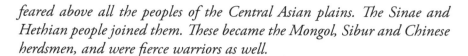

feared above all the peoples of the Central Asian plains. The Sinae and Hethian people joined them. These became the Mongol, Sibur and Chinese herdsmen, and were fierce warriors as well.

* * * * *

Mihaly awoke suddenly. Lajos was standing over him. "What is the matter with you? I have been trying to wake you up for a long time," Lajos said in a loud whisper. He offered Mihaly some stale bread that he and Istvan had found in one of the village garbage cans. The old piece of cloth that he extended to him was torn, and the foul smell made him almost gag, but he quickly ripped off a piece of it to bind his swollen leg. He mumbled his thanks, as he munched on the hard bread. Istvan was standing guard at the edge of the bushes, where he could watch the river and see if the 'man in the white hat' would come for them. Lajos lay down next to Mihaly and fell asleep almost immediately. Mihaly knew he should take his turn standing watch, but Istvan waved him off. The leg began to feel better with the piece of cloth bound tight around it. He found himself drifting off again…

* * * * *

Romans and Huns

Gaelin Alba was a Celtic Sythian, the son of Kraeth Alba, chieftain of a group of Samartians and Sythians, who had migrated from north of the Black Sea to Gaul. When the tribes split in the Second Century BC, part of them went to Ireland and Scotland, and became the Scotti, and the other part went to the Balkans. The family settled in southern Pannonia, but after Gaelin's father died when he was eighteen years old, Gaelin was conscripted into the Roman army that had conquered the Celts and Sythians living in the Balkans. Kraeth had been killed in battle when the Romans took over Moesia when they were living in south central Pannonia. His mother, Fraenuth, along with his sister, Braethen, had been taken captive, the estate where they lived had been razed, his mother was enslaved by the Roman general, Aulus Terentius Gallinius, and his sister taken by a Roman consul of Asia, Apolinius Lucullus. When the battles there were over, Gaelin was taken to Rome along with thousands of other slaves. His wife Brenna and their son had been killed. In Rome, he was trained by the best minds in the empire. He not only studied Greek and Latin, but all the disciplines as well, especially the fine arts. Because of his outstanding native intelligence, Gaelin excelled greatly and, moving up the ladder of instructors and mentors, he eventually was instructed by Marcus Reatinus Varro, the son of the greatest of all Roman scholars, Marcus Terentius Varro. Reatinus Varro had kept the Varronian Institute open after his father's death. Varro was very impressed with Gaelin, and they grew very close in the next couple of years, intellectually as well as emotionally. Gaelin spent many days and weeks in the Varro home, not only in Rome, but also at the family villa in Reata, meeting Reatinus's family and friends, as well as senators and leaders, and going with his family on social outings. After a few years, his master, Reatinus adopted him, and gave him a new Roman name: Onesimus Reatinus Varro. Since he was much sought after as a tutor and scholar, Onesimus was eventually assigned to wealthy Greek residents in Rome. He married again. This time to Cian, a fellow tutor, and former slave. She was, as was Onesimus, a Celt, from Moesia. Eventually, he made the acquaintance of a man named Tychicus from Ephesus. This young man, a scholar himself, was instrumental in helping Onesimus gain employment with the family of a well-known Greek entrepreneur, by the name Philemon, who was well-traveled in all points of the Mediterranean. Onesimus, though a Roman citizen, was nevertheless bonded, and considered, like all other tutors and scholars, an indentured instructor. He was required to instruct Philemon's three young children in all of the literary works, as well as the fine arts. It was rumored that Philemon had become a follower of the young Jewish prophet, Jesus of Nazareth. Philemon had come under the influence of a Jewish Roman — and former anti-Christian himself—whose name was Saul of Tarsus, in the province Cilicia, while he was in Ephesus. Tychicus, too, they said, had become a secret follower of Jesus. It was 60 AD, and many Christians were being killed for their faith…no one dared speak openly of it. Tychicus had insisted that Onesimus and Cian live with him, and his wife Doloriana, in a rather nice part of Rome.

Onesimus had only been employed a couple years, when he received word that his mother (who had been mistreated for years by General Aulus Gallinius) was dying and had asked for "her son Gaelin." There was no possible way to go with her of course, but the more Onesimus struggled with this, the more he became increasingly troubled. He finally decided he had to do whatever it would take, to be by his mother's side before she died. He secretly located a friend of Tychicus, a fellow tutor whose name *was Erastus, who, it was said, was joining a caravan going to Moesia within weeks. While Philemon was away with his family trying to meet with the great Apostle Paul in Rome, Onesimus had full run of the estate. Desperate with worry, he took some of the silver he needed to finance his trip. He left for Singidunum (later called Beograd) in the Balkans, where his mother was being cared for by his sister Braethen, following years of her own mistreatment by General Gallinius. He told no one, not Tychicus, not even his pregnant wife Cian, or his adoptive father Reatinus, now almost 88 years of age. Onesimus was reunited with his sister and saw his mother before she died. They transported her body, according to her wishes, to central Pannonia, near their old home. He felt empty and lost. His father had been killed, his mother mistreated, and now had died. Only he and his sister were left…alone and afraid. Onesimus thought his life was over. His sister had married a Roman who left her, and then was killed fighting the Getae. So, she had gone back to caring for friends of Roman Military families, for whom she had previously worked. Onesimus was troubled, and finally confided the truth in Erastus: that he had run away, broken his bond, and had probably lost his Roman citizenship; that he had left Philemon— even stealing silver from him—all this after Philemon and his family had treated him so well. It was then that he learned that Erastus, like his friend Tychicus, was also a Christian and had been sent out as a missionary intern to Macedonia and Upper Moesia. He spoke of taking responsibility for one's own actions, of confession and forgiveness. He told Onesimus about the young Jewish Rabbi named Jesus, that he was the Son of God, whom the Jews called Yeshua Ha-Mashiach—Christos in Greek—and that he would forgive sins and restore his life. He also spoke of the great Apostle, a man named Saul, now called Paul, from Tarsus in Cilicia. How Paul had helped him come to know this Jesus, and how his life had completely changed. Then he invited him to read some of the letters Paul had written to the new Christian churches of Asia. And he asked him to become a Follower of The Way. Onesimus was suspicious. He knew of Christians being killed in Rome. He knew that Philemon and Tychicus had talked cautiously to him about Jesus, but he always referred them back to his adoptive father, Marcus Reatinus Varro. Scholars don't accept gods other than Zeus and the Roman gods. The Romans said, "only our Emperor is god." Most Romans, and Greeks too, scoffed at this 'Jewish religion.' The more Erastus shared with him, however, the thought of ever returning to*

Rome, where he would surely be killed—and at the very least, lose his Roman citizenship—the more Onesimus longed to have the love and peace that these 'Jesus-people' seemed to have. Then one day, Erastus told him that they were leaving… going back to Rome! Onesimus told him 'no,' that he didn't dare, but Erastus convinced him that they would be with a group of followers of The Way, who would hide him. After a few days of Erastus constantly trying to persuade him, he finally gave in. He had nothing else to live for. They would meet the great Apostle Paul, Erastus said. Paul himself was a scholar, he had studied with the great Gamaliel. Onesimus was impressed. Finally convinced, he actually looked forward to the philosophy they might discuss; they might even stimulate each other's intellect…or so he surmised.

After a few weeks, Onesimus and Erastus arrived again in Rome, where they sought out a group of Christians that Erastus knew, and some others that knew where to find the Apostle Paul in secret. They had covered their heads all along their trip, and now finding friends of Erastus, they quickly hid in a small house near the funeral caverns known as the 'Catacombs.' Onesimus had been there many times as a Roman guide, leading tours for his history students. Erastus introduced Onesimus to various friends, apparently also of The Way, who ate with them in groups of only three or four, and who stood guard nearby while they slept, behind moveable walls. These Christians spoke in hushed tones in the semi-darkness, but they seemed very happy. They said they already knew of Onesimus, and his former employer, Philemon. They mostly slept for what seemed like days. Then, Erastus suddenly showed up…with Tychicus! He told him they would meet with Paul the next day. He said he would bring Doloriana, and Cian… and his newborn son!

Onesimus was so excited he could not sleep. Sure enough, about mid-morning the next day, they arrived. Finally seeing his wife and son was too much. Onesimus broke down and wept for joy. The fear that had gripped him for so long fell away like an old torn garment. He embraced Cian, and his son – she had named him John Mark, or Marcus, after his Roman grandfather Marcus Terentius; and after John Mark, a prior traveling companion of the Apostle Paul, and his friend Barnabas. Onesimus was a little upset (why had she not considered him, the father, in naming the boy?); but, after Tychicus spoke with him, he quickly realized his utter selfishness. After all, had he not left her all alone, with no warning of his departure? And these Christians…had they not supported her, and helped her in his absence? His anger quickly dissipated. Onesimus wondered if Cian had become a follower of The Way herself? Just then, the entire room grew quiet, the door opened, and there stood a short but very wise-looking older man. It was the great Apostle himself, Paul of Tarsus. A great smile was on his face, and all welcomed him warmly. Paul pushed past Tychicus, Doloriana, Cian, and the others. He came along side Onesimus, greeted him warmly, and told him of his visits to the Varronian Institute, his admiration for both his adoptive father, Reatinus, of the reputation of his grandfather, the great Marcus Terentius, and the entire Varro family. Paul had visited the Varro Villa in Reata himself, along with some of his wealthy Greek contemporaries, following his missionary journeys to Asia, and Greece. Cilicia, where Paul was born and grew up, was also a great trading partner with Reata, so Paul was familiar with the entire Varro family and province. They wasted no time in getting acquainted, and when they sat down to eat, Paul made a point of sitting next to Onesimus. Paul broke the bread and prayed, then he handed it to Onesimus. Paul bluntly asked him if he knew of The Way, and the man named Jesus of Nazareth? Cian sat next to him smiling as she ate. Surely Onesimus would not resist the great teacher. Tychicus and Erastus had shown him only love and acceptance, in spite of his insensitivity, hardness, and anger. His heart was broken, he had to admit it. He did want what these Christians seemed to have. Paul spoke to him softly, asking him to release himself to Jesus, believe in his heart that God raised him from the dead, to confess him as greater than the ancient gods of Moesia, greater than the gods of the emperors, greater even than the wisdom of the Varronian Institute. Then Paul prayed, and the coldness in Onesimus' heart fell away. He felt a strange warmth flood over him. "A new creation," Paul called it. Cian cried as she rocked little Marcus in her arms. Paul told Onesimus he had a surprise for him. He told him he had written a letter to Philemon, his former employer, asking him to forgive Onesimus, and Paul had asked if he could pay for the stolen silver himself, but Philemon had refused…just then, the door opened. Philemon walked in. Onesimus fell at his feet, but Philemon raised him up…they embraced. "In Jesus' name, and by God's grace, I forgive you…you are my brother!"

* * * * *

Istvan was shouting at them, "Mihaly, Lajos! Run for your lives, the police have discovered us." Istvan and Lajos each grabbed an arm of Mihaly, and the three of them managed to hobble across the road to an old small shed on the Danube, covered with bushes, where they collapsed in exhaustion, just before the police came running by. It was a false alarm! The police had been chasing a petty thief whom Istvan thought had reported them. By this time Istvan and Lajos were angry and ready to give up on "the man in the White Hat." Istvan could take the stress no longer; he was going to make a run for it. If the bridge was patrolled, he would try to swim across the river. It was almost dark anyway, and hadn't they said "at sunset?" Lajos said he couldn't leave Mihaly by himself. Mihaly's leg was really swollen now. He waved Lajos on. If they stayed, they would probably be caught anyway. Lajos said no, he would wait another hour…just one more hour. Istvan said okay, just one more hour. Mihaly heard whispering…as he drifted off.

* * * * *

In the years that followed, Onesimus was trained personally by Philemon and by Paul. He had already learned Hebrew, in addition to the Greek and Latin he knew from his early days as a slave. He read all of the Scriptures. He read all the letters of Paul to the churches in Greece and Asia, the writings of James, Peter, and all the early Christian leaders. He even met the great Apostle Peter in Rome, just before he was crucified, upside-down. Within months of his conversion, Onesimus and others of The Way witnessed the Apostle Paul's arrest. They were later told of his execution as well. But before his arrest, Paul had called a special meeting. There he had commissioned Tychicus, Erastus, Onesimus, and others as Bishops to the eastern part of the Empire, even as he and Peter had already commissioned Luke, Timothy and leaders of the Greek, Alexandrian, and Jerusalem churches. Cian bore five more children: Lydia, Michael, Stephen, Mary, and Juliana. Marcus grew up to be a fine young man, a scholar and a spiritual leader, like his father. Reatinus Varro had looked the other way when his adopted son became a believer; and he lived to see this only son, Onesimus, become Bishop of Moesia (Ephesus). Marcus and three of the five other children lived for a while with their grandfather at the Villa in Reata, where they opened a branch of the Varronian Institute, teaching agriculture, language, and the fine arts. When Onesimus and Cian were there on a visit, they were overjoyed to see Reatinus embrace Christianity just before he died. Onesimus and Cian lived to see the church in Moesia and Pannonia grow tremendously. In their old age they reunited with Braethen, the sister of Onesimus. Together, they had moved to Singidunum, and Braethen helped care for Cian until she died. Onesimus had commissioned two of his other sons, Michael and Stephen as leaders of the church in Pannonia and the Tiszian plains, between the two great rivers Danuvius (Danube) and Tisza. Marcus had become Bishop in Lower Moesia, and the Eastern Empire church, though still persecuted, was nevertheless producing many great church leaders. Marcus had met a young Grecian Turkic woman named Helene, and her children, Michael and Alexander, were prominent leaders of the church in Byzantium. And thus it was, that Bishop Marcus presided at the memorial of his father Onesimus in Singidunum. It was the fall of 78 AD, and Braethen had sent word to Marcus that only a year had passed since his mother, Cian, had died. Michael, young Bishop in Tisza, and Stephen, who would become the new Bishop in Singidunum, had been there to conduct the memorial for their mother. One year later, Onesimus–the slave who had become the teacher, the runaway mentor who had become a Christ-follower, and the missionary that became the great Bishop under the leadership of the Apostle Paul– died. Bishop Marcus looked at his wife Helene. What great wonders hath God wrought, in his mercy brought about! Between 135 and 226 AD, Michael and Alexander, along with their children, became leaders in the 'Church' which was no longer underground. Eventually the great emperor, Flavius Valerius Constantinus [the great Constantine], along with his mother and sons, brought the Church in Bysantium to prominence as the Eastern Orthodox Church. They also married Sythian women and brought the name Varo (as they spelled it), to the Balkans. By 300 AD, the Eastern Empire was strongly influenced by Greeks, Illyrians, and Moesians. A group called the Cuman people, from northwestern China, through the Black Sea area of the Sythian and Hunnic tribes, had settled in the Pannonian plains as early as 92 AD. They would surely have died out, except that some of these came as mercenary warriors to Bysantium rather than return to their ancient home in Central Asia. There they eventually became part of the ruling class, and intermarried with the Bulgar (Turkic and Hunnic group) Varo family. Other Cumans intermarried with Sythians and other Parthians lived in the Tiszian plains and Transylvania. These came to be called Szekelys ('frontier guards'). Prominent among these were the Roman Varro family of Onesimus and his progeny. Eventually, these Cumans lost their language during the time of the Hun, Mongol, and Magyar conquests, settling in *the Great Plain between the Danube and Tisza rivers. The Bulgarian and Greek part of the family were leaders in the Orthodox Church. The Szekelys and Cuman part of the family in Transylvania and the Great Plains were all active in the Roman Catholic and later the Reformed Church, especially the Anabaptist movement.*

* * * * *

Mihaly woke suddenly. It was very still, and it had started raining. He panicked when he didn't see or hear Istvan or Lajos. Had they left him? He looked around but saw no one. Thinking the worst, Mihaly struggled to his feet. Trying to get out of the shed, he stumbled and fell into the bushes. A hand reached out and grabbed his shoulder, and another hand muffled his cry of pain. Fearing the worst, Mihaly wheeled around, and saw Lajos, his hand restraining him and clasping his other hand over his mouth. "What are you doing?" he whispered, trying not to shout. Istvan stood guard behind him, looking in anger at Mihaly for almost giving them away. "We told you an hour…just one hour, so now we're all leaving together, man in the "White Hat" or not, now let's get going, let's get over to the bridge…Now!"

The Balkans became home to many tribes from the east

'Ancestrial Timeline'

Heth-Sin-Sibur [4000 BC: Hunor/Magor: Akkadia to Mongolia, China...]

Turanian tribes [2000 BC: Altaic, Caucadian, Indo-Europian languages]

Hunnic-Sythian [1000 BC – 500 AD: Greek, Roman, Germanic, wars, etc]

Hunnic-Magyar [500 BC – 1000 AD: Cuman, Celtic, Magyar, Germanic wars]

Magyar-Saxon [1000 AD – 1588, Vitez, Mihaly to Varro, Janos [son: Mihaly]

Cuman-Magyar [1588 – 2023: Varro, Mihaly I – Michael F. [Mihaly X] Varro]

Chapter Two

Magyars, Cumans, Szekelys, and The Story of Michael

The Res Mozar

HE THREE OF THEM TOOK TURNS STANDING GUARD, WHILE THE OTHER two bobbed in and out between the trees on the way to the bridge. Mihaly had tied the cloth tightly around his leg and hobbled as best he could. They used a whistle code to alert each other in case they saw anyone coming. They found another abandoned small building in a riverside park, and one by one they regrouped, about one hundred yards from the bridge, hoping they would see "the man in a white hat" before succumbing to hypothermia. Soon after, they gathered in their new surroundings, Istvan fell asleep in an old wooden box. It was Lajos's turn to keep watch, while Mihaly once again drifted off....

* * * * *

Grandfather had gone to the library to retrieve his old notebook. He looked like "a cat that had swallowed the canary," as he handed Mihaly his notes. Curious about what he would find there, Mihály eagerly opened it. It was only conjecture, but based on research about the origins of the Varro family...and here, in grandfather's own written notes: It's more than 'who Begat whom'. In Grandfather's rough draft of the lineage of the Hungarians, Sumerian, and Sythian people, a pattern of migration began to appear. He called each entry 'House of...' In the margin he had written: "it's about my Sythian family, and our worship of God through history." There he had written the following...* (see Appendix) Here Grandfather Istvan's family historical notes ended. He then began what he called...

The Story of Michael
(Varro, Istvan)

After the Sythian-Roman family Onesimus Varro resettled in upper Moesia (Pannonia), generations of Sythian people spread Christianity and intermarried with Cumans, Bulgars, and Greeks. Waves of central Asian tribes began to migrate and met up with distant family members with similar language and culture. Many became Christians because of the efforts of the children, grandchildren, and great grandchildren of this family; many were martyred. Part of the family joined with the Huns, then the Magyars, Cumans, and other Sythian tribes, settling in the 'Great Plain' between the two great rivers, Danube and Tisza. These were the descendants of the Bishop of Singidunum (Beograd), Marcus Varro, oldest of Onesimus's children. Another son, Bishop of Sofia, Michail Varo 'the Bulgarian,' settled in Lower Moesia and his family became missionaries to the Khazars and others of the Bulgarian Empire. Alexander (Sandor) Varros and his family married Greeks and Byzantines, and became missionaries in Asia Minor, and were active in the church in Byzantium when Emperor Flavius Valerius Constantinus–the Great Constantine–made Christianity legal. Attila, and the Huns, caused great damage to the Romans, and was the primary reason the Empire in the west fell. With Constantine, the **Varro** [and Bulgarian **Varo**, and Greek **Varros**] families, were spreading Christianity throughout the Balkans, Asia Minor and Greece. For more than forty generations, this family was faithful to the call of Christ as followers of The Way. By the time Arpad and the Magyars arrived, and established the Kingdom of Hungary in 1000 AD, Christianity had spread throughout the known world. Celtic, Roman, Magyar, Bulgar, and Greek and Byzantine missionaries went to the far flung corners of the Empire which the Romans had 'opened up' for evangelization. Part of what had been Pannonia, was now Hungary, Transylvania, Wallachia, Moldova, and Bessarabia. Into this setting, with great internal conflict between the various tribes, the Ottoman Turks stepped in to help, then conquered the region. Transylvania was primarily settled by Szekelys, of Hun and Magyar origin, as 'frontier guardians' as they were known.

A young Wallachian prince, Michael 'Prince of the Szekelys' (Besarab, Mihály, also known to Hungarians as Vitez, Mihaly), probably of Cuman and Szekely origin himself), enlisted the help of the Transylvanian Szekelys, to join his cause against a corrupt local government official, Andras Bartholy, and return the former tax-free land rights of the Szekelys, which the Kingdom of Hungary had promised, but had not fulfilled. The proposed conflict against this corruption would return this right to them, drive out the Ottomans, and return Transylvania to Hungary–called the Peasants Uprising. Many of these joined Michael. One such Cuman-Szekely, named Varro, Janos, of Mures in Transylvania (likely Michael's region), became the personal assistant to Michael, and saved his life one day. A captain of the Ottomans broke into the house where Michael was sleeping, and stabbed him three times. Janos, however, had slipped a chainmail jacket onto Michael that morning, and the knife had not pierced Michael's body. Janos was also able to smash a heavy vase over the assassin's head, killing him. Later, Michael returned to his 'Court,' where he granted Janos a tax-free piece of land in Transylvania. He also gave Janos a gift of a 'rez mozar,' a bronze mortar and pestal–the ceremonial symbol of his gratitude *for his service. They were eventually successful in driving out the Turks, but later Michael himself was assassinated by them, the ones whom he had gone up against. Even though Transylvania was eventually returned to the Kingdom of Hungary, the faithful Szekelys were not given back their land rights, as promised. Janos returned to Mures dejected. His wife, Sofi, who, after so many years, had considered him dead, had married another man. His sons by her eventually gambled away the estate. The only thing left was the 'rez mozar,'...but eventually, Janos did remarry. She was Marta, the widow of his neighbor Tibor, who had died in the Peasants Uprising along with Michael, 'Prince of the Szekelys.' Marta and Janos had three more children. The first he named Varro, Mihaly, after Michael Vitez. Before he died, Janos told Marta on his deathbed that every Varro, Mihaly, in every generation thereafter, should receive the gift of the "rez mozar." Eleven generations have come and gone; each Varro, Mihaly, has received this story, and gift—the rez mozar—from Basarab, Mihaly [Vitez, Mihaly],' Prince of the Szekelys.*

Mihaly felt like he had slept forever. The sun was now down completely. Istvan and Lajos were both standing over him looking tired and anxious. "Are we going to do this, or not? Istvan said. Mihaly tried to stand up. To his amazement, his leg was actually feeling much better. He figured the cloth he had wrapped tightly around his leg, not to mention the long sleep, had probably helped him. Without putting full weight on his foot, he could walk...at least slowly. Lajos smiled at him, as he hobbled like a little old man, to the broken-down door, and looked outside. A faint glow from the street lamp cast an eerie shadow in the mist as the three of them headed out toward the bridge that connected the Banat with Serbia. The guard station at the bridge was about two hundred yards away. They had no idea what would happen. Maybe it was a hoax...too late to worry about that now. Going back would surely mean the firing squad. Suddenly, about one hundred yards from the guard station, someone quietly called to them from the other side of the road. He had on a white hat, and wore an old trench coat. Mihaly, who had been in such pain that morning from the fall, had not seen him well, but there was something strangely familiar about him. Mihaly came closer to look at the man's face. Lajos and

Istvan followed cautiously. When all three had reached the stranger, he looked straight at Mihaly...then he slowly took off the white hat...it was his Uncle Mihaly!

APPENDIX

'House of Xiung-nu [40 generations (with gaps)] (he had written 'legend') – All dates approximate

The Xiung-nu descended from Hunor and Magor (sons of Nimrod, Sythians & Sumerians) married Turkic and Iranian people, and nations of these Turanian people of Central Asia, including western China and Mongolia, raided China along the Great Wall, especially during the Han dynasty, migrated to the Great Plains of Pannonia and Balkans. [Zhou-Qin-Han dynasties] "all part of my family": [China] Tan-fu (c.1350bc), Li-wah (1200bc), Wu-fang (1130bc), Mu-wang (1045bc), Li-wang (875bc) and Yu-wang (771bc), whose daughter was Ly-sze, the mother of Dama [600bc] of the [Huns]–Kave (500bc), Kadar (400bc), Bukem (300bc), Beztur (205bc), Ompud (95bc) and Bolug (45bc) [all dates following are AD]"

'Houses of Attila (Huns/Bulgars/Cumans) [21 generations] (here he wrote 'conjecture') [Huns]– migrations west of the great Central Asia basin, led by Kadcha (120ad), Szemen(235) Uldin (290), Basig (330),Donaton (360), and **Attila**, the "Hun" (400-453), who found earlier family migrations of Sythian, Celtic, Samartians, and other tribes, ["all my people"] with similar languages and customs, when they migrated from Central Asia to the Black Sea plains.

[Bulgars/Kumans & the Eastern Roman Empire] – migration with Khazars and Cumans to Balkans. Attila's down-line [with gaps] included the ones who became known as the Magyars. Ernak (475), Chaba (510), Edus (545), Kadiha (580), Chazew (617), Kulchug (647), Edur(680) Vegerus (720),

Elendus (750), Avarius (772), Venedobel (796), Ogyek (823), Gheism (846), the father of Almós (869), who was the father of Arpád [first king of the Magyars]"

'House of Arpád, Cumans, Ottomans & Habsburgs [35 generations] ('Becomes Hungary')

Arpád (880), Zoltan (905), Val (925), Taksony (948), Géza (969), István (985 – Stephen I "First King of Hungary," Peter (1020), *[members of the Arpád family between 1045 and 1300*: Andras I, Bela I, Solomon, Geza I, Laszlo I, Koloman, Istvan II, Geza II, Stephen III, László II, István IV, Bela III, Emerich, Laszlo III, Andras II, Béla IV, István V, László IV, András III, *[members of the Premyslid, Wittelsbach, Capet-Anjou, Luxemburg, Jagellon, Hunyadi, Zapolya and Habsburg dynasties between 1300 and 1575]*: Vencel, Otto, Karoly I-Robert, Lajos I, Maria, Karoly II, Zsigmond, Albert, Ulaszlo I, Laszlo V, Janos, Matyas I-Corvinus, Ulaszlo II, Lajos II, Janos I & II (Zapolya), and Habsburgs: Ferdinánd I, Miksa, and Rudolf'

The Michael Varro [Varro, Mihaly] "line"

[Conjecture, family records, and family oral tradition)

1. Michael S. Varro	IX	Mihaly VIII's son	Bend, OR	1974
2. Michael F. Varro, Jr.	VIII	Mihaly VII's son	Fairbanks, AK	1944
3. Michael F. Varro, Sr.	VII	Mihaly VI's son	Bodo, Timis Co	1913
4. Varro, Mihaly (Pop) [Varro Sandor]	VI	Nephew/Mihaly V Pop's Father)	Piros, Serbia Piros, Serbia	1887 1839
5. Varro, Mihaly [Varro, Istvan]	V	Istvan's brother 'last Cuman'	Karcag, Hungary Karcag, Hungary	1805 1780
6. Varro, Mihaly [Varro, Gesa]	IV	Son of Gesa Son of Mihaly III	Transylvania Transylvania	1750 1720
7. Varro, Mihaly	III	Son of Mihaly II	Transylvania	1690
8. Varro, Mihaly	III	Son of Mihaly I	Transylvania	1660
9. Varro, Mihaly	I	Son of Varro, Janos	Transylvania	1620
10. Varro, Janos		(saved life of Vitez, Mihaly – Res Mozar, estate)		1570
11. Varro		(generations back to Arpad, first of the Magyars)		850
12. Varro		(generations back to Cuman/Szekely/Romans)		450
13. Arpad House		(generations back to Attila and the Roman Empire)		350
14. Attila House		(generations back to Central Asians migrations)		150
15. Sung House		(generations back to Hun–Mongol–Turks)		BC1350
16. Hunor/Magor		(Scythians–Asian steppes, many years back)		BC2400
17. Nimrod/Sumer		(Accadian–Ham/Shem/Japheth and Noah)]		BC3500

Line of Varro, Mihaly

(chronologically,
[*] these are supported by family records)

[Mures]   Janos (1590) [given an estate/res mozar by Mihaly, Vitez, Prince of Szekelys]

[Mures]   **Mihaly I** (1620) [son of Janos, loyal soldier, named for Mihaly, Vitez]

[Mures]   Janos–Bela–Tibor–Imre–Lajos–**Mihaly II** (1660) [son of Mihaly I]

[Mures]   Istvan–Sandor–Joska–Janos–**Mihaly III** (1705) [son of Mihaly II]

[Karcag]   Gesa (1740)–Tibor–Lajos–Bela–Istvan–Janos–Ferenc

[Karcag]   Joska–Lajos–**Mihaly IV** (1780)–*Janos–Imre–Istvan–Sandor

[Vojvodina]   Juliska–Joska–*Istvan–**Mihaly V** (1805)–Imre–Bela

[Vojvodina]   [Uncle] **Mihaly VI** (1845)–*Sandor–Ferenc–Bela–Tibor–Janos–Istvan–Imre

[Timisoara]   Juliana–Ferenc–Joska–***Mihaly VII** [Pop] (1887)–Sandor–Janos–Antal

[Bodo]   ***Mihaly VIII** [Michael F.(1913)–[Istvan-Lajos-Joe-Jim-Margaret-Irene-Frank

[Alaska]   Juli–***Mihaly IX** [Michael (Frank) Varro,] (1944) Margi-Steve-David

[Oregon]   Michelle–***Mihaly X** [Michael S.(Steve) Varro] (1974)–Robert ['Mihaly XI'(?) – if there should ever be one, (from following generations?]

CHAPTER THREE

THE MAN WITH A 'WHITE HAT' AND THE NEW WORLD

The 1908 route from Răducăneni Romania to Manchester England.
Iasi, Lemberg, Cracow, Breslau, Berlin, Hamburg by train.
Hamburg to Grimsby by Steamship.
Grimsby to Manchester by train.

Rail line Europe, c.1913 – the Balkans to Trieste, and on to Paris

The man with a 'white hat'

Mihaly was dumbfounded! He hadn't seen Uncle Mihaly since he was a teenager in Vojvodina. As they followed him to the bridge, Mihaly's mind raced, trying to recall what he even knew of this uncle. His father, Sandor, had mentioned him, especially when the family moved from Piros to Timisoara. Even though he lived in Vojvodina, he had helped Mihaly enroll in fourth grade in one of Timisoara's Magyar elementary schools. Mihaly had had many questions about Uncle Mihaly, but he was always afraid to ask. His father, Sandor, never said much about his brother. But it was rumored that, as an ethnic Hungarian and leader in the Szekely community that migrated from Mures in Transylvania to Vojvodina, he somehow had secret connections with the Serbian government. So much intrigue! "My own uncle…maybe he was a spy," Mihaly mused–thinking on this made Mihaly smile…so much still did not know.

They reached the bridge, where the officials at the guard station recognized Uncle Mihaly immediately. There was a long conversation about…about something, it was hard to overhear everything, but it seemed to be about some Hungarian family business in Serbia that Uncle Mihaly needed assistance with. Many conscripts in the Austro-Hungarian army were leaving. There was so much unrest with Serbia, Croatia, and the Habsburg regime, many Hungarian officials just chose to look the other way; it was called the Balkan War.

Uncle Mihaly handed the guards an envelope. They immediately opened the gate, and Mihaly and his two friends walked across the bridge over the Danube into Serbia…and freedom. Mihaly never saw his uncle Mihaly again. He heard years later that he had died peacefully in his family home in Vojvodina. He was told that Uncle Mihaly had worked in intelligence for many years. He wondered how this dear uncle of his had even known about his plans to leave. How grateful he was for this, his own uncle, who must have risked his own life for Mihaly's freedom. When Mihaly tried to speak of it to his father, Sandor, he smiled and nodded his head, *as he held the resmozar that Uncle* Mihaly had given him, "I hold it for you; some day you come back; I give it to you, Mihaly–keep it for your sons"

They decided to travel at night and sleep during the day. After spending the day in Beograd, sleeping in a park, and sneaking aboard a freight train, they made their way to Sarajevo and then Trieste. There, Mihaly said goodbye to his friends Lajos and Istvan. They had become like brothers to him. They said they had maternal family in Italy, and asked him to go there with them, but Mihaly had his mind set on the

United States, where his brother Joska had gone to live, in Milwaukee, he thought. They broke down in tears as they said goodbye. Mihaly promised he would keep in contact with them through their Italian relatives. As Mihaly said goodbye to Lajos and Istvan, he was reminded of his tearful goodbye earlier that month with his wife, Juliana, in Bodo where they were living near Timisoara. She was so beautiful, and several months pregnant with their first child. With tears flowing down her face, she had begged him to go…to find freedom, and then send for them. Mihaly had told her he could not do it…not without her, especially just before Mihaly's birth; they had told him of their plans to escape. It was October, 1912, during the Balkan Wars. In Trieste, after Lajos and Istvan departed; Mihaly suddenly remembered the envelope Uncle Mihaly had given him. He had said not to open it until he arrived there. Now, eagerly tearing it open, Mihaly read the names of friends of a family in Trieste that would give Mihaly a temporary position on the rail line. He quickly called them, giving them the code name and number that Uncle Mihaly had written in the letter that he was to share – *"Bela Ladislaus 765"*. The voice on the phone said he would be at the station shortly. Mihaly had waited almost an hour when he noticed a car blinking its lights. He went over to the car. "Get in," the man said in Hungarian, *"Bela Ladislaus 765"* – don't say a word." They traveled in silence to a small shed by the tracks, about five miles from the station. "Lock yourself in the shed, someone will come in the morning, there is food, water and a blanket." Then he drove off. For the next eight months, the shed was Mihaly's home. Someone named Imre had shown up the next morning. He handed Mihaly a letter. It gave him instructions on what he was to do each day, how he would be paid, where to leave the money for the food and water, and where to send the money each month. It would be forwarded to Juliana, the letter stated. He spent Christmas alone on the train, where he was a brakeman. Someone named Barta, from the local Serbian Orthodox church in Trieste, showed up after work to take him to Midnight Mass. It was cold and Mihaly came down with the flu in January, but he didn't dare to miss any days of work.

On February 14, 1913, Barta called him on the station telephone, "Meet me at the church at 5:00." Mihaly walked the ten blocks to the church and Barta was waiting for him. "Your son Michael was born this morning; Julia and son are both well, they will join you as soon as he is old enough to travel." They stayed for Mass, then Barta left and Mihaly walked back to the shed. He cried tears of joy, and he promised God again, like he had so many times before, that if she joined him safe and sound, with their son Michael, he would join Juliana's church: a Reformed church, the Nazorean sect of Anabaptists. She had attended this church in Timisoara growing up with her adoptive parents. She was part Saxon, and part Jewish Hungarian, and the Kis family, kind Hungarian art teachers, living in Timisoara, had adopted her. Mihaly had been working for the station manager there, and her church group had gone up to Alba Ilulia for a Magyar history trip, and church visit. They met on the train, since the station manager had asked him to act as tour guide. He took them to the town square in Alba Iulia when they arrived, and she asked him where the church was. He thought she meant the Orthodox church he sometimes attended; she laughed, "No, I'm Reformed, are you Orthodox?" After they got back, he wanted to see her again, so he went to her church. As it turned out, the Kis family knew Sandor, his dad, because they were both artists, and after several months of seeing her at her church, and the families getting together for art shows, Mihaly and Juliana had decided to get married. Many of their friends and family members, sensing the urgency of the times, were also getting married. That fall, they married at the Orthodox Church in Timisoara; but in deference to her family, they had agreed to have the reception at the Nazorean Church. Three months later, the station manager called him in; He informed Mihaly they would relocate them to Bodo, about halfway to Alba Ilulia; Mihaly and Juliana moved the next month; and Mihaly began work at the station there. A cousin from Mures helped them find a small place to live…two months later Julia said she was pregnant.

Things did not look good for the Austro-Hungarian Empire. Unrest was everywhere. In the Ottoman Empire, Bulgaria, Bosnia, Greece, and especially Serbia, things were very dangerous. The Balkan Wars had broken out, and the 'Empire' was drafting all able-bodied men. Mihaly had hoped to escape the draft, but in early 1911 he was called up. He was fighting in the Banat, and there was talk of them being sent to Bulgaria. Many of his friends had been killed. He had been wounded three times. Remembering this narrative brought Mihaly great sorrow…again and again. He knew he needed God in his life. Juliana seemed to have such a strange sense of peace, a peace he didn't have. He didn't think he could endure this time apart much longer.

World War I borders of Central Powers and Allied Powers

In June, Barta met him at church and handed him a letter. In it were instructions on how to take the overnight train from Trieste to Paris, small boat passage from Calais to London, and then to Southampton, with steerage-class tickets from Southampton, to New York. A brother of Andras Kis, Juliana's father, would meet him in Trieste and help him take care of passports, tickets, and overnight accommodations at the home of a friend of the Kis family. Juliana, and son Mihaly, who was now three months old, would be arriving by train in two days. The money for train, ship, and incidentals, were in another envelope. Mihaly had worked hard, and now his dream was coming true! Two days later, Mihaly finished his job, took his regularly-assigned freight train to Sarajevo, and then waited at the train station for the passenger train arriving from Beograd. He knew then that Uncle Mihaly must have had something to do with this. Mihaly learned later that Julia was on a three-day tourist's pass 'visiting family' in Beograd–an 'Uncle Mihaly idea' for sure–accompanied by her new son Mihaly (Michael). What a joy to see Juliana (Julia) again after so long! They quickly went to The travel office in Trieste and secured the right documents. Uncle Mihaly had thought of everything…they were traveling as 'Serbian tourists.' Everything was in order. He had even made arrangements for them to take a passport picture that afternoon. That evening, they took the train going to Paris from Trieste, and from there took a ferry over to England. They purchase steerage-class passage on a tramp steamer in Southampton going to New York. Many boarding the ship were also from eastern Europe, desperate to find a new life during the terrible war.

∗ ∗ ∗ ∗ ∗

The New World

On board ship, Julia met some Hungarians from Vojvodina that had attended the same church as she. Even though she was feeling seasick, she managed to attend some of the prayer services they were conducting on board. Mihaly attended with her, but made excuses to take Michael back to the staterooms (which they shared with twenty other people!), even though he never seemed to fuss or was fazed by the rough seas. And then…they arrived!

America! They docked July 1, 1913, and New York was getting ready for the festive celebration of their Independence Day. Joska, Mihaly's brother, and his wife, Katie (Benko), met them. Uncle Joe— they called him, had married a Hungarian woman in New York after his arrival, three years prior to Mihaly's arrival. The Benko family was from Budapest, and Joe had actually met her there before he came to America to study agriculture. After they all met each other, Joe introduced them to Gyorgy Serly, the Pastor of a Serbian Christian Church in Syracuse, a sister church of one that they had been attending in Milwaukee. He had come down to assist Joe and Katie in meeting Mihaly's and Julia's ship, and had also offered his church as a place for them to stay, on their way back to Milwaukee. Joe and Katie had met Pastor Gyorgy at a church meeting that he had conducted in Milwaukee the previous year. They all boarded the train, and several hours later arrived at the church near Syracuse. They stayed there a week to help in Pastor Gyorgy's church, staying temporarily in one of the church classrooms. Joe and Katie said it was time for them to leave and return to Milwaukee and his job at the library. They had sent letters back to Budapest to Katie's family, and also to Piros, to tell Joe's folks of the safe arrival of Mihaly, Julia, and Michael. Julia had also written to family in Timisoara telling them the good news as well. After Joe and Katie arrived safely in Milwaukee, Mihaly and Julia stayed a couple more weeks and then joined them. They were hoping to find work there, but nothing was immediately available. In August, Katie's brother, Ferenc, in Saskatchewan, Canada, wrote that there might be harvest jobs around Regina and southern Saskatchewan, and that he had taken the liberty of signing Mihaly up for work there. Later that month, Mihaly, Julia, and Michael, who was now six months old, left Joe and Katie in Milwaukee for Regina. Ferenc told them they could stay on the farm near Gravelbourg, about one hundred miles from Regina. They would stay in one of the bunk houses, but not with the other men; at least it would be a warm, safe place to stay. With almost no money left, Mihaly, Julia, and Michael, left Milwaukee by train to Minneapolis and from there to Regina. Ferenc and his wife Margit met their train, and introduced them to Parson Samuel Watson, and his wife Marta, of the Gravelbourg Anglican Church, who was kind enough to drive the church bus to Regina to pick them up. Ferenc and his wife had visited the church a few times, and Parson Watson's wife had told them that if they ever needed anything, to be sure to ask for help. He drove them to Gravelbourg and invited them to visit their church.

After they settled in at the bunk house where Ferenc and Margit also stayed, they were introduced to Carl Norberg, the owner, and the rest of the farm hands. They all ate together—Carl's wife, Sharon, was a wonderful cook—and then they retired early. The rooster crowed at 5:00 a.m., and the long work days began. They spent the next few months this way, but made enough money to pay their room and board, managing to save a little money from each pay check. Parson Watson stopped by for them every Sunday for church, but some weeks they were so exhausted they spent the weekends just resting and writing letters to Joe and Katie, their families back in Timisoara and Piros, and friends from Julia's church. Julia missed her Nazorean fellowship back in Timisoara, but she prayed, gave a small offering faithfully at Parson Watson's church, and attended services and prayer meetings as she was able. Marta and she became close, and was an encouragement to her in her loneliness.

The following May, Julia told Mihaly that she was pregnant again. They had been allowed to stay in the bunk house for the winter and help with the farm chores, but the one-room bungalow was already cramped. Ferenc quarreled with them over a number of things, but mostly over the fact that Mihaly did most of the work, and he allowed it but still received more per-hour pay because of his seniority; so Mihaly had tried to work extra hours, ending up making more than Ferenc anyway. Ferenc also wanted Mihaly to pay him for getting him his job, but Mihaly resisted this. They wanted to save as much as they could to rent or buy their own place someday. Things got worse when Istvan (Stevan) was born at the end of 1914 (even though his birth certificate said January of 1915). There was hardly room for the three of them, and now, with another baby, they could hardly turn around. Mihaly had built a small box with straw and a blanket as a bed for Michael, but had to keep Stevan in the bed with them until he was six months old. The next August, Ferenc and Margit left for another farm, where they found a harvest job, with a place to rent, near Fort Qu'Appelle. By Christmas, Margit had decided to leave him, and moved into Regina for a job at a laundry. He heard that she met a rodeo cowboy and ran off with him later that year. Parson Watson stopped by after the new year to visit with Mihaly and Julia. He told them one of his parishioners had died. Since the man's wife had died five years prior, and they had no children, he had bequeathed the small farm he owned to the church. There was about four years left on the mortgage; the bank gave Parson Watson a little time to see what he could do. The church could not pay the taxes, so Parson Watson wondered if Mihaly and Julia were interested in farming it for the church. There was a small house there, and a shed they had used in the farming. Mihaly knew that this must be a result of Julia's faithful prayers – and an opportunity – but he also knew that there was no way he could acquire this without help. Julia said they could do it, and that with God's help, she knew a way would be provided. She said they would fast and pray until God showed them the answer. Parson Watson was doubtful, but he said he would wait. If the bank did not repossess it, maybe God was answering their prayers. After three days, Julia said she was going to write Joe and Katie in Milwaukee, and tell them about this. Mihaly knew this would do no good, since Joe would never leave his library job, and Katie had worked for years as a cashier for them to even make it. Mihaly was alarmed, though – Julia had eaten nothing, no solid food – in three days. She had drunk only the juice from the saskatoon berry bushes that grew wild there on the farm. She had written Joe and Katie, but it was already a few weeks, and they had heard nothing back. Mihaly pleaded with her to eat something, but she just smiled and asked him to pray with her. By the end of the week, Mihaly decided he had to call Joe on the telephone. She said they didn't have a phone, but that Pastor Gyorgy might have one, and she agreed to let him try to reach Joe on their behalf. After the evening chores, and feeding the baby and Michael, Mihaly tried calling from the farm house phone. Carl and Sharon didn't want to lose them, but hoped for their sake that their dreams might be fulfilled. They were members of the Church of the Assumption, the Catholic Cathedral there in Gravelbourg, and Sharon's family, who were French, had helped to found the Catholic community there. She had told Julia she said the Rosary daily on their behalf. Mihaly was able to get through to Pastor Gyorgy. Before he could explain why he was calling, Pastor Gyorgy told Mihaly that Joe had lost his job at the library, and Katie had slipped and fallen on the ice, and hadn't been to work for a month. Gyorgy told Mihaly that they had told him they considered moving to Fort Qu'Appelle to help Ferenc, who was devastated by Margit's leaving. They had some life's savings that had accumulated in Milwaukee, but were worried that Ferenc, who wanted them to invest it in some risky venture, might squander it. They were thinking of helping Ferenc later, and maybe moving to Saskatchewan anyway, to see if they could get employment there and start over. Mihaly dropped the phone. Sharon asked him what was wrong…that he looked as white as a sheet. Carl handed the phone back to Mihaly, who asked Pastor Gyorgy if he could kindly try to explain to Joe and Katie, on his behalf, the opportunity that God might be opening up for them, if only they could see their way clear to going ahead and coming to Saskatchewan, to all live together, to share the cost of homesteading a small farm. Julia had been praying for this, and now it was coming true! He could not believe it. He cried, he embraced Carl and Sharon, then he ran to the bungalow to embrace his wife, this prayer warrior with a faith he didn't understand. It scared him.

The next month was a blur. Joe and Katie sold their house, converted most of their savings into liquid funds, and moved to Saskatchewan. They agreed to go in together on the small farm, sight unseen, fix up the little house and shed, and move there. They would add onto the house and arrange it so they had separate quarters. Parson Watson and Marta came by and helped them go to the bank. They let them use their church attorney, and with Carl's help also, they signed the papers to homestead the small farm, just northeast of Gravelbourg. The back taxes were reduced since the property had been bequeathed to the church. The church board needed to approve turning the property over with an outstanding balance—which they did. The bank agreed to convert the remaining amount on the contract for the two Varro brothers. The four years remaining were converted for a reasonable rate. Joe and Katie were able to give a modest gift to her brother Ferenc, who moved into Regina, taking a job selling insurance.

Carl and Sharon let Joe and Katie and their three children move temporarily into the unused quarters on the farm. Joe helped with the farm chores, and Katie helped Sharon and Julia with the canning business. After Stevan turned a year old, Julia began helping with the commercial canning, and sometimes covered the store in town where they sold these goods, along with some of Sharon's homemade kitchen and household items. Mihaly and Joe spent all their free time at the newly acquired property, fixing up the house, repairing the shed, and adding on the new living quarters. It was the end of summer, and the harvest was about to start. Michael was almost four, Stevan was crawling, and pulling himself up by a chair; he was nearly two.

Julia and Katie started a new Bible study and prayer group. Carl and Sharon allowed them to use one of the rooms in the barn, and many of the farm hands would come in the evening after work. Mihaly's English was still very broken, as was Julia's, and Katie's was not much better, even after living more years in the United States and Canada than they had, so they were all pleasantly surprised when some Hungarians and Romanian farm hands from the area showed up at their Bible study. Julia began to inquire about churches that might be more similar to her church back in Timisoara, but found none. She decided that God had placed her here for a special reason. Mihaly supported her efforts, but seemed unable to live the kind of faith-filled life she did. She began to pray for his salvation.

Even before the harvest had finished, Julia announced to Mihaly that she was pregnant once again. They would finish the harvest, wrap up the construction of the house and shed on the new property, and then move before winter. Katie got word that Ferenc was in a serious accident and was in the hospital in Regina. Parson Watson offered to take her there to see him, but Joe felt he couldn't get away; the project on the new property was almost finished, so he stayed and worked with Mihaly to finish it by the end of the month. Katie made arrangements to stay with a cousin of Ferenc near the hospital, during her time there. Eventually, Ferenc got better, but part of his foot had to be amputated, and the doctors said he would never be able to sire children. Margit came to see him in the hospital. She said the rodeo cowboy had taken all her money and left. She cried, and then she told him that she had accepted Christ in a little Romanian Baptist Church in Regina. She said she still loved him; she was sorry she had cheated on him. He said he had moved on. Later, when his insurance business failed, he started going to church with Margit, and had a similar conversion. He was baptized, and they remarried. He came to Gravelbourg to tell Mihaly how sorry he was he had treated him badly. Mihaly dismissed it, but he wondered about Ferenc's new found life.

They moved to the little farm before Thanksgiving. The move was hard on Julia. She was seven months pregnant, and she felt badly about letting the others do most of the hard work. She continued to go into town to help Sharon with the store whenever she could, but they had to make plans for their first planting in the spring, so she stayed busy with that after they finished moving in. They had a nice Christmas, and despite the cold and the cramped quarters, everyone seemed to get along well. They had received a great deal of canned goods, corn meal and flour, and even some meat and produce, from the Norberg's as a 'going away' present, part of which they shared with Joe and Katie. In January, Louis (Lajos) was born. It was cold, and the little clinic in Gravelbourg was not well equipped, with only one doctor and a couple of midwives who volunteered when they were needed. The birth went easily enough, but Julia had secretly hoped for a girl this time. Still and all she thanked God for this precious little boy. She sometimes wondered how she would get them all in school when the time came. They lived in a small farm town, but she knew God would work things out for them. She continually prayed for Mihaly's salvation.

The first couple of winters on their new farm were difficult. The land had not been worked in a while and their root cellar wasn't sealed, so some of the canned goods were ruined. The rooms were small and drafty. Katie started coming over to Mihaly's and Julia's side of the house, to borrow things, instead of stockpiling their supplies better. Both families came down with the flu, and Joe and Mihaly lacked experience in working the farm, frequently asking Carl for help. Julia found herself spending more time in town at the store. She didn't really like the farm after all, she had to admit, but Mihaly thought they could be successful if they learned more about how to do it. The second spring planting was delayed because of weather. They lacked the manpower that the Norberg's farm had enjoyed. The Bible study and prayer meetings were going well, but Julia wasn't bouncing back as quickly from her last pregnancy, and Louis took a lot of her time. Michael had turned six, and they had to start thinking about schooling. Stevan was like glue to Michael; they did everything together. Baby Louis crawled, then started walking, and was getting into everything. He and Stevan showed an early talent in art, and loved charcoal, crayons, or pencils, anything they could play with. Despite the cramped quarters, and Julia's exhaustion, Mihaly still wanted more children. He said the boys would grow up and help work the farm, or work on the railroad (his experience with the railroad was still not out of his system), but of course that was all in the future. It was now 1919.

Between spring planting and summer, Julia thought she was pregnant again. She didn't feel well, and decided to go to the doctor in town. Katie said she would take care of things when Sharon stopped by to take Julia into town, to the store. Julia told Sharon she thought she was pregnant again, and could she just drop her off at the clinic. Sharon agreed to take care of the store while Julia stopped in to see the doctor. After examining her, Dr. Stan Nichols confirmed what Julia had suspected. He congratulated her and Mihaly on another baby, but he didn't look happy. She asked him what was wrong. He said everything looked fine with the pregnancy, but she seemed run down. Maybe it was just the aftermath of the flu and the strain of the move, but he thought it probably wasn't a good time to be pregnant again, so soon. He said he would check up on her in couple months after she was further along. She hadn't experienced 'morning sickness' with the first three pregnancies, but now she was very ill every morning. The summer was hot, and Julia could not handle the chores and take care of the three boys. Though she prayed every day, she couldn't manage the Bible study, and Sharon and Katie said they were not up to it without her.

Soon it was harvest time, and Julia, five months along, was still violently ill every day. Mihaly didn't know what to do. The harvest had begun without her, and Joe and Katie were demanding all of Mihaly's time. It was their first full harvest. The prior year could hardly be called a harvest, and if they didn't succeed this season, they wouldn't be able to pay the lease as required by the homesteading arrangement. That would allow the bank to take the farm back. Sharon took Julia to see Dr. Nichols again. He said things didn't look good. Julia had a bad infection that may have harmed the fetus. He thought he might have to take the baby, and frankly he said, the baby might not even still be alive. Sharon said they had to take her into the hospital in Regina immediately and called Carl to come help. Carl was tied up with the harvest, so he agreed to send Julius, his new foreman, with the truck. Dr. Nichols said wait – he was the one making the decisions here, and there wasn't time to make the hundred-mile trip to Regina. He would go ahead and take the baby, then treat Julia's infection. Mihaly was called to come immediately. The midwife came to help. Julia said, with God, all would be well. They went into surgery, took the fetus which was stillborn, and then started to treat the infection. Julia went into sepsis shock. Mihaly was frantic, demanding that Julius take him and Julia to Regina. The trip was more than three hours, and Mihaly cried and prayed all the way there. Julia was not breathing when they reached the emergency room. The doctors finally came out, after what seemed like an eternity. They sat down with Mihaly …they said they had tried everything…the sepsis shock was too much…they hadn't gotten her there sooner…Julia had died. She was only twenty-nine.

Mihaly sat there, frozen and in shock. He felt like his life was over. She was his guiding star. Julius could not console him…he cried uncontrollably. The greatest gift he'd ever had was now taken from him. He wanted to blame someone…maybe Dr. Nichols…or maybe Julius or himself…or even God, for taking a gift back that he hadn't 'taken care' of? Julius had called Carl and Sharon. Joe and Katie were taking care of the boys, and the harvest had ground to a halt. Mihaly said nothing all the way back to Gravelbourg. What was he going to do? Three small boys with no mother. He would probably lose the farm. He, Joe, and Katie, just weren't experienced enough to turn it around. He remembered how Julia always trusted God for everything. Her faith was so strong, and she had prayed for him to turn his life over to Jesus. He just hadn't listened to her. Now she was gone. Suddenly Mihaly knew what he had to do. He had to find the people from Julia's church. He had promised her he would become a Christian, that he would pray and read the Bible, like she did. Joe and Katie couldn't help him, they had stopped going to Pastor Gyorgy's church a few months before they left Milwaukee, and had started going to a small Lutheran church. Mihaly decided he would find someone in Julia's church and tell them he wanted to become a Christian, like Julia had wanted him to do. Then maybe he could forgive himself for letting her slip away. Maybe she would forgive him for not being the kind of husband and father he should have been. There was so much on his mind.

When they got back, Carl and Sharon met them. They had arranged for Joe and Katie to be there with the boys. All the farm hands, from both farms, had gathered at Carl's and Sharon's house. Sharon said a Rosary, Joe read some scripture, and Katie tried to pray, but broke down and wasn't able to finish. Sharon had fixed dinner, and everyone ate in silence, except for the occasional sounds of weeping. Michael only understood a little of what was going on; and Steve and Louie looked bewildered, and kept asking for their mother. Not being able to understand what was going on, they cried because everyone else was crying. Michael tried to console them, but he was crying too. The boys had begun calling their dad 'Pop,' which was what Carl and Sharon's boys, Bert and Sammy, were calling him. So, Joe and Katie's kids, Becky, Jim, and Lizzy, called him 'Pop' too. In addition to that, the farm hands had started calling him Mike, so he dropped the name 'Mihaly.'

After dinner, Carl took Mike in the other room. He asked him about the arrangements for Julia's burial. The hospital had told him they would help him by discounting the morgue and emergency room costs. With what little money Mike had, he arranged for a simple box and a small memorial stone, but he didn't have the money for a cemetery plot. Carl hadn't been able to give Mike a 'severance' when they leased the little farm, but asked Mike to accept a gift now for that purpose. Mike was so grateful to Carl and Sharon for helping them already, and now he was offering him a way to lay his precious Julia to rest. He broke down again and embraced Carl. Sharon came in and embraced him as well, assuring him his wife was with her Jesus, whom she had served so faithfully.

The next few weeks were agony for Mihaly. Without being able to prepare the body, they needed to have the memorial in Regina within the next couple days. The morgue would not keep the body in cold storage any longer. Parson Watson came into town and conducted the graveside service. Julia was buried at a small cemetery where many Hungarians and other eastern Europeans were interred. Most of the folks from both farms attended, and many others from Gravelbourg that had known Julia, also attended. Parson Watson conducted a lovely service. Many brought flowers for the grave. Friends of Parson Watson and his wife, from another Anglican church in Regina, held a nice reception. Mike and the boys were surrounded by love from so many whose lives had been touched by this beautiful person ... Julia, now safe in the arms of Jesus.

The harvest resumed, but Joe, Katie, and Mike were very short-handed, even with the help of some of Carl's workers. It didn't look good for Joe's and Mike's homesteading venture. After they paid off the workers, there was not much left for the bank. Things looked bleak for getting through the winter. Mike went through every day in a trance. He couldn't get the thought out of his mind that he had to find people from Julia's church. When the harvest was over, unknown to anyone, he asked Julius to take him into Regina. He would not stop until he found someone who could point him in the right direction. In his broken English, he went from church to church asking about the "Nazoreans." He had to find them. Finally, he met up with Ferenc, of all people, at the Baptist church. Ferenc had come to the graveside service at Katie's invitation, but was curious about seeing Mike there. Ferenc bought both of them a cup of coffee, and they sat and talked about Julia and her great faith, her life in God, and her servant heart. Margit joined them, and she and Ferenc tried to explain that the church Julia had attended in Timisoara was really Baptist more than anything, it was part of the Anabaptist movement, and the closest thing to her Hungarian Nazorean church was an Apostolic Christian Church, and there were none of those in Regina. He said the closest one in fact was in Akron, Ohio. What? Akron, Ohio? Surely that could not be true! So far away! What about the sign he had seen there in Regina on one of the churches: Church of the Nazarene? Ferenc explained that it was not the same Nazorean church that Julia had gone to. It was a 'holiness' church, a new denomination, like old-fashioned Methodist churches, starting in Texas, he thought – just a few years ago – in 1908, but it wasn't Julia's church. Mike thanked them as Julius reminded him that if they didn't go very soon, Carl would be very upset. He didn't even know they were gone, and it was more than three hours back to the farm. Ferenc and Margit prayed with Mike, and then they left. He wanted to leave for Akron, Ohio, right away, as unrealistic as the thought was.

When they got back, it was almost dark. Carl met them, and Mike asked him not to blame Julius. He had to visit the grave again, that he needed to find 'Julia's church.' Carl was upset, but he shook Mike's hand and told him to get some rest, they would talk about it in the morning. The next day, Mike told Joe and Katie he had to leave. He wanted to leave the boys with them. He would go to Akron, Ohio, to find Julia's church. He would become a Christian …in the same church she had gone to in Timisoara. Joe blew up, and said, no, they would not even consider helping him with this outlandish scheme. He could become a Christian anywhere. Katie was more reasonable, though, realizing Mike was obsessed in his grief, and needed to find an answer to this spiritual need in his life. They argued for a time, and then Mike said he didn't care about anything, and he was backing out of the homesteading deal. He said that if the farm failed, as was probably going to be the case, it wouldn't matter anyway. Katie said she would keep the boys. Mike didn't like the way that she was so harsh with her own three, but he didn't say anything. He had just started Michael in first grade in Gravelbourg a few weeks before, and a small bus came to pick them up, and return the students to the farms in the area, every day. They had all started calling Stevan, who was now four, Buddy, or just Bud for short, and they were now calling Louis, Louie. The two younger boys kept themselves entertained with drawing, carving wood, and creating objects made of old paint, charcoal, and the like. So, it was all set...he would leave in the morning. The next day, Mike was up early. He kissed his sleeping sons goodbye...and rode his bicycle in to Shamrock, where Julius lived, in order for him to catch a ride with him into Regina... since Julius had to work his own farm sometimes on weekends. He waited until a train was pulling out, and then hopped on board. He had checked the route of a Canadian National freight train, and knew it was going east. He slept awhile, and then when the train was pulling in to Winnipeg, he jumped off and looked for the train going south to Minneapolis. He jumped on board another train, this time going south to the U.S. and Canadian border. When they got near the border, Mike jumped off and went into the woods. He waited until dark, and then, finding an opening in the border fence, he crossed over into the U.S. He hitched a ride south to Minneapolis, and from there he hopped on a train going to Cleveland. From there he hitched a ride to Akron. He inquired as to the Apostolic Christian Church, but no one seemed to understand his English. He was very hungry as he started walking, not knowing exactly where he was headed. Someone noticed him walking toward the bus station, and stopped to pick him up. Probably because of the way he looked, the man, who looked European himself, asked him in English where he was going. When Mike didn't seem to understand, he asked him again, this time in Hungarian. Mike was delighted, and responded in Hungarian! He told him he needed to find the Akron Apostolic Christian Church. The man said, with a smile, there was no such church...but there was a 'West Akron' Apostolic Christian Church... and he was a member there! Mike was breathless, knowing God had answered his prayer. Mike introduced himself. The young man's name was Bela. He was probably about twenty, he was from Szeged, and had been in America only five years. They drove to the church, and there Mike met Pastor Katona, who introduced him to several of the members that were there that day. They were shocked that he had come all the way from Saskatchewan…that he had lost his wife, and that he was here to become a Christian…in the same denomination that she had been in, back in Timisoara. Then they said the same thing Joe had said: 'one didn't have to become a Christian in the same denomination in order to be a believer in Jesus,' just to trust him as one's Savior. However, they were very impressed that he had come all this way to honor Julia's faith and Hungarian heritage! They also expressed great sorrow for his loss, concern for his small boys, and prayed for their safety and well-being. Then they went in to the church. Pastor Katona asked Mike to kneel at the altar, and the others gathered around and placed their hands on his shoulder. Pastor told him he must confess his sins, put his complete faith and trust in God's saving power in Jesus alone, by dying on the cross for him, and then to receive the gift of salvation, and power of the Holy Spirit, to live his life as a Christian. Mike said he did. They waited. Finally pastor Katona told Mike he must confess his individual sins. Mike said, 'like what?' Like, 'how had he treated his children, his wife, his family; had he cheated and lied in his business? Had he come to the country illegally?' Mike told them he had been a good husband and father, but he probably could have done better. He said he had left Austro-Hungary without permission, but only to seek a better life in the U.S. and Canada. How had he gotten from Canada to the U.S. this week? He confessed to them that he 'had crossed the border without papers.' When he had finished 'repenting,' they prayed, and then asked Mike to pray, to ask Jesus to forgive his sins and to receive Him into his life. Then they all rejoiced with him in his new found life in Christ. They applauded. Mike cried. Julia would be overjoyed, he said. They invited him to stay, to eat with them. They said Mike could stay a couple nights in one of the classrooms. The next day, after feeding him some breakfast, they had a prayer meeting, and Mike gave his 'testimony,' which was expected, they said, after a new convert gave 'his heart to Jesus.' Mike talked mostly about Julia and her life, and what an inspiration she had always been to him in spite of the hard times in Hungary, escaping from the army there, and life on the farm after coming to Saskatchewan.

As they were finishing lunch, they heard a knock on the church door. Looking out, they saw the Akron police. They came in, and took Mike away in handcuffs. Someone had evidently reported his illegal border crossing to the authorities! Mike was very upset, and couldn't understand how trusting these people – in 'Julia's church' – had resulted in his being thrown in jail. Pastor Katona came to visit him the next day. He told him how sorry he was that his confession had been reported to the police. He said he had not done so, but someone in their church must have overheard him, They found out that it was the young man Bela who had first given him a ride. Pastor Katona said he knew someone in the church who worked for an attorney and sometimes did immigration work. He would speak with her. Erzebet Sabo was able to get her boss, John Barta, an attorney, to accept Mike's case as pro bono, and obtained the right border pass. Unfortunately, this took almost a month, and Mike became very discouraged. He wrote Katie and Joe, but he sensed that things were not going that well…with the boys, or with the farm. It looked like they would lose it. After one month, they released Mike from jail. John Barta corrected his record and accepted Mike's expression of heartfelt gratitude in lieu of payment. He said he did it as unto the Lord, and because he was a Christian, and longtime friend of Pastor Katona. After a farewell service, Mike said goodbye and hitched a ride with someone going to Minneapolis. There he bought a bus ticket for Regina, with the offering the church had taken at his farewell service. He was nervous when they arrived at the border, but they accepted the legal papers that John Barta had prepared. Many hours later, he arrived in Regina.

Julius was waiting for him at the bus station. Mike was very grateful because he had called to tell them he was returning, but didn't expect anyone to meet him. Joe and Katie had said they could not come because, as they later told him, it was too difficult to get their three plus Mike's boys, ready, and bring everyone. Julius said he had some very tragic news. Carl had had a heart attack and was in the hospital. Sharon was with him at the hospital in Regina, but Julius said it didn't look good. Carl was not expected to live. Mike said they must quickly go by the hospital to see him. Sharon met them at the hospital. She was weeping. Carl had just passed away. He was only fifty-eight. Their two boys, Bert and Sammy, were away at college, and couldn't take over the farm. Besides, they had both already made their own plans. Sammy was in Saskatoon, at the University of Saskatchewan; and Bert, who was ahead of him two years, was also at the University of Saskatchewan studying to be an engineer. Sharon said she could not run the farm, but if Julius helped, she might just be able to make it, but only if they scaled down their operation. She hoped her boys might change their minds and come back to help her. But in the meantime, she would move into Regina and live with a niece, try to get another job, and help to keep the farm operational with the savings she and Carl had put away in Norberg Farms, Inc. When Mike asked if Bert and Sammy had been told, Sharon assured him she had just called them, and they were on their way. Mike asked if there was anything else he could do, and Sharon said no, but expressed her concern for him and the family. What would become of them, would Mike and Joe lose their farm, and where would he live? He didn't know, he said. He didn't know yet how to trust God like Julia always had. Sharon said she was so happy he had become a Christian. She would pray for them, and asked him to trust God like Julia always did.

Mike and Julius returned to the farm in silence. Mike's mind was anything but quiet…another blow. What was the use of becoming a Christian? Everything that had happened to him since he 'gave his heart to Jesus,' just like Julia said, had turned sour. He had lost his dear wife, the light of his life. He had been thrown in jail after he confessed his wrongdoing, like he was told to do. He would surely lose the farm, his only means of income. His best friend and mentor had died, and he couldn't even go back to his original employment. They arrived at the little farm, and Julius dropped Mike off. As he said goodbye, Julius told him God was with him…things would work out…he didn't even know that Julius was a God-fearing person. Julius never said much, but he was a good foreman, and went somewhere to church, Mike thought, but he didn't know much about him. Mike thanked him and said goodbye. The boys saw their dad coming and ran out to greet him. "Pop, we're so happy you came back," Michael said. "Me too," said Bud, and Louie just yelled, "Yay!" Joe and Katie came out with their kids, and they all went in the house to hear all about Mike's trip. The only thing in the house to eat were some left over chicken and vegetables, which they all ate heartily. After eating, Mike took the boys to their own side of the house. As he was getting them ready for bed, he noticed a strong smell coming from Bud. He smelled like an Italian kitchen! He then undressed him and noticed some marks on Bud's legs. Then he took off Michael's shirt, and also Louie's. There were marks on all three of their backs or legs…Mike was getting very upset, and demanded to know what had been going on. Bud said they had made Aunt Katie very angry, and when he repeatedly refused to do what she said, she put him in the shed for two days! 'And the smell? Oh, there was nothing to eat,' he said, 'and he got so hungry that he started eating the 'stuff' hanging from the rafters.' Michael laughed…he said it was the garlic that Katie had hung there to dry in the shed. And the marks on their legs and back? She had whipped them with a rope when they wouldn't give their toys to her children, who didn't have any toys. They wanted the ones Michael, Bud, and Louie had made by hand…for themselves. Mike burned with anger. He wanted to go next door and confront Katie and Joe immediately. Instead, before he tucked the boys in bed, for the first time in his life, he asked them to kneel at their bed like Julia had taught them. When he tried to pray, he started to cry. Michael put his arm around him. "Pop, Mommy's in heaven, right? Maybe she can ask God to help us." The next morning, Mike went over after breakfast and confronted Katie and Joe about the abuse of his children. They were defensive, and said his boys were lying. Mike took a deep breath. He told them it was over. He would not live there with them any longer. The bank had already said they would end the homesteading contract by the end of the month, and the harvest had been meager… 'just in time for Thanksgiving'…Mike laughed sardonically. He needed Julia's faith, because…well, because right now…he didn't have any of his own. It seemed like prayer didn't work, and he admitted becoming a Christian had really been more about pleasing Julia than it was about his own need. Yet, something inside him said, if he had no other choice, he might as well trust God. Trusting himself surely had not worked. After all, God had gotten him

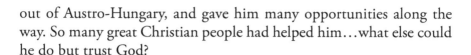

out of Austro-Hungary, and gave him many opportunities along the way. So many great Christian people had helped him…what else could he do but trust God?

Mike and the boys packed up what they had. Julius took him into Gravelbourg. He and Joe ended the homesteading lease with the Gravelbourg Commerce Bank, who wrote off the remainder of what they owed. Joe and Katie had called his brother Sandor in Pittsburgh, Pennsylvania, who had immigrated recently. He said he could get him a steel plant job. Katie used her contacts to become a seamstress. Sandor let them stay with him in the meantime. They parted ways a couple days later. Mike said he forgave them, but they didn't say much, except goodbye. Sandor had said to say hello to him. Ferenc and Margit said Pop and the boys could stay with them, but only temporarily, and they would all have to sleep on the floor, because they rented only a small one-bedroom place. Pop and the boys moved in that afternoon after attending the funeral for Carl Norberg. Sharon was so encouraging, but was apologetic…she just couldn't help them more now that Carl was gone. She promised she would pray for them and said some wonderful things again about Julia, and how good she and Mike had been together. Ferenc and Margit attended the funeral also, made supper for them, and helped them put away the few things they had, before they all retired for the night.

Michael would have to enroll in another school. Pop wasn't sure how long they would be staying with Ferenc and Margit, and with it being almost Thanksgiving, there were only a few weeks left before the semester break. He wanted to find a school where Michael would be able to stay more than a few months, as they had at the Gravelbourg School. Caldwell Grammar School wasn't too far from Ferenc's and Margit's rental house, so he took him there to meet the Principal and inquire about the school. The Caldwell administrator couldn't understand Pop's English, and was quite rude to him, but she said Michael could attend for a few weeks until they found a place to stay. They didn't have any books for him, so Pop tried to go to the library to get some books. They told him he had to have a library card, but without a utility bill, he would have to come back with proof of permanent residence. Michael ended up attending Caldwell only until the Christmas break. Sharon had suggested St. Theresa's Catholic school, but there was a long waiting list. Finally, the Alba School, old and run-down, just blocks away, said they were full but would take a few more immigrant children, and Michael was able to enroll there. He could start after the new year. Bud and Louie were boisterous, so Margit made them play outside. It was cold and they didn't have any winter clothing, so Mike visited Salvation Army thrift shop. There he found shirts, pants, long underwear, and jackets. Seeing how little money he had, a Captain in the Salvation Army overheard them and decided to help them. Mike came home with clothes, proud of himself.

Christmas came and went quickly. Mike and the boys went with Ferenc and Margit to the Romanian Baptist Church, and some of the people there gave them small gifts and some Christmas dinner. Things began to unravel after the first of the year. Mike knew they couldn't stay with Ferenc and Margit any longer...but they really had nowhere else to go. The boys began to fight with each other. Mike and Margit began to argue about his boys' behavior, and Ferenc wasn't around much because he worked odd hours. Ferenc tried to stay out of it, but he finally said he would talk to Pastor Chesciu and see if he could get some help for them. Ferenc and Margit said they were so sorry, but that Mike and his boys would have to leave; they simply didn't have room for them.

That was how Mrs. Sullivan came into their lives. She had lost her husband two years before, and met Mike and the boys at the church at Christmas time. Pastor had talked to her about another matter, and the 'Hungarian widower' and his boys, had come up. In the meantime, Mike had gotten a job–selling coal on the streets of Regina for Foster Coal and Wood Company. Ferenc had heard about the opening through his friend, a plumbing apprentice, who had also previously worked for Norberg Farms, Inc., as a part time book keeper. Sharon Norberg had put in a good word about Pop and his boys. So, Esther Sullivan let Pop and the three boys stay in a small room above her garage. Michael walked to school with some Romanian boys from the church. Pop started selling coal on the streets. Mrs. Sullivan watched Bud and Louie, and helped feed the family when Pop didn't have enough to buy food. He shopped at the Salvation Army store every now and then, but the boys didn't care much for the 'quality.' Pop told them to be grateful for what they had. He had been wearing shoes that were little more than cardboard; when he came in every night, his feet were half frozen. Mrs. Sullivan loaned him a little money to buy a decent pair of used shoes and some boots to go with them. She had offered to buy them, but Pop said no, he would pay her back…it was only a loan. Bud had already turned five, and Louie was having a birthday in a couple weeks…he would be turning three. Michael hated it that he had already attended first grade in three different schools, and next month he would be seven. It was a tough winter, but they made it, by the grace of God, the kindness of Mrs. Sullivan – a God-fearing and kind Baptist lady – and the perseverance of Mike Varro and his orphaned boys.

At the end of March, when Michael and his friends arrived at the Alba School, they saw a sign reading 'The Alba School is closed until further notice.' Michael was able to read since he was five, but in Hungarian only, and struggled to learn English well enough to read everything. He asked what was going on. They told him the school was closed. The principal was there, explaining to parents who had gathered that they ran out of money and didn't have the funds to continue. Where would they send their children? Hamilton, and McKensie were taking as much of the overflow as they could for now, the principal explained, and that they were taking the students over there right now. Michael didn't know what to do, so he returned home, and Mrs. Sullivan sent word for Mike to come. The next day Pop took Michael over to Hamilton. It was several blocks further, but he was able to finish the school year there. In June, Pop asked for Michael to be placed in the second grade, but they said no, he hadn't finished more than four months in any one of four schools: Gravelbourg, Caldwell, Alba, and Hamilton. Pop pleaded with them to teach him in the summer, but they refused. Instead, they said if he finished a full year of first grade at Hamilton the following year, they would evaluate him; maybe he could test out of second, and go on to third grade. He had no other choice. They weren't even sure they would have a home in the Hamilton area the next year.

Mike and the children sometimes attended the Romanian Baptist Church with Ferenc and Margit, but Mike kept writing the church in Akron, hoping they would send someone to start an Apostolic Christian Church in Regina. When he tried to pray, he would think of Julia and start to weep. He wished that Parson Watson was closer, maybe he would go to his church, like they had done in Gravelbourg.

He didn't like selling coal, and could only work that job in the winter anyway. In the summer he would have to get odd jobs just to keep things together. Mrs. Sullivan was a dear soul, but her health started turning for the worse in the spring. Her children said she would have to come live with them in Calgary. She didn't want to, but they said she could not live alone, and were coming in April to sell the house and move her out. Mike didn't know what he was going to do. Pastor Cesiascu was out of resources, Ferenc and Margit could not help them, and Sharon had run out of resources.

Mike cried out to God to help him. He had come to the end of his faith... and honestly, he had run out of hope, too. He often took a walk to look in the store windows and clear his mind. Suddenly, as he walked, he knew what he must do. He would go to the Salvation Army for help. Later, when he went to their facility, they prayed with him, and began asking among their membership if there was anyone that could help. Major Chapman McPherson, a retired Major in the Salvation Army, heard about Mike's desperate need and asked him to come visit. Mike had to bring the boys with him because Mrs. Sullivan was leaving the next day. Major McPherson listened to Mike pour out his heart. He told the Major about meeting Julia and leaving Austro-Hungary under cover of darkness, about getting from New York to Milwaukee, and then to Gravelbourg, and finally Regina. The boys played outside while they talked. Major asked him what kind of work he had done. Mike told him about farming, selling coal, and odd jobs wherever he could get them. Major McPherson was confused and asked Michael if he was working for the railroad when he met Julia. Wasn't that what he had told him? Then 'Chap' told Mike an amazing story...He had been an alcoholic and had lost everything – his family, friends, job, everything! He turned to God at a Salvation Army mission meeting, and then lived in a Salvation Army residence facility for a year. It came out in their weekly prayer meetings that, before he was delivered by God from drinking, he had been a brakeman on the railroad. He left his wife in Illinois for a woman he met who worked with Great Northern. She worked in the front office in Billings, Montana. They were both alcoholics but when the bottom dropped out, he spent two years trying to find his wife again. He found out she had committed suicide, and his children were married and gone…where, he did not know. He didn't even remember how he got to Regina, but God was waiting for him there. Major McPherson told Mike something else…that changed his life forever. Chap had a ministry…with the railroad! Canadian Pacific Railroad was one of his missions, and he happened to know that they were hiring experienced brakemen. He wondered if Mike would be interested? Not only that, but Salvation Army was running a summer school; so his boys could stay in the facility for the summer, and Michael could be tutored in English to prepare him for the first grade curriculum. By fall of the next school year, Michael might be able to start first grade and then test out to complete second and third grades. That way, he would catch up with his class. Chap knew the principal, and he thought she could do some basic testing. Since Bud would be turning six in November, he could also start preparing for first grade. Mike listened carefully to Chap's story. He was truly amazed at God's work in his life. Everything sounded too good to be true. His first job, and his memories of it…back in Timisoara… were still so pleasant. There was just one problem. With Mrs. Sullivan leaving tomorrow, they still had no place to live. Chap smiled. He said, "Let's get you a job first. God is working all of this out, he will provide the answers to all of your questions." They all went by trolley to the train station. Chap introduced Mike to the Canadian Pacific representative while the boys played in the station. In the end it was his experience that got him the job. He answered all of their questions and proved how knowledgeable he was. The supervisor was impressed…and offered him a job. After thanking the supervisor and the representative, Mike and Chap called the boys and turned to leave. Mike was so grateful… but still, how could he possibly afford a place to live? Chap held up his hand, as if to stop him. "How much money do you have per month now?" Mike answered that he had 'about enough to feed his family, but nothing left with which to pay rent.' Chap motioned for them to get back on the trolley; he wanted to show Mike and the boys 'something.' They took the trolley toward the rail yard… and right near where the line ended, Chap showed them what he was talking about…it was a ***boxcar*** on the siding, just north of what was called 'Germantown.' "Now that you work for the Canadian Pacific Railroad, let me show you *your new home.*" And this is how a boxcar became their home for the next few years; as long as they maintained it well, they could live in it without paying rent, Chap said. God truly had answered Mike's prayers! Pop called the boys. Michael came running up to the boxcar, with Bud and Louie close behind… *a home of their very own?* Major McPherson and Pop smiled, then they bowed their heads and thanked God for his mercy. That summer, Mike worked to make the boxcar livable, and several from the Salvation Army mission donated small pieces of furniture, beds, chairs, tables, and bedding and towels, as well as food. Michael began summer classes at the Salvation Army School; he was tutored in English and other subjects. Bud and Louie spent their days playing in the area around the boxcar, but Bud also took classes that helped prepare him for his first year at Wetmore. It was close enough to walk to, but in the winter, trudging through the snow the few blocks in the bitter cold, was very difficult. It was a small school, but it housed grades one to eight. primary–the first three grades; intermediate–the next three grades; then finally middle school–grades seven and eight. High school students were bused to Regina High School. Michael started first grade again; by Christmas he had tested out and advanced to second grade; Bud started first grade, and Louis was able to stay with a neighbor lady during the day: Aneta Cicansky. She had two younger children of her own, Eli, and Katina, so Louie had someone to play with. Alex, her husband, worked with Canadian National Railroad, so he was gone quite a bit of the time. So – after attending six different schools – Michael finally 'finished' first grade. He progressed very quickly after that, much to his father's pride. They lived in the old boxcar by the rail yard, near Germantown, until Michael was ten, Bud was eight, and Louie was six. Germantown was really a ghetto. Not just Germans, but Austrians, Romanians, Polish, Ukrainians, and Hungarians lived there. The city of Regina wasn't able to provide even basic services. Many families lived in shanties of wood, metal, and even cardboard. The winters were brutally cold, many became ill, or died. Many more immigrated from eastern Europe. It was years before the terrible living conditions improved.

'Mihaly VI', Juliana, Michael, 1913

Juliana Kis Varro (1892-1919)

Pop, Michael, Louis, & Stevan

During their time in the old boxcar

a wealth of stories and

lessons of life were

learned

Chapter Four

From the boxcar to the cross

Life on the Prairie

EVEN THOUGH LIFE IN THE BOXCAR WAS NEVER EASY, IT REALLY FELT LIKE home for the first time since Pop had arrived in the new world. Michael and Bud were coming home from school one day when they saw a black dog with its leg caught in one of the old ties by the tracks. He had gnawed at his leg trying to free himself until his skin was all wounded and bloodied.

Michael approached him cautiously, but the dog growled menacingly, baring his fangs. Bud got a stick and was going to hit him if he bit Michael, but he told Bud to put away the stick as it would make things worse. He talked softly to the dog, and then darting suddenly into the boxcar, he brought some bread and a cup of water, and put it within reach of the dog, continuing to talk softly to him. The dog was a black Labrador, and Michael had just learned that afternoon how to say the English word "blacksmith." In Hungarian, the word for blacksmith was 'kovacs,' so Michael said to Bud, "Hey, let's call him "Kovacs," because he looks black like a "blacksmith." Bud yelled, "Hey, Kovacs, nice doggy, nice doggy." Louie heard them from Mrs. Cicansky's, and he came running over. Michael was finally able to get Kovacs to drink a little water. As he inched closer, Michael was able to touch him without being bitten. He carefully pried the wounded leg from the railroad tie. Getting an old piece of cloth, he wrapped the wounded leg, after using a little of the water to clean it. Kovacs wagged his tail...he even let Bud and Louie pet him as well. When Pop got home, he said they could only keep Kovács if nobody claimed him, and if he acted like he wanted to stay. Well, of course you know what happened...no one came for him, and he stayed around. The boys fed him and gave him water. They even made a little bed for him to lie in. Kovacs was the first of several dogs they had over the years.

Our first dog at the boxcar, Kovacs

Pop had never been happy with the Romanian Baptist Church, and he finally found an Apostolic Christian Church, one that had just started, after a new wave of Hungarian immigrants arrived. Ferenc and Margit were still attending the Romanian Baptist Church, but offered to pick up the boys for the Sunday School at the Baptist Church if Pop wanted to go to his own church. Pop had always said he didn't want them to attend there anymore, and that he really wanted them to go to a "Nazorean" Church and Sunday School, like Julia had. Ferenc told Pop he was willing to take them to the "Nazarene" church that they had talked about before. Pop thought about it a long time, then said maybe that would be okay, but only to the Sunday School, because the Apostolic Christian Church didn't have one and his boys should be with other young people. Besides, he assumed the two churches must be similar since they had the "same name." So it was that Ferenc started taking the boys to the First Church of the Nazarene in Regina. Pop would wait until they finished Sunday School, and then they would all attend the worship service at the Apostolic Christian Church together.

Michael was particularly interested in learning about the Bible, and they taught it thoroughly in both Sunday School and in the Worship Service at the Nazarene Church; they invited Michael to their junior youth meetings, but Pop would not allow it at the time. He didn't want them to forget their Hungarian, so he used that as an excuse to spend as much time at the Apostolic Christian Church as possible where the services were in Hungarian. Michael learned many of the old-style hymns in Hungarian, so when they sang the same ones at the Nazarene church, he would get confused. Bud and Louie were at a difficult age, and Pop often seemed distracted by all his 'old-country' friends, so it was up to big brother Michael to be 'father and mother' to them most of the time.

Louie turned five, and wanted to start first grade at Wetmore with Bud and Michael. He had learned English more easily than they because the Cikansky's spoke English in the home, even though both she and her husband were Polish. They had grown up speaking English since they had immigrated earlier than the Varro's, and Eli and Katina spoke English as their native tongue, so when Louie played with them, he learned English quickly. Pop finally was able to get a library card, and he checked out books for himself, and the boys, to try and improve their English; so Louie was reading even before he started school the following year. Michael was an avid reader and insisted on speaking English at home with Bud and Louie, even though Pop would speak to them only in Hungarian. Pop continued to try and furnish the boxcar with things he would pick up at the Salvation Army store, along with clothing that Bud and Michael were embarrassed to wear, but since it was the only clothing that they had, except for hand-me-downs Ferenc and Margit would give them from time to time, they accepted it. Ever since Ferenc's accident they hadn't been able to have children, so when Wetmore School announced that two boys had been orphaned…that a terrible fire had claimed the lives of their Romanian parents, Margit suggested to Ferenc that they adopt them. It was a big decision, but Ferenc and Margit had taken them in last year. The eleven-year-old was Sandor, and the nine year old was Zoltan. They became like cousins to the Varro boys. Ferenc had been like an uncle to Pop's boys, and whatever clothes Sandor and Zoltan outgrew were passed down to Michael, then Bud, and finally Louie. Pop worked long hours on the railroad and often got home to the boxcar long after the boys had gone to bed. Ferenc and Margit had moved to their side of town and lived in another small rental house, like the one they had had, but with one more bedroom which Sandor and Zoltan shared. Pop's boys often stayed there until bedtime and then would walk home if it wasn't too cold.

It was 1923, and Michael had just turned ten, Bud was eight, and Louie six, and would start first grade at Wetmore in the fall. Their lives were becoming comfortably routine, but Pop couldn't seem to advance in his job. He still had little to show in his savings. People at his church began to ask him when he would remarry. 'When would the boys have a mother? When would they move into a more decent dwelling?' Some suggested a few of the single women in Pop's church, but he didn't seem even the slightest bit interested in any of them. He had almost no social life, even though the boys had become active with the pre-teen group at the Nazarene church. Pop had allowed them to go on picnics and birthday parties at the church; but they mostly stayed at the boxcar or were over at Ferenc's and Margit's place, playing with Zoltan and Sandor.

Pop had made contact with friends back in Timisoara (which was now part of Romania), in Budapest, and some distant family in Karcag, in the Great Plains area of Hungary. A Novi Sad cousin had mutual acquaintances in Budapest who suggested he start corresponding with members of the Dornyei family. Julius and Imre Dornyei were friends of the Balla and Varro family. Ferenc Balla wrote Pop that Julius and Imre had a sister, Maria Gold, that they thought would be a good person with whom to correspond. She had been employed in the city government in Budapest, and was looking to correspond with Hungarians in the U.S. and Canada. Pop was not interested, but when Ferenc kept writing him about the matter, he said he would at least give it some thought.

Memories of the old country flooded his mind from time to time, and even though he had never been very musical, he loved the old Hungarian folksongs and gypsy songs. Back in Timisoara, Julia sang so beautifully, and he tried to play a harmonica. There was one gypsy song he had taught the boys, which they all loved to sing together:

Szép asszonynak kurizálok	**The beautiful lady I'm wooing**
Szep asszonynak kurizalok, kurizalok, kurizalok,	It's a beautiful lady I'm wooing, wooing,
Az uranak fittyet hanyok, fittyet hanyok, fittyet hanyok	To her father I pay no attention,
Jaj, jaj, jaj, jaj a szivem, meg ne tudja senki sem	Ay, yay, yay, yay, my heart, no one knows
Hogy en magat olyan nagyon szeretem,	How much I love her,
Csak a cigány egyedul, aki nekem hegedul,	Only the gypsy who plays me the violin,
Csak azt tudja egyedul.	He alone knows.
Hazuk elott van egy arok, van egy arok, van egy arok.	Before their home is a ditch, a ditch,
Minden este arra jarok, arra jarok, arra jarok.	Every night I go there, I go there, I go there.

Jaj, jaj, jaj, jaj a szivem, meg ne tudja senki sem, hogy	Ay, yay, yay, yay, my heart, no one knows
Azt a kislanyt olyan nagyon szeretem,	How love his daughter, Only the notary
Csak a jegyző, meg a pap, aki minket osszead,	And the priest who will marry us, knows.

Pop was at the Salvation Army store one day, buying some old clothes like he usually did, and he found an old harmonica. He was so excited he bought it, brought it home and announced to the boys that they were going to make some special food that night…and sing some of the Hungarian gypsy and folk songs. They all pitched in and made a wonderful dinner together. Pop had also gone to the European bakery down the street, and picked up some Poppyseed Cake. So, when they had finished eating their *chicken paprikas*, fresh beans, and poppyseed cake, Pop pulled out the mysterious little box he had bought and proudly presented his 'new' harmonica. The boys were delighted and began singing *Szép asszonynak jurizálok* (the song above), The boys squealed with joy when moments like this happened, they all felt so content. The boys would ask Pop to tell them the stories about the 'old country.' He loved telling them the stories of their heritage; they would fall asleep like a bunch of contented puppies. Pop knew that he had to think about getting them a stepmother. He sat down and wrote his first letter to Maria Gold. He also knew that he couldn't bring a new mother into their lives and live in the boxcar. The time had come to think about another home.

Chap McPherson had checked in on the Varro family from time to time. He was happy that the boys were becoming active with the young people's program at the Church of the Nazarene, and he had secretly hoped that Pop would join them. Many of the eastern Europeans were more and more comfortable with a less European worship environment. He had stayed busy with his work with missions, and his retirement had been prior to his turning fifty years old. Since then, he'd been elected President of the Regina Interchurch Council, and worked along the chair of Regina Christian Missions group, Marilyn Chandler. Their contact, at first just cordial, had become more than just a business relationship. They dated a couple years, and then he had asked her to marry him. He did not know that she had come from a Methodist background, but her mother had joined the Nazarene Church after her father died, and Marilyn had chosen to care for her, and not to marry until after she was already over forty years of age. They were married at the First Church of the Nazarene in June of 1923. It was one of the few times Pop ever came to the Nazarene Church, but he was so grateful to Chap and Marilyn for all they had done for him and his family, and he felt he had to be present. Michael was a junior groomsman, and the two younger Varro's brought the ring in on a pillow to the howls of all their friends. Pop cried, remembering his dear Julia, and Marilyn was so gracious at the reception.

By this time, Pop had written several letters to Maria Gold, and her brother Julius was planning to leave Budapest and immigrate to Canada. Everyone was kidding Pop about being an 'old bachelor,' and told him it was time for him to remarry as well. Marilyn was the one, as chair of the Regina Missions, who had found a place on Elliott Street where Pop and the boys could live and told Chap about it. He went to look at it. It needed a lot of work, but between Pop and Ferenc, Chap thought it could be fixed up very nicely. He had formed a non-profit entity, McPherson Christian Missions, Inc., and he helped them finance it as part of a mission project. The three boys could have some of the old bunks the Salvation Army had stored at their old warehouse, and they could move everything that was salvageable from the old boxcar to their new house. Marilyn went to garage sales and picked up some old kitchen and household items.

They moved in a month later. The bunks had arrived and the boys no longer had to sleep in makeshift boxes that had been their beds in the old boxcar. Pop took the other small bedroom. Someone that Marilyn knew from the Nazarene Church donated a small icebox, and the wood stove was moved from the boxcar as well. In the meantime, Pop had been writing Maria Gold a couple times a month, and her brother Julius had arrived and was living with a cousin in Regina. Pop met him and talked about visiting Budapest to meet Maria. She had sent a picture, as had Pop, but Julius was able to show him pictures of the whole family and shared a little family background. Maria's mother, Erzebet, had worked in the city government building in Budapest as an elevator operator. The Jewish-Hungarian mayor, who saw her daily in the elevator on his way up to his office, had taken a liking to her. When she did not reciprocate his advances, he forced himself on her one day in his office. She became pregnant, and Maria was born of that union. The mayor would not marry her; he had not told her he was already married. Erzebet thought she would have to remain single, but a kind man, Zoltan Dornyei, who knew her, because they worked together in the Budapest government building, had always been fond of her. They began a relationship and eventually married. Julius was the first-born of the Dornyei children. His younger brother was Imre. They discovered they had common family roots in Voivodina, in Serbia, and Karcag, the Great Plains between Danube and Tisza rivers.

Pop decided the boys needed a mother, and it was time for him to move on. It was hard to believe Julia had died five years previously. He told Julius he wanted to marry Maria and bring her back with him to Regina. He had already suggested it to Maria. Julius was happy. He would help bring his sister to Canada. Chap McPherson told them he would help as well, and that it would be much easier if they married by proxy, and then Pop could go back to Budapest and bring her back with him as his wife. Julius said they needed to change their names to the Canadian way: his name would stay the same but Maria would be called Mary – Mary Gold. They started making plans for the new family that they would become. Pop told the boys one night at supper they would have a new mother. They were very excited. Michael remembered his mother Julia, but Bud had only the slightest memory of her, and Louie – who was only two at the time – had no memory of her at all. It was all so wonderful! A new mother…in a new home. It was hard to believe! With her approval, following Pop's arrangements and Chap's directions, Margit stepped in as proxy, and Ferenc was Pop's best man. Chap McPherson met them at the courthouse, and Pop and Mary Gold were officially married – albeit by proxy. It was the summer of 1923.

Later that month, Pop traveled to New York on his rail pass with Canadian Pacific, and then sailed on a freighter to Amsterdam. Canadian Pacific allowed him a few weeks of "family leave" in order to travel, but he wouldn't be paid for that time off. The boys stayed with Ferenc and Margit. From Amsterdam, Pop traveled to Budapest by train. It was his first time back to Hungary since he had left in 1914. He was moved to tears. All his memories of Julia, his time in the Army, the difficult circumstances…all flooded his mind. Imre Dörnyei met his train, and introduced himself. They went in Imre's car to Zoltán and Erzebet's home where he met Mary. She was just as he had imagined; she looked just like her pictures. They all teased them: 'since they were already married, they could stay together in her room.' This embarrassed them both. They would rather get to know each other a little before sharing a room. The next day Mary and Mike went around Budapest seeing the sights. Mike hadn't been to Budapest since he and his father Sandor had visited distant relatives when he was just a young child living in Voivodina. *Most importantly, Sandor gave the Res mozar to Mike!* Because it was still risky for him to visit Voivodina and Timoşoara, so soon after World War I, (he had, after all, left 'without permission'), some of his family came up to Budapest to visit him. It was a joyful and tear-filled reunion. They were so sorry to hear about Julia, but happy that Pop was remarrying. When Mary and Pop had spent a few days together, she packed up her things and they traveled to Amsterdam. From there they sailed to New York, where they both used Mike's rail-pass to travel safely home to Regina. He had been gone about five weeks, and Pop was anxious to see his boys and get back to work. Since he had used up his money, and with no income during that time, it was important for Mike to help Mary settle in and get back to work quickly. *He made sure he put the Res mozar safely away.*

The boys didn't know how to act when they met their new stepmother, but Margit helped them with some lessons in proper manners and etiquette, and this helped them all become a family quickly. Mary liked the boys, especially Michael, who was more quiet and polite. It took some time for the younger boys to get used to having a woman in the house. Mary's family went to the Hungarian Reformed Church, but she was okay with attending church with Pop. She didn't like the idea of the boys going to the Church of the Nazarene, and she said so. Pop was not harsh with her, but he bristled a bit at her stern ways, and had to force himself to stay out of her way when she constantly corrected the boys' unruliness. She helped set up the house on Elliott Street. It was a huge change having 'a woman's touch' in the house, cooking decent meals, and helping to raise the boys. In the fall, all three boys were attending Wetmore. It was a little further from Elliott than the boxcar, but still close enough to be their neighborhood school. Louie started first grade, Bud was in third, and Michael was in fifth. They always had had only a piece of stale bread for lunch, but now Mary, their new 'mother,' would fix them sandwiches of peanut butter or leftover meat from the previous night's supper. Pop, who had always gone without any lunch, was now given the same kind of lunch as the boys.

It was a cold winter, but Chap and Marilyn McPherson gave them some wood that had been donated to the mission for their stove. So, they were able to cook their meals, and have wood left over to burn for warmth, in the little house on Elliott. Ferenc and Margit continued to stop by to take them all to church. Pop and Mary attended the Apostolic Christian Church. Against the strenuous objections of Mary, Pop said he had decided to allow his sons to stay for the worship service at the Church of the Nazarene rather than require them to come to the Apostolic Christian Church. Michael had won a scripture memorization contest there, and was on a team competing with other churches. As former president of the Interchurch Council, Chap McPherson set it up. Even though Michael was only eleven years old, he came in third place. By the end of the next school year, Mary told Pop she was pregnant. At first, Pop panicked, thinking the tragedy that had befallen his beloved Julia would somehow strike them again. He made sure she saw the doctor regularly. They didn't live too far from Regina General Hospital, where Julia had died. Mary could walk there, but Ferenc and Margit frequently drove her. When Michael turned twelve that February, Pop wanted him to try to get a job to help out with expenses. Mary wanted to work too, but fearing she'd get sick, *like Julia,* Mike allowed her to work only part-time, as seamstress, and in a laundry nearby. Bud became friends with some of the eastern European families, and many of the boys were from single parent homes, and kind of rough. Bud had picked up smoking occasionally, drinking, and foul language from the boys, and even from their dads, uncles, or cousins. Because Pop was gone much of the time, Michael, who had acted as both 'father,' and even 'mother,' was quick to correct Bud's, and eventually Louie's behavior. Their care for personal hygiene was already minimal, but bumming cigarettes and drinking from used beer bottles increased the problem. Michael had always been a serious-minded boy who didn't want to be influenced by the bad neighborhood. So he felt he had to be harsh, even mean, to steer his younger brothers in the right direction. His stepmother was a God-send, as far as he was concerned, and welcomed her taking charge and correcting Bud's and Louie's behavior. But Mary's job, and her pregnancy, had taken her away from spending much time with the boys, especially after school. Pop did not understand this, and put more and more pressure on Michael to find a job to help meet expenses. Again, Chap and Marilyn McPherson stepped in to assist. Regina Photo & Portrait needed a person to help in the back room with photo finishing. It was run by a Ukrainian Orthodox man, Anton Sirko, whom Chap had known from Interchurch Council days. Michael liked the idea but Pop wasn't so sure. He wanted Michael to work, but it was a long walk. Michael said he could take the trolley, and now that Mary was their stepmother, he didn't have to help with the boys and supper as much. Finally, Pop said okay. Michael started his first job – at Regina Photo & Portrait. He worked after school from 3:00 until 8:00, and in the summer, he worked all day. He started the next week. It was cold, and he was very hungry by the time he got home, and still had homework to do. He finished work promptly every evening, took the trolley home, ate his cold supper by himself, and did his homework before going to bed. He was a good student. By the time school was out in June, Mary, who was now nine months pregnant, depended even more on Michael to help her out. In July, Mary's and Pop's first child, of the 'second family,' was born. Pop and Mary named him Joska, but he was known as 'little Joe' from the beginning. Michael, Bud, and Louie were overjoyed with their new little brother. Mary and baby were healthy, and the delivery went well. He was born in the same hospital where Julia had died. Pop cried, and thanked God for his gift of life. Mary wanted baby Joska christened in the Apostolic Christian Church, so they had it done there the next Sunday. And so, the second family began. Two years later Jim (Imre) was born, then Margaret (Margit) a little over a year after that, then two years later Irene (Iren), and finally Frank (Ferenc) two years after that. They all went by their 'anglicized' names. In all, Mary had five children in seven years! Of the entire eight children, four of them –

Bud, Lou, Joe, and Jim – were artists or architects…it was their hobby. The others all dabbled at it. All of them became active in either the Apostolic Christian Church, or the Church of the Nazarene, at some point. Michael had gotten back to work as soon as Joe was born. He worked long hard hours, like Pop. He even took a few photo-finishing jobs on the side, but didn't think to report it as personal income to his boss. They liked his work, and didn't question anything that he did but he was also running around with some boys in the neighborhood that were…from 'okay families' but typical teenagers. Sometimes they got in trouble. One weekend, several of them went out to the edge of town by the train trestle. They put small stones on the track to watch the train shatter them when they passed by. One particular day, the boys wanted to see how big the stone would have to be that might shatter without stopping the train. Michael was just going along with them, and merely watched. When the train came by, instead of shattering the stones this time, the train wheel jammed… and derailed a couple of cars. The train stopped, the boys ran away, and the brakemen came running after them, but they were never caught. Except for this, and other minor infractions, Michael was really an exemplary student and son.

After a few years, the Nazarene church got a new young pastor, Rev. Neil Reynolds, and it began to grow, reaching out especially to the immigrant population of Regina. By the fall, Rev. Reynolds announced that some special weekday evening meetings were going to be held… called a 'Revival'…and a special speaker from Texas was coming, whom they called 'Uncle Buddy Robinson.' Michael made sure that he didn't have to work that Wednesday night, because he wanted to sing in the choir. They had said that everyone who wanted to sing could join them. Michael was only sixteen, but he loved music. He said, "As a true 'Magyar,' I love the violin the most", but he liked singing as well. He especially liked the gospel hymn he had heard them sing last Sunday, 'His Eye Is On The Sparrow.' He was interested in the fact that the lyricist was a Canadian. The choir director recognized him, and welcomed him to sing with them because she knew he had a nice baritone voice. Uncle Buddy preached his heart out, and then he did a strange thing…at least to Michael, who had not experienced this before: he asked everyone who wanted to be 'saved,' to come and kneel at the altar rail. They sang another nice song, 'Just As I Am,' and before he knew it, the girl in front of him in the choir got out of the loft and went down and knelt at the rail. The nice man next to him asked if he wanted Jesus to come into his heart. Michael just nodded, because he didn't know what that meant. The man asked him to follow him, and the two of them went and knelt at the rail while everyone kept singing. Bud and Lou, who always sat with Chap and Marilyn on the front row, started to laugh, watching Michael go forward. Chap sat with the boys while Marilyn, and the man who had sat with him in the choir, began praying with Michael. He was very moved. Marilyn sounded so loving, and the man prayed too. Michael found out later his name was George Coulter. Then Michael prayed as they told him to, repeating after them. They asked him if he believed God had saved him, through Jesus' death and resurrection. Michael said he did. He felt a great love coming from these people. They said he was now 'saved'…that he had become a Christian. Just like Pop had when he went to Akron, Ohio. Just like they told him his mother Julia had. Then everyone was singing, and crying, and smiling at him. Everything felt so wonderful! Right away, Michael began to feel guilty about keeping the money from his extra photo finishing job. He also felt bad about participating in the train derailment. He told George and Marilyn about it. They said it was good that he had repented, but that Jesus had forgiven him; Jesus knew he was truly sorry. Bud and Louie came up and slapped him on the back. They said they wanted to be 'saved' someday too. Years later, they did profess Jesus as Savior as well, but didn't understand those things at that time. Michael couldn't stop talking about how bad he felt for having taken the extra photo-finishing jobs and pocketing the money, so Chap offered to go to Regina Photo & Portrait with him to make it right. When they talked to Mr. Sirko, he was angry at first, but when Chap offered to pay him, he started to laugh, and said Michael was such a good worker, he would just consider it a 'bonus.' He even offered Michael an extra twenty-five cents per hour, which was a lot in those days. Michael still had a stirring inside of him. The next Sunday evening, Rev. Reynolds preached on John Wesley, and his views of the 'sanctified life' and 'scriptural holiness.' He said those who wanted to experience a 'second work of grace,' and going on with the Lord, should come to the altar and pray. Michael came forward, hungry to receive this heart of perfect love. He said the Holy Spirit moved in him, 'like John Wesley.' Michael became even more active in the Church of the Nazarene. He had kept the photo-finishing job, and helped his stepmother even more at home with the cleaning and cooking. Bud and Louie also took on more of the chores. Bud was still sneaking around getting cigarettes from the neighbors. Lou sometimes went with Bud, because Mary, their stepmother had her hands full with little Joe. Pop was still gone quite a bit, and the next year Mary was pregnant again, but the baby, a little girl they named Mary, died a few days after she was born. She was buried next to Julia. Pop went there to visit often. Mary was soon pregnant again, this time with Jim, and very shortly after that, with Margaret. The house on Elliott was just too small. It had only two bedrooms, so Joe now slept in the boys' room, and Jim, and the new baby, Margaret, slept in Pop and Mary's bedroom. Pop started looking again for a larger place…but would he be able to afford one?

Rev. Reynolds and Chap McPherson stopped by one day. It was Pop's day off. They said they knew he was looking for a larger home. Rev. Reynolds, with the help of Chap, had found a place, and wanted them to come see it. They drove a few blocks toward Victoria, turned right, drove a few blocks, and pulled up in front of a small two-story A-framed house. It was 123 Victoria. Pop and Michael got out and went into the house. Alec Bronsky, a retired Captain who had been in the Salvation Army for several years with Major Chap McPherson, had lived there until last week. His wife had died a year ago, and his health recently took a turn for the worse. His daughter had insisted that he move in with her and her husband, which he had finally done a few days earlier. Pop had gotten another raise with CPR, Mary was doing alright as a part time seamstress, and Michael was helping with his photo finishing job after school. Chap said he had figured it out: they might just be able to rent this house, and even own it, if they chose to. They certainly needed the extra room. Jimmy was two, and Margaret was a baby. Michael was already sixteen, Bud was fourteen, Lou was almost twelve…that meant Joe was four already. They were running out of space… and beds! Although Pop was doubtful, Michael, who had always been good with numbers, was very positive. He told Pop he thought they could make it. Chap asked Pop what he thought.

It would be on the market only a few days. If they didn't take it, it would probably be gone. Someone else had already made an offer, but hadn't put any deposit down. Pop said he would ask Mary. She didn't like the pressure of quick decisions, but asked her brother Julius, who liked to use the local idioms, said with his thick Hungarian accent, "Mary…you jump on it," and laughed. Julius had also gotten a job with Canadian Pacific, and wanted to move to Regina, but had had to settle for living with a friend in Swift Current for the time being. Rev. Reynolds and Chap came by the next day, and Pop said they would do it; they would take the house…the Lord had brought them this far, he would take them the rest of the way.

So Pop, Mary, and their 'mushrooming family,' started packing up again. This time they were renting a two-story house, and might even own it someday. Pastor Reynolds gathered the family together in their new home, and offered a prayer of blessing for protection and guidance. God had brought them through the worst times, but now had blessed them with a new home. Pastor Reynolds gave thanksgiving to God that he would carry them through, to enjoy all the things God had in store for them in the future. Chap also offered prayer for Michael's new found faith in Christ, and that God would lead him into new adventures with God.

Michael, who had attended six different schools before he finished first grade at Wetmore, went on to finish fourth grade by the time he was ten. He caught up with his classmates and finished middle school by the time he was fourteen. He started at Regina High School, but Pop, who had had only a fourth-grade education, made him drop out. He said the 'family needed him' to work – to help meet expenses. He promised he would let him finish high school in a couple of years. It was a constant source of strife between Pop and Michael for the next several years. Rev. Reynolds and Chap wanted him to continue to be active with the church, but Pop opposed that too. He wanted Michael to get a job with the railroad, and work with him. There were many paths to follow, and a lot of pressure on Michael. His heart was not in his work at Regina Photo and Portrait. He wanted to follow God… wherever that might lead.

The call upon Michael's life was leading him…away from the prairie

CHAPTER FIVE

YOU WANT ME TO GO WHERE?

Leaving the prairie

ICHAEL STARTED TEACHING A SUNDAY SCHOOL CLASS FOR YOUNG people at church. Bud and Lou had professed faith in Christ and had joined the Nazarene Young People's Society that Michael was leading. Rev. Reynolds suggested that he preach occasionally when they went on 'mission opportunities' to some of the small farming communities on Sunday afternoons. Michael felt awkward speaking in public, but loved the Bible, and diligently prepared the short sermons that he would deliver with Rev. Reynolds' help. In fact, Michael was considered the pastor of the church in the little town of Boyle near Regina for almost a year. Chap and Marilyn sometimes went along to preach and lead singing. George Coulter, the man from the choir, had gone away to Calgary Bible Institute. He wrote Michael several times about considering the ministry. Michael sometimes led the music, and even sang solos. Of course, whatever Michael did, Bud and Lou had to copy, so they went along on some of these mission trips as well. Pop and Mary started taking Joe, Jimmy, and their little sister to the Apostolic Christian Church. Although her name was Margaret, they had started calling her Mugs (Bud said it rhymed with 'bugs,' because she was as 'cute as a little bug'). Irene was born when Margaret was two...and the baby of the family, Frankie, came two years later.

Bud and Lou both showed promise as artists, and had enrolled at Prairie School of Art after finishing middle school, but both left to get jobs after a few months. Bud became an electrician's apprentice, and Lou worked for a buyer at Regina Art Institute. They both finished high school a few years later, but in the meantime, their income helped with expenses.

Michael did not like the idea of Pop and Mary attending a different church than the rest of the family. Joe, Jim, and Mugs had been attending the Apostolic Christian Church, but he, Bud, and Lou were attending the Church of the Nazarene. Michael asked if they could all start attending the Church of the Nazarene together. After all, hadn't they first started attending there because of Pop, who thought it was the same as, or similar to, the church he had attended with Julia in the Old Country? Pop was stubborn, and wouldn't even listen to the idea. He also thought the Nazarenes were too strict about things like smoking, drinking, their mode of dress, and other social issues. Pop himself was very fond of his brandy, especially during the winter months...and wine. But would he allow Michael to pick up the rest of the family, so they could attend the Church of the Nazarene together? Pop and Mary finally agreed to let the ones who wanted to, to attend with Michael, Bud, and Lou. The others would attend Apostolic Christian with them. Joe was the only one who wished to stay, except the smaller children...

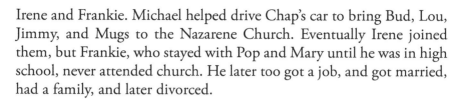

Irene and Frankie. Michael helped drive Chap's car to bring Bud, Lou, Jimmy, and Mugs to the Nazarene Church. Eventually Irene joined them, but Frankie, who stayed with Pop and Mary until he was in high school, never attended church. He later too got a job, and got married, had a family, and later divorced.

Michael became a regular singer in the choir. He was almost nineteen, and was not only leading the Young People's Society, but was also teaching a Bible Study. Rev. Reynolds and Chap McPherson had agreed to mentor him, but Michael mostly read the Bible on his own, and then asked questions about what he had read. Rev. Reynolds was soon called to a Nazarene Church in Manitoba, so he and his wife Shirley packed up that spring, and after General Assembly, moved to Winnipeg. Chap McPherson had taken the Nazarene 'Course of Study,' after serving as a licensed minister with the Salvation Army, so he was certainly qualified to teach Michael. But he was often busy with Interchurch Council and other commitments, so he didn't meet with him as often as Michael would have liked. Chap eventually decided against entering the ministry with the Nazarene Church. He felt his ministry in Regina was now really as a Lay Leader. Marilyn started telling Michael she was praying that he would prepare for the ministry, and she started writing letters on his behalf to Calgary Bible Institute. She was informed it had just moved to Red Deer in Alberta. She had decided to obtain an application for admission on Michael's behalf... just in case.

Pop argued more and more frequently with Michael about his responsibilities at home. Mary was compassionate...and she often favored Michael because he was responsible and helped her with the children, the cooking, and the cleaning. Bud quit his apprenticeship and returned to high school. Lou decided he wanted to go to the United States someday as an artist, but he knew it would be better to finish high school first, and so he, too, returned to school. Michael, who had gone to Regina High School for one semester, was able to attend summer school and finish his freshman year. He decided he would finish high school, one year at a time, alternating a year of work with a year of schooling. He was also tired of working at Regina Photo and Portrait, even though Mr. Sirko wanted to teach him photography so he could run the store and take over the portrait aspect of the business.

The new pastor of the Church of the Nazarene came in the fall. His name was Rev. Albert Fleming. His young wife Bonnie and he were from Idaho, and he quickly showed how dynamic and productive a church leader he was. Michael liked him, even though they had different personalities. Rev. Fleming treated him with respect, as the youth leader and assistant to the choir director. A few months after they arrived, Rev. Fleming announced that they were having a Missions Emphasis Week. A missionary from China, Glennie Sims, was coming to tell them all about the new Nazarene hospital in north China, Bresee Memorial Hospital. They had nightly meetings, just like a Revival. She showed 'slides,' pictures projected on a screen, and gave them 'flannel graph lessons,' in which Miss Sims told a Bible story, with figures cut out of flannel, and displayed on a board. She also introduced them to some of the missionaries, showing pictures of the Kiehn's, the Wiese's, and Dr. and Mrs. Fitz and their four children: Elizabeth, Irma, Maxine, and Guilford. Michael noticed that Elizabeth was just a few years younger than he. By the third night, while Glennie was speaking, Michael bowed his head, looking troubled. Rev. Fleming came over to him and asked him if he was alright. Michael told him that he was greatly moved…that God was asking him to respond to a call to go be a missionary to China! While Miss Sims was still speaking, Rev. Fleming and Michael came down and knelt at the altar rail. The pianist started playing 'O Zion Haste', the choir sang, and Rev. Fleming asked for others to respond to God's call for missionaries. Michael, and five others, came forward that night to dedicate themselves to God's mission work around the world. But Michael was the only one called, as he said, "to China, the land of my ancient ancestors." Rev. Fleming told him he had met Dr. Fitz once at Oklahoma School of Medicine in Norman, Oklahoma, where his wife's parents lived. His wife Bonnie was only six years older than Elizabeth, the eldest of the Fitz children. Glennie Sims told them she had helped babysit Elizabeth and her sister Irma, when they first arrived in China in1920. Rev. Fleming and Glennie Sims concluded the Missions Emphasis week with a final commissioning service after the Worship service

Sunday morning. Everyone offered prayers of blessing on those who had answered God's call to go as missionaries. Pop and Mary would not attend, but they did congratulate Michael on following God's call. Chap, Marilyn, Rev. Fleming, and Bonnie all offered prayers of commissioning for the five people called to be missionaries, including Michael. After the service, Marilyn came to Michael; she was smiling, and told him how mysteriously God moves in our lives. She had in her hands a response from Northern Bible College (which they all just called Red Deer Bible College), the same one that had been Calgary Bible Institute, but had moved to Red Deer in Alberta. It was a letter accepting him as a new student. She had done this on her own, albeit with Michael's permission, but neither of them expected a response so quickly. God had been working in their hearts all along, and now this was a confirmation of it. Michael knew what he must do, but he dreaded confronting his father with it. Both Rev. Fleming and Chap McPherson had written letters strongly recommending him. Now, they also offered to go with Michael to talk to his father. Michael said no, this was something he had to do on his own. They said they would be praying for his meeting with Pop.

In the morning, Michael said he wanted to speak with his dad, but Pop said no, he knew what Michael was going to say. Michael said he wanted to take Pop to the cemetery to visit his mother's grave. Would he go with him, and visit little Mary's grave also while they were there? Pop did not like the idea, but agreed. Michael had borrowed Chap's car, so they drove to the cemetery. They both stood in silence for a long time. Then, Michael asked Pop if he thought he had been a good son. Did he think his mother would want God's will for his life? He had become 'saved,' like him, then sanctified, and then called to be a missionary to China. Did Pop think he had worked hard for the family? He needed to pursue the path God had planned for him. He was going to go to Northern Bible College, in Red Deer, Alberta. Rev. Fleming had a college friend in Red Deer with a farm. Their name was Zumwalt. The Zumwalt's had offered Michael a place to stay in exchange for being a farm hand. Michael would also attend carpentry school in Red Deer, so he could learn a trade to put himself through high school, after he finished the two-year Bible course at Northern Bible College. He planned to quit his job at Regina Photo and Portrait.

Pop didn't say anything. When Michael was done, they got in the car and sat in silence until Michael drove home. Neither spoke a word all the way home. Michael had already gone by to see Mr. Sirko, to tell him he was quitting his position. Mr. Sirko was upset, but was happy for Michael, and wished him well. He even gave him a gift of twenty-five dollars as a severance. Michael suggested that Bud might be able to work there, and Sirko said he would contact him. Rev. Fleming and Bonnie offered to drive Michael to Red Deer to register, and then to the Zumwalt farm. He packed up his things. Mary looked very sad, but she patted Michael on the back. She said Bud and Louie needed to take their turn with some of the financial responsibility. Michael kissed all of his siblings goodbye, and invited them to come to Red Deer sometime to see him, and play on the farm, to which they all squealed with delight. Bud and Lou were in class at the high school, and Joe was in second grade at Wetmore, but Michael asked to stop by the house to say goodbye on the way out of town. Pop was waiting outside. He told Michael not to do this, that he was a disobedient son. He was abandoning his responsibility. Then he grew very angry, and lost control. He said 'don't bother to come back,' that Michael was deserting them… *he should not consider himself to be his son any longer.* He told him to *never* come back. Michael stood there, stunned. He hadn't meant to wound his father, and he didn't know what to say, or do. He knew God had called him…and he must obey God. He still believed his father was a man of great faith and courage, or he wouldn't have been able to get to this point in his life. All he could say was, "I will pray that God helps you see why I must 'obey God rather than man, like Acts 5:29 says; please forgive me if I offended you, so that I am no longer your son…but I must choose to follow God. Goodbye, Pop."

Rev. Fleming and Bonnie were waiting in the car. They didn't feel they could interfere. They just prayed for courage for Michael, and for Pop to see his error. They drove by Wetmore to say goodbye to Joe, then to Regina High where Bud and Lou came out to say farewell. After many long hours of driving, they finally arrived in Red Deer, with Michael and Rev. Fleming trading off driving. They got there shortly after midnight, but Ethel and Myron Zumwalt got up and fixed them something to eat, then showed them their rooms, where they retired for the night. In the morning they went to the Bible College, registered Michael, and also the Alberta School of Carpentry.

Michael found it exhilarating to get up early, do the chores, eat breakfast with the Zumwalt family and then go to class until 4:00 in the afternoon. After classes, he studied carpentry in Red Deer. After eating supper, he did his daily chores. It was a grueling schedule for two years, but he was enjoying himself. One day their golden retriever had a litter of pups. Michael assisted with the delivery, then helped the mother clean them up. One very small one tried numerous times to get in to feed on the mother, but was always pushed aside. "Come on little runt," Michael would say, as he tried to help the little one feed, but to no avail. The mother would not help, and the other pups finally got their fill and left, and before the runt could get back in, the mother would get up and leave. Michael thought the runt would die if he didn't do something, so he pushed some of the fat little ones aside, to let the runt in, but it would never last very long. He finally separated the runt from the others and hand-fed him until they were all weaned. Michael was always like that…all his life, helping the underprivileged, sometimes at great personal sacrifice.

One morning at breakfast, the Zumwalt boy, Earl, who seemed to always be in a bad mood, wouldn't eat his oatmeal. His mother asked him what was wrong. It's the 'wrong flavor' he answered. So, she made him some cornmeal mush, to which he turned up his nose. *Now* what's wrong, she said. It was the 'wrong texture.' So, she served him some dry cereal. He didn't know what to say against it, so he simply said, "it's… it's…the wrong color." Michael stifled a laugh. He could remember eating boiled millet growing up in Gravelbourg…which was all there was to eat. Iris and Elmer, who were the Zumwalt's other two children, constantly teased Earl about his finicky behavior. Michael learned many lessons in gratitude living there, and he was a good Student Preacher at Innisfail Nazarene.

The two-year course went by very quickly. Michael was a good student, and had a good grasp of the Bible, many books and writings, and basic foundational church administration. He looked forward to preaching on a regular basis, and served as student pastor for the nearby church in Innisfail; but most of all he dreamed of going to China as a missionary. It was time for graduation. Michael and his class stood on the steps of Northern Bible College for a picture. Two days later he said goodbye to the Zumwalt's.

Michael had also received a certificate in carpentry, and he looked forward to returning to Regina, and working as a carpenter. After the explosive departure he had had with Pop, he had written Bud and Lou about the possibility of the three of them living together. Bud and Lou had dropped out of high school again to work, but since Michael was coming back to finish school himself, he wondered if the three of them could work part time and finish up together. Pop had not written to Michael during his Bible School years, but Mary had, and had kept him up to date. She thought Pop would come around, but it might take a while. Both Bud and Lou gave some of their earnings to the family to help out, so she didn't think it was a good idea if the three of them lived elsewhere without continuing with at least some financial support. It was finally decided that Michael, Bud, and Lou would live together, split the rent on a place, and continue to help the family out with their finances. When Michael got back, he found a place near Regina High School, with the help of the McPherson's. It was a small two-bedroom house, where Bud and Lou could share a bedroom, and Michael would have his own. Michael quickly got work as a carpenter. Regina was growing fast, and he was able to work inside, putting up walls and lathing and plastering them. Bud had taken Michael's old job with Mr. Sirko, but as a photographer, rather than as a dark room developer. Lou got his old job back as an Art Supply buyer. The three of them did their own cooking and cleaning. Bud had become more active at the Church of the Nazarene, and wanted to go to the United States after he graduated. He wanted to become an artist where all of the good schools were.

Michael had bought a used car in Red Deer, so he had driven to Regina on his own. He even gave a ride to two other graduates, one student on his way to Winnipeg, and the other on his way to Michigan. He stopped by the old house on Victoria to say hello to everyone. Pop was not back from work, but Mary said she had talked to him about the three of them living elsewhere. As long as they continued some financial assistance, she was sure Pop would be okay with it. When Bud and Lou left, they did not have the same explosive departure with their dad that Michael had, but Pop was still sullen about them all sharing another place, even if it meant the house on Victoria would not be so crowded any longer. Michael finished high school in two years. He felt awkward going back as a twenty-one-year-old Bible School grad, and he towered over his younger classmates at 5 feet 10 inches. Regina High School had allowed him some credits from Northern Bible College, and he also took summer school classes as well. Bud had about two and a half years left, so he finished up about a semester after Michael, and went to Northern Bible College (He had told Michael, "Anything you can do, I can do,"). Lou had stayed in school when Bud went off to work with Sirko, so he finished up about the same time, even though he had started two years later.

Rev. Fleming gave Michael several chances to preach, mostly on the mission outreach on Sundays. Bud was interested in Bible School, but he didn't care too much about giving up his Sundays for outreach. Lou and Bud had made professions of faith, and became more active in the Youth program at the Nazarene Church, but they had a minimal commitment, and were more interested in the girls that they met there. Jimmy and Irene had become active in the Sunday School program, and Bud would stop by for them, but Margaret and Frankie ended up going with Pop, Mary and Joe to the Apostolic Christian...now that they had a fledgling youth program... and had started having their services in English instead of Hungarian. Chap and Marilyn McPherson began to help Michael research to find the best four-year Nazarene Colleges. If he was going to be a missionary, he would need a liberal arts college degree. He wanted to be ordained in the Nazarene Church, and he should think about getting married...

The family started growing up, getting jobs, moving away, and getting married. Pop kept his distance from Michael, and they didn't reconcile for many years. But he was cordial when the three boys would come over for a home cooked meal. Michael graduated from Regina High in 1935. Marilyn had done her homework again, and suggested Pasadena Nazarene College in California. Many of the Nazarene missionaries had attended there...or Bethany College in Oklahoma.

Michael liked the idea, and started the application process right away. Rev. Fleming and Chap McPherson wrote letters of recommendation. George Coulter was now District Superintendent for Canada West District, and he was happy to write a letter of recommendation also. Michael's car was not in good shape, and rather than take a chance he decided to sell it to Lou (Bud already had a used car he bought while working for Sirko). Lou said he would fix it up and use it in his job. Rev. Fleming said he was going to Calgary for District Meeting, and Rev. Coulter had someone else going to Northwest Nazarene College in Idaho, so they made arrangements for Michael to ride with Rev. Fleming to Calgary, then with Joe Porter, who was driving to Idaho. From there Michael found someone transferring from Northwest Nazarene to Pasadena College he could ride with.

Before Michael left, Rev. Albert and Bonnie Fleming, Chap and Marilyn McPherson, many of his friends from Regina First Nazarene, and other well-wishers, gathered at the church to pray for Michael. Bud, Lou, Joe, Jimmy, and Irene showed up. Even Ferenc and Margit came for this special send-off. They laid hands on him, blessed him on his way, and asked God's protection, for God to open doors, so Michael could follow the path God had chosen for him; There was a tearful goodbye from his family before the trip to Calgary. Then Michael rode with Joe Porter to Idaho, and with Richard Jordan, who was transferring to Pasadena. Several days later they made it to California. After Michael registered, he found a room to rent above a garage of a long-time member of First Nazarene Church in Pasadena. He had written the Carpenters' Union there, who gave him a lathing job, based on the recommendations of the Regina Carpenters Union (he liked to say he "lathed his way through college"). Now he was ready for college, he was ready to prepare for the mission field, and he was ready to pursue ordination; but most of all, he was ready to serve God...wherever that might lead him.

Northern Bible College, 1933

Michael Varro ['Mihaly VII'] (second row, right) graduates

The next book is about Elizabeth Fitz Varro:
her heritage; China, Oklahoma, Alaska, Pasadena College,
meeting Michael Varro, and more...
Stories from the Boxcar!

BOOK II

Wheelbarrows & Firecrackers

The Journey from the New World to Cathay

CHAPTER SIX

BEN FRANKLIN, THE AMISH, AND LORD BALTIMORE

Benjamin Franklin

Lord Baltimore

Ben Franklin, meet the Amish

Esther Finnette Coleman had just met Edgar Howard Fitz at a Methodist Church in Minneapolis. It was at an MYF (Methodist Youth Fellowship), a weekend retreat for all area Methodist Youth. She was secretary-treasurer of the Anoka Methodist MYF, and Edgar was president of the Minneapolis First Methodist MYF. Anoka was not far from Minneapolis; in fact, Edgar and his parents had lived in Anoka when they first moved to Minnesota from Pennsylvania. She and her friends loved to tease him, calling him 'Eddie,' because they knew he hated that name. He went by E. Howard, the name his mother had always called him, because her maiden name was 'Howard.' She came from a long line of Coleman's on her dad's side, and claimed to be a 'first cousin of Benjamin Franklin;' she had said she would tell him the story someday. He bragged that his grandfather, Jacob Fitz, had built the first bridge across the Mississippi River when they lived in Anoka; he promised to tell her *his* story someday; Esther said she wanted to hear *that* story too. So, he gave her his address, and she gave him hers. They agreed they would write each other and tell their stories. The MYF conference ended that Sunday afternoon, and both returned to their homes.

The next week Edgar wrote Esther and asked her about her claim that she was the 'cousin of Benjamin Franklin;' she replied by writing him, "not so fast, 'Mr. Smarty Pants,' you go first," So it was that he told her the story of his grandfather, Jacob Fitz. [He had been part of the Amish in Pennsylvania that came from Germany, but he had gotten tired of being so 'different,' with all the black clothing, hats, and old-fashioned stuff; one day, he announced that he was leaving to go to the Northwest. The family said for him not to go; that if he did, he would be 'stricken from the family Bible.' He said he didn't want to be shunned by the Amish community and family, but he needed to find the life we wanted for himself. Grandfather Fitz was brilliant, and he worked hard to make enough money to go to Pennsylvania State College where he became a civil engineer. He ended up in Anoka, Minnesota, where he and his firm built the first bridge across the Mississippi. He met Susanna Herr at Penn State; they married and moved to Minnesota to homestead a place on the Mississippi River. He joined the civil engineering firm that built the bridge across the river. His son, Rudolph Herr Fitz was born in Anoka, and went to school there, marrying Elmina Forbes Howard who had come there from Kentucky]. So, what was *her* story, Edgar asked Esther. She wrote back; [The Coleman's had come from England and lived first in Boston until some of them moved to Nantucket Island and became Quakers' her fourth or fifth great grandfather was John Coleman' his future father-in-law, Peter Folger of Nantucket, was a prominent Quaker leader who had two daughters; one married into the Franklin family and one married John Coleman. Both had sons named Benjamin; these two were first cousins: Benjamin Coleman and Benjamin Franklin, the famous stateman]. "That makes me," she wrote, "the first cousin–about 'sixth removed–of Benjamin Franklin." Well, he wrote back, you've got me there...Uh, are you going to the next MYF meeting in St. Paul? Yes, she replied. They met several times and after dating for several months, they got married; Esther and E. Howard had eight children. The oldest was Essie, then Rudolph. He went to grammar and middle school in Anoka where they lived until Essie was ready for high school; like his dad, Rudolph did not like his first name; and he didn't particularly care for his middle name either. So, 'Rudolph Guilford' became...just 'RG' which he was called all his life. His mother and dad bought a small farm just outside of Fairmont, a stone's throw from the Iowa state line. His older sister, Essie, started Fairmont High School. After a few years, he and Essie had six new siblings: Dudley, Vera, Howard, Dulcie, Nellie, and Irma. Sadly, Dulcie lived only a few days. They were all active in the Methodist church in Fairmont, where Esther was the choir director, and E. Howard was lay leader. All of the siblings were part of the MYF. Dudley and Howard played baseball for Fairmont High. RG was on the debate team, but had never been interested in sports. He was well-read, and had a great desire to travel and see the world. His humor was infectious, and he always had everyone 'in stitches.' He loved to write too, and his stories were laced with imaginary places and people. He wanted to learn other languages and cultures, so he started a book club at Fairmont High. His favorite book was the Bible, and he asked Rev. Peter Jacobsen, their pastor at Fairmont Methodist, many questions. At the beginning of his senior year, his older sister Essie married Gus Malchow and they moved to Colorado. Nellie tragically died of a rare illness as a teenager, Howard was the editor of the school newspaper, and Vera and Irma were becoming popular with all the farm clubs and Fairmont civic leaders. His mother Esther asked Rudolph – she still called him that even though everyone else called him RG– if he would sing in her church choir. He loved his mom, but he didn't think he really sang that well, so he made some excuse about needing to help Mrs. Grady with the youth Sunday School class. His dad, E. Howard, was helping Rev. Jacobsen get ready for the fall Revival, and asked RG if he would offer the prayer that Sunday evening. RG was terrified. He didn't like to pray. He hated the written prayers. They sounded phony and not from the heart, but the way his dad was looking at him, he felt he had no choice. He said 'okay.' Some of the girls in his book club also went to Fairmont Methodist and sang in his mom's choir. RG thought he could get out of praying if he sang in the choir, and his dad thought that would be even better. Trudy and Darlene teased him, but it didn't bother him because he wasn't really that interested in girls, even though he *had* dated in high school, but only Darlene, and Trudy–one date each!

So, it was set: Rev. Jacobsen would lead the service and the singing, Esther would have the choir sing, E. Howard would make the announcements, and RG would pray before Rev. Jacobsen introduced the revival speaker, Rev. Alonzo Hansen, from Illinois. It went as planned. After the choir sang 'Love Divine,' RG came from the choir loft to pray. He had decided to pray his own words, but when he was in the middle of the prayer, he suddenly choked up. He began repeating the words that the choir had just sung: "let us see thy great salvation perfectly restored in thee, changed from glory into glory…" but he couldn't finish. He quickly said, "in Jesus' name, Amen." He was embarrassed, especially seeing his dad's face. Esther smiled, Darlene and Trudy kind of giggled, then Pastor Jacobsen introduced Rev. Hansen, who shared a great sermon on: 'Knowing God Saves Us.' At the end of the sermon, the choir sang 'Pass Me Not, O Gentle Savior,' and the evangelist, Rev. Hansen gave the invitation for all who wished to accept Christ, to come to the altar rail. Several came forward, but RG sat there motionless. He couldn't sing because he was choked up. Darlene and Trudy suddenly both went forward. Esther told the choir to keep singing, and she came over to RG to ask him if he was alright. He nodded, but wouldn't move. She said it was okay if he wanted to go forward. His dad looked back at him sternly, then he nodded his head at RG. Finally, he got up and went to the altar. A neighbor lady came and prayed with him. The service ended and they sang a closing song. RG went outside by the back door, pushing past his dad, Pastor Jacobsen, and Evangelist Hansen. They returned home in silence. The other kids went to the kitchen with mom for their normal bedtime snack. E. Howard was in his office, and RG went to the front porch. He sat in the porch swing for a long time. Finally, after everyone else had gone to bed except his mom and dad, RG was still on the porch swing. Esther must have heard the 'squeak, squeak, squeak' of the swing. She came outside and handed RG a cup of hot chocolate. "Do you want to talk, son?" He said nothing. "I noticed you went forward tonight," she said, "Did you receive Christ into your life?" He said he wasn't sure, he didn't feel anything. She explained that it wasn't about the feeling. Did he read in the Bible that we are 'new creatures in Christ Jesus,' but not because we feel something? He knew the Bible well, he said, and he knew in his mind that he had become a Christian, he just didn't have the assurance of it. He felt unworthy. His mom encouraged him to trust God to give him that assurance. He thanked her, and they retired for the night. In the next two days, he wrestled deeply with this doubt of his salvation. The second night, he went for a long walk after he finished the chores. He ended up in the barn, where he kept a Bible, and sat down in the hay to read. He opened to Jeremiah 29:13-14, "And ye shall seek me, and find me, when you shall search for me with all your heart...and I will be *FOUND* of you, saith the Lord." He closed the Bible. He had found the assurance he needed, trusting God that he would grow into faith.

RG finished high school with high marks. His dad wanted him to stay and help with the farm, but his mom wanted him to go on to college, maybe in Mankato, and become a teacher; but RG had already been making his own plans. He told the family he was going to Oklahoma Holiness College. He had already applied and had been accepted. Dr. CB Widmeyer, the President, had already written him. He would work his way through school with the student work program they provided. E. Howard stood up saying he absolutely forbade it. Esther was saddened by his decision, but was open to him finding his own way. Eventually E. Howard said to go wherever God was leading him. All his siblings were sad that he was leaving, but also excited for him. First, Essie had gotten married and moved away, and now RG was leaving too. Dudley, Howard, and the girls were envious, but wished him well.

That fall, RG took the bus to Bethany, Oklahoma (just west of Oklahoma City) and began college. He knew little of what God had in store for him...that he would be ordained in the Nazarene Church, become a medical doctor, and go as a missionary to China... that he would marry into an historically prominent family–and his wife and he would share similar life's goals.

Lord Baltimore and family

Katherine Stagg was just minding her own business. She didn't have time for boys or a job. She was going to be a *teacher* after she graduated from Normal School in St. Louis. She had grown up in a good home of Presbyterian refugees that had escaped the persecution of Mary Queen of Scots. [They had migrated from Scotland to Holland, and from there to New Jersey. Over the next several generations, the family moved west, from New Jersey to Pennsylvania, then to Kentucky, and finally to Missouri]. Because there was no Presbyterian church where they lived in Kentucky, her grandfather Daniel had 'converted' to the Methodist church. Her father, Henry, had become a 'local pastor' (not yet ordained) in St. Louis by the time Katherine was born; so, she grew up going to Sunday School, and was a member of the Methodist Youth Fellowship. Her brothers Daniel and Elijah also attended MYF.

One day, Katherine's father came back from a trip, telling her all about attending the new Missouri Conference as a local pastor. He had been assigned to a new mission church a few miles from the downtown church they attended, but he didn't want the family to be disrupted, so he suggested they stay at the St. Louis First Methodist Church, and he would begin preaching at a branch church several miles away. He talked all about the 'Witten boys:' [Rev. James Witten and his brother Rev. John Wesley Witten; both had been instrumental in starting the Kentucky, Tennessee, and Missouri conferences of the Methodist Church. Their grandfather, Rev. William Stanley Witten, had four sons that were all Methodist preachers, as well as daughters who married Methodist pastors... whose sons also became Methodist preachers! Some of them even went on the expeditions to the Pacific Northwest with Lewis and Clark, including one with Methodist missionaries who went to Oregon, where they founded Willamette Methodist College. The Witten's were originally Catholics who had come to America with Lord Baltimore (Calvert). The family included Calvert's, Cecil's, and Witten's, all of whom had come from England. Lord William Cecil was

Secretary of State to Elizabeth I, truly a long line of British statesmen!].
Hmm! Katherine was not impressed; her father was so excitable, and
overstated everything…in her opinion. She just wanted to finish
high school, and become a teacher. Henry wanted to tell her more,
but she just walked away. Her mother, Elizabeth, was in charge of the
Methodist women's group in their church, and wanted Katherine to
get involved; but she was always busy with her school work, and often
spent long hours at the library. One Sunday morning, Rev. Harold
Beckham, their pastor, introduced a young man from Virginia. He was
a member of the Witten family. [His father Zachariah had married
Mariah, a cousin of Davy Crockett, but she died and so he remarried,
to a woman named Julia Freeman]; their son was Charles Witten, and
he was visiting Witten relatives in St. Louis, hoping to move here if
employment became available. Katherine had to admit he was a very
nice-looking man, even though he was a few years older than she. She
thought he looked like her brother Daniel. Charles was staying with
his uncle John Witten, but would soon return to Tazewell County,
Virginia…if he didn't find employment. Pastor Beckham suggested he
work with his cousins, the Witten preachers. Charles said his father,
Zachariah, was a Bible teacher back in Clinch, Tazewell County,
Virginia. He was not interested in becoming a preacher, and he told
his sons there were "already enough Methodist pastors to go around."
Charles was in the glass business, and hoped to find a position with a
glass company in St. Louis. He wanted his uncle John to help him. By
the time uncle John left for Texas again, he had found a position for
Charles. So, he started attending First Methodist Church every week.
That is how Charles Witten met Katherine Stagg. One day, he was at
the library after work, and ran into Katherine, whom he recognized
from church. He was a real gentleman, and offered to carry the books
for her. She said "No thank you." She *did* let him talk to her for a while
though. When the library was about to close, they walked out together,
and he picked up her satchel of books without asking. She was still
talking and didn't realize they had already gotten on the street car, and
he still had her books. He asked if he could walk her home, and she
said "No thank you," again; but as they kept talking, they walked all
the way to her house, which was near the church, before she realized
he *had* walked her home. The next Sunday, she heard he had joined the

choir, and that he had already been offered a solo. This disturbed her very much, and she went to the choir director to complain. Charles was practicing with the choir director-organist. She listened to him sing the most beautiful rendition of 'Lead Kindly Light' she had ever heard. When he was finished, he smiled at her, and asked if she sang in the choir. She started to say no, but the choir director said, "Katherine has a lovely voice, and she has been thinking of joining us, *right, Katie?*" Katherine blushed and mumbled something like *"well, yes…maybe;"* she started singing in the choir that very next Sunday. She was angry with herself; how could she be taken in so easily by this pretentious young man?

They started seeing each other…and not just at choir rehearsals either. She finished high school, and started 'normal school' (teacher training) in St. Louis, but her mother became ill, and she had to drop out. Her father finished the Methodist 'Home Course of Study' and served a three-year 'trial appointment' at a new parish called Gethsemane Methodist Church. He was ordained at the Annual Conference following a three-year assignment. Charles and Katherine dated, but her mother Elizabeth died during the final year of Henry's probationary period, and they buried her in St. Louis. She decided not to return to normal school, and she and Charles were married by her father at First Church. Daniel and Elijah were happy because they liked Charles. When Katie's and Charles' first child, Eldon, was born, she had to drop out of the choir and the Methodist Women's meetings.

Charles had written his uncle John in Texas, who told them of a 'glass store in Henrietta, in Clay County, Texas…did they want to move there,' he said? Henry had become ill and had to give up the pastorate, so Katherine did not want to move yet. Charles said they could keep her father with them in Henrietta… and Eldon was already a couple years old. So, they moved to Texas, became active in the Methodist Church there, and after a while found a small farm in Clay County outside of Henrietta. Charles worked part time in town at the glass store until Charles got the farm up and running…and it was making a profit.

A year after they arrived in Clay County, their next child, Lura Katherine, was born. Her sister Irene was born two years later, and Max a year and a half after that. Lura was born at home, but Irene and Max were both born at the new Clay County hospital in Henrietta. The family became even more active in the Methodist Church. John Witten decided to sell the glass store and move to Dallas, where the rest of the Witten family in Texas had been living. Because Charles had brought the farm to a profitable position, he decided to change his career, and gave himself entirely to farming. Lura and Irene were schooled at home through grammar and middle school, but after Henrietta began busing area school children, they attended, and graduated from Henrietta High School. Lura was active in Four-H Club, and won several awards for prize sheep. Irene focused on Home Economics and started a food club in her senior year. Eldon had dropped out of school his junior year–against the advice of his mother Katherine, to help his dad manage the farm. Max was interested in cars from an early age, so assisted with farm machinery. Eldon promised he would finish high school later.

The family enjoyed the ministry of such outstanding evangelists as 'Uncle Buddy' Robinson and Roy Tilman (RT) Williams. The 'holiness movement' had been spreading throughout the Methodist Church, and both preachers had been to the Henrietta church for revival meetings. During a spring revival with Rev. RT Williams, Lura came forward to profess Christ as Savior. She began making plans to attend Texas Holiness University in Peniel, Texas. The pastor of the Henrietta Methodist Church, Rev. Todd Billings, was asked by the District Superintendent to leave, because of his refusal to refrain from preaching 'biblical holiness.' Most of the membership then decided to leave as well. The Church of the Nazarene had recently been formed in Chicago, and they founded the Henrietta Church of the Nazarene. Rev. Billings eventually came to be their pastor, and they were able to buy back their former church property. Texas Holiness University ended up joining Oklahoma Holiness College that same year, becoming Peniel-Bethany College, just west of Oklahoma City. Charles and Katherine were not happy about Lura having to move so far away from home, but they believed God wanted her to attend a holiness Bible college like Bethany-Peniel. Katherine's father, Henry Stagg had lived with them for several years, and he died the year that Lura graduated from high school. Lura was very close to her grandfather, and she took it hard when he passed away. He had always told her that Proverbs 3:5-6 should become the guide for her life: "*Trust in the Lord with all thine heart, and lean not unto thine own understanding. In all thy ways acknowledge him, and he shall direct thy paths.*" As she thought of Grandpa Henry, 'the old Scotsman,' (a man of holiness, if there ever was one); she told her parents that she was committed to pursuing God's leading; she would go to Bethany-Peniel. Charles and Katherine had to agree. They got a letter the next day from John Witten, the 'guardian angel' in the family. He wrote that one of the Witten cousins lived in the western part of Oklahoma City–Thomas Witten, and his wife Ann. If Lura was going to be living in the dormitory, they would be happy to keep an eye on her, and she could even stay some weekends with them if she liked. So, Lura left for Bethany, and Irene started her senior year at Henrietta High.

That fall, Eldon was tragically killed in an accident with the farm machinery. Charles and Max tried to keep the farm going, but they didn't realize that Eldon was the one who really had the knack for farming. Without him, the farm started going down. A year after Eldon died, they sold the farm to the Henrietta Cooperative. Irene graduated from high school, and Max made arrangements to get back in school after they moved to Bethany. Lura could live at home after all. Irene said she was going to start a restaurant instead of going to Bible school like Lura. Like lots of other 'sooners,' Charles and Katherine were able to stake out a claim, and started over in Bethany. Max started high school, working on cars at a body shop after school. Lura started her studies at Bethany-Peniel Bible School.

Lura met a young man from Minnesota one day after chapel; he was the student speaker whom Dr. Widmeyer had introduced as: Rudolph Guilford Fitz, but he laughed and told them all to not call him that. He said he went by 'RG'. After chapel, RG spoke to several of the students who had stayed to ask him questions. He told Lura, and the others gathered there, that he was interested in studying medicine following Bible School. Lura said she might be interested in medicine as well. Did he know of any good nursing schools in the area he might recommend? He said he didn't, that he was still new in the area, but he would be happy to find out.

Dr. Widmeyer announced that RG would speak at each of the Wednesday morning chapels that month. He also told them that RG wanted to be ordained in the Church of the Nazarene because they believed in holiness. RG had come from a Methodist family, and he wasn't sure what they believed about 'holiness,' but he longed for the fullness of God in his life. The next week, RG finished speaking at chapel, closed with prayer, and Dr. Widmeyer dismissed the students to their next class. Lura came to the front again to talk to RG about a nursing school. She reminded him she was Lura Witten from Texas. Her family had just moved here. He remembered their discussion and said that he had found out that Oklahoma Medical School, where he was going to enroll, also had a nursing program. He told Lura that this was his second year here, and that he also hoped to complete the course leading to ordination in the Church of the Nazarene…at the same time he was studying medicine. She said that she wasn't sure to what career God was calling her, but she was open to nursing school if God led her there. Dr. Widmeyer, who had been speaking with them, excused himself, saying that he had to go teach a class. RG and Lura went to the student kitchen for some 'Texas tea' and continued their discussion. They talked about their backgrounds, the Methodist Church, and their favorite parts of the Bible. When it was time for their next class, RG suggested that they meet again after chapel next week and talk some more. Lura said maybe they could meet at church on Sunday. Her family's friend, the Evangelist, Rev. James Dobson, Sr., was speaking at Bethany First Nazarene. RG said he knew of him, and yes, if they saw each other maybe they could sit together. She said she would be with her family – they had just moved here – but he was welcome to sit with them. Sunday came. They all enjoyed the singing and wonderful worship with the evangelist, Rev. Dobson, who introduced his new wife. After church, Charles met RG and they started talking about going fishing in Minnesota; he said he had been there, with some of his relatives, on a trip a few years ago. Katherine and Irene met RG also. Max was playing with some of the other boys. Before she knew it, Charles had invited RG for dinner at their homestead. They made their way to the farm after church, and ate a wonderful meal Katherine had prepared and was keeping warm on the old wood stove. This fine meal, that included fried chicken and buttermilk pie, must have made everyone '*sufficiently suffonsified*,' as RG liked to say, because after a long talk about growing up in Minnesota and Texas, they all fell asleep under the big oak tree; by the time the sun started going down, it was time to go back for the Sunday evening service. Lura reminded them that RG, Irene, Max, and she had to get there early for NYPS–Nazarene Young Peoples' Society before the evening service. Some of them piled in the old truck with Charles, and the rest went with Katherine who followed Charles in the car.

Over the next year, Lura started seeing RG as often as their studies allowed. E. Howard, Esther, and some of the family came down from Minnesota for a visit and met Lura. In the spring revival, he had experienced 'sanctification' (which John Wesley had taught was: a second work of grace, and a heart of 'pure love,' as he called it); they weren't in complete agreement with this, but thought this new 'fervor' in his spiritual life might help to bring him more assurance of salvation, which he was desperately in need of. He had begun the process toward ordination in the Nazarene Church. He had also decided to complete a liberal arts degree at Oklahoma College in order to be considered for medical school. This meant an additional two years beyond Bible school. E. Howard and Esther also met Lura and her parents, Katherine and Charles Witten; they all seemed to get along quite well. RG and Lura had now been seeing each other regularly and were anticipating getting married after he graduated. She planned to finish the 'One-Year Bible Certificate' before they married, and then move to Norman, where Oklahoma College was located. Lura had also sought a 'sanctification' experience. Dr. Widmeyer had spoken to her, following chapel one morning, about a month after RG claimed sanctification. She was not sure of her future plans, but she told them God would lead her. RG graduated with the 'Two-Year Bible Certificate.' Irene went on to cooking school after she finished one year at Bethany-Peniel. She had gotten a job at a German restaurant in Oklahoma City, where she met a young man from Germany by the name of Carl Solts; he kept the books for Vienna Gardens where Irene worked.

Lura and RG got married after the spring semester of 1914. E. Howard and Esther were not able to come down from Minnesota again, but Aunt Essie attended from Colorado. Lura's mother and father, Katherine and Charles Witten, were there, as were Max and Irene. Carl came in and sat down with Irene; he introduced his family to RG and Lura. Dr. Widmeyer seemed to take personal credit for having introduced the young couple, and the wedding was held on the campus of 'Bethany College,' as it was now being called. The week after their wedding, the newlyweds moved to Norman where they rented a small cottage near the college and medical school. Lura got a job in a laundry, and RG began to work in a book store. Their two jobs paid for his schooling and a little more, just enough to cover rent and living expenses. They attended the Church of the Nazarene on the north side of Oklahoma City where RG was an intern. He finished an undergraduate degree in science, and was ordained in the Nazarene Church that same semester.

Lura surprised RG with some big news: they were going to have their first baby! He was so happy, and told her, "Well, if our life right now were a cake, this would certainly be the icing on the top!" Elizabeth Finnette Fitz was born the next March; she looked like a little princess, and she cooed like she was already trying to sing. Lura was completely delighted with her new little girl; her mother and father came down from Bethany, and brought Irene and Max to see little Elizabeth Finnette (named for her two grandmothers: Katherine Elizabeth Stagg and Esther Finnette Coleman. RG was as proud as a peacock, and beamed from ear to ear as he held his little daughter. First Nazarene in Norman had a reception for Lura and RG. They were celebrating the birth of Elizabeth, the ordination of RG, and also his acceptance into medical school at the University of Oklahoma. It was announced at the reception that Glennie Sims, and two other pioneer Nazarene missionaries, Rev. and Mrs. Wiese, were going to be with them for a 'Missions Emphasis Week' the next month. They were raising financial support for medical missions, and hoped to build the Bresee Memorial Hospital in north China. Rev. AT Gordon, the senior pastor, had asked their new associate, Rev. Rudolph G. Fitz to help lead the meetings (they had tried calling him 'Pastor Rudy,' but that didn't go over very well). The week began with a great stir in the congregation. RG led the opening prayer and Pastor Gordon introduced each of the missionaries, who gave a wonderful presentation, challenging the congregation to support medical missions in north China; at the end of the week, the appeal was given, for all: *'to give, or to go!'* It was at these mission meetings that God put his hand on RG, and told him he had a special assignment for him. At the end of the final service, Rev. Gordon asked everyone to pray about what God was asking each of them to do. It was then that RG realized that God was calling him to become a missionary to China. He wept; he now understood why God had led him from his home in Minnesota, to Oklahoma, to study Bible in preparation for the ministry; and then led him to Oklahoma Medical School to prepare to become a medical doctor. The two 'careers' didn't seem to go together at first; but now, God's Holy Spirit was putting it all in one basket for him: God was calling him to be a medical missionary!

Later that night, after the final service, RG was pacing in the woods next to their cottage, singing 'O Zion Haste Thy Mission High Fulfilling;' filled with emotion, he ran to the house, grabbed Lura around the waist, and told her they were going to China to be medical missionaries! She looked at him aghast; she had worked hard to put him through school so he would be ordained as a Nazarene pastor; now she was putting him through medical school; they had even borrowed money from her parents so he could finish. Lura was hoping for a good medical practice, part-time church assignment; he didn't understand her reluctance; why did she not share his excitement? God would 'supply all their needs in Christ Jesus,' right? She didn't know what to say (how do you reason with 'a brick,' she thought). Then she had another thought: she told him she could be happy for *him*. God had called *him* to be a missionary, right? But God had not called *her*; didn't she need a call too– to go to China *together*? RG's face fell; she was right…Lura had to have a call too! He asked her to pray. They asked the whole church to pray. The Nazarene Church mission board asked everyone to pray. They wouldn't make their decision until God spoke to Lura. She prayed; she cried; she sincerely wanted to follow God's will, but *CHINA*? The deadline for the mission board was in a week. Lura went to the woods…she prayed some more, but her spirit heard nothing–no call from God. The church was near despair, but RG just turned it over to God. Lura prayed all night in the woods. In the morning, RG and the church – and the mission board–wanted to know: 'what had God told her?' Lura said: "God did *not* call me to be a missionary to China…but", she said, "God told me that he had *already* called me to be the wife of 'Dr. Rudolph Guilford Fitz,' and I had promised God I would follow my husband, to China or wherever God called him. So, I will go with him, and be a good missionary wife!"

The Nazarene mission board praised Lura, her devotion to God, and to her husband, and they were appointed as missionaries to China, effective completing medical school, and tenure as associate pastor at First Nazarene Church in Norman. Soon after receiving the letter of acceptance from the mission board, Lura announced she was pregnant again; just before graduation, Irma Irene Fitz, a beautiful little redhead, red-faced little girl, was born. She had a voice like an angel! RG and Lura spent two years sharing their vision and call to medical missions. Lura loved going on their trips and showing off her two little girls; two years apart, but they might as well have been twins. Inseparable all their lives, they did everything together. Their lives intertwined, and God worked in them in amazing ways...

Dr. RG and Lura Fitz, 1920 Pioneer China Missionaries

CHAPTER SEVEN

WHEELBARROWS AND FIRECRACKERS

Taxi…taxi!

D R. RG FITZ AND HIS WIFE LURA FINALLY RAISED ENOUGH MONEY TO GO to China with their two little girls – Elizabeth age four, and Irma age two – medical missionaries with the Church of the Nazarene! Raising their financial support involved several months of 'deputation,' which were meetings in many churches, where they raised the awareness of the need for medical mission work. Offerings were collected to cover ship passage, and monthly support was pledged, in faith. These funds were sent in to the Nazarene Mission headquarters, to be credited to their necessary support. And now, everything was completed, and RG and his little family were ready to depart for China. The General Assembly of 1920 was convened in Oklahoma City that year, and the Fitz's from Minnesota, and the Witten's from Bethany attended. There were tearful, but also joyful, goodbyes. They drove from Oklahoma City to San Francisco in October where, after loading trunks and personal effects on board a Japanese freighter, the Kashima Maru, the Fitz family sailed for China by way of the Hawaiian Islands, and from there, to Shanghai. The seas were rough and Lura was seasick, so RG had to help with the care of Beth and Irma. He was seasick also but stayed in the cabin and read his Bible to take his mind off his discomfort, while Lura and the girls mostly slept.

They arrived in Shanghai after twenty-three days at sea. Nazarene missionaries, Rev. and Mrs. Deale and Rev. and Mrs. Osborn, who had arrived earlier that year, met their ship. Arrangements had been made to stay at the Assemblies of God mission compound in Shanghai until their trunks arrived and were processed through immigration. After two weeks in Shanghai, RG and family took the train to Beijing. The Deale's and the Osborn's were in language school, and Lura and Dr. Fitz soon enrolled there as well. The family of four lived in a small dormitory comfortably for a year. Next to their room was a small nursery where Elizabeth and Irma slept. They ate their meals and studied with a number of other foreign nationals also learning the Mandarin dialect. At the end of the year, Dr. Fitz took the medical exam in Chinese… and passed! They left Beijing and went to Daming, in southern Hebei province, the location of the Nazarene mission compound.

Arriving at the train station in Handan, they were told that it was the end of the train line; they would have to travel by other ground transportation in order to get to Daming, still several miles away… but there were no cars, no buses; how were they to get from Handan to Daming? Brother Wiese had not told them about this. Instead of a traditional rickshaw, two men, pulling wheelbarrows, arrived. One would take Lura and Irma. The other one would take Elizabeth and RG in *Wheelbarrows*? With ox-drawn carts piled high with their trunks following behind, the Fitz family bundled up in the cold October weather; they were off to their first big adventure in this new land. Lura worried about the girls being frightened, but they laughed and giggled as they took off in this new mode of transportation. As they were leaving the station, a wedding party preceded them, complete with firecrackers and noisemakers—a 'missionary entourage:' an ox-drawn luggage wagon, following a noisy wedding party complete with wheelbarrows! They had arrived in a foreign land; God had many surprises in store for them,. but they knew one thing: God.had promised to always be with them and go before them!

They lived in one of the missionary houses next to the church facility which was called the 'tabernacle.' Dr. Fitz went to work with three Chinese doctors. The medical facility was barely adequate, nothing more than a clinic really. Dr. West and Dr. Sutherland in the United States had been appointed to the work in Daming, but weren't scheduled to arrive for another couple of years. In the meantime, Dr. Fitz and his Chinese colleagues were very shorthanded, having to care for a great number of medical cases and surgeries. The funds were still being raised for the new facility, Bresee Memorial Hospital, and the first phase of the construction was already underway. Lura helped in the clinic preparing bandages, laundry, and patient care.

While Lura and Dr. Fitz were busy with the hospital, an 'Amah' (the traditional Chinese *nanny*) took care of Elizabeth and Irma. They had brought children's books with them, and Elizabeth and Irma started learning to read at a very early age. Ma-Li, their Amah, was trained, not only as a caregiver, but also as a tutor, so she assisted in their home schooling for years.

[Lura supervised their learning in China, so that by the time Beth was ten, and the family went on their first furlough in seven years, she had already finished the equivalence of grammar school; Irma was also advanced in her education and she finished the equivalent of fourth grade before they left China in 1927 for furlough; Irma

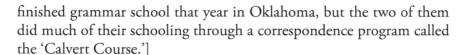

finished grammar school that year in Oklahoma, but the two of them did much of their schooling through a correspondence program called the 'Calvert Course.']

In China, however, Beth and Irma also studied the Bible which was taught at the church and learned all the wonderful stories of God's love. They had both picked up Mandarin easily since they heard it every day, and could speak equally as well in either English or Chinese. At age five Beth asked her mother if she was "too little to give her heart to Jesus?" Lura said 'no, of course not,' and led her little daughter to salvation at that early age. In church services, they used both an old pump organ and a piano, but Beth was particularly fascinated by the piano, and started to play on it on her own. So, the young Chinese woman who played for worship services started to help her learn how to play. By age eight, Beth was playing simple melodies, and by age eleven, she was playing for worship. Irma had made her own profession of faith in Christ at an early age, and was fond of singing while Beth played the hymns. By this time, Beth could read music, and started to harmonize the hymn melodies that Irma would sing. The only problem was: Irma was thrown off by the harmony part Beth was singing. Beth had a plan. She would start singing alto on one side of the room, while Irma would start singing soprano on the other side of the room. As they got closer together, they learned to sing the two parts without the other being thrown off. It was a big hit when they sang their first duet in church just before they went on furlough.

They had been in China about three years when Lura came to the house one evening feeling faint and out of breath. Someone ran to call Dr. Fitz, thinking she had come down with some illness. R.G. arrived and carefully checked his wife's condition. What strange disease had she contracted? Something she had ingested, or maybe a family condition?

The concern on his face turned quickly to a smile. Beth and Irma asked, "What is it Daddy, what is wrong with Mommy?" Dr. Fitz announced to all those assembled that Lura was indeed going to have another baby. Seven months later Vera Maxine Fitz was born. A little sister, born in China! All their Chinese friends and the missionary community had a special celebration for this newborn little 'Chinese' baby. Ma-Li, their Amah, had her hands full now, with, not two, but three, little girls. Maxine, as they called her, fit in well with the already-established routine. After nursing her for six months, Lura went back to work full time at the dispensary.

Maxine began reading at age four, just like Beth and Irma had, and by the time the family went on furlough in 1927, all three girls were very popular with the entire Nazarene mission compound. They played together, read to each other, sang together, even for church, in both English and Mandarin.

It had been a long seven years. Most missionaries went on furlough after five, but R.G. and Lura stayed two extra years because Dr. West and Dr. Sutherland hadn't arrived until it was time for the Fitz's to return to the United States. First, they had to be schooled in Mandarin, and then Dr. Fitz needed to acquaint them with the medical routine of the new hospital. Bresee Memorial wasn't finished until 1925, so they were busy moving the operation from the old clinic to the hospital. The Nazarene mission board also sent Rev. Harry Wiese, and his wife Katherine, to be the new superintendent for the mission in Daming, and this helped alleviate the work load.

The Fitz family arrived in Bethany after a long ocean voyage and cross-country trip. Lura's family was overjoyed at seeing them again after so many years. Dr. Fitz's family in Minnesota said they would look forward to a trip the family might make to Fairmont to see them later that year. They stayed with Lura's family for a few months, but didn't schedule any deputation meetings outside of the state until later. Times were hard and the stock market eventually crashed, so money was tight for them. RG looked around for another place to stay, and found out that the little cottage, where they had stayed during medical school days, was available for rent. The three girls were able to stay in one bedroom, and Lura and RG in the other. After six months, however, things became too cramped, with two nearly-teen girls. Beth was now twelve, Irma ten, and Maxine was five, and ready for kindergarten.

Bresee Memorial Hospital, Daming, Hebei Province, China, 1925

RG began to receive requests for out-of-state deputation meetings as well. So, when he was visiting Bethany College one day, Dr. Widmeyer suggested that he teach a few classes there part-time, and they could stay in faculty housing. "My, how the Lord does provide," RG's said. They moved to Bethany, lived at the college, and started making plans to stay longer than a one-year furlough. Lura was able to get her old laundry job back at the college too. The Mission Board said it wouldn't be possible to send them back to China any time soon, so they started making plans for the girls' schooling in Bethany. Beth and Irma had finished courses by correspondence through sixth and fourth grades, but when Lura visited Morten Grammar School, they told her the girls would have to attend a year first, and then show their standing as sixth and fourth graders, even though the girls had received certificates of completion from the Calvert Course program. Dr. Fitz decided to meet with Mr. Schmidt, the principal, who only backed up what the administration had told them. When Dr. Widmeyer heard about this, he reminded Mr. Schmidt of his standing on the Bethany College Board of Trustees, and also his membership at Bethany First Nazarene. Mr. Schmidt reviewed the Calvert Course certificates, and then told Dr. Fitz he was 'most happy to welcome them all' to Morten. The girls were enrolled in seventh, fifth, and kindergarten respectively.

The family began attending Bethany First Nazarene on a regular basis. Delores McLeary, who was on the piano faculty at Bethany, and the regular accompanist for Sunday morning worship, heard Beth playing piano for Sunday School. She was so impressed that she spoke to Lura, offering to give Beth piano lessons for free. and Irma was asked to sing solos occasionally. The greatest delight, however, was a special feature of the Sunday evening service, billed as 'The Three Misfits' ('Miss Fitz's'). The three Fitz girls sang in three-part harmony. Beth had taught Irma to sing the alto part, while Maxine sang the melody, and then Beth added a tenor part above them. They were a big hit. Beth began visiting the Bethany campus once a week to take lessons from Delores McLeary, and even played occasionally for noon recitals with Miss McLeary's college students, and other students in town from her piano teaching studio.

Before the fall semester started, the family took a quick motor trip up to Minnesota to visit the Fitz side of the family in Fairmont. Charles and Katherine loaned RG their other car for the trip. Dudley, Irma, Vera, Howard, and Nellie, and most of their families, showed up for a grand Fitz family reunion, and all had a chance to meet grandparents, in-laws, siblings, aunts, uncles, and cousins. They feasted on wonderful farm-grown vegetables, chickens, plenty of bread, dessert and lemonade, as they talked, laughed, sang, cried and prayed. The family stopped to visit Essie in Colorado on their way back to Bethany. By then, it was time for school to start. The girls struggled socially at first because they were not at all used to American culture, having grown up in China, and lessons were by correspondence only; they were ahead of their class academically, even if not as well socially.

Beth progressed quickly on the piano, and started playing for church services when Delores could not be there. She even played duets with Miss McLeary and it was suggested that when she returned from China, they hoped she would choose Bethany for her higher education and, of course, that she would major in music studies there.

The mission board finally approved the return of Dr. Fitz and his family to China. Despite the stock market crash, the funds for the hospital and their return fare, which had built up slower than they had hoped, were, nevertheless, available. Dr. Fitz had worked diligently over the previous three years, preaching in churches, speaking at Christian organizations and independent mission societies, and writing letters and news articles about the work of the Bresee Memorial Hospital.

The mission board also had a great concern, and they needed Dr. Fitz to assist them in solving it; one of the missionaries, Rev. Peter Kiehn, with whom they had had great difficulties in the past, was now again causing unrest with the mission in Daming. He had assumed authority at the hospital, against the direct orders of Rev. Harry Wiese, the new superintendent. A standoff ensued, since some of the Chinese doctors said they would not stay unless Rev. Kiehn left, but one of the older Chinese doctors who had already retired, sided with Rev. Kiehn. The mission board authorized Rev. Wiese to handle the matter, but wanted Dr. Fitz to get back to China as soon as possible to help with the conflict. After saying goodbye to family and friends, the Fitz family sailed from San Francisco once again. This time they sailed on the American merchant ship, 'Ocean Wind,' and arrived in Shanghai within twenty days. The family had brought fruit and crackers, snacking continuously, in order to counter the seasickness. Reading and sleep helped also. They spent a good deal of time sleeping, and Dr. Fitz had brought along some seasick medicine this time. Immigration went smoothly, and they were back in China after three years. It felt like they had come home.

Bethany-Peniel College, 1935

Dr. RG, Lura, and Beth, Irma, & Maxine

A national depression dampens…
but does not defeat...
and a new missionary spirit is rekindled

Chapter Eight

Elizabeth and her amazing piano

The *real* 'great wall' was the challenge to faith in Christ

THEY WENT STRAIGHT FROM SHANGHAI BY TRAIN TO ZHENG ZHOU, AND then to Handan, arriving late in the night and exhausted from the trip. Rev. Harry Wiese met them at the train, and took them to Daming in the car the mission had recently purchased. Irma and Maxine were asleep, but Beth helped Lura and Dr. Fitz get everyone to bed when they arrived. Morning came, and

Ma-Li had fixed breakfast for everyone. But Dr. Fitz, with only five hours of sleep, had already had his devotions and left for the hospital. Lura and the girls took most of the day to re-orient themselves, and get their 'land legs.'

Before they left the United States, they had made sure they once again enrolled in the Calvert Course. Beth had finished seventh and eighth grades at Morten School; Irma had finished fifth and sixth grades; and Maxine had finished kindergarten and first grade. The school materials they now had, presupposing another four to five-year term, would take Beth through high school, seventh through tenth for Irma, and grades two through five for Maxine. It didn't take long to readjust to life in Daming, even with the three-year absence. China was home.

Beth began playing the piano regularly for worship, Bible studies, and other mission meetings. During the Sunday morning worship shortly after they returned to Daming, God spoke to her while she was playing the piano for the closing hymn. It was one of her father's favorites: "O Zion Haste." She felt God was calling her to be a missionary to China, and to use her music talent to win the Chinese to Christ. She wasn't sure at first that she could fulfill that call. She was frustrated because there were few piano books and materials to which she could avail herself, in order to advance very effectively. Lura saw this, and decided that they somehow needed to find a piano teacher for her. RG and Lura mentioned this to Rev. Wiese, who passed it on to Pastor Timothy Chao, the Music Director at the Mission. He returned to Rev. Wiese the next day with the report that their staff pianist, Miss Rachel Chen, had studied music with someone at Shandong University in Jinan, by the name of Henry Sung. He had also studied piano briefly in the United States at the University of Southern California. He now lived in Handan, but he had other students in Daming, and taught piano lesson there two days a week. Lura couldn't be more pleased. She asked Pastor Chao to get in touch with Henry Sung, to see if he would accept Elizabeth as a piano student. Pastor Chao told them later that day that Henry Sung would be in Daming the next day to teach his piano students, and he would ask him to come to the mission to meet Beth, and listen to her play. They gave the good news to Elizabeth before evening Vespers.

Beth was so excited! She began praying, "Lord, I know you called me to become a missionary to China, I want to equip myself to serve you. If you will help me to be able to study with Mr. Sung, I will answer your call for me to be a missionary to China, and to share the gospel, especially through music. In Jesus' name, Amen." The next day, Henry Sung came to the Mission after his teaching schedule. He talked with Pastor Chao, and then asked to meet Beth. She met him in the Tabernacle. He was amazed that she spoke flawless Mandarin, and was so well-mannered for a thirteen-year-old. He sat down and asked Beth to go to the piano and play something. Henry was expecting some simple hymn, but she played "Für Elise" by Beethoven, from memory and with a very sensitive touch, so much so, that Henry and Timothy Chao sat there in silence for a moment. Lura and the two other sisters, who had slipped into the back of the Tabernacle to listen, thought maybe they disliked it. Then Henry said in Chinese, "Oh my, you have already accomplished a great deal for such a young lady; yes, I would be honored to teach you! Maybe you should teach *me*." Pastor Chao smiled and told him that was why Rachel Chen felt so confident in allowing Beth to substitute for her. They set a time during the week when Beth would study with Henry. They would be allowed to use the Tabernacle piano, because in the middle of the afternoon there were no meetings or services that would interfere. Dr. Fitz offered Henry a fair price for the lessons, but Rev. Wiese said that the Mission would be happy to pay it since young Elizabeth was really music 'staff' now.

That night, Elizabeth offered the family devotion after supper. She chose the words from Psalm 33:2 "O praise him with the lyre, and the ten-stringed instruments, and harp…" and she prayed this simple prayer. "O God, I will go where you want me to go, I will praise you on the lyre, the instruments…with my voice…and with my piano. Amen" Dr. Fitz and Lura hugged her with tears in their eyes. Irma and Maxine hugged her, and said, "We'll go, too!."

The Nazarene Mission began to grow rapidly. Soon more young men were answering the call to ordained ministry. Prayer services were scheduled and many were experiencing the presence of the Holy Spirit in profound ways. The altar rail was filled almost every Sunday. Daming was experiencing a real revival of the Holy Spirit. Soon all-night prayer meetings were breaking out at the tabernacle. People that had never come to church before, showed up and responded to the invitation to accept salvation in Christ. This lasted for weeks, some said even months. This was the first year back for the Fitz family, and since evangelism was the priority for Dr. Fitz, this was an answer to his prayers. Lura began a ministry with women and children, which took a great deal of her time.

In the meantime, Dr. Fitz was faced with a problem, the one Rev. Wiese had already indicated. Rev. and Mrs. Kiehn had been sowing discord at the very peak of spiritual renewal. It finally came to a head, and Rev. Wiese called a meeting. He asked the hospital staff, as well as all Mission personnel to come together for a time of prayer and discernment. After that they would vote on the Kiehn's position with the hospital and mission. All of the Chinese doctors and hospital staff gathered in the tabernacle. All of the mission personnel gathered as well. Following a time of scripture and prayer, Rev. Wiese said he would allow each speaker five minutes to tell their side of the conflict. They spoke in Mandarin and in English, both interpreted. Several of the Chinese doctors and nurses spoke, telling of the autocratic, and "unchristian" manner of Rev. Kiehn, and the gossiping way in which Mrs. Kiehn spoke behind their backs. Rev. Wiese asked for speeches in favor of the Kiehn's, but only one retired Chinese doctor spoke for them, a doctor who had been in trouble with many of the other Chinese doctors himself. Some had complained that he was guilty of the things that were said of the Kiehn's. Rev. Wiese appealed for more speeches supporting the Kiehn's.

Dr. Fitz stood and told them he was sure that "all assembled here today love the Kiehn's," but that the morale and the spiritual life of the hospital and ministry *had* to come before the personal feelings. Rev. Wiese then called for the vote, and it was nearly unanimous that the Kiehn's be asked to step down from their positions of leadership. It would be up to the Nazarene mission board whether or not they were recalled. The next morning everyone awoke to the sound of singing and shouting. The Kiehn's, and several of the families and friends of the retired Chinese doctor, had gathered on the steps of the hospital where they sat and refused to leave. They were singing, "We shall not be, we shall not be moved..." Despite the sad humor of the situation, the hospital security people eventually ushered them off the grounds. Rev. and Mrs. Kiehn did not live on the mission compound. Rev. Wiese had 'reluctantly recommended' to mission headquarters that they be recalled. The Nazarene mission board sent a letter recalling them, and they left by ship from Shanghai a few weeks later. It didn't seem to dampen the spiritual atmosphere in Daming; and many baptisms were frequent at the river close by.

Elizabeth began to build quite a repertoire, and lessons with Henry Sung were going well. Every few months, he would host recitals by his students, and Elizabeth was one of the favorites of all. She also accompanied the Nazarene mission choir which sang each Sunday. Rachel Chen liked playing for worship, but preferred that Beth accompany the choir. They presented special concerts at Christmas and Easter, and Rachel felt she was busy enough just preparing for worship. Eventually, she ended up playing for worship as well. Rachel Chen married Brian Tang, and they went off on their honeymoon for a few weeks. Brian was a Bible School graduate, and one of the pastors helping in worship. He was to be ordained following his internship there at the mission. Beth not only played for worship while they were gone, but she also played several times when Rachel and Brian took a Sunday off to guest-preach at one of the other mission churches in the area. She was asked to accompany Irma when she sang, and some of the other Chinese young people formed a youth choir. Irma and Maxine both sang in the new choir called Zan-Mei (*Praise!*)

When the weather was nice, the Fitz family often went with other missionaries from the Daming area, to the northern resort town of Beide He. There they stayed at resort cottages and swam in the ocean. It was refreshing and renewing. Many of the Nazarene missionaries held retreats there, and some of the best Bible studies Beth and her sisters ever experienced were at Beide He. They had all just come back from such a retreat, and Lura seemed aglow with the time of relaxation they had all enjoyed. She had given up on having any more family.

Beth was already almost fifteen, Irma was thirteen, and Maxine was eight. The Chinese had said the family needed a 'little prince' but Lura always laughed and waved them off. So, she was surprised when she discovered after returning from this wonderful vacation, that she was pregnant again. She was even more surprised when she delivered: she had given birth to her 'little prince' after three girls! He was red-haired like his sister Irma, and wiggly? He couldn't stay still for a second! Of course, all of their Chinese friends said, "I told you so," God truly had blessed them with an 'extra blessing.' They named him Rudolph Guilford Fitz, Jr, after his father. Dr. Fitz allowed Dr. Li, Zhi Guang, one of the Chinese doctors to do the honor of delivering him. He *did* assist, however, and enjoyed every moment. Rudolph Guilford, Jr., grew up in China, but in an American missionary environment. He seemed to have the colic more than his sisters... and one day it probably saved his life. [Even though the last Chinese dynasty had ended in 1912 with Sun Yat Sen's Nationalist revolution, 'war lords' still fought among themselves for dominance of the culture; they would bomb each other's fortresses from time to time, and stray shells sometimes damaged, injured, or even killed, innocent people, who had the misfortune of being caught in it]. The mission was in such a situation as this, shortly after Guilford was born. Lura and the children were staying indoors when they heard the shelling begin. They lived in a two-story house on the mission compound, and Guilford had been sleeping upstairs that afternoon. Because he had the colic, he started to cry, to the point where Lura called out to Beth, "please go tend to Guilford, he isn't feeling well again." Beth went upstairs and into Guilford's room, picked him up, and rocked him in her arms as she descended the stairs. In that very moment, a shell landed exactly in the middle of Guilford's crib; it exploded, demolishing the crib. Beth screamed and everyone came running. Both she and Guilford were unharmed, 'by the grace of our Lord,' as Beth said. Lura and the girls cried for joy because God had spared their lives in that moment of certain death!

Christmas was a special time for the Fitz family. They didn't spend much money on Christmas presents because they handcrafted most of the items they gave each other. They loved all the hustle and bustle...even the Chinese got caught up in the festive time that was essentially an American holiday. They taught everyone at the mission that Jesus' birth was for 'all the world,' especially since Jesus himself was an 'Asian.' They particularly enjoyed the live manger scene, the choir concert, the hospital party, and family time. The mission went into other parts of Daming to give gifts to those that had come to the tabernacle for services, especially those that had become Christians during the past year. The Fitz children loved when their dad brought the Christmas tree in, and they decorated it—even putting real candles on the branches. They had finished the Christmas Eve service and were gathering at the tree to begin opening presents. Lura called Beth and Irma in to the kitchen to help serve the cookies and hot 'wassail' while Maxine watched Guil; they took turns blowing out the candles when they left the room, so they wouldn't be used up before they opened their presents. When Lura called, Beth thought it was Irmas's turn, and Irma thought it was Beth's turn, to blow out the candles. Dr. Fitz was on his way back from the Christmas Eve service.

Maxine and Guil were still in the bedroom. As Lura was pouring the wassail, they heard Maxine scream; she had smelled smoke and came into the living room. The tree was on fire! Beth and Irma ran to get a blanket to smother the flames. Lura ran to the kitchen to get water. RG had heard Maxine scream and came running up the walk… but it was too late. The fire totally consumed the tree. Fortunately, Beth and Irma had managed to get the blanket in time to put the fire out. All the presents were burned. Lura and the girls cried. RG looked at the burned tree; thinking he would be angry with them, Beth and Irma looked at him and hung their heads. Dr. Fitz just said, "Thank you God for sparing our lives…presents are nothing compared to the *greatest* gift ever given, your dear son, Jesus." They all held each other, and started singing, "Silent night, holy night, all is calm all is bright…" It didn't seem to bother anyone that they had no presents that year; Jesus was the only *present* they needed. Lura cooked a wonderful Christmas dinner and they enjoyed the young Chinese singers who came by to serenade them early Christmas morning. After a 'long winter's nap,' everyone agreed that this was the *best* Christmas they'd every had!

It was 1935. Beth had finished the high school correspondence course, and Irma had finished tenth grade, the same way. Lura and RG began making plans for the two oldest ones to go back to the United States. They would stay with Katherine and Charles Witten in Bethany where Beth would begin college. Irma would enroll in the Bethany Academy and finish high school. The rest of the family would follow a year later. The hospital was in fairly good shape, and the Chinese doctors were taking over much of the responsibility for the patient load. Dr. Fitz began reading more and spending time alone with God. He was experiencing a depression after so many years of overwork with little respite. Guil was four years old... Maxine was twelve; she wanted to go with her older sisters, but she knew it would not be possible.

It was time for Beth and Irma to leave. They had a special farewell service, and commissioned them as 'missionaries to the United States;'(everyone had a laugh about that); and they stopped to take a family picture before leaving for Shanghai to catch their ship.

The Fitz family: Irma, Lura, Maxine, Guil, Dr. Fitz, Beth, 1935

CHAPTER NINE

THIS HUNGARIAN'S GOING TO CHINA

L-R: Irene & Al Solts, Lura & Guil Fitz, Beth,
Maxine, Irma, Lura Solts, and others

The Fitz family homestead – Fairbanks, Alaska

THIS TIME, UNCLE MAX MET THEM IN SAN
FRANCISCO. AFTER immigration and customs, they drove
the long trip to Oklahoma. Grandma Katherine had stayed in Bethany
to care for Grandpa Charles who was gravely ill. Uncle John Witten

had passed away years ago, but his son John had come up from Dallas to see his cousin before he died. Beth and Irma were disturbed by this news. Their grandfather had always been so much fun. [He told them stories of the Witten family adventures, from the American Revolution, to the stories of their Methodist Church in Virginia, to the westward movement, all the way until they got to Texas and Oklahoma. Max reminded them, as they drove, of all these and many other stories, until they arrived in Bethany]. Grandma was there to greet them. They were tired after the long voyage and road trip to Bethany, so she gave them something to eat, then they all went to bed. In the morning, they tried to talk to Grandpa Witten, but he was unresponsive. Grandma thought he had suffered a stroke…about two weeks ago. She tried to get him to the doctor, but he seemed to get better, so she called the doctor and he stopped by. Doctor McIntire was a member of First Nazarene, like so many others they knew in Bethany. He thought the stroke had been light and he should recover, but a few days later, he took a turn for the worse. Irene and Carl stopped by. Max got off work to come by. He was able to awaken briefly and had spoken to Katherine. His nephew John had visited and assured him of God's care for him, and the family's love. Beth and Irma went in to talk to him; Irma started to sing: "Ye-su ai wo, wo zheng zhi(r)…" (Jesus loves me this I know…), Beth joined in, singing the alto part. Grandpa smiled. "We love you Grandpa, mother and daddy love you…please go on ahead of us; we'll join you later," Beth said. Grandma hugged the girls and cried softly. Grandpa slipped away with the smile still on his face. [He had become a Christian before he married Katherine in St. Louis. He had served as one of the leaders in the Henrietta Nazarene church, and cared for Grandpa Stagg there like he was his own father, until he died. After they moved to Bethany, he had taught a Bible class at First Nazarene there. He loved to sing, read the Bible, and everyone loved to hear him pray]. He was buried there at Evergreen Memorial in Bethany. Katherine grieved, but rejoiced that they would be reunited again…as she said: on 'That Day.'

Beth registered as a freshman at Bethany College, and Irma registered at Bethany Academy for the eleventh grade. Delores McLeary had gotten married to one of the music professors at Bethany, Dr. Tim Porter, and they had moved to Illinois to teach at Olivet Nazarene

College. She had heard that Beth was to attend Bethany College and Irma the Academy, so she had decided to recommend that Beth play for the services at First Nazarene Bethany. She had written Beth in China to tell her about this, so Beth began playing for services almost from the day she arrived. Classes began and Beth met so many people that knew of her and her parents. The adjustment was harder than she had anticipated. Boys began asking her to go share a "soda" at the student center. She had only been on group social outings in China with other foreign missionary children. The Daming missionary community got together for joint Vesper services in English twice monthly. Several teenagers from Methodist, Baptist, Lutheran, Presbyterian...and others, knew each other socially, but never had gone on any 'dates.' Beth didn't know what she was supposed to say. [During the very last week before boarding the ship, her mother said to Dr. Fitz, "you're the doctor, if you don't tell her about the 'facts of life,' I guess I'm going have to do it," and she just blurted out everything, without any gracious way of saying how loving and beautiful the whole subject was; that God had ordained a married man and woman, truly in love, to be part of God's plan. Beth was so naïve, she was horrified, and dreamed for three nights in a row that some Chinese man was 'running after her.' This experience did not help her with her social skills]. Guys began to wonder how strange she was...that she always said: "I'm not dating anyone; I'm not getting married now, and God will lead me to the one he wants me to be with." She told Irma, who was sixteen, to say the same. They didn't know what to wear when it was announced that the college and academy were holding a group social gathering. They wore something that had been given to Grandma Katherine for them. It was very out dated and totally inappropriate. When they arrived, everyone was staring at them with the strangest looks on their faces. Beth and Irma were mortified. This, and other embarrassing moments made it difficult to adjust; they felt very homesick most of the year. Their other grandparents had written them from Minnesota while they were still in China. Grandpa E. Howard had died the year after they returned to Daming. Grandma Esther had lived four more years. They hoped to visit cousins sometime after Dr. and Mrs. Fitz returned in a year. The year went quickly, though, and Beth and Irma found that the Calvert Courses they had taken, had equipped them well, and their grades reflected their good schooling. Some of Beth's classes were music, but she decided not to major in music; getting her core classes out of the way first, would prepare her for a liberal arts degree. This would be more acceptable to the mission board when she fulfilled her call to be a missionary to China. Irma did not feel called to be a missionary, but rather to teach elementary school. Both Beth and Irma prayed that God would send them the right partners for life that would honor God. Beth prayed especially that God would send someone who wanted to be a missionary to China. They improved greatly in social skills, and one of the dorm mothers at Bethany, at their church graciously offered to 'coach' them in the proper mode of dress and decorum for young 'Nazarene girls.' They even double-dated a couple times...but only after Grandma Katherine had made sure they had some up-to-date dresses! Beth was busy with her piano lessons and Irma sang in the choir. She even sang a solo now and then, and everyone was enamored with her beautiful voice. Beth studied piano with Phyllis Ludwick, since Delores had married and moved to Illinois. Bethany College had a new president, Dr. Peter Grayson, because Dr. Widmeyer had retired. He had stayed on to teach Bible and a few music classes, but he also traveled as a short-term missionary with his wife Rebecca, for the Nazarene mission board.

Back in Daming, Lura and RG were finishing the five-year commitment they had given the Nazarene mission board. The hospital now used Dr. Sutherland, Dr. West, and doctors from the U.S. who came for short-term assignments. Chinese doctors took more and more of a leading role. The outreach part of the mission was well operated and a number of young pastors attending Bible school starting up churches across the three-province area of Hebei, Henan, and Shandung. Lura helped in the dispensary and taught women's and youth Bible classes, but much of her time she was helping Maxine complete a correspondence course for third grade, and Guilford was in a pre-school program. Dr. Fitz began reading everything he could get his hand on about the farming and frontier living. He had grown up in Minnesota, and with all the pressure of running the hospital, he began saying to himself, "if I don't get my hands down in the soil again, I'm liable to have a nervous breakdown." As he explored the United States frontier, with 'God's Word' and challenges lying ahead, he began to feel called to pioneer missionary work in Alaska. He read up on it, and found out that there were homesteading opportunities there. Land in and around Fairbanks…claims to be staked. He prayed…seeking the Lord about this…then he talked to his friend and co-missionary Harry Wiese. Rev. Wiese told him they would love to have him come back after a rest and furlough, but he knew in his heart that RG felt he had completed his medical missionary work in China for this 'time in his life.' Lura was delighted. She loved China, and the Chinese had loved her, for her hard work, and her love and care of them; but she missed her family, and had spent so much time away from them. She felt it was time to leave. Maybe Rudolph could practice medicine in Bethany… and preach once in a while. Then RG explained to Lura that God was calling him to open up missionary work in Alaska. *ALASKA?* She cried out loud; she ran to her bedroom…and cried; she ran to the tabernacle, to the altar rail…and cried. She sought God's face; she prayed, "O God, I put him through college after we married, following Bible school, I put him through ordination, and through medical school. I came to China… twice…without a call. I need to spend time with my mother and family. How can I do this, Lord?" Before she heard any answer from God, she got up from the altar. She went to RG and said, "I will *not* go to Alaska, I will stay with my *mother* in Bethany. You can go where you want…but you can go without *me*!" It was final…as far as she was concerned.

Over the next few weeks before they left to return to the United States, RG wrapped up the business of the mission. He stepped down as Head of Bresee Memorial Hospital and turned that over to Dr. Sutherland. Dr. West had decided to return to the U.S. Harry Wiese would continue on until they replaced him with a new district superintendent. RG prayed each day that God would show him what to do. He felt the Lord calling him to Alaska, but he also recognized how unfair it was to Lura to have to continue to give up her family. His mother-in-law had now lost her husband, meaning Lura had lost her father. Her sister Irene, and her brother Max, also needed her. He sought the Lord…he prayed for God to show him what to do. Finally, just weeks before they were to leave, he had his answer. He spoke to Lura, "if I could convince your mother, sister, brother and families to go with us to Alaska, would you go?" Lura laughed excitedly…her prays had been answered! She knew that her mother would *NEVER* agree to go to Alaska. She smiled, and said, "Rudolph, I didn't have a call to China, but I went; and now you have seen fit to *'give up your call to Alaska,'* (because she knew her mother would NEVER agree to go…or so she thought). Thank you, RG, you truly are a man of God… the Lord has really been working in your life!" She put her arms around him. She felt that everything was going to be alright. Maxine and Guil came in to see what was going on. They laughed when they saw their mother and father hugging and laughing. RG bowed his head, and they thanked God for their time in China, a blessing upon Beth and Irma in Bethany, and Grandma Witten who was keeping them.

Beth finished her freshman year. Irma finished her junior year at the academy. Uncle Max fixed up the big roadster for the long trip to San Francisco. Irene and Carl Solts decided they needed to stay with Grandma Witten who said it was too far for her to go. They would all be coming back there anyway. Beth had a substitute replace her at the piano at First Nazarene Bethany for a couple weeks, while they went out to meet the ship coming from China with her folks. The USS President Garfield came sailing in under the Golden Gate bridge, and docked at the terminal in San Francisco. Beth and Irma waved excitedly when they spotted their mother and daddy. Maxine and Guilford started jumping up and down, waving frantically. When they finally got through immigration, they claimed their trunks at the cargo dock. These would be sent by rail to Bethany, because there was no room in the roadster; it was tight…with five adults plus Maxine and Guilford. They drove to Temple City, California, and stayed with George and Stephanie Macgregor, who ran a home for furloughed missionaries. From there they drove to Flagstaff, then to Albuquerque, then on to Bethany… staying each place with Nazarene pastors or church members. They arrived home tired and hungry, but happy to be 'home.' Grandma Witten had fixed a nice meal. Irene and Carl had come over and helped, and the whole Bethany First Nazarene family had brought things by…to welcome them back. The following Sunday was a glorious reunion of friends and family, and Dr. RG and Lura were given a 'hero's welcome.' Beth and Irma sang, the choir sang; Dr. Peter Grayson, guest preacher, spoke; they allowed Dr. Fitz to share what Nazarene medical missions had accomplished in China.

They had settled in a few days later, and were having breakfast. RG had gotten up early and was having a cup of coffee with Katherine, his mother-in-law. He asked her what she knew about Alaska–Lura heard them talking at the breakfast table and quickly joined them. Katherine was telling them about the homesteading they had done when they arrived in 'sooner territory,' from Texas, in the early nineteen hundreds. RG asked if what was going on in Alaska in 1936 was anything like what they had experienced then. Katherine went on and on about the excitement of marking their own claim in 1906 prior to their moving there, when Lura was a teenager. Lura came in and poured herself a cup of coffee...she did not like what she was hearing. Rudolph was at his most eloquent best, and her mother was falling for it! She politely interrupted and said she was *not* going to Alaska, but would stay in Bethany with her mother, Irene, and Max. Katherine turned and looked at Lura...then Irene looked in the door and said, "Hello, got room for one more?" There was a cold silence in the kitchen. RG looked away... Katherine was looking at Lura with a quizzical 'what is going on here' look, not aware of the announcement that RG was about to make. Irene said, "shall I come back later?" Lura said, "no, Irene, come in, I was just telling mother that RG wants to begin missionary work in Alaska, and I just told them here I had decided that I am *not* going. I am staying here with you and mother; I couldn't be here when Dad Witten died, and I have given enough; supporting RG through schooling, ordination, and twelve years in medical missions in China." Irene looked at RG who stood up to get another cup of coffee. Then she sat down and looked at Katherine and Lura. RG turned around with his cup of coffee. "The Lord asked me to go to start missionary work in Alaska; we would homestead like Dad Witten and you did in 1906. I promised Lura I was willing to *not* go...but if we could convince you, and Carl, Mother Witten, and Max to go with us and our whole family..." His voice trailed off. Beth and Irma had gotten up. Katherine stood to start breakfast. Max and Carl were already outside working on the roadster. Beth and Irma went to help make breakfast with Irene and Grandma. Lura left to go check on Maxine and Guilford. RG decided he would leave too...for the moment. He needed to go spend sometime reading his Bible and praying. He went to the church and knelt at the altar rail. He opened his Bible, and the pages fell open to

Psalm 73. There he read in verses 25 and 26: *"Whom have I in heaven but thee? And earth has nothing I desire besides thee. My flesh and my heart may fail, but God is the strength of my heart, and my portion forever."* He said, "Lord, I feel you have called me now to a new task in Alaska, but Lura needs her mother and family, if you will show me what I am to do, I will be willing to follow you wherever you ask me to go…or stay. Amen." When he got back, Lura had gone to the store with Maxine and Guilford. Grandma Witten was sitting at the breakfast table with Irene, and Max. "Hello Dr. Fitz, we were just reminiscing about when we moved from Clay County in Texas to our new homestead here in Bethany in 1907. Dad Charles was such a trooper; he staked out our claim all by himself, and waited for us to join him; we came a few months later…so, *when do we move to Alaska?"* RG was stunned. He said he wanted to wait till they all talked to Aunt *Lura*. "Oh, we already talked to her…she said if her whole family was going, God must be preparing her for her *next adventure*; she said how could she say no! She went to the store to pick up some things for Maxine and Guilford." RG knew God had worked his will again; the Lord works in mysterious ways… his wonders to perform!

Beth and Irma were totally on board with the idea; everyone began planning the big move to Alaska. In June they went to Seattle; the Nazarene District Superintendent, Rev. Elmer Smee, arranged for them to stay with people there until they raised the money and shipped the supplies to Fairbanks. RG and Carl went up to Fairbanks from Seattle and signed the homesteading papers and made the arrangements to stake out a claim about twelve miles northeast of downtown Fairbanks; according to the terms of the homesteading agreement, they had to clear between three and five acres per year. The plan was Beth would attend her sophomore year at Fairbanks College, and Irma, Maxine and Guilford to be homeschooled again. They would organize a church in their log cabin and ask for it to be recognized by the Church of the Nazarene in the Alaska Territory. The Nazarene mission board had turned down their request to be sent as missionaries to Alaska, *but* allowed the Northwest District to 'expand' its mission, and raise money to send the Fitz family there. From there they would 'live off the land,' or find employment in Fairbanks. The group included: Dr. and Mrs. Fitz, their four children, Irene and Carl Solts, and their two children; Max, Grandma Witten; in all, it was a total of twelve. The Northwest District agreed to take on the responsibility of helping them raise the funds for: 1) one-way travel between Seattle and Fairbanks, 2) four tents, twelve sleeping bags or bedding, 3) machinery to be purchased in Fairbanks for setting up camp and building two log cabins, and 4) food, cookware and tableware for two months until the cabins were built. Churches in the Seattle and Portland area were very excited about this venture, and the funds came in quickly. In June and July, they completed raising the money, and left by boat for Alaska. From Anchorage they went overland by truck and bus to Fairbanks. The truck took them the rest of the way to their land that Dr. Fitz and Carl Solts had staked out as their homestead. They pitched the tents, built a fire, and enjoyed their first meal of: fresh vegetables, beef jerky, and coffee. They began felling trees for the logs that were to be used to build the cabins. At night they slept in their tents, and took turns standing guard with the shotgun, watching for any bears or other wild animals. The important thing was to keep the fire going, and the coffee pot full. RG and Carl had had a heated discussion about the method of building the cabins. Carl insisted that his cabin needed to be built first, and he would decide the manner in which it would be done. RG disagreed, but in deference to Carl, and because Grandma Witten and Max would join Irene and Carl in the second cabin, RG gave in. Grandma Witten was still quite spry, but her age was nevertheless a concern. They built the second cabin according to Carl's plan. They had finished supper that evening, and retired to their tents. In the middle of the night there was a loud crash…Carl's cabin had come tumbling down! RG could have said "I told you so," but instead they rebuilt Carl's cabin *again*, before the Fitz cabin…but they *did* build it according to R.G.'s specifications! They dug a well, built a 'privy,' and installed some kerosene lamps.

By this time, it was almost September. The ground was beginning to freeze, and they were still living in the tents…they were thankful for the heavy blankets they had brought along. Carl's cabin was finished and they quickly assembled the Fitz cabin as well. The final step in the process was 'chinking' the roof with moss. The surface was thatched with small wood and branches, and then the moss was placed on top; one problem…the frozen ground included the moss they were to use!

Beth and Irma were placed in charge of digging the frozen moss squares out of the ground, plunging them into the large incinerator barrel full of boiling water, with the fire underneath. They would then carry it up to the roof and slap it on; another problem…it then immediately froze. They thought this would be fine… until spring arrived; when everything thawed, the moss, which had not had a chance to dry and "chink" in the thatching properly, began to drip muddy water…right into Lura's nice white linen, the only fancy things she had to show from her years in China. That was the 'last straw!' She broke down and wept, and no one could console her for a long time. She felt China had never been this difficult. Beth and Irma tried to wash them by hand, but they were so delicate and the mossy, muddy, murky stains never came out. The first year was very hard. After the roof was repaired in the spring, they dug trenches in the fields and buried pipe with hot water running through them to thaw the ground for earlier planting of potatoes. These were sold in Fairbanks at the open market. They grew berries and some corn and fresh vegetables; all of this helped pay the bills. They also felled more trees and built a small barn. They were able to bring electricity in from Fairbanks on lines that had been installed by the city. The big news as far as Beth was concerned was that they were able to buy an old upright piano which they kept in the front room. Here they held their first worship service. After several weeks of visiting neighbors in the area, the living room could barely hold the fifteen to twenty people that joined *Fairbanks First Church of the Nazarene*. They petitioned the Church of the Nazarene General Board to be recognized, and after some delay this was finally granted. Dr. Fitz and Carl Solts went in to Fairbanks and looked for land where they might build a church facility. The Northwest District again was very helpful. Dr. Fitz received twenty new members for this new congregation. Nine of his own family were full members and three were preparatory members. Four other families had eight adults and seven additional children as preparatory members. Of the six families all together, they were able to raise the ten percent required to qualify for the District funds. They built a simple church facility close to downtown Fairbanks. Beth began her sophomore year at Fairbanks College and Irma attended Fairbanks High School. Maxine and Guilford continued their home schooling for the time being. Lura, Irene, and Grandma Witten were kept busy

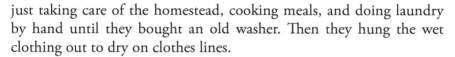

just taking care of the homestead, cooking meals, and doing laundry by hand until they bought an old washer. Then they hung the wet clothing out to dry on clothes lines.

The family became quite good at hunting. They bought rifles in town to add to the shotgun they already had. RG, Carl, Max, Beth and Irma were able to bring in deer, elk, pheasant, quail, wild boar, and a number of other smaller animals. They raised rabbits and chickens as well. They teased Beth—they called her the 'Butcher of Fairbanks'— she hated this name, *but her skill at ringing the necks of chickens so quickly was well-known in that 'neck of the woods,'* Ha! They dressed out game, wrapped the meat in butcher paper, and stored it on shelves in the porch; it would freeze overnight, so keeping it was no problem. [Jumping ahead, Frank shared a story about Irma after she married and had a son named Larry. The family was enjoying a Sunday afternoon, when Larry came in, telling them all about the 'goggy' he had seen. Since there was no "goggy" around, they quizzed him about this; turns out that the 'goggy' was a black bear cub that had wandered on to the property; fortunately, they had a friendly encounter, and the cub went back to its mother, or this might have been a tragedy]. Of course, they were *not* without fear in the wild, but always trusted in God's protection daily. Their first potato crop did *not* do well, and Lura was forced to get a job in Fairbanks at a laundry. She and Irene took turns at the laundry, and the schooling of her two, Alvin K., and Lura Frances, as well as Guil, and Maxine. RG, Carl, and Max, also found odd jobs to tide them over. The church grew from the original twenty members to nearly sixty, so R.G. had to spend more time with the church. Beth finished her sophomore year, and began to make plans to go to college. Grandma Witten reminded her of her plans to go to Bethany, but Beth had also written to Pasadena College in California. There was a report that a number of students there were planning to go to the mission field, and she knew that the Nazarene mission board was no longing sending primarily single women missionaries, but rather married couples. She prayed that God would lead her to a godly man that felt called to be a missionary to China. Irma wanted to finish high school at the Pasadena Nazarene Academy, so the two of them again began making plans to travel together, and make a new life for themselves in California. They both applied to Pasadena College and Academy, and were accepted. Because Dr. and Mrs. Fitz had already been on the mission field, Beth and Irma were offered scholarships.

RG and Lura decided to stay in Alaska, and Maxine started high school in Fairbanks. Guilford started first grade. Grandma Witten, Irene, Carl and their two children, Alvin, and Lura left and found a new home in Nampa, Idaho. Beth and Irma traveled to Pasadena, and were able to live with retired missionaries their first year there, and then later in the dormitory. They made friends quickly and their studies went well. Crusaders was the Pasadena College mascot, and Beth quickly felt welcome in the Crusaders Missionary Fellowship which she attended regularly. Many of the students attended Bresee Avenue Nazarene Church, but the College President, Dr. Orton Wiley, who was a favorite professor of Beth, attended Pasadena First Nazarene, and she loved to hear him preach as a guest there. She was asked to play the piano from time to time, but they had a regular pianist, Lily Graham, who also taught piano at the College. Beth was able to study piano with her for one semester. She also met up with the former President of Bethany, Dr. Widmeyer. She had taken music classes from him at Bethany.

One Sunday at First Nazarene Pasadena, Beth noticed a dark-haired student from Canada who was attending Crusader Missionary Fellowship. He was talking to Dr. Wiley. She knew he had dated Helen Reiten, a missionary kid from Hong Kong. One of Beth's first dates was with Uri Chandler, and she and Uri had run into the two of them at the Student Union building, where they were showing the film, 'Wesley.' Beth was considered an 'old China hand,' and Helen's father had founded the Peniel mission in Hong Kong, so Helen introduced Beth to him. Helen told her his name was Michael Varro from Regina, Saskatchewan. Uri seemed to know him as well, because they had both preached at a street mission in Los Angeles. Uri was planning to go to China and had already learned a little Mandarin. Beth was fluent, and the two of them 'chatted' a few words here and there…so he could practice, he said. Beth thought that Michael and Helen were somewhat serious, but she found out later that Helen was already interested in another Senior named Robert Hammond, who wanted to go to Hong

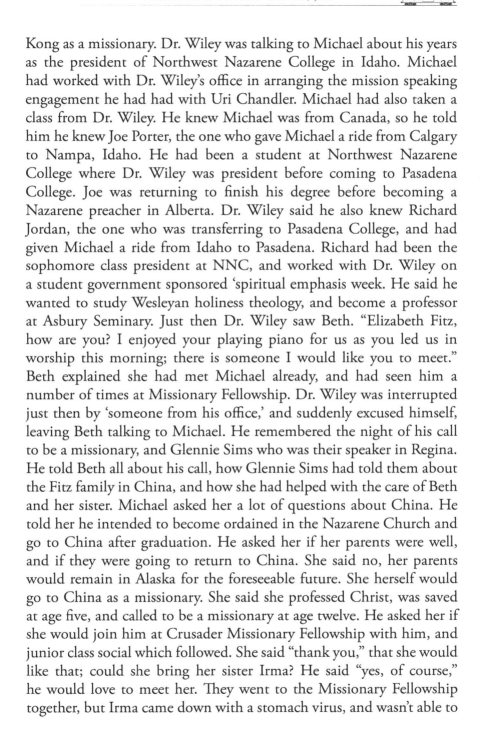

Kong as a missionary. Dr. Wiley was talking to Michael about his years as the president of Northwest Nazarene College in Idaho. Michael had worked with Dr. Wiley's office in arranging the mission speaking engagement he had had with Uri Chandler. Michael had also taken a class from Dr. Wiley. He knew Michael was from Canada, so he told him he knew Joe Porter, the one who gave Michael a ride from Calgary to Nampa, Idaho. He had been a student at Northwest Nazarene College where Dr. Wiley was president before coming to Pasadena College. Joe was returning to finish his degree before becoming a Nazarene preacher in Alberta. Dr. Wiley said he also knew Richard Jordan, the one who was transferring to Pasadena College, and had given Michael a ride from Idaho to Pasadena. Richard had been the sophomore class president at NNC, and worked with Dr. Wiley on a student government sponsored 'spiritual emphasis week. He said he wanted to study Wesleyan holiness theology, and become a professor at Asbury Seminary. Just then Dr. Wiley saw Beth. "Elizabeth Fitz, how are you? I enjoyed your playing piano for us as you led us in worship this morning; there is someone I would like you to meet." Beth explained she had met Michael already, and had seen him a number of times at Missionary Fellowship. Dr. Wiley was interrupted just then by 'someone from his office,' and suddenly excused himself, leaving Beth talking to Michael. He remembered the night of his call to be a missionary, and Glennie Sims who was their speaker in Regina. He told Beth all about his call, how Glennie Sims had told them about the Fitz family in China, and how she had helped with the care of Beth and her sister. Michael asked her a lot of questions about China. He told her he intended to become ordained in the Nazarene Church and go to China after graduation. He asked her if her parents were well, and if they were going to return to China. She said no, her parents would remain in Alaska for the foreseeable future. She herself would go to China as a missionary. She said she professed Christ, was saved at age five, and called to be a missionary at age twelve. He asked her if she would join him at Crusader Missionary Fellowship with him, and junior class social which followed. She said "thank you," that she would like that; could she bring her sister Irma? He said "yes, of course," he would love to meet her. They went to the Missionary Fellowship together, but Irma came down with a stomach virus, and wasn't able to join them. After the missions meeting, they went to the junior class get-together, and everyone started talking about that 'Hungarian preacher' from Canada with the well-known 'Dr. Fitz's daughter from China.'

Beth wasn't able to transfer all her credits from Bethany College and Fairbanks College (now University of Alaska-Fairbanks), she would have to take an extra year. Michael was able to begin his senior year because he had transferred most of his credits from Northern Bible College. He was a philosophy major with a Bible minor. Beth was a psychology major with a music minor. He lived with some other Canadian students in the 'international house' off campus, and Beth and Irma transferred from Crabbe, a private residence, to 'Auntie Mac's' home. Ethel Macpherson, *Auntie Mac,* had been with Peniel, but was now with World Gospel Mission. She opened her home to missionary children, and Beth and Irma were fortunate to be invited to live there. Michael took morning classes, and was able to 'lath his way through college,' as he teasingly said, with a carpentry job in the afternoon. ['Lathing' was the process of nailing 'laths' or small horizontal boards, up on the wall and smearing the plaster over them to complete the wall; 'lathing' became a common joke among carpenters]. Irma and Beth ate their meals with Auntie Mac, but were able to get jobs in the dining center—Irma on the serving line; Beth helped prepare the food. Irma finished her senior year at the Academy, and began her freshman year at Pasadena College as an Elementary Education major. Michael preached once a month at the mission in Los Angeles with Uri Chandler, Bob Hammond, and some of the other ministerial candidates. He and Beth had started dating regularly, and Beth returned home in the evening with so many endless stories of: *Michael this, and Michael that,* but Irma just rolled her eyes, and smiled.

Beth was working hard on her piano recital. She invited Michael to come sit with her during the program. The recital ended with a duet, which Beth played with Nancy Merton, a senior music major. They played 'British Grenadiers' to the rousing applause of everyone. Michael was beaming from ear to ear, and everyone acted as though they were already married. Beth introduced him to everyone following the recital, telling them 'Michael is a candidate for ordination in the Church of the Nazarene, and plans to go as a missionary to China.'

This pleased him, and he started praying about them marrying… and going to China together; Beth was planning on finishing her degree the following year.

Michael graduated with an Arts Bachelor, AB, in Philosophy, June of 1939. He enrolled for an additional year, finishing a Theology Bachelor, Th.B. This gave him, with theology credits he had from Northern Bible College (now Canadian Nazarene College}, a better standing with the General Assembly, to recommend him for ordination in the Nazarene Church that next year. He had also applied to the Nazarene mission board for appointment as missionary to China. He attended District Assembly with Beth and Irma, and other candidates for ordained ministry. When it was over, he received the news he was praying for: he would be recommended by Los Angeles First Nazarene for ordination at the Nazarene General Assembly the following year. In a few months, he also received word that he would be appointed as a missionary to China 'with spouse.' This seemed to be the impetus that Michael and Beth needed. So, Michael made his plan. He would attend a spiritual retreat at Laguna Beach that Dr. Wiley was conducting; Beth, Irma, and several others were also planning to attend. The last night of the retreat he asked Beth to have dinner with him. After dinner he asked her to marry him…to fulfill their call to be missionaries to China… he said he loved her; he wanted to share their lives together. She said she'd be 'so happy to marry him,' to go as missionaries to China… to serve God like she had always planned. The word got to Dr. Wiley that Michael Varro and Elizabeth Fitz were 'engaged to be married.' He surprised everyone by announcing it in the retreat's final gathering. They all sang 'Love Divine,' then applauded, as Dr. Wiley asked them all to bless Michael and Elizabeth in their future together. As he prayed, they all lifted their hands and prayed together out loud. It was a joyful evening. Beth wrote her folks with the news. Dr. and Mrs. Fitz made plans to come down from Alaska for the wedding. Lou Varro, who had moved to Los Angeles, and enrolled at Pasadena College, said he would be happy to accept Michael's invitation to be Best Man. Irma and Maxine were to be Maid of Honor and Bride's Maid…and Michael and Beth asked Dr. Wiley to officiate at their wedding. Their wedding was held June 6, 1940, at Pasadena First Nazarene Church. Later they took pictures in the church with the wedding party.

Beth graduated with an Arts Bachelor, A.B, in Psychology. Michael graduated a second time with a Th.B., a Bachelor's degree in Theology. Rev. R.T. Williams, General Superintendent, who sponsored him at the District Assembly at Los Angeles First Church of the Nazarene, ordained him at General Assembly, which was in Oklahoma City two weeks later. Their appointment as missionaries to China had to be revised to read: 'Rev. Michael F. Varro, and his *wife* Elizabeth Fitz Varro, as missionaries to China.' (there was irony, in that Lura Fitz, mother-in-law, went *with* them on the bus, on their 'honeymoon,' ha!). The traveled together in order to attend General Assembly, because Dr. Fitz had already gone on ahead.

It seemed as if their dream had finally come true...graduated, married, appointed to China as missionaries, starting a new life together; but God had other plans for the moment. The war of China with Japan was intense. They had gotten back from General Assembly and the funds had been raised for them to go to China. They had booked their passage on the General Meigs. The telegram said simply: "Delay passage to China, war too intense to leave at this time." They postponed their passage until the next trip the General Meigs sailed for China. The Fitz's returned to Alaska with Guilford. Maxine stayed in Pasadena to finish high school at the academy, and Irma started her senior year. The week before they were to sail, the Nazarene mission board sent another telegram: "War still too intense to leave at this time." Once again, they postponed their passage. Michael and Beth were living temporarily with Auntie Mac, but they couldn't stay there indefinitely. Michael had to get a few carpentry jobs to make ends meet; Lou was in Art School in Los Angeles. Still, they believed God would work things out. Then the fateful day came. The Nazarene Mission Board wrote a letter this time. *"Due to the intensity of the war between China and Japan, it is necessary for you to cancel all plans to go as missionaries to China, at this time; your appointment is hereby withdrawn until further notice."* The news cut like a knife. Michael and Beth Varro cried themselves to sleep that night. They prayed one prayer: "You are God, we are yours, our hearts are broken, but we will trust you."

Maxine, Edna Maude (and children),
Irma, Beth, Michael, Lou and friends Kyu & Mark

Book III begins with the great disappointment of canceled plans to go to China, raising their family in Canada, North Dakota, and Washington, finally arriving in China as missionaries, even if ever so briefly.

BOOK III

The Long Way Home

The Journey with many Detours

CHAPTER TEN

NOT THE ARCTIC CIRCLE BUT YOU CAN SEE IT FROM HERE

Now try crossing it when it's frozen

THE PASTORAL APPOINTMENTS HAD ALREADY BEEN MADE...EVERY District they wrote said the same thing: They didn't have anything at this time. Michael wrote the Districts in Saskatchewan, British Columbia, Manitoba, and finally Alberta... nothing. Then George Coulter wrote back. An appointment they had made for northern Alberta had come back 'refused.' High Prairie Nazarene Church was open after all. Would he take it? Newlyweds, married four months...what choice did they have? Michael wrote back...they would take it...with broken hearts! Still, God works in mysterious ways...

Michael and Beth packed up all their things. Michael had saved some from his carpentry work and had bought a used 1935 roadster after his graduation in 1939, so he had transportation during his fifth year for the second Bachelor's degree. Irma and Maxine were able to move in with Auntie Mac. Dr. RG and Lura Fitz had returned to Fairbanks with Guilford, by way of Nampa, Idaho. Now Michael and Beth made the same trip with a visit to Irene and Carl, and Lura's mother. They all cried and prayed together. Grandma Witten said, "it is not for us to understand God's ways for us, we need only trust Him." They drove on up from Nampa to Calgary. There they stayed with George Coulter and other Canadian friends. George gave them the information on the church in High Prairie, and gave them encouragement that China would open up again when things died down. The Nazarene mission was moving from Taming to south central China. Rev. Harry Wiese and the Pattee family had located a place for the Nazarene mission in Ji An in Jiangxi province. He encouraged Michael and Beth to apply every year until they received an appointment. When they got to Edmonton, they met the chair of the board for the High Prairie Church of the Nazarene, Chuck Garfield. He remembered Michael as a student pastor in the Innisfail Nazarene church during Red Deer Bible School years. Chuck had to stay in Edmonton on business, but he gave him the key to the church and parsonage, saying he would return by Sunday. It was already late September and the ground was frozen. They had to cross a few rivers between Edmonton and High Prairie because the gravel roads were not completed in a few places. In all her years in China, Beth had not experienced this kind of travel. They had traveled by ox cart, wheelbarrow, rickshaw, train, and many other means of travel, but never by car over a *frozen river*. When they got to the first crossing, Michael got out of the car and told Beth to drive slowly, following him to the creek's edge. Beth said, "Michael, I'm afraid...I cannot do this...what if the ice breaks and we perish?" Michael assured her it was frozen to the bottom, but he just wanted to make sure. He said God was with them, and that everything would be okay. With her 'heart in her throat,' Beth drove the car slowly behind Michael. He jumped on the ice several times, then motioned for her to drive onto the ice. He moved forward…then jumped on the ice again, and again…until they made it across the frozen river. He laughed, jumped in the car, and they drove on. They did it two more times. Each time Beth was frightened but trusted her new husband that he would get them there. It was already almost dark when they pulled into the gravel drive in front of the church and parsonage. They unloaded the car and opened a can of beans that had been left on the shelf in the kitchen. They found some blankets and slept their first night there.

Michael opened his Bible in the morning to Lamentations 3:22-23, *"it is of the Lord's mercies that we are not consumed, because his compassions fail not…they are new every morning, great is thy faithfulness…"* Elizabeth," he said, *"It's not the Arctic Circle…but you can see it from here!"* He laughed, and then Beth laughed and said, "what else do you have for us, Lord?" There was a knock at the door. Evelyn Foster, the wife of Bert Foster, another member of the church board, had brought some eggs, bread and milk. They visited a bit while Beth made some breakfast, giving them some information about the church and High Prairie.

Michael preached a good sermon his first Sunday there. Beth played the piano, and led them in some of their favorite hymns. After the service Chuck Garfield, who had returned from Edmonton, and his wife, the Foster's, and several others, came up and greeted them. Chuck had collected the offering, and handed Michael some change. They had agreed to pay Michael and Elizabeth a dollar fifty per week, but what he gave him were a few dimes and nickels. When Michael asked him about it, he said, "Well Reverend, we have to pay the electric bill first, and then the other utilities, you get what is left." [Michael loved to tell the story that when their first child, Lurabeth Julia, was born, they doubled their salary…from a dollar fifty a week to three dollars!!]. Times were very hard. The church had left a sack of potatoes, a sack of onions, and a sack of carrots, in the root cellar. They had not tasted meat for over a month. One day, there was a knock on the door. It was freezing cold and they asked the man to come in. He said "no, Reverend, I just wanted to give you some meat that I have here for you." He wasn't a member of the church, but he said he had heard they needed some help. He shifted from one foot to the other, and acted nervous, but Michael thanked him and asked him to leave it on the porch. He did so and left abruptly. Michael suspected that he had shot it out of season, and felt guilty for accepting this gift, so he went to the Bible to see if there was any "word from the Lord." In I Corinthians 10:25, he found the answer: "… and ask no questions for conscience's sake." Beth laughed and said, "Michael, isn't that reading into God's Word? Hmm?" But she quickly prepared supper, and with the fresh venison and vegetables, it was the best meal they had enjoyed in months. There were many stories like that, but with Michael's carpentry skills and odd jobs that he and Beth were able to find, they got through this difficult time, and God brought in believers too through their ministry.

At the end of their second year in High Prairie, Beth told Michael she thought she was pregnant. They had a doctor in town, and a small hospital. They had made several friends in the community by that time and most everyone thought well of Dr. Einar Gunter. So, Beth went to see him; he confirmed what she thought: she was pregnant. When their daughter, Lurabeth Julia, was born, though, it was January 1, 1943, and it was sixty-three degrees below zero! Dr. Gunter had sent in the information to the Department of Statistics for the Province of Alberta, and they received an award for the first child born in Alberta in the year 1943. It was so cold that when Beth and Lurabeth arrived home after five days in the hospital, they had to keep her in bed with them; but in order to not suffocate her, they kept her under the blanket only a few minutes at a time, providing a small opening so she could breathe. They kept the furnace as low as possible so they wouldn't deplete their meager coal supply.

By the end of their third year in High Prairie, World War II was in full swing. Michael had been born in old Austro-Hungary, but all of his siblings had been born in Canada. They were considered Canadian, but Michael's passport read *Romanian*, since the Treaty of Trianon, after World War I, had made the former Hungarian areas around Timisoara part of Romania. He had applied for United States citizenship, but because Romania, *and* Hungary, were part of the World War II Axis Powers, his application had been delayed, and then made "inactive until further notice." Elizabeth told him she was pregnant again. They both felt they had done all they could at the High Prairie Nazarene Church. Michael had asked the new District Superintendent of Canada West for another assignment but nothing seemed to be available at that time. George Coulter had been moved to Kansas City, and was thought to be in line for General Superintendent. Michael decided they needed to leave High Prairie, whether he got another appointment or not. He wanted to go live in Edmonton and work on his U.S. immigration, while working on getting an assignment in the Northwestern U.S., in the Seattle area, if possible, in the fall. He was sure the Nazarene mission board would not send them to China if he didn't become a naturalized U.S. citizen. Beth had not seen her folks in Fairbanks for three years, and didn't want to wait until they were too old to enjoy their grandchildren. So, Michael suggested she take Lurabeth and go visit her family in Fairbanks for the summer, and then he would join them when the baby was born. After they prayed about it, Beth agreed that this is what they should do. Michael wrote Rev. Samuel Johnson, the District Superintendent, telling him that he had resigned as the pastor in High Prairie. Every year, they had also applied again to go to China as missionaries, but were given no hope of doing so until the war was over. Beth and Michael clung to the hope that they were in God's hand, and he would hear their cry. A new chapter in their ministry was about to begin…

Rev. Michael and Beth Varro and daughter, Lurabeth Julia

Chapter Eleven

A Towhead...and mosquitoes 'that'll take down a moose'

The old homestead, and another re-start

EFORE LEAVING FOR EDMONTON, MICHAEL HAD WRITTEN MYRON AND Ethel Zumwalt, who were still living on their farm near Red Deer. Myron had become a part time pastor in a small independent church after graduating from Northern Bible College, but he had never become ordained. His children had moved into Calgary, and he ended up teaching a Bible Class in a Nazarene church in Red Deer. He had called his brother, Rev. Kenneth Zumwalt, in Edmonton. He asked him if Michael could stay with him for a few months. Ken Zumwalt was a pastor in the Pilgrim Holiness church. He said he would be delighted to have Michael stay with him…even have him preach once in a while in his church…and that way he wouldn't even have to pay rent. So, it was all set. Michael would stay the summer with Ken Zumwalt. He said he could help him make contact with the U.S. Immigration office in Edmonton, and advise him on the best way to pursue U.S. citizenship. Michael made contact with the Nazarene Church in Edmonton, and they said they would have pulpits to fill during the summer as guest preacher, even though they still had no churches to offer as pastor. Rev. Samuel Johnson in Calgary allowed Michael to use the resources of the Canada West District office to contact the Mission headquarters in Kansas City. Even with free board…if it weren't for the carpentry jobs, he wouldn't be able to make it. They hadn't been able to save anything in High Prairie; the airfare for Beth and Lurabeth had depleted their savings.

Beth had come to Edmonton with Michael to take the plane with Lurabeth up to Fairbanks. They said a tearful goodbye. Michael told her to give his love to her folks and to have a good visit. He would be there as soon as he could. It was the first week of May, and she was already eight months along. When she arrived in Fairbanks, RG and Lura met her plane and they went straight to the Homestead. It had changed quite a bit. The potato crop was coming in very well now, berries and vegetables were in abundance, and they were getting a good price at the Farmer's Market in Fairbanks. She hadn't forgotten how to use her rifle, nor how to drive the tractor, and she pitched in with a fair amount of the chores while her mother took care of Lurabeth. She was still driving the tractor nine months pregnant. It pleased her mother for them to combine two names in naming their first child: [the first part of 'Lurabeth,' was Elizabeth's mother Lura; the 'Beth' part of 'Lurabeth' was Elizabeth's name; her second name, 'Julia,' was for Michael's mother 'Julia,' who had died when he was six].

They had to keep constantly covered with repellant. The mosquitoes were in such abundance…*a black swarm of them could cover an entire moose, bringing him to his knees!* They had hired a part time worker from their church, a Klingit named Sconto. He had professed Christ as a young man in the Nazarene church where RG was pastor. He married a young Klingit woman who took on the name Ruth after she was saved in the Olivet Baptist church across town. She had come over to Fairbanks First Nazarene after her mother died. Lura had met her when they both worked at the laundry near the church. Sconto and Ruth had three children, and the job of foreman that RG had given him probably saved his life. It kept him from going back into alcoholism and petty theft; he had spent time in prison. Beth learned from Sconto how to trap small game, and after he told her about how far he had to commute, she suggested that his family move to *Denali Sunrise,* a new housing project near their homestead. It would be closer to work, and Ruth could apply for the laundry job there. Ruth applied for the job, and Lura wrote a letter of recommendation. Three weeks later Sconto said Ruth got the job…and they were moving to *Denali Sunrise!* "The Lord be praised," she told Lura. She was able to get the job largely on Lura's recommendation. Sconto had bought a radio. He played it loudly as he worked at the homestead. June 6, 1944, Sconto came running in to tell Dr. Fitz that the American and European military forces were invading France at Normandy. Beth was driving the tractor, but she stopped and had come into the cabin to check on Lurabeth. She started to cry, and Lura thought she was upset about D-Day; she knew Beth had several former classmates that were fighting in the war…or maybe the baby was coming early. No, she said, "I don't care if this is D-Day, or A, B, or C Day; today is our fourth wedding anniversary, and I miss Michael so much, I can't stand it that he is not here with me." RG said, "well, daughter, you need to just bake him a cake, then call him, and tell him you are celebrating 'D-Day…that's 'D' for 'Darling,' and you miss him." Beth stopped crying and hugged her daddy, and then her mom. Sconto shut off the radio, and started laughing; he pointed to the phone. "Call your husband! Tell him he needs to get here soon, you are going to have the baby! Lurabeth came into the room. She was only a year and a half, but she always sensed when her mother was upset. 'One to walk-two to talk,' they always said, but she was already almost walking, and not only said several words, but was already speaking in simple sentences. "No cry, mommy," she said and hugged her mother.

Beth went to the phone, but since they were on a party line, she couldn't get through at the moment. Michael had written faithfully every week. He was speaking almost every Sunday, either in Edmonton, or in one of the surrounding cities… either in Nazarene or Pilgrim Holiness churches mostly. He had made enough money to wire Beth something a couple times already. He had said he planned to leave soon and come to Fairbanks by the end of June…in time for the baby's birth, but if it were not for the generosity of Rev. Zumwalt, and Rev. Johnson, the only money he would have would be from the carpentry he was able to get once in a while. He had nothing saved up for airfare to Fairbanks, and wasn't sure how he would get there. The U.S. Consulate had given him little hope if any… being born in Hungary, but now *Romania;* it was holding everything up.

The days came and went, the party line was either busy or down, and this made Beth feel very discouraged. When they went into town the next day, they learned that Michael had sent a telegram, and wired some money…he had remembered their fourth wedding anniversary! And this brightened Beth's day. The next two Sundays Beth still played the piano and led the music at the Nazarene church in town, and RG preached two good sermons about the "Sower of the seed; some seed fell on dry, thorny, or good ground." Beth wondered if this was the *dry and thorny ground* of their lives, would China ever open up to them? Michael wrote that he was working on hitching a ride with anyone coming up the Al-Can highway, but nothing had shown up to date. The bus service was primitive and unreliable. There was no money for airfare, and boat passage was impossible because of the war. Dr. Fitz offered to pay for the trip, but money was very tight, and they wouldn't have enough for the winter if they drew from the profits from the farm, and banks were not loaning money. They prayed earnestly that God would show them what to do. They had finished the service Sunday morning, June 25, and had returned to the cabin where Lura had fixed dinner. They invited Sconto and Ruth to join them. They had moved in to *Denali Sunrise,* and everything was in a mess, so Lura suggested they have dinner together. If they stayed in the little room in the barn, and the kids stayed in the loft…(Peter, Thad, and Miriam, their three, loved to stay with the Fitz's and play in the barn), then on Monday they could all go together to help them finish moving in. After a Sunday afternoon nap, they were getting ready for a light supper, and then go to the evening service, when Beth knocked on her folk's bedroom door. "Daddy, Mother…we need to go to St. Joseph's…the baby is on the way. Dr. Fitz asked Sconto if he could take the evening service; Ruth watched Lurabeth and their three children. Lura and R.G. went to St. Joseph's Hospital. Beth's contractions were already close together, and by 10:45 p.m. Michael and Beth's second child, their son, Michael Franklin Varro, Jr. was born…After their five-day stay, Beth and 'Franklin,' returned from the hospital. Before going out to the homestead, Beth insisted they stop at the telegraph office. She sent the following telegram to Michael:

Son Michael Franklin Varro Jr born 062544 at 2245 hours [Stop)

All is well with all my love Beth [Stop]

CHAPTER TWELVE

LEARNING CHINESE...AND FINALLY SETTING SAIL

All the pretty flowers, learning Chinese…
and becoming a U.S. citizen

THE MONEY MICHAEL HAD BEEN SENDING EVERY TWO WEEKS WAS intended to help pay for Beth's stay with her folks in Alaska. Everything that was left, paid a little rent to Ken Zumwalt, and helped buy groceries for the two of them. He had intended to set aside something toward airfare or a bus ticket to

Fairbanks. The used car they had driven to High Prairie from California lasted about three years, with a few repairs, but currently was not drivable, and sat out in front of Ken's place. He had not been able to fix it, so until he had the money to have it fixed, or traded in, Ken loaned Michael a car that could get him around Edmonton to preach, or to his carpentry jobs, but was not road-worthy for any long trips. This was one from an older gentleman in Ken's church that was not being used. Michael intended to save a little money, and trade the car in on something else, and then drive to Fairbanks in a few weeks. Beth was getting increasingly upset about their extended absence from each other, and asked her dad if she could send Michael's money back, in order to get the car repaired. The only problem with Michael coming up to Fairbanks would be not having the preaching or carpentry jobs during his absence from Edmonton. They prayed about what to do. It seemed to them that the best thing to do would be to wait on the Lord, and take it a week at a time. In a few weeks, Beth was back on the tractor and helping with the harvest of potatoes, berries and vegetables. Lura watched Lurabeth and Franklin, or Ruth did, whenever Lura had to go into town. Beth also went in to market their produce, as well as playing for Sunday worship. The Kimble family stopped her after church one Sunday and asked if she would teach their two children piano lessons. Rebecca and Albert Kimble were in middle school in Fairbanks, and had been trying to learn piano from their mother, Shirley Kimble, without great success. Beth didn't want to charge them anything, as members of the church, but they insisted, so she started teaching them after school at the church, on Wednesday afternoons, before choir practice. Dr. Fitz thought that would be okay, and she could also save the money Michael was sending her for her stay. He said he would no longer accept it. She and Michael were family, and besides that, she was helping him without pay on the homestead. Beth began saving up for airfare to return to Edmonton.

September came, and they had worked hard to adequately prepare for winter. The freeze came, and then the snowfall. Beth was diligently preparing the choir for Thanksgiving and Christmas. It appeared that she and the children would spend Thanksgiving with her folks. Sconto, Ruth and their children hadn't been able to keep up the rent at Denali Sunrise, and the small two-bedroom house there was inadequate. Dr.

Fitz decided they needed to move into the cabin that had been the Solts' cabin when they lived on the homestead. But now that they had left to live in Nampa, the old cabin was not being used except as a shed for farm machinery and drying venison and other foodstuffs. They cleared it out after building another more functional shed. There was more room for their three children and Ruth was able to help with the laundry and care for Lurabeth and Franklin when Beth was not able to be there. Thanksgiving dinner was a beautiful spread of roast turkey, venison, vegetables, Lura's fresh baked bread and pies, and fruit. Beth and the children joined in with Sconto, Ruth, and their children. Dr. Fitz prayed a wonderful prayer of thanks for health, God's 'providence, and the witness of the Lord's love and protection.' Beth spent the afternoon in her room trying to hold back the tears. Enough was enough…she wouldn't be separated from Michael any longer. She started counting the money she had saved from her piano lessons… and the money she had held back from what Michael had sent. Dr. Fitz knew how distressed she was from being absent from Michael for so long. He had decided to give her some money for the 'extra work she had done, helping clear out the Solts' cabin.' He said he wouldn't "take no for an answer." She had checked with the airlines in Fairbanks. She had just enough for the airfare for a one-way ticket to Edmonton for herself, Lurabeth and Franklin. She had called Florence Berryman, who had played the piano for services before she and Lurabeth arrived, asking her to "take your old job back." The day after Thanksgiving she wrote Michael, "I've been so lonely without you, won't spend Christmas without you. Franklin is almost six months old. I and the children are flying to Edmonton next week." Michael had been busy, too. He had written the District Superintendent of the Washington Pacific district, Rev. Richard Morgan, every month asking for an assignment in the Seattle area. He had also written the University of Washington about enrolling in the Chinese language program. Rev. Morgan had written back every time telling Michael there was nothing open. After Michael was accepted as a graduate student at the University of Washington, he told Rev. Morgan that he would even accept an associate pastor position. The first week in December, Rev. Morgan wrote back that he had an Associate position at the Eli Hill Nazarene church near Tacoma. When Beth wrote about arriving the next week, he told Ken Zumwalt

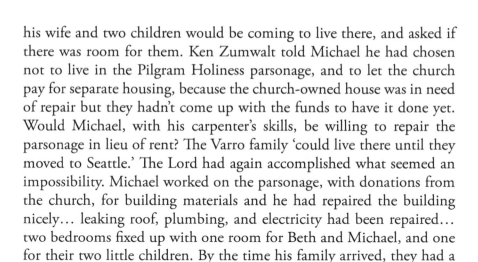

his wife and two children would be coming to live there, and asked if there was room for them. Ken Zumwalt told Michael he had chosen not to live in the Pilgram Holiness parsonage, and to let the church pay for separate housing, because the church-owned house was in need of repair but they hadn't come up with the funds to have it done yet. Would Michael, with his carpenter's skills, be willing to repair the parsonage in lieu of rent? The Varro family 'could live there until they moved to Seattle.' The Lord had again accomplished what seemed an impossibility. Michael worked on the parsonage, with donations from the church, for building materials and he had repaired the building nicely… leaking roof, plumbing, and electricity had been repaired… two bedrooms fixed up with one room for Beth and Michael, and one for their two little children. By the time his family arrived, they had a place to stay.

Two weeks before Christmas, Beth and the children arrived… reunited, a place to stay, preaching, and carpentry jobs to support them, while they took the next step in their quest to become missionaries to China…to which God had called them. They spent the first part of 1945 in Edmonton. Michael guest preached wherever he could find assignments, and was an ace carpenter wherever he found jobs. Beth kept up the parsonage and taught a few piano lessons at the church. They attended the Nazarene church in Edmonton when they could, but went with Michael when he was guest preaching. Rev. Zumwalt stayed in the little house he and Michael had been living in. After Beth and Michael, and the children, left for Seattle, he moved back in to the parsonage, with great thanks from the Edmonton Pilgrim Holiness congregation for the repairs. With the money Dr. Fitz gave them, Michael was finally able to get the parts for the car that were needed, and he quickly repaired it. They were able to drive around Edmonton until the spring, and then drove it to Seattle without any problems. Michael and Beth found a small house in Sumner, just a few miles from the Eli Hill Church of the Nazarene. Michael drove into Seattle to the University of Washington three days a week, for classes in Chinese, and taught a Bible study on Wednesday evenings at the church. He also preached once a month, either at Eli Hill, or as a guest preacher for one of the other district churches needing someone to fill the pulpit. He made contact with the U.S. Naturalization Bureau in Tacoma, just a few miles from where they lived. He filed all the appropriate papers… but was told the wait-time to become a U.S. citizen was about two years. In the meantime, he wrote the Nazarene mission board asking about their postponed appointment as missionaries to China. They received a letter three months later telling them, Rev. Harry and Mrs. Wiese, Rev. John and Mrs. Pattee, Mary Scott, and Ruth Brickman, were reopening a Nazarene mission in south central China within the year. They were told they would be considered after the next General Assembly.

Classes at the University of Washington were going well, but the Eli Hill Nazarene Church did not like the idea of having an associate who was studying Chinese, and working as a carpenter on the side. Michael reminded them that they were not providing a parsonage or paying them for a full-time position at the church; conflict became very heated. The Pastor, Rev. Ronald Cramer, was an Elder in the Free Methodist Church, who was serving Eli Hill as a 'crossover' since the last District Assembly. He had not been appointed to a church in his own denomination, so was willing to accept this church until he received another assignment in his own denomination. He and Michael became good friends, but the church board was unreasonable. Michael actually received some invitations to speak in Free Methodist churches because of Rev. Cramer's friendship and contacts with other church he knew of. The church wanted Michael to leave, but Rev. Cramer prevailed and asked Michael to teach Bible classes and had the church pay him accordingly. Beth tried to teach piano lessons but only a few students signed up. Michael came home from a carpentry job one day, and saw a big smile on Beth's face. She was pregnant, she said. She also had found a neighbor who asked her to help with some light farm-work. She and the children had spent the day gathering straw that could be used for decorative purposes and sold by the neighbor, Mrs. Fred Perkins, to a floral shop; they would put together dried plant arrangements. She had also given them a chicken which Beth prepared for their dinner that evening. "I thought I smelled something wonderful," Michael teased. Lurabeth and Franklin showed him the pretty flowers they had picked. They sat down to the meal Beth had fixed, thanking God for again providing for their needs. Beth was able to help Mrs. Perkins for the next five months.

Three months later, Uncle Lou came and stayed with them. They had such fun with him; he loved to tussle with the children in the hay from the neighbors' harvest. Jumping down on him from a big box, Lurabeth cried "bombs over Tokyo," and Franklin echoed, "bobs ober Toko," showering Uncle Lou with hay. [Irma and Maxine had gotten married in Alaska right after Beth left. Two young men from the U.S. Army stationed in Fairbanks had come to the Nazarene church. It was near the end of World War II and romance was in the air. RG and Lura liked the young men and both Irma and Maxine were soon married. They shipped out and were stationed elsewhere before the war ended. Maxine and Harvey Ishman had a daughter, Katherine (four months before Franklin), then he was stationed elsewhere. Irma and Ralph Adcock had a son Ralph Lawrence (born about a month after Franklin). Harvey ended up leaving Maxine, so she decided to finish up at Pasadena college. Beth offered to keep Kathy until she and Michael and the family left for China]. And that is why Kathy ended up staying with the Varro family, and they were all just like 'brother and sisters.' It was a houseful alright, but everyone enjoyed it. Lurabeth heard Kathy call Louis one day. "Uncle 'Nouis'," she called; taking exception to this 'mispronunciation' of her favorite uncle's name, Lurabeth called out indignantly to Kathy, "Kathy, it's *not* Uncle 'Nouis,' it's Uncle 'Wouis'!" Beth and Michael had to hold their sides laughing; there were many other fun times during their stay in Sumner.

By the fall of 1946, Beth and Michael finally received the news they had waited for, for so very long. The Nazarene mission board, 'upon the recommendation of Rev. Wiese at the Nazarene Mission Station in Ji An in Jiangxi,' were reactivating *"their appointment to be Nazarene missionaries in China,"* When Beth opened the letter, she cried for joy. Michael was at the Eli Hill church, but she called him to come immediately…she said she had some wonderful news! Michael drove quickly home, and they laughed and rejoiced together. This was what they had prayed for…for seven years! They were to 'book passage on a ship leaving from San Francisco to Shanghai, after going on deputation to raise their required support as a credit with the mission board, and then report to the mission station no later than the end of October of 1947.' Rev. Harry Wiese would see to their training and orientation. Michael was in his last semester at the University of Washington, and

Beth had to laugh… she said 'not *AT* him,' but '*WITH* him,' in his pronunciation of Mandarin; he said, "No fair, I'm Hungarian, I had to learn English growing up, and now Chinese is my *third* language! It's not the same as you native Chinese-speaking people." He practiced daily with her, and not only passed the exam, he got one of the *highest grades*. The others wondered how he got the best grade on oral pronunciation, and he told them he had a wife who was a 'native speaker … they all thought he had married a Chinese woman, and he never set them straight!

A week after his exam, the U.S. Naturalization Board letter arrived. He had been approved for citizenship! The neighbor lady, Mrs. Perkins watched the children while he and Beth went into Tacoma. Michael, and twenty-three others were sworn in as new United States citizens… his dream, and long wait, had finally come true!

It was December 16, and they were getting ready for Christmas. It was cold and rainy. Michael had the day off, since there were no carpentry jobs for him, and he didn't have a Bible study that evening. After supper, Beth lay down, saying she felt tired. Just before going to bed, she called out to Michael, "I think the baby is coming very soon now," There was no hospital in Sumner, so they went in to Puyallup to Pierce County Hospital…and that evening, Margaret Finnette Varro was born…'then there were three.' The Varro family was growing!

The deputation went better than expected. Michael was able to book meetings in churches throughout the Seattle, Portland, and Nampa, Idaho, areas. Some of their college friends had taken churches all up and down the West Coast, and Canada. Beth had to stay home most of the year to take care of the baby, plus Lurabeth and Franklin; many meetings, however, were in the Seattle and Portland areas, so she could bring the children along, and even had them sing. Lurabeth was nearly five, and Franklin was three, and she had taught them 'Jesus Loves Me' in Chinese…it was a big hit. Of course, everyone wanted to see the new baby, and she proudly presented her at every stop. A trip to Canada gave Michael's family a chance to meet the children. They had met Beth during their time in High Prairie, and she had also met family in Calgary, Regina, and friends from Pasadena College that were from British Columbia, Alberta, and Saskatchewan, but this time they met the whole family.

The big day arrived. They had driven to San Francisco the week before, and stayed with distant cousins, and some friends. They packed trunks for the time that they thought they would be in China; these were loaded on the ship's cargo hold…they would be processed through customs in Shanghai. Beth and Michael were to stay at the Assembly of God Mission compound in Shanghai near the docks that had been the German quarters called the '*Bunt*.' Mary Scott and Ruth Brickman were returning to China, so, they and a mission board representative, met them the night before at the Nazarene Church in Palo Alto. They had dinner together, then stayed the night with families of the church, arranged by their pastor, Rev. Herbert Chisholm. The next day, they stopped to take pictures before boarding the ship. It was the General Meigs, which had been converted from a troop carrier during the war, to a passenger ship. Beth remembered how she was prone to seasickness, so she had brought along some travel sickness medicine.

Before the ship set sail, Michael called his family together in their state room. He had found a scripture he wanted to share with them. He opened to the book of Romans, Chapter 11 verses 33.: *O the depths of the riches both of the wisdom and knowledge of God! How unsearchable are his judgments and his ways past finding out!* Then he held each of the children, Lurabeth, Franklin, and Margaret. He said, "I knew this day would come, I just didn't think it would be seven long years; God had to teach us some lessons, because His ways are not our ways–they are truly unsearchable." Then he prayed, and they all went out on deck, and waved goodbye to all the people that had come to see them off; the streamers and loud horns created an exciting setting for their trip across the ocean. They were finally fulfilling the call God had given them to go be missionaries to China.

The seas were rough. It was October and the trip took twenty-four days. They went ashore briefly in Yokohama, but no one was feeling very well… except Michael of course, like his dad, he never got seasick. After a few more days, they arrived in Shanghai. Missionaries from the

Assembly of God mission compound met their ship, and they went through immigration; the trunks would be processed later, and in about three weeks, they returned and went through customs.

Beth felt like crying. She was home! The children stared at everything; it was all so new and different. Margaret had slept a lot on board ship, and now she was fussy with all the noise and clamor. The people at the compound were nice, and showed them their quarters, which were very comfortable. Michael kept silent most of the first day there. He was still pinching himself. A young Hungarian-American... 'who would ever believe he could finally arrive in the land of his ancient ancestors?' He was here to preach the gospel of Jesus Christ as a missionary; he had come from such humble beginnings...so poor they despaired of every making it through some days. Now with a college education, married to a missionary's daughter, an ordained minister in the church that 'sounded like' the humble Hungarian apostolic Anabaptist congregation, where his late mother had found the Lord. He couldn't believe it. The 'stories from the boxcar' flooded his mind— and he praised God for it!

Rev. Michael Varro, Beth, Franklin, Margaret, and Lurabeth

The prayer of their hearts had been answered.

Only God could do this...

CHAPTER THIRTEEN

A REALLY 'COOL' SLEEPING PORCH AND SQUEALING PIGS

The 'Old, old Story' at a New mission station

BETH AND MICHAEL VARRO AND THEIR CHILDREN WERE MADE TO FEEL at home while at the Assemblies of God mission compound. They attended mission church services, where they met a young professor of music from the Shanghai Conservatory of Music named Jeremiah Ma. He had just returned from the United States; he had finished his doctorate in choral music at the University of South California. He had married one of the conservatory professors by the name of Amy Huang, who was an outstanding soprano, and also a good pianist who accompanied the choir; they were fine Christians. On Sundays, he conducted the Assemblies of God mission choir. He was told that Beth Varro was a fine pianist, so he and Amy wanted to meet her. He told Beth he had met the well-known Haldor Lillenas when the USC Choir toured Portland and Seattle. Michael and Beth were very impressed with his testimony as well as his fine musicianship. Garland Benintendi and his wife, Florence, were newly arrived Assemblies of God missionaries from Oregon, and were also in language school. They were very interested in the new Nazarene mission that had relocated from Hebei province to Jiangxi province, where Beth and Michael were headed. Mary Scott and Ruth Brinkman were staying at the compound too, but they weren't used to their hosts' style of worship, so stayed in their rooms and read their Bibles and prayed.

The three weeks went by quickly. The trunks, that had been held up in customs, were now ready to be processed. Michael and Beth were told to buy their train tickets to Nanchang, in Jiangxi Province, with a transfer to Ji An, where the new mission compound was located. Mary Scott and Ruth Brinkman had already departed after a week in Shanghai. They were returning to Ji An after a furlough, so most of their baggage was already there. Beth and Michael's trunks were processed and marked for shipment from Shanghai to Ji An by train as unaccompanied baggage. Early morning a week later, they had breakfast with their Assemblies of God hosts, and then took a taxi to the train. It was already November and the air was clear but chilly. As they arrived at the Shanghai train station, Beth was holding Margaret, but noticed as the children got out of the taxi, that Franklin had no shoes on. The train was leaving in forty-five minutes. She cried out, "Michael, Franklin must have kicked his shoes off again (like he often did) under the breakfast table!" Michael quickly called a cab, but Beth yelled, "No, Michael, we don't have time." He got in the taxi anyway, explaining that they would have no opportunity in the interior part of Jiangxi province to obtain another pair of shoes…he promised her he would make it in time. Beth frantically prayed, and asked those that were seeing them off, to pray. They simply *had* to get the shoes and return in time before the train left. Michael raced through the traffic, explaining to the driver in his newly acquired Mandarin Chinese, the importance of driving fast, but without endangering his life. The Assemblies of God missionaries had discovered the shoes under the breakfast table, and were standing outside the mission compound gate with them in their hands. Michael took them, thanked the missionaries profusely, and the taxi raced back to the train station. Fortunately, the mission compound, which was near the shipping docks, was also close to the train station. Beth, with the children, had decided to *not* get on the train until she saw Michael, for fear that, pulling out of the train station without him, would be disastrous. As the whistle was blowing, Beth began to cry, and prayed, "Lord, you called us to this place, we trust you to help us now…bring Michael back in time with the shoes. Amen." As she, and the others that had come to see them off, together said "Amen," Michael ran through the crowded station with the biggest grin on his face, holding the shoes up high so everyone could see. They all got on the train– as it was literally pulling out of the station. The others seeing them off, clapped and waved, lifting their hands in praise to God for His care for this young beautiful family. Franklin hid behind his mom. He started to cry when he saw the look on his dad's face. Michael knelt down and talked to him. "Franklin, you can *never* do that again; always, always, keep your shoes on; Daddy almost missed the train. You can *never* do that again." Franklin cried, and Michael held him close. Beth and Lurabeth cried too, but out of relief that all was well. Beth told Michael she and the others had prayed. He knew she had…he knew she always would. Then they praised God again for his loving kindness.

Several hours later, the train pulled into the Nanchang station. The family was able to get off the train for a while and have something to eat… the AG missionaries had packed them some sandwiches, and a thermos full of soup, and another one full of fruit juice. It was good to be able to stretch their legs, since the cramped quarters on the train made it almost impossible to move their limbs much. Just as they were finishing up their meal, the whistle blew, and they all got back on the train. It was several more hours before they pulled into the Ji An train station. Rev. Harry and Florence Wiese met their train. They had all met at General Assembly, but had never met the children of Beth and Michael, so everyone was introduced all around. The sun had just gone down, and they had been traveling all day, so they were very tired.

The Wiese's drove them to the mission compound and showed them to their home. The tabernacle was on the left as they entered the gate, and the missionary homes were in the back, behind the tabernacle. The Varro's residence was an older-style Japanese house near the front of the compound, adjacent to the pig slaughtering house, (just over the wall from them). They were greeted by the rest of the mission compound residents…both Americans and Chinese, who all applauded when they arrived. After a reception of some pastries and fruit, they bid them goodnight, and the travel-weary Varro's bedded down for the night.

Thanksgiving was especially meaningful to Beth and Michael that year of 1947. All the missionaries gathered to celebrate together, and the Chinese staff joined them. Some Christian friends from a little church down the road came also. [It was a China Inland Mission group. The well-known Dr. James Hudson Taylor had founded the mission in Henan province, and C.I.M. churches had sprung up in all the surrounding provinces: Shandong, Anhui, even south-central China– including Jiangxi]. They had good fellowship with the Nazarenes who were less than a mile away, so Florence Wiese and Beth Varro had invited them to join them. There was plenty to eat: turkey, fish, ham, vegetables, and bread. They sang 'Come Ye Thankful People Come,' in Chinese and English; they sang several other songs together; then Michael and Beth sang, 'Whispering Hope,' and the Chinese choir sang, We Gather Together.' Harry Wiese gave a reflection, 'What Thanksgiving Really Means.' Beth and Michael gave testimony to God's working in their lives for several years in bringing them to China–Beth saying she was thankful for being able to 'come back home.'

Christmas was just as exciting. Beth was particularly excited during this time. Her childhood playmate, Mary Xu, the daughter of their Amah in Daming, had escaped from the communists in the north and joined them at the Nazarene mission in Ji An. Her mother, Ma Li, had become a Christian. She married one of the Nazarene Chinese pastors. Their daughter, Mary Li was Beth and Irma's playmate. She had gone to the Nazarene Bible College in Daming, and later married a Chinese pastor, Peter Xu. During the war with the Japanese, her husband had been killed. When the Communists took over north China, Mary herself was imprisoned; God delivered her, and she found the Nazarene compound just before Christmas. Beth and Mary hugged each other and cried. "God helped me find you," Mary said. Mary needed a job, but Rev. Wiese said the only thing that was available was becoming the 'governess for the Varro children.' Beth said, "O no, I could never have this very educated woman, and my friend, be a maid," but Mary insisted, saying she was not insulted, but instead, would be honored to take care of Beth's children. She said her mother had taken care of Beth…it would be so fitting, and a privilege to take care of Beth's children. So, Christmas was a time of reunion, as well as the joyful celebration of Christ's birth. Michael was busy with Bible studies, and preaching occasionally—in Chinese as well as English (they had started an English service at the request of some young Chinese U.S. educated business people). The children were experiencing their first Christmas outside of the U.S., and were excited about the gifts that Beth and Michael had found on the open market. Michael found a tree and they were able to decorate it with homemade ornaments. Most of all they loved singing the carols in both Chinese and English. The mission children, in the tabernacle, performed the Christmas story, and Lurabeth and Franklin were shepherd and villager.

With the coming of the Chinese New Year, and other special feast days, the slaughter house next door was especially busy. Franklin ran crying to his dad with the ear-shattering squeals of the pigs being slaughtered. It was hard for Mary, as well as Beth and Michael, to explain the necessity of killing these animals. Franklin had nightmares after he saw them slit the throats of these pigs, and then dress them out. At Chinese New Year time, they were informed at the mission that Dr. R.G. Fitz, and Lura, would be coming to Ji An to assist with the medical ministry which the Nazarene mission was attempting to start up again. Beth was, of course, thrilled. Her parents could live in the small apartment on the second floor, adjacent to the tabernacle. A small but efficient hospital, close to the compound, had given permission for them to practice medicine there. It was a short-term assignment. Dr. and Mrs. Fitz had decided to lease out their cabin in Fairbanks; after Rev. AB Morgan and Rev. G. Murton had served as pastors there, they felt they could afford to take a one-year assignment to help with the

Nazarene mission in Jiangxi. They had been such an important part of the medical team when it was located in Daming in northern China, so it was a natural move.

Summer came to south central China, and it was uncomfortably hot and humid. Some nights, Beth and Michael, and the children, couldn't sleep... even with an electric fan. Even though they had limited electricity, there was little to no running water. [Michael loved to tell people in America, 'we had *running water* in China.' Then he would show his slides of a man running with a pole on his back with buckets on each end of the pole—"You see the man running, he had water...we had 'running water;' and everyone would laugh"]. One day, Michael decided to visit a lumber yard in Ji An; there he found wood of every kind, though it was a bit rough-hewn. He drew up plans and went to Rev. Wiese; he explained to him that the Japanese style home they lived in was older, and held the heat from the day...he proposed building a 'sleeping porch' above their house. Harry looked at the plans; he had done some carpentry work himself growing up in Kansas, and decided this was a reasonable request. Within a week...with the help of some of the Chinese workers on the compound, Michael fashioned a 'sleeping porch' above their house. It was open on the sides, and had a simple roof in case of rain. The breeze blew through it, keeping them cooler; and it came complete with railings and a staircase. Beth and the children brought sheets and a light blanket for padding. They slept better than they had in weeks! All the other missionaries were envious, but were only able move their bedrolls to the balcony. Even though Irma was teaching in the U.S., and Maxine was trying to alternate between working and finishing her Bachelor's degree in education in Pasadena, Guilford had come with his folks to Jiangxi. He was a teenager, and was only eleven years older than Lurabeth. When he heard about the sleeping porch, he of course had to join the Varro's. Michael said 'okay,' and he started that very night sleeping in the sleeping porch that Michael had built for his family. The next week, Beth called Michael to come quick, and bring his camera upstairs to the sleeping porch. He ran and got his camera, ran up the stairs and joined Beth and the children, and Guil. As they looked out on the skyline of Ji An, they saw not one, not two, but three other sleeping porches above the line of houses. Guil said, 'copy-cat,' and Lurabeth and Franklin echoed, laughing, 'copy-cat!' They all had a good laugh. Michael had started a trend. He had always said he was the 'Carpenter from Regina,' whose only desire was to be like the 'Carpenter from Nazareth.' If his sleeping porch could be an 'evangelistic tool' to bring them to Jesus, he was all for it.

Brother Wiese had obtained permission for the mission to pitch a tent on the outskirts of Ji An. Rev. John and Lillian Pattee, who worked in Ganxian, came up to Ji An for a Revival, so Ruth Brickman and Mary Scott stayed in Ganxian while the Pattee's were in Ji An. Beth played her accordion, calling them to worship, Michael and some of the other Chinese workers passed out gospel tracts on the street, inviting people in to the tent for the evangelistic service. Michael and Beth Varro sang, 'Bringing In The Sheaves,' Mary gave her testimony also, about her escape from the north. John and Lillian Pattee gave testimonies, Dr. and Mrs. Fitz spoke, Florence Wiese gave her testimony, and Rev. Wiese gave the message; some Chinese pastors spoke too, and the choir sang 'Just As I Am,' as Brother Wiese invited them each night to accept Christ; many of those walking by, committed their lives to Christ in the Revival.

The Chinese youth group was also growing, and Beth wanted to help them grow and have an important place in the ministry. Beth helped lead the group,and Mary Xu assisted too; some of the Bible school pastors got together and told her they wanted…'to go on a picnic.' They decided on a small lake close to Ji An they called: Xiao Ganjiang Hu, a kind of 'runoff' from the large Ganjiang River that formed 'little lakes' as the river traveled toward the Yangtze River at Nanchang. The Youth Council voted to let them go, as long as they had written permission from their parents; they said they wanted to take picnic baskets and eat together…they also wanted to swim. Mary had to stay and watch the children, but Beth and a Chinese pastor's wife, Esther Zhang went along, and Guil went too. They all piled into the small church bus that the mission rented from one of the mission church members, Liu, Feng-hui. Mr. Liu worked for the assistant to the mayor of Ji An. They arrived before noon and had a nice lunch of two meat and vegetable dishes and rice, and some fruit juice. They had a Bible study, and then were supposed to rest for a while before going in swimming. As Beth was cleaning up after the Bible study, and others were resting under the trees by the lake, she noticed that some of the Chinese young people were laughing and pointing at the lake. Beth thought nothing of it…until she heard them laughing and calling out: 'Xiao Fei' (Dr. Fitz had been given the family name 'Fei,' so he was called 'Lao Fei' ('older Fei,' but Guil was referred to as 'Xiao Fei,' or 'younger Fei'). Guil was always showing off and 'clowning around,' but in that split second, Beth suddenly realized the Chinese thought Guil was clowning around…she froze momentarily in her tracks…Guil did not know how to swim! She dashed to the shore and jumped into the water; she frantically swam out to where Guil was thrashing the water and flailing the air…he was going under for the third time. Each time she grabbed him he pulled her under. She realized they were both going to drown…unless she could save herself; she slugged him with all her might, and he let go. As she swam to shore, the Chinese young people gathered at the shore. Suddenly, they all started to clap and shout. Guil, slapping the water and churning around, had made his way to the shore on his own. She started to cry, thinking her only brother, age sixteen, was lost. A couple girls and a young man helped her out of the water, just as two other guys jumped into the water and were helping Guil make it the rest of the way. She ran over to him and hugged him, bawling him out as she did. "I thought we had lost you; I'm sorry I hit you so hard, but we would have both drowned." In his bragging kind of way, he said, "Nah, Sis, I was just kidding around with you," but with that guilty 'look in his eye,' she knew he would have drowned without her. She slapped at him, both of them knowing God had intervened to spare him. He put his arms around her so she couldn't see his tears. Guil had never professed Christ as Savior, but that night after they told their 'folks' what had happened, Guil's dad spoke to him. "Guilford, the Lord spared your life today; since He let you keep it, don't you think you should turn it over to Him?" Guil couldn't keep the tears from coming down his face this time, and as his dad prayed, he let Jesus come into his life. Guilford had been a typically rebellious MK (missionary kid), but later he spent his whole life serving the Lord. [Like his father, he went on to seminary, became an ordained minister, then a missionary doctor…but not to China…to Swaziland, in Africa! After going to college and marriage, he and his wife, Doris, and all their children became missionaries, teachers, artists, musicians, or church workers]. Beth told Michael about Guil's near-drowning, and he, and the whole mission family, rejoiced in God's mercy in sparing Guil's life. The youth group made new rules about their outings: each person had to be paired with another; and their whereabouts had to be known to the entire group at all times.

[The Chinese communists, led by Mao Zedong, had started occupying Manchuria right after the close of World War II; then sweeping south, they occupied one province after another. The Nationalist, led by Chiang Kai-shek, had successful resisted at first, but then they lost more and more territory to the Communists, moving the capital from Beijing to Nanjing, then Qung qing, and finally to Taiwan. In the fall of 1948, the United States government ordered all women and children out of China. Some single woman, and a few families, who refused to be separated, stayed; but ultimately, many of them found this to be foolish. Some were imprisoned or killed; other families experienced concentration camps].

It was yet another heartbreaking time for the Nazarene missionaries. They had been forced out of Daming in Hebei province, and now again from their new south-central China mission station. It was particularly heartbreaking for Beth and Michael, who had waited seven years to come to China, only to be there for less than two years. In consultation with the Nazarene mission board…it was decided that Michael Varro and Harry Wiese would stay as long as possible at the mission station in Ji An, but Katherine Wiese, Beth Varro, and their children, would all leave before Christmas, going through Shanghai; John and Lillian Pattee, who were already in southern Jiangxi province in Ganxian, would leave through Hong Kong. Mary Scott and Ruth Brickman would stay in Ganxian until spring… if possible. Dr. and Mrs. Fitz would leave after the first of the year, and Guil would leave with Beth and the children.

The day of departure arrived. Trunks had been transported by truck to the 'Bund' to be put on the ship at Shanghai. A special service of farewell and prayers for the safety and well-being of those left behind. Many tears, and cries of anguish were shed by both the Chinese workers staying, and from those who were leaving. They sang "Blest

Be The Tie That Binds," and the altar in the tabernacle was filled with those praying and crying. Those in Ji An, and across the province, and all over China, those that could afford it, were leaving by any mode of transportation possible. Michael Varro and Harry Wiese decided to stay at the mission compound instead of accompanying Beth and Katherine and their children to Shanghai. They were concerned that the mission could be vandalized, or overrun by looters, if things got bad enough. They got on the ship in Shanghai, and settled into their staterooms. Beth had left the two older children with Guil on deck, while she took Margaret to the restroom. Lurabeth came running in the room yelling, "Mommie, Uncle Guil is holding Franklin over the rail by his feet." Beth ran out on deck. Sure enough, her prankster-brother, while not meaning any serious harm, had grabbed Franklin by the ankles and was holding him upside down over the rail above the water. Not wanting to startle him suddenly...and drop Franklin in the bay, she steeled herself and walked quietly up to him, grabbed Franklin's leg, and putting her other arm around his waist, hauled him in to the safety of the deck floor. Then she turned on Guil, ordering him to stay in their stateroom until the ship was under way, yet another few hours away. She also told him she would report this to their dad. Guil pleaded with her not to do this, as he knew how severe Dr. Fitz could be, as a kind but 'ruthless' disciplinarian. She said, "Guil, you meant it as a practical joke, but you could have been responsible for the death of my son, and I know you would have never forgiven yourself for that." Guil was very humbled and assured Beth he meant no harm, but that anything like that would never happen again. Dr. Ma, and some of the Assemblies of God missionaries saw them off, after letting them stay again at the AG mission compound. The mood was somber and most of the passengers were quiet and kept to themselves. Many of them were Chinese nationals...that had the means to pull up roots and escape.

They landed in San Francisco and Irene and Carl met their ship. They said Beth and the children could stay with them until China either fell to the Communists or the Nationalist got help from other countries. Grandma Witten had died a month after they left in 1947, but their children Lura Frances and Alvin Kay had married and would be visiting while they were there. Irma and Ralph had left Alaska, and were living in Seattle, but she and her two boys, Larry and Ron, would be with them in Nampa for Christmas. Maxine and Kathy were living in Pasadena. She had finished her degree and was teaching there, but wouldn't be able to make by Christmas. Dr. and Mrs. Fitz would not be able to be there since they would not be leaving China for at least another month. It was a quiet and somber Christmas, but they spent a lot of time praying for Michael, the Nazarene mission in China, and the Chinese people. They believed God would work out his perfect plan for them.

[The inflation in China became very volatile. By the end of the first quarter of 1949, the Republic of China dollar was worth almost nothing. Michael went out on the street in front of the mission compound. He saw a beggar pushing a wheelbarrow full of money. He calculated that the value of everything the man had in his wheelbarrow was worth less than one U.S. dollar. Conditions were getting worse and worse (with nothing to eat, it was said some even resorted to eating their own children). Crime was rampant. Word on the street was that the Red Chinese Army was just across the Ganjiang River from Ji An. When they looked through the binoculars, they saw Communist troops looking back at them through their own set of binoculars]. Finally, Brother Wiese received a reply from his telegram that there was little hope of keeping the mission station. Even if the mission in Ganxian were not overrun immediately, it wouldn't be wise to 'shelter in place,' as it was only a matter of time before it too would be taken... the time had come to go...*China was closed.* They began making plans to abandon the property and try to make it out of China alive. They gathered the Chinese preachers together for a farewell meeting. After the time of prayer, they gave them, yet again...the assurance that Jesus had given his disciples, "And lo, I am with you always, even to the end of the age." There were tears and hugs. Brother Wiese placed Pastor Xu and Pastor Liu in charge, and gave them the last three thousand U.S. dollars the mission had, hoping this would somehow help them carry on the work. In retrospect this was a *terrible mistake:* It was reported that they were found with the money on them after Michael and Harry left, and this immediately branded them a 'American Imperialists.' The ones who escaped told the missionaries that these two dear preachers were executed. Brother Wiese and Michael grieved they had done that, but were assured that many were killed regardless of the circumstances, and that it was all in God's hands.

It was July 1949. Brother Wiese and Michael took the mission's old 1947 Chevrolet sedan, and managed to have it chained to a flatbed railcar. There was no passenger service. All natural resources from the north–coal, gasoline, kerosene, etc., had been confiscated by the communists. Banks were frozen, businesses shut down. Members of the Nationalist Army were sent out to cut down trees, but this wood was 'green' and the locomotives could not burn the wood, so the trains could not get up a 'head of steam.' Had it not been for the relatively flat terrain, escape by train would have been impossible. As it was, getting a head of steam would only get them near the top of a hill sometimes, only to slide back down; they could not move until they stoked, and stoked, and stoked the boilers until they got enough steam to take them over the top of the hill. They slept in their car with only the belongings they could carry. All around their car...and underneath... and hanging on the sides of the flatbed, were refugees. Everyone, it seemed was leaving in fear of the communists.

They finally made it to Hong Kong. Shanghai had fallen and escape from there was now impossible. Ruth Brickman and Mary Scott, along with Dr. and Mrs. Fitz had managed to escape a few weeks before. They all met up in Hong Kong, and booked passage on an American freighter. They sailed in under the Golden Gate bridge in San Francisco, where they went their separate ways...to be with their families. They'd served faithfully; they didn't know if they'd ever serve in China again or not, but they knew the future was in God's hands.

Michael was allowed to 'own' the 1947 Chevrolet from the Mission in lieu of the money they still owed him for Beth and the children, from the prior December to July of 1949. Rev. Wiese, Ruth Brickman, and Mary Scott stayed in Temple City, California, near the missionary retirement center. The Pattee's had already moved in there. Dr. and Mrs. Fitz went with Michael to Nampa. [They had made arrangements to sell the homestead in Fairbanks, and buy land in Nampa, near Irene and Carl]. They pulled up *unannounced* in front of the house on a bright July morning. Guil, Beth and the children ran out to meet them, praising the Lord for their safe arrival. With little money left, they had driven straight through from San Francisco. Lura was exhausted, and RG wasn't feeling well. They got them inside and gave them something to eat and drink. Michael had driven most of the way, and only had ten dollars left in his pocket; they had driven in the evening, and rested during the day. This meant less traffic, it was cooler, and economized on gas too. It was a houseful, but everyone was so relieved that all were safe that everyone pitched in and shared the space, and did whatever they could to assist with the eating and sleeping arrangements. God had spared their lives. They all believed that the ministry they had planted, would somehow continue...to God's glory. Nampa First Nazarene invited Dr. and Mrs. Fitz, and Michael and Beth, to be the special speakers for the next Sunday service. The entire family went to church together, and it had been many years since they had been able to do that. They gave a report on the mission work in Jiangxi in south central China, and the altar was filled at the end of the service, with young people committing their lives to go as missionaries. China *would* open again someday, but in the meantime, there were many other mission fields. They had a wonderful Sunday dinner together that Auntie Irene fixed following the service. They spent the rest of the week relaxing, showing pictures, telling stories, and catching up on their rest., The Nazarene mission board had asked Dr. and Mrs. Fitz, and Rev. and Mrs. Varro, to come to Kansas City at their convenience and make a report on the mission work they had done in Jiangxi; so, the next week, they began scheduling deputation tours. Irene said she would be happy to keep the children while they were gone. They also made plans for Guil to enroll in high school in Nampa. Before they left, Carl took RG over to the property he had located for them. It was a basement house, but they would be able to eventually build on it, and it was less expensive than a regular two-story house (it was only seven blocks from the Solts' place). It would be good for the two sisters to be able to live closer together. They hadn't been able to do this since they first went to Alaska. RG took Lura over to see it—she didn't like it as much as the log cabin in Fairbanks, of course, but it was functional and less expensive. When they were not living there, they could rent it out. They decided to take it. Dr. Fitz had always been against a mortgage, so it was decided they would use the money from the sale of the homestead in Fairbanks. They didn't believe it would take three years to sell the cabin in Fairbanks, so in the interim, Carl helped to hold it by renting the basement house. It was owned by a member of the Nampa First Nazarene, and they were willing to wait until the house in Fairbanks sold before buying it. Students from Northwest Nazarene College could rent it until the sale was complete.

Beth and Michael went on a deputation tour, primarily to churches in Canada, and the western United States. Dr. and Mrs. Fitz did limited deputation, primarily in the Pacific Northwest and Alaska. Guil started high school in Nampa at Christian Academy, and the children stayed with Auntie Irene and Uncle Carl. Lurabeth had turned six shortly after they returned from China, and so Beth visited the closest elementary school to inquire about enrolling her in first grade. They said that wouldn't be possible, since it was already the middle of the year. Beth prevailed on them to test her reading ability and readiness. They refused her request. Uncle Carl visited the Pastor of First Nazarene Church to see if he could get some help. He was informed that Mr. Brogton, the Principal of Garden Ranch Elementary was a member of the Nazarene Church board. After a talk with him, they agreed to test Lurabeth's reading ability. If she could read at the attained level of the presently enrolled first graders, she would be allowed to start first grade at that level. After they tested her, the first grade teacher Mrs. Smythe informed everyone she had never seen anything like it. Lurabeth could not only read at the first-grade level, she exceeded the reading level of even *third-grade students*! She was quickly enrolled and Uncle Carl dropped her off, and picked her up, every day from Garden Ranch. Franklin and Margaret stayed with Auntie Irene during the day, and Guil, Lurabeth, Franklin, and Margaret fared well during the several months Beth and Michael were away. [Two interesting side notes: Auntie Irene, like her sister Lura, believed in salting everything quite liberally. Lurabeth and Franklin grew up telling everyone they had 'high blood pressure' as adults because things were *salted* so richly, Ha! Which of course was untrue—everyone knew what a great cook Auntie Irene was! Another side note: Uncle Carl was from the old 'German school of discipline;' if there was an infraction of the rules: *'the more severe the punishment, the better behaved the child.'* Franklin, and Lurabeth—even Guil, at age sixteen, felt the 'razor strap' on their backs numerous times. When Beth returned however, this 'more than adequate' punishment was revealed to Beth by Lurabeth, and Uncle Carl was strongly reprimanded for unjustly punishing her children. Uncle Carl never touched the children again in such a manner! And they always continued to believe him to be a kind gentle man, despite this severity of discipline].

By late summer of 1950, deputation was over, but the possibility of being appointed, or called to a church, seemed rather remote for Rev. Michael Varro and his family. Nothing had shown up in Canada, or the Pacific Northwest. Finally, the District Superintendent of the Dakotas District, Rev. Harry Taplin, wrote with an offer of the Sawyer, North Dakota, Church of the Nazarene. It was a small-town church, fifteen miles from Minot. Rev. Taplin also needed a caretaker for the district camp grounds; one problem: there was no compensation for the caretaker's position—it came with the call to the local church, in a farm community that could barely maintain the church and parsonage facilities. The pastor's salary was in fact inconsistent, and was currently behind by three months. Beth said to Michael, "it sounds like shades of High Prairie to me;" but without any other real possibilities, they felt they had no other choice. They prayed about it, and then, fearing they would once again be without any call, wrote Rev. Taplin that they would take it. They loaded their trunks, that had finally arrived from San Francisco, onto an old 'hay wagon,' since nothing else was available or affordable. It was already August, and it would be getting cold in North Dakota. Guil had finished his first year of high school by correspondence in Jiangxi, and then his sophomore year at Nampa High School. The homestead had not sold, so RG and Lura decided to have Guil return to Fairbanks to begin his junior year there. Bidding farewell to Irene and Carl, Beth and Michael and their family headed out for their next great adventure.

In Montana, the axle on their 'hay wagon' suddenly broke! Fortunately, the wagon did not overturn. While Beth was preparing a lunch of sandwiches and soup Auntie Irene had provided for them, Michael was praying, "O Lord, we thank you for how you have always delivered us from the 'lion's den,' well, we need you again to show us your way…as we strive to serve you again…in your name. Amen." At that *very moment*, a car pulled over. A man got out and introduced himself as a rancher who owned the adjacent property. "Looks like you snapped an axle, mister," he said. Michael told him they were returned missionaries from China, on their way to a pastoral assignment in North Dakota near Minot. "Isn't that interesting," the man said; he told them he was a Mennonite, in a church near Butte, close to where they were broken down; he said not to worry about anything...they could stay with him at their ranch a mile away. He would have his men unload the wagon onto a truck, weld the broken axle, and they would be on their way...in a day or two. *How could this be!?* Michael had *just* finished his prayer to God. Like 'manna from heaven,' there was their heavenly Father again providing for their every need. Mr. Dornfelt and his wife, Susanna, were the very picture of Christian love. They made them feel welcome, they fed them, let them rest, and bathed them in love...like Elijah and the widow of Zarephath. The children had a wonderful time playing in the barn, feeding the animals, and even trying their hand at milking the cows. It was a respite...provided by God himself. The workers welded the broken axle, reloaded the wagon, and Mr. and Mrs. Dornfelt prayed for them, and their new ministry. They went to bed early so as to get a good start in the morning, and as soon as the sun was up, Beth bundled up the children, and Michael checked the axle before pulling out. Mrs. Dornfelt had made sandwiches and a thermos full of coffee for Beth and Michael, and milk for the children. They stopped for an early lunch in Billings; they found a park and rested awhile. After several hours they saw the North Dakota state line... this is where they would live for the next three years. Rolling hills and groves of trees would make a grand playground for the children. Beth and Michael would be the best 'home missionaries' there ever could be...if they were *not* to return to China at this time...then Jeremiah 29:11–God had a plan for their lives. They committed everything...all that they were, all that they had...to Christ Jesus.

Ship arrives in Shanghai, 1947

The General Meigs, ship to Shanghai

Nazarene Tabernacle in Ji An

Frank & Mr. Hu in Ji An Bible class

Guil & Beth & Nazarene Youth Retreat

Grandad saying goodbye

Doors close, windows open,
but God's mission goes forward

A Spiritual Journey begins

Book Four begins the story of Michael Franklin Varro, Jr. [Frank],
His schooling in North Dakota & Washington;
profession of faith, baptism, death of his brother Stephen;
life in Hong Kong, Taiwan, and Seattle;
meeting and marrying Margo after college, and Taiwan

BOOK IV
Boys, Men, and Dreams

The Journey with Many Hurdles

Chapter Fourteen

Rolling Dakota hills...
and meeting the 'Good Shepherd'

Turning a 'heartbreak' into a mission field

IT WAS ALMOST SUNDOWN WHEN THEY PULLED INTO SAWYER. A neighbor, George Rheinholt, and his wife, Marta, came over and gave them the keys to the church and parsonage; he introduced them to some neighbors that helped unload the wagon. No one offered to get them anything to eat before they all left for their homes, and Lurabeth turned to Michael, "Daddy, we're hungry," she said. Franklin and Margaret said, "Daddy, Mommy, we're hungry." Michael looked at the overgrown garden full of weeds. He had seen the same kind of weeds when he lived with the Zumwalt's in Red Deer; these were not your ordinary weed, they were fresh 'lambs-quarters.' Michael called the children over to him. "See all those beautiful green weeds?" He showed them a sample of what he was referring to, "I want you to pick as many as you can, and bring them to Mommy." Beth had eaten these delectable greens in Oklahoma, but also in Alaska. The children brought a huge pile of the greens into the parsonage, and Beth had, in the meantime, found some wood for the old range, and started a fire. Soon she had boiled some water in a pan she had found in the basement. The greens were soon tender…in bowls with spoons that Michael had scrounged up from a box he had also found in the basement. When they finished, Lurabeth said, "best meal I ever had." Franklin echoed, "best meal I ever had," and Margaret just smiled and licked her chops. While Beth was cooking the greens, Michael had unpacked the wagon, and set up bedding on the floor. They made do as best they could and slept soundly in their new home.

The next day, Michael and Beth set up a small dining room table and chairs, a sofa and side chair, and the beds. Lurabeth and Margaret shared the bedroom upstairs on the west side, Franklin used the bedroom across the hall on the east side, and Beth and Michael used the bedroom downstairs. There was a small country store a few blocks away, and they were able to buy a few things for meals there. After lunch, there was a knock on the door. A man introduced himself as Otto Schmidt, the chairman of the church board. He said he owned a farm just north of Sawyer. He said he and his wife, Eleanor, and the Forthen and Rheinholt families were basically the church board. He said the others in the church were inconsistent in their attendance. He welcomed them and gave them the keys to the Nazarene district campground. Michael thanked him, and then asked about the salary arrangements. He shifted from one foot to the other and said they would "do the best that they could." If the pastor would 'pay the utilities' out of what they gave him, and they provided vegetables and meat periodically, in lieu of the money they were unable to pay them, it would come to a few dollars a week, which included being caretaker for the district campground; but, they couldn't *promise* they would always meet this obligation. Michael asked if there were any carpentry or construction jobs around Sawyer...he told Mr. Schmidt he was a carpenter. He said he didn't know anything about that, and suggested Michael go visit the Ward County carpenters union in Minot. He said the Forthen's had some chickens for them and they would drop by later. They would have to dress them out themselves or cage them for later use, but they were welcome to them. He had a sack of potatoes, onions, and carrots in his truck. He went and got them and put them in the basement, then he said goodbye. Hazel and Richard Forthen dropped by after a while. Richard said he would take Michael to see the district campground, because he was the one who had done some of the maintenance with the previous pastors. Hazel visited and helped Beth dress out one of the three chickens while their husbands left to see the Nazarene campground; the children went along too. They didn't stay for supper, so the Varro's ate their first full meal alone that evening.

In the morning, Michael and Beth went into Minot. Michael found the Ward County carpenters union and found out they were planning to build a new grain elevator right there in Sawyer. He signed on for the project, which would pay him enough for the family to live on, given the fact that the income from the church was very tenuous. Beth was also able to enroll at the Minot State Teachers' College that same day. The credits she could transfer from Pasadena College would allow her to complete her teacher's certificate in one year. Then they would be able to apply for a teaching job in the area. It was a good day! So, Michael, who *NEVER* stopped at any restaurant, said they were going to celebrate! They pulled into Velva (six miles east) to a Dairy Queen, and to the squeals of delight from the children, he ordered ice cream cones for everyone. Beth had that quizzical look on her face like, 'can we actually afford this, Michael?' but, with his eyebrows twitching up and down, like they always did when he was emotional, he nodded his head as if to quell her concern (the family later named this the 'eyebrow alert'). That was the first time Franklin remembered his dad teaching them the Hungarian song, 'Szép asszonynak kurizálok,' which they learned to sing...and sang all their lives, and even taught to their children, and grandchildren. As they licked their cones, they sang and laughed. All they had been through seemed to *melt* away (ha,ha) going home from Minot to Sawyer.

Michael preached his first sermon, and they all had their first Sunday at the Sawyer Nazarene Church. He preached from II Corinthians 5:17 *Therefore if any man be in Christ, he is a new creature, old things are passed away, behold all things are become new.* A *new* assignment, a *new* task God had given them. That Sunday, the Forthen's, Schmidt's, Rheinholt's, and a few other families came to church, including the brother of George Rheinholt: Rasmus Rheinholt, who brought them a few pounds of venison. George and Marta Rheinholt told them that if they ever needed anything, to "just stick your head out the back door, and holler." A neighbor lady, Mrs. Hoy (Evangeline Hoy), who was a Lutheran and did not ordinarily attend the Nazarene Church, also showed up that Sunday, and introduced herself. She seemed to like Beth, and was respectful of Michael, but the children were afraid of her. She was very stern, and later on, complained to 'Pastor Varro' about every little thing the children did. She was an older single woman and let everyone know they were not to come into her yard. When the children built a 'tree house' that hung over into her yard (but the tree was on the parsonage property) …she complained, telling Michael this 'wouldn't do.' Michael explained that they were 'children…no toys to play with, and so they became very creative; we should be happy it keeps them out of trouble.' She wasn't having any of it, and mumbled as she turned and went back in her house. That Sunday no offers were made to have them to their homes for a welcoming Sunday dinner, but they all did seem to be happy they finally had a new pastor, after almost a year without one. They said Rev. Taplin had promised them a pastor two years ago, when the previous pastor left to go to Williston Nazarene Church, and the next 'pastor' was only a Bible school student, and didn't stay more than five months.

It snowed the first day of school. Lurabeth entered third grade, Franklin started first grade, and Beth took Marta up on her offer, and left Margaret with her while she went into Minot to attend Minot State Teachers' College. She finished each day by mid-afternoon, so she could drive back to Sawyer and pick up Margaret. Michael also began construction on the new grain elevator…the same day school started, but the cold weather that came the next few months made their work sporadic at best. Michael often went to the campground, sometimes with Richard Forthen, to do repairs and replace broken windows, change light bulbs, and do minor plumbing work. If there was no construction work, Michael watched Margaret until Beth got home. Lurabeth and Franklin finished class by 3:00 p.m., and would walk home by the time Beth arrived. They made friends with the Reading family children— Carol and Wayne. Shirley and Robert, their parents, didn't go to church, but let Carol and Wayne come to Sunday School, Vacation Bible School, and church parties once in a while.

The church grew gradually over time. Beth led the Sunday School, played piano for the worship, sang duets with Michael, taught the children to sing together for church, Sunday School, and Vacation Bible School. Michael preached, taught a Bible Study, called on the sick—even those in hospitals, in Minot. They invited neighbors and their friends. Michael visited everyone he could, in the little town of Sawyer, with its population of a grand total of two hundred thirty five people. Mr. Tallerude, the school principal, told Michael, "these people are mostly German and Scandinavian…they are Lutheran; the others: Baptists, Methodists, Presbyterians, Nazarenes and Pentecostals go into Minot, but I like you… and your children, so I'll help you all I can; just don't ask me to join your church," he laughed.

The hills around Sawyer were a wonderful playground for Lurabeth and Franklin. Sometimes Margaret came along with them, but she was only four, so she mostly stayed at home. The Souris River (French for 'mouse'), often overflowed its banks, but that seldom deterred Lurabeth and Franklin from their regular routine of exploration. The Nazarene campground was in fact right on the river, and had been known to flood. During those times, Michael and Beth were careful not to let them go too far away from the house or the campground. There was no running water, but the parsonage had a good well, and a big hand pump. All the washing of clothes, cooking, cleaning, and bathing depended on this sturdy pump. At times Michael was not available, so Beth taught Lurabeth and Franklin to use the pump to assist her with cleaning and meals. There was a 'privy' about five yards from the back porch. [Michael used to 'brag' to the newcomers around there about the 'first-rate facility' they had. "Why, it's a two-seater, complete with Sears catalog, and all the up-to-date spools and gadgets anyone could ever want;" in forty-below-zero weather, his first chore was to, literally, cut a six-foot-high 'path' to the *old outhouse*]. Franklin hated his chore of emptying the 'chamber pots' every morning. "I don't like it," he said, "why can't Lurabeth do it?" He was told that she had to help her mother with cooking and cleaning; his protest: 'then-let-Margaret-help-me,' fell on deaf ears, telling him she was 'too little;'

He loved the little wild animals he found out in the hills–prairie dogs, chipmunks, rabbits, and the like. One day, he came upon a lair of wild rabbits; not finding the mother at home, he assumed she had died...and he was only trying to 'rescue' the little infant bunny. He proudly took it home to show to his mother. She was happy for his excitement, but immediately chastised him for separating the baby from its mother. Knowing it was probably hopeless, Beth tried to nurse the bunny all night long, anyway... with an eye dropper full of milk; but in the morning, the bunny was dead. Franklin's joy turned to grief. He cried, and Beth held him close and cried too, reminding him he needed to ask questions about things he didn't understand. George Rheinholt had given them a speckled Cocker Spaniel, they named *Sandy*, and she had pups. The kids were overjoyed, but Michael couldn't find a home for all of them...he said they could only keep *ONE*. Franklin liked the little chocolate-colored one... he called it *Brownie*. While they were playing with Brownie upstairs, Michael had the sad responsibility of drowning the last three he hadn't been able to adopt out; he told them it was more humane than letting them starve. It seemed so cruel, but years later the children finally came to understand how merciful it really was. But one day, tragedy struck. Sandy started chasing chickens and the neighbors said they had to get rid of her. Beth cried all the way to Minot, taking Sandy to the pound. Well, at least they had Brownie, right? Two months later, they came home from school to find Brownie had been struck by a car out on the highway. Lurabeth said they couldn't wait until Mommy and Daddy got home...they had to have a 'funeral' right away. She ran and got a shoe box and found an old rag to wrap him in. Franklin dug a hole by the porch next to the old pump. Lurabeth said 'girls can't be preachers,' so Franklin would have to be the 'preacher;' she said they had to sing a song. Just then, Beth and Michael arrived home as they were putting Brownie in the box, lowering him into the hole, as they sang, "Where, O where has my little dog gone?" Trying not to laugh, Beth and Michael joined in singing, "...O where or where can he be, with his tail cut short, and his ears are long, O where of where can he be?" Then they covered the box with dirt; they cried, and hugged each other, then they found an old brick for a gravestone. No dogs for a while, but it made a lasting impression on the family, and was a favorite story for generations.

It was spring...the crocuses were pushing up through the melting snow. The kids had put their sleds away, and none of the town's teenagers or smaller children were sledding on their favorite hill just south of the parsonage; Lurabeth was over at Carol's house, and Wayne was at Butch's house; Margaret was still at the Rheinholt's. But, Franklin was bored, and wanting to explore his favorite grove of trees, so he set out by himself... with just a light jacket on. He went a little further south than he had ever gone, but he wanted to check out the melting snow, and the trail of blooming crocuses he saw in the distance. What a great time he was having...the air was brisk, and the sun was warm. Forgetting the time, he didn't notice the clouds were getting heavy, a slight wind was picking up, and the sky was getting white and hazy. It started to snow. How strange, he thought, since winter was supposed to be over. Maybe he should turn around and go back. The snow started coming down harder, and the wind had picked up a lot... suddenly, Franklin was frightened; he turned around and started back. By the time he got to the back side of their favorite hill, he couldn't see anything. The snow was now coming down in 'sheets,' and the wind was howling; he couldn't see the hill or even the ground; he wasn't sure which way to turn. He got down on his knees, but the snow melted and chilled his skin through his jeans; he thought he was at the top of the hill, so he decided to roll down, but the snow was cold, and the wind blew against his ears, further chilling him. He wasn't quite seven years old...but he decided he was going to die. Dad talked about God helping us whenever we need him, but he only knew the prayers that he said before bedtime, and the ones he heard his dad pray in church. "God, I know I'll be with you if I leave here, but I don't want to go yet, will you help me?" After rolling down the hill, he reached out, with his bare 'glove-less' hands, to what he thought was the gravel road, a couple blocks up the alley from the parsonage. Feeling desperate, and freezing cold, he crawled on his hands and knees along the alley. When he couldn't feel the gravel, he adjusted his direction until the gravel road took him north. He finally saw Mrs. Hoy's garage, and he knew he was almost home. He crawled the remaining one hundred feet or so, until he could see the light from the back porch. Lurabeth had come home from Carol's, Beth had picked Margaret up from the Rheinholt's, and Michael was just pulling in the driveway. He stopped the car and ran to Franklin as he called for Beth to come quickly. Lurabeth brought a blanket, and jokingly said, "Franklin, it's not Christmas, but you look like Frosty the Snowman," Beth had hot water on the stove, and they quickly removed his cold wet clothes and, after first wiping him down with a towel with lukewarm water, they put him in the horse trough that they used as a tub for bathing, and soon he was 'good as new.' Of course, Franklin told them the whole dramatic story of how he 'almost died,' and how he asked God to 'come and help' him. He could see that Lurabeth was jealous of all the attention he was getting, and he relished the moment.

The Nazarene camp started that summer, and special speakers; the college choir from Northwest Nazarene College brought people from all over the Dakotas, for not only a very spiritual time, but also a lot of fun, friends and fellowship. It also was a time for Michael and Beth to meet other Nazarenes who were visiting from other states, and tell their story of being in China, the hope of returning to the Philippines, Hong Kong, Malaysia, or *any* other place where ministry to the Chinese people might be possible. Rev. Taplin introduced Michael and Beth as the caretaker of the district camp, but said nothing about being host pastor, or 'returned Nazarene missionaries from China.' Michael suggested he could give a welcome, or pray, or even address the delegates in one of the business sessions. Nothing was said about it, but Rev. Taplin was quick to call on Michael if there were any plumbing, electrical, or missing bedding or pillows. Franklin came in with some of his friends during the week, and some of them gathered around Rev. Taplin, saying "Hi, Uncle Harry," so Franklin did the same. "Hi, Uncle Harry," he said. Michael called Franklin outside and said, "don't *ever* call him 'Uncle Harry,' he's *NOT* your uncle;" though Franklin was allowed to call some of the other pastors, or their wives, 'Uncle,' or 'Auntie,' the Varro children were not allowed to address Rev. Taplin in that manner, but they were pretty perceptive, and quickly figured out how 'hurtful' he was to their father, and how badly Rev. Taplin treated him, but quickly taking credit for all the other things that had to do with the success of the district.

Beth had graduated with a teaching certificate from Minot State Teachers' College, and had hoped to get a teaching position in either Minot, Velva, or hopefully, even Sawyer. Such was not the case; by August, she was getting discouraged–nothing had shown up. She called around to several of the schools where she had applied, but everything was already taken. She was over at George and Marta's one day, helping her do some of the canning, while Michael and the children were helping George shucking corn, and she mentioned it to Marta. She said, "George could call his brother Ras? He lives out in the country south of Minot and Sawyer, he might know of some of the small farming communities…whether they need a teacher or not." She called George in and he called his brother Ras. A couple days later, Marta stuck her head out the back door. Michael and Beth, and the children were harvesting what little they had been able to plant in their own garden. "Hello there, Beth. Ras says Benedict needs a teacher, and the job of principal is open too." The next day, they piled into the car and drove to Benedict, about twenty miles south and east of Sawyer. Eleanor and Fred Randall met them at the school; they welcomed them, and said they would be the ones conducting a short interview. After talking about thirty minutes, Beth was offered the position of principal and lead teacher in a little three-room school. Eleanor taught first, second, and third grades in one room. Phyllis Grender taught fourth, fifth and sixth grade in the second room, and Beth was to be the principal, and would teach seventh, eighth, and ninth in the third room; high school students were bused into Minot. Beth didn't know if she could do this. She knew they needed to know something right away, so she asked if they could have some lunch and talk it over, and then try to come to a decision before they went back to Sawyer. Michael drove them a few blocks to the little store in Benedict. Beth went in with the children and bought some luncheon meat, bread, and a little jar of pickles. She made sandwiches, and they talked. Michael said it was important that she teach; he would continue work on the grain elevator in Sawyer, or any other carpentry jobs he could find, he would preach on Sundays, and go in on Wednesday for Bible study and prayer meeting. They would have to move to Benedict, but he wasn't sure where they could live. They would have to pray about that. Beth agreed; she was not at all sure of her ability to handle preteens and teenagers. They went back to the school. Michael said Beth had agreed to take the position, on one condition—they had to have a place to live; it was too far in sub-zero weather to commute every day. Eleanor smiled; she said they were good Lutheran Christians and believed God had sent the Varro's to Benedict. 'As it turns out,' she said, she and her husband had a little house on their property that her father had been living in. He could no longer live by himself, and they were going to have to move him in with them. They could move the little house to the corner lot the Randall's owned which was one block off the main street and the highway, across from their farm. Beth would have minimal administrative responsibilities, and she was the only one with a teaching certificate, so no one else was qualified. They only had one week to dig a storm cellar, and move the little house over top of it; Michael added a little porch. Since Michael had helped Fred move the house, then he asked Michael if he would mind helping him butcher a steer. He said sure, it was the least he could do. They butchered the steer…and Fred gave him one quarter of the meat. He didn't want the head, so Michael took it and it made some of the best ground beef he'd ever had. They wrapped it in butcher paper and kept it on the shelves in the new porch Michael had built…O, don't worry about keeping it frozen. It turned five degrees below zero the night they finished up, and they had meat all winter! School started the day they moved in, and they had some of Marta's canned vegetables and fruit, and, yes you guessed it…'potatoes, carrots, and onions.' Lurabeth was in Mrs. Grender's fourth grade room, Franklin was in Mrs. Randall's second grade room, and Margaret stayed with Michael, except for days he worked construction Those days he would drop her off at Marta Rheinholt's.

One very cold night after Wednesday Bible study and prayer meeting in Sawyer, the kids had fallen asleep at the church; with the wind howling and near-blizzard conditions outside, Michael carried the children one at a time to the car. Beth told Michael she thought they wouldn't make it back to Benedict…it was snowing too hard. He told her they had to try. She had to open up the school next morning at 7:30 a.m. 'What if they got stuck in the snow?' What if they had to close the school down? He told her to remember High Prairie… this could never be as bad as that, right? They made it to the junction, going south from the road to Minot toward Benedict. Highway 52 was paved, but going south toward Benedict was a gravel road. Michael knew that there was a small lake they had to go around just five miles off the main highway. Since it was fresh snow, they wouldn't be able to see the road. When they started to round the curve, he stopped the car, and got out, telling Beth to drive, following him. He walked toward what he thought was the road; if there was gravel, he knew they were on the road. He told Beth to follow his path through the fresh snow; they had good snow tires so, despite how frantic Beth was about going in the ditch or into the lake, he told her to just drive slowly, following the path he made. Beth prayed out loud, and told the children to pray. Margaret started to cry. Lurabeth told Margaret "mommy knows how to follow daddy, so it will be fine." Franklin wanted to go walk with his dad, but Beth said "stay still…and pray." Once they made it around the lake, it was a straight shot for fifteen miles. Michael got back in the car. He was grateful for the heater; even with his heavy overcoat, his lips were blue, and his teeth were 'chattering.' They could follow the telephone lines now, even if the road was obscured by the fresh snow. The wind had died down and the 'white out' was over. They had made a forty-minute trip…in two hours! Beth bundled the kids up in bed and Michael restarted the fire in the stove they had left several hours before. Beth felt like calling school off, but despite the huge snow drifts, the roads in town were mostly passable, and those that were not, Fred Randall and others had already plowed out before noon. The harvest had been good, and so the whole town showed up for the Halloween Festival at the Community Center the last Saturday in October. Beth found an old sheet and cut out two 'eyes,' so Franklin could be a 'ghost.' The two girls went as 'witches.' Mrs. Randall was holding a 'Fall Festival,' in place of Halloween, a couple nights before Halloween, so instead of going in to Sawyer, the Varro's enjoyed their Benedict neighbors' kindness, and attended the Randall's church close by. It was fun bobbing for apples, eating roast corn, and of course there was candy for all the children. Michael and Beth *did* go in to Sawyer for the Wednesday night prayer meeting that week, but it was nice to enjoy a little country hospitality first. The children were asleep at the Randall's when they returned, letting them stay the night there, picking them up in the morning in time for school. They had Thanksgiving and Christmas services in Sawyer. Evangeline Hoy had given them a turkey and some other things for Thanksgiving, but she was going out of town to her sister's place in Bismarck, so she didn't join them. George and Marta Rheinholt decided to bring them Christmas dinner. Beth and Michael and the children had opened presents following a Christmas Eve service in Sawyer, so they stayed the night in the parsonage, had Christmas dinner, and then went back to Benedict later that afternoon. The Rheinholt's were having family over so they cooked for the Varro's, wished them a Merry Christmas, but didn't stay. [Beth and Michael always felt that the Rheinholt's were probably the best thing that ever happened to them in Sawyer].

Beth was having trouble controlling her classroom. She had never been much of a disciplinarian, and Michael had to come often to help her with 'these unruly country boys.' She had grown up in China where respect and order were taught from an early age and it was difficult for her to adjust, and teaching was beginning to wear on her; she had taught Bible classes and English in China with no problem; and the commute was beginning to take its toll on Michael and the children too. The grain elevator had been completed and he was looking for other carpentry jobs.

One day, Franklin was out playing with his friend Butch Randall. The snow banks were still very high, but they loved hiking around the area. Butch knew the terrain and the rules of nature much better than Franklin, but he didn't say much about it. As they explored one afternoon, Franklin got a little further ahead of Butch than he should have. Trees were hung up in snow and caused a dangerous situation of which Franklin was unaware. He went toward the tree, and the large snow bank began to shift. This was referred to as a 'snow well,' and could result in suffocation and death if a person fell through. Butch yelled at him to stop *IMMEDIATELY!* Franklin laughed and kept going, unaware of the grave danger he was in. Butch ran and tackled him. He dragged him back just before the entire bank gave way. They were both covered from head to toe with snow. Butch said they had to go home right away. On top of this, Franklin was not wearing a cap, and a covering for his ears like he was supposed to. Butch looked at his ears and yelled at him to come quickly. He saw that Franklin's right ear was beginning to freeze, and he was unaccustomed to weather-related dangers such as these. Fighting him all the way, Butch finally got Franklin to the Varro's house. Thankfully, Michael was home with Margaret; Beth and Lurabeth were still at school, as was Eleanor Randall, Butch's mother. Michael thanked Butch for his quick attention to this danger, and applied cold water to Franklin's ear, then warmer and warmer water, massaging the ears until the color came back into them. Michael had grown up in Canada and was familiar with such things, but had failed to share these things with his wife and children. He bawled Franklin out for getting so covered with snow and not wearing a cap, and for not covering his ears. Franklin lied, and said Butch had pushed him down in the snow... failing to mention that Butch had saved his life; and he said nothing about the 'snow-well.' Not having any reason to doubt his son, but unhappy that he had not listened to the neighbor boy, Michael dismissed it, and asked Butch to go on home. They would 'talk it over with his mother' the next day. Beth and Lurabeth came home shortly after Butch left, had supper, and went to bed. The next day, Franklin's teacher, Mrs. Randall, told Franklin to stay after school; she told him Butch had told her what happened; she said Franklin must have been unaware of the danger he had been in, and how Butch had saved his life. She then told Franklin she was going to spank him...not because he had not listened to Butch in a life-threatening situation, but because he had *lied* about it to his father. She spanked him hard and sent him home; she had told Beth what had happened and that she was going to spank Franklin, but Beth still didn't quite understand what had transpired, so she let it go. They went home, and Franklin cried all the way. Beth told Michael what had happened at school, and that Eleanor Randall had spanked Franklin. Michael became very angry and talked to him about the entire situation; then he *also* spanked Franklin. He repeated what Eleanor Randall had said: he *must not lie*, especially when Butch had saved him in a life-threatening situation. Franklin never forgot the lessons he learned from that day on.

It was the end of March; it was still cold, but not snowing so much. Michael built up the fire till it was nice and cozy in their little house. They still hadn't run out of frozen meat from the porch, and also had vegetables in the root cellar. Beth made a special dinner for the family. Franklin did the dishes–as he always did, Lurabeth made the beds, and Margaret helped her pick up the laundry for their mother to wash; after the children had gone to bed, Beth sat down on the bed; she smiled at Michael…then she told him she was pregnant. He laughed… surely, she was making a poorly-timed joke; but she wasn't. She said she would give birth in less than seven months; during these difficult years in North Dakota while they waited, longing to return to the mission field, it seemed ironic, but nevertheless they committed themselves again to God.

The school year ended and Beth talked to Michael. She said that they had offered her another year's contract, but that she did not want to accept it. Sawyer had been a very hard assignment, and Michael admitted he too wanted to move. First, they prayed, then they wrote the Nazarene mission board again…as they had done before, and again asked to be sent to the Philippines, Hong Kong, Malaysia, even India, or even some other mission assignment. There was always the same response: 'China is closed, seek other ministries.' So, they decided to look for another church in the Dakota District, but nothing was available. Regardless, they knew they had to leave Benedict. It was becoming too hard on Michael: doing carpentry in Sawyer, or anywhere else in the area, and then Wednesday night prayer service, going in again on Sunday to preach…every week. Beth was a good teacher. This was obvious in the offer of a renewed contract, but she simply could not handle the rough behavior of the students. They moved back to Sawyer in time for district camp. They tried to talk discreetly to Nazarenes that were visiting from other Districts. Harry Taplin found out about it and threatened to have the church 'vote them out.' After camp meeting, Michael and Beth poured themselves into Vacation Bible School; Michael did a lot of calling, even going to

Velva, six miles away, and other communities around Sawyer. Some new families had moved into the Sawyer area, and taken up farming. They visited a few times, but like most farmers, it was hard to count on them being in church, with the farm taking so much of their time. One day, when one of the young men that he had called on, named Albert Sorenson, met Michael at the grain elevator to talk about giving him the job of building on to his shed, and Michael took the children along. While they talked, Lurabeth and Franklin got out of the car. They were bored, and were looking for something to do, so Margaret followed them. Lurabeth told Franklin that 'daddy built this grain elevator,' and Franklin wanted to know where they put the grain. Lurabeth told him they put it in the elevator; the train would come along and move the grain from the elevator to the train. Since he wanted to see where they did that, Lurabeth said she would show him. She began climbing up the metal ladder alongside the grain elevator; Franklin followed, and of course Margaret, now only six, followed them. Lurabeth had just about made it to the top; Franklin was a few feet below, and Margaret was about another five feet below. Suddenly, Michael came out of the grain elevator office; he had finished his talk with Albert. As he looked toward the car for the children, he of course didn't see them. In a panic, he looked all around the grounds for them, but did not find them. Then he heard their voices…above him. His heart froze! Looking up, he saw Margaret a couple rungs from the top. Not wanting to startle them and have her fall, we walked quickly over to the metal ladder. He let Margaret reach the top, and then he called out their names. With fear in his voice, but forcing himself to sound calm, he ordered them to, "come immediately down the ladder… slowly, slowly…daddy will help you." They knew they were in *big* trouble, but they all came down slowly, and quickly got in the car. No one dared say a word all the way home; Michael went in his bedroom, and then called each one of them in; they each got a spanking they never forgot…but after each spanking, he held each one tightly and said he loved them, that he didn't ever want to lose them, and that he wanted them to remember how important it was to '*always* tell Daddy where you are, and where you are going.' The spanking helped them remember. Beth came in and added her support for the spanking, but also hugged them and said she loved each one of them. Margaret was particularly broken up about it, realizing she might've fallen off the ladder or into the grain; and Franklin and Lurabeth were appropriately self-incriminating, promising never to do such a foolish thing again.

School started, and it snowed again on the first day. Lurabeth liked her new fifth grade teacher, Mrs. Gardner. Margaret started first grade... with the same first grade teacher that Franklin had had – Mrs. Lubbers. She seemed to like her. Franklin was eight, but had not yet adjusted to his left-handedness. At District camp, two well-intentioned ladies, watching him eat with his left hand, had remarked, "Oh, look at the little 'south paw'." Thinking this must be some kind of 'strange animal,' he immediately began trying to use his right hand. It was easy enough to relearn how to eat with his right hand, but learning how to write? Well, that was another matter; he secretly worried about it, and when school started, sure enough, his new teacher, Mrs. Stephanie Haynes, asked him to switch from his left to his right hand. He thought she was the most beautiful woman he had ever seen, but he was so nervous about his poor handwriting, and afraid she would not like him...if he did not switch; he started to run home when school was out. Wayne Reading caught up with him, saying, "what is the matter with you?" Then he saw that Franklin had wet his pants, and was embarrassed; he had decided he had to try to finish the job, so he opened his pants to urinate in the ditch, but Lurabeth and Carol caught up with them, and Lurabeth yelled, "Franklin, stop! What are you doing?" Now totally mortified, Franklin sat down on the edge of the ditch, so no one could see his wet pants. Lurabeth realized her little brother was having a hard time for some reason, so she told Wayne and Carol to go on home. Just then, Lloyd Putney, the town bully, came along and taunted Franklin. "preacher boy...wet his pants... he's in love with his teacher," he taunted. Lloyd was quite tall for his age, and very overweight, and no one wanted to 'scrap' with him, especially because of his bullying; but Lurabeth went straight over to him and said, "if you don't shut up, and go home, I'll knock out every tooth in your head!" Lloyd ran away as fast as he could; he never messed with Franklin again... and he avoided Lurabeth like the plague. Franklin did not want to go to school the next day... Lurabeth had told her mother about the wet pants incident as soon as they got home, and Beth told him it was 'okay' to have an accident once in a while; was there something that was bothering him?

He denied it and went to bed. Lurabeth had also told her mom about the attempted switch to write with the right hand, and Mrs. Haynes had already spoken with her about it. They were not going to force the switch, but would attempt it only if it was comfortable for Franklin. [Stephanie Haynes and her husband were new to Sawyer, but she was a first cousin of Hazel Forthen, and in fact had heard about the teaching position in Sawyer through Hazel; her husband, Mark, had attended the Church of the Nazarene in Fargo, where they met at North Dakota State University; she had been a psychology major there and understood the stress of trying to switch 'left-handers' to the right hand; she had told Beth she would not force the issue; she also understood young boys' 'crushes' on their teachers. Mark had told her that Franklin came over once to see her at their home; Mark had caught him 'peeping in their trailer-house window; and of course, this was inappropriate, and Mark had told him to come back some time, with his father or mother, or visit at the school]. When Franklin returned to school, there was no pressure to switch hands. There was no mention of the incidents of wet pants, nor 'visits' to the Haynes' home, and things were much better for Franklin from then on.

In October, a baby boy, Stephen Howard Varro, was born. Beth was still in the hospital for a few days after the birth, so Michael thought he would have to hold the Sunday service without the benefit of Beth's playing the piano for services; he mentioned this at a board meeting that was held following the previous Wednesday night prayer meeting. Hazel Forthen asked why they 'hadn't asked Stephanie Haynes to play.' Michael told Hazel that he was not *aware* that Stephanie *played* piano. "Oh yes, she may have been a psych major," Hazel told them "but, her minor was music, and sang in the University Chorale at North Dakota State; she and Mark also sang together in the Nazarene church choir in Fargo," So it was that Stephanie Haynes ended up playing the piano for the service on Sunday. Beth came home Tuesday, and all the neighbors came by to see the 'little addition' to the Varro family. The Rheinholt's, Mrs. Hoy, even the Schmidt's, and Forthen's, came by. Stephanie and Mark came over too. Everyone brought food, welcoming the new baby, and Beth and Michael didn't have to cook for a week!

Michael had written the Nazarene mission board about returning to the Far East as missionaries. He had also asked for contacts in other Districts… for any possible pastoral openings, in case they could not return as missionaries. Just before Thanksgiving, a letter arrived from Dr. EE Zachary, the district superintendent in the Northwest District. He wrote that the Nazarene mission board had given him Michael and Beth's address. He said he had heard of their missionary experience in China, from a mutual friend of theirs in Canada, Rev. Lawrence Hoff, who knew of the Fitz's work at Bresee Memorial Hospital in Daming. He told them that the Ephrata, Washington, Nazarene Church was going to be coming open for a pastor the following year. The current pastor was retiring and moving back east. Michael wrote back saying that he might be interested. They made arrangements for Michael to drive the several hundred miles out to Spokane, Washington, to interview after Christmas. Beth was staying home to take care of Stevie instead of teaching that year, so it made it easy for him to drive out to Spokane early Monday morning, after Sunday services, the first week in January. He discovered that his old friend, Lawrence Hoff, from Northern Bible College days, now pastoring in Ritzville, close to Spokane, was the 'mutual acquaintance' of Dr. Zachary. He was able to stay with them and go to the interview. Rev. Hoff gave a good reference, and had others from the Canada West District give good letters of reference also regarding his pastorates in Alberta and Saskatchewan. It seemed that God was finally answering their prayers. In God's time, he and Beth still believed that they would be sent to China as missionaries. After a good interview with Dr. Zachary and the Northwest District board, Lawrence and Edith Hoff drove Michael to Ephrata to visit the Nazarene Church. They had a chance to introduce Michael to Rev. Homer Stuart, the retiring pastor there. Because no official word had been given yet about Michael's interest, they simply told him Michael was visiting from North Dakota where he pastored the Sawyer church, and that they were old friends from Canada. Rev. Stuart bluntly said, "Oh, I already know they selected you to replace me; I'm retiring to Kankakee, Illinois, where my wife's family lives; they know all about you through Dr. George Coulter; he told Dr. Zachary that 'if they weren't going to send you to be missionaries in the Far East, they'd better replace me with you…if they had any *sense* at all!" Michael's 'eyebrow alert' started up, and he almost burst out crying; instead, Lawrence and Rev. Stuart began to laugh. Then Michael laughed too. God had heard their prayers! He felt that this new assignment would lead them one step closer to completing their 'preparation time,' before returning to China, or somewhere in the Far East (*Deo volente–if God wills it*, as Michael put it). Rev. Hoff dropped him off at his car in Ritzville, and they said their goodbyes; Michael drove straight through, back to Sawyer. 'What if Rev. Stuart was wrong,' he began to wonder. Lawrence assured him that he knew Dr. Zachary well, and if he told Rev. Stuart that Dr. Coulter had put in a good word for him, it was almost a 'done deal,' right? As he drove, Michael started singing "…for his eye is on *'Michael Varro,'* (rhymes with *'sparrow*, he would always say), and I know he watches me…" Michael never let anyone see him cry (except Beth a few times), and he rarely cried for sorrow; he only cried when he was moved by joy, which he always kept controlled… the Hungarian-and-reserved-person that he was, of course; this was one time he did, though…Sawyer had been a rough three years, but God had heard him and said, 'well done, good and faithful servant.' He turned on the radio when he got to Billings, and a Christian radio station was playing some George Beverly Shea. He was singing the very song he had just been singing himself…the one that had always been Michael's favorite. He finally pulled up to the parsonage in the middle of the night, but Beth heard him pull in, and got up. She fixed some Chinese tea, and they talked about the trip. Beth said she had prayed, and knew in her heart that God was moving them on. Stevie slept through the night, and the other children were sound asleep, too, so they just let them be. In the morning, the phone rang. It was Dr. Zachary. He said he had decided not to wait until the district clerk sent the official notification, he wanted to let them know that the Ephrata Nazarene Church, upon his, and several others' recommendations, had voted to call him to be their pastor. Dr. George Coulter, his dear old friend from the time he was saved in Regina, had helped him again. "God certainly seems to know what he is doing, doesn't He?" Beth said. Knowing this would be their last year in Sawyer, Michael and Beth poured themselves into the ministry. Beth had to care for Stevie, and others began to pitch in when they realized that she had to run the

Sunday School, play piano, and the women's and youth ministries as well. Lurabeth was also learning how to assist with Stevie's care...Marta said 'Beth made her tired'...just watching her!

Franklin was very proud of himself, first, the little garden he had planted that spring; he loved washing the dishes daily; he took out the 'chamber pots,' although he still hated *that* job (he never let on that he really liked washing the dishes; but in sub-zero weather, it was the only chore that kept his hands warm!). Margaret also began taking on extra chores, like feeding Stevie. She also learned to help Lurabeth and Beth with diapers, and other laundry items. Franklin wanted to go with his dad when he wasn't in school (Michael never took him). Michael didn't get many carpentry jobs that winter, so he hired on with some of the farmers; hauling and other jobs like that; whatever Richard Forthen could line up for him.

The sledding had been good. It seemed like the whole town showed up for the annual sledding contest. They would line up on the hill next to the Sawyer schools, and sled down alongside the schools—elementary, and the high school, which was next to the gym. The winner that year made it all the way from the top of the hill, down past the stores, and all the way to the highway. Even though Franklin's best friend was Wayne, he had made friends with some of the other boys as well. Elmer Long seemed to like him, and they started hanging out together. Phyllis and Maxine were friends of Elmer, and they said they wanted to meet Franklin. One day, after the sledding contest was over, and all the snow had melted, Elmer suggested that Franklin and he and two other girls all go down to the 'giant culvert under the train tracks...and kiss!' Franklin wasn't sure what he was getting into, but it sounded like fun, and he had always been a daredevil. Phyllis Porter was the smartest girl in third grade, and Maxine Ferguson was her best friend. Maxine only had one full arm...they said it was because she got the other one caught in some farm machinery...her right arm had been severed at the elbow. She never let it bother her, though, or let anyone treat her differently. Anyway, after school, Elmer told the other three to meet him down by the train station...they would go under the tracks in the giant culvert. When they got there, Elmer put his arms around Phyllis...so Maxine put her arms around Franklin; they were supposed to kiss, but just then, the station master, who had seen them go into the culvert, came running toward them, yelling, "I'm going to tell your folks what you are doing here." Elmer, Franklin, and the girls ran out the other side, and down the tracks. It was cold and they were bundled up, so no one could tell who they were. They split up, and each went to their own homes. Elmer made them swear they would never tell anyone; Franklin told Lurabeth, of course (they always told each other *everything*), but only if she swore she "would never tell a soul," It got around that the Varro family was leaving Sawyer to go to Washington state. One day the Principal, Mr. Tallerude, came over to Franklin's table at lunch time. "They tell me you are leaving…to go to Ephrata, Washington." Franklin didn't know Mr. Tallerude very well, even though he came to see his dad some times; it made him nervous that he was so friendly all the time. "Let me ask you something, Franklin." Now he was *really* nervous, especially since Mr. Tallerude was smiling, and acting like he was going to tell him a joke. "If you're 'Afraid-a Washington'… then don't go!" And he laughed so loud, all the people at lunch thought Franklin had told *him* a joke! The problem was, Franklin didn't even *get* it! Other students and teachers gathered, and Mr. Tallerude told the joke again…and again. He thought it was very funny…so did several teachers, apparently. They came to Franklin and repeated it over and over. Lurabeth had a different lunch time, but she had heard about the joke too, and asked Franklin why Mr. Tallerude was telling this joke so much. When she found out Franklin didn't *get* the joke, she explained it to him ['afraid-a-Washington,' she said, 'sounds like 'Ephrata, Washington'], then he laughed…he *got* it! So, he told all his friends too…they all laughed! Franklin was very pleased with himself.

Michael wrote Rev. Taplin that he was resigning to accept a position in Washington state as the pastor of the Ephrata Nazarene Church. Then he announced to the church that he was leaving. They were sad, saying he had been one of their best pastors ever. That Monday, after Sunday service, Michael and the children were working in the garden. Marta Rheinholt yelled from her back porch, "Rev. Varro, please come quickly." He told the children to go in the house, and stay there. He said for them to tell their mother to come right away; he heard the fear in Marta's voice, and he knew something tragic had happened. Beth came running; Michael had already gone in the house with Marta.

George had had a heart attack after cutting the lawn. He had just gone into the house to rest in the recliner. He never regained consciousness. It was the first personal experience with death the children had ever had, and it moved them deeply. Michael conducted the funeral within the next few days. The entire community turned out. George was well-known as a very kind, generous man. Marta was able to continue living in the same house until she could no longer care for herself. After that, she lived with her daughter in Minot, until she too passed away.

Michael had been asked to help with the revival at the Ritzville Nazarene Church before the school year ended. They were told that taking the children out early would not affect their academic standing, so the decision was made to pack up and leave before the end of May. They managed to get their same old 'hay wagon' as before. They had given it to Ras Rheinholt for his use on the farm when he said he would make sure they had meat and vegetables from time to time. They said goodbye to all their friends in the church and community; they even heard from other churches in the district with whom they'd served. Everyone realized it had been a hard assignment, and they had done a great job.

They arrived in Ritzville a few days later. The Hoff's were very gracious and let them stay with them in the parsonage. One of the parishioners had a garage that was not being used, and they were able to park the wagon with their trunks and furniture there. The Evangelist was Rev. Timothy Merton, but Rev. Hoff and Rev. Varro led the service and prayed. Edith Hoff played piano, but she wanted Beth to play, so it was agreed they would trade off. Each night the message was about 'those who die without Christ, after the last trump had sounded,' and those who don't believe 'would go to hell.' Both Lurabeth and Franklin, and later Margaret, had gone 'to the altar to get *saved*,' every night sometimes, during revivals in Sawyer (they didn't want 'to go to hell'), but this evangelist seemed to greatly emphasize 'the last trump' sounding before the end, so people must become believers. This frightened Franklin very much, so he went to the altar again (just to be sure), because he was so frightened about the last trumpet sounding. Lurabeth and Margaret stayed put this time. Michael came to pray with him, but he told him, "Franklin, you already accepted Jesus as your Savior." Franklin told his dad he didn't want the 'trump to sound' before he got 'saved!' Later that evening, they were all having pie and ice cream at the parsonage (as was every Nazarene clergy family's custom), following the revival service. Franklin and the girls were told to get ready for bed first. Franklin opened the window to get a little breeze. All of a sudden, he heard it! The 'trump' was sounding...he heard it, off in the distance! He was *sure* of it. He ran downstairs in his pajamas yelling, "the trump sounded, I heard it!" They all laughed. Rev. Hoff asked him, with a twinkle in his eye, if he was 'sure it really was a trumpet, maybe it was a French horn?' Totally taken back by this insincere reaction to what Franklin thought was a 'sound theological announcement,' he ran back upstairs embarrassed. [Actually, it turned out to be a neighbor boy, practicing his trumpet]. After everyone had a good laugh at Franklin's expense, they asked him if he wanted some pie and ice cream. He was hurt and angry...so he refused it (and he never would have *ever* refused pie and ice cream). Later, Beth came and talked to him. She said that she and all the rest of them were wrong for making so light of what she came to realize was a sincere concern on his part. She put her arms around him and said, "I have something *for* you," and she brought in some pie and ice cream she had put on the table in the hall. He accepted it this time, and smiled...he thought his mom was the *most sensitive and understanding woman in the world.* Then, Lurabeth and Margaret came in, and they all laughed and tickled each other...after a good pillow fight, of course.

Some of the Ephrata church people had repaired the parsonage in Ephrata, and they moved in after they finished the revival in Ritzville. That summer they had fun: swimming, and meeting new friends... both in the church, and other churches they visited; soon it was time for school. Dad decided it wasn't fair for Franklin to have to sleep on the couch, since Lurabeth and Margaret shared one of only two bedrooms, and Beth and Michael used the other. He quickly got permission from the church board, and dug out underneath the parsonage, set up the forms and the walls, for the basement. Mrs. Ellen Thornton, Mrs. Evelyn Dodge, Mr. and Mrs. George and Ruby Haight, Bob Alexander, and Mrs. Florence Shragg, all thought it was a wonderful idea, and they even helped raise some money for the project. Now Franklin had his own room. Never mind that they ran out of money before they dry-walled it, it didn't matter–he had his *very own* room. Lurabeth and he played Chinese checkers by flashlight under the covers, many a night, even after Dad said "lights out."

Lurabeth was the world's greatest 'bookworm,' and since both their schools were just a block apart, she insisted on reading her book on the way to school in the morning...guided only by seeing the 'shoes of her little brother' as they walked together. Franklin got sick of being thus taken for granted, and decided to teach her a lesson: one day he walked out into the middle of the road as she was reading her book. She of course followed, guided by his steps. Someone driving down the street, honked their car horn at them. Lurabeth jumped, and then screamed at Franklin, "You little devil." The teenage driver laughed his head off while Franklin ran for cover; Lurabeth ran after him, hitting him on the head with her book.

Franklin was allowed to join the Cub Scouts. He learned to make a 'hobo stove' out of an empty tuna can, rolled up corrugated cardboard in a can filled with candle wax. He told Lurabeth they had to 'camp out' in the back yard so he could cook meals for them. They didn't have a tent, but Beth went along with it, and let them drape a blanket over the outdoor clothes line, and then slept under the blanket, pretending it was a 'tent.' In the morning he didn't have the pan high enough above the flame, so he burned their eggs and bacon. The girls said that was 'enough,' and went inside to ask mom if it was too late to leave Franklin's 'campground,' and get a little breakfast!

Thanksgiving was a fun time. Michael had been elected the chairman of the Interchurch Council, and so he led the Community Thanksgiving. They had a combined service and Thanksgiving dinner. Everyone met at the Lutheran Church, and so he led the service, all the clergy of other churches assisting. Rev. Merlin Norris, who nominated Michael, closed in prayer; they became lifelong friends, and supporters of their future mission work. They ate together, had wonderful fellowship, and the children made new friends too.

For Christmas, Franklin was a 'wiseman' in the Nazarene Church Christmas pageant. He and DG Thornton (Delbert George, but they all just called him DG), and one of the Haight boys, were 'wisemen,' too. Lurabeth was Mary, and Margaret was one of the 'shepherd girls.' DG had taught Franklin a new 'spoof' version of 'We Three Kings,'– *"we three kings of orient are, tried to smoke a rubber cigar, it was loaded and exploded..."* Well, you know what happened ...they sang it wrong so many times, the night of the performance...yes, they sang the *wrong* words...then they got so tickled with themselves, they started laughing! Michael called Franklin out by name, and you know what happened. Yup, after the pageant, he got a spanking. So did DG, from his mom (DG had no father; they had divorced, and with no dad, DG floundered a bit). He and Franklin were always getting in trouble together, so Michael tried to keep Franklin away from him as much as he could. [One Sunday afternoon, DG wanted to do something, but Michael wouldn't give Franklin permission to go with him. DG and some others broke into the school, poured tempera paint everywhere, and turned on the fire hose. Two of the other boys, that had been habitual juvenile delinquents, went to 'reform school' for a while. DG would have gone, too, but Rev. Varro appealed on his behalf. The point is: Franklin could have been with them, and Michael reminded him of that; another time, both Lurabeth and Franklin got in trouble on a Sunday afternoon. They slipped under the metal gate and fence of the next-door Shell Oil Company, which was behind the Nazarene Church; they were always exploring somewhere, and they knew Mrs. Slonecker, the owner, had not been nice *at all* to their dad, and the church people; she had told them that if they didn't sell the church property to her, she would make it very rough for them, and they would *regret it*. Once inside the gate, Lurabeth and Franklin heard someone coming, and jumped inside the giant tires; they lay stretched out in the curved position of the tires, until the oil company people gave up searching and left; she called the police, but they were long gone by then. They never told their mom and dad, so when he was questioned, he said truthfully, he knew nothing about it. Another time, the three of them were in the basement of the church. Lurabeth decided they were going to have 'church.' Like the time when they were in Sawyer, she told Franklin he had to be the 'minister,' because *girls can't be 'ministers.'* She had found some grape juice and stale bread wafers, left over from the last communion. The problem was: of course, *the grape juice had fermented.* Franklin said all the 'liturgy and prayers' that he remembered his dad saying; they drank the 'juice' and ate the stale bread. If a little is good, then more must be better, right? *They finished it off!* When they returned to the parsonage, they were, well...a little 'tipsy.' Beth discovered her three children were not in 'proper Nazarene decorum.' She didn't tell Michael, but she figured out what had happened; they were so silly and giggly. Lurabeth said Franklin had done a communion 'shervice, zhust like d-d-daddy.' She had some coffee, so she put milk in it and called it 'chocolate milk.' She didn't have the heart to spank them, and she had to hold her sides to keep from laughing].

The school year ended and they decided to take a trip to Canada. It had been years since they had been there, and the Varro family had aunts, uncles, cousins and grandparents that many hadn't met. Mary Varro had passed away years before; Michael's brothers and sisters had married, had children, and even Pop had remarried...a third time! [This time to: Novenka, was her name; he had gone *again* to the 'old country' for a bride. Novenka was only six years older than Michael. She, like Mary Gold, was from a Hungarian family; but they were not from Budapest, they were from Karcag, where the original Varro family had come, migrating from Transylvania; and part of the family was Ukrainian]. Michael and Beth got the children up early and left first thing Monday morning, the first week in June. They had some car trouble in Spokane; but they fixed it and were soon on their way again. They raced for the border before closing, just minutes after midnight, and the border patrol would not let them go through... until the next morning, they said. Short on funds, and planning their lodging only with family, they decided to sleep in the car. The only trouble was, with two adults, three growing children... and a new baby, it appeared that someone was going to have to stay outside of the car. Michael decided that would be 'the men.' Franklin took exception to this, and didn't consider himself, a ten-year old boy...to be a man, yet. Michael handed him a blanket and they crawled under the car. The night was *cold*, and the gravel was *hard*. Dad might have thought of it as 'male-bonding,' but Franklin called it 'torture;' early in the morning, the two of them got back in the car, went through the border without incident, and then on to Cranbrook, Alberta, where they stayed with their friends, John and Muriel Fox; then Calgary, and Regina... two weeks, before returning to Ephrata. They were able to see all of the

Canadian brothers and sisters: Bud and Helen, Joe and Josie, Jim and Ollie, Margaret and Glen Wood, Irene, and Frankie, and their families. They stayed with Pop and Novenka two nights, Bud and Helen… all the others in the Regina area. Most had not yet moved to other places, except Louis, who stayed in the U.S. after World War II, and lived in Los Angeles. Later, Bud and Helen moved to Calgary, Joe and Josie moved to British Columbia; the others had stayed in the Regina area, Michael had gotten Rev. Hoff to preach for him in Ephrata. Lawrence was able to have a visiting seminarian to preached for him in Ritzville. Before leaving, Novenka showed them pictures of the family back in the old days. It brought back memories–their get-together in Regina was a time of healing, reacquainting with each other, and a common heritage. Most were now parents and grandparents. Michael and Beth and family left with a great sense of oneness. Most had become active in church, and had chosen to follow Michael into the Nazarene Church. When they left, there were tears…of joy. All of them were very proud of their 'big brother' Michael, and followed his example. It was also an opportunity for Michael to repair a strained relationship with Pop, too. They left with really warm feelings. They drove straight through to Ephrata…and no problems at the border. Things had gone well, but everyone seemed happy to have the Varro's back. They got back just in time for Lurabeth and Franklin to go off to Pinelow Nazarene Camp–the girls', and boys' camps just a week apart. At the end of the week, all joined together for family camp. They found it spiritually uplifting, and the kids made some new friends in the district. When they got back from camp, they let them keep a dog George Haight gave them. She was a Terrier mix, so they called her Terri, and Franklin and Margaret were the ones that took care of her mostly. School started–Margaret and Franklin at Broadview…but Lurabeth was at Ephrata Intermediate on the west side. Lurabeth and Franklin had learned to swim at the Grant County Park, near Franklin's school, and the whole family enjoyed taking picnics and swimming there, even after school started. Stevie celebrated his first birthday in October; so, they took a picnic, cake, and some ice cream in a cooler to the park. Mrs. Estes was Franklin's teacher, and he saw her with her husband at the park. He wanted her to meet his family, so he called them over to meet her. She was very gracious, and told them her brother was a Lutheran minister in Wenatchee. She told them she had been in a life threatening auto accident a few years ago, and her brother, and another preacher in Wenatchee (and a former Nazarene), came and prayed with her in the hospital. She had become a Christian after her accident...but she had lost the use of her left arm. Franklin had noticed this, but he never knew why she used her right arm only.

Things went much more smoothly than in Sawyer. Michael did do some carpentry work, but mostly helped others out with various projects, including adding on to the grain elevator in Ephrata. As chair of the Interchurch Council, he made a lot of calls on families in the Soap Lake, Moses Lake, and Quincy area farms and communities. They took a trip in the fall to Sun Lakes Resort, and went to Nazarene 'zone' meetings in central Washington. Beth stayed busy with women's, youth, and music groups, but most of her time was taken up with the care of Stevie.

That fall, a new family arrived from Phoenix, Arizona. They had attended a small Nazarene Church there. Mr. Richard Kinnersley was a very outspoken man, and had lots of ideas about how a church should be run. He was very strict with his children, but Marian, his wife, was very quiet. They all seemed to do everything he demanded. He thought he should be the chair of the board, but Evelyn Dodge was chair, and she told him he had to be there at least a year before he could even be elected to the board, and serve a few years before he could become chair. He didn't like that. He criticized everyone...and everything. He wanted everyone to say 'Amen' loudly when Rev. Varro preached; he said Rev. Varro should preach loudly and say 'Amen' more; he didn't like Rev. Varro...'he was not dynamic enough.' He wanted someone like his pastor in Phoenix, Rev. Bob Gruber. Michael found out, through a friend in Phoenix, that everyone was happy the Kinnersley's left the Nazarene Church there. He had run the pastor off, a young Pasadena College graduate, in his first five years of ministry. Tim Sherman, their previous pastor, had asked the District Superintendent to find him another church because Mr. Kinnersley had implied that Tim's wife was not qualified to be in ministry...she had *not* become a Christian until she was in college; he said she had been 'in the world,' after growing up as a missionary kid, in Mexico. But she had greatly assisted her husband in his ministry, because she was bi-lingual and most in their church congregation were Spanish-speaking. Mr. Kinnersley didn't like that either; he thought the Nazarene Church should be *white*, and send missionaries to save the 'rest of the world.' Mr. Kinnersley started stirring up trouble in the church; he wanted the church to have a different pastor. Michael wrote Dr. Zachary telling him about the problem, but Dr. Zachary was already aware of this 'trouble maker,' as he put it; he later admitted that...as it turns out, Rev. Sherman's wife was a cousin of his; but things went well despite Mr. Kinnersley's behavior. Lurabeth started taking violin lessons. She was already playing piano...and Franklin wanted to study piano and violin just like 'sis.' She finished the Michael Aaron Piano Series, and gave it to him, and he learned to play everything *she* did. She finished the John Thompson Piano Series, so he took up *that* piano study too. She graduated to a larger violin, and gave it to Franklin, so he took that up as well; but he was not studying with a *teacher* like she was. Beth had started both of them on piano, but Michael's dream was for his 'Hungarian children' to be able to play the violin; they could only invest in one child's lessons at that time, and Lurabeth...showing the most promise, was bused to Cashmere, about forty miles away. Margaret took up piano too, and after Franklin gave her the Aaron and Thompson books, she did quite well too; but neither she nor Franklin pursued violin like Lurabeth; she was the one that showed the most promise in music.

The Ephrata Nazarene Church was growing, about ten to fifteen percent each year. They had averaged between forty and fifty for several years, but after a year and a half with the Varro's, it was averaging about fifty-five to sixty in attendance; for special services like Christmas and Easter, they got up to seventy...even seventy-five sometimes. Michael decided to bring in an evangelist for the 'spring revival' that he hoped would help them average seventy-five or more. They were still applying every year to go as Nazarene missionaries to 'Asia somewhere, anywhere.' The Philippines and Taiwan, called Formosa or Free China at that time, were good mission fields, but some in the Nazarene Church that believed ministry among the Chinese was a 'thing of the past.' Still, others were pushing for a presence in Hong Kong, Formosa, Malaysia, and even the Philippines, which all had large Chinese communities. Other mission boards had accepted former missionaries among the

Chinese who were Nazarenes (but not serving under the Nazarene mission board). Michael decided to invite Rev. Marvin Cunningham, and his wife Sylvia…he was the brother-in-law of Free Methodist missionaries in Hong Kong…to be the evangelist for the spring revival. If the church showed steady growth, and spiritual development, he believed this would assist them in building a resume that would result in an appointment to go to some mission field. This revival was like many of the other revivals the Varro children had experienced, but rather than focusing on 'fear and avoiding hell,' Rev. Cunningham focused on the 'great love of Jesus' and *gaining heaven, without losing one's own soul.'* The first night, several came forward to the altar, including two new young couples, and Barbara Merkel. Barbara was already active in the youth group, and Beth had been grooming her to take it over. Lurabeth told Franklin they didn't need to go forward any more. Dad had told her, after the 'last trump' incident in Ritzville… that he didn't want them coming forward again 'just because it was a revival;' but Margaret went forward the second night anyway, and told Lurabeth and Franklin that she didn't do it because she was 'afraid of going to hell.' She said Rev. Cunningham had said we shouldn't become Christians because we are *afraid*, but because *we love Jesus*, and what he did for us on the cross. That night, Franklin and Lurabeth got into one of their famous arguments; they loved to discuss anything … and everything. Franklin said it didn't matter why someone becomes a Christian, just as long as you do it. Maybe he was still suffering from the embarrassment of the revival in Ritzville. Lurabeth said anything that anyone does, needs it to be 'for the right reason.' He asked her if she had gone to the altar because she was afraid of going to hell. She said no, it was to confess her sins, and ask Jesus' forgiveness, asking him to come into her heart, and thanking him for doing so. The next night, he didn't tell his dad or mom, and he didn't tell Lurabeth or Margaret. He went forward again…as soon as Rev. Cunningham gave the invitation. He had changed his mind–it did matter why one does what ones does. He understood for the first time, when Rev. Cunningham said we 'cannot even imagine how much Jesus loves us'… and Franklin swore he looked *straight at him*…he was *not* afraid, just sorry…and thankful. Rev. Cunningham and Michael came over. They asked him a strange question: "Why did you come forward?" Franklin looked straight at his dad, and said, "I'm not afraid! I want to invite Jesus into my life…because He loves me so much." So that was always the time Franklin pointed to, as the time he became a Christian. The revival ended the following Sunday night. Beth had prepared the three older children, and they sang 'I Need Thee Every Hour,' which was Franklin's favorite song. The girls sang melody, and Franklin sang the alto part his mother had taught him. Marvin and Sylvia Cunningham also sang a song. They sang 'Leaning On The Everlasting Arms,' and Beth played for them. More came forward the closing night. Everyone agreed this was one of the best revivals the church had ever had. With these good results, Michael wanted to schedule a Baptism. He decided on Lake Lenore, just a few miles north of Soap Lake in the Ephrata area. Michael held a class for the seven baptismal candidates: his three children, and four others. Lake Lenore was a small fresh water lake, one of the several lakes left over when the ancient Columbia River changed its course. The four others to be baptized were first, then Margaret, Franklin, and finally Lurabeth. [She loved to make up stories, and one of her favorites was that her dad tried to 'drown her;' she said, with a twinkle in her eye, that he 'dunked her'–in the name of the Father– 'praying five minutes over her,' then he 'dunked her' again–in the name of the Son, another five-minute prayer, of course, then he 'dunked her' again–in the name of the Holy Spirit, another five-minute prayer… "see," she said facetiously, "he tried to drown me." They always laughed at this 'tall tale,' but loved hearing her tell it again and again. The three Varro children showed a real change in their lives, and began finding ways to not only be the 'preacher's kids' but truly live out their faith as new 'followers of Jesus.'

Stephen Howard Varro born Minot Oct 22, 1952

Lake Lenore

"Pop" & Novenka Varro

Michael & Bud

1-Jim, Irene, Maggie, Frankie…
2-Pop, Mary, Joe, Beth, Michael

CHAPTER FIFTEEN

MISSIONARIES AND MUSTANGS

'Angel-On-Loan'

Stephen Howard Varro (1952-1956)

HE SCHOOL YEAR WAS COMING TO A CLOSE. THE CHURCH WAS AN exciting place to be, and more young people were joining. Mr. and Mrs. Kinnersley had come to the revival, and he had made sure everyone heard him say 'Amen'…loudly, every time it seemed appropriate, and a few times even when it was not. His wife, who was always silent, seemed nervous and uncomfortable about something. They had a daughter, Rachel, who had a mind of her own, and Mr. Kinnersley was always trying to explain her to everyone. She had done well in high school, and she and Barbara Merkel had become good friends. Richard didn't want to seem like he was alone in his dislike for Rev. Varro. He would try to 'speak for' Marian, his wife, and when he couldn't manipulate her, he himself decided to go to Evelyn Dodge, chair of the board. He reminded her that a vote on the pastor was required every spring. In Nazarene polity at that time, a simple majority was not enough. A two-thirds majority was required. She called for a vote on the pastor…to be done following the service in two weeks. Richard Kinnersley began his campaign to 'vote Rev. Varro out.' He went to unsuspecting couples that he could intimidate, lying to them by telling them the vote was to dismiss the pastor, and to vote 'no.' He told his wife to vote 'no,' and he told his daughter to vote 'no.' He knew she was best friends with Barbara Merkel, so he told Rachel to tell Barbara to vote 'no,' as well. Neither Barbara, nor Rachel would do what Mr. Kinnersley was 'dictating to them' to do. Barbara Merkel was a real fan of Beth and Michael, and both voted 'yes.' Most of the young couples were new, and not familiar with the two-thirds majority requirement anyway, so they thought it was not a big deal anyway. Mrs. Dodge asked Rev. Varro to wait in the parsonage while they voted. Of those eligible to vote, Ellen Thornton, Evelyn Dodge, George and Ruby Haight, Bob Alexander, and Florence Schragg, plus Rachel, and Barbara–all the leadership in the church–voted for the Varro's to stay. With such a small church however, a 'no' vote by Mr. and Mrs. Kinnersley…and two other couples thinking they were voting NOT to dismiss the Varro's…this came to eight 'yes,' and six 'no' votes. Mr. Kinnersley was quick to point out that the two-thirds vote was not attained. Mrs. Dodge declared, reluctantly, that the pastor's vote failed. Franklin ran to the parsonage to tell his dad. Michael's 'eyebrow alert' was off the map. He prayed…and then he returned to the church to face them. In the meantime, Barbara Merkel had stood and said that neither Beth, nor Lurabeth, who was eligible to vote as her next birthday was twelve, hadn't voted. They called for a second vote. The two couples that had voted 'no' because they did not understand the vote also objected. Mr. Kinnersley reminded them they could not vote twice. Rev. Varro entered the church, and said that no second vote would be taken. He dismissed the service with prayer, and everyone was stunned, and left quietly. Evelyn Dodge resigned on the spot; some cried. The vote was reported to the district and the circumstances of the two-thirds vote–all due to one disgruntled man. Dr. Zachary told Michael that in cases like this the District Superintendent can intervene and declare the vote invalid. Michael said that he would not stay under these circumstances, and he never wanted to be a pastor in the first place–God had called him to be a missionary. Did Dr. Zachary have a church plant where he could do a 'missionary assignment?' Dr. Zachary looked at him a long time, he started to smile...how could Michael possibly have known what he had been praying for? Only God could do this...then he told Michael they had been looking for 'someone who would be willing to plant a 'mission church' in the area...in fact, right next to Ephrata–in the town of Quincy–just several miles away. No one, not even a retired or seminarian candidate wanted to touch it with a 'ten-foot pole.' Michael said he would have to consult with Beth, but he thought they would take it. When he got home from Yakima (the district office was about forty miles away), he told Beth about the offer. She looked down...she sighed...then she began to laugh. She said, "when we finished deputation and realized we could not return to China, I prayed "Lord I'll go anywhere you want me, just *never* send me to North Dakota," and so *that* is where God *sent* us... and when we finished there and went to Ephrata, we visited Quincy on the way to a 'zone' meeting in Wenatchee–we made a rest stop and I saw nothing but dust and tumbleweeds–and I prayed, 'Lord I'll go anywhere you want me to, just *please* don't send me to Quincy!" Then they both laughed. God has such a sense of humor. Michael called Dr. Zachary right away...they would plant a new 'mission church' in Quincy, Washington... this would be their new 'mission field.'

Before they finished their last month there, they invited some Chinese airmen from the Larson Air Force Base in Moses Lake to the parsonage for a meal. Michael had been told by one of the other pastors in Ephrata that the U.S. Air Force was doing some training at Larson for the Republic of Chinese in Formosa. A few of these young men had somehow found out about Beth and Michael having been in China;

they were very homesick. Michael met with the chaplain at Larson and arranged for them to come to Ephrata to be their guests, at the parsonage, for a visit and meal…Beth cooked some wonderful Chinese food. The Air Force van dropped them off and said they'd be back in three hours to return them to Larson that evening. When they arrived, they were very cautious, but when Michael and Beth spoke to them in perfect Mandarin, they relaxed and had a great time. They visited, enjoyed the meal, and promised to come back and go to church. Even though they never *did* return to go to church, Beth and Michael had enjoyed a little 'taste of home.' The children entertained everyone with singing, piano, and violin playing, and even a few 'Chinese songs and sayings' Beth had taught them. It was a great time with these Chinese airmen.

As soon as Pinelow Camp was over, they packed up again and moved to Quincy. Michael had found a few families there that were Free Methodist, and because there was no Free Methodist church in Quincy at that time, they said they would attend a Nazarene Church if one were planted there. Another Nazarene family had just moved there from Idaho. They were Bill and Eleanor Smith, and their three children, John, Morgan, and Susie. Bob Alexander and Florence Shragg decided to leave the Ephrata Nazarene, and join the Quincy Nazarene as 'charter members.' With four eligible members of the Smith family, Sharon and Harry McMullen (former Free Methodists), Bob Alexander, Florence Shragg, and the four eligible members of the Varro family, the total number of charter members of the Quincy Nazarene Church, came to twelve (fully one-third of the total Ephrata membership right off the bat!). Bill Smith helped Michael locate a house they could rent. This house had a garage that was quickly converted into a church 'sanctuary.' A thrift store donated a rug, a small table and a podium. Pioneer Elementary had a surplus of folding chairs, so they were able to borrow twenty-five. The school also loaned them a piano from storage. Dr. Zachary approved a one-year 'district plan' for planting the Quincy Nazarene Church, but the congregation had to commit to fifty-percent of the pastor's salary. The five 'giving' families (including the Varro family) could not afford the district pastor's minimum, so Dr. Zachary also approved a supplement for one year; the opening service was Labor Day Sunday. They advertised in the Quincy Quest, and printed door hangers and flyers. A few guests showed up, so with the six Smith family members, the McMullen's and their two children, Bob Alexander, Florence Shragg, six Varro family members, and three guests, they had twenty-one in the opening service. Michael preached a good sermon, and all were very happy they had attended. [Franklin told his friends he was a '*charred* member of his dad's new church!']

Stevie made friends with one of the neighbor boys, Stevie Berger, and they became inseparable. Michael and Beth had decided to give each of the children twenty-five cents a week as an allowance...as spending money. The idea was to teach savings, and Lurabeth and Franklin let their 'allowance fund' grow so that after several weeks, each could buy something more significant than just candy or donuts. Lurabeth was better about it and saved about ten cents a week, Franklin didn't do as well because he liked to buy donuts or candy, like his friends did. He saved only about five cents a week. Margaret did about the same. Stevie Berger had convinced Stevie Varro he should 'share' some of his money with him. Stevie was always running out of money, so Beth decided to see why all of his money was being spent on candy. She overheard Stevie Berger persuading Stevie he should 'take turns sharing' their money, but she knew Stevie Berger didn't get an allowance. This kind, generous nature of her little son impressed her, but she put a stop to it, because it wasn't fair to him. Lurabeth told her mother the Berger children were all 'cons.' She, Franklin, and Margaret had made friends with all three of them: Laura, Ben, and Stevie. They even formed a 'club,' complete with clubhouse, rules, and ranking of members. They found wood, and dug a pit, covering it with the boards in the vacant lot next door to the parsonage/church. They rigged up a 'tetherball' pole and played competitive tetherball. The highest ranking members were called 'privates' because they had earned a 'private' room, and the lowest ranking members were called 'generals' because they were 'regulars,' and not special, they were just 'general.' They took the first part of the family name Berger, and the first part of the family name Varro, and put them together to form the name of their club—the BeVar club, or the 'Beaver Club.' Laura insisted she had to be president, and private first class. Ben said he had to be vice president and private second class. Lurabeth asked why, since she had come up with the name; Franklin and she had built the clubhouse; Margaret, even Stevie V., and Stevie

B. had helped. What had Ben and Laura done? The whole idea quickly fell apart, and Lurabeth told her mother the incident with Stevie Berger 'conning' her brother Stevie out of his money was the last straw. 'The Beaver Club met its demise as quickly as it was founded," Beth and Michael were truly impressed, so they had a good laugh.

School started, and Lurabeth wanted to play in the band like her friends; the band director asked her what instrument she played. She told him it was the violin...and the piano. He laughed and said she couldn't be in marching band with a violin, or a piano, on her back! She asked him what she had to play in order to be in the band. He smiled and said, 'well, maybe a clarinet, a trumpet, or a flute...' Before he had finished, she interrupted and said, 'flute.' He said, 'but you don't play the flute.' She told him she would, and when did they start marching. He laughed and told her it wasn't that easy. She said 'when?!' He said two weeks. She borrowed a flute from a friend and taught herself to play in two weeks. For years, Mr. Ben Calloway, the band director told that story as an inspiration to aspiring music students, as the mindset each of his students needed to have in learning how to play an instrument. They marched...and Lurabeth played her flute. [She also didn't like her friends calling her every name in the book, except her correct name: Lurabeth. They called her 'Lulabell, Loribeth, Lollypop,' etc. She decided to be called by her second name, like her brother Franklin. She became known as *Julie*, from then on]. Anyway... about the band, Franklin did not like this; he competed with his older sister in everything, and complained to his mother that it was not fair that she could play an instrument, and that he could *not*. Beth was sharing this story with her brother Guil, who had just graduated from Northwest Nazarene College. He told Beth he had an old trumpet he wasn't using. He had played for a few years in high school, and when Dr. and Mrs. Fitz moved to Nampa in 1952, he finished up there and planned to play it in college, but never did. He said Franklin could have it. The bell was bent, but it could be straightened. So, Franklin started on the trumpet in Sixth Grade. The kids made fun of his 'trumpet with a bent bell,' but he ignored them. He even marched with the middle school and high school band for 'Jackrabbit Days.' Margaret didn't seem to care about playing any instrument, except the piano. When the Apple Blossum Festival was held in Wenatchee, they all went there to play for the concert. Franklin was sitting with the trumpets and needed to release the spit-valve, but not being fully acquainted with the mechanics of it, blew as hard as he could, but didn't hold the valve open long enough. Julie loved to tell the following story: "we had worked hard all day on one passage, and we finally got it right; suddenly...there was a loud blatting sound that came for the trumpet section; the conductor rapped his baton on the music stand... wonderful, flutes, you finally got it, just right...and then some 'idiot trumpet player' blats his horn in the quietest, most serene moment!" She told Franklin this story on their break. Franklin hung his head; he had to admit that the *idiot* trumpet player...was *he!* Beth and Michael came to the concert and were so proud of their children, and especially loved the Festival Choir that sang 'This Is My Country.' Both Margaret and Stevie clapped loudly for them, too.

Franklin had also started a paper route. He 'threw' the newspaper printed in Spokane – the Spokesman-Review. He didn't like walking the route and Beth suggested he save his money and buy a bicycle. If he would earn half, they would kick in the other half, and buy a good used bike. He would get cold, and asked his mom if she would drive him. In the worst weather she gave in and did so, but most of the time she reminded him of his goal, and urged him to discipline himself to complete the task unassisted. He did for a while, then he 'found' a hamburger stand that was right in the middle of his route. He got so hungry, he started using some of his money on 'just a little snack.' Soon all his savings were literally 'eaten up.' Michael helped him remember his goal by telling him his own stories of perseverance and hardship, but this didn't help much. He became discouraged and wanted to quit his route. Julie told him 'Varro's don't quit,' and he started thinking about it. Beth suggested that maybe he needed an intermediate goal. She found his old Cub Scout catalog, and found a 'hand warmer.' It lit like a lighter, and you put it in a sleeve that could fit in your pocket. They made an arrangement with Franklin's paper route supervisor. He could have credits build up. Instead of payments, he earned credits toward a hand warmer. It arrived, and he liked it very much. It reminded him of washing the dishes in Sawyer. He loved to keep his hands warm. After he got the hand warmer, the credits kept building up because Franklin didn't notice it and his mom and dad 'forgot' to cancel the arrangement. By the time he noticed it, he had almost enough money saved up for his part of the bicycle. 'Close enough,' Michael and Beth said, and unbeknownst to Franklin, they bought a used bicycle in Wenatchee and surprised him.

The church was growing very slowly, so Michael still got carpentry jobs. He helped the Free Methodists build a small A-frame church building. They had organized right after the Nazarenes, and some of the local Free Methodists went back to their own denomination. Michael dreamed of buying land and building a new church facility, but it was still too early. They had started with a dozen or so, and now after a year it was up to almost twenty-five, but it was slow, and very discouraging at times. But at 'zone' meetings they were highly thought of. Ephrata had faltered, and some talked of coming to Quincy. Mr. and Mrs. Kinnersley left and went back to Arizona, but were not welcomed at the church that they had left previously, and they ended up...so it was told, going to a pentecostal church. Michael committed to finding a way to get to Hong Kong or Taiwan, or sticking it out until the church grew and they could serve God there in Quincy. They began making plans for the District Assembly, which was to be held in Walla Walla. Bob Alexander's wife had 'left him' in Ephrata, and she had taken the children. He now was driving from Ephrata and picking up Mrs. Schragg in Soap Lake, then driving to Quincy and back for Sunday Services. Mrs. Schragg's health got worse and could no longer come to Quincy. So Bob decided move to Quincy, but he had no job.

Michael had built out the basement just like he had done in Ephrata. Franklin now had his own room in Quincy, the same way as before! Michael finished out a couple other rooms downstairs also, so he invited Bob Alexander to come live there with them. [Bob arrived with some furniture...and a television set! It was the first TV the Varro family had ever had. They all enjoyed watching TV together]. Julie had won the 'zone' Bible quiz contest, so she was going to go with them to compete for the Bible quiz District championship. Bob would stay and take care of Franklin and Margaret. Michael, Beth, Julie, and Stevie, would all go to Walla Walla for District Assembly. The third day of District Assembly, Bob had called the children to come sit down and eat supper. As they bowed their heads to pray, Franklin looked out the window. Mrs. Smith got out of her car…she burst into tears, then got back in the car. They prayed, then started eating. Mrs. Smith got out of the car again, crying; she came slowly to the door and knocked. Franklin ran to the door. He had always liked Eleanor Smith and he was smiling as he started to invite her in. She was as white as a sheet… she blurted out the words she had obviously rehearsed many times: "I'm so sorry, but I have to tell you that *your little brother Stevie was killed in an automobile accident in Walla Walla* at the District Assembly." Then she burst into tears. Bob, who was always quiet, cried out, "O no! Lord Jesus, please, No!" Franklin burst into tears, hardly knowing what this all meant. Margaret cried out loud too, asking where mommy and daddy were, and if they were okay. Eleanor sat down, and in between sobs, explained what had happened: they were having a business meeting after the Bible quiz, Stevie was fussing, so Beth suggested Julie take him to the car…that he couldn't rest in the nursery…with babies crying so much. Julie was reading her book, and Stevie was so restless, he finally said, "I'm going to go see mommy." Dad had always drilled it into them to be sure to lock the car door. As she turned to lock the door, Stevie darted into the street just as a car was coming through the intersection. It struck Stevie…he was killed instantly… Julie turned to cross the street. Two Nazarene preachers on the church steps, who witnessed the entire scene, ran into the street. The woman in the car thought she had hit a rock, and was continuing down the road. The preachers ran after her yelling for her to stop. Julie crossed the street, burst into tears, and women from the church came running to her. Another came and put her arms around Julie, took her into the bride's room, and had someone watch her while she ran to get Beth. Michael was called out of his meeting and told the tragic news. The woman who had assisted Julie, got Beth, and told her, "I think you need to come quickly; your daughter needs you right now." Thinking something had happened to Julie, she ran to her in the bride's room. Another preacher had called an ambulance, as soon as the other two got the woman driver to stop. As Michael and Beth joined the others, the ambulance pulled up. The woman driver was hysterical—they learned that she had a little boy…exactly the same age as Stevie. District Assembly shut down, and all the delegates, preachers and their wives, and others attending, gathered in the sanctuary for prayer. Michael and Beth got in the ambulance with Stevie's body and attendants. They quickly got to the hospital and watched as they took the broken little body of their son to the emergency room. The woman, Mrs. Jane Harmon, had to be sedated by the doctors. Then she joined Beth and Michael sitting on the lawn, crying and praying, *"O Lord, you gave us a little angel for a little while…we loved him so much…maybe he was just a temporary gift, so now we give him back to you…thank you that we will join him again someday…with you, and all those gone ahead of us."* The doctors arrived. "I'm so sorry, Rev. and Mrs. Varro… Stevie is gone," Dr. Max Trumble said. Beth and Michael held each other and cried. They called Jane Harmon's husband to pick her up, but not before she stopped to thank Beth and Michael. "I was the one who ran over your child, but *you* took the time to comfort *me*, and didn't say one unkind word to me; only people that love God like you do could ever do that for me; thank you, may God comfort you." She left with her husband, but they both came to the funeral; it was decided the District Assembly would conclude early, Beth and Michael would be excused to return to Quincy and pick up Franklin and Margaret, then return the last day of the District Assembly for the funeral. It was almost surreal as they drove back. Beth was in no shape to drive, and Michael drove silently, his face like a stone. He thought of Job, and all that *he* went through. Michael was alone in his thoughts as Beth wept, finally falling asleep from emotional exhaustion. "The Lord giveth, the Lord taketh away…"he couldn't finish it. He felt hollow. Then he remembered, "and lo, I am with you always, even unto the end of the earth," Jesus had said. His mind drifted back to the time when his father rejected him before he went to Bible School, "and you became my only Father," he remembered…"you were with me then…and you are with me now!" Then he looked at Beth, who had just awakened, and he said, "and *blessed* be the name of the Lord"; say it Beth, **say** it with me." They both cried, and said, "and…blessed be the name of the Lord."

They picked up Franklin and Margaret. Beth held her three children close to her and wept. Julie had tried to jump out of the car twice on the way back. Her guilt was so profound, even though Beth and Michael comforted her, assuring her that there was nothing that could have stopped the car, or anything she could have done to stop Stevie from entering that street [note: many had demanded that a traffic light be placed there because of other close calls, without success; it took the death of one little boy, to save the lives of countless others– they put a traffic light there after Stevie's death; he may have saved scores of other lives]

The funeral was beautiful. The entire District Assembly stayed to honor Rev. and Mrs. Varro, and their family–and their sweet little son, Stephen Howard Varro. Most of the Quincy Nazarene Church family, including the Smith's, Bob Alexander, and several others from both the Quincy and Ephrata churches, came. They sang 'Safe In The Arms Of Jesus," and 'Precious Jewels.' Dr. Zachary preached a beautiful memorial to Stevie, called 'God's Precious Angels.' When it was over, the hearse took Stevie's body, with the family following behind, back to Quincy, where he was laid to rest in the small Quincy cemetery. Eleanor Smith, and other friends, had arranged a reception at the parsonage. Many assured the family of their continuing prayers and love. God helped them somehow to make it through the next several weeks and months. The burden was crushing…but God was *there*.

Michael prayed every morning, now more earnestly than ever, that God would show him what to do. God had called them to be missionaries to China. They waited seven years (like 'Jacob…and got Leah,' he said), then he waited seven more years (would he not, like 'Jacob, finally get the promise of Rachel?'). He got a letter from an old Pasadena College school mate, Robert Hammond. He had heard about Stevie, and offered his and Helen's condolences and prayers for them (remember Helen Reiten? She had dated Michael briefly, then married Bob). He wanted to know if the Nazarene Church was ever going to appoint them to a Chinese mission field. Michael answered him that they had not. Bob wrote back, "Come to Pasadena; I will pay your way; Voice of China and Asia, Inc. needs you to consider becoming missionaries in Formosa." Michael told Beth about it. She admitted she wasn't sure. They had heard many things about their old nemeses, the Kiehn's, and their 'more than questionable' involvement with Bob Hammond, the Nazarene Church, and legal trouble in Formosa, but she said, "if we commit it to the Lord, and he opens a door, well…?" Her voice trailed off. By the end of June, Bob Hammond had sent

Michael a round-trip ticket – Seattle to Los Angeles. He flew back after five days…with the full backing of the Voice of China and Asia board approval, even for Beth, sight unseen, because many already knew her, with a promise of financial backing. Beth could not believe the swiftness with which everything was happening. Could this dream really be happening after all this time? She wrote to her family and friends to pray about this with them. Everyone she wrote said the same thing: put it in God's hands, and let him decide. Despite their doubts, one thing was sure: God had clearly called them to be missionaries to China…at least missionaries to the Chinese people. They decided to seek the face of God in their devotional time, and believe God would reveal Himself to them again concerning their life' work. They reviewed everything: 1) they had prepared themselves in college, Bible training and certification for this work, 2) they had served briefly in China after waiting seven years, and 3) they had applied to the Nazarene mission board every year in good faith, to what they had already appointed them. They prayed…they searched the Scriptures…ironically, they found the answer in the same Scripture passage that Beth's father, RG Fitz, had found in searching for God's will. It was Jeremiah 29:13-14, *"And ye shall seek me, and find me, when you shall search for me with all your heart, and I will be **found** of you, saith the Lord."* They felt that God was showing them to be true to their call, and not necessarily to any one mission board. God sometimes calls to a work, but does not specify how that call is to be fulfilled. Suddenly they had their answer. No church, or work, may be perfect…but God's *plan* for each of us is perfect, even when *we* are not perfect. They prayed…and then thanked God for the answer! They would accept the appointment of Voice of China and Asia, go to Formosa as missionaries with Peniel, and start work there.

Michael wrote Dr. Zachary that they were accepting an appointment to go to Formosa with the Voice of China and Asia. He also announced to the Quincy Nazarene Church that he was resigning as their pastor. Dr. Zachary wrote back that he would like to first appeal to the Nazarene mission board for an appointment, on their behalf, but nothing came of it. They left most of their furniture and other things at the parsonage, and sold the rest. They spent Thanksgiving in Quincy, but made arrangements with Maxine to spend Christmas at her house in Gladstone, Oregon [she had married again...to a wonderful Christian man, Henry Fritz; he had accepted Kathy (born Ishman) as his own, and they had birthed three other children: Cheryl, John, and Jerry. Irma and Ralph had divorced after twelve years; she had three boys. Besides Larry, and Ron, who have already been mentioned, Tom was also born]. So, they had a big Fitz family reunion at Maxine and Henry's house. It was a time of healing. A few of the family had been able to attend Stevie's funeral, but not the entire family. Dr. and Mrs. Fitz, Guil, Irma and her three boys, Maxine, Henry, their four children, Beth, Michael, Julie, Franklin, and Margaret, were all in attendance. They sang, prayed, cried, reminisced... Daming and Jiangxi, Canada, North Dakota, Seattle, Pasadena, Cyprus, and all the other places they had been. They were all excited that Beth and Michael were finally going to be missionaries to the Chinese again. They cooked Chinese food, had wonderful devotional times...and even found enough space for everyone to sleep (many of the young people on the floors), and went to church together at the Oregon City Nazarene Church, where they sang—the 'Fitz Family Singers.' Henry offered to buy the Studebaker, and because some repairs were badly needed, Michael let him have it for a modest price. They finished the reunion with prayer and all the hopes and best wishes for their ministry in Formosa. Henry went with them to Pasadena, and then drove back to Gladstone...and it was very cramped with six of them in the small car! VOCA provided transportation while they were there, and Bob and Helen kept them at their place for three weeks, before they flew out to Hong Kong. During that time, they had a chance to meet the staff, stuff letters, and help with the 'relief food and clothing' in the warehouse. Michael and Beth were introduced to many of the 'regular supporters' of the ministry in the Los Angeles and Pasadena areas. They saw the Rose Parade, and visited some of the Pasadena churches. It was an exciting time, and God seemed to be preparing them for a great adventure.

The first week in January of 1957, they departed by plane and flew up the West Coast, stopping in San Francisco for a couple days, where they spoke in a couple of 'supporting churches.' Then it was on to Portland, where they had a last chance to say goodbye to Maxine and family. After that, they stopped in to Seattle, saying goodbye to Irma and family. The long haul came when they departed Seattle by

Northwest Orient Airlines for Tokyo, with refueling in Anchorage and the Aleutian Islands. They spent a couple days in Tokyo with friends of the mission, and then arrived in Hong Kong, where they met the Hinshaw's, the Sweet's, and the Morgan's, all newly appointed VOCA missionaries to Hong Kong; and they stayed at the mission compound on Waterloo Road–their home for the next four months. Julie finished her freshman year by correspondence. Margaret attended half-day at St. Teresa's primary school on Waterloo Road, next to the mission compound, and Franklin attended Diocesan Boys' School with Paulie Sweet; and the Morgan boys attended KG5 (King George Fifth) School, but they were unable to accommodate Paulie and Franklin (all dressed out in their blue blazers, grey slacks, and red and blue striped ties); he and Paulie, with their sack lunches in hand, boarded *Number-Eight* bus every morning, and returned every afternoon the same way, all on their own. The youth group from Peniel Church provided great opportunities for Julie and Franklin to experience a Christian atmosphere in an international setting; they went on 'launch parties,' to other islands in the Hong Kong Bay. These were small boats, or *launches* where they visited such places as Lan Tau, Cheung Chow, and other area islands, eat their lunch together, and often see "films" at the YMCA in the evening; adult chaperones went along from Peniel church to supervise; Franklin said his 'first girlfriend' was the daughter of one of these Portuguese-Chinese chaperones; her name was Portia Yip, and she made sure she sat with Franklin for the YMCA movies. They started teasing him about being with 'that *Portuguese Fisherwoman*,' and they all had a good laugh about it, but he was 'clueless.' Richard and John Morgan did not speak much Cantonese, so they always sat in the balcony of the Peniel Church on Sunday mornings and played games, or had some other 'diversion' during the service. Franklin sat with them, and asked them "where are you going," when they suddenly departed the church. They simply said, "watch, and don't tell anyone what we are doing." They went out into the busy street where they purchased two green banana leaves, and took them back up to the balcony. There they 'placed bets' on: what was in each banana leaf. To Franklin's utter amazement, they opened the banana leaf where he saw two male spiders; these spiders then suddenly attacked each other, and fought 'to the death,' and, depending on which spider 'won,' the bets were settled up. Franklin was so naïve. He didn't tell anyone else, but of course he told Julie, and she said, "don't you know the Morgan boys have a bad reputation, and that is why Paulie Sweet is not allowed to sit with them in church?" Franklin told her about the spider fights, only after she swore she 'wouldn't tell mom and dad.' Mom and dad never found out about it, but the Morgan boys got into a lot of trouble. Nobody would say, but the Morgan's later returned to Canada with their parents, and their missionary appointment was cancelled. Julie had met some guy in the youth group too. His name was Peter Shek, and he later went to high school in Formosa, where they dated each other. Hong Kong was so much fun, and the Varro children didn't want to leave, but Michael said they would depart in May and go live in Taipei in Formosa. 'You mean no adding-subtracting, multiplying-dividing *pounds, shillings and pence, and French lessons?*' Franklin said; he was having the time of his life, but the English school system, and only four months in Hong Kong had been like a bizarre dream. One minute, he was in seventh grade at Pioneer School in Quincy, the next minute he was going to an Anglican school and learning French and the English money system. One day, the 'Master' (what they called the classroom teachers in Hong Kong) left the room for a minute. The class immediately began to throw erasers, chalk, and books at each other, laugh, and carry on. A tall Chinese boy, Lon Sit, who liked Franklin, handed him an eraser; he, Lon Sit, and two others, began throwing these at their classmates. Suddenly, Master Lam appeared in the doorway. The class scrambled to their seats, but not before Master Lam grabbed Lon Sit, four others…and Franklin. He hauled them into the Head Master's office where they were 'caned.' Lon Sit was struck four times, on his open palm, with a bamboo stick. The other two were struck the same. Franklin, it was determined, was not a ringleader, so he was only struck once. Franklin cried out in pain—he couldn't imagine how four strikes would feel. He never forgot the experience. From then on, he evidently was some sort of a 'hero' to the 'naughty element' at Diocesan Boys, and when Lon Sit and his friends came around, the others laughed and called Franklin '*soy-jai.*' He never could get anyone to tell him exactly what they were saying in English, but it evidently had to do with '*naughty boy,*' or similar, but he enjoyed the attention. Those at the mission weren't sure what to make of it.

There was a scandal, or a rumor…some said it was a court case…in Formosa that involved VOCA and the Varro's (and Fitz's) old nemesis, Peter Kiehn. It consumed Michael's attention early on in Formosa. Peter Kiehn worked for Bob Hammond, or so they said, and purchased land in the name of VOCA, then he tried to give it to the Nazarene Church. A suit followed, but the local Chinese court awarded the case to Kiehn. When the Nazarenes realized it was 'tainted,' they refused it. Peter Kiehn tried to build a school there, but it failed. He tried to sell it, but no one wanted to buy it, so it finally was auctioned off by the Republic of China government. By the time Michael came back to Hong Kong to pick up his family and move to Taipei, all the missionaries had turned against VOCA. They didn't think much of Peter Kiehn either, who finally left Formosa…for good. It was into this situation that Michael and Beth Varro made their entrance as missionaries. They moved into a Japanese-style house on 'Xin Sheng South Road, Second Precinct, Number Eighty-Four.' They had a neighbor lady, Mrs. Esther Lawler, who lived next door in the mission compound. They shared a cook, Ella Xun, and a gatekeeper and pedicab driver Xian, Shifu. The Varro's maid was Mary Zheng. They located the Taipei American School, and the children were all evaluated. Julie qualified as a sophomore, and Margaret qualified for sixth grade. Franklin was approved for eighth grade, but they recommended that he take summer school because, as he put it, his math skills had been 'scrambled' by the English monetary system! Summer school started right away, and he was dropped off every day for the six-week period of mid-June to the end of July. There he met the children of the Assembly of God missionaries, the Benintendi's (that had lived briefly in Shanghai, who had kept the Varro's before they went 'interior'). He played at Ken's and Eddie's house, where they made fried rice and played *Clue* and other games. They found out they had much in common, even though they didn't remember the China experience. They all went down-island to Sun Moon Lake for Taiwan Missionary Conference at the end of July. They made many new friends. Everyone seemed wary of them at first, but when they got to know them, as one longtime friend put it, "we didn't think much of your mission board, or the president of your mission, but we grew to love you, and know that you are God-fearing, wonderful and ethical people, so we overlooked the rest of it!" The first families that the Varro's got to know well, were the Hunker's, Southern Baptist missionaries, and the Valder's, Lutheran Brethren missionaries. All three families lived within a few blocks of each other, in kind of a triangle– the Varro's to the north; the Hunker's, southeast; and the Valder's, southwest. Joyce Lynn Hunker and Becky Valder were both one year younger than Margaret, David Hunker, and Danny Valder were the same age as Franklin, and Julie was a year and a half older. Franklin assumed Danny and David would attend Taipei American, but this was not the case! Not only David and Danny, but the Benintendi boys and others, were headed to Morrison Academy, a missionary boarding school, five hours away by train, in Taichung. Franklin was miserable that year. He said it was the worst year of his life. Even though they got him a bicycle to ride to school, none of the children at TAS seemed to be his kind of friends. He made friends with Butch Walters...and quickly got in trouble. They were 'just climbing the ladder to the gym roof for fun', they said, but the Principal, Mr. Nesbit, took exception to that, and they were in detention for two days. After Butch and his family were transferred 'stateside,' Denny Meiers was his friend. He invited Franklin to his house in Tianmou, which the missionaries called the 'American Ghetto.' These were all U.S. military, business, or government families, usually stationed there two years or less, and generally isolated themselves from the Chinese people. Some of them tended to look down on the missionary community. Franklin wore mostly 'missionary barrel' clothes that were hand-me-downs, given as 'relief' clothing, along with flour, cornmeal, and other relief items from Church World Service, and other Relief organizations. Denny liked Franklin and wanted him to stay at his house, but never would accept Franklin's invitation to stay with him. Denny's family was soon stationed elsewhere too. Franklin was miserable. He wanted to go to Morrison...where his friends were. Franklin was somewhat short, and slight, and everyone thought he was in seventh grade instead of eighth. A girl, Susie Dearborn, had a locker next to his, and she treated him like he was a little kid from elementary school. Franklin was trying to get his books out of his locker one day, and was more in front of her locker than his. She said to him, "move your 'carcass' little kid;" she was being flirtatious but he was humiliated and felt he had no friends. At his dad's suggestion, he decided to make friends with the Chinese students at TAS. Frank Shen, Danny Yang, and Ruby Yu all hung out together, so Franklin decided to hang out with them. Frank Shen asked him why he had a funny name like 'Franklin.' He said it became his dad's middle name, after becoming a U.S. citizen–that he had named himself after Benjamin Franklin. They laughed, thinking it was a joke. He decided then and there...he was never going to be called 'Franklin' again; his name was now *Frank*...just like Frank Shen. It was a cool name and he would be cool. He was known as Frank from then on, even though his folks always called him Franklin. He always tried to be the class clown, and cut up in class. He thought his homeroom teacher Mrs. Genevieve Gregg, was the most attractive woman ever, and he wanted to get her attention. Once, she said to the class, "I'll be 'frank' with you..." so Frank came up to her desk. She stopped talking and looked at him. "What is it?" she said. Frank said, "you called me;" the class started laughing; it took her a second, then she put her hand on her hip, and she said to him, "you're so 'bright,' no wonder your mother calls you *'sun'*." The class roared, and she put her arms around Franklin, but instead of hugging him, she marched him over to his seat, and sat him down...hard. It was a moment he cherished for a long time. He decided he had a crush on Mrs. Gregg; he loved the attention she gave him.

Julie was active in the MAAG Chapel (Military Assistance Advisory Group), and Bob Harding, a fine Christian U.S. Navy guy (they all called him 'Uncle Bobber Sir,') was their sponsor. He told them they were all going on a hiking party. He said they would hike up Yang Ming Shan (which the U.S. military all called 'Grass Mountain'), have hot dogs, chips and ice cream, and then hike back down. The MAAG bus would take them home. Well, all went well until they stayed too long at the top of the mountain (only about three thousand feet). Bob told them three times it was getting dark, and they had to leave 'pronto,' but when they all finally left, it was really too dark to complete the trip as planned. Bob said they had to change the plan. Instead, they would wait for the bus to come to the top of the mountain and pick them up. Julie and several others had already run off, and didn't hear the change of plans. They hiked down a bit, and then completely lost their bearings. Bob, and the other adults tried to call, and even went down after them, but they were too far ahead, and didn't hear them. The last several ones, who *did* hear, went back and waited for the bus.

They went down the mountain to wait for them at the bottom. By this time, Juli's group was completely lost. They stumbled and scratched themselves on some rocks. They saw something slither across the trail and realized they had just encountered a very deadly bamboo snake; but, they figured, if they kept going *down*, they would eventually get to the bottom of the mountain. They didn't realize they could easily go around the mountain without ever finding the location where they were headed. It was now hours since the sun had set, and they were beginning to experience hypothermia, even though the night was not that cold. Without any jackets or outer clothing to speak of, this could be dangerous. Then they smelled cigarette smoke; out of the shadows came a Formosan farmer; he was as frightened as they were of him, "Wai-guo ren!" (foreigners), he exclaimed. Julie, who was the only one who spoke even a few words of Chinese, said, "wo men shi Mei-guo-ren, qing bang wo men (we're Americans, please help us)." He figured something was wrong, and they needed his help. He led them down the mountain to the waiting bus. Bob and the others were frantic, and had called the MAAG Military Police. They hadn't arrived yet, so Bob called them back to say his party had been found. It was 5:00a.m. in the morning. "Uncle Bobber Sir, we are so sorry we didn't listen to you, and we don't want *you* to get in trouble for this, please don't make a report." He said he would have to account for the MAAG bus getting back so late, but the driver made a report…they had had 'vehicular delay' and anything else would be what the kids themselves told.'

By the time missionary conference came around the next year, Frank had already decided he would go to Morrison…no matter what! The girls were okay with staying in Taipei, but Frank said nobody could make him go back to TAS. He was going to go to school with his friends at Morrison. Michael informed him it was 'not his decision,' and enrolled all three of them, for the next year, at TAS. Everyone had heard about it…the missionary community was really pretty small… and Frank was a manipulator, he had already given his 'sob story' to a number of missionaries. They all started working on Michael. Beth was ambivalent; she saw the advantage of a Christian environment, but wanted to keep Franklin at home longer if she could. Her grief over Stevie was still profound, and Franklin was now her only son. They had moved from Taipei to Mushan, across from the Zhengzhi

University, and they had built a beautiful mission compound with a two-story Student Center-Worship facility, a bamboo chapel, and two other small buildings for their staff and relief distribution. [She had miscarried once already, and one of her best friends, knowing how deep Beth's grief was still, told her one day, "Beth, I hate to see you grieve; you told me you desperately need to have another baby to 'take the place of Stevie' but…only because I love you so much, listen to me… you have three *living* children that *need* you, let God fill your void, listen to Him." Lillian was right]. When they arrived at Missionary Conference Beth was again six-months pregnant. As much as she wanted Franklin home with her, she knew she couldn't hang on to any of her children. They belonged to God, and he would work His will in each of their lives. Michael's stubbornness was not as easily tamed though. Franklin had told David Hunker and Danny Valder to request a room together with him. They had preceded him at Morrison by one year, so they knew Mrs. Culver and some of the other teachers and staff. Mrs. Culver was the dining hall 'mom,' and she said she would see what she could do…but only if they all roomed together with her grandson, Jon. These were all Orient Crusades missionaries, and were one of the missions sponsoring the school; [it was started in 1952, with just eight students and two teachers, on the west side of Taichung, in the Oriental Missionary Society compound. Orient Crusades came in and helped, with two other mission boards, and the school grew quickly, relocating the year before Frank arrived, to a new beautiful campus]. With everyone working on him, Michael didn't have a chance. They laid it on thick, saying things like "our children need a strong Christian environment, not be led astray by the things of this world." After that, Michael made it seem like it was his idea all along. He told Beth, "we need to protect Franklin from the kind of influence that got him in trouble this last year." Beth smiled. She would miss him very much, but felt good about having him in such a school as Morrison (she had never had such an opportunity herself in Daming). Frank was elated, he helped sew the number '18' on his clothing for laundry purposes. They went down with him to enroll him in class at Morrison, and Julie and Margaret came too; Julie whispered in his ear, "you know of course…you'll be smoking and drinking in a month." He laughed, "let's see how you do at TAS next year." He knew he was the 'scout,'–they were both there by the next year.

Dad had brought a dog home just a couple months before school started. A beautiful tan Boxer-mix, and everyone knew it was Frank's dog. They went everywhere together. Frank had taught him to 'sit,' 'shake hands,' 'roll over,' and 'stay,' by the time he left for Morrison. Frank told Margaret she had to take care of Koko for him. Classes were challenging. Frank was more homesick than he thought he would be. And then the island had a terrible typhoon. Sports practice was grueling, and Coach Holsinger and Coach Brown worked them pretty hard. Mrs. Marge Brown was the choir director and she was very exacting. Frank's voice hadn't changed yet, and he was still only four-feet eleven-inches when he arrived…'skinny as a rail.' Going by his audition, and what she had written on his sheet, she placed him as an 'alto.' He could already read 'the spots off the page,' but everyone laughed when they saw that he was the only boy in the alto section. Marge Brown was very perceptive, and quickly moved him to the tenor section, where he eventually became the leader, and even 'assistant to the choir director,' according to her (but no one denied the truth of it). After the big typhoon, Frank heard from his mom, who wrote almost every week, even if she were tied up in Bible studies, choir practice, or teaching at Zhengzhi University–Margaret had taken Koko for a walk after the big storm, over by the Chinese grade school, some electric lines were down; and just before Margaret went forward, Koko stepped on one of the live wires and was electrocuted. As she lunged forward to 'rescue' him, the Chinese workers screamed at her, "Tui! Ni tui bah! (stand back, stand back!). Margaret would have been electrocuted, no doubt, had it not been for Koko. Frank cried when he read the letter, and said he was going home, he didn't want to go to this school any more. Beth assured him this was a difficult time, but he must take courage and stay with it. They had a long weekend every six weeks, and the first one was coming up that next week. They took time to memorialize his dear Koko, and thank him for being a hero by saving his sister's life. Having the long weekend gave them all time to stave off their homesickness.

Beth was now nine months along, and could go into labor anytime. Dr. Dale was concerned that, because she was already age forty-two, there might be some risk, and suggested she might want to come early to the hospital. It was a long weekend for Frank, so Beth arranged for Julie to play the piano, and Frank to conduct the choir Sunday. They had decided to call the baby Irma Katherine if it was a girl, and David Edward if it was a boy. Michael checked Beth into the hospital early, and arranged to stay at the hospital himself. It was the weekend of October 11, 1958. Frank slept in his mom and dad's bed, praying all night it would be a boy. The girls stayed in their own room. Beth went into labor the same night that Frank came home. Everything went well, with no complications at all. Michael called midmorning to tell him *he had a little brother*. A little brother! Frank was elated, as were Julie and Margaret (they changed his name to 'David Bruce' at the last minute). God had blessed them once again!

Frank started feeling out of place. He had grown only one inch in several months. He had not played more than a few minutes in any soccer game. His classes were hard. The only thing he looked forward to was choir; but he *had* started piano lessons with Marge Brown, which was good. By Christmas he had been selected as the first tenor for the Morrison boy's quartet. He had his devotions on the roof every morning, and one day he read in Joshua 1:9, *"Be **strong** and take courage, be not dismayed, for the Lord thy God is with thee, withersoever thou goest."* He said to himself 'be *strong*...not *'be tall.'* He went to breakfast; he went to class; he went to the laundry room...where they had a new set of weights; he began warming up and stretching. Then, he did the press, then the curl, then the squats, with the weights. Then he went to soccer practice, supper, study hall, and went to bed after their snack. Every day he increased the weights a little, and the number in each routine. He was so sore he felt sick at times...but he kept it up every day... and then he increased the number of times per day from one to three. Soccer season ended, and he had played in almost every game, and his number of minutes per game had doubled. The Mustangs won four, and lost six, his first year there. He made the junior varsity basketball team. He shot free throws in between classes. He developed an outside shot. He played every junior varsity (Broncos) game, and half of the varsity (Mustangs), as a substitute. He didn't play baseball, but he came in fifth in the hundred-yard dash. At the All-Island Track & Field Meet in Taipei, Coach Holsinger came to him and said, "we don't have anyone else to run the mile, so you're going to run it. "Coachie, I've never run a mile; I don't think I could even finish." Coach said, "you can, and you *will*," he laughed, "because we don't have anybody else." Frank started out 'even with the pack,' but by the second of the four laps, he was last, after two guys dropped out with cramps; by the end of the third lap, everyone had forgotten the mile race, and had gone on. Frank was far behind…the rest had already finished; he thought about quitting all the way around the last lap; nobody else was running; this wasn't even his race…and besides, he had never run it before, so he had nothing to prove, right? Then Julie's words came to his mind: "Varro's don't quit." The last hundred yards were grueling, and he couldn't think about anything except just finishing and collapsing. He quietly crossed the finish line…the entire grandstand stood and clapped wildly. His mom and dad were there, and so were Julie and Margaret. Coachie came over and put his arm on his shoulder. "That was sensational, Frank, thank you." Frank said, "Coachie! I came in *last!*" "No, Frank, it's like *life*, you finish the *race*…you win the *crown*." By the end of the year, Frank had grown three inches – he went from 4'11" to 5'2," and he bulked up even more. He continued this regimen three more years and got up to 5' 5" by the end of sophomore year, 5' 7" by his junior year. He graduated at 5' 8 ½" and 152 pounds. He was varsity soccer by the end of his sophomore year, and captain and star center forward by his senior year, tying for the most goals for the season. In basketball, he became the star shooting guard. He was co-captain of the track team by his senior year, and his 'four-by-one' relay team record wasn't broken for fifteen years…and only then by his own brother Dave's 'four-by-one' relay team!

Everyone started calling him 'Frankie Avalon' by the time he was a junior. He had never heard of him. So, one of his girlfriends showed him a picture…sure enough. Then they all started calling him 'Frankie,' and singing 'Venus' every time they saw him. The student body bragged about getting all the latest songs and movies from the States within a week, and the Stars and Stripes (the newspaper for the U.S. Armed Forces)? –well, it wasn't even a day late; it was printed in Tokyo and overnighted to Taiwan. In Taichung they had a snack bar even missionaries could go to, and all the latest fashions kept Morrison and the entire missionary community fairly in-style at all times. Michael and Beth maintained their opposition to 'worldly things' which their Nazarene background did not allow. The 'Ten Commandments' movie came to the U.S. military theater in Taichung. Some missionary children were planning to go, while others were 'not allowed to go' by their parents. The faculty decided to require written permission from parents for any student planning to go off-campus to see this movie. A long weekend was coming up, so students whose parents did not object would have the opportunity to obtain the permission slip required. Frank found out that most of his friends were going to be able to get permission, and he did not want to be left out. He knew his dad and mom still maintained their Nazarene standard against certain 'social sins,' but he also knew that his family allowed seeing 'films' that were shown in facilities other than theaters. He had in fact attended several; they were Christian films in churches, secular films in Hong Kong, that were shown in the YMCA, and the like. He had a discussion with his dad about it, explaining that 'all his friends' were going to see a really great 'biblical film' called the 'Ten Commandments,' and he was sure that it would be good for him to see it also, and all that he needed was the written permission from his parents. His dad asked him where it would be shown; would it be shown in a military 'theater?' Franklin told him: 'not exactly… the room where the 'film' would be shown, was used for military briefings, parties, meetings, and other social events… very wholesome events!' His dad ended up signing the slip, giving him permission to see the 'Ten Commandments!' Although many in the Morrison student body were unable to see the movie, Frank was pleased that his father and mother were reasonable about seeing worthwhile movies, and that the movie theater was not always the raunchy, risqué, burlesque theater that their generation envisioned, and the *quality* of the movie itself was the choice, rather than the location.

By the end of the school year, Julie was ready to transfer to Morrison, even if it meant it would only be her senior year there. Margaret was allowed to come to Morrison also, and she started eighth grade there. By the time they arrived, all her friends, her brother, even her sister, were going by their nicknames, so she had to have one too. She didn't like Marge, Margie, Maggie, or Peggy, and Margot seemed too 'French,' so she finally settled on 'Margi,' (with a hard 'g'). She was known as Margi, at least by Morrison friends and siblings, from then on; and Juli(e) dropped the 'e,' making it Juli. [so, it was: Juli, Frank, and Margi…from then on].

[The summer before, the Varro siblings had spent time at Bitan (Green Lake), in the Xindian District of Taipei, not far from their new home; here they rented boats, sometimes taking a picnic…sometimes even with the whole family. It was some of the most enjoyable times the family ever had together; and sometimes they hiked up to Zhinangung–to the so-called 'Thousand-Step' temple (Taoist)–on the mountain close to their mission compound].

Two strong storms that summer, Typhoon Billie, in July, and Typhoon Ellen, in August, hit the Varro mission compound, only two months before school started. Over seven-hundred were killed in the flood, thousands were homeless, and there was over five hundred thousand US dollars in damages. At the height of the storm, the Varro's, living upstairs, heard the cries of their maids, Jiao-jun, and Sun-yuan, on the grounds in separate quarters. "Jiu ming!" (save us!), they cried . Michael called Frank, and the two of them went downstairs, wading through chest-deep murky water through the Worship-Student Center, past the piano floating on its side, and then outside to a raging torrent. The current by the Student Center was swift, so Michael and Frank formed a human chain, and swam upstream so they would end up across from the porch to the small house where the young women lived. Getting them back was even more precarious…the maids were desperate, and wouldn't listen to instructions…which would keep them from drowning. Frank stayed, holding on to the door of the small house while Michael crossed over, then Frank tried to hand off each hysterical woman to the other side. Finally, they got the two across and Frank crossed back over. The water was rising, and the current was becoming even more dangerous, but he made it back. They took them upstairs, and Beth, Juli, and Margi helped them dry off and drink some hot tea. Suddenly, Sun-yuan began wailing, "Wo de shou biao!" (my wristwatch). They calmed her down by promising that Frank would go find it…'this is a joke, right? I'll be swept away,' Frank said. Michael said, "go find the watch, Franklin, it's the only thing she has in this life, you can do it." Frank muttered something like, "my life for her watch," to himself, as he descended into the murky water once again. The rest of them stayed to mop up as much as they could, and taped the windows so no glass would blow in. As he left the porch this time, he heard the 'death squeal' of a pig trapped in the water against the mission compound wall (it reminded him of his horror, as a child in Jiangxi, hearing the pigs being slaughtered next to their house in the mission compound). Now he was cold...he really wasn't sure he could get across... every slimy, bilge-water step he took, he thought he would be swept off into the dark night. *"O God, I can't just disappear into the night like this, I need you to help me get across."* He searched the Student Center. He went to the platform, now under water. He remembered they always roped off the last few rows. He found some cord, tied it to the drain pipe alongside the Student Center, made a big loop, then threw it over the door of the little house, and pulled it tight. Hoping the door would not come off, he pulled himself through the raging water, over to their quarters. The water was almost up to the upper bunk. He felt around for the dresser, and then went under water to feel around inside the dresser, one drawer at a time (she had been hysterical, and couldn't remember which drawer!), starting at the bottom, he worked his way to the top drawer...it was his last chance ...and there it was. He put it in his front pocket, returned by way of the rope, and went upstairs. [strangely enough, no one had offered to go with him, you know, in case he was just swept away?] He was now cold, shivering, and wet. He wondered if her watch would even work! Sun-yuan cried with delight, and mother and dad were appropriately proud. Juli and Margi helped him peel his wet clothes off, and covered him with a blanket, gave him some hot tea, and then they all went to bed. [Frank thought what it would be like for them all to be reading in the China Post... about a young missionary kid being one of the seven hundred drowning casualties, and dreamed that he was under water...and couldn't find the top]. He awoke with a start. The wind and rain had died down, so he crawled out of bed, and went into the living room. Beth was in the kitchen with Sun-yuan and Jiao-jun fixing breakfast. They hadn't slept more than a couple hours. Dad was already out in the yard assessing the damage. The pig Frank had heard squealing was bloated and lying upside down on the broken-down wall which was covered with mud. The water had receded in the past few hours, but there were still large puddles everywhere, the entire yard in the mission compound was covered with mud. It was already getting warm, and there was a stench starting to rise in the air. Michael had thought before about relocating the mission compound. There had been just too many typhoons, costing too much in repairs, by living so close to the river. He often told about his being tempted by the devil, "you should be higher up, maybe on the mountain," Satan laughed; but then Michael had remembered...yes, he was called to where 'the people are,' and wouldn't let the devil tempt him. He would *stay* ... 'where the people are.' He hired the brick layers again, but this time he had them fashion a cross-shaped opening every few feet in the walls. It still provided security, but it left an opening so the flood waters could get through. In the next month, the entire staff and Frank and his sisters worked to repair the typhoon damage. Beth, the girls, and staff worked mostly with the relief clothing. The bales and boxes had not been moved upstairs in the building in the front of the compound, and everything had gotten wet. It all had to be washed and then hung out to dry before it could be donated. Frank and all the men on the staff did the clean-up in the yard. Michael spent his time hauling material to and from the store and the dump. The weather was unmercifully hot and humid. They had to haul all the mud and debris out of the yard... exhausting work; they had to take breaks, and drink lots of water, to keep from getting sun stroke. They *did* take time to go to Missionary Conference; it was good to get away; the spiritual uplift was worth it; returning to Mushan, Frank seemed lethargic and tired, but pushed on; they finished what they could...but now it was time for school. Juli and Margi joined Frank this time at Morrison. They sewed the numbers into their clothing, packed their bedding, clothes, and toiletries, and took the train down to Taichung to begin another school year. They met some new teachers, and a newly arrived boys-dorm 'mom,' Carmen Ashby. Michael, Beth, and Davie returned to Mushan after helping them move into the dormitories. The first day of class went well, and the soccer team began its workout. It was still stifling hot, and taking the last lap after a grueling workout, Dan Valder turned to Frank and said, "Hey, man, your nose is bleeding," Dan threw him a towel to put over his nose as they finished the lap and said, "I get nose-bleeds all the time, here, put your head under this." Frank put his head under the large pipe by the men's showers…it had icy cold water coming out of it. The bleeding stopped, they went to supper and study hall, then they got their evening snack, and Mom Ashby said, "lights out." Jon, David, Dan, and Frank had hardly said goodnight, when a "rush" came out of Frank's head…like a giant faucet had just been turned on. He yelled, and David turned the light on. Frank was covered from head to toe with blood. They held his head back and wiped his face with a towel. Mom Ashby came to see why the light was on, and suddenly the whole dorm was awake. They got the bleeding to 'stop' again, by plugging his nostrils, but it was really just running down his throat into his stomach; this went on for most of two days…by then, the sinuses and stomach were filled. As he lay back in his room while everyone else went to class, Gay Olson, the wife of Marlin Olson, Frank's math teacher, looked in on him. She pulled the 'stoppers' out immediately. It looked like Frank was going to explode, his sinuses were so full. Thomas Means, the principal, was called; he chastised Gay for 'taking matters into her own hands,' but everyone defended her, because anyone could see the blood was not stopping…only backing up. They rushed Frank to the MAAG Infirmary where a Navy Corpsman thought 'this young man' was going to die, and kept injecting his nostrils with adrenalin, and shouting hysterically, "come on, man…come on, man, don't die on me." Juli had come to visit Frank at the Olson's house on the Morrison campus, and told Frank she had called Mom, and Dad, thinking yet another brother was going to die, and she wanted to say goodbye before it was too late. They 'life flighted' him in a Chinese 'C-119' to Taipei. Mr. Means sheepishly accompanied him, then quickly disappeared back to Taichung to his office. Norm and Muriel Cook, and Hans and Alice Wilhelm, met the plane and rushed him to the Seventh Day Adventist Hospital. Now barely conscious, Frank lay like a limp rag on the curb while Hans came with the car [this was 'pre-ambulance service' in Taiwan]. Dr. Donald Dale, and Frank's parent, met them there. Frank was rushed into surgery, with whole blood, Vitamin K, glucose, and antibiotics flowing into him from both arms and legs. A tearful Michael and Beth Varro, and Davie, agonized in the waiting room in prayer, with other missionaries that had come to be with them, thinking they would lose yet another son. The minute Vitamin K and the other IV's hit his system, Frank sat up in bed, threw up a two-pound 'congeal of blood' from his stomach (sorry, gross), and asked for a hamburger. They thought he was in shock, or delirious… especially in a Seventh Day Adventist Hospital (no meat!) Dr. Dale said, to the relief of all, that thanks to the replenished Vitamin K, the blood was now clotting, and he was going to be fine…after they cauterized the two little burst-vessels high up in his nose…and cleaned the sinuses out! Ouch! Frank had not realized how close to death he was, until Dr. Dale said, "one more pint, Frank," moving his hand across his neck with the 'cut-throat' sign. Michael and Beth came to visit him twice a day. When he told them he "couldn't eat one more soybean burger," they snuck a real hamburger in, from the MAAG Snack Bar. ['My kind mother Broke-A-Rule!']

But now, Frank was very bored. They had told him he must stay in the hospital, for observation(?) *after* they cleaned his sinuses out. He felt perfectly fine and wanted to leave…they said no! He hopped in a wheelchair and started doing 'wheelies' in the hall. The nurses bawled him out, and told him to stay put. He took his wheelchair and decided to go 'exploring.' He went out of the main hospital building, found a piano in the adjacent building, and he was playing 'Moonlight Sonata,' when a Chinese nurse came in shreaking, *"you out of dormitory, American boy, you back in room…staying there!."* They had to admit, when Frank was finally discharged at the end of the week, that he had provided the only entertainment they had had…in months; he had chances to see Davie, Mom, and Dad several times.

It was Juli's senior year at Morrison, and her last year in Taiwan. She was vice president of the Morrison Student Council, editor of the Echo, the student newspaper, member of the Morrison Mixed Ensemble, on the track team, and one of *four* seniors in her class! Frank improved in soccer, basketball, and track. Margi was junior varsity cheerleader and then junior and senior year she was varsity cheerleader. It was a good year, but it was time for Juli to go to college. She needed to be with family, dad had said, but where should that be? They settled on the University of Saskatchewan in Regina. She could stay with Michael's sister Irene, and Jim (Michael's brother), would act as 'guardian.' It was a tearful goodbye, but Beth and Michael felt Juli was strong, and she would do well. She flew back with some other missionaries going home on furlough, and then took the train from Seattle to Regina. The rest of the summer Frank and Margi spent a lot of time with their friends at Thirteenth Air Force swimming pool, visiting Morrison friends, going to the USIS Library to read, and Missionary Conference. He and Davie played together at the mission compound.

Frank's junior year was very eventful. He made starting position on the soccer team as the center-halfback, and made his first goal, with a key pass from Bob Suessmuth, beating TAS. He had a starring role in the production 'HMS Pinafore,' and became the Student Body Vice President. He had a number of girlfriends, mainly in the choir, and in sports. He brought in the record bid in the Sadie Hawkins 'slave day.' Determined to beat out Frank's then-girlfriend, Margaret Latane, some girls pooled their money until Margaret topped out. She cried, and Margi, Margaret Latane's best friend, pooled their money so she could win the bid for her boyfriend; everybody had a good laugh seeing Frank dressed in 'drag,'...being Margaret Latane's 'slave' the whole day...but for a good cause, of course.

[The senior's made good on their get-away, for their 'sneak' in the spring. Caught off-guard because the juniors showed up at track practice... but, voila, no seniors! Coach Brown, being the junior class sponsor...and taking exception to this...showed up at the boys' dorm, after 'lights out,' via the balcony. Not waking the others, Coach Brown took seven junior boys, down the ladder, to a mission van...assuring them he had checked with Mom Ashby on this and went down-island to where the seniors were. Forgetting that the government-approved gasoline stations would be closed, they suddenly realized they were running out of gas...with apparently no prospects for filling up. Fortunately, Ken Benintendi, who spoke both Mandarin and Taiwanese, was with the group, and managed to help Coach Brown inquire as to the whereabouts of a gasoline station. Well, it wasn't exactly a 'station,' Ken told him. The 'gasoline resource' turned out to be... what some would call a 'black-market outlet,' located in a...well, 'house of ill-repute.' They pulled up in front of a two-story building... young women, who were scantily dressed were...umm, 'hanging themselves out' of the open window. Seeing the 'prospect-for-business'

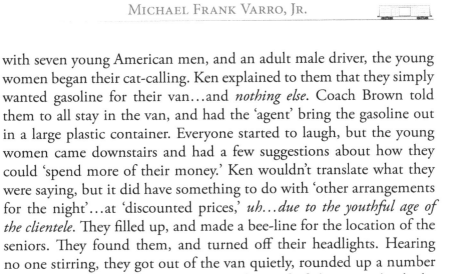

with seven young American men, and an adult male driver, the young women began their cat-calling. Ken explained to them that they simply wanted gasoline for their van...and *nothing else*. Coach Brown told them to all stay in the van, and had the 'agent' bring the gasoline out in a large plastic container. Everyone started to laugh, but the young women came downstairs and had a few suggestions about how they could 'spend more of their money.' Ken wouldn't translate what they were saying, but it did have something to do with 'other arrangements for the night'...at 'discounted prices,' *uh...due to the youthful age of the clientele*. They filled up, and made a bee-line for the location of the seniors. They found them, and turned off their headlights. Hearing no one stirring, they got out of the van quietly, rounded up a number of small stones, and placed them on the roof of the seniors' vehicle, spelling '*Class of '62 was here!*,' then quickly departed before anyone stirred. They drove back, stopped to buy some 'Mahn-tow' (steamed bread), for breakfast, and arrived in time for their 8:00 a.m. classes. The campus was a-buzz with the wild story of their adventure. It was a long weekend, so everyone left. One of the juniors, from Hong Kong, shared the story...with a slight exaggeration...telling everyone that *she* was the only female in a van full of seven males, and Larry Brown! Whoops! The stuff 'hit the fan,' and all returned to the Morrison campus to find out the following: Larry Brown and Carmen Ashby had been fired! And all seven boys had been expelled. When Cathy admitted she had lied, all seven boys, including Frank, were reinstated, but placed on probation. Mom Ashby and Larry Brown were also put on probation, and the sponsorship of the junior class was taken away... but they could keep their jobs. The seniors never admitted they knew the juniors had been 'found-out,' and graduated with the largest class since the school started in 1952...thirteen graduates!]

Summer came, and David Woodward with the China Sunday School Association contacted Michael about hiring Frank. He needed a... 'librarian' to clean up old books for the library that Bethany, a new Christian school in Taipei, would need before they opened that fall. Frank took the public bus every morning from Mushan to CSSA on Zhungshan north road, and cleaned up books. Chinese students were always looking for any-and-every opportunity to practice their English. One such student got on the bus one morning, and sat down next to him. Frank was tired, and really wanted to sleep a little bit more, but when the young man spoke to him, he didn't want to be rude. The student said, "Accuse me" (meaning 'excuse me'), may I 'plactice' my 'Engrish' witch you?" Frank said 'sure, go ahead, what did he wish to talk about?' The young man replied, "Plesident Eisenhar ('President Eisenhower') say, 'I want 'piss' for the ho' ward!" ('I want peace for the whole world'). Taken aback slightly, Frank, (very irreverently under his breath), said, "If President Eisenhower wants to 'piss' for the whole world, I think we should let him." Not realizing what Frank had *so rudely* said, the young man beamed from ear to ear. Frank smiled…and got off the bus…it was his stop. [Frank had made friends with someone from Washington State. Allen Peterson (whose friends all called 'Pete') came to Morrison. His father was a visiting 'Professor of Agriculture' at Taichung Agricultural College. He was going to be a junior, but most of his close friends, like Frank, David, and Dan, were going to be seniors (Jon Culver and his family hadn't returned from furlough yet). Even though they lived in town, his parents let Pete stay in the dorm. Pete was friends with everyone, but Frank and he had hit it off pretty well, and Frank wanted to get to know him better, so he invited him that summer to come stay a few days with him in Mushan. Pete came up on the train, and Frank and his dad met him and took him, after Frank's work at CSSA, to Mushan. The next day, Frank's mom and dad had a celebration in Wanli, where they had a church and school, and they needed Frank's help. They took Pete along, and after the meeting, they all sat down for a banquet…a twelve course meal, the likes of which Pete had never experienced! After they got back late to Mushan, Frank and Pete retired for the night. It wasn't very long before both were violently ill… 'running off at both ends' so to speak, a real bad case of dysentery. Pete was such a joker, he told everyone that Frank had taken him there to 'poison him…so he could take his spot on the soccer team!' Ha! They found out it was shrimp that had been deep fried and then put out on the back porch before serving it. They had a good laugh, but both loved telling that story. Later chapters tell of Pete and an *amazing lifelong connection* between him and Frank]

Missionary Conference came. Frank knew this would be the last one before he went off to college. After the family checked in at Sun Moon Lake, the youth all gathered together to hear from their leaders,

Norm and Muriel Cook, and Hans and Alice Wilhelm. All of Frank's closest friends were all there: David, Dan, Pete, Liz, Martha, Les, Randi, and others. They had a full slate of activities planned…besides the regular swimming and boating that they always did…someone always swam to 'the Island' for the first time (about a four-hundred-yard swim; Frank had swum it as a freshman; every year following, he just tried to see if he could improve his time). This year the Varro family was not staying in the 'Lodge,' but in a cabin, a short distance from the main Conference Center. After supper they heard the speaker, Dr. Timothy Glenn, visiting from the United States. He had been in India growing up, and then as a missionary in South America with the Navigators. He was very good, and received a warm welcome from the Taiwan missionary community. The youth had their snack and devotional time afterward, and then all went back to their lodging… much later than the adults, of course. The next day after breakfast, the adults had a time of worship, but the youth met separately. The special speaker for their Bible study was the son of the well-known missionary legend, the great Hudson Taylor, Dr. James Taylor. They all assembled in the wooded amphitheater down by the lake. He told them that people sometimes asked him what they should call him; he had earned a D.D. (Doctor of Divinity), but in Chinese, a 'di-di' was 'little brother', and he said he liked that: he was a *little brother* in Christ to all his co-workers. Then he prayed and gave a wonderful lesson on the call to service for young people: Mark, Timothy, most of the disciples…even Jesus…all young men when God called them into service. After the Bible Study they had lunch and then it was time to go swimming and boating. Liz Lovejoy and Martha Richie were splashing and horsing around with Frank, so the three of them decided to get a boat and row out to 'the Island.' Frank was rowing, and they had gotten out about two thirds of the way when the clouds started getting dark, and it started to rain…really hard! He was hoping to make it to the island, but the girls said they were frightened and that they should turn around. Frank thought they should make the island, wait out the storm, and then return back to the dock. They said, "no," that it was getting dark, and they were cold. They pleaded with Frank to turn around. Against his better judgment, Frank turned the boat around, and started rowing for shore. The rain started coming down so hard they couldn't see the shore...or the island. They realized the boat was filling up with rain, and they had nothing to bail with. The rowing was becoming extremely difficult, and Frank was starting to get exhausted from the rowing. The girls began to get a little frantic because of the situation. When he felt he could not row any longer...even after stopping to rest periodically... he gave it everything he had...but, he felt something 'give' and he *had* to stop. They were adrift for a few minutes 'while Frank caught his breath,' and suddenly the sun came out, the rain and the wind stopped, and they could see the dock and the shore just a few hundred feet away. After resting a few more minutes, Frank thought he could make it to shore. Liz and Martha said they would row, and this time Frank let them. They made it to shore, put the boat away, and saw that everyone was leaving to go to supper anyway, so they ended their traumatic afternoon. Liz went on, but Martha took Frank's hand and helped him up the hill. Everyone knew that Martha was Alan Tharpe's girlfriend, so this was a new 'wrinkle' in things. Martha and Frank had supper together and he joined his folks later; he told them about what had happened; His dad said it sounded like he needed to find Dr. Dale, or Dr. Nicholls, and be checked out. He might have had a slight hernia, or strain. Frank said he felt fine, but promised he would see Dr. Nicholls the next day if it got worse... he thought Dr. Dale had stayed in Taipei, but he knew Dr. Nicholls was at the conference. The music was exciting, and some of the youth, including Frank, made up part of the conference choir. Martha sat with Frank, but neither of them said anything about Alan (he was with his parents for the summer in Hong Kong where they served with the Southern Baptists, but they did not attend the conference). Martha's father was a Colonel in the U.S. Army in Taichung, where they were stationed. Liz looked over at them disapprovingly, especially since she thought Frank was available...and she knew Martha was *not.* Martha acted like they were 'just being part of the youth group.' After the service, Frank and Martha joined the rest of the youth. They were going on a hike, down the road about a mile, have a devotional time, with snacks before bed. As they started walking, Frank started feeling pain in his lower abdomen again. He and Martha were walking slower and slower, but he didn't want to tell everyone what was going on. They sat down a few minutes, and he felt a little better. They caught up with the rest of the group as they were having the devotional. They had their snack, but in the meantime Pete, who wanted to go with Leslie Rodd, caught up with Frank and Martha, and the foursome decided they would leave the group and go take a boat to the island. Frank said there was no way he could row the boat, and they laughed. Pete said he would be happy to row this time. Long story short, they made it to the moonlit island. It was past curfew, but Norm, Hans, and their wives, thought the four had retired for the night like the rest of the group. Well, teenagers were doing what teenagers do, and after an against-the-rules romantic outing on the Island, the four of them returned to shore, and sneaked into their respective quarters. Frank tried to sneak in without his dad knowing it…whoops! big mistake. His dad met him at the door, a strong tongue-lashing ensued, and, in more than a whispered bawling out, he said, "Don't you care about what people will think about you, etc.," at least that was the gist of it. But 'no bones were broken' (ha!), and seemingly a new relationship with Martha had started. Everyone left Sun Moon Lake thinking 'what a great conference!' Michael and Beth had decided to stay over a couple days, so after everyone left, except for about thirty others with the same idea, they settled in for a few extra days of relaxation before returning to Mushan. [Frank had let Martha know, and everyone around her, that he was willing to 'fight Alan' for the right to call Martha his new 'girlfriend.' The rumor mill started cranking out wild tales of romance and intrigue]. Frank was bored; all his friends had left, and most of the ones that had stayed had children that were not his age. Margi was more interested in reading or writing letters like her mom, and Davie was willing to play by himself. The next day, the wind started picking up. Then the rain started up. By supper time, Anna, a full-blown typhoon, was in force. Hotel management told them to 'batten down,' or move to the 'Lodge.' They decided to stay in their cabin, but the wind increased and the rain, even stronger than the wind, pelted everything very hard. By morning, they were able to see mudslides everywhere. They also saw that lines were down…meals at the 'Lodge' had to be cooked by wood stove…soon they ran out of food. Frank, Margi, Davie, and their parents, went down the hill into the village. So did all the other missionary families…all the staff and other Chinese families, too. They were told that the mudslides had been so bad, they were marooned up there at the lake; this meant no supplies could get in…and no one could get out; then the food ran out. All they had left was flour and a few staples. They made 'Mahn-tow' but realized that even that would soon be gone. One of the Presbyterian missionaries, Sydney Bradford, who was familiar with the Sun Moon Lake area, knew someone with a short-wave radio. He called the U.S. military base in Taichung, and they made arrangement for a seaplane to come in, land on the lake, and transport all of them out. The plane arrived to the cheers of all. There was only one problem: the plane only had enough room for about twenty-two of them, but there were almost thirty-five missionaries, including their children. It was finally decided that women and children (except several of the older children who stayed back) would go. The rest would hike over the mudslides and catch ground transportation down the road. Margaret volunteered to walk out with her dad and Frank, but there was room for one more adult, so she went with her mom and Davie, and they flew out with the other twenty-one people in the seaplane. Chinese workers were hired to haul most of the luggage that couldn't fit on the plane. Then with backpacks and the best hiking boots and shoes they could muster, a group of a dozen or so missionaries and Chinese co-workers took a boat to the southwest end of the lake, and started walking out. Frank and his dad walked out with the group. When they came to a big mudslide, they walked over it, or around it. Small buses from villages met them and took them as far as the next mudslide. They repeated this over and over…walking over the mudslides, taking a bus or truck, whatever was available, until they arrived at Shuili. From there, they were able to take a bus all the way to Chiayi, where they got on the train going north to Taipei. They were able to contact Rev. Jesse Pan, the pastor at the Da An Peniel church. He was able to loan them a car (they had driven up to Sun Moon Lake in their own car…which was now stranded there). They drove to the Sungshan airport, picked up Beth, Davie, and Margi, and arrived home in Mushan late that night. Michael and Pastor Pan drove the mission vehicle back up that week, and picked up their car.

Frank's senior year started well. He was elected student body president and captain of the soccer team. Les Rodd was elected vice-president, and president of the senior class. Martha Richie was editor of the yearbook, the 'Morrisonian.' David Hunker was associate editor of the yearbook, and editor of the newspaper, the Echo. Jon Culver came back from furlough and was soccer goalie after Gordy Herring left; they had a winning season. The big music and drama production had been during their junior year. ['HMS Pinafore' had been a great hit, and it was an all-school production. Marge Brown did the music, Jim Montgomery did the drama; they worked extremely hard putting it all together; several had primary roles in it, mainly juniors and seniors. Frank was Ralph Rackstraw, Molly Green was Josephine, Bob Suessmuth was the Admiral, Gordon Herring was the Captain, Martha Richie was Cousin Phoebe, Pat Roberts was Buttercup, David Hunker was Boatswain, Dan Valder was Dick Deadeye, and everyone else in the Morrison High School were choruses of sisters, cousins, aunts, and sailors. It was sold out every night, and the American and international community loved it]. Because they only had a big drama and music production 'every two years,' they decided there would be no 'senior play.' They did, however, have a special Christmas program, and sang the DuBois 'Seven Last Words of Christ' at Easter, complete with soloists. The men's quartet Frank's last two years at Morrison was Frank (tenor 1), Dan Valder (tenor 2), David Hunker (baritone), and Jon Culver (bass). They performed for Chapel, MAAG Worship Services, Evening Vespers, and for several social events on and off campus. They went with the choir on tour to northern Taiwan, and both the choir and quartet made recordings at the Overseas Radio and TV studio. Frank and his friends continued to see movies, both at the U.S. military theaters as well as the Chinese theaters (permission slips were now not required by the school). They also spent time at the 'New Compound' which was where the U.S. military lived, and they sometimes stayed overnight with the military students attending Morrison; some decided they would learn how to dance! This was considered a 'big no-no' by most, so everyone kept it quiet. Despite his sometimes 'curiosity-killed-the-cat ways' Frank became conscience-stricken (because of his strict upbringing: *no dancing, theater, smoking, drinking, or gambling, called 'the forbidden-five'*), and he ended up 'ratting' on everyone. He thought Mom Ashby could be trusted to keep the secret, but she told him, "Frank, I wish you had not told me, now I have to report this." Everyone was furious with Frank, and it took a long time to live that down. Alan Tharpe started dating Margi (some said in order to get back at Frank for 'stealing' Martha), Allen and Les dated most the year. Frank and Martha broke up when Frank started dating Carol Latonen from TAS. Several other couples dated and then broke up and dated others (one of the teachers said '*everybody dates everybody at Morrison*'); everyone was close; so, relationships…well, shifted!

The end of the year was filled with exciting things. Frank and David performed a 'Senior Recital.' They performed Beethoven's 'Sonata Pathetiqué.' David did the First Movement, and Frank did the Second Movement. David performed several pieces by himself, as did Frank, and then they played a four-hand finale, 'Arabesque' by Anton Arensky. 'Senior Sneak' was another exciting event. Remembering the experience as juniors chasing the seniors, a small group of the now-seniors had to have a 'plan' that would throw the current year's juniors off…like a diversion. Marge and Larry Brown had been reinstated as sponsors, so with their help, a 'decoy plan' was leaked purposely to throw them off. Sherman Dam was the decoy site, so when the seniors left, they had one of the sophomores, with information purposely 'planted on them…led the juniors to Sherman Dam…instead of Oluanbi, at the southern tip of Taiwan. Because Martha Rickie's dad had contacts, they 'snuck away' in a Deuce-and-a-half truck, stayed at a military-type 'quonset-hut' accommodation, had all their meals there, and stayed all day on the beach. The juniors followed the false lead, and realized they had been had, hauled a commode up to the senior 'suite' (the end of the boys' dorm, converted into two-person rooms), but Mom Ashby hauled it back down, thinking this was going too far. After a wonderful 'sneak' they returned with accusations of 'stealing girlfriends' again (this time Pete accusing Frank of 'kissing his girl, Les'), but then everything blew over. The year ended with a wonderful graduation. Frank, Margi, Dave, and his parents left for Hong Kong, where they boarded the HMS Himalaya for the United States via Hawaii.

Sailed HMS Himalya Hong Kong-San Diego June 1962

Ephrata Nazarene Church

Rev. Varro, Quincy First Pastor

Stevie Varro, Quincy Memorial Pk

Hong Kong

Sun Moon Lake, Taiwan

Frank Morrison Soccer

Morrison Senior Year

Frank's and David's Recital

Morrison Madrigal Singers

The 'warm bath' is over…
weigh anchor…it's a big ocean

CHAPTER SIXTEEN

MUSIC...AND THE HALLS OF IVY

Frank and Margo meet as music majors at Seattle Pacific

AFTER A FEW DAYS IN HONG KONG VISITING PENIEL MISSION missionaries, and some of their missionary friends from Taiwan, they boarded the HMS Himalaya. [Frank had done a rather confusing and insensitive thing; he had been dating Carol Letonen fairly regularly...she was American military, and attending

TAS. Muriel and Norm Cook, and several others close friends, had told Frank that 'many in the missionary community' were concerned about two things: whether or not Carol was a Christian, and whether she shared the same values as Frank. Muriel said many were praying that he would not make a big mistake by continuing this relationship until he knew for sure; he 'thumbed his nose' at this 'invasion of his privacy;' but his parents got involved, saying they shared the same concerns; Frank basically cut himself off from any and all advice, swearing he'd continue the relationship...whether they liked it or not. Everyone was fairly shocked at this, since Frank had not only been a leader in the areas of academic, music, sports and social life, on and off campus, but also as a spiritual leader, taking charge in the leading of Vespers, spiritual emphasis week, in his devotional life, and by example. He was faithful in his weekly prayer and personal Bible reading, probably as much as anyone on campus; after study hall his senior year, with his friend, Joy Trachsel, he told her he had felt a call to ordained ministry; but he was seventeen, and like Jonah, said, "No, I'm going my own way, thank you," and made plans to be a world-renowned choral musician. When it really came down to it, though, he just could not deny his sensitive heart to God. But...he had still 'failed to tell Carol the changed time' of their airline departure from Taipei to Hong Kong, and she arrived at the later time to find Frank had already departed without 'saying goodbye.' Broken-hearted, she wrote Frank a letter swearing her continued love for him...and wanting to continue the relationship in the U.S., after her own graduation the following year, but Frank had moved on; he broke it off...to the quiet approval of many in the missionary community].

Frank made friends easily on-board ship, including a young British girl, Veronica, in first class. His mom and dad shared a suite with Davie and Margi, but he shared a small two-bunk cabin with a British man, Nigel Burns. Known for his independence and love of exploring, Frank found out that by going to the bottom of the ship, he could walk across to first class, and then taking the stairs up to the top deck, he could visit Veronica whenever he wished. The problem was...the steward followed him, and found out he was tourist class, and kicked him out, telling him if he caught him there again, he would be reported. Frank stayed out of first class, forgoing any relationship with Veronica, and made some friends with other people his age in tourist class instead. He was particularly concerned about Davie 'falling overboard.' He was exactly the same age as Stevie was when he was killed, and Frank watched him like a hawk. Someone noticed Frank's concern, and suggested they could purchase a 'harness' for Davie, that they were for sale in the galley. Frank used his own money and bought one, and Beth was very grateful. Margi and Michael were impressed. Frank spent a lot of time reading and sunbathing by the pool, and got a good suntan. When they got to Hawaii, he noticed two girls that got on board. When they saw Frank, they smiled and came over to him. "Hi, Frankie, are you taking a trip?" they said, "Yes, I'm with my family; I'm going to the U.S." he said, "but how did you know my name?" They laughed: *"everyone knows your name, Frankie,"* and they put their fingers to their lips, *"...O, you're incognito...we won't tell anyone!* Now whispering, they said, *"we love your voice."* Now Frank was very confused; he thought maybe someone had put these two girls up to something...they knew his *name*... they liked his *voice* (after all, he *did* sing, and was in fact going to be a music major!). He told them he was with his family, but they kept saying they 'wouldn't tell anyone.' Then it took a strange turn—"we've seen *all* your movies, too," they said. Then it dawned on him...they actually thought he was *Frankie Avalon*, and this wasn't just a joke! They went on to talk about Annette Funicello, and all the beach movies 'he had done with her and the Hollywood crowd.' They suggested, if he wasn't tied up with his 'family,' would he be interested in a 'midnight swim?' He jumped at *that* chance, of course. They met at the pool after supper (they were in tourist class, but they ate in different dining halls), and after a bunch of splashing and flirting, Frank decided to show off a little. He got up on the railing around the pool, dove off into the moonlit pool...before checking the cord on his swimsuit... and dove straight through his swimming trunks! As they laughed hilariously, Frank retrieved his swimming suit, and crawled out of the pool...very embarrassed (after putting his trunks back on of course; he suggested they, 'call it a night,' despite their protests to the contrary. They looked for him several times again, but he was on the 'lookout for them,' and avoided them at all costs. He had told Margi about it, telling her to tell no one, especially mom and dad, and sent her ahead of him to warn him of them if he ever saw them again. In a few days, the ship arrived in Vancouver. Frank was not feeling well, but he disembarked anyway, and the family spent the day with Uncle Joe, Aunt Josie, and their children, Tim, Ken, and Lisa. Juli had come out from Regina to meet the ship, and spent the day with them. She was staying with Joe and Josie for a week, and she planned to spend some time later with her family in Washington and Oregon [she told them she had met, dated, and was now *engaged* to Larry Boxall, a graduate student at the University of Saskatchewan in Regina]. Josie fixed one of her fabulous meals, and they left after a great visit, for the ship. Joe was in charge of raising funds in Canada, for Michael and the family, with VOCA, and so he was very familiar with their ministry. Frank didn't eat much, but by the time they returned to the ship, he was feeling better…probably just the twenty-four-hour flu. They got off the ship again in San Francisco. It was Frank's eighteenth Birthday! They asked him what he wanted for his birthday…he didn't hesitate for one second, he said 'Chinese food!' They were in the best Chinatown in America, some said; they got off the ship, and took a bus to Chinatown where they watched which restaurants the Chinese patronized…it turned out to be a little 'hole in the wall' called Hunan Gate. They let Franklin order in Chinese…'jiaozi (dumplings), of course, hot-sour soup, beef with qingcai (Chinese broccoli), and gungbao (kungpao) chicken. When Dad was paying the bill, he told the proprietor, in Chinese, "that was the best Chinese food I've had in three weeks!" The proprietor asked, "and where was that?" Dad laughed and told him, "China, of course" (at least the Taiwan-part of it, he said to himself). The proprietor laughed, thinking Dad was making a good joke. In San Diego, they got off the ship. Bob Hammond had sent a car for them to drive for the summer, and they drove to Pasadena, where they worked with the staff for two weeks, and spoke in area churches. At the end of their time there, they had driven up the coast, across western Canada, and then back down to the States. After three months of deputation, Michael, Beth, Margi, and Dave returned to Taiwan. Margi spent two more years at Morrison, Dave started Chinese kindergarten, then transferred to Bethany for first through sixth grade, and then transferred to Morrison for junior high and high school.

[They had visited Guil, Doris, and Karla, before they left for Swaziland in Africa; he had finished medical school at the University of Washington, and was in an internship in southern California; while they were in Portland, staying with Maxine and Henry, Juli joined them, and there she told them all about her college years: she had stayed with Aunt Irene while she matriculated to the Canadian school system, and then did her freshman year in Regina at the University of Saskatchewan as a pre-med major. Uncle Jim had paid the bills, and Michael and Beth had sent monthly payments to him for Juli's tuition and fees, and some for room and board to Irene; at first, she attended the Nazarene Church with Jim, Ollie, and Irene–when she *did* attend at least; she was active in the youth group, but many of them did not have much in common with her; she was 'homesick' for Taiwan, and missed her family and the kind of people with whom she had an affinity at Morrison. She met a group of Christians on campus, who were more like her Morrison friends; most of them attended a United Church of Canada there in Regina. A graduate student from Edgeley, named Larry Boxall, joined the group and attended church with them; she and Larry ended up dating that year, and then he asked her to go with him to Edgeley…to meet his mother, Leata, his father, George, and his brother, John. Then, after several months of dating, Larry asked Juli to marry him; she asked her dad, Michael, to officiate, and asked Frank to sing. Margi was the Maid of Honor, John was the Best Man, and Dave was the Ring bearer; at first, Michael and Beth had resisted the whole idea… there was the question about whether Larry 'was a professing Christian.' Jim was willing to support the idea, but Irene was completely against it, and refused to even attend the wedding. Beth and Michael prayed; Juli had said Larry believed 'in his own way,' and they felt it had to be her choice anyway, not theirs. Michael pleaded with Irene to support him–to attend the wedding, but she refused…it put a strain on their relationship that wasn't fully resolved for many years. Juli traveled with them as far as Seattle for their visit there. Irma had returned from Cyprus where Ralph had worked (they weren't supposed to know, but everyone in the family knew it was the CIA). Ralph and Irma divorced after Larry, Ron, and Tom were born; she had met someone named Mike Palalus from Cyprus, but in the Seattle (where she taught following her return) she and Mike married… but when they got back to Cyprus, she found out Mike was already married! Feeling cheated and tricked, she returned to Seattle again, and the marriage was annulled; she had no money, so her parents, Dr. and Mrs. Fitz, funded her travel; she got a teaching job, and was doing fine, when Michael and Beth and the family visited her there, and they had a wonderful time catching up, cooking Chinese food, and visiting Seattle Pacific College for Frank's sake. He applied and was accepted to SPC... 'pending his parents' decision on SPC' (and three or four other choices, including Pasadena College, Westmont College, and Moody Bible Institute)...at least 'according to dad,' as Juli put it...Frank had already decided on SPC (they just needed to lock horns again, as she put it, until Frank's stubbornness won out again, ha!) They visited the campus; Frank arranged for a music audition, and met some of the staff and a few of the faculty, and the college president. Juli left the next day and returned to Regina to make preparations for the wedding in August. The rest of the family visited and spoke in churches in Idaho, Montana, North Dakota, British Columbia, Alberta, and Saskatchewan. After the wedding, they visited relatives in Minnesota and South Dakota; by the time they returned to Seattle, they had *made the decision, based on the fact that Frank could live with Irma to save expenses.'* (Juli just said 'yes, okay, whatever, ha!)].

At the end of August, Beth, Michael, Margi, and Dave said a tearful goodbye, and they flew back to Taiwan. Frank had been on his own before, but 'home' had been only a few hours away. Now a new chapter began. 'Home' was no longer with his mother and father, or siblings. 'Home' was where he was *headed*...to try to make it on his own. The freshman orientation weekend did not help...it made it worse! They went to Camp Casey on Whidbey Island...a lot of fun, but it didn't prepare him for the culture shock he was going to experience. When they got back from the weekend to the campus, Frank was so bewildered, he didn't call Irma to come get him; he started walking...he walked...and walked; he started to pray; he didn't really know where he was going, but with the supernatural sense of direction he had always had (he had only been from Irma's house to the SPC campus once), he had walked *seven* miles from SPC to Northgate where Irma lived, and showed up looking like a lost puppy! "What's wrong, Frank?" Irma asked. He didn't really know at that time. She knew though...she had been through it years ago herself, when she and Beth returned from China in 1935. She fixed supper...Chinese food, of course, and then

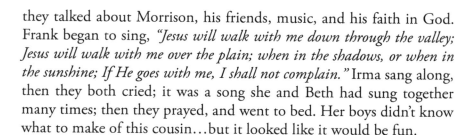

they talked about Morrison, his friends, music, and his faith in God. Frank began to sing, *"Jesus will walk with me down through the valley; Jesus will walk with me over the plain; when in the shadows, or when in the sunshine; If He goes with me, I shall not complain."* Irma sang along, then they both cried; it was a song she and Beth had sung together many times; then they prayed, and went to bed. Her boys didn't know what to make of this cousin…but it looked like it would be fun.

Frank started his freshman year at SPC; his audition had gone well…and he was offered a music scholarship (which was renewed every year of his four years at SPC). The first week of classes he tried out for the Victory Quartet. Few freshmen ever made one of the two college men's quartets; they usually sang in one of the gospel teams before trying out for the Victory Quartet, or the Clarions, the two top quartets. The Victory Quartet particularly had a long tradition of excellence. Three of the four singers from the previous year's quartet had graduated, and a fourth dropped out, so there was a completely fresh slate of singers trying out. The tryouts seemed to be inconclusive… going on and on for over two hours. Frank finally landed the tenor I spot in the Victory Quartet, beating out a junior for the top spot. The final result was: Frank Varro, tenor I; Byron Gjerde, tenor II; Don Brumfield, baritone; Glen Settle, bass; and Neil Craig, piano. Frank auditioned for the A Cappella Choir, and made that also. As a declared music major, he was required to sing in the Oratorio Society, so he had to stay late Monday evenings to rehearse, plus he was studying voice with professor Phil Mack, the conductor of the A Cappella Choir. With all the music classes, he thought he would not have time for any of his core classes, but he was able to fit many of those in as well. Irma told him, 'under the circumstances, he needed to take her car to school' because, with all the music rehearsals and private lessons, he would never make all his classes trying to ride the bus. So, Frank dropped her off in the morning at Green Lake Elementary, then drove himself to class at SPC and stayed there all day. Irma got a ride back home with a fellow teacher that lived at Northgate. Her boys got rides to school; she took the car on weekends and went to church. Tom went with her, but Ron and Larry usually slept in. Practically every weekend was taken up with singing in churches with the quartet. After the first year, however, the schedule really got hectic…trying to share the car for Irma's special school events, Ron and Larry's school functions, Tom's frequent doctor's visits, and Frank's academic and musical extra rehearsals and events... so Frank decided he needed to move on-campus, and he moved into a dorm. Irma and Tom still went to hear them almost every week. They were by far the most faithful supporters of the Victory Quartet, so the guys voted them 'honorary members' of the Victory Quartet's fan club!' One weekend, the quartet was informed by the SPC administration that they were to get themselves to a Free Methodist youth conference in Idaho. They almost weekly took one of the college cars, so Glen, as the only senior in the group (Don and Neil were sophomores, and Byron and Frank were freshmen); he checked it out for the weekend as usual. They had planned to leave Friday after class, drive to Fruitland, Idaho, stay the night with the youth conference sponsors, sing Saturday and Sunday for the conference, and return late Sunday evening to Seattle. Something must have gone wrong with the signing-out of the car, because when Glen went to pick up the car, it was gone, and he was told that another member of the SPC administration had signed it out; they had already taken it...they were already on their way to Vancouver, B.C. Norm Edwards, the Alumni director found out about this...and it all 'hit the fan.' They tried to get another car unsuccessfully. The youth conference people were called, and were upset that the Quartet might not show up, and started calling other Alumni board members. The guys had eaten supper; they had gone to bed... waiting to be told what to do. They were awakened out of a dead sleep about 4:00 a.m. Norm told them to get in his car; he took them to the Seattle-Tacoma Airport where they got on a small 'rattle trap' of a plane... in their suits and all...and found themselves a few hours later at the Boise airport. They piled into a station wagon driven by a wild woman who called herself the Free Methodist pastor's daughter, from the conference. She drove ninety miles an hour...on snow-covered roads, to Fruitland. Glen had his finger nails embedded in Frank's and Don's knees the whole way. She played a Christian station on the radio full volume, while she shouted above the radio the entire way, telling them about the church, their youth ministry, and her family. Without any shower, shave, or breakfast...after three hours of sleep...they arrived just in time to sing for the conference morning worship. They had missed the Friday night opening, but that had not been in the plan anyway, because they were supposed to have been driving…on their way there from Seattle. They made it through the day, yawning and napping whenever possible, in between worship, Bible studies, activities, lunch and supper. Following the evening service, they were shown to their room…in the attic of the small parsonage! Glen and Don shared one double bed, Byron and Frank shared another, and Neil slept on a twin bed. After a freezing-cold night with only a light blanket on each bed, Glen awoke in the morning, exhausted from the whole ordeal, and sat on the edge of the bed rubbing his eyes. He put his feet on the floor… *each foot right on top of two bumble bees!* As he cried out in his pain, Don jumped. At that very moment, the slats in the bed gave way, and the two of them went crashing to the floor! This woke up the other three guys, and all five were shouting and yelling, trying to figure out what was going on. The pastor and family came running upstairs to see what the commotion was. After fixing the bed and putting something on Glen's bee sting, they had breakfast, and had another full day of singing and entertaining young junior high and high school kids. They started thinking about how they were going to get back to Seattle; no one had any ideas of how they might accomplish this…they had no money, and the college had no money or car they could arrange for them to drive back in. Frank told them that his grandfather, Dr. Fitz, lived in Nampa…about forty-five miles east of Fruitland; he volunteered to hitchhike into Nampa… to see if his grandfather might let them use his car? Not knowing how far they might be able to drive it, or how they would get it back to him, they said, "Yes, Frank, go ahead, we don't have a lot of choices here, we'll just have to play it by ear." Frank called his grandfather, Dr. Fitz, who agreed to let them take his car as far as Walla Walla. He would take the bus there and drive the car back. Don remembered that Linda Marbut, who sang in Choir, was from Walla Walla. He called and found out she had gone home for the weekend. 'Yes', she said, she would arrange for them to have a Sunday evening service, and they could take an offering. With the offering, they could buy train tickets to Seattle. Frank hitchhiked into Nampa (you could actually do that in those days without being mugged or killed!); he drove the car back to Fruitland, they sang their final service, drove the car to Walla Walla, and Linda, true to her word, had arranged for an evening service. She asked the church to be generous in their offering because the Victory Quartet 'needed to get back to Seattle!' After the service, they had just enough money to buy five one-way train tickets from Walla Walla to Seattle. They slept on the train, and some friends picked them up at the station, taking them back to the SPC campus in time for their 8:00 a.m. classes!! "Wow! What a weekend," Norm said, when he heard this incredible story; he couldn't believe how resourceful they had been. Needless to say, he 'had words' with the administration about the 'blackeye' SPC had been given because of it; with great thanks to the Victory Quartet, and some resourceful alumni; the administration eventually apologized. The second year the Victory Quartet joined the Carillon Trio to form the first Seattle Pacific Ensemble. They toured together to a number of places, and made several appearances on campus, and in local, statewide and regional churches and events. A highlight was an appearance at Winona Lake, Indiana, for the Free Methodist General Conference. They got back to Seattle in time to be a part of Myrtle's wedding. Frank moved back in with Irma for the summer and took a couple of summer classes. He attended Crown Hill Nazarene with Irma, and took in a short Fitz reunion in Portland before classes resumed.

Auntie Irma

Victory Quartet '65

Victory Quartet '64

Margo & Gospel Team

Victory Quartet '63

Frank conducts Falcon Men's Chorus

First date photo

Finding his stride with the books and music... but missing a 'beat or two'...in searching for the 'rest'

Chapter Seventeen

Driving Miss Margo and a 'Slow Boat to China'

Whadda ya mean Seattle's 'halfway between Taiwan and Michigan?'

LL BUT ONE SINGER, FRANK, AND THE PIANIST, NEIL, DROPPED OUT OF the Victory Quartet the following year. Dan Michelson, Tenor II, Glenn Bowerman, Baritone, and Doug Bartlett, Bass, were all added. The Bowerman twins, Mary–soprano, Myrtle-alto, and Arlene Nordlund–mezzo, became the Carillon Trio, with Mary Anne LeCompte as accompanist (and also as alto when singing with the whole ensemble). Frank's third year, the Ensemble stayed intact as far as the Quartet was concerned, except for Dan Michelson and he was replaced with Wes Anderson. The Carillon Trio had a complete turnover, since Mary, Myrtle, and Arlene were graduating. Taking their place was Arnola Etulain, Darlene Janke, Pam Wetzel, and Judy Shull. This Ensemble toured to a Christian camp in Colorado, with several other on-campus off-campus appearances. Frank's final year was taken up with student teaching, and so he, and all the others, in both the trio and quartet, were replaced, except Pam Wetzel.

The SPC choir toured each year: Pacific Northwest (first year), Oregon-California (second year), and Idaho-Utah (third year). They sang many times on campus and in area churches. They gave a concert each quarter in each of the three years Frank was a member. He was elected president the second and third year. They sang many classics as well as standard sacred choral literature, including works by Howard Hanson, Brahms, Bach, and Beethoven. They were well received by the Puget Sound Choral Directors, Music Educators, and other college and university audiences. Frank was a soloist with the choir several times. One of the unique things that the choir had was a fall retreat, and a weekly prayer service at noon, where they would pray for each other, and the ministry of the choir. They gave personal testimonies each night of their tours as well. Most of Frank's dating life at SPC was with girls from the choir, with others associated with the choir or ensemble, or mutual friends of the choir or ensemble. Frank also studied voice with Phil Mack and gave a junior recital with Gayle Moran, whom he had dated before she became a well-known performing artist, (and wife of jazz musician Chick Correa). Having studied with a baritone, and voice teacher for most of the top singers on campus, Frank decided to make a major change in his focus. He wanted to study with a tenor, another tenor that had studied with Edison Harris...that had studied with the great William Vennard...who had studied with a leading 'Belle-Canto School' representative in the United States: Madame Schumann-Heinz! The new voice instructor was Ira Jones, and he took Frank in a new direction with his voice. Frank gave his senior recital with Ira after studying with him just one year. The results were dramatic, and well-received.

Frank had become president of the Falcon Missionary Fellowship, a campus missions group whose members were interested in becoming missionaries. Even though Frank was pursuing his own interests in music outside of ordained ministry, he wrestled with a call of becoming a missionary…as a teacher of music, and this included the area of radio and television ministry overseas. He had enjoyed dating a number of girls, but most of them didn't regard living overseas as *one of their high priorities, ha!*. Frank was torn between a career in Seattle, (or at least the United States), or going back to Asia, or somewhere overseas. He had been steady with a couple of girls, but these relationships didn't last. He came back from a summer tour with the SPC Ensemble–between his junior and senior year, ready for his final year of college, but still confused as far as any life partner was concerned. He had made contact again with Allen Peterson (remember, Morrison, sports, etc.?) Art Peterson, Pete's dad, had promised him a harvest job in Pullman, Washington. When the Ensemble arrived back in Seattle, Frank went to Pullman to be with Pete for the month of August. When he got there, Art told him he had some bad news…and some good news. As it turned out, there was only *one* harvest job…and Pete had taken it. At first Frank was very upset…after all, he could have gotten a job in Seattle, if Art hadn't promised him the harvest job in Pullman; then Art told him the good news: he had arranged for him to be on the Washington State University 'water crew.' These were the ones who changed out the sprinklers, and hand watered the corners, for the grounds at the University. That, and painting his other house (they had just moved the previous year, and were renting out the old house), would come to the same amount Frank would have been paid for the harvest job. Frank didn't have to breathe the dust and hay all day like Pete, and he was paid the same. Pete drove the combine all day, and then he 'drove it again'…every night. The sun was unbearably hot, and Pete was exhausted every day. He told Frank his dad had given him the best of the two options. Frank made enough money to trade in an old Chevy which was falling apart, on a Buick that he would use in his student teaching and senior year. Frank took it; he returned to Seattle, spent the last two weeks with Irma before moving back to the dorm, and had enough money left over for some clothes.

Frank had just finished moving into the dorm with his roommate Neil Craig. Even though Don Brumfield had dropped out of the Victory Quartet, he and Frank had stayed close. They had double-dated once in a while (and often 'broke up' at the same time too!), they found themselves still connecting once in a while. As Neil and Frank were getting ready to go to Gwinn Commons for supper, Don showed up at their dorm room and told them, "everyone, get in my car, we're all going to St. Mark's Cathedral for the dedication of the new Dutch *Flentrop* pipe organ." Neil asked who was going–that he was hungry…and they should eat first. Don said they didn't have time to eat; they could eat later. Gayle Moran and Margo Moore were fellow 'Michiganders;' and the two of them had just arrived back on campus from the train station, and they were the next to show up after Don, Neil, and Frank. So those five and Judy Shull, all piled in Don's car. Don told Neil, Gayle, and Judy, to get in the back, and Margo to get in the front seat with Frank and him. [Margo Moore was a piano performance major, and hung out mostly at Crawford Music Building, while the *rest* of the music people hung out at the Student Union Building, or somewhere else. Frank thought she was a very serious student, and acted like she 'owned the practice room schedule.' Once, she had kicked Frank out of '*her* practice room,' when he tried to tell her it was *his* time. She showed him the schedule; sure enough, she was right. He also knew one of her good friends, Karen White, that he had dated briefly]. Don pulled out in his 'hotrod' Ford, heading for Capitol Hill, and St. Mark's Cathedral. Frank talked to Don, thinking Margo wouldn't have much to say. She started asking Don what the dedication of the new pipe organ was all about. Don didn't know much about it, but Gayle did. She knew about Peter Hallock, the 'compline choir,' and the *Flentrop* organ. When Gayle finished, Margo turned to Frank and asked him about the SPC choir. She had been first flute in the SPC band, and she and Frank had talked briefly in Spokane at a joint performance of the band and choir, when the band and choir tours had intersected there for one night. She had also studied voice with Wadad Saba, who said she should also sing in the choir. She didn't want to be in the band in her junior year, and asked Frank what he could tell her…as 'past president of the choir'…about Prof Mack that would help her get in. Frank said he would look at the audition lists and talk to him about it…if he had the chance. Frank was interested in Michigan and what growing up there was like; he told her about Taiwan, and she said she had already heard about him, and the stories of his musical experiences at Morrison. She had attended his junior recital, mainly because she was friends with Gayle, with whom he had shared the recital. Don kept trying to add stories of the quartet and their famous 'tour of Idaho,' but by the time he got into the best parts, they had arrived at St. Mark's, and they all went in together for the organ dedication and choral concert. Everyone was sitting on the floor facing the back, where the stunning pipe organ was. The cathedral choir was there too. Frank sat down with Margo, and they talked during the breaks in the concert. They both loved hearing the choir and the organ very much, and learned about the installation and history of the Dutch *Flentrop* tradition. Peter Hallack was a very interesting speaker, as well as choirmaster-organist. Margo had not heard of 'compline,' the sung service there at St. Mark's Cathedral, which was each Sunday night at 9:30. Frank told her about it, and asked her if she would like to join him the next Sunday evening. She said 'sure;' she said it would be interesting. They rode home with Don, but went to the Student Union Building for something to drink, then Frank walked her to her dorm.

Classes started the next day, so Frank made a point of getting to breakfast at Gwinn Commons early. He knew Margo was a server in the food line, and he wanted to talk to her briefly in the line before it got busy. He thanked her for the fun time at St. Mark's, and reminded her of their date the coming Sunday. She asked him if he could stick around the Crawford Music Building after her audition…to see if she made choir; he told her he would meet her there after her 12:00 audition. He went to his first half-day student-teaching orchestra rehearsal at Magnolia Elementary. Margo went to her first junior-year classes, and then her choir audition. Prof Mack said he would post the first day's 'preliminary' audition results after the 12:00 auditions. Frank met Margo after her audition and suggested they go to lunch at the SUB, since the results wouldn't be posted until 1:00. They had lunch, and then went back to Crawford. The list was in longhand… Margo's name was *not* on the list! Prof Mack was going back up the stairs to the choir room, and Frank called out to him; he said he just wanted to say 'hi,' and thank him again for his 'help on the junior recital [because Frank had switched teachers, he was on Prof Mack's 'black list;' so Frank needed an excuse to 'bury the hatchet,' but *not* in Prof's head, ha! Prof Mack had *retaliated* by giving Frank a 'B' in choir, since he could hardly give him a 'B' on the junior recital, which was outstanding…it would reflect on his own teaching as well]. "Hey, Prof Mack," Frank said, "I wanted to thank you again for the outstanding experience of singing, and soloing, in choir for the three years I was with you," (pretending he didn't know about the 'B' he had been given in Choir [how do you get a 'B' in choir anyway]). They talked briefly, and then Frank said, "Say, I have a new friend, Margo Moore, I don't know if you know her, she's a friend of Gayle Moran, and from Michigan too; she's an outstanding soprano, and studied with Wadad Saba; I noticed she's not on the 'preliminary' list of those who made the choir—do you think there might be some mistake?" Prof Mack looked like steam was coming out of his ears, and he turned beet red. He mumbled something about 'checking his notes again'…as he fled to his studio, so embarrassed that his evaluation might have been wrong. "When we finish the…ah, the…ah, the…auditions, well, uh, you can come check the final list, okay?" Auditions were finished by 5:00 p.m., Tuesday afternoon, and the final list was posted, Frank and Margo ran over there and read it together… 'Margo Moore, soprano I,' [*Yes!*]

Classes went well the first week. Frank got some good experience conducting the Magnolia Elementary orchestra and assisting the strings teacher, Sylvia Graham, in teaching beginning orchestra students the strings and other orchestral instruments. Margo attended her first SPC choir rehearsal—the first choir she had sung in since the Methodist church choir in Quincy, Michigan, having been *only* in band her entire four years of high school in Quincy, Michigan…and Okanogan, Washington. Education classes consisted primarily of student teaching methods and lesson plans. Sunday came, and it was the first time in almost four years Frank hadn't been on the road with the SPC Ensemble or Victory Quartet. He visited some other churches with Irma and Tom for a few weeks in the fall. Margo was still in the 'Ambassadors' gospel team, either singing or accompanying. Frank stopped by for Margo that evening for their *first-real-date*. It was the first time she had heard a 'sung service' such as this, and St. Mark's Cathedral Compline Choir was particularly moving. After the service, they had a chance to meet Peter Hallock and some of the choir members, all men. Following the service, they went to Dick's for hamburgers, fries, and a coke. After walking across campus back at SPC, they got back in Frank's Buick. As they talked, the most horrible smell arose from the car. Both were embarrassed of course, and it became apparent that the smell was not the *cologne* from either of them. Frank turned on the light and looked around the car. To his rising consternation, he discovered he had stepped in some 'dog-deposit,' and, worse than that, he had ground it into the rubber padding on his brake pedal. He managed to find a stick and remove the 'stuff' from his shoe, as well as the brake pedal. Margo laughed, and reminded him that she was 'the farmer's daughter' from Michigan. They got out of the car and he walked her to her dorm. He told her he had had a really good time. He asked her out for the next weekend. She said she was 'busy.' He said 'how about the following weekend?' She shifted feet, and cleared her throat. She said she was 'kind of' going with someone else. Not willing to take 'no' for an answer, Frank said he thought he knew something *about* that (SPC was a small community, and most everyone knew 'who was going with whom'). He was already good friends with Howard Elseth, and knew Howard had dated Margo...they were both involved in the Gospel Team program. Frank said Howard and he were good friends, but he didn't know she and Howard were currently dating. If she didn't want to go out, 'it was okay (not really), just say so.' She didn't like Frank pressuring her...but she'd really had a good time too; and she thought Frank was a BMOC ('big man on campus'), and felt a little nervous because of all the girls he had dated. She said she really *did* want to go out with him; she really appreciated him helping her get into choir... did he have anything in mind? Frank said he wanted to take her to dinner at the 'Beach Broiler' at Alki Point (Frank had not taken anyone to the Beach Broiler before; it was a place guys supposedly took their dates when things were 'getting serious,' but he didn't tell her that). He hugged her; Frank didn't kiss her goodnight (uncharacteristically, he did not try...and 'characteristically,' she would not have *let* him!) It was to be on the night of an Alumni board meeting...at the SUB. Frank had formed his sixteen-voice men's choir, called the Falcon Men's Chorus, sponsored by the Association of Students of SPC. The Seattle Pacific College mascot was a Falcon, and they all wore maroon sweaters—the college colors…a very male collegiate look of the 1960's. They sang really neat male chorus kind of music…like 'If I Ruled The World,' and other Perry Como, Frank Sinatra, and others of the period, along with some sacred selections. The Alumni board had asked Frank to have the Falcon Men's Chorus sing for their fall meeting. It was the same night as Frank's date with Margo at the Beach Broiler, so they said they would have their dinner first, followed by their meeting…which included the Falcon Men's Chorus. Frank said he would be back from his date after dinner, and they would sing. Dave Baker, another 'BMOC' on campus, was also on the program. Frank told Margo they should leave by 5:00 since it was about a twenty-five-minute drive, around Elliott Bay, to Alki Point. They could eat by 6:00, and leave by 7:00…so his men could sing by 7:30. 'Yes, that would be fine.' Margo always spent a lot of time in the practice room and Crawford Music Building, so Frank did not know she hadn't heard of the Falcon Men's Chorus; nor did she understand about the Alumni board and their dinner program. Frank showed up at 5:00. Jerry Donahue, the dorm proctor, called her room. She said she would be right down…at 5:15, Frank asked Jerry to call again… 'she would be a few more minutes'…at 5:30, Frank asked Jerry to remind her they had a tight schedule, and would she be able to be down soon? 'Yes, of course, she would be right there'… at 5:45, Frank is getting a little nervous about the tight schedule, but determined to have this special date with Margo Moore…ten minutes later, Margo came down, they got in the car, drove like crazy to Alki Point, ordered immediately…but the food did not come. At 6:45, their food came, and Frank asked Margo if it would be alright if they took it 'to go.' He explained what she had *not* understood; she thought: a nice casual evening…with 'Mister BMOC,' Alumni board meeting? Big bucks for the college, and a 'feather in his cap' (and 'call it macaroni'?), 'By the way,' she said, 'what is the Falcon Men's Chorus?' They dashed to the car, got caught in traffic, arrived at the campus at 7:50. All the guys ran over to Frank, who was now a *basket case*, Margo was almost in tears, and they both smelled like smoked salmon… 'Oh, that was what was coming from that to-go box.' Wes Anderson, one of Frank's best friends from Victory Quartet days, who also sang in Frank's Falcon Men's Chorus, came running out to tell them Dave Baker had just finished singing…not just his part, but the *whole program*–uh, they were saying the benediction! Frank apologized profusely to Bob Screen, the MC…traffic, and all that, etc….but Bob said 'no harm, no foul.' The guys left, all of them with that smile that said, "look at Frank's new girl." Wes said to not let it get to him, and left too. Frank came over to Margo; she was so embarrassed, and said she was so sorry. She figured Frank would never ask her out again; but he said, "Hey, let's go up to the Hill lounge (Margo's dorm) and eat our salmon!" She laughed, and they ran to Hill, found some forks and napkins, and ate their dinner. Jerry rolled his eyes. Frank had 'lost his mind…or was it his heart?'

Frank started working on his senior recital with Ira Jones. The vocal technique was completely different from what he was used to. He introduced the 'Belle Canto style to Frank. The focus was on 'singing into the mask,' proper breathing, and 'release of the tone on the breath,' and the results were very exciting. Some of the students listened in, and told other music faculty members (but not in front of Prof Mack or his wife Marcile Mack, head of the piano faculty); but some music faculty members listened in as well, and were quite open in their praise of the fine results in Frank's voice. Diane Lippold had been Frank's accompanist, beginning in his sophomore year, throughout his junior year…including his junior recital, and Frank assumed she would continue through his senior recital and graduation. He was beginning work on a Handel solo cantata, the Schumann "Dichterliebe," and several contemporary songs. After several lessons, Diane said she needed to talk to Frank. He thought there was something wrong, but she said 'no, she just needed to talk to him.' After the next lesson, Frank started to walk out with Diane, but she said she needed Ira to approve of what she was going to say. Ira and Frank looked puzzled. Diane said she knew Frank had been dating Margo Moore..and they seemed to be 'going steady' now. She said she felt awkward playing for Frank, when Margo was such a fine accompanist, and Frank would probably prefer if Margo accompanied him for his senior recital. She said she wanted Ira's approval as well. Frank hadn't said anything, or indicated that he wanted to switch accompanists. Ira asked Diane about Margo's ability and she admitted that Margo was… 'frankly' a more skilled pianist then she. Ira and Frank laughed at the pun. Ira said he had no objection if Frank didn't, after all, he actually could have anyone he wanted…it was *his* senior recital. Frank thanked Diane

275

profusely for her fine work the past two and a half years, and for being so gracious about Margo and her ability. Frank only asked one thing: he didn't want this change to have any effect on Margo's relationship with Marcile Mack, her piano teacher, or with Prof Mack in choir. Ira came a little 'unglued' on that one, saying that would be ridiculous and said it should *never* be a personal thing…that all of them needed to be professional (he had refused to comment on Prof Mack giving Frank a 'B' in choir after switching voice teachers). So, it was settled. Margo showed up at the next lesson, and began working with Frank on his senior recital repertoire. Margo and Marcile Mack never mentioned it in her piano lessons, and Prof Mack never mentioned it in choir.

Frank and Margo had several fun dates. They went to Ivar's Seafood Bar, took a roundtrip ferry ride across Puget Sound to Bremerton, took a photo-booth picture, and went to dinner several times. Margo made sure she was on time, trying to overcome Frank's first impression of her! Christmas came, and Frank saw Margo off on the train to Michigan. She and Gayle Moran traveled together whenever they went home for holidays. Gayle left to go find their seats, she said, so the 'lovebirds' could be alone. The whistle blew and Frank turned to kiss Margo goodbye…she had held off up until now, except for hand-holding and hugging, but this time she enthusiastically kissed him, he jumped off the train just in time, laughing, as he 'pretended he had missed getting off, and would 'just have to go with her to Michigan.' They wrote letters during the Christmas break, and she played the SPC Choir recording, 'My Eternal King,' which featured Frank's solo voice, for her parents several times. She told them he was the one she was dating. When they got back and the winter quarter commenced, the choir went into full gear, and they took their annual choir tour. Margo's junior year, they toured inland, to eastern Washington, Idaho and Oregon. Her senior year, they toured western Washington and Oregon. She was happy to give her personal testimony, but she was quiet and didn't like public speaking, especially on concert nights of tour, but she soon learned that the Wednesday noon prayer meetings, and personal testimonies on tour, were expected of *every* member of the choir, and Prof Mack put pressure on each one of them, as 'good members of the choir,' to participate in these practices. Frank attended some of the area choir concerts on tour and encouraged Margo to 'just go ahead and do it.'

He learned quickly that Margo wasn't one who could easily be 'pushed' this way. They got into a few 'fights' over things, especially things she strongly believed in, and he had to learn when to 'back off.' One night, at the opening of the second half of the concert, as was the practice, Frank was surprised to hear Margo lead off with the opening personal testimony. She just said simply, "I have learned, in my walk with Christ, that the most encouraging scripture for me has always been Proverbs 3:5-6, *"Trust in the Lord with all thine heart, and lean not unto thine own understanding, but in all thy ways acknowledge him, and he shall direct thy paths."* Frank said "Bravo," under his breath. Don Brumfield, who was sitting with him, said, "what did you say?" He said, "nothing, I'm just proud of her for doing what she said she would prefer not doing;" she had resisted saying anything when Frank suggested she 'just give her favorite verse,' but now she had done exactly that... word for word! She had to go on with the rest of the tour, but Frank and Don had a chance to at least talk with her after the concert, and Frank and Margo were now noticed as 'an item.' They finished the rest of the tour, and winter quarter soon ended. During the break, Frank told Margo there was someone he wanted her to meet. He had told her all about his family in Taiwan, and all the Varro and Fitz stories; and she had also told Frank about the Moore's, and the Wickman's—Margo's father and mother's sides of the family. [Interesting note: they discovered Margo had a grandmother named Lura...exactly the same name, with the same spelling, as Frank's grandmother Lura, except that his was maternal...and hers was *paternal*. They also discovered that he had attended school in Quincy, Washington; and *she* had attended... and graduated from: Quincy, Michigan...so they had *both* marched in the 'Quincy marching bands' as well]. One of his relatives Frank talked about a lot was...Aunt Irma, his 'other mom'...and he was her 'other son,' since his parents were so far away; he said he wanted to take her to meet 'someone' very special' to him...to see what she thought of Margo. He called Irma, and asked if she would make one of her famous Indian curry dinners...he wanted her to meet someone he was going with; he wanted to see if she thought she might be the *'one.'* She said 'yes, of course,' and they went out to Aunt Irma's house. After dinner, Irma wanted to take a picture of them 'cheek to cheek;' then he went into the kitchen to help her do the dishes, while Margo looked at the wonderful collection of pictures that Irma had of China (he said "I'll wash, you dry."). She smiled and said, "what's wrong with you, Frank, I can see it in both your eyes; get ready...you marry this girl, you hear me; she is 'the one,' so why have you taken so long... where have you been hiding her from me?" Frank smiled and hugged Irma. He felt like he had his 'family's' approval...he knew that whatever Irma liked, his mom and dad would like! That Saturday, they went to the Seattle Center (the site of the World's Fair in 1962), they took in a matinee performance of the opera, 'Cosi von tutti,' at the Seattle Opera House [they could always wait until ten minutes before curtain time, and get five-dollar tickets], then they lay out on the grass on the 'Center Field,' listening to their favorite music. They took the Monorail downtown. There they visited Zales' Jewelers...just for fun, *a little 'window shopping to get some ideas of what she might like...just in case.* They took the monorail back to the Center and took the Buick to Chinatown, where they picked up some fabulous 'jiao-ze's' (dumplings), and a couple of their favorite dishes. It had been a long, but very good day. When they got back on campus, Frank walked Margo back to the dorm. He got back to his dorm, Ashton Hall, to find Neil and Wes talking to Howard Elseth about a 'big project.' Howard was always up to something; he told Frank he took all the credit, of course, for 'introducing him' to Margo, and said he was so happy things were going so well...he wanted Frank to know he already had another girlfriend...but that was *not* what he wanted to talk to him about; he had found a *great deal* for them for the spring quarter...they could live at the Olympic Apartments, on the other side of Queen Anne Hill, close to the Seattle Center...and they would have *free rent!* Wow! It sounded great. He failed to tell them– Neil, Wes, and Frank–that they would be...*managing* an 'old folks' home.' and he didn't tell them that *he* would be living somewhere else! And...George Carlson, the elderly man that was the current manager, was going on a three-month vacation...before they had a chance to even learn the ropes! In other words: what was *expected* of them...for 'free(?).' It sounded too good to be true...and it *was!* But the three of them fell for it. They checked out of the dorm before the end of the quarter, including their meal ticket (at least breakfast; Howard said it would be easier to cook for themselves). It looked like Frank's spring quarter was going to be different than anything he'd ever experienced in his entire college career!

Frank's student teaching was in high gear. He had been assigned to Ingraham High School, and was supervised by Jerry Semrau, the choir director. Wally Golicke, the previous Ingraham choir director, had built up the program, and Frank had been requested by Wally, (since Frank was the winner of the Puget Sound Choral Conductors' Guild scholarship that year). He was also known to John Morgan, the principal at Ingraham, who had been the choir director at Seattle First Nazarene (the denomination of Frank's early life). Frank learned a great deal from Jerry, and conducted some of the selections on the choir's spring concert program. Margo attended one of the concerts with Irma and Tom, so she had a chance to meet Jerry and his wife, and several other musicians. [When Frank wasn't involved in his student teaching, he was part of the SPC student government as the senior class representative, and he was also elected to the Centurions, a men's honorary, and Who's Who in American Colleges and Universities].

Voice lessons and preparations for his senior recital were beginning to build to a 'high pitch' (pun intended, ha!), Margo and Frank began working weekends to learn the German, and other languages, that were necessary to pull off the recital before his graduation. Frank's Falcon Men's Chorus was in demand and was featured at the Seattle Arena for SPC's Homecoming, singing 'If I Ruled the World,' to thunderous applause. Some Sundays were taken up with the Falcon Men singing their sacred repertoire in churches. As plans for graduation were being developed, Frank's parents informed him they would be coming to the U.S. for a summer furlough, and his graduation. When Frank informed the 1966 SPC graduation planning committee of this, they invited Rev. Varro to offer the benediction for the 1966 SPC graduation ceremony. In the meantime, the job of managing the Olympic Apartments was getting almost unbearable. Every morning the phone would ring; some little old lady would invariably say the same thing every time: *"Aren't we going to have any heat this morning?"* Frank or Wes usually were the ones who started banging on the hot water radiators to try to get them back on. They were finally so upset with all the griping and shouting from these persnickety people, they called Howard and said to get a hold of George: 'they wanted to quit!' Howard said he didn't know if George was back from his honeymoon. *Honeymoon?* They thought it was a vacation! No, at over seventy-five, George had met someone, and they had gotten married! The good news was…he and his new bride would be returning in three weeks. They weren't sure they could stand it, but, somehow they made it, until George arrived with his new wife, Maude. They moved out before graduation, telling Howard he would have to take care of things the last week. Frank started commuting again from Irma's house. He wrapped up his student teaching, did a great final concert with Jerry and the Ingraham choir, and wrote up his evaluation and finished the requirements for his Bachelor of Arts in music education.

The big night had arrived! His senior recital was May 24, 1966. Ira Jones, most of the music faculty, numbers of students and other faculty, and family, were in attendance. Irma and Tom came, as did Gayle, Don, Neil, Wes, and several other good friends. Frank had served as the West Seattle Presbyterian Church choir director two years prior, and then as Highland Park Nazarene Church director of music, and licensed minister in the Nazarene Church. Frank was pleased to see some of these churches' members and friends in attendance as well. The recital began with a Handel solo cantata; it was in typical 'A-B-A' song form; but when he got to the end of the first part, his mind went completely *BLANK!* Without batting an eyelash, he started the first section again. Margo scrambled to figure out what was going on, but quickly jumped back in after the first four bars. Picking up from there, he completed the first section again, and went on to the second section, concluding the cantata with the repeat of the first section. There was momentary silence, wondering if there would be *yet another repeat?…* then great applause, led by Professor Carl Reed, who commented later at the reception that the 'A-B-A' song form was sometimes performed with an *optional* repeat of the first part…and he thought Frank had done the repeat on *purpose*, even with the first few bars of the repeat being unaccompanied! He went on to sing the Robert Schumann song cycle, 'Dichterliebe' ('Poet's Love,' in German–made so popular by the great Fischer-Dieschau), The second half he sang several contemporary classical songs, and folk song arrangements. It was received very well, and many who knew his voice, made note of the 'greatly-improved sound and technique.' [Ira refused to take the credit, but he beamed from ear to ear… that he had had something to do with it; and several new music majors later signed up for Ira's instruction]. The reception that followed was very nice; many asked Frank about his future plans...a career in teaching music was certainly likely they noted. Irma and Tom, church music people, and friends wished them well, and the lovely evening concluded ...*but the evening was not over!* After the reception, Frank took Margo up to their favorite place at the top of Queen Anne Hill (he had made *plans* for this special night!); after talking awhile about their relationship, Frank prayed with her, he told her he loved her, and wanted to spend the rest of his life with her; then he took out the ring...the one that she had liked best, when they went to Zale's a few weeks before. He asked her to marry him; she thought he was asking her to marry him that coming June, and not finishing college before graduating... she said she didn't think that was a good idea *at that time.* He laughed, and said he had 'no thoughts at all' of changing her plans for graduating from college before marriage; he said he meant: *a year and a month from then!* She put her arms around him. "Yes, yes, I'll marry you, Frank Varro." She put the engagement ring on. It fit perfectly (she had tried it on at the jeweler's, of course). They kissed goodnight and he drove her back to her dorm. They kissed in the Hill Hall lounge in front of everyone, and she flashed her ring to all those hanging around. Jerry Donahue rolled his eyes, and smiled...like he had 'seen this coming all along.' It got around fast that Frank and Margo were engaged, and those in the Hill Lounge all clapped. They said goodnight after this very *eventful* evening.

Graduation time was so exciting: Beth and Michael Varro arrived with Dave from Taiwan; they stayed with Irma and the boys. [Margaret had come two years before with them when they took a ship, the Holland American, through the Middle East, Hungary and the rest of Europe, then New York, where Frank had met them, and traveled across the U.S. and Canada with them; Margaret finished her freshman year at SPC, but lived with Irma for a while, then went back to Furman University to live close to Alan Tharpe's family, until he graduated; she then came out to be with her family for a few months, including Frank's graduation, before getting married to Alan the year before Frank and Margo. Her mom and dad, Wilma and Francis Moore, had been berry farmers and career school teachers in Quincy, Michigan; they had spent a one-year sabbatical in Okanogan, Washington, before returning to Michigan to finish out their required years before retirement; they were in the process of selling the farm, where they had lived for twenty years, but now took time to come to Seattle to celebrate Margo's and Frank's engagement, and his graduation; they were able to meet Frank's parents, sister, Irma and her boys, and Frank and Margo's friends; several of them—a year later—were in the wedding party in Wenatchee, where Wilma and Francis would live for many years]. The Class of 1966 graduated two-hundred-ninety-three; many of them were strong leaders and gained levels of excellence unequaled by many of SPC's classes. Rev. Varro offered the benediction, and Frank introduced his parents to as many friends as possible. Seattle Pacific College, now University, was founded by Free Methodist pioneers in 1891, it had become one of America's leading Christian academic institutions, and Frank was privileged to have graduated from there; he became active in Alumni activities, and served two years on the Alumni board and was the chairman of the 1972 Alumni Banquet. There were many pictures taken of Frank, Margo, her family, his family and many other friends.

That same weekend, the two families…The Varro's, and the Moore's… gathered at Ivar's Restaurant for an 'engagement dinner,' hosted by Francis and Wilma Moore. After dinner, Wilma offered a special engagement ceremony and toast. The two families shared the following together: a bite of a hard roll…for the hard times that would come. This was followed by a sip of bitter cranberry juice…for the bitter times; this was followed by a sweet roll…for the sweet times; which was followed by a cup of tea with honey. "Though the hard, and the bitter are hard to swallow, They are but for a moment,' the sweet will always follow," she said. Then Francis read from Psalm 128: *"All those that fear the Lord and walk in his ways will be blessed; you will eat the fruit of your labors, and blessings and prosperity will be yours; your wife will be like a fruitful vine in your house, and your children will be like olive shoots around your house; this is the way a man is blessed when he fears the Lord; and live to see your children's children."* He closed the Bible. Then Michael and Beth stood and laid hands on 'Franklin and Margaret' and prayed a blessing on their engagement and future marriage. It was very moving, and everyone left feeling unified as a family. Margaret returned to South Carolina after her marriage to Alan Tharpe and the

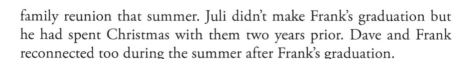

family reunion that summer. Juli didn't make Frank's graduation but he had spent Christmas with them two years prior. Dave and Frank reconnected too during the summer after Frank's graduation.

The next day, Michael and Frank got a ride with a friend and left for Portland, where Frank sang for the wedding of good friends from SPC, Dave and Sherry Abbott. They stayed with Maxine and Henry on their way down to Pasadena to pick up a car from VOCA, the one they would use during the summer's deputation tour. Frank and his dad had some good 'father-son' time. It had been a long time since they had done that, and they took advantage of the opportunity. When they got to Pasadena, they spent a day or two with the staff again, and Michael gave the VOCA board his report. They headed back to Seattle in what Frank loved to call the 'green bomb.' On the way back, Michael said he wanted to talk to Franklin about his summer. Franklin was driving the first leg, and Michael suggested they stop for lunch at a place called the 'Split Pea.' After ordering, Michael said he wanted to make a proposal…he knew Franklin planned on staying at Irma's while Margo went to summer school at SPC…but he really needed him to consider going with them on deputation to help with driving, singing, and leading their deputation meetings. Franklin said 'no,' he and Margo had already made plans to spend the summer together. Michael asked what would Margo be studying? He said she would be taking a couple of electives that she would need to graduate, plus piano lessons. Michael said, if they spent the time together that engaged couples usually spend, wouldn't this hinder her study time? If she stayed with Irma, wouldn't some of her time be in visiting, going out, and practicing piano? Franklin had to admit it wouldn't be the most ideal situation for mixing romance and study. Franklin asked where they were planning to go? What route would they take? Michael said they would probably go up from Seattle to British Columbia, go across the Rockies to Calgary; then go to Regina, Winnipeg, drop down into Minnesota, and work their way back through North Dakota, Montana, Idaho and Washington. They would have meetings all along the way, but most of their time would be spent in Canada where they had the most contacts. Frank said he would think about it. They finished lunch…Frank let his dad pay the bill…it was nice to have VOCA pick up the expenses for the summer, but they were also expected to cover these expenses with the offerings they received. Dad drove and Frank slept for a little while. When he woke up, they needed to fill up with gas again. Michael said he would drive, and as soon as they took off, Michael asked Frank how much he had to pay for the engagement ring–it looked really nice on Margo's finger. Frank said he had to put fifty dollars down, and Zale's let him finance the rest…about three hundred dollars. Michael told him he knew that with his training, and now with a degree in music, some people would have to pay a lot for his services…and now Frank could see what his dad was doing: he was 'spinning his web,' and drawing him in. Frank laughed out loud…he knew what was coming next. Michael said, "If you go on deputation with us, I can't pay you for your services…but I will pay off your ring." He *knew* it! Dad was at least *half* Chinese. He could bargain better than anyone he knew; but Frank knew how to 'suan jiang' (bargain) too! He said, "I'll tell you what, Dad…if it is alright with Margo of course, I'll go part of the way with you…let's say, across Canada, then Minnesota, to see the Fitz's…then take the train back to Seattle from Fargo, North Dakota." Michael almost ran off the road…he had 'created a monster'…he had taught his son *too many* of his own secrets! He paused, and then he said… "deal!" They got back to Seattle, and everyone was happy they had made it safely. Frank explained what they had talked about…he waited for Margo to answer, and Frank was surprised…she said it was a 'good idea;' this way, she wouldn't be tempted to spend time going out, she would have time to study, and she had decided to go only the *first* summer session. When Frank returned, they could spend the rest of August together. So, it all worked out; Michael looked like he'd swallowed the canary, and his 'eyebrow alert' was off the chart!

They were off…they spent time in British Columbia and Alberta in meetings and visiting friends. They even went up to High Prairie and Innisfail, and Franklin had a chance to see all the places they had talked about. He helped with the meetings and led singing and sang solos. They had a mini-family reunion in Regina, and most of the family was there. In Winnipeg, they visited friends and had a meeting. After they finished their visit with the Fitz family in Fairmont, Minnesota, they went on to Fargo, North Dakota…and another meeting. There they said goodbye to Frank. He got on the train going to Seattle where Margo and Irma met him. She was so happy to see him–it had been almost a month. Irma and she had talked non-stop. Margo said she was so fascinated with all Irma's stories of China. They laughed... then fixed the best Chinese food she had ever eaten...she was having a wonderful time. Irma was teaching summer school, so Margo drove the Volkswagen and dropped her off at Ravenna Elementary; then she went on to class at SPC, and picked Irma up on their way home. They had many wonderful talks together and had become very close. After Frank got back, they took picnics, or ate out, and started planning for Margo's senior year, including her own senior recital. Frank had already started the process of getting a teaching contract, before he left with his mom and dad on deputation, and some of the responses had started coming in. He narrowed his choices down to two: Goodman Junior High in Gig Harbor, and Kent Junior High in Kent, just south of Seattle. Graduates of SPC from both schools had contacted Frank; they knew of his musical reputation, and both were offering competitive salaries, and both had outstanding musical programs; but, Frank didn't want to be that far from Margo and the SPC campus, and Kent was offering a stipend for conducting the pep band for football and basketball games. In the end, he chose Kent. This was 1966, and he made a whopping forty-eight hundred dollars per year salary...plus the stipend of four hundred dollars for the pep band, which brought it to a total of fifty-two hundred dollars, and that was more than Gig Harbor could offer...plus they were a ferry ride away, more than a one-hundred-mile round-trip. He also planned to keep his minister of music position at Highland Park Nazarene which was only a twenty-minute drive from Kent. Having made the decision on where he would teach, he decided to take Margo to see the apartment he had found near Highland Park Nazarene; he had found an inexpensive one-bedroom apartment in Burien, less than two miles from the church. During his senior year, Rev. Dean Dace had suggested that he become a licensed minister in the Church of the Nazarene; it would help him in his music career, and it certainly would help the church. The church had voted unanimously to sponsor Frank, the application was completed, and approved at the District Assembly. Frank preached a few times at Highland Park, primarily for the Sunday evening 7:00 service, and Margo played for the service. She had grown up a Methodist and wasn't sure she knew how to play in the 'gospel style,' but she had fun learning; soon she switched to the organ, and she, and the church pianist, Shirley, played together–to the delight of all. They called them the Highland Park 'Don Hustad and Tedd Smith' (of Billy Graham Crusades fame). Margo approved of his choice of apartments and he paid the deposit. They also took time to enroll for the fall quarter at SPC, and paid the deposit for her stay in Hill Hall again. The old Buick had given out, and Frank had traded it in on a blue Toyota. They went on several dates to Golden Gardens, a beach that faced the Olympic Peninsula. It was so beautiful at sunset, and they liked to go there often. When they got back for supper, Irma said she'd heard from Beth and Michael. They were in eastern Washington, and would be arriving tomorrow night. The summer was almost over and they had to get back to Taiwan. The next night, Beth, Michael, and Dave showed up in time for supper. They showed them their pictures...some of them with Frank in Sumner–where they had lived before going to China; also, High Prairie, Regina, and several other places they had visited after Franklin left on the train. The next day, Frank drove them to Kent to see his new school assignment, and then to Burien to show them his apartment. It was a tearful goodbye, but they knew God was with Frank, and would be with them also, as they completed the work in Taiwan to which God had called them. Frank couldn't believe Dave was now going into third grade at Bethany in Taiwan, and would soon be going to Morrison like the rest of them! They flew out the next day, and later wrote that they had arrived safely. School started at Kent Junior High. Even though Frank wore a coat and tie, he looked so young, people at the office tried to send him to class, because they thought he was a student! Bill Deffries, an SPC graduate himself, and vice-principal at Kent, who had hired him, had promised him 'one choir and three bands.' Frank met with the three bands as scheduled, but asked Bill where the choir was. "Oh, you have to organize that," he was told. Frank's jaw dropped. [He'd been a music education major, but was not really a band person. His expertise had always been choral-vocal, even though he had played trumpet ('meagerly' he always said), even into college...and he had been in the Chamber Orchestra, conducted by Winifred Leighton, with whom he had studied instrumental conducting]. Undaunted, Frank went to the study hall. He said: 'you-you, you-you-and-you' (the whole study-hall), come with me." He selected seventh, eighth, and ninth graders, and checked them out with the teacher there. He told all of them to go to the 'band-choir hall;' they would all be his new choir! He took about twenty-four kids, told each of them which part they would sing...soprano, alto, tenor, or bass...and to the ones that protested, "we can't sing," he told them, "I will teach you, and we'll switch parts later after we test your voice." Many of these were his ninth-grade band students...who could already read music anyway, since some of them also sang in church choirs. He started with the fundamentals, taught them the basics of choral singing: balance, blend, projection, sight reading, and vowell-modification. They were inspired and worked hard. By Thanksgiving, they sang for a school assembly, 'Jesu Joy Of Man's Desiring.' By Christmas, they had elected officers, purchased uniforms, and sung a full concert of both classical and favorite Christmas songs; they visited nursing homes; they registered for the region competition, where they performed for a committee of judges; this included: Rodney Eichenberger, head of choral music at the University of Washington (with whom Frank later studied for his doctorate in music), Barbara Reeder, also of UW, and Neil Laurance, Western Washington University, representing the Puget Sound Choral Conductors Guild, (which had granted Frank their annual scholarship in 1965). They sang a Bach chorale, 'From Heaven Above' ('Von Himmel Auf'), unaccompanied in four-parts. When they were finished, Barbara Reeder came down to talk to them; she said it was 'highly unusual for a junior high choir to sing a cappella, begin with a pitch pipe, and sing as accomplished as they did.' In the past, the best any Kent Junior High choral group had ever done was a III (3), but the judges had voted two to one that they receive a One (1), the top rating. Stan Haynes, who was the Kent Schools music superintendent, and Kent-Meridian High School choral director, came down to talk to Frank. He said he was very happy to have Kent Junior High represent the district so well, and he was proud that Frank had come to Kent as their music director; then he pulled Frank aside to tell him, confidentially, that the Kent-Meridian High School choral position was coming open the following year; he could no longer do *both* jobs, and he had been asked to be the music superintendent full-time. Frank asked him if that meant he was offering him the Kent-Meridian High School choral position? He said he was, but of course they would have to go through the 'selection process' first. He said he was the one who would make the final decision though (and he could assure Frank that he would be the one chosen). Frank did not tell him at that time (but his plans were to marry Margo Moore in June and accept the position of music director with Overseas Radio and TV, Inc. and go to Taiwan as missionaries). He couldn't wait to tell Margo...he also reasoned that his draft board would be classifying him IA (One-A), within a few months; the Vietnam War was at its height. He and Margo would have to raise their own monthly support, and ship passage, after they got married. He talked briefly to Rod Eichenberger and Neil Laurance; Barbara Reeder introduced him to them. He told Rod that if he ever had the chance, he would love to study with him at the University of Washington...he said he had heard such great things about him. Then he called Margo to tell her the good news. Frank was spending almost every evening at SPC. [After getting something to eat at Gwinn Commons or the SUB with her, he would do lesson-planning, and reviewed music, while she studied at the library; then he would drive the twenty miles back to Burien Gardens to his apartment, catch a few hours of sleep, and then get up and drive, through morning traffic, to school]. He left one afternoon before dinner to go see Margo; but suddenly he 'threw a rod'... right on the Alaskan Viaduct. He somehow managed to get it out of traffic, and a tow-truck came along and towed him to a 'used car dealership.' He called Irma to see if Ron could give him a ride, but Ron said there 'wasn't anything they could do.' The guy at the used car dealership said he couldn't give him anything for the Toyota, but it *had good tires*, and he would give him 'an old ranch wagon...straight across...the Toyota, with its tires...take it or leave it.' Frank had no choice. The back was full of tree cuttings and leaves; he looked like a farmer in an old car. He had to park it on a slope and 'pop the clutch,' to get it started. When he showed up to take Margo out... (they were supposed to go to Golden Gardens that weekend), she laughed, "I'm not getting in that rattle-trap," she said (but she did). They got some fish and chips at the Windjammer, near Golden Gardens, and parked just above the beach like they often did. It was Saturday, and the sunset was breathtaking as usual; Frank made sure he parked on an incline so he could start the car again. After they ate their fish and chips, and enjoyed the sunset awhile together, Margo reminded him that the in-hour, even on weekends, for women at Hill Hall, was 10:00. What? He couldn't believe it was already almost 9:30. They broke their embrace, and Frank went to start the car…but the car didn't start. He couldn't 'pop the clutch' if it didn't even turn over; he turned everything else off, turned the key…nothing. He let it roll down the slope anyway, and popped the clutch. It rolled down the slope… but nothing happened. Now Margo was getting upset. It was almost 10:00, and she would get in trouble if she came in even five minutes late. Frank had an idea. He walked next door to the Windjammer, and called Wes, who was now head dorm proctor…he would help them. Wes laughed, and said something about 'lover boy and his girl,' but Frank let it go; he said he needed his help…he wasn't kidding. Wes came and got them, and informed Hill dorm proctor, Jerry Donahue (yes Jerry, who said, 'I might have known,' since it was Frank and Margo *again*). They were going to be late, and Wes said he had approved it… because it really *was* car trouble. They left the car there, with a note on it. Wes took them back to campus. Margo made it back to Hill by 10:30, and Wes said he would take them both in the morning; he knew Margo was supposed to play for the service too, right? Frank could sleep in the other bed in his room…since Wes didn't have a roommate at that time. Frank called Margo, and told her the plan. In the morning, Wes took them to Highland Park, telling Frank he'd have to get Margo a ride back to campus on his own, and go get Frank's car later; getting to and from school might be a 'bigger chore.' They had a good service, and Rev. Dace, and his wife Loretta, talked to several friends about Frank's transportation problem. Glen Embree and his wife, Sharon; Percy Dean, and his wife, Dorothy; and Frank and Margo, 'should all get together sometime.' Margo and Frank stayed to lead the evening service. Frank had called Larry Overstreet, who was in charge of scheduling gospel teams at SPC, and asked him which team 'might possibly be in the West Seattle area that day.' Larry said, in fact, the Ambassadors–Margo's old gospel team–had been at a Baptist church that morning in West Seattle, and was singing at their evening service that night as well. 'God works wonders doesn't he, Larry,' Frank said, and told him what had happened. Larry and the team, swung by Highland Park that evening, met Rev. Dace, and some of the congregation, after their service; they took Margo back to the campus.

Margo said she was praying that Frank would work something out… about *getting to Kent in the morning.* Glen and Sharon were standing there and overheard Margo. What *about* Kent in the morning? Frank explained to Glen about the car, and Glen offered to take him and pick him up, and drop him off, *for a couple days…* until he could get another car. True to his word, Glen stopped by for him, took him to school, in Kent, and then stopped by for him that afternoon… Glen sold insurance, so his time was not really committed; after a couple days, Frank was supposed to have contacted a car dealership, but he was having a hard time figuring out how he was going to finance something that would 'last more than a few months.' [His brother-in-law, Alan, had convinced him he 'couldn't go wrong on a Buick,' but during Frank's student teaching, he started having to put transmission fluid in, at the bottom of Magnolia hill…just to get to the top…and this ended up being every morning, before he traded it in on the Toyota, which only lasted six months]. He needed someone to help him. He prayed; he had Margo pray with him. Now Glen had told him he couldn't keep doing it daily, 'just let him know…but only if he couldn't find another car soon.' A couple days later…after school, he saw his friend, Melissa, the English teacher; he asked her where she lived, and if she could give him a lift to his apartment in Burien. She said "sure, hop in, I'll take you home." He told her it was Burien, where did she live? He told her he didn't want to impose on her. She told him it was *no problem.* They got to his apartment, he thanked her…and got out of the car. She shut off the motor, then got out too. She said, "Hey, I want to see your apartment," and followed him upstairs. He opened the door and laughed, "Well, this is my humble abode." She came in and sat down, so he offered her a coke. He sat down too and they started talking. After a while, she scooted over, took the coke out of his hands…put it on the coffee table…and put her arms around him…it was obvious she was offering 'more than just a ride home.' He pulled back; he told her he was engaged to Margo, and they were going to be married in June; she said that didn't matter to her. He stood up; he said he was sorry if he had said anything that led her to believe he wanted anything else but a *ride.* He offered to pay her for the gas. She smiled, and looked inside the bedroom… then she went to the door. Frank said he hoped this wouldn't ruin their 'professional-only' relationship. She promised she wouldn't tell Mr. Deffries ...or anyone else. As she left, he told her he *needed to tell Margo* what had happened; he told her it was his fault... he shouldn't have imposed on her; she left. Frank called Margo right away; she reassured him he had done nothing wrong, and thanked him for telling her about it. Then Frank called Dean, who told him, as his pastor, that there would be many who might try to break them up, but God would keep him strong. Dean suggested Frank call Glen about getting a car, and have Glen call him, that he knew someone at the bank that might help them. Glen took him to school the next day... but when he picked him up at Kent Junior High in the afternoon, they went straight to the Burien branch of Seattle First National Bank; Dean met them there, and Glen introduced Frank to James Harper, the branch manager; Glen had already stopped by the Buick dealer in Burien to talk to his friend, Joe Strong. They handled Opel...and Buick, and he said he had found a sky-blue Opel Kadett that he thought Frank would like. He laughed and said, "I had to go ahead and do this for you...I can't continue to take you every morning, and fetch you every afternoon; besides how can you date Margo... with me driving." They all laughed. Frank was so embarrassed, but were very grateful. Dean and Glen were so good to him...and God had answered his prayer. Dean said he would make him a deal: the church would advance Frank the down-payment, and then take back a little each month from his church pay-check. Joe, at Seattle First, had agreed to make the loan... on the word of the church, and make the monthly payment low enough, that Frank could handle it. Frank almost cried he was so grateful. He didn't *call* Margo, he just *showed up* in his new *CAR*. It was nothing fancy, but it would last...at least until they got married, go on their deputation trip, and get on a ship going to Taiwan. She was thrilled. It didn't need to be fancy, or sporty, she said...it was 'functional' and it would make them look 'international,' even sort of 'European.' They went to Golden Gardens to retrieve the Ranch Wagon...but it was gone. It had been impounded by the police for auction they reasoned. He hadn't seen Melissa for a few days, so when he ran into her in the faculty lounge, he discreetly tried to avoid her, but she came over to him and said loudly, for the whole room to hear: "Frank, I heard the choir's doing really well; hey, I wanted to let you know that my boyfriend, Jim, asked me to marry him;" she flashed her ring for everyone to see, but Frank thought she was sending him a message that 'she wasn't on the prowl' anymore. It turned out she was *not* engaged at all, and she didn't renew her contract after Jim got her pregnant...she went back to graduate school! The rest of the year went fast. Frank's pep band played for all of the football games, and then for the basketball games as well. Even though Frank was able to get his choir the first 'One' rating ever, the best his bands–all three, could manage were 'Two's.' Kent-Meridian High School posted the choral director position, so Frank went to see Stan Haynes; he told him he was so honored to be offered the choral position at Kent-Meridian, but he had been called to be a missionary and would be doing radio and television ministry in Taiwan, after Margo and he got married. Stan was disappointed, but he said he himself was Minister of Music at Auburn First Baptist, and knew Frank was a Christian; he couldn't blame him for answering God's call.

Margo was working hard on her senior recital. She was taking eighteen hours in her last quarter, and she had been nominated for Homecoming Queen...she was very busy. Her parents had moved to Wenatchee, Washington, the previous year, and they had invited Frank to spend time with them, whenever Margo and he came to visit, and they had fixed up a room in the back of the house. It was kind of their "junk room" and the slats in the bed had fallen out, never mind that the boxes of apples that they kept there had gone a "little ripe." Hey, it was a warm bed, and their warm hospitality made up for it (actually, it reminded Frank of the first trip to Idaho that the Victory Quartet had made, with the slats in the bed gone... but no bumble bees here, Ha!) [His first visit was actually the most memorable. Francis had sold the farm in Michigan the previous summer, and he had loaded a trailer full of whatever they couldn't sell; the trailer must not have been packed very well; it swayed back and forth all the way to Wenatchee...days and days of going less than fifty miles per hour; they had bought a house above the Columbia River on Sunnyslope from a Seventh-Day Adventist pastor, Rev. Lewis Peters; they arrived on a Saturday forgetting that they would not be allowed to unload! The pastor let them pitch a tent and sleep in the back yard; this is where they were resting when Margo and Frank arrived (Wilma and Francis had returned to Michigan after the engagement dinner in June of 1966, sold the farm, and then arrived in Wenatchee two months later). There would be room for Margo to stay in the tent, but it wouldn't be 'permissible' for Frank to stay in the pastor's house, or in the tent...but where would Frank stay? 'Sorry Charlie, you'll have to figure that one out yourself!' Frank had *three bucks* in his pocket...even then, you couldn't get a room for that. Sleep on a park bench? Someone help him cash a check on Saturday afternoon after banks were closed? Margo pleaded to no avail. Frank said he would figure something out and left; he tried several places, but none of them would take a check, and no 'credit cards' in those days. He finally found a room above a bar in downtown Wenatchee; no supper, paying his three bucks up front, he tried to sleep. The noise and smell from the bar kept him up until it closed; then the sound of breaking empty liquor bottles did it...he wasn't going to be able to sleep...thinking someone might stagger upstairs and mug him. He was glad when Sunday morning arrived, but rather than going to church, he waited until nine o'clock, and then went up to Sunnyslope to see if they had started unloading...he'd had no supper or breakfast, but Rev. Peters wouldn't even let Frank go around the house to their tent. Francis heard the commotion, and he and Margo showed up in the driveway. Francis was an 'old Scotsman,' and took exception to any perceived unfairness. He came unglued, telling Rev. Peters how he had driven days to get there, had to wait all day to unload, and now his daughter's fiancé *couldn't even join them* for some fruit and instant coffee? Then Wilma arrived and calmed Francis down; but now Margo had also 'stepped into the fray.' In the end, Rev. Peters told them they could start unloading everything in the family room and patio. He hadn't meant to offend, he said; they were supposed to be moved out before the Moore's arrived, but the people helping them move hadn't shown up the previous week. After everything calmed down a little, Frank told them how bad it *really* had been...no supper or sleep the night before in downtown Wenatchee...did anyone know where he could cash a check? His car was now riding on empty (this was the blue Toyota, before the Opel Kadett). After they were all moved in... and the Peters had moved out of course, things settled down. Francis and Wilma later got involved in the Wenatchee Methodist Church. Wilma got a teaching job, and taught at Sunnyslope Elementary for three years, and then joined Francis in retirement. They also found the local CFO ('Camps Farthest Out') in which they had been active in Michigan (this was a camping and retreat program for developing a deeper personal spiritual life). Margo and Frank came to Wenatchee several times during her senior year...Thanksgiving, Christmas, and other special weekends].

Now it was time for her senior recital, planning their wedding at the Wenatchee Methodist Church, and doctors' examinations for both Margo and Frank. She spent hours practicing piano, especially the Schumann 'Davidsbüundler,' an eighteen-section cycle, similar to the 'song cycle' that Frank had performed for *his* senior recital, and several other classical and contemporary works; and she had to have the whole thing memorized (the same as Frank's recital). They went to Dr. Frederick Strach for their pre-marital exams. Dr. Strach discovered a small heart murmur for Frank, but he said he didn't think it was of any serious consequence; he also examined Margo and found her to be well, both generally, and as to any 'female' health issue. He prescribed birth control pills, which he said she should start taking a month before they married. They returned to Seattle, and now all she had to do was: *finish eighteen academic hours, memorize a senior recital, and take birth control pills...* which nauseated her. She hadn't made the 'homecoming court,' but she was honored to have even been nominated. Wilma and she spent weeks planning the wedding... buying her wedding dress, deciding on the bridesmaids' dresses, arranging for the cake, reception, and all the myriad details of the ceremony, including booking the church, and arranging for cousins and friends to have places to stay when they came to Wenatchee...one hundred fifty miles from Seattle. At one point, she was so overwhelmed she told Frank, "I can't take anymore, let's just elope," and burst into tears; Frank told the Moore's they wouldn't be back for supper...he took her out to 'dinner' to Smitty's and ordered *breakfast*. Frank knew a blueberry-pancake-breakfast would calm her down. Sure enough, after eating breakfast, and taking her to their favorite view of the Columbia above Wenatchee, she was 'ready for anything.' On their way back, Frank stopped in front of the church and prayed. They arrived back at the house with smiles on their faces. They were ready to finish the quarter, the recital, and the wedding. Wilma met them at the door; she looked quizzically at them but said nothing; she smiled and squeezed their hands...it would be fine. The night of the senior recital, Margo was very nervous. She waited a long time before she could get herself out on stage. About ten minutes after the scheduled start time, she walked out on stage, sat down and played the opening Bach piece flawlessly; she played the Mendelssohn piece with great sensitivity, and after accepting the warm applause, walked quickly off stage. She stayed in the lady's room so long that Frank finally asked one of their mutual friends to go check on her. She came out…but nothing anyone could say could get her to go back out on stage. Frank finally figured it out…it must be the Schumann piece she was so nervous about. She had spent most of her practice time on it, and she felt the most unsure of it; he took her hands; they were icy cold…he rubbed them vigorously; her muscles were like iron bands. Finally, he prayed with her, asking God to allow her to let go of everything, and place it in God's hands. He whispered in her ear, "it's not for your teacher, it's for *you* and all of us…your *fans*, God loves you, and so do I." Then he literally pushed her out on stage, past the curtain. She walked to the piano as people clapped; she looked back… but Frank made her keep walking to the bench. She sat down…and began to play; Frank knew that if she could get past the first five pieces, she would have it. As she played, he thought, "I have never heard her play with such sensitivity." She finished the last twelve pieces with a flourish! The final section ended with the contemporary Hoiby piece, and she finally relaxed and even looked like she enjoyed herself. When she finished, the audience burst into applause. She sat there a moment, and then stood to receive the ovation. At the reception, Marcile Mack was 'proud but reserved' in her praise. Frank did not like this, and steered her quickly away to her parents, friends and family. The Highland Park folks had come, and they were wild in their enthusiasm… Irma and Tom were there and overjoyed; Margo finally relaxed…she was among friends and family. It didn't matter that her piano teacher was holding back…because, nobody else was! Graduation and the weeks leading up to the wedding were a blur. Margo's dad had addressed all the invitations by hand. Aunts, Uncles, and Cousins came. Auntie Ruth, Wilma's sister, arrived, and made the wedding cake. The organist couldn't come at the last minute, and Margo panicked… until one of her bridesmaids, Gayle Moran, suggested …herself! She could do it; so, Margo chose another to be a bridesmaid; what a God-send. Margo always thought of Gayle as a great vocalist, or pianist, but having Gayle play organ was one of her dreams come true. [All Frank's plans were set–a private cabin near Hurricane Ridge for their honeymoon spot… the place where his family always stayed, compliments of a preacher friend, Rev. Wilson Lieby in Port Angeles; plans also included going to Victoria, B.C., to see Butchart Gardens…]. After the wedding rehearsal, and rehearsal dinner in the Moore's back yard, Frank and his groomsmen–all members of the quartet–stayed together; Margo, and Carol, her maid of honor, three bridesmaids, and Gayle, all stayed at the Moore's (Doug Bartlett, assisting minister for the wedding, and bass in the quartet, arrived the next day. Wes Anderson, Neil Craig, and Glenn Bowerman, and Frank 'cut up all night' at the Apple Inn, and then had breakfast together at Smitty's in the morning. They took pictures *before* the ceremony, while Gayle practiced. Frank Whitt, the Wenatchee Methodist associate pastor, filled Doug in, after his arrival (he had to do another wedding in Oregon that morning), and Jackie Pratt, and Bev Buob, met Carol Simpson, maid of honor (also Margo's best friend from Michigan);they all got dressed, then took more pictures. It was a great ceremony, including Frank singing 'Ich Liebe Dich' to Margo, before her dad walked her down the aisle. Margo and Frank sang 'Wedding Prayer' to each other, and took communion… just the two of them; they also had a recorded prayer from Frank's dad in Taiwan (since his parents could not be there, his two maternal aunts, Irma and Maxine, stood in their place). When it was all over, the quartet sang for the reception at the church; then they had the punch and cut the wedding cake. After greeting all their guests, the wedding party, and extended family, went up to the Moore's house for more to eat and fellowship. Frank and Margo left for Bellevue… …but wait, there's more! They had a *flat tire* just one mile from their hotel! Still in his tuxedo, Frank changed the tire; and they showed up with the decorated car, his hands all greasy and dirty, and Margo still in her wedding dress, at the hotel in Bellevue, to the laughs and well wishes of the other hotel guests! The next day…before they went to their cabin near Hurricane Ridge, they had breakfast at Denny's. He told their server they had just gotten married, and that 'today' was his *birthday*. His server said, "Oh, today is your birthday, too? What would you *like* for your birthday?" Without batting an eyelash, Frank looked at Margo, and said, "I already got it yesterday!" The server laughed and started singing, "Happy Birthday and Wedding to you, Happy Birthday and Wedding to you" …by this time, everyone in the restaurant joined in, "Happy Birthday and Wedding to you, Happy Birthday and Wedding to you." It was so beautiful, Frank asked her if she had had any training…turns out she was a *voice major* at the University of Washington, a transfer student from Michigan State–she was putting herself through college by waiting on tables, but hoping to get a scholarship. Margo brightened; from Michigan? Then they both held up their palms…like all 'Mishi-ganders' do, to show each other where they're from on their hands; her name was Berta Doerne, and she pointed to the part of her hand where Grand Rapids was…she had to turn in their order, but not before Margo showed her where Quincy was, near Coldwater! And Grand Rapids was close by! What are the chances? They ate, and waited for her to come back, but it was the end of her shift (she had been there all night), and unfortunately, she had to leave. They cleaned up their car and took the Kingston Ferry from Edmonds, and drove up to Lake Dawn to their cabin. Frank had made arrangements with Rev. Lieby to leave the key in the same place as always, and they went in. Frank had to show off–he got up early the next morning, took the boat out and caught three silver trout for breakfast. Margo didn't think she'd like 'fish for breakfast' but she had to admit it was tasty with bacon and eggs…the way Frank fixed it anyway. They had a wonderful time, and stopped to thank God for bringing them together for a lifetime together… marriage, family and ministry. After three days, they took the Blackball Ferry to Victoria, saw Butchart Gardens, and then took the ferry at Nanaimo across to Vancouver, and stayed with Frank's Uncle Joe and Aunt Josie. They returned to Wenatchee for a short visit with Margo's folks before they started new jobs in Seattle. Frank had resigned from Kent Junior High. Percy Dean, who used to be a pastor in the Nazarene Church now had a successful construction business, and Dean Dace had recommended Frank to Percy…for a job in construction; it was to be just until Frank and Margo could go on a 'deputation trip' and raise their funds for their ship passage, and monthly support, with Overseas Radio & TV. Glen Embree knew someone with Coast Mortgage in downtown Seattle, and Margo was hired there as an administrative assistant.

Overseas Radio had an office in Seattle, and Frank and Margo were able to meet with their board there. They interviewed them and approved them, subject to raising the necessary 'support and ship passage.' Frank had received a letter from his draft board...sure enough, changing his status to IA ('One-A'), which many guys, in those days of the Vietnam War, called 'the death sentence;' he was to report to his draft board, and 'make arrangements for a physical examination prior to being assigned to 'boot camp.' Frank called the ORTV office and told them he had to have a 'letter of appointment' immediately; he would take it with him to his draft board to show them he qualified for a deferment as a 'church religious worker.' They were happy to do this, and Frank drove to Bellevue to pick it up personally. He met with his draft board representative the next Monday. The rep was easy going, but asked him a lot of questions about his background, upbringing, education, and 'church stuff.' What would he be doing, 'how was radio and television work in Taiwan a church ministry,' and what about his wife, his parents, and the schools he had attended in Taiwan? Finally, he smiled...*deferred* he said, and stamped his registration booklet. Frank breathed a sigh of relief, and called Margo. She had started her job at Coast Mortgage, which was only a mile away, so he picked up lunch for her at a Pike Place Market seafood place; they had lunch, and then he reported for his first day with Dean Construction in Belleview. It was very hard work. He had to dig down to the footing and put in the drainage around each newly framed-up house. He was exhausted every evening the first week, and he had a hard time getting up in the morning because he was so sore. He and Margo still did the music at Highland Park every Sunday too. Overseas Radio gave them a 'promotional film' they could use to introduce their work in Taiwan, but was unable to book any churches for them. Frank and Margo started writing letters, calling family in Canada and the U.S., and had a 'prayer card' printed up for the promotion of their ministry. They saved what they could for the car payment, the rent, and living expenses, but they were going to have to stay with friends and family on their 'trip' because they didn't have anything left for meals and lodging. Three months after their wedding, they quit their jobs, and 'went on the road.' In faith, Frank called and booked tentative departure on the SS Washington Mail for December 20, 1967...for Taiwan...but they only had *one* service booked, and seventy dollars in travelers checks; that service was Calgary First Church of the Nazarene; when they got there, the Zumwalt's, old friends of the family, the ones that had agreed to the service, had left town. The pastor, Rev. Hermann L.G. Smith was gracious; and he was an old family friend. The service went well, and Frank and Margo received an offering of: two pledges for monthly support of ten dollars each, and twenty dollars in cash, for ship passage. Rev. Smith, assuming they had lodging with the Zumwalt's, prayed with them and left. Frank called Elmer Zumwalt, son of Myron. He said he was 'happy to hear that Frank and his new bride were in town; no, he had had to work and couldn't come to the service; no, he wouldn't be able to have them come over, or stay with him; he was leaving town… maybe next time?' Frank thought…'and you agreed to the service; but you can't host us? Frank didn't want to spend the ship passage money' he needed to find a cheap room, and by this time, he's thinking Margo must be wondering what kind of a "crazy person had she married?" They found a room…guess where? Above a *bar* again. It smelled of disinfectant, it was loud downstairs…at least until they closed; the bed sank to the floor in the middle, but it had a warm comforter, recently laundered, and smelled fresh; they slept well, and only paid five dollars for it—'hey, better than Motel 6,' and they had a few bucks for breakfast at a little cafe across the street! They drove to Regina, and Juli and Larry welcomed them into their little trailer. Frank wondered if they would even have room for them, but Juli showed them a couch that folded out, and they had a great visit. Juli had arranged for a service in the United Church of Canada in Regina, but it turned out to be only a chance to talk to their Sunday School class, and a place in the Worship service, at the announcement time, for Frank to tell them about the Radio and TV work they would be doing…and to pass out their prayer card. So…nice visit, no offering or support, but Juli said she thought Uncle Bud and Helen, Jim and Ollie, and 'maybe' Margaret, might help them, but they were already giving what they could to Michael and Beth in Taiwan, and they gave that through Joe, who ran the VOCA office in Vancouver…out of his own home. They had dinner with Pop and Novenka. Bud and Helen, Jim and Ollie, and Margaret came into town from Balgonie to see Frank 'and his new bride;' they all stopped by, but didn't stay to eat. They had a great visit with Pop and Novenka. He said he liked Frank's wife, 'Margit,' and that she reminded him of his first wife, Juliana, Michael's mother, and he started to cry again. He told Margo stories of growing up in Hungary, raising the family in Canada, and…and…his voice trailed off. Novenka gave Margo some of her famous pickles and some sweets, and they returned to Juli's and Larry's. Debbie, her three-year-old, loved singing with Uncle Frank, and so they sang, "If we all will pull together." She was little, so Frank knelt down to be on her level, but then she knelt down…because 'Ugga Swank,' and 'Ugga Maggo' did it; they laughed, and then Juli called them all to breakfast. Margo and Frank left feeling good about their visit with the family, but there had been no progress toward their goal. Margo said she disagreed; how could they minister in Taiwan before she got to know his family? They probably would have the same situation when they got to Michigan with *her* family. Connections were important… and she wouldn't have it any other way. Frank said, "Come to think of it, we've got to let God do this, instead of me worrying about it." He smiled, and pretended to slap his own face – 'thanks, I needed that.' She tried to tickle him, and he acted like he was going to run off the road. They crossed back into the U.S. in Minnesota, and came over into Wisconsin at Duluth. After they had something to eat there, they drove until it was late. They stopped for the night in Ironwood, just into northern Michigan. They drove across Mackinaw bridge, to Traverse City; Margo wanted them to visit Interlocken music camp, where she had been on staff and a camper during her high school years. They had lunch there and then worked their way down to Battle Creek and Marshall, where Frank met some of Margo's family, Aunt Nina and her cousin Harley. Margo had made arrangements to stay with her parents' good friends: Harold and Gloria Gates, their longtime neighbors, and spiritual brother and sister with CFO. They welcomed them warmly and allowed them to use their place as a base for visiting friends and relatives. Frank met many of Margo's family in the area, visited the farm, and the young man and woman, and children, who had bought it [a fire destroyed everything, a neighbor bought it, leased for crops]. Many friends and family were impressed with the idea that Margo and Frank would go to Taiwan as radio and television missionaries, but only a couple of meetings, and meager cash offerings and monthly pledges were obtained. Margo said she wanted Frank to meet just one more friend, before they left for Kentucky (to visit Margi and Alan); she said they needed to see Bert and Vita Wilson, and their son Bill Wilson, who still pastored the Baptist church where Margo had first made her profession of faith at age eight. After a quick visit. Bert, Vita, and Bill, they said they wanted to gift them thirty dollars, and both Bill and his parents made monthly pledges of twenty dollars each. They said they would promote it in their church...and more support might come in later. They prayed with them, and then Frank and Margo headed out for Louisville, Kentucky to see Margi and Alan at the Southern Baptist Seminary. They arrived in time for supper. Margi and Alan lived in married students housing on the seminary campus. Like Juli, they had one bedroom and a couch that folded out. They insisted that Frank and Margo take the bedroom. The problem was: the only bathroom they had...was just off of the bedroom. Four people used the same bathroom! And the couch they used took most of the living-dining area, so there was barely enough room for the table, and their small kitchen barely had enough room to fix meals. Alan was generous and suggested they eat their meals out, but breakfast was still 'interesting.' They were fairly conflicted as a newly married couple, and Alan made no bones about the fact that he had gone to seminary, and had become a Baptist minister [his parents had been Baptist missionaries in Hong Kong], solely *to avoid the draft*. He wanted to 'educate everyone' on his new liberal theology. Margi and he argued, but she did not want them to do this openly, so she was continually escaping to the bathroom with him to argue, not realizing that Frank and Margo could hear most of what they were saying anyway. Since both were very stubborn about their own views, this might go on sometimes for very 'extended periods,' and Frank and Margo knew Margi was embarrassed. But in the end, it was a fun visit, and they all went down to Mammoth Caves in central Kentucky near Park City. They drove down there, toured the caves and stayed overnight, sharing a room at Motel 6. Margi said they wouldn't be able to send any support, but would ask others at the seminary to remember them and pray for them, and took some of their prayer cards...some support might come out of it. Margi said she planned to finish her undergraduate degree after Alan went on to graduate school, but it might have to wait until after the Vietnam War. Alan helped with pastoral duties in some Baptist churches; he reported this to his draft board. They said goodbye and headed for Wilmore, home of Asbury College and Seminary. Frank's good friend from Morrison, Jon Culver, had married and he and Judith were teaching in a high school in Indiana, not far from his parents; Weldon and Sylvia Culver had been Overseas Crusades missionaries in Taiwan, and Sylvia was now the executive secretary for the Asbury College President. Frank wanted to see them at Asbury before Weldon passed away—Welden was in the last stages of cancer. Sylvia was finishing the day in her office and came home to visit with Frank and Margo who were already visiting with Weldon. It was a short but very inspiring time. Weldon wasn't expected to live more than a few weeks. Frank prayed with them. There were tears, but a great sense of hope and triumph knowing Weldon would be going 'home' and would see many of his fellow missionary friends and family. Weldon followed them out to the car. He told Frank to fill his car with gas, and handed him a five-dollar bill. He said he didn't have anything to give them for support or boat passage, but he wanted to do what he could. Frank accepted it with gratitude. 'This will get us one step closer to Taiwan, and I know that is what you want, Weldon; God love you for this.' They drove on to Jon and Judy's in Milan, Indiana. They were getting back from their school day as Frank and Margo arrived. Judy asked if it would be alright if they grabbed something to eat over at the high school. They told them they had agreed to be chaperones at the Milan High School dance that night… maybe they could visit at the dance? Good idea thought Frank…until they got there and discovered the music was SO loud, they couldn't even hear each other talking above the din. They laughed and waited until the dance was over, went to their house and had some ice cream and pie Judy had made. Jon and Frank reminisced about Morrison, while Margo and Judy got to know each other. They asked about what they would be doing with Doris Brougham and Leland Haggerty… and his family in Taiwan. Jon and Frank had been roommates and went to school with the Haggerty children. Then Jon and Judy pledged a surprisingly generous monthly amount, given the fact that they were living on teachers' salaries and were already supporting other mission outreaches. Jon said, "My dad taught me the importance of missions, and God may yet lay it on our hearts to serve as missionaries ourselves someday." [Jon and Judy years later *did* serve as missionaries for years in Indonesia]. Frank and Margo were moved almost to tears. They thanked them and blessed their work in the school and their church there in Milan. In the morning, they had breakfast before Jon and Judy went to class, and Frank and Margo got back on the road. This time they headed to Minnesota. It was already November, and they were planning to spend Thanksgiving at a 'Fitz reunion' in Fairmont, Minnesota. Frank had written Aunt Pearl, his maternal aunt who was the wife of Frank's late Great-Uncle Dudley. [Aunt Pearl was kind, and sort of a 'favorite aunt,' who had written Frank in college...in the course of things, had taught him a valuable lesson: she enclosed a small check from time to time..."to help with your college expenses." Frank was very appreciative, but like many young *immature* college students, he told all his friends, "Wow, look what my Aunt Pearl sent me," without writing back and thanking *her!* She didn't write for a long time; when she did, she did *not* enclose any money (one of the great things about her was that she was not only very kind, she was also not afraid to speak her mind...when appropriate). She wrote Frank, saying, "My dear nephew, Franklin, I would like to pass on some advice to you. I have written to you, and often sent you something to help you with your college experience; I am very happy to do so, but if you ever thought about it, you would receive a lot more...if you ever learned to say 'thank you.' Frank was very embarrassed, and in the future always wrote her back his sincere appreciation. He learned many valuable lessons from her...he loved to call these: "*Pearls of Wisdom.*"]

When they arrived in Fairmont, Aunt Pearl showed them their room and let them settle in for a little bit; she said dinner would be ready shortly; they came down ready for dinner in a few minutes. She said for them to sit down, she had something she needed to tell them. She told them she had been contacted by her brother-in-law, Dr. Fitz (she always called him Rudolph). He told Pearl the sad news that *Lura had succumbed to the Parkinson's disease* she had had so many years... she had just passed away. Frank was sad, but at the same time, his dear grandmother had suffered so long, he was relieved that she now suffered no more; she was now in heaven with so many other family and friends. Frank and Margo were scheduled to be in Nampa in a couple weeks anyway, and now looked forward even more to staying with Grandad to help comfort and bless him in his loss. They knew he had a great hope of seeing her again. They enjoyed the great meal Aunt Pearl had fixed and looked forward to sharing Thanksgiving with the rest of the family the next day.

The whole Fitz siblings and families met at Clarisse's home (Clarisse was the daughter of Vera and Claire Musser, who was Rudolph's sister). There were members of three, even four, generations of aunts, uncles, and cousins. They all 'loved Margo to death,' as they said, and there was an amazing 'spread' of Thanksgiving food, drink, breads, and desserts. It was sad to see Aunt Vera so advanced in her senility, but she acted as though she remembered 'Franklin,' but she obviously thought he was 'Michael' and kept calling him that, and talked to Margo like she had known her for years, calling her 'Beth.' The others apologized for her, but Frank just hugged her and acted like being 'Michael,' which he actually *was*, was just fine. Margo, who had only spent a few weeks with Beth, was honored for Aunt Vera to keep calling her 'Beth.' After another day of relaxed visiting and going to some of the other Fitz's homes, Frank and Margo were invited to the house of Doris, Uncle Howard's younger daughter. She hosted them for a meal, and they stayed the night. They had a good time, and then left early the next morning for Colorado. They had received a letter from a minister in Denver that had hosted the SPC Ensemble in a summer camp. He had received Frank's prayer card and wanted to help, but they were not in town. He went on to say that he had contacted a pastor who knew of the Overseas Radio and TV ministry, as he did, and wanted to host Frank and Margo for a service. They drove to a lovely little country church near Sterling, Colorado. Country Bible Church was one of the most loving, warm, and mission-minded churches either Frank or Margo had ever been to. They stayed with the pastor, Rev. Ernie Johnson, who knew Doris Brougham and the Heavenly Melody Choir. They were already supporting the ministry, but wanted to add five new families of supporters. Frank and Margo had a wonderful service, and sang and played their music, and spoke of their vision for using music in missionary radio and television. It was cold, and snow covered the ground as well as the roads, but the church was filled. Frank and Margo stayed the night and then drove on to Nampa, Idaho. They drove all day, and pulled in to Grandad's driveway in time for a late supper.

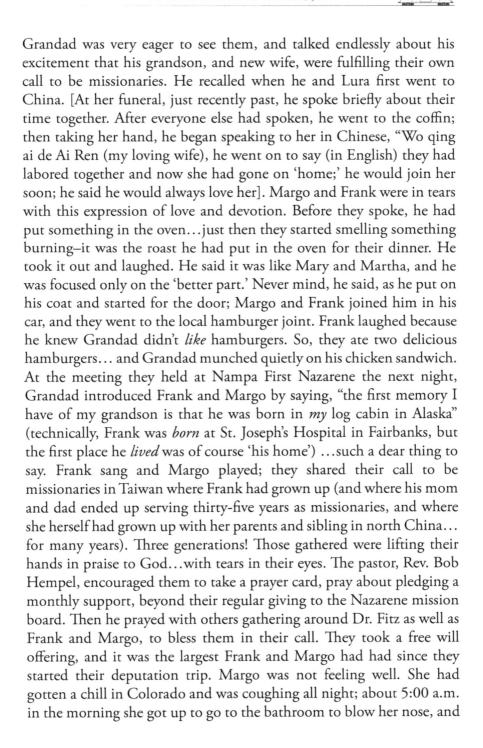

Grandad was very eager to see them, and talked endlessly about his excitement that his grandson, and new wife, were fulfilling their own call to be missionaries. He recalled when he and Lura first went to China. [At her funeral, just recently past, he spoke briefly about their time together. After everyone else had spoken, he went to the coffin; then taking her hand, he began speaking to her in Chinese, "Wo qing ai de Ai Ren (my loving wife), he went on to say (in English) they had labored together and now she had gone on 'home;' he would join her soon; he said he would always love her]. Margo and Frank were in tears with this expression of love and devotion. Before they spoke, he had put something in the oven…just then they started smelling something burning—it was the roast he had put in the oven for their dinner. He took it out and laughed. He said it was like Mary and Martha, and he was focused only on the 'better part.' Never mind, he said, as he put on his coat and started for the door; Margo and Frank joined him in his car, and they went to the local hamburger joint. Frank laughed because he knew Grandad didn't *like* hamburgers. So, they ate two delicious hamburgers… and Grandad munched quietly on his chicken sandwich. At the meeting they held at Nampa First Nazarene the next night, Grandad introduced Frank and Margo by saying, "the first memory I have of my grandson is that he was born in *my* log cabin in Alaska" (technically, Frank was *born* at St. Joseph's Hospital in Fairbanks, but the first place he *lived* was of course 'his home') …such a dear thing to say. Frank sang and Margo played; they shared their call to be missionaries in Taiwan where Frank had grown up (and where his mom and dad ended up serving thirty-five years as missionaries, and where she herself had grown up with her parents and sibling in north China… for many years). Three generations! Those gathered were lifting their hands in praise to God…with tears in their eyes. The pastor, Rev. Bob Hempel, encouraged them to take a prayer card, pray about pledging a monthly support, beyond their regular giving to the Nazarene mission board. Then he prayed with others gathering around Dr. Fitz as well as Frank and Margo, to bless them in their call. They took a free will offering, and it was the largest Frank and Margo had had since they started their deputation trip. Margo was not feeling well. She had gotten a chill in Colorado and was coughing all night; about 5:00 a.m. in the morning she got up to go to the bathroom to blow her nose, and

Dr. Fitz was there (he got up every morning to have his 'devotional time;' he had given up the master bedroom for them, and so when Margo found that he was using the bathroom, she went ahead and used the one in their room. He started to sing, and it scared her; she ran back to the bedroom frightened...Frank couldn't help but laugh. They slept later than usual because they were so worn out from their long trip, and because of Margo's cold. When they finally emerged, Grandad smiled and said he had learned that "the younger generation is ready to rise, about the time that the older generation is ready to retire." They had some breakfast, prayer, and then went on their way again. They drove to Wenatchee; Wilma and Francis were very happy to see them; they had missed having them for Thanksgiving, and so they invited several of their friends, and had 'another Thanksgiving' for Margo and Frank. They stayed there a few days while Frank prepared his report for the ORTV board. They were going to have to postpone their December 20 sailing date. They had about three fourths of their ship passage, and about the same for their monthly pledges. While they were staying with Margo's parents, they took a trip to Seattle and met with the board. They were very excited about the success of their trip, but they had heard from Doris Brougham, who said they were way short. The amount they had raised was close to what the board had authorized, but she said she would ignore the board, and placed an additional amount for them to raise, saying that *half of everything they had raised* 'went to the mission.' Whoops! Thing were not off to a good start. They hadn't helped with any deputation, the board apparently did not have the authority they thought they had, and the communication in the entire matter was lacking. Frank postponed their sailing, and got on the phone, wrote letters, and prayed. Wilma and Francis had good friends in their neighborhood that were members of the Brethren Church in Wenatchee, and *they* agreed to a service; friends from the SPC Ensemble said, 'why didn't you tell us that you needed help in getting to Taiwan,' and they arranged for a service at the Queen Anne Presbyterian Church, in addition to offering a very generous monthly pledge. Frank counted up the offerings and 'cash on hand' again. It was enough to rebook passage after the first of the year. The SS Oregon Mail was leaving January 16, 1968. Frank smiled, hugged Margo, and said, "I'm taking you on a *slow boat to China*," and they danced around the room. Wilma and Francis came running to see what the squeals of delight were all about. It was better this way: they would be able to spend Christmas with Margo's folks! They sang, *"God is so good, God is so good, God is so good, He's so good to me,"* Christmas was bitter-sweet. The Moore's were having to let go of their only child to this 'wild Hungarian,' but in their hearts they trusted God to taken care of them. Francis, who never cried, broke down when they left to go to Seattle to catch their ship. He thought he 'would never see her again.' Wilma was quiet and prayed a lot in the days leading up to their departure. They would not be able to see them off, it was just too hard. They said goodbye, and Wilma prayed before they went out the door…for God's blessing to be upon them, return them safely again, and that many souls would be won through their witness. She ended by saying, as she always did, *"Deo volente"* (as God allows it). They drove to Seattle and stayed with Margo's cousin, Jim and Christine. Jim had agreed to sell the Opel for Frank and put the money in their account. Two of the board members of ORTV came to see them off, giving them the official letter appointing them as ORTV missionaries. SPC friends, Arlene Nordlund, and Roger and Maryanne LeCompte West, from Ensemble days, came to see them off, and even came on board ship and took some pictures. They met the captain and crew of the SS Oregon Mail, and the other passengers. It was a joyful time; a fantastic fulfillment of a 'three-generational' call to service as missionaries. Frank's heart was in his throat; Margo was both scared to death, and excited beyond words… 'newly-weds on a slow boat to China!'

Frank graduates SPC

Frank's Kent Jr. High Choir gets 'No.1' rating

Frank and Margo are married June 24, 1967

Honeymoon and fishing

309

On SS Oregon Mail

On the set of ORTV

BOOK V
Kicking the Slats Out of the Cradle

The Journey, then Shipwreck,
then Victory!

CHAPTER EIGHTEEN

I LOVE THIS PLACE...LET'S JUST STAY HERE

Taiwan – 'Ilha Formosa' (beautiful island)

THEY PULLED OUT OF THE HARBOR AND UP THE STRAITS OF JUAN DE FUCA, out into the Pacific Ocean. It was very rough sailing all the way to Japan. Frank and Margo became very seasick the first three days. It was so rough they had to put up the slats on their beds to keep from rolling out. They had to pull up slats on the tables in the galley to keep the dishes and food from sliding off. Each of the twelve passengers...six couples all together...were paired off: four people at each of the three tables. Margo and Frank were paired up with a nice older couple from Spokane, Washington, George and Naomi Keller. The other two tables also had four at each table, and all of them were from Spokane. They all seemed to know each other, and all of them were over seventy. They loved to drink, and 'happy hour' in the lounge-library was what they looked forward to every day. Frank and Margo were still 'teetotalers.' They were only age twenty-three and twenty-two, so they made friends with the black steward who was forty, and he was the closest person on the ship to their age! Meal time came and George and his wife were sitting at their table. They had already had too much to drink, but Frank and Margo were making jokes with them and having a good time. George ordered more drinks at the table, and ordered his steak 'rare,' and Frank ordered his 'medium.' Margo and Naomi ordered chicken. The sea was rough, and they had the slats up, but everything was moving around on the table anyway. The crew ate with the passengers, and the steward acted as their server. He told them they would have to hook their chairs to the table to keep from falling backwards. George started to hook himself, at the same time he was trying to take a sip of his drink, just as the ship lurched to one side. George went tumbling backwards. Everyone had a good laugh, and the steward helped George back into his chair. They finished their salads, and the steaks and chicken came. Without checking who had what, they started eating. Frank soon realized that George had gotten his medium steak, and he had gotten the rare steak. He ate it anyway but later, as they were going to their staterooms, the ship made a violent pitch. The 'up-staircase' was suddenly the 'down-staircase,' and Frank, who was feeling seasick again anyway, found that his meal was coming *up* as well. Margo was not well either, but managed to get the steward who helped them with the 'accident' and got them safely to their room. They had taken crackers and oranges during the 'happy hour,' and instead of alcohol, they drank Seven-Up, and took some of it to their room also. In the morning, they didn't feel well enough to come to breakfast, but snacked on the oranges, crackers and Seven-Up. The steward came knocking on their door. "Mr. and Mrs. Varro, you *must* make meals; the ship has no doctor, and you must eat something." Frank told him they hadn't skipped breakfast, but had eaten the crackers and oranges instead of bacon and eggs with the passengers in the galley.

He said 'okay' and told them to just be sure to keep something in their stomachs. They got up a little later and went to the lounge where Naomi was working on a jigsaw puzzle. Frank loved jigsaw puzzles, and so he and Naomi worked on the puzzle, while Margo read in the library. The others talked or read also, except for 'happy hour,' of course! This was the way they spent the ten days on their way to Yokohama. Finally, in the safety of the harbor there, they waited overnight for a berth. In the morning they disembarked. They had arranged with Doug Bartlett (yes, the bass who had officiated at their wedding), had taken a missionary assignment himself…in Osaka, Japan; he met them in Yokohama. Even though the ship planned to call at five ports in Japan, they were allowed an 'overland pass' as long as they met the ship at Sasebo, the last port in Japan, southwest of Osaka. Frank and Margo were overjoyed to see Doug serving as a missionary, and talked endlessly of his experiences as a new missionary. They got on board the 'bullet train' which went from Yokohama, through Tokyo, to Kyoto and Nara. Frank spent most of the time on the train talking with Doug about his ministry and new experiences as a young missionary in Japan. He was very excited, and Frank listened intently to him. It paralleled Frank's experiences growing up in China, Hong Kong, and Taiwan. At each stop, Japanese schoolgirls pressed their way onto the train, in their black and green school uniforms. Margo's eyes were as big as saucers. She finally turned to them and said, "Look at all the Japanese!" Frank and Doug held their sides laughing before they realized Margo had never been outside the continental United States, except briefly in Canada and Mexico. This was a brand-new experience for her. Before they even had a chance to take a short nap, they were arriving in Osaka. They took a taxi to the mission compound where Doug lived. He introduced them to several of his Japanese friends. They visited briefly, then Doug showed Frank and Margo their room…an elevated room with hard 'tatami' covering. Inside was a large padded comforter with another comforter to cover themselves with. They took off their shoes and wore slippers around the living quarters. They slept well; it was cold in January but the comforters kept them warm. In the morning, they walked across the cold floor to the bathroom, where they lit the small water heater above the sink, as they had been instructed. Soon there was hot water. They finished getting ready and went to breakfast with Doug and his Japanese friends; this consisted of hard-boiled eggs, pastries, and coffee. It was more of a 'western breakfast' than Japanese, but many modern young Japanese had adapted themselves to an American way, while keeping many of the traditions of their parents. After breakfast, they went to meet the church elder that Doug was working with, Kan-Ga Sensei. He was a delightful pastor, and was responsible for bringing young American interns like Doug to work with him for the last twenty years. It was an invaluable experience that helped prepare Free Methodist, and other denominational men and women, preparing for the ministry. They did all of the sights in Osaka, Kyoto, and Nara. They had lunch in a Chinese restaurant. When Frank was puzzled about this, Doug told him that Chinese food was very popular there, especially among the young people. Then they did more sights; they went to an open market, which Frank loved; he said it reminded him of the markets in Taiwan. It was like a 'preview' for Margo of what to expect in Taiwan. They did more sightseeing the next day, and took in a prayer meeting with the church group Doug was working with. At the end of the day, they had a simple Japanese supper that was made in their quarters. It was called 'sukiyaki' (pronounced ski-yah-kee), meat, vegetables, bean curd, and transparent noodles…it was wonderful. Then they took a walk through the cold streets to a bathhouse. Doug had made sure they all had the proper 'swim attire' for a Christian group! Inside they went into hot tubs… so hot you didn't want to jump right in…just one step at a time to adjust to the hot water gradually. At the end of the night, they were so 'toastie-warm' you could see the steam coming off everyone as they walked back to their quarters. It was a fabulous experience, and Margo couldn't stop talking about it. They slept that night so soundly they had trouble waking up in time for breakfast. They did more Bible study the next day, sight-seeing, then returned early for supper and went to bed by 9:00 p.m. because they were told they would catch a plane at 4:00 a.m. the next morning, fly across the Inland Sea to Fukuoka, and there they would catch a train to Sasebo, where they would pick up their ship again. Frank said 'okay,' Doug would go with them, right? No, Doug told them…he would teach them a few words of Japanese…so they could go from the airport, to the train station in Fukuoka, and buy train tickets to Sasebo. What?? "We can't do that," Frank said. "Oh yes you can, Frank," Doug said, and laughed (what seemed like a sadistic chuckle). The instructions were these: 1) the plane would arrive in Fukuoka, a bus with a picture of a train on it, would be there, 2) take the bus to the train station, go to the ticket booth, then hold up two fingers, and say "Sasebo…'ni' (two)," 3) get on the train marked 'Sasebo' and take the three–hour trip to Sasebo, take a taxi to their ship, the SS Oregon Mail; easy…you can do it! So, Frank and Margo got up at 3:00 a.m., Doug took them in a taxi to the airport, they caught their flight at 4:00, arrived at 5:15…no problem. They took a bus with a picture of a train on it to the train station in Fukuoka…no problem. Frank went to the ticket booth, got his money out, held up two fingers and said, "Sasebo…'ni' (two)." The Japanese lady *asked him a question*, but he had no idea what she said; he held up two fingers again, and said 'ni' (two), and she handed him two tickets! Wonderful, it worked. They caught the train going to Sasebo, and the conductor directed them to their car…ten cars back! [Frank figured out quickly what the ticket booth lady had asked him…they got on the train in what was obviously *not first class!* She had asked him 'what class would you like?' He had held up two fingers and said '*ni'-second class!*]. There were live chickens on board; there were screaming babies, and motion-sick people standing…with vomit running down the aisles! Margo grabbed Frank's arm with a look of terror in her eyes; Frank covered her eyes and forced her to sit down next to the window, as far from the aisle as they could get; she covered her head with part of her coat, and the two of them braced themselves for the three-hour trip. Frank got his Bible out of his luggage and started reading to her from the Psalms. Before long, the train pulled out…Frank was reading, and Margo's eyes and ears were covered; almost as soon as they got under way, the baby stopped crying, the freezing-cold car started warming up a little, and a 'steward' came along and cleaned up the mess. Before long, an elderly Japanese man sitting across from them said, in perfect English, "have you been to Japan before?" Frank was taken aback, but responded, "Yes, I grew up in China, Hong Kong, and Taiwan… with my parents and siblings… we visited Japan many times; but my wife has never been to Japan before; we are going to Taiwan to be missionaries." He smiled, saying he had gone to school in the U.S., returned to Japan as a businessman, and when his business failed, he worked in Sasebo as a vendor for U.S.

merchant ships. They visited, and Margo fell asleep, Frank read a bit, then fell asleep himself. The three hours went quickly; they pulled into Sasebo. The elderly man said his 'English name' was Timothy Ryuyu. He offered to help them get to their ship. He knew the SS Oregon Mail and the entire Mail fleet. Wonderful! God had sent him to care for them. As they arrived and took a taxi to the ship, they noticed a large crowd had gathered near the docks…it was a protest group! The USS Forrestal was in port…a nuclear aircraft carrier. Timothy helped them navigate through the crowd. He laughed, gave them his card, and bid them farewell. They were very relieved to be back on board. Ben, their steward friend, said, "it's about time you showed up; they were going to leave without you, but I begged them to wait" he teased. The ship wasn't scheduled to leave for another five hours, and Frank knew he was joking, but Margo was worried. They got under way on schedule, and Frank and Margo were happy to go to 'happy hour' this time, and tell their friends all about their adventures in Japan. George offered them some champagne. He said that one of the couples was celebrating their forty-eighth wedding anniversary. They needed to show their 'respect' by toasting Betty and Charles Martin's big event with the rest of them. Frank politely refused, then realized 'this wasn't necessary,' like the Apostle Paul had said, to hurt their feeling over a minor 'legalism,' and he and Margo lifted their glasses and drank one sip each to show their respect. George wanted them to drink more, but Frank said one toast, in order to honor Betty and Charles, was sufficient and they put their champagne glasses down. To Frank's surprise, George came over to him and thanked him for honoring their friends, the Martin's. Then Betty and Charles came too, and thanked them. They said they knew Frank and Margo were 'religious,' and appreciated them not unnecessarily offending them. George didn't try to force any alcohol on them for the rest of the trip. George *did*, however, drink a little too much that evening. When they went to supper, and Frank tried to rearrange his silverware which had slid to the sideboard, he said in his slurred speaking, "I think your m-manners are… attro-cioushh." Naomi was embarrassed and kicked him under the table, but Frank just laughed good heartedly, and said, "why thank you, George, I should have learned some from you." Margo, who started to leave, sat back down when Frank grabbed her arm, but Naomi was not laughing, and said under her breath, "he means well....," then to George, "George, you should apologize." Frank just smiled...he got the last laugh, because George had made such a fool of himself. They ate the rest of the meal in silence, but at the end, George asked them, "you are going to Taiwan with a church, then?" Frank and Margo explained it was a Christian radio and television ministry. Naomi told them she and George sometimes attended 'Fourth-Memorial' in Spokane. What? Why hadn't she said that earlier. Did they know Neil Craig? She said 'no,' but she'd seen the young man who played piano and conducted the choir. Frank told them that was *Neil*, his 'best man!' Wow, what a coincidence? God used even that awkward moment to His glory! They slept well that night. The sea had calmed down a great deal, and they pulled into Pusan, in the southern part of Korea by the next morning. They visited a pastor from Frank's childhood in Taiwan, Rev. Jiang, An-hui, who came there from Taiwan to minister to the Chinese community in Pusan. Frank's dad had written and told them how to find them. They took a taxi, and had lunch with them after a brief visit; the ship was only in port for less than ten hours, then they were on their way again; next stop: Inchon, Korea. In the morning, they pulled in, but did not dock until later. The bay was very rough; they had planned a tour of Seoul, so a launch came out to take them ashore. The waves were treacherously high, and Margo and some of the others said "No," they absolutely would not dare to get on board the launch. Ben, the steward, said for them to trust him. When the waves brought the launch up, he would pass each passenger over to the man receiving them on the launch. They *MUST* step out the moment he said *GO!* And 'if they didn't,' one of the passengers asked? Ben said they had *about thirty seconds to live!!* The water was so cold, they might die of hypothermia. Frank had Margo go ahead of him in case anything happened...she wouldn't move; Ben grabbed her and pushed her into the arms of the Korean man on the launch; then Frank did the same on the next wave. They were both successful, and were shaking...not from the cold, but from thinking about the 'alternative.' When they got to shore, they witnessed small children sweeping up whatever spilled grain they could, from ships docked there. The poor children were barely clothed and had nothing on their nearly-bare feet except rags. Their noses were running, and Frank and Margo and the other passengers felt such pity for them. Some of the other passengers gave them a few U.S. dollars...in spite of being told *NOT* to. There was a bus waiting for them; the ship had arranged a bus tour of Seoul including the Royal Palaces and lunch at the Samgakju (they didn't have time to go to the DMZ, so they toured other sites such as the Namdaemun Market, and other sites; by evening, they were all miserably wet and cold...it had snowed or rained all day. They were ready to quit and go back to the ship, but the tour guide Kim said she had a *surprise* for them. The bus arrived at the Dure Restaurant; they went in, took off their coats in a private elevated room with the tatami straw matting; they sat at a table on the floor, but were told to put their feet under the table. To the great delight of all, they found that their feet were resting on a heater under the table! An audible gasp could be heard. Then they had hot tea to warm their insides, and food that was delicious, with entertainment by local Korean musicians. By the time they got on the bus and headed to Inchon to get back on the ship, the wind had died down...and they had no trouble pulling alongside and climbing the stairs up the side, to the upper decks and their staterooms. Wow! what a great tour, and a quick exposure to the best of Korea. They couldn't stop talking about it all the way to Okinawa. They set sail before midnight, and made it to Okinawa in a day and a half. They had breakfast on the ship and were told they had one day there, with the option of staying on their own overnight in Naha, or coming back to the ship, but they were leaving by noon of the following day, and they needed to be sure to be on-board. Frank and Margo took their own short tour and had lunch at Rukie's, an American restaurant (the U.S. had occupied Okinawa since the close of World War II). They returned to the ship, because they didn't have unlimited funds like some of the other passengers. By 11:00 a.m. the next day, they were to leave...but Sam hadn't reported back. They talked of leaving him...they had heard nothing from him. Suddenly, at exactly 11:26, Sam showed up at the dock...it was obvious he had had a little too much to drink; he was ranting about something, but nobody could tell what he was talking about. He told them to "go on...get the [blank] outta here...here...I'm fine without this!" Another member of the crew, Shiba (they thought was his name), from down below...no one seemed to know the relationship between the two of them, came out from one of the lower doors, and talked to him a little while; suddenly, Sam pushed him aside, and got on board through the same door; Shiba got back on, and they weighed anchor within a few minutes. Nobody saw Sam at supper, but the next day he was in uniform and was his usual 'gentle-giant' self; he denied everything, and finally George and the others gave up teasing him. He pretended he knew nothing of what they were speaking. Captain Reynolds refused to answer anyone's questions about Sam. Frank and Margo were not interested in this, however; they started getting excited…because Keelung, Taiwan, was the next port! They would be there tonight (but the ship would not come into port until the next morning; never mind, Frank and Margo were so excited, they packed everything up, lay down in their beds…but they couldn't sleep. They went out on deck to see the lights of Keelung. The seas were calm, and it was cold, with only a little wind…it had been a nice voyage. They went back inside and slept a little until the sun came up.

As they pulled into port, Frank and Margo immediately spotted his parents, Dave, and three members of the Overseas Radio and TV staff. Doris Brougham and Leland Haggerty *could not make it*, due to a 'previously scheduled radio broadcast.' Frank and Margo unloaded their things and went through customs. They had fewer trunks than most, so they were able to declare it as unaccompanied baggage, and loaded it up on a truck, which would follow them later. The staff directed them to the ORTV compound and they unloaded their things. Doris and Leland had finished their broadcast and met them at the offices and Globe Theater. The trunks and suitcases had been stored temporarily on the grounds, so Doris suggested they all go to lunch first. Frank's parents and Dave came with them and they went to a little restaurant there in Dazhi; they asked Michael to thank God for the safe arrival of Frank and Margo; they ate together, and then returned to the office. Doris mentioned that they had come out 'under supported,' but when Frank challenged her, and produced the letter from the ORTV board in Seattle, she waved it aside and said, "they meet the needs of our non-profit status, but we call the shots here in Taiwan." Frank's face fell; he looked at his dad, who looked like he might interfere; Frank gave him that 'don't you dare open your mouth; let me handle this' look. Frank's mom interrupted to say they had to be getting back to the student center in Mushan. They thanked Doris for the lunch, welcomed

Frank and Margo again, and excused themselves. Frank didn't want to get off on the wrong foot, so he simply said, "we came here to serve God, what would you like us to do?" Doris explained that Frank and Margo could stay in her apartment above the Globe Theater, until they built some 'staff apartments' in the back. They would 'absorb the cost' of housing, language study, and other things that would have been covered by the 'support that Frank and Margo *should have* raised.' To Frank's amazed look, she said the board should have told them that 'half of everything they raised went to the mission first!' So, of the three hundred per month they had raised…on their own, half of that would go to the mission first? Frank queried; 'Yes,' she said; 'and, so, what if not all of the hundred fifty—'*their half*,' came in? 'Well, they would have to live on whatever came in!' They were *stunned*. They had given up jobs, raised their own money without any help, sailed over six thousand miles, with no communication from them…about how they would live or do their jobs? Doris walked out…she showed them her apartment, and they put their things away…but, outside her office, to the welcoming Chinese staff, she acted as though God himself had come down and handed them a 'gift-wrapped blessing' in the arrival of Frank and Margo; but when no one was looking, they were talked down to, treated like 'junior missionaries,' and disrespected;' Frank and Margo went by themselves for supper, then went back to the apartment to pray; they cried out to God to show them what to do. They couldn't throw themselves on the mercy of Frank's parents; but they weren't sure how they could live on less than a hundred a month either; they went to scripture again; immediately Matthew 6:23-26 jumped out at them, *"Look at the birds, do they plant or reap, or gather into barns? Yet our Father feeds them; are you not fed better than the birds…or clothed better than lilies?"* Frank started to sing, "I sing because I'm happy, I sing because I'm free…" Margo had been in the bathroom crying; she came out and put her arms around Frank; he wiped her tears, and they sang together in harmony,"…for his eye is on ('Michael Varro—rhymes with sparrow,' like his dad always sang), and I know he watches me." They laughed, and Frank put away the Bible, and pulled out his 'surprise' (while Margo had been in the bathroom at lunch, Frank had slipped outside and bought some peanut brittle from one of the street vendors; he pulled it out now, "Tah-dah," he said, and gave her some, and ate some of it himself; they munched on it until they fell asleep. The next day, they ate with the staff downstairs; they met several of the staff, but one young woman in particular took a liking to them…she was the announcer for their Thursday evening television program–her name was Gloria Fan (same Chinese surname as Frank–pronounced *fawn*). Her Mandarin was almost as beautiful as she was; her English was good too, and Margo felt comfortable around her, because Gloria would be her 'interpreter.' She 'hung out' with Margo and Frank, especially after her apartment was built…just down the hall from them, and they eventually entrusted her with their honesty, and their feelings…without showing disrespect for 'management.' Frank started a morning radio program, 'The Taipei Breakfast Club,' but his studio time…the recording time of the program…was just after Gloria's…11:00 at night! He would 'pour coffee' (actually a glass of water) on air, and ask people in the English-speaking community to call in. ORTV operators would record their comments or requests, and then pass them on to Frank who would respond on the next program as though it were 'live.' Leland Haggerty conducted the 'Tianyin Gesheng' ('Heavenly Melody') choir,' and conducted the on-air show; Frank sang (in Chinese) with the choir, every Thursday night on television. Frank was the music director, and did much of the 'wood-sheading;' but he also sang in the men's quartet, consisting of: John Wang (first tenor); Frank (second tenor); Jeff Huang (baritone); and Dennis Wang–John's brother (bass). Frank had to relearn many songs he had sung before, but in Chinese! Every Thursday night, the choir, men's quartet, and women's trio (Ruby Yu, Anna Ling, and Linda Huang), sang…from memory, in Chinese, on television. Frank played trumpet sometimes in the band…and sometimes in a trumpet trio. When the Chinese French horn player didn't show up, Doris told Frank to play horn." (he was so glad he had been a music education major (and he even got an 'A' in brass too!). On Sunday afternoons, Frank produced a 'talent show,' which consisted of vocal, choral, keyboard, and instrumental solos; they would also do trios, duets, quartets, and sometimes choral pieces… without script or narration. Margo played piano accompaniment, electronic organ, or keyboard solo. It was hard work, and they were often exhausted. One night, about 3:00 a.m., management came knocking on their new apartment door. "Get up, everyone has to assemble in the Theater." When Frank asked what was going on, he was told that a big donor from the U.S. had arrived, and they had to put a 'show' on (the time difference didn't matter, since it was about 3:00 in the *afternoon* in the U.S.), they had to impress them with a 'big splash,' so they could receive big donations for the mission. The band played, the choir sang, the quartet and trio sang; Gloria pretended she was introducing the parts of the 'show,' and Doris and others spoke in Chinese. The guests from the U.S. were very impressed, and promised a big donation. Frank wanted to capture the moment and the look on everyone's faces...it was priceless! He thought this was so 'pretentious,' and from the looks on all the staff's faces, he evidently was not the only one; everyone went back to bed, and the next day nobody spoke of it; when Frank asked John and Dennis Wang in rehearsal about it, they shrugged their shoulders...this sort of thing happened all the time. After lunch, it was announced that there would be a big youth rally on the coming Saturday evening. Frank and Margo would be introduced after the opening section. The choir, band and all the groups rehearsed for it. Saturday night came, and the Globe Theater was filled to capacity. After the first segment, Gloria Fan asked for a big 'drum roll,' and Frank and Margo were brought out on stage; after she introduced them, she turned to Frank and said,"I told them you grew up here across from Zhengzhi University, and went to Morrison Academy in Taichung; now take the microphone and speak to them in Chinese!" Frank was floored; he had forgotten all the Chinese he ever knew in the five years he had been away! He held the microphone a minute, then he remembered...he remembered how to say 'who he was, where he had been in college, and that he was happy to be in Taiwan again.' They clapped and cheered; Frank beamed from ear to ear; then he called Margo over to the microphone, and said, "Wo na-lai i-ge tai-tai." They erupted into hilarious laughter; thinking he had done very well, he turned to Gloria to receive his 'well-deserved' praise, but she couldn't stop laughing; finally, she got ahold of herself enough to tell him that instead of saying "I brought back a wife with me," she said that he told them...he said something like, *"I dragged this woman here...by the hair!"* Gloria explained to them what he had intended to say in Chinese, but Frank and Margo fled the stage in embarrassment. Doris and Lee Haggerty brought them back out, to cheers from the crowd. Doris told them they were going to be working with the staff, and said, "anyone that can make this youth rally have this good a time, laughing, means we're off to a great start."

Ruby and other members of the Choir had been going up to 'Shu Linkou' for several months already...so they invited Margo and Frank to join them Sunday mornings. It wasn't a very well-kept secret this was a 'Chinese communist radio interception unit' for a U.S. Tri-Service Base, thirty miles from Taipei, on Linkou Hill. It had a base Chapel; Captain Tom Bush, the Chaplain, and his wife Bonnie, were in charge of the worship and music. Margo was invited to be the organist, and Frank was to be the choir director and worship leader. Frank and Margo connected quickly with Tom and Bonnie, who wanted to offer them the paid positions there, and dispense with the ORTV team. It was a godsend, and they accepted right away. When they got back, Ruby and the choir had already told Doris, who called Frank and Margo in, and said this was an answer to prayer. Frank smiled and agreed; it would cover the deficit in their support–right now they were living on less than the Chinese staff, who were paid directly by the mission...and they hadn't had to raise their support in deputation. Doris said, "Oh no, that is not what I mean, you have to turn in everything you make outside the mission, and we pay it out where it is needed." Margo burst into tears, and ran out of the room; it was too much for her; she had married Frank, and had gone on deputation with him, with 'nothing;' they had raised the money, put up with the raging ocean, and now the 'raging sea' in her own life...the culture shock of an 'only child living far away from her parents,' and after God answered their prayers... having it snatched from them! Frank turned to Doris...he said, "we're keeping the money Linkou Chapel is going to pay us; if that is not okay, then we'll leave now," and he walked out and went to find Margo. Doris told him as he was leaving, "let me consider this, and I'll let you know tomorrow." They left and went to the little "hole in the wall," where they always went, to lunch. Margo's favorite was 'beef curry;' they both ordered it, savoring the fine taste of it. After a time of prayer back at their apartment with Gloria, and some of the staff, they took a nap. Later, Frank told Margo he had a surprise for her...he had made arrangements for them to celebrate their first three months in Taiwan at the 'River Barbeque' in Dazhi. They invited his parents, but they were tied up with a Bible study; so, they celebrated on their own, and Frank showed why Mongolian barbeque was one of his favorites, and the favorite of all the American military in Taiwan. The next day, Doris called them in. She told them she had "decided to let them keep the money" they made at Linkou. This was the answer they were praying for; she also told them they were planning an 'All-Island Tour.' How exciting, they thought. She said Frank could go to rehearsal, but she wanted to speak with Margo alone–she had already spoken to Frank... without Margo present; but Margo and Frank compared notes later, against her wishes; [they discovered that she had spoken with Frank about him being the 'veteran missionary,' having grown up in Taiwan, and she having been his trumpet teacher at Morrison; they would need to be 'patient with Margo,' since she didn't understand the ways of missionary life, etc.; however, she had spoken with Margo too... 'Frank didn't understand the 'ways of a woman,' and the value of 'feminine input,' presumably offering herself as Margo's ally.' It wasn't enough to just sew discord between them and 'management,' which they had thought *they were to be a part of,* but triangulation now was being attempted between Frank and his new bride. Frank told Margo they wouldn't be a part of that...they were together, God was with them, and they would follow His lead, and consult with each other in prayer before they went to anyone else]. They focused on doing a good job in the morning radio program, in Margo's accompanying, and in the television broadcasts and music. The All-Island Tour was next; it was probably the highlight of their entire time with ORTV. They left in early summer, just before Margo and Frank's first anniversary. They started in the northern part of Taiwan, went down the east coast, crossed the island in the south, and then worked their way back to Taipei. They performed concerts in several cities, including Keelung, Hualien, Taitung, Kaoshiung, Tainan, and Taichung...and then back to Taipei. Everywhere they went they played to capacity crowds, all of whom had heard them on the radio, or seen them on TV. The reception they received was very enthusiastic. The men and the women stayed in separate dormitory-style accommodations. They ate well, it was a lot of fun, and it was a good time to bond with each other, both socially and spiritually. They took pictures... Margo and Frank dressed up in Ami tribe costumes (Ami were one of several Malay aborigine people in

Taiwan), a watermelon-eating contest, and several of the performances. Frank came back to his room one afternoon to find the guys in the quartet looking at his open 'shaving kit.' They were curious about the contents, so Frank took each item out and showed them. John and Dennis liked the 'American toiletries,' so Frank gave them each a sample. They were willing to try the cologne, hair spray, and even the spray deodorant. Jeff turned down all of it. He finally accepted a bit of the cologne, and hairspray, but would not even consider the spray deodorant. He turned to Frank and said, "No, thank you, I like the 'natural smell.' Without thinking, Frank teased, "We noticed." John laughed, and then even Dennis got it, and laughed. Jeff looked puzzled at them, before he realized they were teasing him, and they all had a good laugh. The tour was very successful, and Frank and Margo were able to bond with the staff. Gloria, the trio, and the quartet, all seemed to really enjoy them. God blessed it.

Michael and Beth said they had to celebrate Frank & Margo's First Anniversary, so they invited them to come out to the Mu Shan Student Center overnight. Beth had made both a peach pie, and an 'anniversary cake.' They had a pork roast with vegetables. Dave said he had a special present. After dinner he gave Frank and Margo a package; inside were "wam-wies," dried salty plums, which he knew were one of Frank's favorites! He insisted that Margo have one. She screwed up her face the minute she did, and everyone laughed. "Takes some getting used to, I guess" she said, as she took it out of her mouth...to 'save for later," she said. Beth had to go to the Student Center choir rehearsal, and Frank came with her, while Margo looked at all the Varro picture albums. The choir warmly welcomed Frank, who enjoyed conducting them as well.

The Taiwan Missionary Fellowship Conference was in July, and Frank introduced Margo to all his missionary friends. Margo was a good sport, and listened to the wild adventures and stories about Frank at Morrison and other places in Taiwan. They had already served with Dr. Dale and Triple 'C' (Christ Can Conquer) as counselors at the winter retreat...for all the children of missionaries and others serving in Taiwan, from Morrison as well as Taipei American; she had met many of them already, so they already knew her. It was held at Sun Moon Lake, and Margo was intrigued with finally seeing one of the places

Frank had talked about so much. They didn't stay with Frank's parents, but had a little room above the Conference center that overlooked the lake. Margo loved it. She finally had a chance to be away from the strain and the stress; she felt spiritually refreshed. The Bible teacher, Winton Mallory from England, and the featured Speaker, Dr. Luis Palau, were particularly inspiring. They felt relaxed and inspired in this time of renewal…and she and Frank had been talking about 'starting family.'

Dr. Dale asked Frank to serve as the high school Camp Director after missionary conference. They were able to get permission from the U.S. military provost to get supplies from the PX and commissary because many military families sent their children to the camp. Both military and missionary communities provided staff to work with Frank. He composed a theme song, 'Happening,' which they used in the worship services. Members of the staff took turns speaking in the morning and evening worship, teaching Bible studies, chaperoning, and supervising the swimming and activities. It was held at Wan Li, not far from Frank's parents' mission school and church. It was a great success, and many campers made professions of faith because of it. Margo stayed at the ORTV compound, where she and Gloria 'hung-out' together. When they got back from camp, they had a television performance that caused a great controversy. Each week, they chose a 'theme' for the program. Taiwan Television allowed them to sing Christian songs, but only if they were sung along with other American 'popular' songs. They could invite viewers to come to their youth rallies, and enroll them in their 'Studio Classroom' (teaching English on air), but they could not directly 'preach' or invite people to make professions of faith on the Thursday night program. The theme for that week's program was 'Pirates,' and the men were asked to do a 'pirates dance.' One of the choir members was a Nazarene seminary student, Jerome Sung; he refused to perform the men's dance, because of his religious convictions against dancing in general. He was told he must perform it, or be fired. Some of the others then also refused to dance. They were told to do so or be fired. The others changed their minds and went along with it, but Jerome stood by his convictions; he was fired immediately after the performance. He said he was sorry he had caused them to be angry with him…he needed the money to finish seminary, but they would not relent. Frank was upset and called his father, who hired Jerome immediately, as one of the CEF student preachers. This caused a problem with Doris, and before the choir left for an engagement, that Saturday, there was a confrontation in front of the Globe Theater. Doris said this was going directly against their orders (to side with Jerome…and now his father). They said they were in charge, and Frank had put them in an embarrassing position with the missionary community. Frank was not willing to back down this time, and refused to go with the choir to their engagement. No one would say anything against Frank and Margo, but neither were they willing to sacrifice their only income. They left for their engagement, Doris left and went to her office, but told Frank she would inform his draft board that 'he was not under appointment with ORTV' if he quit. Frank and Margo went to their apartment. They prayed. They knew they couldn't stay, but what would they to do about a job, and income. Frank called his dad. Michael wouldn't say anything against Doris or ORTV, but he just said, "Come work for VOCA for a while." He said he would send a letter to Frank's draft board, vouching for their 'missionary appointment.' They went to Linkou that Sunday, and Chaplain Bush said, "why so sad?" Margo had been crying, and it was obvious. Frank just poured out his heart. Tom listened while Margo and Frank let it all out. Then, without saying a word, he picked up the phone; he 'knew someone' at Taipei American School. He wouldn't say who, but some Air Force Captain knew Bob Brown, the TAS business manager. Bob told Tom that Dean Kaufmann, head of the music at TAS, was looking to replace Ken Swanson, who was 'going stateside' on a sabbatical. Bob said he was willing to set up an interview with Bob and Dean Kaufmann; they were overjoyed…God had come to their aid again. Tom wouldn't tell them whom he knew. He just pointed upward, and said, 'somebody likes you guys.' They said nothing until after the interview. Dean Kaufmann was a fine Christian man, and his wife, Sharon, and he, had a Bible study in their home. After the interview, Bob Brown said, "Dean, if your recommendation is to hire Frank, let's do the paperwork right now, and then we're ready to go; I know Ken will be relieved, music positions are not that easy to fill." They took care of everything on the spot. Frank had brought his Washington State Provisional Teaching Certificate with him, as well as copies of his transcripts. Dean said he wanted to meet Margo; and Frank said she was with Tom at the Snack Bar. They called Sharon, and Bonnie, and they all met there. I guess you could call it a Joy-Fest…at the very least! It was the biggest miracle God had ever done in their lives; they liked to call it 'from rags to riches.' Frank was to be high school band director (since they already had a choir director), and teach intermediate school classroom music. Bob Brown had called Chaplain Steve Jones, and told him he had someone to fill the choir director vacancy at the HSA (Headquarters Support Activity, U.S. Navy Chapel. Tom said fine—with his blessings; he and Bonnie had found an Airman with a music background that could take their place; this also included PX, APO, Commissary, and Officer's Club privileges. Bob wasn't sure, but he thought all of that would be in the neighborhood of thirty-six hundred a year, plus the hundred a month from the HSA Chapel job, more than his first-year salary at Kent Junior High! School would start in just three weeks, so they had to find an apartment and move. Frank wrote a letter to Doris and ORTV, thanking them for the opportunity to work with them, and offered to come help out when needed; he also asked about the money that was being 'put away for their return to the U.S. after two years,' as agreed. They were packing their things up when Gloria stopped by and told them Doris had gotten their letter and wanted to speak with them. Frank went to her office. She was smiling and friendly; she said it was better this way; they could stay on with ORTV part-time. This way they would be able to buy them things at the Commissary and PX. Frank explained that they 'were *not* going to be with ORTV anymore. They would live on their own…near TAS. They could help out on a voluntary basis…but would not share their salary with ORTV. Her face fell; she said what they were doing was wrong, after 'all we did for you.' Frank didn't even try to bring up any of the things they had argued about so many times. He thanked her, and left. They had found a two-story apartment in Shilin. A short taxi ride got him to TAS in ten minutes. Michael and Beth loaned them an old washing machine, and Frank bought some wicker furniture and other things with an advance from his dad. Michael had written him a letter, taking them on as 'local-hire' with VOCA (like Jerome Sung), with a copy to Bob Hammond, and Frank's draft board. In their new home, Margo fixed some supper, and then Frank opened the Bible. He opened to Jeremiah 29:11-12 *'I know the plans I have for you…to prosper you, and not harm you...plans to give you hope and a future;'* They held each other and cried. God had come to them in their greatest need ... and prospered them. School started; Frank's Navy Chapel choir started. God had not abandoned them; rather, He had given them a new lease on life!

Frank and Margo made friends with Ellie, who sang in the Navy Chapel choir; she told them her husband, Jack, was a Navy Corpsman and worked for a doctor with the U.S. Embassy. His name was Dr. Steve Beckman. Steve Jones, the Chaplain, was a 'kick in the pants.' He was a big joker and a tease. He said, "it's time for a choir party, and we should have it at Ellie and Jack Kingston's place–they have a swimming pool." They lived on Yang Ming Shan (called Grass Mountain by most). So, they set a date for a week from Saturday. It was September, and Frank was getting into the swing of things. He came home and told Margo he had gotten the lead in the Taipei Drama Club production of 'Oklahoma.' He told her he had also 'offered her talent' to play the piano for the production, and the director was very excited about it...they couldn't wait to meet her. She was not feeling, well, she said, and had talked to Ellie about it; could he wait until she had seen Dr. Beckman first? Sure, no problem, but please put the choir party on the calendar–Jack had already said 'okay' Margo went to see Dr. Beckman the next day with Ellie. Frank was at the chapel after school, and Jack called him. "Hey man, how are you feeling...*Papa*?!" he said. Frank did a double take. "What? Papa? Who?" Jack told him to shut up, and listen...he was going to be a 'daddy!' Margo was three months pregnant! Stay right there at the chapel, Ellie and he were bringing Margo to him; they were going to celebrate at the Snack Bar with banana splits!! While Frank was waiting, he called his mom and dad. "Guess what? I'm going to be a 'daddy,' and you are going to be grandma and grandpa again!" Chaplain Jones was there and heard the big news, so he passed it along, and before the day was over, everyone in the HSA choir, TAS, and most of the missionary community, Frank presumed, by then had heard their big news!

Margo started playing for "Oklahoma" rehearsals, and both she and Frank joined the Taipei Drama Club. Terri Johnston, the Drama teacher at TAS, was Director for the production, but a couple of delightful British women, Sondra White, and Lilian Grimes were president and secretary-treasurer, and responsible for putting it on. They were happy to meet Margo and Frank and invited them to the 'curry party' that the Taipei Drama Club was having at their house. It was a large British imperial-type house near the Grand Hotel. They had 'giant vats' of both chicken and beef curry; each guest served themselves curry and rice, with generous portions of chutney, coconut, and every other imaginable condiment. Wine, and other alcoholic beverages were plentiful as well. Tea, coffee, and Chi-shui (Chinese '7-Up'), were also available. It was a great party, and Margo and Frank added this great social gathering to their list. Later that month, Steve Jones gathered everyone in the HSA choir together at Ellie and Jack's place. They went swimming, had barbeque…with 'some' rehearsal, but everybody was so stuffed, most said they couldn't even 'sing a note.' Chaplain Jones had invited some guests to the party. He introduced Frank to Rear Admiral Paul Stevenson, who asked him why he hadn't joined the Officer's Club yet. He wanted to put him in touch with Captain Jim Partin who was in charge of the Club. He told Frank he also needed to visit the provost's office and register with him. [At that time, TAS was the largest non-DOD (Department of Defense) school in the world; in other words, it was an independent school, started by missionaries and business people in 1949, but contracted by the DOD for military dependents; all instructors there had U.S. military privileges: Post Exchange (PX), Commissary, APO, and Officers Club membership… all included in this, and military orders were also required]. Frank was glad to learn about that. Bob Brown had told him, but he didn't know how or where to join–the Officer's Club that is. Paul said, 'come see him the next week and he would help him take care of it.' An important contact was made at the HSA Chapel choir party: Sara Mae Eckstein, who attended chapel, and was a friend of Steve Jones (an accomplished soprano from Seattle, but tied up during the week so she couldn't sing in the Chapel choir). Sara had met Margo at a 'Women of the Chapel' luncheon and had asked her to play for the Nightingales, a women's chorus, conducted by Mazel Anderson. Sara Mae wanted to get the TAS Drama Department, the Taipei Drama Club, and the Chapel to put on 'Amahl and the Night Visitors' for Christmas; Frank thought it was a great idea and wanted to jump on it right away; Sara Mae said she had discovered a ten-year old Chinese-American boy in Taiwan, (who had sung with the Vienna Boys Choir, and was quite accomplished), by the name of David Wang. If he sang Amahl, Sara Mae said she could sing the mother's part, and Frank could sing the King Kaspar part; Steve could sing Balthazar, and the HSA Chapel choir could be shepherds and shepherdesses. The only part she didn't know about was Melchoir. Frank immediately suggested Dean Kaufmann. Sara Mae said they would need to start on it soon. They finished the evening with the choir singing the Lutkin 'The Lord Bless You And Keep You,' and Steve giving the closing prayer. Wow! What a productive evening. Frank talked to Dean Kaufmann about putting on 'Amahl' and he loved the idea, but he and Sharon were going to be in the States for Christmas. Frank remembered a young Airman that had sung in his choir at Shu Linkou: Mark Thomas. He asked Tom if Mark was still around; Tom told him Mark was no longer stationed at Shu Linkou, he was at Thirteenth Airforce in Taipei, which was even better. Frank called Mark; he said he didn't feel he could do the part, that he was just a 'choir kind of guy' and didn't do solos. Frank convinced him he would teach him everything he needed to know, so Mark said he was willing to try; but his feelings wouldn't be hurt if they got somebody else; Mark learned his part, with Frank helping, and with that they began rehearsals, building sets, and the early production process.

Frank's folks met them almost weekly at the snack bar, or the Officers Club for dinner. Mondays were Michael's day off, and so it was a good time to get together. They had started by coming out to Mushan, but it was a long bus ride, and since Michael and Beth still had the Hillman they'd had for years, they agreed to come into town instead of going out to Mushan. Taipei Drama wanted to start another show: 'Oklahoma,' So now Tuesday and Wednesday afternoon or evenings, were taken up with both 'Amahl,' and 'Oklahoma' rehearsals. Thursday evening was Chapel choir rehearsal; Friday and Saturday they often had 'Oklahoma' scene rehearsals. As accompanist, Margo had to be at 'Oklahoma' rehearsals most of the time. They would try to take in a movie or dinner at the Officers Club one of those nights too. Soon Margo had added Nightingale rehearsals on Tuesday afternoon, too. This also meant that some evenings the Nightingale performances pre-empted, or this affected the start time of other rehearsals. The production of 'Oklahoma' was well received. Frank had to get three-inch heeled boots to make his character 'Curly' look tall enough alongside the girl playing 'Laurie.' The only snag in the show was when some were told they could 'ad lib' the last night, Steve Jones, as 'Judd,' broke three ribs when things got out of hand. The trouble makers were told by Taipei Drama Club that they weren't allowed to play any future shows.

Their good friend from SPC, Judy Shull had taken an intern assignment in Japan, and was working with Doug. She wrote and wanted to spend Christmas in Taiwan with Frank and Margo. She hadn't heard that they had left ORTV, so Frank wrote her to tell her the good news, and he said, "let's meet instead in Hong Kong." Christmas in Hong Kong! It sounded like so much fun...and it was. Margo was almost five months pregnant; she had gotten over her 'morning sickness,' and she was very excited. Frank had told Margo about growing up there, and she looked forward to it. They flew there and stayed at the YMCA. Judy said that that was also where she was staying! They took in Tiger Balm Gardens, the Star Ferry, The Peak, and all the other sites, and they ate the best Russian 'borsht' ever, at Rikki's Russian Restaurant. They visited the Peniel church and Frank introduced Margo and Judy to Rev. Fred Leung and all the rest of the staff; they had to get back, but it was a wonderful respite from their busy schedule. Judy left to go back to Japan, and Frank and Margo said to be sure to greet Doug and their Japanese friends.

Frank had a band concert when they got back, and Margo had a Nightingales concert the very next night. The HSA Chapel choir also gave a concert...the week just before the 'Amahl and the Night Visitors' presentation; it was a very full schedule. 'Amahl' came off very well. Mark had worked very hard on his part, and he did very well. The Kings' parts were the favorite of many. When China Television found out about it, they asked for the opportunity to put it on television. The makeup artists made them look like authentic ancient 'Chinese kings,' especially the beards which took an hour every night to put on with glue. After all the concerts, Frank and Margo went out to Mushan to help his parents with the student center Christmas production. Frank conducted the choir, and Margo played the piano while Beth supervised the pageant. Michael preached and told them the story of Jesus' birth in his sermon, 'The Greatest Night,' and three students came forward to profess faith in Christ. After the concert, there was candy for the children, and small gifts for the university students and adults. Beth had fixed a light supper before the program, and now they went back upstairs for dessert and coffee after it was all over. They opened presents...as was their custom, on Christmas Eve. It was hard on Margo, who was celebrating the first Christmas in her life without her parents; but they had sent presents in the mail, and now she had her in-laws, and Frank and Dave, to share all these together. They tried to sleep, but some of the Chinese young people came caroling after midnight, so they had to get up and invite them in for rice cakes and tea. The next day Margo helped Beth fix the Christmas turkey...after 'stocking gifts,' of course (Dave was only ten years old then, but he and Margo were already developing a special relationship, and it started at that time). He was like the younger brother she had never had. They all sat down to a fabulous feast of turkey, dressing, yams, potatoes, and all the rest. Beth had learned to make the most interesting dishes out of whatever she had on hand...lily root salad, for instance, and many other 'western' cuisine items made from local produce. It was always good; but most famous, of course, was her pie (which Margo later learned to replicate with precision). When people asked Frank the 'trick question,' "who makes the best pie...your mother or your wife?" [he wasn't 'stupid,' so of course he said, "my wife, *and* my mother; because my mother taught her"]. Margo, with the secret of Beth's pie crust, perfected it! So...their pie, *with ice cream*...then naps...a great Christmas!

The next four months went quickly; but not without tragedy. Frank had come home from school one day before Thanksgiving; his dad and Dave had arrived...with a little dog. The rice farmer in Mushan, from whom Michael bought the mission property, had given it to them. Dave already had a dog, so he thought of Frank and Margo. About the time they moved from ORTV, a Cantonese lady met them in Shilin, and offered her help in finding an apartment; prior to this, Frank, who had already seen several 'for rent' signs on his own, and toured some of them, thanked her, 'but,' he told her, 'he didn't need any help;' Frank said he had already decided on one, and was going to the office to put the money down on it, and complete the deal. He asked her name, and whether she was the proprietor or not. She said she was 'Leung Tai-tai, from Canton,' in broken English. She was not the proprietor, but an 'introduce-you person,' she called it. She refused to speak Mandarin–only English. Frank smiled and thanked her again; he said he didn't need her help; 'see, we are already here at the rental office,' 'he told her. He paid his rent and signed the papers. Margo and he were moved in when Mrs. Leung came by and said they owed her two hundred NT ('new Taiwan dollars' about fifty USD. He said 'no, he did not,' and had told her that when he rented it; she cursed him, and said 'he knew nothing of Chinese ways.' He forgot all about it until after the Chinese New Year celebration. They had named the little dog 'Cinder' (a little brown and gray female dog...like 'Cinderella!'). He called Dave, and asked him: 'had he come over and taken the dog back?' He couldn't find her anywhere. Dave helped him look when they all got together at the Officers Club the next Monday; they all looked for about an hour– nothing. The following Saturday, Frank and Margo were sleeping in when Frank overheard their nice Chinese neighbor, Mr. Feng, talking with someone. [Mr. Feng was very nice, and always let Frank use his phone, and had a cousin in America he always wanted to talk about]. Frank heard a woman's voice. Mr. Feng said in Mandarin, "you should never have put my nice American neighbor's dog in the stew pot." Sure enough...as Frank peeked out the upstairs balcony window, he saw Mrs. Leung talking with Mr. Feng. Frank flung open the sliding door, and confronted Mrs. Leung, who quickly ran away. He asked Mr. Feng about what he had told Margo that he had heard. Poor Cindy, their little dog, had met the same fate as many little dogs did during the 'Fragrant Meat' season of Chinese New Year [only among Cantonese, however, and sometimes other people from south-central China]. Margo cried, and said she didn't want to talk about it...it was so cruel she thought. Frank went next door and thanked Mr. Feng for standing up for them, but Mr. Feng tried to ignore it; he changed the subject... but gave Frank and Margo a 'gift' for Chinese New Year. It was some special marinated pork (Frank didn't tell Margo it was from the same pig they had butchered next door one night the previous week; the squeals had brought back horrible memories of Ji An as a child, living next to the slaughter house where they lived]. Margo fixed it up nicely, and they had their own celebration of the Chinese New Year; they had already had a big celebration with Frank's folks and some of the students from Zhengzhi University, where Beth taught English (she was considered faculty there). At dinner that night, Margo held up a letter from her mom, and said, "Guess what? My mom is coming to Taiwan when the baby is born." Frank said that was great, and was her dad coming too? No, just her mom, she said. She wants to stay in a hotel; they all agreed that it was 'out of the question'…she would stay with them, and Margo said she would write her back immediately.

Frank had been studying Chinese with David Chen for almost a year. David had been on the ORTV staff, but continued to teach Frank even after they left there. His mother was a well-known professor at the famous 'Beijing Language Institute' in Taipei. Frank had grown up speaking Mandarin, but he never did read or write much. He studied with David so that he could at least have a minimum reading knowledge of…let's say 'simple newspaper articles,' as David put it (around two to three thousand semi-recognizable characters). Frank had progressed to the point where he was about halfway there. One lesson right after Chinese New Year was about food. Frank and Margo loved to cook, and bought the famous 'Pei Mei' cookbook. He learned that there were 'four main cuisines of China: West (Chuan), North (Lu), South (Yue), and East-Coastal (Huaiyang),' Frank remarked that his favorite was the West (spicy). David immediately said, "since you like it spicy, I will make a deal with you." He told him about the 'Uh-Mei Restaurant' in downtown Taipei. He bet him that he wouldn't be able to finish the meal he was going to order for him. If he did, he would give him 'six weeks of free Chinese lessons!' Obviously, David didn't know that you 'never make a bet with Frank'. He and Margo met David at 'Uh-Mei' the following week. David was with his wife, Xi Mei, and they had already ordered. After Frank offered prayer, they began to eat. Each dish was hotter (spicy = 'la') than the one before. Margo and Xi Mei stopped eating. David laughed, and kept eating. Frank started turning red, his nose ran, tears streamed down his face, he was perspiring… but he wouldn't quit. They had already eaten 'jiaozi' and hot 'noodles swimming in red hot sauce.' Flushed, with tears running down his face, David finally lay down his chopsticks. When Frank claimed victory, David reminded him the deal was 'not if he (David) stopped,' but if

Frank *finished* the meal. Margo told him to stop, he would be sick, and she didn't relish cleaning up the mess! There was one 'jiaozi' left, two bites of 'ma po dou fu' (a spicy bean curd dish), and the bowl of what's called the 'mother of all habañera' noodles. Xi Mei said in Chinese "close enough." David responded in Chinee, "a deal is a deal." Frank ate the last 'jiaozi'…and kept it down. He ate one bite of 'ma po'… then the next; he looked at the noodles, and thought he was going to be sick. Margo yelled, "stop!" but he paused for a few minutes, and then suddenly just wolfed down the entire remaining three bites or so of the noodle soup. They looked at him…beet red, tears flowing down his face, blowing his nose, and wondering if he was going to be sick. Margo looked at David. He laughed and said, "Hao ji le!!" (very excellent). He paid the bill while everyone in the restaurant cheered, and Frank ran to the bathroom, while they all clapped (no one asked him if he threw up [confidentially, he did, but there were no witnesses]). He had won the bet! They all went home, wondering about this strange 'wai guo ren' (foreigner) who loved Sichuan food as much as the Chinese.

The TAS band was doing well, and improving in their performance under Frank's direction. He started students on instruments and gave private instruction for sixth graders and then put them in the beginner's band; they worked their way up, until they could audition for the top TAS band, which included juniors and seniors. Many of the missionaries sent their children to TAS instead of Morrison, and Frank taught many of them in band—the Melgren's, the Rench's, the Raley's, and other military and missionary children. Some of them kept in touch with Frank for many years; Frank also performed for the missionary community.

[Speaking of performing, the first week he and Margo had arrived in Taiwan, they were in Mushan visiting his parents. Dave asked Frank to get on his swimming suit, they were going down to the river for a swim; though Dave had swum there before, Frank, in all his years he had never swum in the Jingmei River by the mission compound (remembering the horror of the flood when he almost drowned); Dave said it was completely safe now, so they went straight to the river; though Frank usually checked before diving, Dave had said it was safe, *so* Frank just dove in immediately; he immediately hit his nose on some *root* sticking out from the bank; Dave took one look at him and said, "we better get you out and see if everything is okay;" Frank had to perform that night for a group of missionaries, so they got ready, and Margo, Dave, and Frank joined Beth and Michael; they drove into town to the Community Center on Xinsheng Road; a group of missionaries were gathered there and welcomed Frank 'back to Taiwan' and met Margo…but, the first thing Margo noticed was: there was *no* piano. (whoops! no one had checked on that; the set-up team was so embarrassed); anyway, after dinner and remarks, they introduced Frank, who sang four or five songs 'unaccompanied!' but something about Frank's demeanor caught Dr. Nordhoff's eye; he asked Frank if he was feeling alright (Frank was turning his head very gingerly and acting a little strange); Dr. Nordhoff asked what he had been doing that day, and Dave and he confessed about the diving incident; "I need to see you in my office first thing in the morning; and be very careful how you sleep on your neck tonight," he warned; Margo, and Frank's parents, were now alarmed, and asked Dave about it. Dave acted a little sheepish, but Frank wouldn't let him take the blame, after his dad kind of tore into Dave; Frank said it was completely his fault; he hadn't checked before diving; in the morning, Michael took Frank to see Dr. Nordhoff, and after the examination, Dr. Nordhoff told Michael and Frank, "It is as I feared, you have a hairline fracture in your neck." "What? You've got to be kidding me," he said; he showed him the X-ray; sure enough, there was a slight fracture; he had to wear a neck brace for a while].

Another 'singing story' was the one about a trip south, following 'Oklahoma;' 'Coachie' Chuck Holsinger, from Morrison, now superintendent, called Frank at TAS one afternoon; he wanted him to come to Taichung and sing for the Morrison Trustees board banquet. They would pay him for travel and an honorarium. 'Sounds great,' Frank had said, until he found out there were no trains back to Taipei after 10:30 p.m. and he had to teach the next day; 'Coachie' called him back later to tell him they would pay for a taxi from Taipei to Taichung, wait for him till after the banquet, and then drive him back to Taipei. Unbelievable! Frank said if they wanted him that badly, he would agree to it. Margo couldn't go, so Sylvia Knapp played for him; Frank sang several selections from 'Oklahoma,' and other sacred songs, like 'All

That Thrills My Soul,' 'Wonderful Lord,' and 'How Great Thou Art.' It was very well received, and many of the board members wanted to talk to him about his ministry, and why 'wasn't he teaching music at Morrison instead of TAS!' He laughed, and said he wouldn't touch that with a ten-foot pole! He got back about 3:00 a.m., slept a few hours, and showed up in time for his sixth-grade music class. The Spanish teacher next door saw him yawning before lunch, and said 'Señor Franc,' why so tired?' He told her and she laughed. He said, "Hey, by the way, I want you to give me one of those long Spanish names," she said she couldn't do that, without all those 'paternal, and maternal names.' Frank had an idea: what if he did 'Michael' and 'Frank' and then the diminutive of each? She said, *Bueno!* then that would be: *Miguel Miguelito Pancho Panchito Varro.* Frank smiled; some in the lunch room applauded...or just rolled their eyes].

Margo was due the last week in April. She had gotten a letter from her mom, who said she was planning to come to Taiwan, in time for the baby... Margo was very excited. Frank asked if her dad was planning to come, and she said 'no,' just herself. She wrote that she would plan to stay in a hotel; Margo wrote back that it was 'out of the question, completely' she would stay with them at their Shilin house; Margo asked for her dad to 'please come too,' but he said he was not up to it. Dr. Beckman had made arrangements for Margo to deliver at Country Hospital on Ren Ai Road. It was a Chinese hospital, and Dr. Andrew Chen would assist him. This would be much better than the HSA Navy Hospital, which was smaller and older. Country Hospital was *first class* and Frank could be there for the birth as well...even stay with them in the room if he wanted to. Wilma arrived by April 20, and Margo and Frank met her plane at the Sungshan Airport, and took her to the Officer's Club for something to eat before they went home to their Shilin apartment. Michael, Beth, and Dave joined them. She was tired from the long flight so they saved visiting until the next day. Ellie, and Martha Melgren, had planned a baby shower for Margo and invited all her 'American military...and missionary, and Chinese, friends.' They had wonderful appetizers and things to drink. An array of American and Chinese goodies covered the table at the Melgren's house. At the shower, their Chinese friends claimed they could tell *the gender of the baby...* with a wedding ring and a necklace. They said the way the ring swings when it is held over the pregnant stomach determines the gender…if it swings in a back-and-forth manner, it is a boy; but if it swings in a circular manner, it is a girl. So, they set it up, and everyone watched to see which way it would swing. It looked like it was swinging back and forth, and everyone cheered, saying it was to be a little 'prince,' a boy; but then the ring went into a kind of circular fashion. They started disagreeing on which one it was. Frank stopped everyone, and came into the middle of the room; he said he was going to tell everyone 'what the gender of the baby would be;' they listened carefully to him as he said, "I know *one hundred percent what it will be*; it will be a boy…*or* a girl!" Everyone laughed, and agreed that Frank was right. They went back to the food, the drinks and the games. Margo introduced her mother, and Frank's mom and dad. It was a fun time.

Margo had been playing the organ for the HSA chapel, but she made arrangements for a substitute because the coming Sunday, April 27, 1969, was her due date. Frank wanted to be there for the birth as well, so he had made arrangements for someone else to conduct the choir too. By Friday, she was miserable, and her feet were very swollen. Dr. Beckman told Frank to make sure she kept her feet up level with her waist. Wilma helped with the meals, and Frank went to TAS every day that week, but came home for lunch daily to check on her. Wilma was a big help, and Margo thought it was *so special* to have her mom there with her. It was already **hot** (since they had had no air conditioning at the Dazhi apartment, they made *sure* that their first purchase at the PX was an AC window unit). Wilma went with them Saturday evening for dinner and insisted on paying the bill. They told her she was their guest while in Taiwan, but she was stubborn, and said she had saved up for this very special trip, and she wanted them to let her pay, so they said 'okay.' They took a taxi back to their apartment and she tipped the driver *forty NT* (on a forty NT taxi trip!). Frank and Margo had to get cross with her; they said that was a hundred percent tip! She said it was only one US dollar, but they finally prevailed on her, and helped her understand that they lived there, and if the tourists 'spoiled' the locals, it would make it harder on them (Frank 'allowed' her to give him ten NT, which was still twenty-five percent; the cab driver left grumbling about the 'haggling skills' of Frank). Wilma was *sure* the baby would come that night. She was staying in the front room upstairs, but she insisted on remaining fully dressed...even with her hat on! She said she was afraid they would leave her there if she didn't have time to dress. "Mom, we would *never* leave you here!" Margo said, but Wilma stayed dressed anyway...but nothing happened; Frank and Margo slept soundly...suddenly, about 4:30 a.m., Margo started labor. Frank was nervous...it was his first child...so he woke up Mr. Feng next door and used his phone to call Dr. Beckman; but, he said, they needed to let the contractions progress a little bit longer; if they were still far apart, they needed to wait...and, in the next two hours, things started to happen more regularly, so, Frank decided to go ahead and take her to the hospital. Everything slowed down again, and they waited all morning. Wilma was happy they had gone ahead and left for the hospital. She read a magazine in the waiting room, and Frank kept her up-dated. By mid-morning, the labor got to be more regular again. Frank called his mom and dad after their church service, and they said they would leave Mushan in a couple hours. Margo had already gone through prep, but she was nervous, and Dr. Beckman said Dr. Chen could handle things for a while... he would be there in a little bit. Finally, Dr. Beckman arrived. It was almost 4:00 in the afternoon. Labor was good by then, and he said they would do the 'saddle-block' shortly. He had Dr. Chen and the nurses get the rest of the prep taken care of, and told Frank to 'scrub up and get your gown on' and get ready to assist him. "What? I'm not assisting you...I'm watching." But Dr. Beckman, who liked to tease, said for Frank to 'count the vertebrae so I can administer the saddle-block;' Frank was acting like 'what if I do it wrong,' when Dr. Beckman had it all under control anyway; when things weren't as fast as he thought they should be, Dr. Beckman got the forceps out; he pulled so hard, Frank thought he was going to 'pull the baby's head off.' No, everything was fine; the baby finally popped out; it was a little girl! Margo was groggy from the medication but, after they got her all cleaned up, she was able to hold her. Frank was in awe! This little gray *blob* with a 'cone-head' (from the forceps) was now a beautiful pink baby! They all went out into the next room... Wilma was there...Michael, Beth, and Dave were there. Wilma, always thinking she had to assure everyone that the '*worst* is behind us,' said of her new little grandchild (that still seemed a little misshapen to her), "well, she's not a *beautiful* baby, but she certainly is *alert*." Margo quickly said, "Mom, she IS a beautiful baby." Michael went into his 'eyebrow alert,' and looked like the proudest grandpa possible, and Beth glowed like she had just seen an angel; Dave beamed from ear to ear. In the room, Margo turned to Frank and said, "look what we did, this is fantastic! I still can't believe it." They thanked God for this miracle of birth, and then talked again about the names they had thought about: they both loved the name Michelle, and all of Margo's dolls, while she was growing up, were named Elizabeth, which was also Frank's mom's name. (Frank's dad always thought they had named her the feminine form of Michael, and they just let him believe that…it might as well have been true anyway). So, *Michelle Elizabeth Varro* it was. They told everyone; Margo had friends stop by every day; and she was able to keep Shelley in the room with her (Frank was invited to stay there too but he let Wilma stay instead; he stayed at the apartment and visited after school every day. After five days in the hospital, Frank brought Margo and Shelley home to Shilin. Wilma wanted to give Shelley a 'welcome home' gift, so Frank took her to the PX, and she was able to buy a little pink outfit for her. That night they celebrated at the Officers Club. Wilma wanted to stay longer, but she said she 'couldn't leave Francis alone too long…that she was planning to leave the next day.' Margo and Shelley said goodbye at the house, and Frank took her in a taxi to the Sungshan Airport. Before they went to sleep, Frank reflected on their time in Taiwan. How wonderful God had cared for them– from near disaster…they had found paradise. Margo said, *"Let's just stay here, you can teach at TAS, and we'll raise our family here. God is so good."* Frank agreed, "Sound's good to me, we can be missionaries, teachers, and minister to the military…all at the same time." They planned to stay as long as God would allow them–*Deo volente!*

Taipei Breakfast Club

Frank conducts TAS Band

Margo & Beth, Taipei park

Cross Island Trip

One bite-'Hundred-Year-Egg'

Michael and Beth Varro

Taiwan – Gem of the South Pacific

*The **rest of the world** — and a new plan develops!*

CHAPTER NINETEEN

THE WORLD ON A SHOESTRING... AND 'THE SCHOOL OF HARD KNOCKS'

Promise me we'll come back

IT GOT AROUND THE NETGHBORHOOD, THAT THERE WAS A NEW ADDITION to the 'Fan' (Varro) family. Mr. Feng, their next-door neighbor, came to visit, with his wife, and then spread the news that a new little 'bai wa-wa' ('white baby') had arrived, and there was a steady stream of visitors. HSA chapel choir rehearsal was that night; after rehearsal, Steve Jones said, "when do we do the baptism?" Frank wanted his dad to do it, but he knew he would never agree to 'infant baptism' so he asked Steve if his dad could do an 'infant *dedication*' instead. Steve said, "what's a little *theological difference* among friends," so Michael and Beth came in the next few weeks to HSA Chapel and did an 'infant *dedication*.' Frank never knew that Chaplain Steve, who was ordained in the Congregational Church before joining the Navy, had put in the chapel record that it was an 'infant baptism,' when what Pastor Varro *really* did was an 'infant dedication'. Just before Steve left the Island the next February, he told Frank it had been recorded that way because he had to go by the Navy rules that require that the 'theology of the current chaplain' be the one that is used. It was fine with Frank and Margo, and Steve said what mattered was what it was in the eyes of the parents, and the child's baptism *or dedication,* to 'God's glory;' they agreed. Frank soon got a letter from the U.S. Embassy reminding him he had not registered his 'foreign born' child; he quickly called Dr. Beckman about the birth certificate; he wanted to thank him again anyway for all he had done for them, and asked him how much they owed him. Dr. Beckman was always so gracious, and he loved to tease; he said, "you don't even begin to have the money to pay me what that kid is worth!" Frank laughed and said, "okay, so what would you settle for?" He said, 'truthfully, embassy doctors are only able to receive payment from U.S. military and state department people...because they are sent by the government, but not U.S. civilians living overseas.' What? God had done it again?...he wouldn't even accept an 'honorarium;' but Margo and Frank gave him two Chinese vases as a gift...before he and his family left Taiwan the next year. He said he was going to go back to Michigan and retire as an anesthesiologist; he said he was just...going to *'retire...and 'pass gas.'* Ha! Frank and he really laughed hard. He asked him for a birth certificate, which the hospital provided, and Frank took it to the U.S. embassy, and registered it with them. They kept it, and issued the official U.S. document showing a 'live birth' in Taipei, Taiwan...of two U.S. citizens living in Taiwan, and this was Shelley's *birth certificate.*

Taipei Drama Club sponsored another show, 'South Pacific;' Frank was cast as 'Lt. Cable.' Margo played for the production, which was very well received. Shelley stayed with grandma and grandpa, or the Melgren's, during times of rehearsals and the production. They attended the production and all really enjoyed it.

Another event that had happened in Frank and Margo's life was Linkou Chaplain Tom and Bonnie Bush being reassigned 'stateside.' They said they wanted Frank and Margo to have their house in Tianmu. It was a two-story suburban house with a nice yard, a balcony, and easy access to TAS…all they had to do was 'take over the rent,' he said; he wasn't even going to change the 'name on the rental agreement, or the electricity contract.' Frank asked if that was 'official, or unofficial;' Tom said the U.S. military did this all the time; local contracts with Taiwanese landlords and power companies, etc., were just 'rubber stamped'…as long as everyone got their money–they didn't care (the provost didn't like it, but let it go). So, they moved into their second home, this time a nice suburban two-story house, close to what many called the 'American ghetto.' They even inherited 'Duke,' their German-Shepherd-mix dog; in Tianmu, there was a bowling alley, snack bar, theater, and tennis courts, and swimming pools… 'a little slice of America,' you might say.

[Right after the previous New Year, Bob Brown had called Frank into his office. Frank wondered if he had done something wrong. 'No, not at all,' Bob said. The K-2 music teacher was not working out, and they were going to have to let her go. He wondered if Margo could teach; Frank told him she did not have a teaching certificate, but she did have a B.A. in music; he asked if she wanted the job; Frank said he doubted it (this was when Margo was almost six months pregnant), but he would ask her if she was interested. Bob said it would almost double their income; Frank said he would talk to her. Bob mentioned that the K-3 assignment would only be a 'morning-plus' assignment. Frank promised he would pray about it, and talk with Margo to see what she wanted to do. Margo decided she could do it, but only for four months; when the baby came, she would have to stay at home, even if she got an 'amah' (maid). So, Margo taught K-3…and when the big typhoon came, and they lost all their books in the flood, and the mud, including the singing books…all the teachers sent all the students to… you guessed it–to *MUSIC*; the pianos were ruined, the books were gone…

but they expected K-Three students to go to Margo's music room... and Four-Six students to go to Frank's music room! The clean-up took forever, and the elementary, junior high, and high school campuses were forced to do an abundance of improvisation. TAS, being in a U.S. military community, however, had a great advantage, and there was money and personnel to help with the clean-up. The chapel got a little water but little other damage. The mission compound in Mushan had damage too, but nothing like when Frank was growing up there].

The school year ended, and they had the summer to finish fixing everything up. Tom and Bonnie left, and Frank and Margo had moved into their Tianmu house. Duke was a little guarded at first, but he took to his new owners very well. The next task was to get an 'amah.' The Americans living in Tianmu told Frank that a live-in 'amah' would cost too much, an English-speaking amah would also cost too much. They knew Frank spoke Chinese, so they recommended a young Taiwanese woman whose husband had left her. She had a little girl, a year old, and she needed to bring her with her. Margo thought that would be fine...she could teach her Chinese, and Margo could teach her English! Shelley was almost six months old, so they thought this would be a good fit.; her English name was Amy, and she had named her little girl Susie. She came every morning by 9:00 a.m., and left by 7:00 p.m. She fixed meals, did laundry, helped with the care of Shelley, and ate her lunch and supper with Frank and Margo; it was also a great setup when Margo and Frank wanted to go out sometime with Ellie and Jack, or over to the Melgren's, to a movie or something else. They took Shelley with them to the chapel, Officer's Club, or anything that wasn't a 'date night.'

Frank got a letter from the Taiwan Missionary Fellowship asking him to be in charge of the music for the missionary conference, and assist with the youth. He was excited and accepted right away; the conference that year was going to be held at Morrison, and those attending could stay in the dormitories. Frank wrote a play, and the youth loved putting it on. It was called 'The Rev. Dr. Preachwell...And His Mission'—a satire on missionary life, from an MK (missionary kid) point of view. Many of the older missionaries were offended and walked out. [Unfortunately, Frank was beginning a new phase in his spiritual journey (this will be the theme of the final chapters in this book)]. Frank conducted a choir which some of the missionaries joined, including both his mom and dad; he sang solos, and a duet with Bill Ury, the head of the Methodist mission in Taipei. It was very hot, and Shelley cried a lot; they tried to get a room with A/C but were unsuccessful. Margo played the piano for the conference, so grandma had to help with Shelley's care some of the time. Everyone was so proud of Frank for marrying such a 'fine Christian girl, and returning to Taiwan.' They seemed to understand about the trouble they had had with ORTV, but thankfully, all but a few chose *not* to ask about it. The speaker was Dr. Clyde Narramore, a well-known Christian psychologist, and many missionaries who had read his books, enjoyed hearing him speak as well. After missionary conference, Frank and Margo returned to Taipei to find that a new associate chaplain had come to HSA Chapel. His name was Lowell Malliette; he had come from a Nazarene background, and many of the evangelicals at the chapel were very excited about his arrival. Two families in particular were close to the missionary community. One couple was Dan and Ann James, with the U.S. Embassy, and the other was Alan and Sharon Elliott. They, and several teachers from TAS, met weekly for a Bible study…which Ann taught; then they met with Frank and Margo, and Chaplain Lowell Malliette, and his wife Shirley, about starting a 'Sunday evening evangelistic' service. With no resistance from Chaplain Steve, they started it that month. Frank led singing, Margo played, and Chaplain Malliette preached. They had some wonderful guest speakers. Sometimes Frank and Margo had attended Grace Chapel on Yang Ming Shan in the past, where Glen Hix was pastor; he was with the Southern Baptists, but most of his ministry was with the American community, instead of the Chinese. He and other preachers in the community, both missionary, and military, and non-military, were invited to guest preach at the evening service. Chaplain Steve, though not himself an 'evangelical-conservative' often attended with his wife, Rose, and even spoke a couple times; they invited guest musicians; they called the Sunday evening meeting: 'Meeting At The Cross,' and it was held at the chapel every Sunday evening at 7:00 p.m. Gladys Aylward, of *'Inn Of The Sixth Happiness'* fame, started attending regularly, and Frank and Margo got to know her well. Frank even met Madame and Generalissimo Chiang Kai Shek (Frank's family had been invited to their church in Beitou, because Beth Varro had taught a Bible study…on breaks, as part of Madame Chiang's 'Troop Comforting' sewing circles; through Beth, Frank had even invited President and Madame Chiang to speak at the evening service, but they declined… "so sorry, busy, unable to attend, etc."). Another special guest was Pat Burgess, a young single Nazarene missionary; she was very talented as a speaker and a singer. The Elliott's and the James's invited many of their friends to 'Meet At The Cross' services, and were very gratified at the good attendance each Sunday evening. Many of the missionaries started coming as well; Frank took the opportunity to invite some of the ORTV band and choir to be a part of the music and worship…they were so popular Frank invited them back several times. One evening, at the reception, which they always had after the service, Leland Haggerty called Frank aside and asked him to come into the chapel with him… he handed him an envelope and asked him to open it. Frank opened the envelope and found two-hundred eighty-five dollars inside; when Leland saw Frank's face, he said, "It's the money we promised we would put aside, for two years, for your return passage to the U.S." Frank called Margo to come see; they were very appreciative, and Margo started to cry…the hurt that they had felt melted away; there was forgiveness and reconciliation, something both sides had wanted for some time. In the months that followed Frank and Margo were invited to appear on China Television, the new color television station. They appeared on the Thursday show as guests, and everyone received them warmly. After Chinese New Year, they received the tragic news that Pat Burgess had been killed in a plane crash in Hualien. Frank was invited to sing at her funeral. The Nazarene Seminary missionaries, the Holstead's and Rench's, had become good friends with Michael and Beth, and included them as 'fellow Nazarene missionaries,' even though they were with VOCA. This invitation of Frank to sing at Pat's funeral…was another one of these healing gestures. A few months later, Gladys Alyward also passed away. This was not only a huge Taiwan event, but a *world event*. Her story of China, and her missionary work there, was well-known; her becoming a Chinese citizen, and adopting a Chinese boy, were part of that story; though the now-grown Chinese son professed to be a Christian, his plans for Frank to sing at her funeral…and for other missionaries to speak, were *put aside* in favor of a Buddhist-style ceremony, to the great disappointment of the entire missionary and Christian community, but the biggest disappointment was: her service was not in a church, but a Buddhist funeral home.

In the spring, Bob Brown stopped by Frank's classroom...the superintendent, Dr. Wire wanted to see him. 'Is there a problem,' Frank asked? 'No, not really, they were very happy with his teaching–Dr. Wire would explain.' Frank went immediately to his office (his wife, Lynn, sang in Frank's chapel choir, so he knew him fairly well). He told him how happy they were with his teaching, and all that he meant to the community; there was only one problem: his Washington State Provisional Teaching Certificate was only good for three years; Frank said he had tried to get an extension. Yes, Dr. Wire said, but without a fifth-year and a Standard Teaching Certificate, they could not continue his contract. Frank said he had thought about that, and had been planning to get a Master's degree, and come back and teach at TAS... for the rest of his career; Margo and he had just been talking about that. Howard Wire leaned over his desk; he told Frank he had a job at TAS *anytime* he completed that step. He told him many at TAS were career teachers, and had done the same thing. Frank walked back to his office with mixed feeling; he was excited that TAS wanted him; he was even hoping he would eventually take over the choral music program there, maybe Ninette Mordant, the TAS choir director, would get married, or go to graduate school...he was disappointed that their time in Taiwan would be coming to a close. He went home; he told Margo that what they had just talked about...was going to be happening sooner than they thought. They began making plans to return to Seattle. Frank would apply to several graduate schools, and see what would come of it. He sat down and made application to Seattle Pacific College, and the University of Washington right away. He also found out that the *GRE* (Graduate Record Exam) could be administered there at TAS; so he made arrangements for that as well. He took the GRE on a Saturday in a few months; he took it one Saturday, and found out in a few weeks he had passed! He also got letters of acceptance from both Seattle Pacific and the University of Washington. [He had intended to apply to UCLA...his music teacher, Dr. Chen, Lu Yuan, wanted him to pursue his private studies on the traditional Chinese instruments: mainly Gu Zheng, but also the Pi Pa, Yue Qin, and the Chinese flutes.

Dr. Chen said Frank *MUST* get his doctorate in 'ethnomusicology;' in the end, Frank decided against that, in favor of a doctorate in Choral Conducting; Seattle Pacific did not have a doctoral program in music, so he would be able to go to the University of Washington after all, and study with Rodney Eichenberger].

Their second Thanksgiving and Christmas in Taiwan were special that year. It was Shelley's first for both, so for these celebrations they went to grandma's and grandpa's in Mushan. The students all made over Shelley, and they took their first family portrait at a studio. For Thanksgiving, Margo and grandma collaborated to make this a special meal. Mr. Li, from whom they had bought the land, gave them a turkey; he had become a good friend of the family; they also had everything else associated with this 'feast of thanks:' yams, mashed potatoes, vegetables, and...you guessed it–pies galore! Pumpkin, Apple, Cherry, even Starfruit. Yum! They had a two-hour nap after that one! Christmas was just as special. Seeing Shelley open gifts was priceless. She was only eight months old, but she tore into the paper wrappings like it was the 'object of the game,' and was even more curious about what was inside! They had the HSA chapel choir performance of course before they went to Mushan, and the Nightingales sang a concert too. [Margo said she would not get caught up in the politics of the 'ladies chorus,' but some in the chorus had decided that Mazel Anderson was 'too old' to continue as their conductor, and against her own wishes, Sara Mae Eckstein was asked to be the conductor. Margo played, and Sara Mae conducted, but many boycotted the concert because they had been so unfair to Mazel]. For the second year in a row, the Taipei Drama Club presented 'Amahl and the Night Visitors.' Sara Mae was pregnant and so she decided to be the stage manager, and let David Wang's mother, Helen, play the part of 'Amahl's mother.' They cast the same Kings, Page, and Shepherds and Shepherdesses. The day before the first performance, Helen came down sick; Sara Mae said she would go ahead and resume the mother's role...but Helen 'did not like losing her starring role,' so she insisted on having them make a very dramatic announcement that she was 'very ill, but would still play the part.' It was all 'very embarrassing,' but everything came together. Steve Jones didn't tell anyone that he had to leave *immediately* for the airport after the final show, and didn't bother to change his costume. He showed up at the airport…still in the role of the 'black king, Balthazar'… and greeted his incoming guests from the U.S. with: "Um gau wah," which he delivered with great gusto! Some people were shocked and didn't know what to make of it. Someone reported it to the authorities at the airport… and he was detained! His friends could not believe it was Steve…the chaplain! In the end, they all had a good laugh; the authorities from ROC (Republic of China) didn't think it was funny though; Steve's commanding officer called to say it was all just a joke, so they let him go. That same week, Frank had had a Christmas band concert; it went well, but, Margo left the concert early to go to the PX; she had promised mom and dad a surprise, so before leaving to go out to Mushan after the concert, she stopped in to get something for them she had promised herself she would get them this Christmas: they loved things like nuts, candy, and other things they couldn't get on the open market in Taiwan [Michael had always wanted to send nuts as gifts to others, and say in his card: "nuts to you!"]; the carolers came again of course, so Christmas Eve was a long night! When it was all over, Michael called their attention to the fact that this year they celebrated a new 'baby;' a gift God had given *them*, much like Mary and Joseph marveled at the 'baby' God had sent into the *world* as the most wonderful gift ever given. It truly was a Christmas to remember. Dean Kauffmann and his wife Sharon came to Frank about the possibility of singing the "Seven Last Words of Christ" with the HSA Chapel Choir as an Easter cantata. Frank had sung it with the Morrison choir and Marge Brown in high school, so he was familiar with it, and he immediately agreed to it. It was decided Dean would sing the baritone solos, Sharon would sing the soprano, and Frank would sing the tenor. They began rehearsals the next Thursday. Paul Sweet, Frank's childhood friend from Hong Kong, had returned to the U.S. to go to college and married Janice after joining the U.S. Army; they were sent to Taiwan, and met up again with Frank and sang in his choir; the choir was excited about the coming performance during Holy Week, and advertised it on Armed Forces Network Taiwan, in flyers and posters at the Officers Club, TAS, the PX and Commissary, and mailers to the community. By Easter, the whole community was abuzz with excitement, and the performance came off very well. Holy Week was celebrated with special services on Maundy Thursday, and

Good Friday… the service in which they presented the cantata. Easter Sunday included an Easter Sunrise Service; combining HSA chapel, and Calvary Chapel (*at* Calvary Chapel); then each had their own 11:00 Easter Worship services, and Frank and the choir presented a special Easter anthem for that.

[During their time in Taiwan, Frank and Margo had some special visitors who stayed with them. Don Brumfield, Frank's Victory Quartet buddy… and 'matchmaker' for Frank and Margo, came on an 'R & R' (Rest + Relaxation) visit from Vietnam [but some *irreverently* called it: 'I & I ([Intoxica----& Intercou---); he came to see them while they were still with ORTV in Dazhi; they waited for him as he processed through the disembarking line, and noticed the number of Chinese girls lined up against the far wall (?); after greeting them (Frank and Margo), he handed them the two hundred bucks he'd been given; Frank said, "what's this for?" Don said, "the rest of the guys turn over their money for the week to the escorts;" (they were all lined up along the wall; Don called them 'USDA-approved'); "what" Don laughed; he said that 'in order to prevent the spread of any STD, the U.S. government (knowing the ones on 'R & R' would drink and sleep with the 'local girls' *anyway*, went to a lot of trouble to certify that the 'only ones they cavorted with' would be at least: 'certified clean' (stifled laughter). Instead of spending his two hundred on booze, or the girls, he was giving it to Frank and Margo. So, they went out to fancy restaurants and spent his money *together*! They went out for 'chateaubriand' at the President's Hotel, and showed him the sights; they had a great time… laughing, crying, reminiscing about SPC, attending a Christian concert by the 'Certain Sounds,' (a US Christian traveling choral group), and about the horrors of Vietnam. The first morning…(Don was sleeping on the couch in the front room); Frank had forgotten to tell Don about the ROC (Republic of China) military maneuvers in the fields behind their apartment. The shelling started at 6:00 a.m.; suddenly, Don came bounding down the hall, yelling, "In-coming!" The door of Frank and Margo's bedroom flew open, and he dove under their bed in a panic mode. Frank and Margo jumped out of bed wondering 'what in the world' was going on! Don sheepishly appeared from under the bed. It took him a few minutes to orient himself, as he crawled out; "sorry, guys—I awoke in a panic…the guns roaring…I thought there was 'incoming fire;' it happens all the time in Nam." Then they all laughed, but Frank and Margo realized how terrible it was for them, and their good friend had given them a taste of what it was like every day. Another visit had been with Doug Bartlett from Japan; they showed him the sights, and took him to the chapel, and TAS, to see where they worked; he loved meeting Shelley and visiting with Michael and Beth in Mushan. They returned the visit by coming to Japan for a week's visit the following summer. Another visit of a very special friend was Bob Sweeney from Morrison days; he had gone into the army after college and was with MAAG (Military Assistance Advisory Group), and was stationed in Kinmen, offshore from the China mainland; he came twice during their time in Taiwan; he was so big, and the bed was so small, everyone laughed, especially their maid Amy, at how little his blanket actually covered on his bed. He too had two great visits with them. After the second visit, he said he had a *surprise* for them: he had made arrangements for them to visit him…on Kinmen! Wow! That was not an easy thing to accomplish; they had to fly, literally, 'under the radar,' to get there. They had to get permission from the provost to leave Taiwan. The airfield there was highly secret (they confiscated cameras, but didn't take Frank's camera…he actually had a 'forbidden picture' of the airfield no one ever knew about). They were watching a movie, when suddenly the Chinese Communist started 'shelling.' (even though it was *just propaganda leaflets*, but they were still *SHELLS*, and sometimes hit local farmers or their water buffaloes). One time, a stray shell had come right through the theater and destroyed two walls. Frank had to go outside and watch the shells breaking up less than a hundred yards above them. They had a wonderful time with Bob and all the other MAAG (Military Assistance Advisory Group) guys there; Saturday afternoon, the fog suddenly came in–no way they would be able to fly back to Taiwan–worse, they would miss the HSA chapel services Sunday morning! They *had* to let Chaplain Steve know, so, Bob got on the radio and called the chapel through his secret code: "this is 'blue fullback'…calling; 'white collar' do you read me?" Steve Jones came on the line and said: "blue fullback, this is 'white collar' I read you, go ahead." He asked him 'if he knew who was with him… 'yes'… and you know *when* they are to return… 'yes'…well, they will return *one day later*,'…copy that, over, out." Frank thought this was so cool, speaking in code like that. Steve got the message, made arrangements, and Frank's and Margo's returned on Monday after the fog cleared... flying just yards above the water].

As things began to wind down that school year, Frank came home one day, and told Margo he had heard about a music position at the International School in Seville, Spain; his friend, Bobby Turner was applying there in math and wanted Frank to think about doing the same...but that was *not* what Frank was excited about. (Frank had told Bobby it wouldn't do *him* any good–his provisional certificate would expire, and he would still need to go to graduate school to get a permanent certificate), but when Bobby told him he could use the money he had saved up...to go on around the world...*that's* when Frank got excited! Bobby told him he had a travel agent that could set the whole thing up. Margo said, "you mean we could take the money we have saved–and go on around the world instead of going straight back to Seattle!?" Frank told her that's exactly what they could do. The agency in Taipei was Cathay Travel, and Bobby's agent was a Hindu named Salil Sveetar, who always planned his travel for him. Frank made contact with him right away and laid out a plan for travel through Asia and Europe, before traveling across the U.S. from the east coast to Seattle, completing an 'around-the-world trip.' Frank and Margo had saved their money diligently with an American Express banking system, with the U.S. Navy 'support group' in Taiwan. A trip like this, however, was still beyond their means...unless they found ways to travel by the cheapest means possible. Salil had several suggestions on how to accomplish this: driving through Europe and across the U.S. would be much cheaper; he suggested that they buy a car; he had previously helped other U.S. military families this way; if they bought a European car through the PX, it would be military rates–they could take possession in Rome for instance, and drive through Europe, staying in student hostels in the summer, which would be as inexpensive as anyone could travel. If they purchased food in a grocery store for some of their meals, that would also save money. What about getting the car to the U.S.? They would have to ship the car and wait for it three weeks to arrive on the east coast before driving to Seattle. They priced European cars at the PX; they could buy an Opel Kadett, the same car they had had before they left Seattle, have it shipped from the factory in Frankfurt, Germany, then take delivery in Rome. Salil planned the first leg of the trip through Asia... Philippines, Vietnam, Thailand, Singapore, Malaysia, and India (since they could not fly directly to Israel, they would fly to Athens, change planes for Tel Aviv, then back to Athens, after their Holy Land visit, they would fly to Rome; there they would take delivery of the Opel, drive through Italy, Yugoslavia, Hungary Austria, Switzerland, to Germany; after Germany, they would see France, the Benelux countries (Belgium, Luxembourg, and Netherlands), and cross over from Calais, France, to Dover, England; from there they would ship the car to Baltimore, stay with friends or relatives on the east coast, and then drive to Seattle. It seemed like an impossibly expensive trip, but Salil promised them they could do it. If they stayed in missionary guest houses in Asia, summer 'private homes,' and 'gasthaus's (rooms above taverns...Frank freaked out remembering his own experience with *rooms above taverns!*). Salil laughed; he would make sure the facilities were acceptable, he said. They ordered a light-green Opel Kadett from the factory in Germany...to be delivered to Rome. They transferred money from their HSA American Express account in Taipei to their Seattle First National Bank account. They booked their air travel and lodging through Asia. They wrote friends in the Philippines, India, Belgium, and Germany; they wrote relatives in Israel, Yugoslavia and Hungary, and Frank's sister, Margi, in North Carolina, and Juli in Colorado. They told them of their 'dream trip' and requested a visit with them; the rest would be booked as they went. It seemed too good to be true. They prayed no unforeseen circumstances would result in them running out of money. They prayed that God would keep them safe.

Shelley was almost a year old, so Frank and Margo planned a special first birthday party for her. They invited Michael, Beth, and Dave to join them at the Officers Club for a special celebration; she'd played with Susie, Amy's little girl, but there were no other children her age that they could really invite; so, it seemed appropriate to just have a family get-together. They got her some new clothes and toys from the PX, and Grandma baked a cake. She opened her presents after dinner and they sang 'Happy Birthday' to her; others at the club joined in...it was a fun time; she seemed to really enjoy it. [Before they left, Frank also had his final band concert; Bruce Raley had a solo, Karen

Benintendi (little sister of Frank's longtime friend Ken Benintendi from Morrison) played flute; Larry Rench played trumpet (he had played guitar for the Triple 'C' summer camp, with Frank as camp director); the Melgren children were in his music classes, as was Richard Monte all of these reconnected and many other military and missionary kids...later on in Frank's life; many military and missionary children who had been in his Triple C camp, also played in his band]. It had been a good two years of teaching music at TAS, and Frank was going to miss it; he hoped to return after his graduate work. Frank had done some recordings, and written articles for the VOCA mission magazine, the 'Flashlight,' but Bob Hammond, didn't use any of his material; so, Frank resigned his position and offered to repay the money they had given him, but Michael told Frank to keep it, because he and Margo had done a lot of good work for VOCA at the Student Center, not only in music, but also guest preaching and Bible Study; his draft board was no longer pursuing him, but Frank wrote them anyway, to tell them he would be a graduate student in music at the University of Washington; Frank and Margo contacted the landlord of the house after Tom and Bonnie Bush had lived there...they finally had a chance to meet; his name was David Zhang (he had thought all alone 'Frank' was 'Tom' since they had never changed the name on the lease). He told him they were leaving to go back to the U.S. Mr. Zhang had already heard, and had found new Chinese renters. Frank thought, "God was working things out smoothly in our lives again." His dad bought their furniture and used it in the Student Center. The provost approved the purchase of the Opel, kept a copy of the letter of his resignation from TAS, and certified the closure of their American Express Banking account, and collected all of the PX, Commissary, and APO cards. [Frank had failed to turn in his Officers' Club card; (friends at TAS said: 'lose it' in your dresser or something–you might need it when you are in Vietnam, Germany, or someplace where U.S. Forces are stationed; they said he could use the club-card in those places, as others had done); the provost asked for it, but was not surprised when Frank 'didn't have it.']. They were ready to go. Amy had gotten another job, thanks to the recommendation Frank had given her. They packed the rest of their stuff, including all the disposable, PX-purchased diapers they could fit into their luggage. Michael, Beth, and Dave–and a group of HSA chapel friends came too. Many of these had come to Frank and Margo's going-away party in Mushan. This included an 'early birthday' (Frank's twenty-sixth) and anniversary (Frank and Margo's third): Steve Jones, Sara Mae Eckstein, Paul and Janice Sweet, and Lowell Malliette and his wife Shirley. The James's had already left for India; the Elliott's had left for Belgium; Frank and Margo were hoping to see them there, and made sure they had their new addresses. Ellie and Jack had left for the 'states' shortly after Dr. Beckman and his wife; the same as Bonnie and Tom Bush; some of the Student center people came, as did the Da An Peniel pastor, Jesse Pan, and his wife, Joy. They surprised Frank and Margo with some of their favorite appetizers, jiao-ze's, xiao-lung-bao, seaweed, and 'sea-slugs,' to the hoots and hollers of the military people who bet Frank ten NT (about twenty-five cents USD) each person, he wouldn't finish them...he did, and collected a hundred NT! They all laughed and presented Frank and Margo with gifts of special Chinese costumes and trinkets; then Beth presented a cake for Frank's birthday and their anniversary; they all sang, and then Michael showed the slide show he had prepared—a collection of 'every birthday from his first through the twentieth.' Michael had captured *ALL* of them on film; [Steve and Sara Mae started cutting up, right about birthday number fifteen. It really got funny when they all chanted together, "and here's Frank on his (blank) birthday," for the last five birthdays; but Michael and Beth took it all in good humor; then they ate cake and ice cream after the 'slide show.' It was time to go; everyone started thanking Michael and Beth and leaving. 'Nice party,' they all agreed.

June 16, 1970, came, and Frank and Margo, and Shelley took off from the Sungshan Airport, bound for Manila, PI. Michael, Beth, and Dave saw them off, along with several other friends from TAS and HSA Chapel; they were met by Dale and Sharon Gregory in Manila. [they had been in Taiwan studying the Fujian dialect of Chinese... called Taiwanese, because many from that province had immigrated to Taiwan over the past four hundred years, a number of these had later moved to the Philippine Islands, and the Gregory's were called to be missionaries there]. Frank and Margo had met them at the English Vesper service in Taiwan, and had become good friends, and promised they would stay with them if they ever got to the Philippines. They spent three wonderful days there; they showed them all the sights, and then took them to the church where they were serving; they introduced Frank and Margo to some of their co-workers—then it was time to say goodbye. They flew from Manila to Vietnam. Even though the war was going on, Tan Son Nhat Airport was open to civilian travel, and it was secure. They had made arrangements with Salil to stay one night at the Hotel Majestique, right on the Mekong River; a short taxi ride, with luggage stacked on the roof, it was an adventure in itself, and Frank and Margo stuffed themselves into a small cab with Shelley on their lap. They used the Officer's Club card for lunch, and some U.S. MAAG officers couldn't believe their eyes: here Frank, Margo, and Shelley looked like carefree *tourists in war-torn Saigon out of uniform*, casually having lunch (they heard that the Hotel Majestique was blown up a few years after they were there, and were grateful for their time there; the beauty of the city, the *oy-dai*, colorful dresses of the beautiful Vietnamese women, and the barb wire around the Catholic Cathedral were in such stark contrast; they marveled that they were given an opportunity to even see it at all; they didn't rest very well thinking about where they were, and breathed a sigh of relief as the plane lifted off and they flew out to Singapore. They stayed in the *TEAM House* (The Evangelical Alliance Mission). The city reminded them of Hong Kong—beautiful, with tall buildings, and a very orderly way of life. They had lunch downtown, and took a bus tour. Later they had a chance to crack a coconut at an open market, drink the milk and carve out some of the coconut meat on their own. They met other missionaries staying there, and had dinner with them; *TEAM House* served simple meals for those who did not wish to eat out…and Marian and Gilbert Schuster from Iowa, serving with Navigators in Manila, had come to Singapore for a conference of other Navigators from other parts of Asia; Frank and Margo shared their own work too, and all had a great time together. They made a brief stop in Kuala Lumpur on their way to Bangkok, had a light meal, and took some pictures at their hotel. They arrived in Bangkok later and checked into the Christian Guest House; the travel agent had arranged for an evening of dinner, a Thai fashion show, and dancing; the next day they took a bus to the 'Floating Market' and toured the temples and ruins of the Angkor Wat culture. It was their third anniversary, so they had a nice place to celebrate it at the Dusit Thani Hotel, recommended by the Christian Guest House in

Bangkok; they had spent most of their allotted budget for Thailand already on the tours, but they ordered a simple meal and shared it, so they could order a piece of cake as an 'anniversary dessert.' The hotel catered to Americans and other western tourists, so when the waiter found out it was their third wedding anniversary, he helped them sing "happy anniversary to you…" and some of the people around them joined in. Shelley sat in her high chair…she was eating cut-up or mashed solid food by now, so she shared part of their dinner, and loved the part of the cake they gave her. They flew out to New Delhi the next day. It was a late flight so they just spent most of the day reading and relaxing at the Guest House before checking out. It was only a four-hour and thirty-minute flight to New Delhi, but they didn't arrive until after midnight; by the time they got through customs and took a taxi to the YMCA, it was after two in the morning. The room was dusty, and the heat was **stifling**…management had forgotten the crib Frank had ordered for Shelley, and when they complained, one of the stewards retrieved a twin-sized mattress, folded it over, and threw it in the crib. It was so hot they couldn't sleep, so they went down the hall to the community restroom, got the sheets wet, and put the wet sheets over themselves. The overhead fan helped them get cool enough to sleep for a few hours. The next day, they took the 'Red Fort' self-guided tour, but their motorized 'pedicab' (bicycle in back instead of in front like Taiwan), broke down…in one-hundred-ten fahrenheit! While he fixed the cab, the wave of horse and cow manure smell was so strong in the heat, Margo started to gag, and had to cover her face. They had written Ann James, who worked at the U.S. Embassy, but she hadn't written back (they had tried calling in Bangkok, but no answer). This time, Ann answered; she said they had been out of the country; she asked them to come for lunch… she had a surprise. They got there and couldn't believe their eyes…not only was the embassy spectacular, the James' house was equally so; and the surprise? She took them into the library; there sat a middle-aged man that they were told was someone they 'knew of very well, and had read his book'–*Brother Andrew: God's Smuggler!.*' This Dutchman (Andrew van der Bijl), who had always aspired to be a spy, and deal in the clandestine, had become a Christian; he ended up smuggling Bibles into Russia, China, and many Muslim and Communist countries; he always prayed the same prayer: "*O Thou,*

who madest blind eyes to see, now make seeing eyes blind!" Officials missed 'seeing' thousands of Bibles he smuggled into many countries…here he was in Ann and Dan's library; unbelievable! They sat down and ate; they heard many of Brother Andrew's adventures. They also spoke of Frank and Margo's ministry…and they told them about last night! Dan said they would definitely stay with *them* tonight. They laughed when Frank asked the 'wrong' servant for another spoon when he dropped his on the floor; he was told that 'another of the servants' was the 'spoon servant;' she was the 'bread-serving servant.' Of the seven servants that day for lunch, not one of them had a cross-over duty. Ann said it was part of the caste system. After a very restful and cool night (their fabulous home was well air-conditioned!), they had a nice breakfast, a tour of the embassy, and then they caught their flight to Agra in a few hours, and flew south about an hour or so to the great Taj Mahal. The tour was spectacular, the clear pond was peaceful, and the adjacent hotel where they had a meal was very nice. On their way over to the hotel, a snake charmer put on a show for them; as he played his 'oboe' the hooded snake swayed back and forth in a sinister manner. He would strike the snake from time to time to keep him aggressive, and to prompt people to give more money. Everyone made over the 'little white American girl' so one of the stewards held Shelley while they took pictures. When their food arrived, it looked as though some metal had melted on top of their food. Frank called the waiter over to complain. "Oh, no my friend," he said, "it is part of the dish, it is silver leaf and you should eat it, it is very special with your sweets." After protesting for some time, they finally tried it. It was very thin and didn't seem to harm them. All the waiters smiled; they were very pleased they had tried it. By then it was time to return to New Delhi. The Air India agent said he was *so sorry*…the flight had been cancelled! What? They had an overnight flight to Athens by way of Tehran! They couldn't miss it. 'Not to worry, please,' the agent said; they would just take a taxi back to New Delhi. A taxi? That would take hours! Yes, but you will get to see some of India. How *true* that turned out to be; they were able to see a lot of the countryside that they never would have seen otherwise. Shelley and Margo had a long sleep; Frank slept a little, but had the driver stop from time to time for him to take pictures of the countryside. God had made another little *detour* part of His plan. They had left their suitcases at the airport, and later they had a light meal, and picked up their luggage before catching the flight to Tehran. Salil had booked inexpensive flights for them... called 'red eye' specials, and BOAC flew the nearly four-hour flight to Tehran; but the layover was considered 'company-paid,' so their lodging was at the *airline's expense*; how clever of Salil, Frank thought. They were arriving again after midnight, but this time it was a very nice hotel room...and it was free! They stayed less than 24 hours, but had a chance to see...a downtown Tehran Bazaar ...the Shah of Iran's Palace (including the 'Crown Jewels')... and take some pictures...all as guests of BOAC! They flew out the next afternoon, and arrived in Athens in a few hours; since there was no direct air service to Tel Aviv, they flew first to Athens, changed planes, and then on to Israel. A taxi took them 'up the hill' to Jerusalem... forty-one miles away. The 'Seven Day War of 1967' had left bombed-out tanks, rubble, and other evidence of the war, that still hadn't been completely cleaned up. They came into Jerusalem, now united under Israeli control, and made their way to St. George's, an Anglican hostel and church with a tall 'spire.' . There was also a group of Christian archeologists staying there; they joined them each morning for a continental breakfast...a hard roll and a cup of Turkish coffee. Each evening they would discuss what they had seen or done. Frank and Margo stayed most of the week visiting all of the important sights of Jesus' life, death, and resurrection. After Jericho, they 'swam' in the Dead Sea—it was so salty, the nick Frank had on his face, from shaving that morning, stung like fire; he tried 'floating' while holding Shelley on his lap, and neither of them could even submerge halfway; they prayed at the 'Wailing Wall' (but Margo and Shelley were *not* allowed in, and Frank had to wear the 'yarmulka' while he went in to pray). They went to 'Gordon's Calvary and Tomb,' then the traditional site of Calvary, the Tomb, and then went to Bethlehem to see Jesus' birth site. Most impressive though was the visit to the Garden of Gethsemane... it was hot, and they were resting by one of the many olive trees there; the gnarled ancient branches spread out over the ground, and Frank and Margo sat down for a moment to rest their legs. A Christian Arab guide asked them if they were part of the tour group they'd seen ahead of them; Frank said 'no, they couldn't afford a guide, so they were 'piggy-backing' on the group ahead of them;' the guide struck up a conversation with them. He told them he had been a believer all his life, and his mom and dad had led him to the Lord when he was twelve; he then asked them, "say, do you know how old the olive branch is... that you are sitting on?" Frank said he thought it must be *really* old, maybe even 'more than a thousand years old.' The guide said, "probably more than *two thousand* years old; *do you know Jesus might have knelt here... right where you are sitting?*" Frank fell off the branch!. A shiver went down his spine...*"Jesus, my Savior, could have knelt right here where I am sitting?"* The night before his *death*, the most important events in *history*, his death and resurrection...he decided to "go through with it right *here* where I sit?!" It was almost more than he could stand; tears came down Frank's and Margo's faces. Youssef took both their hands in his and then he prayed, "God of Ibrahim, Itzhak, and Yaqob, bless these two believers in the 'Name that is above all names, *Jesus Christ*...to Him be all glory, honor, dominion, and power. Amen!" Frank and Margo went on with their tour, but the highlight of their entire time in the Holy Land was that *singular* experience of feeling the actual presence of Jesus in the Garden of Gethsemane. That evening they had supper with their Jewish relatives, Iren and Bela Weisz (Iren was the daughter of Ferenc and Ana Balla, and granddaughter of Julia Varro Balla, a cousin of Frank's dad). Bela had a hardware store in Jerusalem, built against the wall... that had been 'no-man's land' in the 'Sixty-Seven war.' They introduced them to their children Imre and Ana. They had a 'different perspective' on the Arabs and Jerusalem, of course, so Frank and Margo just listened and nodded, and asked many questions about the Varro family. Michael, Beth, Margi and Dave, had been to Hungary and Yugoslavia in 1964, and visited with Iren's parents and aunts and uncles, but had not come to Jerusalem...it was not open at that time. The meal they had there was wonderful, and Iren had made some poppy seed cake for their visit...it was fabulous. They asked Frank and Margo to be sure to greet their family when they arrived in Novi Sad. Iren had converted to Judaism, so Frank asked if Bela could offer a blessing from the Psalms, which he was happy to do. They returned to their room at St. George's and went to bed early; they were going to Tel Aviv, then to Athens the next day. The short flight there was good and they checked in to the Athena Hotel to rest, and then went to supper at the little restaurant in the hotel. They took a bus tour the next day, including the Acropolis and all the famous Greek historical sites. After supper at a little Greek restaurant close to their hotel, they took in the 'light and sound' presentation at the Acropolis. It was inspiring, exciting, and very historically authentic. The next day they took a bus to the Aegean Sea, swam in the clear blue water, in an area designated for tourists, and on their way back, somehow got caught up in a parade; all of them on the bus were putting their heads out the windows and waving...like they were part of the parade! They had a good night's rest and caught their plane to Rome. It was Sunday afternoon, the sun was bright, the flight was short, and they arrived in Rome without incident; after getting their luggage, a bus took them to the train station. They caught a cab which took them to a little *penzion,* just a block from the Coliseum. Frank had gotten some money exchanged at the train station, but they only gave him ten-thousand lira notes...with no change. He told the taxi driver the address for the *penzion;* when they arrived, the meter showed the fare to be: fifty-five hundred lira; with an exchange rate of about six dollars and seventy cents USD, to ten thousand lira, the fare was barely over half his ten-thousand lira note. He didn't have much money, and wanted change from the driver. The driver wouldn't give change...but Frank wouldn't let go of the ten-thousand lira note. He put the luggage back on the roof of the cab, and Frank, even with Shelley in the child carrier on his back, took the luggage back down. The driver then looked like he was going to punch Frank; so, Frank went to the door of the *penzion* to appeal to the proprietor for some change; instead, she bawled Frank out in Italian like he was a 'cheapskate.' Finally, with no other options, Frank surrendered the ten-thousand lira note and the taxi driver got in his cab muttering in Italian—likely something about that 'cheapskate' American tourist...but it probably would have been censored! They went inside, moved into their room, and rested until supper. It was Sunday afternoon...a good time for a nap. They would worry about their budget, getting their car, and how to get a visa to Hungary, in Rome...another day. After supper, they went to bed, and had a good night's rest. After breakfast, Frank called the Opel agent about their car; he didn't offer to pick them up, or take them to the dealership, but rather gave them the address and phone number. They took a taxi there, and met someone who showed them the car; he gave them the papers...he asked them to sign. Not so fast, Frank said, and inspected the car; it had a small scratch on the driver's side, and the odometer read 'over eight hundred miles!' The price of the car had included the shipping cost from Frankfort, which Frank had prepaid in order to take immediate delivery in Rome; it appeared the agent was avoiding him by not meeting him there, and the dealership had been instructed to release the car only upon Frank's signature; it was obvious that the car had not been shipped...it had been driven to 'pocket the shipping cost,' but Frank could hardly refuse the car, and this upset him. He called the agent again, but he denied that it had been driven, and that he (Frank) was responsible for any damage to the car. What could he do? He signed the paper, and wrote on the bottom in the comments section that he should be reimbursed for the prepaid shipping cost. They drove to the address Frank had been given for the Hungarian consulate, in a travel agency outlet. Even though they were there during the posted office hours, they said they were 'closed' after they saw Frank's name: 'Michael F. Varro.' He asked, "Shall I come back later?" She said something which sounded like Hungarian to him; Frank didn't speak but a few words of Hungarian, so he told them he had relatives waiting for him in Novi Sad, Yugoslavia, and also in Budapest. The 'travel agent' told him he could get a three-day visa to see Uncle Imre Dornei in Budapest; Frank said they 'needed to be in Vienna by July 14 to meet a friend who would travel with them to Zurich.' They said 'come back 'tomorrow.' So, they took a tour of Rome, including the Catacombs, Appian Way, and the Coliseum, and then St. Peter's where they saw the famous Pieta; that evening they saw another 'light and sound' show, like the one in Athens...very exciting. They ordered 'pizza' that evening from a little shop near their *penzion*, but it tasted like *a cracker with seafood!* The next day, they returned to the Hungarian consulate; they said, "you...no visa...you go border, three-day pass, okay?" ... You spend more than fifty—no *'forint'* (Hungarian dollar), only US dollar, okay?" Frank told Margo what he thought they were saying, i.e., it would take too long to get a visa, so they should get a three-day border pass instead...but they would *have to spend* fifty (US dollars, *ONLY,* and surrender the pass upon departing, at the border). [They were three days behind schedule; they had promised Joyce Humphries (who had worked at the U.S. Embassy in Taiwan and sang in Frank's HSA chapel choir), that they would meet up in Vienna and travel together in their car...Vienna, Salzburg, then Zurich, where she would meet up with her U.S. Embassy contact; they were also out of disposable diapers, and had had no luck in locating such a thing in local markets; Margo had washed out some cloth diapers, but this was not a good option when they were traveling]. That evening after supper at the *penzion*, they went out to a 'department store' and found some pads that could be used as a lining for the cloth diapers. This would have to do until they got to Novi Sad...where they could do laundry. The next day after breakfast, they checked out of the *penzion*, drove up through the gorgeous peninsula of Italy, stopping only for lunch in Florence (with extreme disappointment that they didn't have more time to visit one of the *world's greatest Renaissance centers of art!*)...and made it to Venice before dark. They had a gondola ride, a visit to the famous San Marco (St. Mark's Church, a Renaissance treasure), and fed the birds at San Marco Square. They stayed in a little 'room, with a view' off the canal, and had breakfast the next day at a wonderful little Italian café. The next morning, they drove on around the bay to Trieste, where Frank's grandfather, 'Varro, Mihaly,' had escaped from the Banat (now part of Romania and Serbia) in World War I, had gathered up his wife and new born son, Michael—Frank's dad, before they immigrated to Canada. They crossed over into Yugoslavia, and went to Ljubljiana (now in Slovenia), where they had lunch. After taking some pictures, and resting briefly, they drove on to Zagreb (they had a Croatian saté-type of meat, and vegetables for supper, which reminded them of the Malaysian food they had eaten in Taiwan). They had hoped to make it all the way to Novi Sad that evening, but it was starting to get dark, so they stopped for the night in a little town named Slav Brod (now in Serbia). They were able to get a small room with only a bunkbed... Frank on the top, Margo on the bottom, and a 'cradle-type' of bed for Shelley on the floor next to Margo. 'It was just like Michigan farm-land,' Margo said, and she loved traveling through the countryside; she felt so peaceful...and happy. They ate breakfast at the little cottage, and then made it to Novi Sad in the early afternoon. They called Ferenc and he told them how to get to get across the bridge, in Voyvodina, to their house. After they freshened up a little, Ferenc introduced them to his wife Ana, his sister Zophi, who was visiting from Szeged, and his daughter Erzebet, and her son Janos. Ana and Erzebet had fixed a big dinner, which they ate outside in the patio area. Ferenc evidently worked for some kind of 'state exhibition commission;' at least that is what Frank gathered from the pictures Ferenc showed him, and a combination of broken English, German, and Hungarian. He showed him around his house; and showed him more pictures of Ferenc with others 'apparently at work somewhere.' [Frank had done a refresher course with his West-German neighbor in Tianmu before they left Taiwan; and he had studied German at SPC with Dr. Breitenbach]. Erzebet offered to do their laundry for them, and Margo tried to help, but she insisted that Margo and Shelley visit rather than take on this 'mundane chore.' Shelley was the center of attention, and she allowed herself to be passed from one to the other, all evening, while they snapped pictures of them; they retired for the night; in the morning they had a variety of pastries, coffee and fruit. Immediately after breakfast, they went over to Ferenc' sister Julia's house; she lived there with her husband Adam; they had prepared another breakfast of Hungarian sausage, veal cutlets, bread, and some kind of juice (or was it 'kirshwasser?' [inside joke, see following chapters]. They didn't say whether it was alcoholic or not...and Frank didn't ask!... That day, they took a short trip to Piros, the place where Pop...Frank's grandpa, had been born. Ferenc pointed out the building where he had lived and schooled through the fourth grade; then they walked down an adjacent street. As they did, people started coming out of their houses; Ferenc explained that they were all named 'Varro.' He told those that came out that Frank was the son of Michael Varro, the son of Mike Varro (Pop–Varro, Mihaly). They were all the cousins, aunts, and uncles of Frank; one after another came over to Frank and Margo, and said in broken English, "me Varro...me Varro; they cried and laughed; Frank and Margo embraced them and said, "me Varro too...me Varro too!" It was quite a moving experience; they wanted to touch and hold Shelley, and she loved being passed from one to another. Following that 'long-lost-family reunion,' they saw some gypsies, *complete with covered wagons*, a block away. Frank wanted to take their picture, but they said *'no.'* Seeing a chance to make some money, the *leader*, 'Boiko,' came over to Ferenc and said (apparently)...they would do it...for a few American dollars. Ferenc was ready to chase them off, told them that they were 'relatives of people here in Piros,' and bawled out the gypsy leader for trying to 'make a buck off the Americans.' Backing off a little, 'Boiko' said, 'okay, he would do it for a few American cigarettes;' Ferenc tried to explain that Frank and his wife did not smoke, and had neither American, or any other kind of, cigarettes. Aunt Zophi stepped forward; she smoked and offered some fancy cigarettes from Budapest. 'Boiko' looked at them…then suddenly he laughed and told his party to all smile, and pose for the camera. Frank snapped a few pictures; they wouldn't let Frank pose with them, but he was happy to have at least gotten something. They left, and returned to Novi Sad. They were having dinner at Julia and Adam's house again. It was chicken paprikas, Hungarian veal cutlets, bread, vegetables, and topped off with pastries… including Frank and Margo's favorite…*yes, poppy seed cake!* They were stuffed, but Ferenc and Adam broke out some 'cherry wine' and coffee. They felt they couldn't turn them down, so they drank a sip or two of the cherry wine and ate a little poppy seed cake. Their laundry was done; Erzebet was so proud of herself–and Margo was profuse in her praise. Now they were out of the pads, but traveling by car made it easier to handle. They slept well; in the morning they bid them farewell. Zophi went with them as far as the Hungarian border; she got out of the car a hundred yards before the guard station, and walked across the border. Frank was ordered to pull over when they got to the border; he was told to get out of the car… and present his passports with visa; Frank told him that in Rome they had told him he could get a border pass since they didn't have time to get a visa. He looked at his passport a long time; finally, he said, "Varro, Mihaly, you no leave Magyarzag legal?" Frank told him he had never been to Hungary before; the guard left and went inside the station; he was gone a long time. He came out and called him by his Hungarian name again, "Varro, Mihaly…you vater, Varro, Mihaly, no leave Magyarzag legal?" Frank knew his dad was only a thirteen-month-old child and had no volition of his own, so he answered truthfully: "he…he was a *baby.*" Why did Frank feel like this guy knew everything about him? Frank smiled and asked his name; the guard said, "Szabo, Andras." Frank said he was 'Magyar' and only wanted to see the country of his ancestors;' he told him an uncle was waiting to see him in Budapest. Andras smiled, "you Magyar, your vater Magyar, …you grandfather? *HE* leave no legal? You know? You don't know?" Frank told Andras that his 'vater' might know–all he knew was that Uncle Imre Dornyei, was waiting for him (Margo was praying, and she knew Frank was praying as he spoke with Andras). He handed back his passport; then he smiled, "you Magyar, yes, but you eyes no Magyar... you Kun, name no Magyar." He handed him back the three-day border pass, with instructions on surrendering it at the border near Nickelsdorf, when heading toward Vienna. They breathed a sigh of relief and drove on toward Budapest. Frank thought he might see Zophi, but she was long gone, and he knew they didn't have time to see her in Szeged. As they drove through the countryside, Margo saw a giant hay wagon the local Hungarian farmers were loading; the old-fashioned pitch forks and hay wagon looked like a 1950's movie at sunset. It was getting dark as they approached Budapest; they remembered the instructions: 'cross the bridge at the Danube, then go into the old city of Buda. They found the apartment building, and Imre, who was expecting them. He introduced them to his wife, Irina, and then showed them the room where they would sleep. He gave them a snack of some pastries and juice. It was Sunday afternoon, so most sites were closed, but he took them to a beautiful cathedral on the hill, and they took in part of a service; the choir sang the 'Theresa Mass' by Haydn; they stayed a while, until Shelley started getting fussy, then they drove around Budapest, with Uncle Imre telling them, as best he could, about the sights. They spoke mostly in English, with a few words, here and there, in Hungarian or German. After they arrived back at their apartment, they ate a delicious supper of cabbage rolls and vegetables that Irina had prepared. Shelley had fallen asleep during supper, and after visiting a bit, they retired for the night. The next day Imre took them to the Danube, evidently to a place where they camped in the summer time. Frank gathered that he and Irina and the Dornyei family came there often, and maybe had just been there a few weeks prior to their arrival? Irina had brought some cold cut sandwiches and fruit for lunch, and some left over poppy seed cake for dessert. It was a fun time. Uncle Imre took them all out for supper, in the business section on the 'Pest' side, after they visited the factory where he worked. Following supper, they returned to their apartment, where he broke out a bottle of wine...he had not offered any to Michael, Beth, Margi and Dave, because Ferenc warned him that they did not drink any alcohol...at all! It seemed important to him that they accept his hospitality, so they gave in, and drank a few sips; he and Irina were very pleased and offered more, but Frank and Margo politely refused. They went to bed early because they had a long drive to Vienna the next day, and had to surrender the border pass, as it was the third day that they had been in Hungary. They left after breakfast, and made a short stop in Esztergom. They still had a few *forint* (Hungarian money) left, and they knew they had to spend all of it, because there was no exchange back into US dollars at the border (nevertheless Frank did save one ten-forint note inside his sock...for memoirs only!). This time they had no trouble at the border. Frank had snapped a picture of the 'three-day border pass, for memoirs also, before he surrendered it, and they drove on their way, much relieved that they were no longer in a communist country. They made good time, even though they stopped to take pictures several times, and were pulling into the eastern side of Vienna just as the sun was setting. As Frank entered the city limits at a traffic circle, an Austrian jumped out in front of his car, bawling him out in German. Evidently, Frank had not yielded to the cars on the right before he entered the circle. Frank acted apologetic, even though he thought he had had the right of way. They checked into Tourist Haus, and found that they were well prepared for them, including a small cradle-like bed for Shelley. Frank had a message at the front desk letting them know Joyce Humphries had arrived and was staying at the Astoria Hotel. She wanted to get together with them the next day following her meeting. They ate at the Tourist Haus, then walked around the park listening to a live band play Johann Strauss. Shelley played on the slide, Frank pushed her in a swing; then they retired to their room, and slept in the cool evening air with the windows open. The next day after breakfast, they met Joyce at the Astoria, and toured the 'Schönbrunn' together (this was the palace of the Hapsburg and Austro-Hungarian empires). They also toured the famous 'Lippizaner' horse show. Joyce was on an expense account, so she suggested she pay for dinner out at the famous Die 'Metzgerei'...and she didn't have to suggest it twice. They visited the 'Mozarteum' on their way, and the restaurant welcomed children, so they had no problems taking Shelley with them. It was nice to let Joyce splurge on them... they had been 'pinching the pennies' pretty tightly the whole trip. They all had typical Austrian and

German fare: weiner-schnitzel and sausage dinners with red cabbage, soup, sauerkraut, bread, and vegetables. They topped it all off with some Viennese torts and coffee. Joyce ordered a bottle of wine, but Frank and Margo told her they didn't drink. She convinced them that a 'half glass' wouldn't harm them, so to be polite, they had a little. She was used to the U.S. Embassy parties in Taiwan, so she had no trouble finishing off the small bottle herself (she said it was a good thing she hadn't ordered a regular sized bottle). They dropped her off at the Astoria, with their profound thanks, but refused her kind offer for them to stay with her in her suite...they had already prepaid at the Touristen Haus. The next day they had breakfast at the guest house and picked up Joyce about mid-morning. They drove toward Salzburg, stopping for lunch in Linz. It was nearly sunset when they arrived in Salzburg. They came in on the Autobahn and easily found the 'Salzburghaus,' a private residence, and like many homeowners in the Alps, they catered to tourists during the summer months, opening their homes for rental-share, and many students and tourists traveled this way. After they checked in with Mrs. Schlosser, their hostess, they asked about getting something to eat. She said it was only a 'bed-and-breakfast' there, but if they went back through town, they would find a number of places where they could eat. They enjoyed seeing the festive setting of Salzburg...lights, parks, music playing, and they found a nice place to eat. They returned early after supper, and Joyce stayed in one room, and Frank and Margo stayed in another, and Shelley had a small crib in their room. They wanted to take in as much as they could the next day before they had to leave, so they retired early. Mrs. Schlosser served them a nice breakfast in the morning, and they toured the city, seeing the cathedral, the places where Mozart and his family had been, and the other tourist attractions.

They got on their way in the early afternoon, and still had time to make it to Landsberg, Germany, after stopping briefly in Munich for supper. They found a ski lodge that was a bed and breakfast in the summer, and it wasn't just a hard roll and coffee in the morning either. It was a full breakfast with eggs, sausage, and pastries, plus fruit, juice, and coffee. After they got on their way, they made it to Liechtenstein for lunch, and to Zurich. Here they said goodbye to Joyce after a light supper with some U.S. Embassy friends of hers. They had contacted

Margo's Quincy High schoolmate, Nancy Warner, before leaving Taiwan. She had married Ted Hadfield, and deployed to the U.S. Army base in Kaiserslautern, Germany. Frank and Margo were almost out of money, and needed help in cashing some traveler's checks; they had gotten away later than planned in Zurich, and didn't feel right imposing on Joyce's friends. When they got to Mannheim, they called Nancy, but there was no answer. They had enough gas to get there, so they took a chance and pushed on into the night. It was almost 2:00 a.m. when they knocked on the door of the little house on base where they lived. At the gate, the Army Post guard had called them, and this time they answered. Nancy and Margo squealed with delight at seeing each other again. Ted was half-asleep, and Frank– with Shelley in the carrier on his back–felt very awkward...but it worked out beautifully. They visited briefly; but because Ted had to get up in three hours to go to work, they agreed to continue everything in the morning; Nancy showed them their beds, and everyone went to sleep quickly...warm and safe with friends. The next day, Nancy took Margo to the Base PX, where they finally purchased disposable diapers! Frank was also able to cash a check, purchase additional traveler's checks, and fill up the Opel with gas. Nancy and Margo made lunch while they visited about their times together at Quincy High School, and Shelley played with her toys; she was beginning to crawl and pull herself up to sofas, chairs and other things, so they had to watch her carefully so she didn't get into things. Frank read and napped; Ted spent most of the time during their visit at work, but joined them for supper. They told Margo and Frank how they met, married, their time together during his military training, and moving from the U.S. to Germany. It was a good visit, and Margo and Frank wanted to spend more time with them, but they had to make the schedule that Salil had made for them. After parts of two days, they moved on; they left the next morning for Bonn. In Bonn, they visited the West German Capitol complex, and Beethoven's birthplace and house; they had lunch at a little German cafe called Schwarzwälder, and then drove through the German countryside toward Luxembourg. Since they would be coming back through Belgium and Netherlands later, they didn't take time to stop except in Luxembourg, where they stayed the night. They found a little hostel that offered 'chambre touristique' on the outskirts of Luxembourg

City, and stayed the night there; they had been able to visit a market earlier, and bought some ham, cheese, and bread ('Schinken, Kase, und Brod'), for supper and breakfast. It was fun trying out Frank's German… and actually being understood! They slept well in their little room, then drove on in to Paris in the morning. They had been told to go to the Paris train station, where they would find the Tourist Information Center…and they spoke English there! They found ads that showed inexpensive tourist rooms; they ended up at a small but quaint hotel in the Pigalle called the 'Hotel Montmartre.' They were warned that the Pigalle… named for a French sculptor Jean-Baptiste Pigalle (who lived there 1714-1785, close to the famous Moulin Rouge), was an area that was a bit risqué. Frank and Margo said they would take it…it was all they could afford, and they could cover Shelley's eyes, ha! They drove out to the Pigalle, checked in, and then took their own 'self-guided tour' of Paris. They were able to purchase a tourist map, and fortunately, take in most of the important sights: Eiffel Tower, Arc de Triomphe, the Louvre, Notre Dame Cathedral, the Bastille, and the Seine River, all close together, and not far from the Hotel Montmartre. They spent four or five hours seeing the sights: the Louvre, and Notre Dame Cathedral, were particularly impressive; and they were able to see the world-famous 'Venus de Milo,' and the 'Mona Lisa.' There were always visiting choirs singing at Notre Dame cathedral, so they enjoyed listening to some of them, particularly one that they thought was from the U.S. They had lunch on the Seine River at a little tourist spot, the Café de Seine, where boats were floating by, and sounds of accordions and singers was delightful. They took a trip to the top of the Eifel Tower, and then returned to their car, and went out to the Versailles. They 'piggy backed' again, as in Jerusalem, and were able to learn most of what they needed to know about the French Revolution, French history, (and especially about the Hapsburgs (and Austro-Hungary). By this time, it was late in the afternoon, and Shelley was asleep in Frank's carrier. They were tired and returned to their room; Frank had found a brochure which advertised a live show near the Moulon Rouge. It was like a dinner theatre (clean enough to pass the family test, included a simple meal… and allowed children!). They enjoyed both the show and meal, and several customers came by…to talk to Shelley. It was still early so they walked to a park close by, then returned to their hotel. Frank heard a noise on the stairway around 2:00 in the morning. He opened the door a crack and saw someone stumbling up the stairs; thinking it was just some inebriated Frenchman, he closed the door quietly and went back to bed; a few minutes later, there was a knock on the door. Frank ignored it, but the knocking continued. He finally went to the door and opened it a crack…with the chain still in place. It was the man he had seen on the stairway. He was Japanese…Frank thought a student perhaps? He was speaking English, but very slurred. He said he thought this was his room…room number 305? 'No,' Frank said, this was their room…room number 205; he suggested that he go up one more flight of stairs…and for him to be careful…to 'sleep it off.' They went back to sleep, but the experience bothered Margo, and she was nervous about the neighborhood they were in. Frank assured her everything would be fine, and they went back to sleep. About 4:00 a.m., there was a loud knock on the door; they kept pounding on the door, and yelling something in French; Frank came to the door, and opened it up. It was the Gendarme's…French police. They said in broken English, "passport.. you.. everyone.. passport.. et maintenant!" Frank grabbed the passports as Margo held Shelley tightly. Frank asked what was going on. Another gendarme who spoke pretty good English stepped forward and said that someone had been killed in the hotel that night. Frank looked quickly at Margo; he didn't want her to say anything about the drunken Japanese student. They checked the passports and left, going on from room to room; Margo wanted to leave right then, but Frank said that if it were the Japanese, their leaving would seem suspicious, and there was no reason to believe he was necessarily the one they were referred to. They slept a few more hours, and then quietly packed up and left, going down the back stairs…just in case. They drove a few hours and then checked into a little 'guest house' on the outskirts of Cambrai. They had been planning to stay with Alan and Sharon Elliott later in Mons, Belgium (Frank and Margo had known them through the HSA Chapel in Taiwan, but they were now working at SHAPE (Supreme Headquarters Allied Powers Europe), just south of Brussels, in Belgium. They knew they would be on vacation sometime in July or August, but were not sure when they would be back, and had decided to take a chance and show up anyway; they spent the night at a guest house in Cambrai. Frank was successful in ordering breakfast in the morning…in French. He had studied French in high school at Morrison, but had forgotten most of it. Margo had studied French at SPC, but not from a French-speaking instructor, just vocabulary. So, Margo told Frank what to say, and Frank ordered for them; the lady was polite, and let Frank struggle through it in French, and then she said in English…with a delightful French accent, "qui monsieur …that will be two orders of eggs, with bread and fruit; you would like them scrambled with bacon, qui?" Frank smiled and then they both laughed (who said the French were nasty? Maybe in Paris, but not in the countryside). Everyone in Cambrai was friendly and welcomed these two American young people and their baby with open arms! After breakfast they drove on to Mons; Frank followed the directions to the address in the letter; when they arrived, it didn't look like anyone was home; he knocked and then went around the house… nothing. He called the number he had for them, but there was no message on the answering machine, and it didn't allow leaving a message. They drove away disappointed; they decided to try and see them another time; a change of plans—they would finish visiting Belgium and Holland, and then go on to London by way of the Calais-Dover ferry—visit Pam and Jim in London a few days, and then ship the car from London, or Southampton. They would stay with Margaret and Alan in North Carolina until the car arrived in Baltimore, or wherever they could ship it, and then pick up the car, drive out to Seattle, and visit Juli and Larry in Colorado on the way. 'Yes, that would work,' Margo said. They had lunch in Brussels. What a beautiful classic old city, they thought. They drove to the Netherlands, and saw tulip fields…but already finished blooming, since the world-famous Tulip Festival was over (they bought bulbs anyway and planted them later in Seattle). It was nearly sunset when they pulled into Amsterdam, but they were unsuccessful in getting a room…anywhere! They drove all around Amsterdam; they bought a tourist map, in order to see at least some of the historic places. After a light supper at Cafe Amsterdam, the manager there directed them to Haarlem, just outside of Amsterdam. They had no trouble finding a little second story room overlooking the canal next to a windmill. It was so very picturesque. The little room was clean and felt like a 'bed and breakfast.' The lady proprietor made over Shelley, welcoming Frank and Margo warmly. She also served a lovely breakfast in the morning. They made their way back through Antwerp and France, to Calais. The police pulled Frank over in Antwerp… again, regarding the right of way on a traffic circle…but when he saw he was an American tourist, he waved him on…but bawled him out in French. They made it to Calais and bought their ferry tickets to Dover. They waited in line, and it reminded them of waiting for the ferries in Washington state. The wind was brisk, and they were happy to be on board ship. The sun was going down as they arrived in Dover, and seeing the 'white cliffs.' Frank broke into song, "There'll be blue birds over, the white cliffs of Dover," but Margo rolled her eyes, and the Brits round them looked at him like: 'just another crazy American tourist.' It was too late to drive on to Pam's and Jim's, so they found a little room there called White Cliffs…another delightful 'bed and breakfast,' and the people there were very friendly. Margo told Frank she was SO happy to hear English spoken again. They enjoyed a typical British breakfast of eggs and sausage with tomato, and some kind of bread with tea or coffee. They checked out early and drove to London. They called Pam…and she told them how to get to Chingford where she and Jim lived. Margo and Frank were determined to made the most of the three days they had to spend with them. [Margo and Pam had been pen-pal friends since fourth grade, but had *never met!* They had looked forward to this visit for a *long time*, but with the time constraints, they were only going to be able to have a brief visit (the plan was to ship the car to Baltimore from London, then go to Frank's sister Margaret's place while waiting for the car). The story of their longtime friendship was an interesting one: Margo had been given an opportunity while growing up in Quincy, Michigan, to select a pen-pal during her time in Girl Scouts; it was part of earning an international pen-pal badge; she selected someone named Pam Jordan from Sunderland near Edinburgh, Scotland; they had written each other all these years but had never seen each other face to face; Pam moved from Sunderland, met and married Jim Black in London (no children yet), but through the years, when either Margo or Pam lost track of each other in the various moves, Margo's mom always served as a 'home address' for both of them]. Frank pulled into their street in Chingford and Pam came out to wait for their arrival. Jim would be back later, so they could see them then, she said. She opened the car door and Margo and she embraced as though they had known each other all their lives…which they had. She held Shelley and made over her as though she were her own. She showed them to their room, and they visited a little while. She pleaded with them to stay longer, but it just wouldn't be possible. Then she dropped a *bombshell*: London had just begun a dock strike and it was paralyzing their economy. *It would prevent them from shipping their car in any case.* Frank felt the blood completely draining from his face. He didn't know what he would do. They were running out of money. They couldn't sustain a crisis like this very long. Pam asked if he was going to be okay. He said they would have to think about this. Margo said she, for one, wasn't going to let this ruin their visit. She asked what they would be able to see. Pam said she had thought about this a lot, and she knew exactly what they could see. She said they would have supper first. Pam had made a wonderful beef stew. They ate supper and visited some more before they went to bed. They heard from Jim in the morning. He was out of town on business but he sent his greetings and regrets he was unable to be there to see them. They went in Frank's Kadett and visited some of the best-known sights: Buckingham Palace, Tower of London, Madame Tussaud's Wax Museum, Piccadilly Circus, and Westminster Abbey. It was like having their own personal guide, because Pam gave them a personal perspective…not just a 'group guide's monotone general' one. They went into a real *London pub* for lunch, but were asked to leave because Shelley was riding on Frank's back in the carrier. Frank had Margo and Pam wait with Shelley outside, and he ordered authentic English fish and chips for everyone…in a newspaper. Pam said they had to have a Guinness, but Frank asked if she ordered one, could they just have a sip of hers to say they had done it. Pam said of course they could. They even had a chance to attend an evensong at St. Paul's Sunday evening. The three days went so fast, they felt like they had just gotten there. Much of the time was spent visiting. Margo and Pam caught up on family news. They rode the 'Underground,' London's subway system. They even took a picture with a 'Bobby' and crossed the Thames River on the London Bridge. It was time to go. Frank and Margo had talked about what to do and then they prayed for God to show them how to get out of the terrible problem they had. It didn't seem like they had any other options except going back to Mons… and pray that the Elliott's had returned. They couldn't get them on the phone, but they would have to take a chance. Frank found the scripture the morning they left that he felt God had shown him. It was found in Deuteronomy 31:8, *"The Lord himself goes before you and will be with you, he will never leave you or forsake you…do not be afraid or discouraged."* At breakfast, Frank and Margo witnessed to Pam of their great faith in God. The London dock strike would not overcome them. They were like the 'children of Israel,' they said. Even though they didn't know if the Elliott's were there, or where they might ship their car…but somehow God would provide the 'way through the desert.' Pam and Margo cried as they said goodbye, and both promised to let each other know how things came out for them. Shelley started to cry thinking she had done something wrong; they just laughed and hugged her. No, 'Sweetie,' everything was okay, mommy and Pam were shedding tears of joy. God was with them. Frank pulled out of the street and went down the road till he found a 'petrol' station. He filled up, and prayed it would be enough to get them to Dover, and then from Calais to Mons to the Elliott's. As he pulled out he looked the wrong way out of habit…his American left-side driving almost did them in; a car whizzed by and they missed it by just inches. They had come into London from Dover by way of Ashford, but they wanted to see a little bit more of the South England countryside; they returned by way of Cambridge. It was very picturesque, and they had a chance to see the King's College chapel on the way. They bought their Dover-Calais ferry tickets and waited. There was a brisk wind and they were glad they had jackets…unbelievable that it was almost August! They prayed all the way to Calais and then disembarked and drove to Mons. It was late afternoon, and they craned their necks to see if there was a car in the driveway as they neared the Elliott's house. Frank stopped the car. He told Margo they were going to pray before they turned on to their street. "Oh Lord, you know the trouble we are in, we are running out of money; we need to ship our car to the U.S; you called us to pursue graduate work, and we will follow you; we are not afraid—please lead us in the right path. Amen." He turned the corner…and there it was! The Elliott's car was in the driveway; they drove up to their house. The girls came out of the house; then Alan and Sharon came out too. They welcomed them warmly. They said they were sorry they hadn't been there when Frank and Margo came through earlier; they had gone to Switzerland, but weren't sure of their dates when Frank wrote them. Frank told them how God had given them the assurance they needed from the Word. Alan and Sharon were strong 'believer's,' and joined them in praising God for the privilege of being a part of God's plan in their lives. They had supper and talked about the good times in Taiwan, the HSA Chapel, and Steve Jones, Lowell Malliette, and their Bible Study with Ann James. The girls, Missy and Debbie, wanted to talk about TAS; and about Frank starrying in 'Oklahoma' and 'South Pacific;' he hadn't had either one in class, but he knew they sang in Ninette Mordant's high school choir. The next day, they helped them do laundry, cashed another check for Frank on his Seattle First account and bought more traveler's checks. Alan knew about the London dock strike, so he was already coming up with plans about shipping the Opel; Frank told him their predicament. Frank asked how much it was going to cost. Alan said, "let's go take a tour of SHAPE where I work, and I'll explain it to you." They toured the huge complex. SHAPE was the military arm of NATO and this was a very important assignment for them. They sat down for something to drink along the way, and Alan turned to Frank. He said, "you can't afford the non-military rates, but I can help you because I work for 'SHAPE.' I will ship it for you from Antwerp to Baltimore, you can pick it up there in three weeks." Frank was stunned. How could this be happening? Instead of being stranded…Frank had had visions of appearing at the U.S. Embassy in London…destitute, and throwing himself on their mercy…God had delivered them yet again; God had brought this wonderful friend in their hour of need. Alan, like Dr. Beckman, said he wouldn't accept payment. He couldn't because Frank was a civilian, and a friend in need…and it was a way of saying "thank you" for all the spiritual uplift Frank had provided during his music, drama, and teaching ministry to him in Taiwan. Margo and Frank wanted to cry; this was more than wonderful… it was a blessing from God.

Frank and Margo packed everything they could in their suitcases. They followed the plan Alan had come up with: he would drive the Opel back to Mons and then schedule shipment of the car from Antwerp to Baltimore, using his military rates and credits, along with other SHAPE shipments. They had breakfast and a time of singing and prayer, then said goodbye to them; Alan took them into Brussels; they bought airlines tickets to London's Heathrow Airport, using the last part of the itinerary Salil had arranged for them; from London they planned to fly to New York JFK, and take a shuttle flight from there to La Guardia; there they would fly to Raleigh-Durham and stay with Margaret and Alan until the car arrived…good plan! They said goodbye to Alan, Sharon, and the girls…with *profound thanks* and checked in. They had to wait a couple hours until flight time, so they had lunch at Heathrow. Then it was announced that the American Airlines 747 had mechanical trouble and would be delayed… another hour. They were told finally that the 747 would not be available, and that they would instead fly a 707 to New York. This delay was a concern, because getting through customs, shuttling to La Guardia, and making the last flight to Raleigh-Durham was cutting it close. They finally got underway and had a pleasant but uneventful flight. Shelley and Margo slept most of the way, and Frank dosed off from time to time. He got up to walk around or read the rest of the time. It took seven and a half hours, but it was an amazing experience to return to the United States after two years and seven months…Frank said that 'once they finished driving the rest of the way to Seattle,' they would prove, firsthand, that *the earth was round!* Ha! With little unaccompanied baggage, they went through customs quickly. Frank had alerted the stewardesses that they had a flight to catch at La Guardia for Raleigh-Durham. They knew that they had already missed the earlier flight, but were hoping to catch a later flight, so they rushed through the airport as soon as they cleared customs, and caught the shuttle leaving for La Guardia. Inevitably, there was traffic, and they got there at 11:00 p.m. (but 4:00 in the morning, London time); they rushed through La Guardia to the Delta gate…but, it was too late…the last flight from La Guardia to Raleigh-Durham had left thirty minutes prior. With no reservations for a hotel, and little time or money to stay elsewhere…and getting back early the next morning to catch the first flight out, wasn't an option either. They decided to sleep in the airport, then fly out in the morning. Shelley was tired to the bone, even though she had slept most of the way from London. Margo held her close and bundled up together with a jacket she had. Frank walked around the airport for a while; he found some coffee for them, and a sweet roll…for everyone to share. They didn't want any, so Frank ate it himself and drank the coffee. He finally dozed

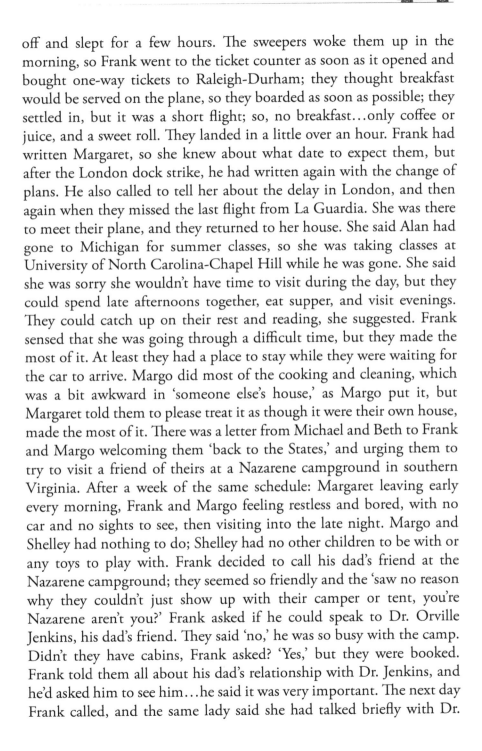

off and slept for a few hours. The sweepers woke them up in the morning, so Frank went to the ticket counter as soon as it opened and bought one-way tickets to Raleigh-Durham; they thought breakfast would be served on the plane, so they boarded as soon as possible; they settled in, but it was a short flight; so, no breakfast…only coffee or juice, and a sweet roll. They landed in a little over an hour. Frank had written Margaret, so she knew about what date to expect them, but after the London dock strike, he had written again with the change of plans. He also called to tell her about the delay in London, and then again when they missed the last flight from La Guardia. She was there to meet their plane, and they returned to her house. She said Alan had gone to Michigan for summer classes, so she was taking classes at University of North Carolina-Chapel Hill while he was gone. She said she was sorry she wouldn't have time to visit during the day, but they could spend late afternoons together, eat supper, and visit evenings. They could catch up on their rest and reading, she suggested. Frank sensed that she was going through a difficult time, but they made the most of it. At least they had a place to stay while they were waiting for the car to arrive. Margo did most of the cooking and cleaning, which was a bit awkward in 'someone else's house,' as Margo put it, but Margaret told them to please treat it as though it were their own house, made the most of it. There was a letter from Michael and Beth to Frank and Margo welcoming them 'back to the States,' and urging them to try to visit a friend of theirs at a Nazarene campground in southern Virginia. After a week of the same schedule: Margaret leaving early every morning, Frank and Margo feeling restless and bored, with no car and no sights to see, then visiting into the late night. Margo and Shelley had nothing to do; Shelley had no other children to be with or any toys to play with. Frank decided to call his dad's friend at the Nazarene campground; they seemed so friendly and the 'saw no reason why they couldn't just show up with their camper or tent, you're Nazarene aren't you?' Frank asked if he could speak to Dr. Orville Jenkins, his dad's friend. They said 'no,' he was so busy with the camp. Didn't they have cabins, Frank asked? 'Yes,' but they were booked. Frank told them all about his dad's relationship with Dr. Jenkins, and he'd asked him to see him…he said it was very important. The next day Frank called, and the same lady said she had talked briefly with Dr.

Jenkins, and he'd said for them to come on; he would find a place for them to stay; so, Frank called Margaret on her break and told her they were leaving. They would be at the Nazarene camp near Richmond, Virginia, and would pick up the car after the camp. He thanked her for letting them stay there. Frank called a taxi, and they went to the bus station, bought tickets to Richmond, and loaded their luggage on board. Before they got to Richmond they stopped in Petersburg, and Frank called the Nazarene camp to be sure they were expecting them for supper, and to check on the lodging situation. They also needed someone to pick them up at the bus station...they didn't know the camp was twenty miles out of the city! He didn't get the same nice lady he had talked to before. When he told her Dr. Jenkins had arranged for them to stay there, she said there was no cabin, tent, or dormitory available. Dr. Jenkins was not available, and the lady named Sherry must have been mistaken. *Another crisis...O Lord, don't let this fall apart now...no car, no lodging, getting low on money again...now* what would they do? They couldn't go back to Margaret's. Margo just wasn't willing to do that. Wasn't there something else they could do? They got back on the bus. It was less than thirty minutes to Richmond. So, now we pray! Who else do we know in Virginia? *Wait!* Les and Allen Peterson had come to their wedding in Wenatchee, and then they had gotten married...in Virginia! But were they still there? Margo had written Les before they left Taiwan, but they hadn't planned on stopping in to see them. Pete was in Vietnam, Frank thought, and they had planned to drive straight to Seattle after they picked up the car. It was a thought though. Now, where did they live? Margo couldn't remember. Just as they were rounding the corner to pull into the bus station in Richmond, Frank saw the church across the street. He turned to Margo and exclaimed. "'church'...something church... church river? No, church falls, that's it." They got off the bus and Frank unloaded the luggage. While Margo and Shelley sat in the bus station, Frank went to the pay phone, and called the operator. She said, "What city?" Frank told her it was for "Church Falls, Virginia..." (pause) "do you mean Falls Church, Sir? There is a Falls Church, Virginia," 'Yes,' Frank told her excitedly...for the Allen and Leslie Peterson residence.' Suddenly, Frank heard Les's voice on the other end; he almost dropped the phone; he was never so happy to hear a voice on the other end, than he was now, hearing Les's voice! God had done it...*AGAIN!* Les said Pete was in Vietnam, but she and their son Michael were in Falls Church in an apartment. They MUST come stay with her until the car arrived, she said, after Frank explained the whole thing. Her brother Rusty could drive them her to Richmond to pick them up. Sorry, but they would have to wait a couple hours. Anything, Frank said. He was just so grateful that they could stay with them. They hung up, and Frank bought some supper with the little cash he had left. They fell asleep again briefly, and before they knew it, Les and Rusty were coming in the bus station. They drove back to Falls Church and made it before it was too late, so they visited a while. In the morning, Frank called the American Shipping Company about the Opel. It had been just over a week. They thought it might arrive on a freighter out of Antwerp in about six days. Great! They went shopping, went to a movie, went into Washington DC to visit the capitol, and had fun watching Michael and Shelley...their 'rug rats' crawling around the apartment. Pete wrote often, telling of the 'absolute horror' of war. He said the only thing that kept him going was his faith in God. Frank had known Pete a long time, but he had never known him to be anything but a 'nominal Christian.' His strong faith in God, now in the midst of horror and devastation, warmed Frank's heart in an unbelievable way. Margo said she was just sad that he hadn't been able to come to Taiwan to see them on an 'R & R.' Randi, Les's sister, came by and visited...a Taiwan mini-reunion. After almost a week with Margaret, and now after just over a week with Les, and Michael, Frank decided to call the American Shipping Company in Baltimore. They said the car had already arrived the day before. The guy was being sarcastic, and said, "I figured if you didn't get here by today, the car would be completely 'stripped!' Frank asked him why he hadn't called him, but the guy just laughed. Frank didn't know if he was kidding or not. He wasn't going to take a chance. He asked Les to take him to the bus station. He would take the bus to Baltimore, and then take a taxi to the harbor and pick up the car. Margo insisted that he pack a lunch, so they quickly made a sandwich and a thermos of coffee, and dropped Frank off at the bus. It was early enough in the day, that Frank made it to the dock before they closed. The car was undamaged, and the dock supervisor that had talked to Frank laughed when he saw him; he said he was just 'kidding,' but

Frank was not amused. He ate his lunch, and then drove the car back to Falls Church. They all rejoiced that everything had worked out so well, and they had supper and went to bed. In the morning, they had an early breakfast, and left Falls Church heading for Colorado. Taking US Highway 40 most of the way, they made it to St. Louis by late evening. They had a simple supper of fast food, and booked a Motel 6 for the night. The next day was an equally hard drive. Even though they drove almost sixteen hours...including 'potty breaks' and food-and-gas stops...they pulled into Juli's and Larry's place, in Ft. Collins, Colorado, about 9:00 p.m.(counting the time difference, it was 10:00 St. Louis time). Juli told them to go straight to bed, they could visit in the morning. She let them sleep in a little, and then they had breakfast about 10:30. Juli said she had planned a picnic supper. Larry had a new teaching position at Colorado State University in Chemistry. Debbie was six and she still remembered the song they used to sing when she was little, "If We All Will Pull Together," and she wanted to sing it. She didn't call Frank and Margo 'Ugga Swank and Ugga Maggo' anymore, but she remembered them coming to 'her house' in Regina. They had a nice picnic and then returned to their house for the night. They left early the next morning and headed for Wenatchee. They were getting pretty weary by the time they got to Boise, Idaho, so they stopped at a Motel 6 again. They splurged a little and ate at a decent restaurant...a Mexican place called Guadalupe's. After breakfast at McDonald's in the morning, they got on the road again, and made it to Wenatchee by supper. Wilma had fixed a special 'homecoming' dinner of steak and corn on the cob...and asparagus that grew wild in their back yard! Francis tried not to cry again. He hadn't seen his daughter in almost three years, and his new grandchild, Shelley...well, he hardly knew what to say...he had never been a grandfather before. Shelley took to Grandma and Grandpa well. Margo and Shelley laughed, and then cried. Grandma took pictures, and Grandpa held Shelley like she was so 'fragile, that if he held her *too* tight, she might break! It was so good to be *HOME*...Margo could hardly believe it. Frank just took it all in and thanked the Lord for keeping them safe these past few years while they were apart from each other. Frank also checked his bank account with Seattle First. It was next to nothing. He told Margo he didn't know how they would rent a place in Seattle and start graduate school without borrowing some money or getting jobs right away. They rested a few days, and let the wonderful trip they had just experienced set in. They showed Wilma and Francis their pictures...which truly were breath-taking. They made plans to go into Seattle the following week and look for rent houses, check on Frank's graduate school status, and apply for jobs. Wilma and Francis showed them off at church, especially their new granddaughter, Shelley. All their church friends made over Shelley a lot. Wilma had invited the cousins from the Tri-Cities: Pasco-Kennewick-Richland, up for dinner Sunday afternoon, and they all came: Gauin and Carol, (their four kids, Christa, Cindy, Cathy, and Gauin; Dick and Katie (their two couldn't come); and Jiggs and Rita, and Janet and John). They had a great Moore family reunion and loved meeting Shelley, Margo and Frank's new baby. Monday came and Frank and Margo left for Seattle early, planning to return by that night. They found want ads in the paper, but soon realized how depressed the economy in Seattle was. They learned that Boeing had just lost the SST contract, and people were leaving in droves. One of the signs said it all, "Will the last person out please turn off the lights." They found houses in the Green Lake area for rent. One in particular caught their eye. It was a small two-bedroom house just blocks from the lake. They asked if they could rent it, and told them Frank was to be a graduate student at the University of Washington. They said they could take the papers, fill them out, and pay first and last month rent... it was seventy-five dollars a month. Frank didn't have the one-hundred-fifty dollars to seal the deal, but they said he could consider it theirs as soon as he filled out the application and gave them the money–they would hold it for just a week. Margo was willing to take even a hotel maid's job, but when they saw she had a B.A. in music, they said 'no, she needed something better than they could offer her.' She next tried a front desk job at the Olympic hotel in downtown Seattle. They interviewed her and asked her when she could start. She looked at Frank...he nodded, and she started the following Monday. Frank followed a lead for retail at Sears... selling men's ties and toys, so he ended up with a job too. Rod Eichenberger welcomed him to the graduate choral conducting program, but said he was sorry the two teaching assistant positions had already been promised. They returned to Wenatchee not knowing how they could secure the rental house.

Francis said he would give them the one-hundred-fifty dollars, but Wilma insisted on it being a *loan*, and drew up the note with interest. Grateful that they would help them out of this bind, they accepted it as a 'loan' and filled out the application for the rental house. They packed up their things and stayed a few more days until Sunday church services again, and then left Sunday afternoon for Seattle. They turned in the application for the rental house with the money, and Frank and Margo started their jobs Monday. They found out Margo had to be on the front desk by Tuesday morning 5:00a.m.! Frank would work at the Sears Men's Store 1:00-5:00p.m., and then the Toy Store until closing at 9:00 p.m. This way they could each watch Shelley 'in tandem' without involving a daycare...for a while; at least until Frank's class schedule changed. After they moved their things in the house, and visited Irma, who gave them some of her used furniture, or whatever they were able to pick up at Goodwill. They celebrated with a 'welcome home' meal and visit with Irma and the boys. Shelley came to know her Auntie Irma as 'Auntie Grandma,' because her 'Grandma Beth' was not able to be there much of the time growing up. Her other Grandma and Grandpa were of course Wilma and Francis in Wenatchee. Frank and Margo were able to make enough from their jobs to at least pay the rent, food and transportation...and Frank's schooling.

Singapore

Taj mahal,India

Garden Tomb, Jerusalem

Acropolis, Greece

Varro relatives

Serbia: Pop's birthplace

Their new life: graduate school at the University of Washington…was about to begin

Chapter Twenty

Having Fun...But Coming Undone

Gaudeamus igitur – 'therefore let us rejoice' (in our new life)

SUNDAY CAME, AND FRANK ASKED MARGO WHERE THEY WANTED TO GO to church. She said she had no idea. They didn't really know any of the Seattle Pacific alums at that time, they were not connected with the Methodists in Seattle, like her parents were in Wenatchee, and in fact, they didn't really know anyone, in any of the other churches in the area either. Since they lived closest to the First Church of the Nazarene on Forty-Fifth Street, they decided they would give it a try. They were surprised that so many people there knew Frank's parents. John Morgan, the principal of Ingraham where Frank had done his student teaching came over and greeted them warmly. He had given up conducting the church choir, and a young man from Oregon was now conducting them he said. The pastor, Don Moore, reminded him of the time he had come to SPC for a gathering of 'Nazarenes' before Frank graduated...yes Frank remembered. They were all friendly and welcomed them to the worship. They were interested in Shelley and made special mention of the fact that she was a little 'Taiwanese.' As the service began, Frank sensed that something was wrong...there was a tension there. At the announcement time, the choir director announced that he and he wife and family were leaving to go back to Salem, Oregon; he broke down in tears and a couple women cried and left the service. Don Moore preached a good sermon, and everyone visited briefly with Frank and Margo after the service. Frank bought some chicken wings and vegetables, and they returned to their little Green Lake house. They had no TV, so they were taking a nap when the doorbell rang; it was Rev. Don Moore. Frank invited him in and they made some coffee, and they sat down. He explained that he was so happy they had worshipped with them that morning; he said he noticed they had worked with ORTV and were Nazarenes. He also knew that Frank and Margo had done the music at Highland Park Nazarene, where Frank had been a 'local pastor'...a licensed minister with them. He then said that Chip and his wife Diana were leaving... there was unrest in the church, and some, including Chip and Diana hadn't liked him since he returned from a 'Youth Ministry Explosion' conference in Florida. Many young people hadn't darkened the door of First Nazarene in years, and had been on drugs; after Don came back from Florida, he reached out to the youth and tried to include them in the service. Many came to the Lord, but they were still 'rough around the edges,' and this upset a lot of people, even their own parents, who didn't want the 'cross-over' music, like ('Jesus is the) Bridge Over Troubled Waters,' and other non-traditional music. Some wanted Don to resign...or they would fire him. He asked if Frank wanted the job as his new 'music director?' 'What?' Just like that? Just 'jump into a hornet's nest?' But God was moving in Frank's heart, and he said *he would take it.* Frank wanted Margo to be able to play the piano, and asked if there would be remuneration. Don said there would be, but they 'wouldn't get rich on it,' he laughed. So, Frank became the new Minister of Music at Seattle First Nazarene, and Margo played piano for the choir...and the worship services. Things went well for a few months. The music was good, the choir anthems were good, and most people knew Frank and his parents. Christmas was a special celebration of traditional carols and choir anthems. Frank and Margo got involved in a new young adults Bible study. Frank was selling more men's ties at Sears than the salesmen on commission, but he was called in by the sales manager to 'back off' a little, and stop 'showing-up' the full-time salesmen. It was close to Christmas, and Frank was selling lots of toys too, so he got in trouble there too...for the same thing. Bill Scott, the sales manager said he was going to have to let him go if he didn't stop 'out selling' the other salesmen, so Frank just backed off and enjoyed the ride like Bill told him to do. Percy Dean, from construction days, called him one day. He said Red Schollers, also a former Nazarene pastor, ran a Wigwam store, and he had Christmas hours available for Frank...he told him he could make some extra money...more than he was making at Sears. So, Frank called Red, and he ended up quitting Sears and going to work for Red; it helped with the extra expenses of graduate school, living expenses, and Shelley's daycare. Margo had had to quit her job at the Olympic Hotel; the late-night hours were completely ridiculous. Frank and she would bundle Shelley up in the middle of the night, drive to downtown Seattle, work while Frank was in class, and then he would have to pick her up and still get to *his* job. It wasn't working out; Margo did, however, have a chance to meet Lloyd and Jeff Bridges one day; they asked for their mail, and Margo said she would check. "No, Mr. Bridges...Mr. Bridges," she said, turning to one and then the other, "no mail; we are so happy you are staying with us at the Olympic Hotel," and they smiled. She quit the next week. She was talking to Irma about what to do, and Irma said she should be a music teacher like she had been in Taiwan. They contacted the Seattle Public Schools, and found a music position at Webster Elementary School as a 'paraprofessional.' Although Margo did not have a teaching certificate, she could still teach music classes...under the supervision of a classroom teacher. This meant putting Shelley in a daycare. They found one just down the street. Mrs. Anna Sorenson watched her for a few hours every day; Frank would drop her off on his way to class. They spent Christmas in Wenatchee with Grandma and Grandpa, but had to work it around their school and church schedules. It was Shelley's first Christmas, and Wilma went all out to make it special. Shelley especially loved opening all the gift wrappings ...even more than the gifts. Frank hardly wanted to even take a break for Christmas because of all the excitement of his music program; he had auditioned and was accepted into the University of Washington Chorale with Rodney Eichenberger. He also sang in the Madrigal Singers with Gerald Kechley; his study with Dr. Demar Irvine on 'Writing About Music,' was the basis for all the graduate papers he would write, and later culminated in the writing of his own doctoral dissertation. Dr. Irvine had said the first day, "look around you, only half of you will finish this class." A 'friend,' John, turned and whispered to Frank, "I guess we know which one of the two of us will make it." True, Frank struggled greatly with the requirement to write a full graduate music paper each week, but in the end, it wasn't Frank that had to drop out...it was *John!* Frank had never been exposed to such great choral classics at SPC as he experienced at the UW, and he soaked it all in like a dry sponge. Frank made friends easily with the other graduate students and a lifelong bond was formed with the members of the Chorale. Margo formed a choir at Webster, performing Webster and performing every few months. She took a class or two herself at UW, especially in African instruments and dance. With the salary she was now getting, and the schedule Frank was now having to keep, they made enough for Frank not to have to work, and some hope was held out for him to eventually get a scholarship, or a 'teaching assistantship.'

When they got back for the next quarter, things were even more hectic. Things at the Nazarene Church were not going well; Rev. Moore was experiencing even more conflict with the church board. His wife, Susan, had had a history of mental illness (which he had shared with the church before he arrived), but it was usually kept in check...as long as she took medication and stayed in touch with her doctor). The stress of the church situation, however, caused her to have a 'meltdown,' and, on the advice of her doctor, he sent her back to Iowa to be with her parents...for a while. While she was gone, he tried to find someone who could assist him with the care of the children. He was busy with the church, especially during times of conflict, and a young woman, whose husband had left her, started coming to the church with her mother, and made a profession of faith. She was with a public relations firm, and had expendable time, so when Rev. Moore announced that his wife was away visiting her parents in Iowa for a while, this young woman, Marianne Fredericks, came forward and volunteered to help with his children; he accepted immediately, and the children took to her right away. She acted only professionally and handled the situation well, even though she had not had children of her own during the eight years she was married; the rumor mill began...as soon as she showed up with the children in church...the pastor must be having an *affair with this 'worldly woman.'* Because of her experience in multi-media presentations, Pastor Moore asked her to head up the Lenten and Easter cantata. Frank was glad for her help. Pastor Moore was trying some different things to attract young people to church, and he was changing the music and worship up a lot. Frank and Margo had joined a Bible study at the church. Bob Prince, the teacher, was a Portland State professor of English, who commuted to the University of Washington three days a week, where he was working toward a doctorate in English Lit; he and his wife, Patty, lived in Portland, where they were members of First Nazarene Church in Portland, but were in Seattle Thursday through Monday taking the classes he needed; they attended Seattle First Nazarene, and volunteered to teach a Bible study there on Sunday afternoons. He had chosen to teach a study called: 'What the Bible says about Jesus Christ *Superstar*,' which was the rage at that time. Don Moore asked Frank to sing 'Gethsemane,' from 'Jesus Christ Superstar,' for Passion Sunday (he left out the middle section... the part that was 'hard rock,'); some people complained strenuously. Interestingly enough though, they came to Frank and said they 'didn't blame' *him*, but the pastor was 'really stepping in it this time.' With Marianne's help, Frank had put together a collage of traditional and contemporary anthems and solo or ensemble selections...including several 'secular songs (or what many churches were calling 'cross-over' songs), ...telling the gospel story using 'marketplace' resources; they darkened the windows of the church by covering them over with black plastic, and projected slides and films to help tell the crucifixion and resurrection story. It was a powerful presentation, and many were very moved, but others decided to report this to Bert Daniels, the District Superintendent, and demanded a 'pastoral vote,'...that Rev. Moore must be 'having an affair' with his babysitter! Marianne told them there was 'absolutely nothing romantic' going on with him, and she offered to leave the church, but Don would not hear of it; his wife was under a doctor's psychiatric care in Iowa, and he had no other option—her leaving would seem to be an admission of guilt, which was not the case. They called for a pastoral vote anyway, and now some accused Frank of going along with Pastor Moore against their wishes. In the end, Don decided to resign in order to not have a negative vote on his record. He sent the children to his In-laws in Iowa, and received a *call* almost immediately from a Friends Church in Battle Ground, Washington—to be their pastor. Ironically...though he had never dated Marianne, they went out after he resigned...and ended up getting married in a couple years. After he divorced Susan, who was hospitalized. Dr. Hugh Benner, a former General Superintendent in the Church of the Nazarene, came in to serve as Interim Pastor. After the first Sunday there, Frank was talking with him in the church office. Dr. Benner remembered Frank's parents from their missionary days in south China, and he said he knew they were "serving in Taiwan with a 'non-Nazarene' mission board." Frank smiled...he continued to copy the material for their Bible study that afternoon. Suddenly, Dr. Benner asked what he was copying. Frank explained it was material for their Bible class that afternoon. He looked at it, and shrieked, "Why, this is not a Bible study...this is that, that... *Jesus Christ Superstar' stuff!"* Frank explained that they were studying what the Bible had to *say about* it, not what 'Jesus Christ Super Star' was saying about the *Bible*. Dr. Benner tore it up in front of Frank, telling him that he was going to 'shut that Bible study' down. Frank joined Margo, who was waiting in the lobby, and said, "that's it, we're out of here." They went home, and he typed up and sent in his letter of resignation. The next Sunday, they attended First Free Methodist Church, the Seattle Pacific College church. Lydia McNichols had been the director of choral music at least twenty-five years, and Frank had even sung there as a soloist and guest choral singer, so he went up to say 'hi' after the service. She pulled him aside, and said she had heard he was a 'doctoral student' at the University of Washington in choral music (it was actually a master's degree). She told

Frank she was retiring, and had already told Dr. Bob Fine, the pastor, that she wanted "Frank Varro, who's studying for his doctorate at the UW," to replace her. Frank's jaw dropped to the floor, Margo looked stunned, and Lydia thought Frank didn't want the job, from the shocked look on his face…here was God doing it again! They hadn't even been gone from First Nazarene a week, they didn't know how they would make it financially on Margo's Webster Elementary job; here Shelley could be at the daycare for *free,* if Frank were on staff! Margo would back up Sylvia Foreman, the organist, and Frank and Margo would find themselves 'at home' in the Samaritan Class with other young adults. God always stepped into the gap, and delivered them 'from the lions den.' Margo started to cry, so Frank explained to Lydia what was going on. She smiled and said, "isn't that just like our loving God." Dr. Bob Fine interviewed Frank that next week, and again with the church board, and they offered him the job. It gave Frank and Margo a great musical outlet which would help with his graduate work, and provide the extra income that they needed for Frank to pay his tuition, and living expenses. God's timing is perfect. That same week, they received an 'eviction notice,' for *non payment of the house note.'* What? They were *leasing*; what was happening to their rent payments which they had faithfully paid every month…and on time! They found out that the young divorcee, who had received the house as part of the divorce, was living with a boyfriend, but spending the Varro's rent money on drugs and personal expenses, instead of paying the house note! Frank produced the six-month lease: October,1970, to March,1971. The eviction notice was cancelled, and they were able to stay there another month…it was already the beginning of 'month six' anyway, so they started looking for another place. They located a rent house on Queen Anne Hill, just minutes from First Free Methodist… and, up the hill from where Frank's church choir job was…and Shelley's daycare…plus two miles closer to Margo's job at Webster Elementary. How's that for God's 'time and place?' Unbelievable! They moved at the end of the winter quarter. Frank's studies were going well, and he was making new friends. Rod Eichenberger accepted his application for a 'teaching assistantship' but, there were only two positions, and both were already committed…to Bruce Browne and Larry Marsh. Rod also wanted him to prepare for his conducting audition in order to enter the graduate choral conducting program. The Chorale had also received an invitation to participate in the Intercultural Exchange in Europe that Summer, and he wanted Frank to go. Six college choirs from the U.S. would spend two weeks in Vienna in August. They would sing the Kodaly 'Te Deum' the first week, and sing the Mahler 'Eighth Symphony' (the *Symphony of a Thousand*), the second week, along with the Staat Oper soloists, Vienna Boys' Choir, and the Bratislava Radio Orchestra, all conducted by the well-known European conductor, Gunter Thöring. Simply put, it was an *opportunity of a life-time*. Frank just *had* to go; but how could they afford it? Even with discounts, it would cost over twelve hundred dollars! In those days, that was a lot of money. Rod said they would raise money with fundraising concerts, donations, and 'selling U.S. flags and other patriotic paraphernalia.' Each participant was told they could pay it in four installments: May, June, July, and August. Margo agreed...he HAD to go. Frank began preparing for his graduate school conducting audition. He chose the 'Libera me' section of the Faure 'Requiem.' His graduate conducting class choir volunteered to be the *chorus* for the audition, and Barney Crouse sang the baritone solo. Frank did well, and all three conductors that auditioned that day: Bruce Browne, Larry Marsh, and Frank Varro, were all accepted into the graduate choral conducting program. Margo and Frank had moved to the rent house on Queen Anne Hill and Shelley started daycare at First FM. Lydia McNicholls introduced Frank to the First FM choir, and many of them already knew him from SPC student days; they got off to a great start. Frank came home from their first rehearsal with Margo. They had a snack and put Shelley to bed. Margo said she had something to tell Frank...she said she was pregnant. [one of the benefits of Margo working at Webster was they had medical benefits with Group Health]. After she dropped Frank off at First FM that afternoon, she had gone to the doctor and he confirmed it...he thought she might be about ten weeks along. Frank laughed, grabbed her, and swung her around. Shelley was coming up on two years in a few weeks, so this was good timing...but she didn't look as excited as he thought she should be...what was wrong? She said she didn't know exactly, but the doctor had told her everything was 'okay'... but not 'fine.' He asked her if she felt alright...and she admitted it wasn't just normal 'morning sickness;' something didn't feel right about it. Frank had noticed she wasn't acting up 'to par,' but he thought she might be having a touch of the flu or something. Dr. Worthing had said to let him know if anything changed; so, they went about their business for a couple weeks. Frank dropped her off at Webster, went to class after dropping Shelley off at First FM daycare, and then picked her up later from Webster; they would usually shop, fix supper, and then go to any evening functions they might have before going to bed. It was a few weeks later, about 2:00 in the morning (by this time she was almost five months along); she woke Frank to tell him she thought she might miscarry…they needed to go to the hospital. Frank asked if they needed to call an ambulance; she said no, but he called the doctor just in case, and the answering service contacted Dr. Worthing; he said for them to drive on their own to the Group Health Emergency Room. Margo miscarried that night; they performed a D & C (dilation and curretage) on her, which was very painful, but she was allowed to go home in a few hours. By this time, it was 6:00 a.m., so Frank called Elizabeth Simes, Margo's supervising teacher at Webster, to tell her what had happened; she was very kind and understanding, and wished Margo speedy recovery, and for her not to worry…that she would take care of everything…she was praying for them. Margo took the rest of the week off, and was feeling sad and disappointed, but ready to return to work by the next Monday. Frank told Bob Fine and the FM staff what had happened, and the church was in prayer for her speedy recovery. Frank dropped Shelley off at the daycare and went to class as usual, so that Margo could rest. Margo called her mom and dad, and they were very understanding and said they would pray for her… 'God has a reason for everything in our lives,' Wilma said. There would be other opportunities for more children…just happy she was recovering well. They wanted to see her as soon as she was able to travel, so Frank promised they would come to Wenatchee in a couple weeks for Shelley's birthday celebration. With any trips out of town, he now had to skip class Thursday and Friday so they could visit and then come back Saturday afternoon in time for Sunday services, because he now had the First FM church choir. Margo taught at Webster the next two weeks, and they picked Shelley up at the daycare Thursday after lunch, and drove to Wenatchee, arriving in time for supper. As they pulled into the driveway, they saw the surprise that Wilma had referred to—

Uncle Al and Aunt Alice, Wilma's adopted brother and his wife from Phoenix, were there visiting. Margo was so excited; she hadn't seen them in years. Wilma had told Alice about her granddaughter, so she baked Shelley a very special birthday cake…Snow White and the Seven Dwarfs! She had placed little plastic figurines on the cake. Besides Snow White, all seven dwarfs: Doc, Bashful, Dopey, Happy, Sleepy, Sneezy, and Grumpy, were all on the cake. Shelley's favorite story at the time was Snow White, so she squealed with delight and threw her arms around Auntie Alice, whom she had just met. She hugged Uncle Al, too, but he wasn't a hugger,' so he looked funny trying not to be awkward. They had a special birthday dinner, and sang 'Happy Birthday' to her, and she opened presents; there were storybooks, including Snow White, with pictures. There was a little 'Snow White' doll, and other little storybook characters. The birthday card had a 'Snow White' theme also; they were so happy to see her so excited on her second birthday; she remembered the experience for many years. Margo and Frank were sorry they couldn't stay over Sunday, but Francis and Wilma understood, and congratulated them on getting such good jobs, and particularly Frank for getting the First FM church choir position. Uncle Al and Aunt Alice left to see relatives on the coast, and Frank, Margo, and Shelley stayed the night, leaving Saturday right after supper.

The Chorale gave several concerts and fundraisers in the spring quarter, and established a scholarship fund. Those that had their own means of funding the trip to Europe, paid into their own account, which didn't require scholarship funds. The others were required to help fund the scholarship from outside donations and participate in Chorale fundraising efforts. Frank had been able to meet the monthly schedule of payments to his account in April and May, and was working on the June and July. They were scheduled to leave the third week in August, so those who hadn't raised the last couple payments still had time to raise the rest. First Free Methodist choir set up an account for Frank, and several donations came in which helped a lot. Many of his church choir members also attended the concerts. The tour program, and their individual concert in Vienna, included the Bach Motet 5, 'Komm Jesu, Komm,' the Bernstein 'Lark,' Brahms…and several folk songs and spirituals. It was an exciting program, and the anticipation of doing the Kodaly 'Te Deum' and the Mahler 'Eighth Symphony' was even more so. Lydia McNicholls agreed to come back for the three weeks that Frank would be gone. By the first of August, Frank still owed three hundred fifty dollars. He didn't have the money, so he asked Rod if there was any more money in the scholarship fund…and what he needed to do to get some help. He also told Bob Fine, and the First FM staff in their prayer meeting. He didn't know it at the time, but Dean and Loretta Dace had decided to divorce; she continued to teach school, but Dean had resigned from Highland Park Nazarene, and the ministry; he had gone to work with Percy Dean as his business manager. Somehow [Frank thought Arlene Nordlund, who sang in the Carillon trio, was on the First FM staff, and also sang in the FM choir, must have told a friend of Percy Dean…or something]. In any case, the word had gotten to Dean Dace and Percy Dean. A letter arrived at the church…from Dean Construction Company, with a check for three hundred fifty dollars…Dean had written a note to Frank, telling him that he was now the business manager for Dean Construction… and 'discovered' they had shorted Frank *three hundred fifty dollars on his last check*… five years earlier! Incredible as it seemed, God had provided for Frank yet again. He told Margo and she said 'by this time, we should believe *anything* that God puts in our path, right?!' Frank told Rod he could give the scholarship money to someone else, and, sure enough, someone else was able to go on the trip that otherwise would not have been able to go… except God provided a way again. Frank hadn't talked to Dean Dace or Percy Dean in five years, so, he called Dean Construction, and Percy answered…he said it was Dean's idea. He had found a 'discrepancy' in the books ('sure, whatever,' Frank said, laughing;' why did they happen to be going back five years, anyway;' he said Dean had heard from Marky Barrett, his insurance agent, who also sang in Frank's First FM Choir, and he said Dean had been 'cleaning up a lot of old financial records.') Percy said, "Stop, Frank; God is good, you did a lot for us, just let God take care of you, okay? Have a great trip…say 'hi' to Margo and that baby for us, okay?" And then he hung up. Frank was dumbfounded. The Samaritan Class had a 'bon voyage' party for Frank (and Margo), and they all promised they would take care of Shelley and Margo for Frank. Some of them had made donations to Frank's 'scholarship fund' …anonymously, so

Margo thanked the whole class, instead of sending individual 'thank you' cards. Margo was on a twelve-month contract so she had income during the summer. Elizabeth Simes had said she would stop by while Frank was gone; they lived on Whidbey Island, but she would say 'hello' after they finished shopping at Pike Place Market sometime.

Margo dropped Frank off at the Sea-Tac Airport the Monday of the second week in August to catch a United Airlines shuttle flight to Vancouver, B.C. There the University of Washington Chorale met to take a chartered British Airways flight to Amsterdam. On the flight from Vancouver, someone handed Frank a gin and tonic to drink, telling him it was a "Seven-Up" because they knew he did not drink alcohol. When he said, "that was good," they gave him another. Realizing it was alcoholic, Frank waved off a third one, while they all laughed. They had supper together and then caught the overnight train to Vienna. It was a wild night, and especially on the train that night. The beer and wine flowed plentifully. Many sleeper cars had several "trades" that night as well, but Frank allied himself with members of the tenor section that wanted to actually sleep, but the laughter and noise of those running from car to car made it difficult to do so. In the morning, they arrived in Vienna and were transported to the Gusser Hotel where they were staying. A few people were absent from breakfast, which they ate at the hotel…presumably in their rooms catching a few more 'winks of missed sleep?' Their opportunity for slumber didn't last long. Rehearsal for the Kodaly "Te Deum" was later that morning. The rehearsal was at the Konzert Platz, but was performed outside of the Hall in Viennese tradition. Each day they would meet with the other five college choirs from the United States for intercultural events, such as tours of the Schonbrunn…or the Spanish Horse Show (with world-famous Lipizzaner stallion horses), or other attractions. Each choir presented an evening concert in one of the several churches in Vienna. This amounted to three individual U.S. university choir concerts almost every night for two weeks…six in all; there was also time each evening to socialize and take in the many 'wein kellers' (wine cellars) that were in abundance in Vienna. Frank had developed his own circle of friends…in particular Kathy Thornton, Roupen Shakarian, Bonnie Blanchard, Dick Sparks, Nancy Zylstra, Greg Vancil, and Nancy Farrell, who helped each other by sticking together most of the time.

They knew Frank 'preferred not to drink,' but they reminded Frank that it was also a fact that the water wasn't safe to drink, and the Gusser Hotel where they were staying…where they ate most of their meals, didn't serve water, or soft drinks, either. In fact, each hotel had their own beer…so, the Gusser Hotel served…Gusser beer! Most of the choirs attended the other choirs' concerts, and there was a reception after each one… where 'weiss wein,' 'eis wein,' and every other '*wein*,' flowed freely. Frank told Roupen he would keep him from getting 'out of control'…if he would do the same for him. Well, that didn't work very well…apparently! When Frank realized that Roupen was 'pulling on his pant leg as he danced on the table top…he realized he had gone too far. In another cafe, Frank sang his gypsy song, 'Szép asszonyak,' along with the Hungarian Ziegeuner band (but they laughed at his Hungarian!). They were having a great time, but they soon realized they needed to 'tone it down,' especially after the owner of an Italian cafe yelled at them, in a thick Italian accent…after spilling red wine on his white linen, "you would do this in America?" They were unintentionally spreading the 'ugly image of Americans.' Other U.S. choir directors were facing the same thing, and met with their choirs and the Intercultural Relations tour sponsors, and asked their choirs to control themselves. At the end of the first week, they presented the Kodaly 'Te Deum,' in an outdoor setting with great response! The Vienna Sinfonia accompanied the U.S. Choirs…Gunter Thoring conducted. The Viennese received it with great enthusiasm. Since they were taking a four-day break, Frank had an idea: on his own, he went to a travel agency in Vienna, which was advertising 'trips to Hungary;' wouldn't it be great if he could visit Uncle Imre in Budapest again while they were there? He hadn't written Imre, but they had the weekend off, and Frank wanted to go somewhere; he asked Bruce Browne and Larry Marsh if they were interested in going to Budapest with him. "Are you kidding? Can we do that?" they asked. Sure, Frank assured them, 'the travel agency was selling roundtrip train tickets for only a few bucks,' he told them. 'And what about lodging? Frank told them he had stayed with his uncle the year before; they could stay there. They jumped at the chance, and before you could say "Blue Danube,' they had purchased three roundtrip train tickets to Budapest; they would leave Friday afternoon, stay two nights with Uncle Imre, and return by train Sunday afternoon. It was all set, so they told Rod what they were doing; they had their passports and their overnight bags, and jumped on the train before hardly anyone else knew what was going on. The train wasn't that fast, and they stopped at several stations along the way. In each place, they had to show their passports, and they were reminded that Hungary was still a communist country. It was just getting dark when they pulled into the station at Budapest. The station manager, who spoke very little English or German, asked Frank where they were staying; he told him he had an uncle living in Budapest…across the river, on the 'old Buda side.' 'What's his name, Frank, and what is the address, Bruce and Larry wanted to know'… they had assumed Frank's uncle would meet them…that he was expecting them… 'Yes?' Frank said, 'well not exactly…but he knew Uncle Imre wouldn't mind. Everyone's eyebrows suddenly went up. In communist Hungary after dark…Frank's uncle didn't know they were there…and no address? The station manager said they would have to stay in a hotel. Frank said no, he would call a cab; he knew where Imre lived–they would see…it would be alright! The cab driver asked (apparently)… 'where to?' in Hungarian. Frank said 'drive,' he would 'tell him the way.' The cab driver said something in Hungarian (probably said something like 'you crazy Americans,' [sure!]), but he drove them across the Danube; Frank said 'turn right'–Bruce and Larry were very quiet in the back seat; Larry kept murmuring something about "communist Hungary, after dark, is there really an Uncle Imre? They drove along the river, and then suddenly, Frank yelled, "there it is," pointing to a couple of adjoining buildings. He jumped out of the cab, ran up to the door, knocked, and waited. Larry and Bruce got out of the cab and waited about twenty yards away; by now they were *very* nervous. A woman came to the door…but it wasn't Irina, Imre's wife! Now Bruce and Larry were in 'total panic' and said they were going back to Vienna! Of course there were no trains at that time of night. Frank somehow managed to let the lady know that he was somehow related to Imre Dornei. When she heard the name 'Imre Dornei,' she smiled and said over and over "Imre Dornei, Imre Dornei." She started jumping up and down; she said in English, "You…go train" pointing to the trolley; holding up two fingers, she pointed to the left and said, "two…you go train…two!" Taking that to mean they should get on the trolley, go two stops, and get off. Apparently, there would be an apartment building, or house. Frank bowed, thanked her, and started to go. She said, pointing to herself, "Maria Sabo… Imre Dornei… mein bruder" (she used the German term for brother). Then she put her arms around Frank. "You…Varro, Mihaly." Frank put his arms around her too. She was the sister of Mary Gold; Varro, 'Mihaly' (Frank) put his arms around her too. She was the sister of Mary Gold, Pop's second wife, and Imre. Wow! A little touch of home in the middle of their journey. The cab driver told them he would take them the two trolley stops. Bruce and Larry were very relieved, and Frank felt proud he had met 'family,' totally on a whim! (or was God just taking care of them again?). They got out of the cab, but told him to wait…just in case. Frank went up to the apartment (Maria Sabo had told the cab driver in Hungarian what was going on), while Bruce and Larry waited. Sure enough, he found the name "Dornei, Imre" on the mailbox, so Larry and Bruce paid off the cab driver and joined Frank at the entrance…but the door was locked. Soon, an inebriated Hungarian man showed up and stumbled to the door, and pressed the code. Voila! They followed him in. They took the elevator to the eighth floor, found the name on the door, rang the doorbell… and waited; by this time Bruce and Larry couldn't believe this was actually going to turn out okay, and started to laugh; there actually WAS an 'Uncle Imre,' they were in communist Hungary after dark, and it looked like they were NOT going to 'end up in jail after all! A very surprised Uncle Imre opened the door. He looked puzzled at first, and then Frank pointed to himself, and said, "Varro, Mihaly." He suddenly remembered last year's visit with Margo and Shelley; he embraced him Hungarian style, and let them in; Frank introduced him to his friends. Then Imre told them to stay there a minute; he talked to someone in the sitting room, and suddenly an older woman moved from the sitting room, past the kitchen to the back room. Frank found out later Imre had kicked his mother-in-law, Kata, out of her bed in the sitting room, to join his wife Irina in their bed in the back. He broke out a bottle of Yugoslavian wine…they polished off the whole bottle; now they were finally feeling better. Imre said something in Hungarian they didn't understand, but between German, and broken English, they figured out what he was trying to say… 'where were they staying?' Frank paused, then pointed to the floor; they would stay here with him…on the floor, if he would let them; then it dawned on him; they had tried to tell him they came from America to Vienna…then on the train to Budapest to see him… they would go back to Vienna…two nights. 'Egen!' (yes); he jumped up; he gave Bruce and Larry another bottle of wine, and motioned for Frank to come with him; Bruce and Larry drank the wine, and Frank went with Imre on the trolley, past their old residence (which Frank had tried to tell him about…"egen (yes), meine schwester, Maria—yes, my sister"), to a storage place, where he picked up camping cots and blankets; they got back, Frank tried to take the cot, but Imre set it up in the kitchen, gave Bruce his mother-in-law's bed, and set Larry and Frank up in the open-out couch. Bruce and Larry had drunk the entire second bottle of wine, and were feeling no pain. In the morning, they met Irina, Imre's wife, and Kata, the mother-in-law, who quickly got their breakfast and took it to the back room… after exchanging greetings with 'Varro, Mihaly and his friends from America.' Imre served them breakfast of sausage, bread, and some kind of clear liquid, (Bruce said it was 'kirshwasser!') After the two bottles of wine the night before, and now 'kirshwasser' for breakfast, Bruce said, "well, I wanted to take a trip with you, Frank, but this wasn't exactly the *trip* I had in mind!" Larry and Frank laughed, and they finished their breakfast. Imre said he would take them on a tour of Budapest, but Bruce said he wasn't feeling well (no surprise *there*), thanked Imre for his hospitality, and asked if it would be alright if he rested there at the apartment. Larry tried persuading him, but to no avail. Larry teased him about not being able to 'hold his liquor,' and Bruce didn't deny that it 'probably had something to do with it.' Alcohol for breakfast was not his usual diet. Frank had drunk only a small amount of the wine the night before, none of the bottle Larry and Bruce had consumed, and only a swig of the 'kirshwasser,' whereas Bruce had drunk most the two bottles of wine the night before, but only a little of the 'kirshwasser' for breakfast. Imre, Frank, and Larry took his car to go to Budapest. Their first stop was the Turkish bathes on Margit Sziget ('Margaret Island') in the middle of the Danube. These were hot springs… and beautiful Hungarian women in bikinis were everywhere. Larry was going nuts and wanted Imre to ask them if they would join them, and a couple of them did. Realizing it wouldn't look good if they were fraternizing too much 'with two married men from America,' Frank suggested that they be friendly, but not get too close, despite the encouragement of Imre, and the willingness of the young women. Next, they went for lunch at a little Hungarian cafe, where they had some cabbage rolls, and some other very tasty things, which Imre described, but Frank and Larry didn't understand or recognize. They went back to the apartment to check on Bruce and he was feeling much better, so they left and went for a tour of the famous Budapest Parliament Buildings, to go see where Imre worked at some factory (apparently), and bought some incidental tourist trinkets in downtown Budapest; by then, it was time for supper. Imre took them to a little place close to where he worked called the Magyar Etterem. A giant vat of seafood soup, bread, and wine came... one after the other; then, expecting to get the check, a huge platter of every cutlet and vegetable arrived; the soup had only been the appetizer! There was every sort of condiment, wine, and sweets, too. They also had cabbage rolls and Chicken Paprikas; they stuffed themselves until they could eat no more, while Imre kept offering them more wine and bread. Even Bruce, who could eat a lot, said he was stuffed and turned down the last attempts of Imre to feed them more. Then Imre ordered coffee...a good idea they thought, after all the alcohol. But poppy seed cake arrived with the coffee. So, they ate a few bites of that 'most delectable of all Hungarian pastries!' They were almost sick, but managed to walk to the car. They needed to return to Vienna the next day, so they asked Imre about the train. He managed to convey to them that the train took over three hours with stops, but the 'boat' on the Danube...called the 'Hydrofoil' (elevated by water jet), would only take less than an hour, even with a stop in Bratislava, Czechoslovakia. They could use their round-trip train ticket and exchange it for the Danube hydrofoil. They jumped at the chance, and went by to exchange the tickets before going back to Imre's apartment. They slept very well...with full stomachs...and it was a beautiful fall day when Imre took them to the Danube to catch their river boat ride back to Vienna. When they got back to the Gusser Hotel and met up with the Chorale, no one believed the great adventure they described; they thought they were drunk, or 'delusional' and just making up 'such a wild tale.' It was the 'talk of the town.' The story spread to all the other choirs, and everyone wanted to toast Frank, the 'Hungarian gypsy' that had introduced them to this 'adventure extraordinaire,' to this day.

Rehearsals began for the Mahler Eighth Symphony. They were long and grueling. Thoring was a task-master. He made them stand for hours, even without 'potty-breaks.' He demanded absolute perfection. When some could stand it no longer, and began to leave to go to the restroom, he demanded they return...he would dismiss them shortly. He said if they didn't return immediately, they would not perform! They returned but finally some of the conductors complained to the tour organizers, but before they could stop him, Thoring suddenly stopped the rehearsal and gave them a brief twenty-minute break. A favorite alto of Frank's in the Chorale (originally from Alabama), was heard saying loudly in the women's bathroom, "may shee-it fall on his hay-ed," to the roar of laughter of all those present. They resumed the rehearsal and worked for another couple hours...a total of eight hours, including short morning and afternoon breaks, with less than an hour lunch break. It was *worth* it though, the Mozarteum Hall was packed. The Bratislava Radio Orchestra, the Staat-Oper soloists, and the Vienna Boys Choir, and the six college choirs from the U.S. combined for this fabulous performance of the Mahler Eighth Symphony, conducted by Gunter Thoring. These U.S. college choirs included: the University of Washington, Ohio State, University of Connecticut, Shenandoah Conservatory, Midwestern University, and Catholic University. Later, when Frank was the choral conducting teaching assistant for Rod, he was in charge of converting a recording of that performance to a long-play record which he sent off to each of the performing choirs. It was a once-in-a-lifetime experience, and the highlight of the 1971 UW Tour. After these two 'life-changing' weeks in Vienna, the UW Chorale went on tour by bus through Austria, Italy, Germany, and France. They went to Venice, Milan, and Como. They sang at the famous San Marco church, took gondola rides, and played baccio-ball in Venice. They lunched in 'Romeo & Juliet Square' in Milan, and celebrated a 'wild' birthday of Suzie Ziatta, their alto friend in the Chorale, in Como. They gave concerts at each place they went. They went through the Alps; they took a cable car up to Mt. Pilatus above Mt. Lucerne. After a very long bus ride, they arrived in southern France, only to find a French-style 'bathroom' the girls on the bus did not, uh…know how to 'negotiate.' Someone told them Frank had grown up in Taiwan, and knew how to do the 'Chinese squat,' so here was Frank demonstrating how to position oneself 'over the hole,' in order to 'take care of business.' Some of the girls shrieked and refused to go; they said they would *wait* until they could get to a 'western style' commode! And they got caught up in a parade as they entered Dijon during the Burgundy Wine Festival. The bus had to come to a complete stop at one place, so, chorale members got off and walked alongside the bus watching the crowd. They noticed that the men had little accordian-head plastic hammers and would "bop the women on the head." If she 'bopped him back,' they laughed and ran off together. It looked like everyone was having such fun. One of the guys on the bus grabbed a plastic hammer and tried bopping one of the local women on the head. When she bopped him back, he just stood there laughing, *not knowing* what to do(?); she then grabbed him by the hand and started taking him toward her residence. Other guys tried the same thing and the girls on the bus got into the act as well. No one bothered to tell them that bopping the girls on the head was 'an invitation to share a romantic encounter,' and if she bopped you back, it meant she accepted the invitation! Wild shrieks ensued and the bus emptied, with Chorale guys and girls bopping each other as well as the local citizens of Dijon! Wine samples were plentiful, which explained the obviously total lack of inhibition of everyone. Rod had to put a stop to it though, since they had to have supper and a concert that night in a local cathedral. The French section of the program was explained by Nancy Farrell from the Chorale… in perfect French. The crowd was very pleased with the concert, especially the songs sung in French, and they exclaimed how authentic they were. After a week of touring, they arrived again in Amsterdam. They arrived back 'home' in Vancouver, B.C., and took the shuttle to Sea-Tac airport. A bus was waiting for them to take them to downtown Seattle to the Olympic Hotel where they disembarked and everyone said their goodbyes. Margo and Shelley met Frank with happy tears and hugs, thus culminating one of the greatest musical experiences of his life.

The fall quarter began. The music building was alive with the news of the great tour… and the many stories that came out of it. Larry Marsh took a choral position at the University of Michigan, and Bruce

Browne took a similar position at Mount Union College in Ohio. They continued to pursue their doctoral studies with Rod Eichenberger at the University of Washington, but they had passed their pre-dissertation exams and would write dissertations following a few years of teaching experience. Ron Kuhn, a choral director from Great Falls, Montana, and Ken Kosche, from Chicago, had already been promised the choral teaching assistant positions, so Frank and Margo continued to fund his graduate work through his position at First Free Methodist and her position at Webster Elementary. Frank was appointed to the Seattle Pacific Alumni board, and Alumni banquet chair. Frank took a full load each quarter, and when courses were not available, he took some of them by permission as 'individual study.' He signed up for 'Asian study' courses as well, and hoped to 'minor' in Asian Studies but was told it was not necessary. He could just take them as electives. He took History of Modern China, and an individual study in ancient Chinese documents, including the 'I-Ching.' Since he was required to pass a Reading-comprehension test in a foreign language, he asked if he could take it in Chinese. Unfortunately, not enough of the test was oral, and Frank did not have enough 'reading ability' in Mandarin; but they would allow him to take the French or German test, since he had had two semesters of high school French, and three quarters of college German. He signed up for a refresher ('crash course') course in German, but it was an 8:00 a.m. class, and the professor droned on and on about Nietzsche's syphilis, and Frank wasn't learning anything, so he dropped it. Dave Schrader, Rod's office mate (and incidentally a fantastic percussionist), told him to buy the primer in German grammar that he recommended, and a box of vocabulary cards; every night, he studied the vocabulary cards and reviewed the grammar book; he set a date for his exam. Dr. John Verrell, his advisor, told him "Don't worry if you don't pass it the first time; most people take it three or four times before passing," he said. On a Saturday morning about a month after cramming for the exam, Frank took the 'German Comprehensive Reading Exam.' He did the best he could, but ended up 'guessing' at a lot of it, and the translations he thought were totally wrong; then he waited…and waited. Finally, the results came in the mail. They hadn't picked up the Saturday mail, so Sunday afternoon Frank picked up a letter with the results. He took it inside the house and showed Margo.

She said, "Open it, Frank." He was sure it was a 'fail,' but he opened it anyway–he would have other chances; someone he knew well had taken the French exam five times, and finally switched to Spanish, and then passed that the *third* time. He thought the grading was based on a hundred points, so when he saw the 'seventy-two,' his heart sank; he thought he had failed. He knew he shouldn't do it, but he called Dr. Verrell…at his home… on Sunday afternoon. He apologized for calling him at home, but he had just gotten the results from his language exam, and wanted to ask him what was the passing score. Dr. Verrell had been taking a nap, and he didn't sound too happy about this impetuous young graduate student everyone was talking about, who was like a 'dog with a bone,' so he didn't take too kindly to the call, but he wasn't unkind about it either. He said, "Frank, you don't call your professors on Sunday afternoons, but since you woke me up from my nap anyway…the passing score is 'seventy-two;' why, what score did you get?" Frank almost dropped the phone. Not 'seventy-one,' not 'seventy-three,' but *'seventy-two'*…the exact mark that was a *passing score*. He told Dr. Verrell that he passed with the exact passing level; he thanked him, and Dr. Verrell congratulated him and hung up. One step closer to finishing his Masters of Music degree on his way to the Doctor of Musical Arts degree in Choral Conducting! He had passed his graduate choral audition; comprehension language exam; and now he could plan for his Masters conducting recital. That is: if he could get passed Miriam Terry. He had gotten a job as a music librarian, and she came in every other day to check in, or check out some 'completely rare' or 'out of print' book she wanted for some research she was doing. Many feared her; others laughed at her for her eccentric ways and mannerisms. Frank had not been able to get the class on Bach that he wanted so he asked Rod to help him get Miss Terry to take him in an 'individual study' class. She said, "no," she didn't know of Frank's work, or reputation. Rod told her he had done well with Dr. Demar Irvine, and 'Dr.'Gerald Kechley. In that case, she said, she would 'give him a try.' Frank put his heart and soul into her class, but he made one fatal mistake: not knowing that she thought Bach to be above all other masters– choral, or otherwise, he did a report on Handel's choral music; but, Miss Terry had no use for Handel, or any of the other great choral composers. Frank did a report on Handel's choral music. Frank's conclusion was that there was 'no question that Bach was the greatest of all the choral composers of his time,' but that others, such as Telemann, and Handel, had been more *widely known* during that period; and thanks largely to Mendelssohn, Bach's music became more widely known. That was it. She gave Frank a 'C' on his report. Frank was devastated, and went to Rod, who went to Miss Terry. She refused to change the grade…under any circumstance. Rod said he had asked her to take Frank, and that he didn't need to even take it for a grade. She wouldn't budge. Rod went to the committee and they voted to request that the Graduate School change Frank's registration from a 'course for a grade' to a pass-fail status. Miss Terry was quite upset, but she could hardly fail him, so she had to change it to 'pass.' Later, she came into the library, and tried to be friendly with Frank. They actually ended up at least 'colleagues' if not friends [Frank had gone home after the 'C' on his report, and told Margo; he felt devastated, but she encouraged him to fight it; that is when Rod told him what the committee had decided]. The next week, Margo told Frank after supper she thought she was pregnant again. She wanted to wait until she went to the doctor, before she really counted on it, but Frank said they would celebrate even before the doctor's report. He had gotten the good news about continuing in his graduate program…and he felt good about the possibility of her going full term this time. Margo and Shelley hadn't even seen her parents during the time Frank was gone; Margo did not like to drive through the mountain pass, so they visited with Irma often, and Wilma and Francis came over one weekend. Frank got back and they celebrated Thanksgiving with the cousins in Tri-Cities, and Margo's folks came down. So, now it was time to go to Wenatchee and celebrate Christmas with her mom and dad. Frank's Christmas cantata at First Free Methodist was the Sunday after the end of the fall quarter exams, so they left that next Monday morning. Margo's school was out also, so they had a full week off, and Lydia McNicholls said she would take the First FM choir the Sunday after Christmas. Monday evening after they arrived Frank said they were going to celebrate Margo's good news…she had confirmed with the doctor before they left that she was, in fact, pregnant again. He said they were going to the Cottage Inn; Wilma insisted that she pick up the tab again; she said they hadn't seen them since Frank went to Europe, and the good news of another one 'on the way,' and Frank's safe return were two good reasons for them to celebrate, and besides, they were 'guests in her house' for Christmas. Margo convinced Frank it was alright, so he let it be this time, and enjoyed Wilma's hospitality. They had a wonderful week off, and went to Leavenworth to see the Bavarian Village, all decked out in Christmas lights, they heard the German band play Christmas carols, and it gave Shelley a chance to play in the snow. They visited Wenatchee Methodist Church, and Margo had a chance to play their newly refurbished pipe organ, the first opportunity to play it since they had been married. It was fun to see Shelley enjoy sledding in the snow with a cardboard box Frank had converted into a 'sled.' Some of the neighbors came over and had cookies and wassail Wilma had made. It was a great time, and fond memories of Christmas at the farm came back to them. They returned to Seattle the next week. Rod wanted Frank to help him plan a tour of the Chorale to California in the spring. Ron Kuhn and Ken Kosche had gone back home for Christmas, and he needed some ideas and advice about the tour. He knew Frank had a knack for that sort of thing and Ron and Ken had been busy with other things. Ken had also been experiencing some health issues, so he needed to pace himself. Rod said Frank could use some of the time to choose a work for his Masters recital in the spring. Rod gave him several choices, but he ended up choosing Ned Rorem's 'Canticles.' Rod said he could rehearse and perform it with the University Oratorio Singers. Nancy Farrell recommended Carol Sams for the soprano solo in the 'Canticles' which turned out well because few sopranos could handle the solo work in the piece. Ron and Ken assisted in lining up the Chorale tour to Washington, Oregon, and California, but Frank volunteered his time to help. They programmed Palestrina, Brahms, Schonberg, folk songs, and spirituals. It was a challenging program, but the Chorale, that by now was a close-knit and talented group of professionals (especially after Europe), rose to the occasion and learned the music well. On spring break, the Chorale went as far south as San Francisco, and sang mostly in churches. Frank was assuming more of a leadership role, even though he had no official position in the Chorale; with Rod's encouragement, he told the Chorale, "we are going to have a 'rallying cry' when we need to gather the group together and get everyone's attention;" then he taught them a Taiwanese street vendor's call...one he had heard growing up in

Mushan (the vendor bought tin cans and the like...then after pressing them out into sheet metal, he sold it on the street for a profit). His street call, which Frank taught them, went like this: *"O lam buay buah, Hai xi gah lah ah lahm buay boo-oo;"* they all just stared at Frank in disbelief! Who was this weirdo 'missionary kid' anyway? Frank repeated it, and then taught them one word at a time...even teaching them how to flick the last word 'up a fifth' at the end. That was it; that street cry became the rallying cry of the Chorale, and when they heard it, everyone came running to the bus, or rehearsal hall, or wherever they were supposed to gather. In later years, other Chorale members used it, and it has been 'sung' on at least four continents. The tour was a benchmark for future Chorale performances, too; they arrived back in Seattle with an even better reputation than before. Spring quarter began with the news that Ken Kosche had gotten cancer; he would receive treatment...the prognosis was good, but Rod did not want to take a chance, and asked that Ken withdraw, for the time being, from being choral teaching assistant; then Rod offered the position to Frank, with strong recommendations from several in the Chorale, for Frank; he took the position by storm, completely revamping the choral library, arranging for the Mahler Eighth Symphony to be pressed into a long-play vinyl record, and sold, at cost, to the other five U.S. choirs that had sung it together in Vienna. He took over organizing the UW-sponsored High School Choral Invitational, and conducted several special rehearsals that Rod was unable to make. Ron and he became very good friends, but Ron was frustrated; everyone checked with Frank about everything related to the Choral program, rather than him, even though he had seniority over Frank. Rehearsals were going well for Frank's Masters conducting recital with the Oratorio Singers... and Carol Sams, his soloist was amazing. The recital was only a part of the program, however, and when it was over, Frank could have left to celebrate, but instead he chose to stay and help sing the rest of the program with the Oratorio Singers. When the program was over, everyone had left. Margo and Shelley had come, though, and so had Irma and Tom, plus several of Frank's friends and choir members of First Free Methodist, so they all went out and had a little celebration of their own. He had exams, which he passed, and then just like that...he had completed his Master of Music in Choral Conducting. Rod wanted him to stay on as his TA, but he also thought Frank should start looking for a choral position while finishing his ABD ('all but dissertation'). Jobs were in short supply but Frank applied for 'anything and everything' from coast to coast, even 'part-time vocal coach' in 'Podunk-Anywhere.' In the meantime, Frank had attended all the SPC Alumni board meetings, and was planning the Alumni banquet, which was held on the campus of SPC, and called: 'On Board the SS SPC.' They decorated Gwinn Commons like a ship, and entrance was by the stairs, fixed up like a 'gangplank.' There were class reunions in the afternoon, including the 1965 SPC Ensemble (in which Frank had sung), which was on the program. They sang some of their old repertoire, but some 'up to date' things just for the banquet. The current Seattle Pacific A Cappella Choir was taking a tour of the Far East that summer, so Frank featured them too. He received many accolades for 'a great banquet,' and Bill Carpentar, the MC, announced that Frank, the banquet chair, had just completed the Masters of Music degree, *that very afternoon*, in his closing remarks, to a round of applause.

Margo was finishing her second year at Webster Elementary. She and Elizabeth Simes had developed a really close relationship, and the last week of classes she came to Margo in the teachers' lounge and asked if she could talk with her. Margo thought she must have done something wrong, but when they sat down, Elizabeth nervously asked her if she could ask her for a personal favor...she and her husband, Carl, hadn't been on a vacation in years, and wondered if Margo and Frank would be willing to come watch their place on Whidbey Island for three weeks while they went on an Alaskan cruise. Margo was so excited! She said she would have to talk to Frank, of course, but she was sure they would be able to do it; she called Frank at Rod's office at UW. Rod answered, but put Frank on the phone. Since it was only three weeks, Frank thought he could work around the summer class schedule. He told Rod, who said, "sure, as long as you invite me to come visit." Frank took him seriously, and told Margo they'd have to have a party, and ask the whole Chorale to come. Elizabeth and Carl invited Frank and Margo to come to get the "lay of the land," and told them to help themselves to anything in the garden or freezer! So, it was all set up. Lydia McNicholls agreed to take the First FM choir for the two Sundays they would be gone. They were so excited about this opportunity. Shelley said it would be her 'new adventure.' They arrived on Sunday afternoon; and Carl and Elizabeth left for Seattle to catch the cruise ship. They immediately began making plans for a 'Mongolian Barbeque...on their second Saturday there. They sent out invitations, planned the menu...and the phones started ringing off the wall ... 'what is a 'Mongolian' Barbeque?' Frank teased them all, and told them facetiously that the hardest part was "finding a Mongolian who was willing to be barbequed!" They explored the island the first week, shopped for their party, swam every day in Puget Sound, napped, read, and studied. It was great. Saturday arrived; Frank had two barbeque grills covered with foil and hot coals waiting. They had set up a table with meat, vegetables, and sauces. Beef, pork, and chicken; chopped celery, carrots, onions, tomatoes, ginger, garlic, and parsley; soy sauce, vinegar, sesame oil, water, sugar, salt and pepper. Frank told them: "watch me now, and do what I do." Margo and he had made a kind of pita bread to take the place of the 'shao-bing' (the pastry one stuffs it all in).' Rod and Sherry, Bruce and Larry and their wives, several of their other graduate school friends; they all came and enjoyed it, after a swim in Puget Sound... those that wished to. They ate their fill, some brought beer and wine, and Shelley entertained everyone with her little songs and poems. She had already learned several sayings in Chinese, and all thought she had 'picked it up in Taiwan,' because they knew she had been born there (uh, no! she was only a one-year-old when they left and wasn't even talking yet! It was fun to watch anyway). It was the 'mother-of-all-parties;' they didn't stop talking about it for months...even years–like the Hungarian trip the year before. Frank and Margo attended a little community church there and enjoyed it so much. Elizabeth and Carl, called after they arrived back in Seattle, and asked if "everything was okay." Frank and Margo couldn't thank them enough. Everything had been so great. For the second summer semester, Frank took some classes at UW, getting a jump on his DMA program. He also took Instrumental Conducting from Vilem Sokel, also some of Rod's choral workshops; and Frank was asked to sing in his previously-mentioned voice teacher's ensemble too. Ira Jones had formed a chamber group and asked Frank if he had any ideas for a name; Frank said flippantly off the top of his head, "why don't you just call it 'Coro da camera' ('chamber choir'). The name stuck, and they sang several concerts together. Frank also sang in several groups in the area, and was soloist for some Bach cantatas and other concerts. His study with Edison Harris was very productive...it showed continued improvement. Frank loved to give his 'voice instruction *pedigree:*' Edison Harris–a student of William Vennard–a student of Madame Schuman-Heinz. He also sang in the Seattle Chorale ('the symphony chorus'), and made his debut as a soloist in their spring concert at Seattle First Presbyterian. They took several trips around Puget Sound, Hurricane Ridge, and Wenatchee to see Margo's folks, and several weekend visits with Irma and Tom. Margo told Frank, after her visit with Irma, that she thought 'she had lost the baby...again.' They went to the doctor who confirmed it...but he said a D & C wouldn't be necessary this time, as she was able to just 'pass' the fetus. Frank asked Bob Fine and the First Free Methodist staff again for their prayers; this time, however, associate pastor Stan Watkins told Frank to talk to Rev. Wayne Henderson...pastor 'on loan' from the Church of God-Anderson; he knew of a baby they could adopt privately; it was due in a few months, a Free Methodist teen on the north side of Seattle who was pregnant; Frank said he'd talk with Margo, and get back with them.

Fall came and the year went by quickly. Frank's cousin Ron offered the services of his wife Terry to type Frank's dissertation, whenever that option came available, and Frank said he would consider it. There were several concerts, including Chorale, Oratorio, and University Singers performances, and Frank, as Rod's 'primary' TA (teaching assistant), had the main responsibility of organizing them. He also performed the three conducting recitals that were required for his DMA. In the Fall, he performed with a hand-picked chamber ensemble of twenty singers–six sopranos, six altos, four tenors, and four basses–they sang at one of the noon concerts before Christmas; he didn't have any problems getting his friends from the Chorale to volunteer. Most of the program was selected from the earlier periods of the Renaissance and Baroque. Winter quarter Frank selected his First Free Methodist choir as his second choral conducting concert; this concert was held at First Free Methodist, where Frank was director of music, and he brought in a string quartet and other instruments to perform Beethoven's 'Elegy,' and other selections, primarily from the Classic period. In the spring,

Ron Kuhn and Frank, who were now on staff, and conducted the University Singers, performed with that ensemble, in a shared concert. This was Frank's third and final conducting recital, and he chose the Brahms 'Vier Zigeunerlieder' ('Four Gypsy Songs, Opus 112), and Ron conducted the Dello-Joio 'A Jubilant Song.' All three conducting recitals went very well. He also now had a 'committee.' This committee would guide him through the doctoral process, consisting of: 1) three conducting recitals, 2) qualifying exams, 3) research and writing of the dissertation, and 4) defense of the dissertation. His committee was: Rod Eichenberger, chair, Gerald Kechley, assistant chair, Dr. Demar Irvine, Edison Harris, vocal performance chair, and Dr. Frank Conlon, faculty member outside of the School of Music–a requirement of each music doctoral candidate.

Rod came to Frank one day and said he had some news that might be of interest to him; there was a one-year sabbatical-leave job at Central Oregon College that was coming open in the fall of 1973. David Evans, the Director of Choral Activities there, was taking a year off to work on his doctorate, and Rod wanted Frank to apply for the job. He felt it would be advantageous to get some choral teaching experience before writing his dissertation. He wouldn't let him skip that part since Frank had a very limited record of academic choral experience. Frank agreed and applied for the position. They called him for the interview and Frank drove down in the spring to Bend, Oregon. Margo couldn't get the time off, so she stayed in Seattle; she said she would pray that, if God wanted them to take this next step, he would provide that opportunity for them; she was kind of excited at the prospect of moving to Oregon…if Frank got the job. Bend was on a high plain with a lot of mountains and lakes all around it. It would be a good place to raise a family, she said. He drove down the next Friday, interviewed, and then drove back Saturday evening. He met Dr. Ord Pinckney (Fine Arts chair), David Evans (Choral-Vocal), Jerry Yahna, (Band-Orchestra), and Gene Wieden, (Theater Arts). He was impressed with the college, the community, and the opportunity for his first college choral experience; they said they would let him know…after they finished the interviewing process. Frank was in the choral library on Wednesday of the following week when Rod stuck his head in the door; he looked down and sighed, "well, we gave it our best shot," he said, "someone wants to talk to you on the phone." Frank asked who it was, but Rod wouldn't say. He just said for Frank to come to the phone in his office. Figuring it was Ord Pinckney, or David Evans, telling him he didn't get the job, he went to Rod's office and picked up the phone, expecting the worst. It was Ord Pinckney. "Hello, Frank, I wanted to call and tell you we enjoyed the good interview we had with you, but...we have decided to...(laughing) offer you the position of Director of Choral Activities, 'anyway'...but you understand that it is just a one-year job, during David Evan's sabbatical leave." Frank looked at Rod; he and Dave Schrader were holding their sides laughing. He had tricked him! He made it sound like he had *not* gotten the job. Ord Pinckney was telling him he would like for Frank to bring Margo and Shelley down to Bend sometime, and meet everyone, maybe look for a place to stay, and tour the campus. No hurry, he said, just let them know when they might be able to come... within the next month he hoped. Frank said he would, of course, and since his 'qualifying exams were to be in the next two weeks, he asked if he could bring them down right after that... 'perfect,' Ord said, and he told Frank congratulations, and to go ahead and call him directly when they would be able to come. Frank hung up, and then acted like he was going to 'smack' Rod; by this time Ron, Joanie Conlon, and others in the music building had gathered, and were slapping Frank on the back; he couldn't wait to tell Margo the good news, but he wanted to surprise her...like Rod had surprised him. He packed everything up, and told them he would celebrate with them later...maybe after Seattle Chorale at the Northshore Tavern (where they always met for pizza and beer after rehearsals Monday night). They waved him on, and he drove toward Ballard to pick up Margo. He made sure he looked 'sad' and appropriately disappointed, before he picked her up. She said, "what's wrong?" and he said, "well, I heard from Central Oregon College, I gave it my best shot" and then he burst into laughter and said, "I got the job in Bend!" She squealed with delight and they drove to pick up Shelley at First FM, bought some steaks at Safeway, and cooked them on the barbeque on their back porch. It was indeed a good day–God had answered their prayers. Now it looked like they were going to be Oregonians for a while. He had done all of his three choral conducting recitals, and all he needed to do now was find out if he had passed his qualifying exams. That good news came the week he got back. Rod told him to enroll each of the quarters for the following year, and then he would need to come up to Seattle…to show his progress during the year absent, by preparing fifty topics upon which he could show competence, before beginning to write his dissertation. Things were falling into place. Rod also said he wanted Frank to join ACDA, the American Choral Directors Association, and go with them to Kansas City for the 'first national convention'…as a separate entity from MENC (Music Educators National Conference). Frank said he would, and booked his flight along with the rest of them for the conference. Bruce Browne and Larry Marsh would be attending, from their respective teaching positions in Ohio and Michigan. Frank had also heard from his mom and dad. They were 'finally' going to resign from VOCA, and switch mission boards after sixteen years; they would come home for a full year of furlough and live in Seattle; then they would return to Taiwan with China Evangelism Fellowship, and move to Xinzhu for a new ministry in Christian films and books…and also work among the aboriginal people in the mountains of Taiwan. [How ironic; after sixteen years of waiting *to live close to them* in Seattle, Frank and family would *leave* to go live in Bend, Oregon, five hours away! They all decided they would have to live with that, and since Frank would be coming up to Seattle often for his 'schooling-in-absentia,' they would still have several times to visit. Frank went off to Kansas City for the convention. It was a great time of wonderful choral music and meeting colleagues from around the nation, and the world…but, it was not without its downside.

[Frank had started 'kicking the slats out of his cradle,' enjoying the accolades for his talents, while allowing his 'spiritual growth' to slide; sure, there were those who were 'bent' on seeing him 'slip and fall,' who were more than happy to 'educate' this missionary kid to the *ways of the world*… but Frank himself wasn't doing anything to prevent it either! He wanted the recognition, which he thought, at the time, he had *never received*…in order to become one of the 'best choral conductors in America,' so he just 'happened' to ignore his call to ordained ministry (just before graduation at Morrison). If the trip to Europe had been the 'foot in the door,' the trips to other conventions, Australia-New Zealand, and elsewhere, in the years that followed, were all further openings of that door; the parties, and new associations with musical artists from all over the country, and the world, started eroding his spiritual life...God would use this 'time of training,' though, and spiritual drought...his 'desert years,' ultimately for God's glory. All of the years of struggle that would come about after that time were part of this maturing process; it was the message of Ephesians 4:12-3, which speaks of "coming into the fullness of *maturity* in our spiritual growth," for God's glory–one must "walk and not faint," before one can "run and not be weary...falling is part of the process...but, Frank did not know that at the time. After the ACDA Convention, they returned to Seattle, and Frank was ready to not only take on the world, he would do *anything* to be a *PART* of it].

He had made plans to take Margo to Hawaii...kind of a surprise for all her hard work and support...everyone told him she was the one who had done all the 'heavy lifting,' They said she was the one that had earned her "PhT" ('put hubby though'), while he had 'all the fun.' So, Frank had secretly saved his last three TA paychecks. He had put them in their savings account, which she never checked, since she paid all the bills...from their *checking* account, and he made sure they were current on his tuition at UW. Someone had told him about 'cheap vacation packages' to Hawaii, and he had been making payments. He didn't know anything about 'Paradise Vacation Trips,' but he figured they couldn't be too bad...three islands in five days, round trip airfare, ground transport and a 'luao' thrown in...it sounded pretty good! They seemed reputable enough, the price was right, and what could go wrong...right? Their sixth wedding anniversary was coming up June 24, 1973. He had finished the spring quarter, the SPC Alumni Banquet was June 9, and his last Sunday at the church was June 17. His folks were in Pasadena, California, and would not arrive until the end of the month; so it was all set. He picked her up from Webster after school, her last service day, the Friday before the Alumni Banquet and told her he wanted to celebrate their anniversary with a special outing on Friday, June 23, 1973.

She asked what it was...he wouldn't tell her, he said, until after their last Sunday at First FM. He made the last payment to the travel people on Monday the eighteenth, and on Tuesday at supper, he told her what he had done. She threw her arms around Frank, but she immediately started asking questions. What about Shelley? He had arranged with their friends, Kathie and Ed Teel, to keep her for the week. What about his folks arriving? They were staying with Irma, and were not expected until at least Thursday, and they (Frank and Margo) would be back by Tuesday. How could they afford it? He told her he had saved up his last three TA checks and had paid 'Paradise Vacation Trips' in installments. He told Shelley she was getting to stay with friends she *liked* from the church, and they were planning a hike... Shelley loved that, and she went to her room to start 'packing.' On Thursday morning, they were all packed up, they dropped Shelley off at Kathie's and Ed's, and headed to the airport. They flew United to Honolulu where they stayed overnight; the next day, they took Aloha Airlines to Maui, and stayed in a little bungalow about fifteen miles from Kahului... with a mango tree right outside their window; they swam in the ocean, she wore a '*mumu*' and Frank a Hawaiian shirt; they ate a simple meal at the lodge on the grounds. They slept with the windows open, and a nice ocean breeze helped them 'sleep like babies.' In the morning they had breakfast at the lodge, and then asked about the mango tree. They were told to 'help yourselves,' so they picked the mango and let it start to ripen. After a few hours of sun bathing, they took a nap, and it was time for supper. They packed up in the morning, and flew to Kuai (which was the site of many movies with tropical settings; their hotel was near there, and they took them on a short tour around Lihue and the surrounding area); it was overcast, but they spent the rest of the day at the pool sunbathing. Big mistake! Forgetting that the worse sunburns can occur on overcast days, they didn't apply as much sun block and tanning lotion as they normally would, and got one of the worst sunburns of their lives. After supper, they lay on their beds with the fan on and only a light sheet covering them (they looked like lobsters, and laughed at each other for their foolishness); the next day they ate breakfast and then retreated back to their room to nurse their sunburns. In the late afternoon, they caught their plane to Honolulu, checked into their hotel and gathered with the other tourists for the scheduled '*luao*.' There was hula dancing, 'sword and fire' dancing, a several-course meal, and lots of '*mai-tais*'...and roast pork. It was fun, but very much in the tourist style, and having lived in

Taiwan, it seemed very '*touriste*.' They told the tour guide it was their 'sixth wedding anniversary,' so they made Frank get up and dance for Margo. They gave them, and several others that were celebrating wedding anniversaries, *lei's* and *mai tai's*. It was fun...and a bit boisterous; they slept well, and in the morning they decided to rent a car and tour the island of Oahu on their own. They went to the USS Arizona Museum, Iolani Capitol building, Waikiki beach, Polynesian center, and then headed to the other side of the island to see the Manoa Falls; they parked the car and hiked up to the falls. It was just so-so, as falls go, but when they returned to the car, the passenger-side window had been broken and Margo's purse had been stolen; she had no money in it, (and no credit cards in those days), but it was upsetting nevertheless. They had barely gotten underway, when a bee came through the broken window and stung Margo; her sunburned arm swelled up; it hurt a lot! Frank said they'd get some baking soda when they got back; he began to worry about the insurance on the rented car. Things went from bad to worse; when they returned the car, the rental place wanted *them* to pay for the broken window, but Frank showed them the contract that confirmed no personal liability since he had purchased the insurance when he rented it. They went to their room, but on the way, someone offered them a free meal. Frank asked what the catch was; they denied any such 'catch,' It was a promotional for tourists, and they hoped some would investigate investing in time-shares... that was all. Frank wanted to see it in writing, so they showed him. He told Margo, no harm in having a free steak dinner, right? Margo remained skeptical, but they had it in writing, so she went along with it. They said they were to meet in a room off the lobby a half hour before dinner. It was the most miserable thirty minutes Frank and Margo had spent in a long time. The pressure to buy after hearing the 'pitch' was very fierce. Then they had them sit at tables as individual couples, and were promised payment plans, 'fully refundable' down payments, etc., ad infinitum; but just when Frank and Margo could stand it no longer, it was over. They had *not* succumbed, and they were ready to walk away from the dinner offer also, if needed. Instead, they were ushered into a small dining room, where they enjoyed a cold 'steak dinner'...no potato or vegetable, a miniscule salad with no dressing, and a roll. Margo ate it quickly and left for their room. Frank got up and followed

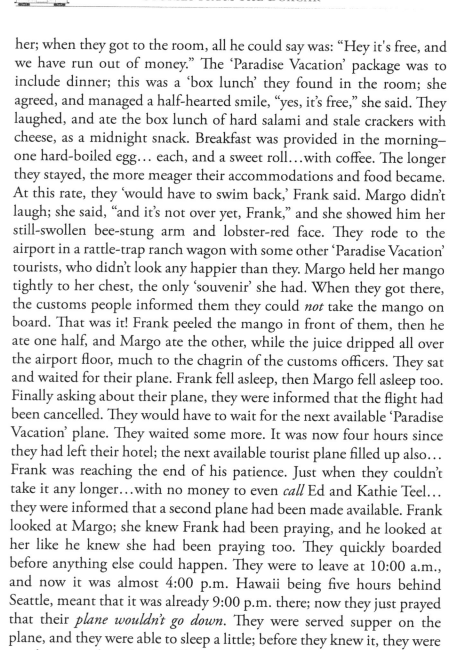

her; when they got to the room, all he could say was: "Hey it's free, and we have run out of money." The 'Paradise Vacation' package was to include dinner; this was a 'box lunch' they found in the room; she agreed, and managed a half-hearted smile, "yes, it's free," she said. They laughed, and ate the box lunch of hard salami and stale crackers with cheese, as a midnight snack. Breakfast was provided in the morning— one hard-boiled egg… each, and a sweet roll…with coffee. The longer they stayed, the more meager their accommodations and food became. At this rate, they 'would have to swim back,' Frank said. Margo didn't laugh; she said, "and it's not over yet, Frank," and she showed him her still-swollen bee-stung arm and lobster-red face. They rode to the airport in a rattle-trap ranch wagon with some other 'Paradise Vacation' tourists, who didn't look any happier than they. Margo held her mango tightly to her chest, the only 'souvenir' she had. When they got there, the customs people informed them they could *not* take the mango on board. That was it! Frank peeled the mango in front of them, then he ate one half, and Margo ate the other, while the juice dripped all over the airport floor, much to the chagrin of the customs officers. They sat and waited for their plane. Frank fell asleep, then Margo fell asleep too. Finally asking about their plane, they were informed that the flight had been cancelled. They would have to wait for the next available 'Paradise Vacation' plane. They waited some more. It was now four hours since they had left their hotel; the next available tourist plane filled up also… Frank was reaching the end of his patience. Just when they couldn't take it any longer…with no money to even *call* Ed and Kathie Teel… they were informed that a second plane had been made available. Frank looked at Margo; she knew Frank had been praying, and he looked at her like he knew she had been praying too. They quickly boarded before anything else could happen. They were to leave at 10:00 a.m., and now it was almost 4:00 p.m. Hawaii being five hours behind Seattle, meant that it was already 9:00 p.m. there; now they just prayed that their *plane wouldn't go down.* They were served supper on the plane, and they were able to sleep a little; before they knew it, they were on the ground at the Sea-Tac Airport; it was almost 2:00 a.m. The 'anniversary celebration' was over, and even though they had moments that they were both anxious, it was still a fun trip, and one they talked about for years. They called Ed Teel to tell them they might as well keep

Shelley overnight, and they would pick her up in the morning. They slept till 9:00 in the morning, then picked Shelley up. Ed said they had taken the 'hike of the century,' and Shelley had out-hiked everyone; Kathie and Ed couldn't stop talking about it. Frank and Margo wanted to share all that they had been through, but now it seemed like 'yesterday's news,' and they saved it for another time. They were just glad that everything had turned out okay. They never forgot their sixth wedding anniversary celebration, though... that was for sure. Shelley was happy they were back and showed them several of her drawings and 'art projects.' She was becoming more independent, and during the past year had loved going exploring with Frank and Margo around the neighborhood. One of their favorites spots was a little park just two blocks from their house overlooking Puget Sound. It was truly one of the most beautiful spots on Queen Anne hill. They went there often; Frank loved doing gardening while Shelley played around the house, so after they dropped Margo off at Webster, Frank often kept Shelley at home during the morning, and then would drop her off at First FM daycare, and go on to his classes by 11:00 a.m. One morning...it was one of those 'most-beautiful-places-in-the-world' days... Frank was puttering around his garden, and Shelley was doing her usual singing, dancing, and generally entertaining herself. After a while, he didn't hear her. He didn't think anything of it at first, and finished up what he was doing. Then he called her, but there was no answer; he went looking for her, but didn't see her anywhere. He looked through the house, calling her name...nothing; this was highly unusual. He went down the alley in the back, around the block, and then looked all through the house again; he looked in closets, in the basement... everywhere; he started to panic. He asked neighbors if they had seen her; 'no... nothing.' Now he really panicked, but getting ahold of himself, he called the police; the dispatcher took him through all the steps, he looked again, he looked under beds, in closets, basement, under desks...again, and again. She said, "look in the refrigerator and oven," then he really panicked, and choked up...but there was nothing. She said she would send a patrol car. They arrived, and Frank gave them her name, age, and description. Now choking up, Frank wanted to go with them to patrol the neighborhood, but they said, "no, you need to be here if she comes back." Frank started to pray: he went into a closet, spread himself out on the floor, and sobbed, crying out to God to spare his daughter; all he could think about was his brother Stevie, who was killed in an auto accident when he was three...the same age as Shelley! It seemed like an eternity, but within minutes, one of the squad cars pulled up and... 'officer George' they called him... met Frank at the door... holding Shelley in his arms; he held her out quickly to Frank who held her tight; officer George teased, "we found her at the little Viewpoint Park overlooking Puget Sound, she acted like she owned it," he laughed; "and she was probably trying to run away from you, thinking she might be in trouble with that load in her pants!" They all laughed...then Frank and Shelley laughed too; they went on their way with the profound gratitude of Frank...and Shelley. He cleaned her up, they had lunch, and he took her to First FM daycare. He made it to his conducting class and Frank told Margo when they got home that night, and she just held Shelley and Frank, and praised the Lord...again...for his grace and protection.

Frank's folks arrived that Friday, and Frank and Margo went out to Irma's house to greet them. They had moved from their home of sixteen years in Mushan, and put everything in storage in Xinzhu in Taiwan. [They had also resigned from VOCA, so they had first gone to Pasadena, California, and officially severed their relationship with them; Irma had offered her home to them for the summer, and during the time that they would travel in the US and Canada. VOCA *gave* them the same green Chevrolet they had driven when they were home in 1966, plus a severance package...of a meager few thousand dollars... amounting to only six months of salary! The plan was for them to put part of this toward a place, to rent in Seattle, until they could buy. Michael and Beth had not told VOCA they planned to return to Taiwan with China Evangelism Fellowship, because, in fact, they had not completed their plans with Elizabeth Evans; they would also have to switch the California board of directors to a new board of directors after Ms. Evans retired; they eventually extended this incorporation to Oregon, formed a new board, and were licensed to do the mission business there. Irma agreed to be the treasurer; Maxine became secretary, and editor of the newsletter, the *Messenger*. Frank took them around the Lake Washington area to look for houses to rent]. Two others that they looked at were not adequate for what they needed, but

Frank found them one in Kirkland that they liked, even though the previous owner had added on to it, but nothing was 'plumb.' Frank's dad insisted that this did not matter to them...he could 'fix it up,' he said. He *was* at least willing to let Frank call his friend, Don Brumfield (who worked for an 'inspection and appraisal' company), before buying it. Michael put money down on it *anyway*, to insure they didn't lose it...and he didn't want to *rent* it–the price was only seventeen thousand dollars, and, with the money in his Ephrata Security Bank account, he could save by buying it outright, saving thousands. Frank was alarmed, especially when Don came back with the inspection report–Don said, "don't touch it with a ten-foot pole," Well... Michael bought it anyway...cash! Years later, after Frank and Margo had lived there (as did Dave and Mar... then her sister Tammy and her husband); it was sold...for seventy-five thousand dollars! Wait! There's more...with Bill Gates as a *neighbor* just south on Lake Washington only three miles away, as 'lakeview property,' it is *now* worth millions! (but back to our story) they now had a place of their own. [They had been given a house in Nampa, by Beth's siblings, and had committed, to Dr. Fitz at least, the 'unforgiveable sin'–a second mortgage, and then built a beautiful house on top of the existing basement structure; this was eventually paid off by renters, and Dr. Fitz had lived in it until Lura died in 1967, the year Frank and Margo went to Taiwan; years later, he remarried (his high school sweetheart from Sherman, Minnesota–Katherine Peebles), when both of them were eighty-one years old! She had lost her spouse also, and her grown children, as well the Fitz children, were, at first, very excited for both of them, until Dr. Fitz accepted a pastorate in North Dakota...at the Williston Church of the Nazarene! She moved there with him, but when winter came, she couldn't handle the forty below zero weather...and in poor health...her children came and got her; they said she needed to live 'somewhere closer to family.' By the time Frank's folks arrived, Dr. Fitz had had a stroke, was living with Irma, and going to the Burien (Seattle area) Church of the Nazarene, close to where Guil and Doris, and family, were living. Both he, and Michael's father, Pop, died the same year...1974, both also born the same year...1887; these two men were part of a great legacy, unmatched as far as Frank was concerned; the 'Stories from the Boxcar' would continue after these two 'giants' were gone, however... through Michael, and then through Frank].

Margo, Frank, and Shelley moved to Bend, Oregon. By the end of the summer of 1973, Frank had resigned his position at First Free Methodist; they replaced him with someone Frank did not think would continue the great choral music program there.

[Dr. Fine's daughter, Laura, had had an aneurism and died suddenly at age thirteen, so the church was already in mourning. Frank and the choir sang a choral arrangement of 'Safe In The Arms Of Jesus' for her memorial service; then not long after Frank left, Bob Fine himself got cancer and died...it was a very difficult time for the church; Frank and Margo had decided to turn down the opportunity to adopt the little girl that pastor Wayne Henderson had told them about, following Frank's acceptance of the choral position in Bend...so, the little girl had been adopted by another family in north Seattle]. They came down to Bend in the summer and found a duplex they could live in for a year; David Evans himself showed them around and introduced them to the staff at the college. He also showed them the church where he was organist-choirmaster, Trinity Episcopal Church; he said it was 'all arranged,' and said he had to leave for another meeting; Frank asked him 'what was arranged?' As David went out the door, he called out to them, "the two of you are also taking over my position here as director of music and organist, too." He said he had to go to a meeting, but Father Granville Waldron, the Rector, would explain everything, and he left. Frank and Margo knew nothing about the Episcopal Church liturgy... 'when to stand, sit, kneel...anything.' As they were fretting, and trying to decide if they should just politely decline this new 'wrinkle' in the scheme of things...in walked Father Granville Waldron,

He was nothing they could have ever imagined in an Episcopal priest. 'He'd been a cop in Los Angeles,' he said; he preached short sermons; 'make that a homily instead of a sermon, (Frank thought he had said 'hominy,' and wondered if that was what they served for communion; Ha!). Granville used a CB in his truck, and punctuated his sermons with things like, "...so Jesus said to his disciples, 'copy that, 10-4, good buddy,' I'll meet you at the lake after the storm, okay? —over, and out." This was definitely going to be different than anything they ever had expected!]

Frank worked hard, and the choral program improved markedly. The COCC choir sang concerts on campus and in the community; he formed a chamber choir that sang for special events and nursing homes; he brought Rod down for a 'choral invitational' of area high schools. When Gene announced the community theater would do 'Sound of Music,' Frank prepared the 'nuns' chorus, worked with the 'Von Trapp' children to sing in parts...he even played the part of 'Rolf,' (a seventeen-year-old Hitler youth...when Frank was twenty-nine! He did his own makeup...slicking his hair back, making himself look twelve years younger!). The show came off very well, and Gene, knowing Frank's position was only a one-year music job, tried to get a 'theater position' approved so they could keep Frank there longer. Ord Pinckney approved it, and found the money to fund it, but the Administration would not approve it. Through the theater, Frank and Margo made friends with Mike and Patty Porter. Patty was one of 'Frank's nuns' in the show, and Mike helped build sets and assisted with 'tech.' They had a four-year-old daughter, Holly, and she and Shelley became best friends. The families did everything together—they went for pizza, picnics, movies, sailing, and other things. They were Catholic, and so they declined the invitation to attend church at Trinity, but were very faithful in their attendance at their own church, St. Charles Catholic (they 'sponsored' the hospital where Steve was born). They did have several 'theater patrons' 'follies' in order to take advantage of the time that the Varro's were there. Margo was Frank's accompanist and played a number of theater and music concerts. They also enjoyed thoroughly their work with Father Waldron, and the music at the church. Margo became active in women's special ministries: quilting, bells, and children's ministry. She started a children's choir, and a bell choir. Father Waldron called them in to his office one day. He said things had worked out so well that, whether David Evans came back or not, they *HAD* to become Episcopalians. He had arranged for the Bishop of Eastern Oregon, to come and confirm them in the spring (Frank could *just imagine* how *that* news would go over with his 'Nazarene parents!'). Margo wasn't even sure that would be 'good news' with her *own* low-church Methodist parents! (Wilma had in fact been a Four-Square Pentecostal before she married Francis!). God seemed to indicate to them that it wasn't which church they were a part of, but whether they honored God *IN* their church. When Frank's mom and dad visited, with Dave, Frank wasn't sure his parents would even go to church with them...to his surprise, they did...and even went forward for communion; Father Waldron took note of it, and made sure he introduced Frank's parents and Dave. When Beth and Michael sat back down, she turned to Dave and whispered, "well, you just had your first taste of wine." [Dave, like Frank and others who had attended Morrison, had never shared with them all the things that happened 'under the radar,' like cross-island camping trips...with no chaperones, and indulging in normal teenage rebellious behavior, that he and Frank, and most MK's ('missionary kids') for that matter, were *KNOWN* for (*despite their strong present faith*). He stifled a wild-eyed denial, and Beth looked pleased with herself for having had a hand in 'educating' him (*Not! And he wasn't about to share that story either*)

[Well, Margo had always wanted to take dance, and she had not been allowed to do so growing up in Michigan; her parents never allowed her to go to any dances...ballroom or rock n' roll...either one. Looking back on it, signing up for a ballet class was one of the best things she ever did in her life, she said. Three months after they arrived in Bend, Margo told Frank she thought she was pregnant. They were both very cautious because she had miscarried twice already. The doctors that Granville and Marty Waldron recommended were great: Alan Toliver and Mark Rogers had been in practice in Bend for a couple years and welcomed Margo as a new patient; Alan was her primary doctor but Mark ended up on duty when the baby was born in June at St. Charles hospital; so, Margo decided to sign up for ballet in Bend...and now jumping forward–and *the story really gets funny here*: when Rob was born in Ohio...when she again signed up for ballet... Frank loved to tell the story (untrue as it was) that he 'wanted to meet these two ballet teachers,' because...*Margo always got pregnant every time she started taking ballet!* Ha! Margo forbade Frank from telling this false story ...especially since both ballet teachers were *WOMEN*, but he loved to tell it anyway! The stress of graduate school was definitely

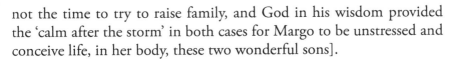

not the time to try to raise family, and God in his wisdom provided the 'calm after the storm' in both cases for Margo to be unstressed and conceive life, in her body, these two wonderful sons].

The big fuel crisis of 1973-74 hit while they were in Bend. People running out of fuel and long lines at gas stations became a common sight. Frank was scheduled to attend a regional ACDA in Spokane but was afraid of running out of gas, either on the way up, or on the way back. Then he had an idea: Margo's cousin was the owner of a gas station in Richland (about halfway). Frank could stay the night there, both on the way up, and on the way back, and since they were 'family,' he could fill up with gas both ways. Margo called her cousin and set it up. Frank left in the afternoon, arrived in time for a late supper, and then headed for bed in the bunk just above their sleeping son; Frank was awakened in the early morning by Margo's cousin, apparently on his way to work, attempting to grope him! Frank kicked him with all his might...the cousin just laughed; and left. Frank now had to go to the station to fill up, but trying to pay the attendant without going in to the office, Frank was told Margo's cousin wanted to *see* him. Frank held the money out, laid it on the desk and attempted to leave. Margo's cousin had spread pornographic magazines all over his desk and tables, and he tried to grab Frank as soon as he came in. Frank dropped the money on the table and ran out, got in his car, and drove off. Neither Frank, nor Margo, knew her cousin was like this, and there was no way he was coming there on the return; he would have to take his chances on filling up somewhere else. From then till his death many years later, Frank nor Margo ever had the chance to reconcile with him. In Spokane, his friends from graduate school were more interested in drinking, carousing, and 'hitting on him' (women *and* men), rather than just enjoying the music convention; Frank was put in a compromising position, and he couldn't understand 'what he was doing wrong' that was attracting this kind of behavior, first from a relative, then his graduate school friends (even faculty). Turning on himself, Frank, rather than remaining strong, blamed his innocence and naïvete for what was going on in his life. After all, it was just part of being 'educated to the things of the world' in order to handle college choir conducting, right? He returned home defensive and angry. He had no strong spiritual friends...nor seem to 'want them' any more.

In April, Frank and Margo were confirmed by the Eastern Oregon Bishop, The Right Reverend William Spofford. He received them in the older 'orthodox way,' which Father Granville had 'informed' them about. Like a new baby receiving life at birth, the Bishop, after confirming them, gently slapped their faces, like a doctor would 'spank' a newborn baby to get it to take its first breath; it was very meaningful, and something Frank and Margo always remembered. They remained confirmed members in the Episcopal Church for almost twenty five years. Two months later, just before they moved back to Seattle, their second child, Michael Steven Varro ('Steve') was born. The night of the big 'Patron's Follies' (a community music and theater show held at COCC), they had scheduled a cast party following the show. It was a week before the due date for Steve, but Margo, didn't play the show, or even attend, thinking Steve might come early. Sure enough, he did. Frank came back from the cast party about midnight, and had barely gone to sleep, when Margo woke him up saying, "the contractions are regular and are closer apart, Frank, I think we better go to the hospital." Beth had come down with Frank, from his last visit to UW the previous weekend, so she stayed with Shelley while they went to the hospital. They had been taking the Lamaze classes, and immediately went into the routine...the 'breathing' exercises they had learned. Margo was in labor for about five hours. Dr. Rogers was very caring and helpful. Frank was allowed in both the labor and delivery rooms the entire time. (Frank always told everyone Shelley was born right on the 'scheduled day,' that Steve was one week *early*, and Rob was one week *late*; Shelley was born at five in the afternoon; Steve was born at five in the morning, and Rob was induced at 7:00 a.m. and born at 9:00 a.m.) At nine days old, Steve was baptized at Trinity Episcopal Church in Bend, by Father Granville Waldron. Frank's mom had been invaluable during the week following Steve's birth; she helped Shelley get off to the Nazarene Vacation Bible School, she cooked and cleaned, and she helped watch Shelley during the day, while Frank finished up the semester at COCC, and Margo took care of the baby. Beth took the bus back to Seattle and helped prepare for Frank and Margo's move to Kirkland, where they would live...together, until Michael, Beth and Dave and returned to Taiwan.

The big move day arrived; they had been planning their trip back to Seattle before Steve was born, but they weren't sure how Frank would drive the truck, Margo would drive the Kadett, and take care of the newborn baby. As they were having supper with the Porter's before the 'Patron's Follies,' they talked about this problem. Mike said he knew someone that worked at COCC, Sally Minton, whose husband Bill worked odd jobs… harvest jobs, transport, delivery…stuff like that. Sally and Bill went to the Mennonite church and could probably use the money; how much was Frank willing to pay? Not very much, Frank said. Mike thought Bill might do it for 'fifty to a hundred dollars', plus expenses. Frank could drive the Kadett, and Bill could drive the truck, and take the bus back. Let's see: truck rental, gas, bus fare back, meals along the way, and an honorarium. He could put the rental and bus fare on a credit card, and cash for meals, plus Bill's fee. Mike and Patty talked to Sally who talked to Bill. Two days later, a week after Steve was born, they said they would do it…and would not accept anything over the expenses! Wow; there it was again! Bill showed up right after breakfast. Frank had rented the Ryder truck, and it was parked in front of the duplex. They quickly loaded the small amount of furniture, boxes of household goods and their clothing. Shelley sat in the front seat with her dad, and Margo, with Steven in the car seat, in the back; it made it convenient for nursing and letting him sleep in a little crib Frank had rigged up, and anchored with the seatbelt. They headed out toward Portland; they made rest stops as prearranged with Bill. After a short pre-lunch stop in Portland they headed up I-5 and went as far as US Highway 12, where they ate again and made a rest stop. It was still mid-afternoon when they pulled into Tacoma. There they made another rest stop, and Frank called his folks. They said they would expect them for supper. When they pulled into Kirkland, Beth had supper ready. Frank asked Bill to join them, but he said he would need Frank to take him to the bus station, or else he would miss his evening bus to Portland, and the connection to Bend. While Dave helped his dad unload the truck, Beth, Margo, and even Shelley, helped where they could, Frank took Bill back into Seattle to the bus station. Frank insisted that they go ahead and eat supper without him. He could warm his plate up after he got back. With Bill safely on the bus, Frank headed back to Kirkland where the family had finished eating and were putting things away. After he ate, they visited a bit and then went to bed. Michael had had his longtime friend, Wes Sage, pour the foundation and do the initial framing-up for the new addition to the house. Henry Fritz came, and did the 'framing up', while Wes was called out on another job; but...nothing was completed to that stage; Frank had agreed to move in for the summer, but there were just bare studs...and no finished flooring: this is what Frank and Margo moved into...and tension arose immediately...this was *not* what they had agreed on, and his folks had not communicated this change in the plan. Beth felt the tension and was embarrassed. Michael couldn't hide his 'eyebrow alert;' they decided to make the best of it (but only after Frank took it on himself to nail a large piece of drywall over the studs to at least give them minimum privacy). They had brought a crib with them... purchased at Salvation Army, which they placed in their room, so Steve could be with them. Shelley was in another bedroom adjacent to them, which Frank also covered with drywall. Michael got up early every morning; the sound of the 'skilsaw' awakened everyone; Beth made breakfast, and Steve woke up crying. Michael and Beth went ahead and ate breakfast without them...letting them 'rest up from their trip.' The only trouble was...they couldn't possibly 'rest' with the 'skilsaw' squealing, with smells and noise coming from the kitchen right next to them, and with bare studs and a piece of drywall barely providing minimum privacy. On top of everything, Frank had to report to Rod at the UW daily, so he couldn't help much with the construction project. Beth was trying to assist Margo with nursing, but neither she, nor even Margo, realized a post-natal kidney infection had also developed; not knowing this, Beth asked her almost every hour "have you tried nursing him again, dear?" This only added to the stress. Frank arrived at UW the second day back, and Rod started talking to him about the 'Australia-New Zealand tour;' he said he had a solo for him, and that Frank was one of his six tenors...they were taking only twenty eight altogether... eight sopranos, eight altos, six tenors, and six basses. 'No,' Frank said, he was *not* going; there was *no way* he could go at this time—new baby, living with his folks, Margo had a kidney infection, etc., etc. Rod just looked at him. "I thought you wanted to finish your doctorate," he said laughing. This was too much pressure; Frank had had to promise Margo 'on his grandfather's grave' that he wouldn't do this. So, he told Rod he really wanted to go, but he 'didn't have the money.' Rod wouldn't take 'no' for an answer...he had already raised the money...for at least the soloists. Frank felt trapped; he called Margo, told her he wanted to take her to lunch, she left Shelley and Steve with grandma, and he picked her up and they went to Farrell's in Bellevue. As soon as they ordered, Margo started to cry; she said she knew what he was going to tell her. Frank asked if someone had called from UW; she said no, but she knew the predicament he was in, and that she wanted to support him...but she was angry that there was this kind of pressure on him. He said, "okay, tell me what you think I'm going to tell you." She said she felt he was going to tell her...that he was going on the Australia-New Zealand trip. He swallowed hard, and then told her...she was right, but how he had refused to go...how Rod had countered every reason for not going, even the cost of it...with more pressure. Frank said he loved her and would never hurt her, and everything that came with it. She stopped crying; she said she had to tell him something: she had gone to the doctor that his mom had suggested, and he had confirmed she had a kidney infection. Frank promised her 'his mother would step up to the plate' and help her. Margo loved Beth, and they got along great; they had become very close in Taiwan. Frank conceded that his mom could sometimes be a little 'overwhelming.' Dave and Margo had also become very close, despite the age difference. So, they ate a little of their lunch, but took the rest of it to-go. They didn't feel very hungry; they didn't talk all the way home. Margo knew it was something Frank had to do, even if he wanted to be with her, especially right after Stevie was born, moving in with his parents, and everything so topsy-turvy. [Frank had interviewed for a choir director's job at First Covenant Church, downtown Seattle, and they had hired him. They said the job could start at the end of August, after he got back]. Michael agreed to finish the drywall and flooring for Shelley's, and their rooms. Rehearsals started in two weeks; the Fitz's, who always got together during the summer, decided to meet for a picnic at Juanita Park on Lake Washington before Frank left. UW Chorale presented a concert prior to departure, and they all attended it. The next day they got on the plane and travelled the five hours to Honolulu, and after a two-hour layover, flew the thirteen hours to Fiji, and then another five hours to Sydney. They arrived on Sunday morning; it was 'early spring' there in the Southern Hemisphere. The Chorale was exhausted from the trip, but they had breakfast and something to drink, and felt better. Frank's friend Kathy Thornton came running out of the bathroom yelling for everyone to go 'flush the toilet...and watch the water 'swirl clockwise'...instead of counter-clockwise, like back in Seattle! Now everyone had to try it. They flushed the toilets over and over, just to watch them swirl. Rod came along and asked 'what in the world' they were doing...he laughed; he couldn't believe they had nothing better to do than entertain themselves 'flushing toilets;' must be the jet-lag he told them; he said for them to finish eating their breakfast and get on the bus. They had a concert that night at the Sydney Civic Concert Hall, and they had one hour to check into the student hostel and rest a little before their rehearsal (they were told to be sure to thank the Intercultural Forum for the meals before their concert). Then they gave a great performance to a packed hall. A reception followed before they retired for the night. The next day they toured Sydney harbor, visited the zoo, and the world-famous Opera Hall. They caught a flight out in the morning for Perth, on the west coast of Australia. It was unbelievable how big Australia was, and most of the Chorale had no idea it would take them almost five hours to get there. On arrival, they were bused to the Perth Concert Hall, sight of the World Conference of the International Society of Music Educators, where they warmed up on stage. They were told initially that they were to sing first on the program that evening. Since the theme of the conference was: 'American styles of music,' they scheduled a contemporary Magnificat by the American composer, Shendin Manesco; but after they had warmed up, one of the ISME officials met Rod on stage and told him there had been a change in plans. Perth, being the host site, had accordingly arranged for an aboriginal dance troupe to perform first... as a 'welcoming' gesture. In the dance rehearsal earlier that day, however, members of the ISME performance committee noted that the women in the troupe danced 'topless!' The host committee had wanted a touch of "local culture," and had engaged the group...without actually having first seen them perform...and did not know they danced 'au natural.' It would be highly insulting to cancel their appearance, bur rather than cloth them in halters, or some appropriate top, they ran out and purchased 'women's undergarments'...white brassieres! Following the opening dance numbers, there was an embarrassed murmur, and only polite applause. The smell backstage of rancid butter, with which they covered their bodies, coupled with the natural body odor of men and women after a strenuous workout... well, we'll just say it was 'overpowering.' Never mind that the Chorale sang the best performance of the Magnificat ever given, or that any of the other American folk songs and spiritual 'brought down the house'...the only thing delegates to the 'thirteenth conference of the ISME' remembered for the rest of their lives, was the performance of the Aboriginal Dance Troupe of Western Australia! And it was great!

The Chorale had a chance to do some sightseeing as well that the tour guides arranged, and the week was filled with concerts, American folk songs, spirituals, lunches, demonstrations, and a lot of visiting with musicians from around the world. The evening after the Chorale's concert, the Kiwi Choir from New Zealand gave their concert. Having just heard the 'authentic' way of singing American spirituals, the crowd audibly gasped when the New Zealand sang 'Gonna Ride The Chariot' in a beautiful...but very stiff and unnatural manner. Having arrived late, and without the advantage of hearing the Chorale's demonstration of the 'correct spiritual style,' the Kiwi Choir had to endure the 'condescending looks' of all the other attendees, who were now 'self-appointed experts;' how funny! And a contingent of nuns followed the Chorale wherever they went; someone remarked it looked like a 'flock of penguins' gathering around them. They stayed in private homes, which was one of the best features of the whole trip. Frank roomed with Brian Trevor (a fellow-alumnus of Seattle Pacific), and every morning, their hostess, Roberta, who was married to Chris Giles (she called him 'the butcher' – and he actually *was* a union butcher!), knocked on their door, saying in her strong Australian accent, "mornin' boys, here, drink this orange juice; it'll take that taste of 'canary shit' outta yer mouths." Since there was a union, sometimes even including butchers and produce workers...striking somewhere in Australia every day or so... she bragged that they would never have to worry about it...since Chris brought stuff home every day: beef, pork, lamb, and sausage: "Wat'll it buee, boys...chops, stike (steak), sowsage...wat'll it buee?" And so, every day they ate eggs, bacon, sausage, and usually a chop or steak. It was '*wonderful*,' and they didn't feel like eating anything else for the whole day! But then, after all the music, visits, tours, eating and drinking, it was time to continue the rest of the tour of Australia and New Zealand. They had been in Sydney and Perth a total of ten days, and were scheduled to fly to Adelaide the next Wednesday evening. When they arrived at the airport, they were told that the airline workers had gone on strike, and their flight would be delayed. How long? They weren't sure. So, someone ordered 'brandy alexanders,' and Frank broke out his Ma-zhang set. He taught them how to play Ma-zhang while they sipped their 'brandy alexanders,' and every hour they checked to see if the strike was over. Some of them fell asleep, others talked, and some played cards. About 5:00 a.m., one of the airport officials came over to them. "The strike is over; you can get on the plane." Just like that, the strike was over, and they boarded the plane, flew to Adelaide, checked into the dormitory at Central Australia University of Adelaide, and slept a little while before rehearsing on stage for the concert that night. They ate in the University Cafeteria, got into their tuxes and dresses, and gave a concert. Brian had the solos in the Brahms 'Ziegeunerlieder,' but Frank had the solo in 'Ain' Got Time To Die,' which always 'brought down the house,' and that night was no exception. Someone said if you closed your eyes, you might think Frank was *not* a 'white Hungarian, raised in China, singing a black spiritual in Australia!' It was fun, and Frank put his heart and soul... and his Nazarene 'gospel soul' into it. They slept 'like babies' that night after so little sleep the night before. They were able to take a short tour of Adelaide before catching the afternoon flight to Melbourne. They had only an afternoon performance at the University of Melbourne for the College of Music, and then supper on campus, and stayed in the dormitories there. The next day was free, but it was cold and rainy, and many of the Chorale members didn't go on the city tour that was provided. They had hoped to take a short trip to Canberra on their way to Sydney and Brisbane, but that plan fell through. They flew out the next day to Brisbane. There they sang another concert, this time at Queensland University, where they stayed in the dormitory, and ate in the cafeteria. The following night they gave their final concert, of the Australian-leg of the tour, in Sydney. This time it was in another part of the city, at the University of Sydney. Again, similar arrangements were made… a concert after supper in the recital hall. The next day they flew out to Auckland, New Zealand; they didn't have a chance to visit the South Island, and Christ Church, but they did have a concert in Auckland that night at the concert hall. The tour guides had made arrangements for them to visit Rotorua the next day, a few hours by bus, to the Maori community and hot springs. There they stayed in private homes, where they enjoyed the hot springs, a light meal, and then were taken to the concert hall where they sang a couple songs for the Maori's…but mostly just enjoying the hospitality of a 'luao-type' of meal, their dancing, and songs. They wanted to do a special dance for Rod; they had 'warned him' that they would dance around him and for him to remain motionless …no matter what they did… with all of the guests and Chorale members looking on. Rod, telling the story later, said the last thing in the world he *EVER* expected… *after dancing and chanting around him for a very long time, was some guy, 'with a painted face, stomp his feet, yell really loudly…and then stick his five-inch tongue out at him, two inches from his face!'* This was, of course, to the hoots and hollers of the entire Chorale. After much food and drink, they retired for the night, and slept soundly. They took the bus back the next day, and after resting up, some went on a tour of Crystal Mountain the following day. To save what little money he had left, Frank and four or five others stayed by the pool at the hotel in Auckland. He had a chance to make friends with some people he hadn't really gotten to know that well; he got a little rest and some sun (some tattled that it 'didn't look good' that Frank spent so much time at the swimming pool with Carol, one of the altos, but Frank seemed oblivious to appearances at that time in his life). The next day, they flew out to Fiji, where they had a chance to unwind, shop in the villages, and swim in the sea. They spent the night there, and then got on the plane, and flew the thirteen hours back to Hawaii; from there to Seattle…an exhausting but wonderful trip. Margo met Frank at the bus station. It was late, and Shelley and Steve just stayed at home with Grandma and Grandpa Varro.

The tour was the talk of the town. The Chorale's Australia-New Zealand trip made the news all over the University of Washington campus, as well as in Seattle's music circles, and especially in the national choral community. Like the 1971 trip to Europe, it set a new standard for choirs all around. When it got around town that Frank was part of a doctoral program in choral music at the UW, someone said...'hey, Church of the Epiphany Episcopal is looking for an organist-choirmaster.' He had already started at First Covenant Church downtown, but he agreed to at least call the Rector, Jack Gorsuch, to find out about the job. [Here he did an insensitive thing: having only served at First Covenant Church for four months...when offered the position at Epiphany, he accepted it right away, giving less than two-week's notice; Margo was also offered the organist's position (only on the condition that she study with a well-known organist at Phinney Ridge Lutheran, Alma Onckley, professor of music at University of Puget Sound; Margo had been a piano performance major but had never studied pipe organ); the First Covenant people were hurt—they thought someone in the church had been unkind to them]; nevertheless, it was a great opportunity, and it fit into Frank's final year in graduate school while he wrote his dissertation; but he hadn't considered the feelings of the people there, and he felt badly; thankfully Phil Mack was able to accept the position.

Beth had to leave by August to return to Taiwan in time for Dave's schooling. Michael decided to stay an extra month in order to finish up the dry wall, plumbing, electrical, and paint the new addition inside and out. It was during this time in Frank's life that a very important thing happened. It was while he and his dad were finishing up the house. Dad was downstairs finishing the plumbing and electrical. Frank was sanding and painting the rooms upstairs...their relationship most of Frank's life certainly had not been what it should have been. Michael had always tried too hard to teach his son what he himself had never had a chance to know. His own father-son relationship had been broken. Even though there was 'forgiveness,' it had only recently been really restored. Frank was angry and had spent as little time with his dad as he could; his opinion was: [*Dad loved the Chinese and wanted to 'save' them, never mind spending time with HIM, never tell him he was proud of him, if he had to choose between being his father and a spiritual mentor, he had said he would have to choose the latter, Wow! Heavy... really heavy!*]. Frank's spiritual problems, he would later recognize, stemmed from Frank's unforgiving attitude...but that one day...the 'father-and-his-son' found the beginning of an important, connection. As Michael worked, he suddenly started singing a Chinese song, one that had become a *family favorite*: ...*Da shan ke i no kai, xiao shan, ke i quen i*... ['though the mountains should fall, and the hills be brought low']... (Frank heard him, and started singing in harmony)... *Da ce di ce ai, yung bu li kai ni* [but my love will never depart from you,' (Isaiah 54:10), and then they sang it again together. Frank yelled out, "Hey, Dad, we're pretty good, we'll have to take it on the road!"...no response; he repeated what he'd said, but still nothing, so Frank swung himself down to the basement level...Michael was wiping his eyes, and turned away; he didn't want Frank to see that he was overcome with emotion; then tears came to Frank's eyes...neither man would admit something had *happened* there...*but a precious special connection had just taken place.* The father-son thing...the thing that had eluded them for so long...the ice melted, and they both knew it. Even though many miles would still be traveled before the restoration was complete years later, ***that*** was the moment Frank always said Michael became his *Dad*, and Frank actually cared about being his *son*. When both men 'recovered their composure,' Michael said, "Say, I think we should celebrate finishing the work with an open-house!" He said he wanted to turn the keys over *ceremoniously* to Frank and he wanted the people from the Kirkland Nazarene Church to come...maybe Margo could fix food...a party! *[the 'boxcar-res-mozar' thing!]* So, they planned everything together; people from the church came... Margo baked a cake, and Michael made a big deal of turning the keys over to them. The next day, Frank and Margo took his dad to the airport and he returned to Taiwan. He joined Beth in Xinzhu in their new home in Taiwan. The bookmobile and film ministry became their new mission project. They would labor with China Evangelism Fellowship for sixteen more years. Beth taught at Qinghua University, and later both of them would teach at Sheng De Bible College until she began having dementia; Michael could no longer leave her unattended, while his own health remained robust until years later.

During the year in Oregon, Frank enrolled in each of the three quarters, plus the summer quarter that he was on tour with the UW Chorale to Australia and New Zealand. He had been required to prepare fifty topics, on which he would be prepared to discuss in detail on a qualifying exam. From these, each member of his committee chose one or two topics for Frank to discuss. If he passed this hurdle, he could choose a dissertation topic, write the paper under the supervision of the chair...with input from his committee, and then defend his dissertation, prepare it according to the graduate school specifications, and have it published. Finally, he would receive the Doctor of Musical Arts in Choral Conducting. It was a long year's project; included in the paper would also be the write-up of his three conducting recitals. He easily passed the qualifying exam, because he had prepared diligently and covered all of the material. Next, he set out to select a topic for his dissertation. He had wanted to write on the contribution of Hungarian school of musical thought, but Rod felt this had already been completely covered; much had already been written on Kodaly and Bartok, Rod said. Frank said he wanted to do original research on the next generation of Hungarians. Like what? Rod had asked. Frank had already given it some thought and initial research led him to a man who had become a good, but relatively unknown composer, a teacher of composers, an eclectic, as well as eccentric, man, that had traveled the world, was loved by many, and who was well-known in Europe, Asia, and Africa, but hardly known at all in North America. He had been a student of Kodaly at the Budapest Academy, and stylistically he was in the mode of Bartok. This man's name? Matyas Seiber (or Matthew in English, the last name being pronounced *shy-bear*). Frank was finally able to convince Rod that this was the subject upon which he should write. So, Frank's dissertation was set: *The Music of Matyas Seiber*. It was the project that consumed Frank's attention for a year. They enrolled Shelley in Kindergarten, and Margo found a baby sitter just a few blocks away. She was Sherry Ashton Towers, the granddaughter of Dr. Ashton from SPC. Margo got a job as a para-professional again at Lakeview Elementary. She carpooled with Irma, who had moved to Kirkland a few years before (and the year with Beth and Michael was so enhanced by these sisters again being close). Irma was able to take Margo to work on the way to her own school. Frank needed the one car they had, so he would let Steve sleep awhile before taking him to the babysitter. Shelley played till it was time to catch the bus to Juanita Elementary (sometimes Frank was so intent on typing his dissertation, that, had it not been for the neighbors, and Shelley's independent spirit, he might have failed to get her on the bus on time (Shelley liked to tease that this 'warped' her life, ha!). No question about it, though… it was a very hard year for them. Margo was stressed out all the time worrying about the organ job at Epiphany, for which she felt ill-equipped. Steve had one ear infection after another, so Frank, in his effort to keep the fever down (the doctor had said to keep him in the bathtub in lukewarm water to get the fever down), many nights Frank fell asleep holding Steve while he bathed him with the water. The drainage for the property, of the new addition to the house, had never been done right, and water leaked into the house; sheetrock and studs were spoiled, and there was a constant damp smell in the house. Frank was in the Seattle Chorale, and began partying again with graduate school friends. Margo started to pull away. She tried to talk to Irma, but she couldn't really say too much. Frank had applied for every job posted: vocal instructor, choral director…anything; Frank's mom had gone to Minot Teachers' College, now Minot State College, so when he saw a job posted for teaching there, he applied, and they offered him the job…without even calling him for an interview! He asked them if it was because of his 'great credentials and references;' they laughed and said, "no, not really; we saw that your mother attended Minot State;" then he asked them what he would be doing; they said he would be 'supervising student teachers in *forty-below-zero weather* on icy roads all around northeast North Dakota! Frank remembered living there…he thanked them, but turned it down. They laughed and said Frank was the *fourth person* to do so thus far. [The choir at Epiphany responded well to Frank; the search committee had warned him about one married couple, a tenor and a soprano John and Ellen Boyce…they were known to have run off almost every previous choirmaster-organist…but Frank had them 'eating out of his hand' by Christmas…anything they complained about Frank would ask them to bring it before the choir for 'discussion,' but most of their complaints had to do with other choir members, or things the church had, or had not, done…so by bringing it into the open, which they did not like, they thought that Frank was siding with them, when in fact he was exposing what they wanted kept secret; Frank put them *in charge* of 'correcting' problems, or going to Father Gorsuch if they thought the parish was not handling the choir, the organ, or music purchase, etc., correctly]. Father Jack just

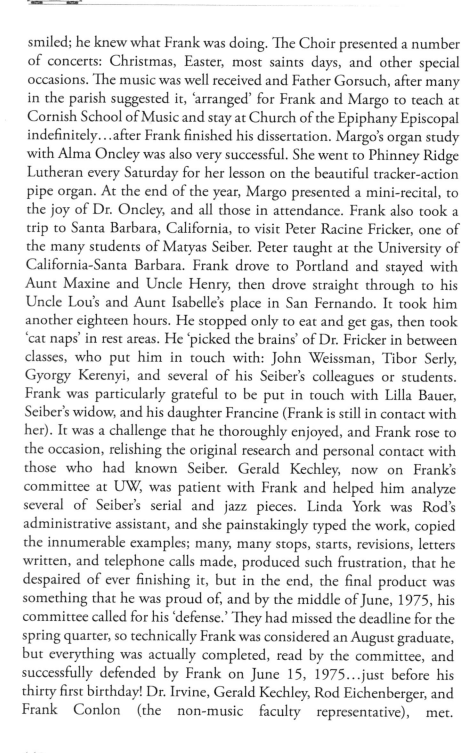

smiled; he knew what Frank was doing. The Choir presented a number of concerts: Christmas, Easter, most saints days, and other special occasions. The music was well received and Father Gorsuch, after many in the parish suggested it, 'arranged' for Frank and Margo to teach at Cornish School of Music and stay at Church of the Epiphany Episcopal indefinitely...after Frank finished his dissertation. Margo's organ study with Alma Oncley was also very successful. She went to Phinney Ridge Lutheran every Saturday for her lesson on the beautiful tracker-action pipe organ. At the end of the year, Margo presented a mini-recital, to the joy of Dr. Oncley, and all those in attendance. Frank also took a trip to Santa Barbara, California, to visit Peter Racine Fricker, one of the many students of Matyas Seiber. Peter taught at the University of California-Santa Barbara. Frank drove to Portland and stayed with Aunt Maxine and Uncle Henry, then drove straight through to his Uncle Lou's and Aunt Isabelle's place in San Fernando. It took him another eighteen hours. He stopped only to eat and get gas, then took 'cat naps' in rest areas. He 'picked the brains' of Dr. Fricker in between classes, who put him in touch with: John Weissman, Tibor Serly, Gyorgy Kerenyi, and several of his Seiber's colleagues or students. Frank was particularly grateful to be put in touch with Lilla Bauer, Seiber's widow, and his daughter Francine (Frank is still in contact with her). It was a challenge that he thoroughly enjoyed, and Frank rose to the occasion, relishing the original research and personal contact with those who had known Seiber. Gerald Kechley, now on Frank's committee at UW, was patient with Frank and helped him analyze several of Seiber's serial and jazz pieces. Linda York was Rod's administrative assistant, and she painstakingly typed the work, copied the innumerable examples; many, many stops, starts, revisions, letters written, and telephone calls made, produced such frustration, that he despaired of ever finishing it, but in the end, the final product was something that he was proud of, and by the middle of June, 1975, his committee called for his 'defense.' They had missed the deadline for the spring quarter, so technically Frank was considered an August graduate, but everything was actually completed, read by the committee, and successfully defended by Frank on June 15, 1975...just before his thirty first birthday! Dr. Irvine, Gerald Kechley, Rod Eichenberger, and Frank Conlon (the non-music faculty representative), met.

[Unbeknownst to Frank…ultimately a successful 'ploy,' Frank Conlon immediately picked an 'argument' with Dr. Irvine on the wording Frank had used in the second chapter, relating to the phrase: *'it is not contended that'* versus *'with no intent to show'* (when discussing Seiber's 'periods of composition'). In the end Dr. Irvine, while pointing out that either usage would be acceptable, agreed that Frank should make that one slight change to *satisfy* everyone; Frank Conlon successfully *deferred* any further discussion, and they all voted to accept the dissertation. "So clever," Frank whispered to Frank Conlon later. They finished the final copy, turned it over to the Graduate School who had it sent to be microfilm published at the University of Michigan. Rod took Frank out for lunch, and a drink, to celebrate. Margo took Frank out that night for a *real* celebration. They got a babysitter and went out—just the two of them; they went to Black Angus in Bellevue and had a steak dinner…went dancing, then long year was over, …the goal had become a reality:

The Doctor of Musical Arts in Choral Conducting had been achieved!

Family in Ohio

CEF Retreat Son Village, Oregon

Family arrives in Texas

St. Helen Catholic

Last CEF Retreat with all Fitz family children

St. Andrew's Faith Alive

Annual CEF (China Evangelism Fellowship) meetings,
ala family retreats, were the highlight of many summers
in the Pacific Northwest

Chapter Twenty-One

Top of the Mountain.....Really?

President of the Houston Life Underwriters

OD TOLD FRANK ABOUT THE CHORAL JOB BRUCE BROWNE WAS LEAVING in order to come to Seattle, to write his dissertation, and finish up his doctorate. It was Mount Union College, in Alliance, Ohio, and Bruce had sent a letter of reference after Frank applied for the position. Rod also sent a letter of recommendation. They called two finalists for the job, and Frank flew back to Ohio for the interview. After the two interviews, they called to offer the position to Frank. They started packing up again and rented a truck for the pieces of furniture, books, and clothing they had. Margo and Frank gave notice at Epiphany, much to the consternation of Jack Gorsuch and the church. Frank had made arrangements with his brother Dave, and Marlene, to live in the house in Kirkland. Irma and Tom came over to help pack up. After they packed the truck, Irma invited them over to stay the night and have one of her special curry dinners. In the morning, Margo put Steve, now one year old, in the child seat, and Shelley up into the truck with her daddy, and they were off. They stayed in either Motel 6, or Best Western motels, and ate at McDonald's to save money. Mount Union informed them the position they were offering was 'instructor,' but when he objected, they asked him to have a letter from the UW graduate school stating he had successfully completed the DMA, even though it wasn't official until the end of August. He was successful in this and they changed the offer to 'assistant professor.' Even so, the salary ended up being less than Frank had received at Central Oregon College as instructor...the difference being, they said, was: one was a private Methodist College, but COCC was a state community college. They made it to Alliance in three days. The night before they arrived, a thunderstorm was so severe, they had to pull over and wait until it stopped; it was so late, and with no available motels in the little towns in Iowa where they were holed up, they broke out some blankets and slept in the back of the truck that night. They pulled into Alliance the next afternoon. They had been instructed to contact a 'Bert Couchie,' the College business manager, when they arrived. Frank called him, and he let them into the college rental house where they lived for the next two years. It was a beautiful two-story white house with a porch and big front and back yard. Margo loved it because it reminded her of the houses in Coldwater, Michigan, where she had grown up. Though it looked nice, it was not well insulated, and they couldn't keep it warm in the winter, or cool in the summer. There were three bedrooms upstairs; Shelley slept in one, Steve slept in the bedroom next to it, and Margo and Frank slept in the master bedroom next to those two. They spent the next week moving in and furnishing it. They went to downtown Alliance and picked up some furniture at a second-hand store; they already had a table and three chairs, plus a high chair for Steve, and some dishes and pans. They bought an orange-brown sofa, (which Shelley and Margo made fun of for years, much to the consternation of Frank, who said it was the only one they could afford at the time). They also found some material at a cloth store and Margo began making curtains. Frank went to faculty meetings…and held auditions for the college choir, the chamber choir, and show choir. He met Cecil Stewart, the choir director prior to Bruce Browne, and he was very helpful in giving him the 'lay of the land.' A student committee met Frank and gave him some background on the choir. Classes started and Frank taught a full load: voice, choir, chamber choir, show choir, and classes in music literature, and music theory. Frank quickly became friends with one of the other voice teachers: Rachel Kimball. Cecil Stewart and she were good friends and both were 'good Methodists;' she had a strong church background; she was interested in Frank and Margo's own spiritual journey, and said she had a similar history. She said First Presbyterian in Alliance was looking for a choir director, so Frank applied for that position, too, and was hired. Pastor Eby seemed helpful and introduced Frank and Margo to members of the church, while Mrs. Eby made Margo and Shelley feel comfortable with women's and children's ministries. The first year flew by like a whirlwind. Frank planned a choir tour to Florida. They stayed in homes and sang mostly in Methodist churches. They went to Disney World and had a great time there in between concerts. [just before the tour, Margo told Frank she was pregnant…*after starting ballet again…* so she would stay home with the children she said; that's when the story…the one of Margo taking ballet in Bend (see chapter twenty), now again in Alliance… this story was 'hatched.' Having miscarried twice in graduate school, and getting pregnant (after taking ballet in Bend), then moving to Ohio and taking ballet *again*, was what made the story so funny]. So, Frank had to go on tour without her. The tour was great fun, and they were well received in all of the places where they sang: Tennessee, North and South Carolina, Georgia, and Florida; and their home concert was well received too.

Several of Frank's voice students did well in competition, and Frank became a member of National Association of Teachers of Singing, and also Phi Mu Alpha, the Men's music fraternity. In the spring, the drama department recruited Frank, and members of the choir, to assist with the theatre production 'Marat-Sade,' which included 'singers in a mental institution.' All were insane–even the conductor. Many of the lyrics were inappropriate, especially for a Methodist college, and Frank was criticized by some, for his participation; for this effort he became an honorary member of Alpha Psi Omega, the drama fraternity. And some students seemed to enjoy 'corrupting' their missionary-turned-worldly choir conductor. Trying to be *one* of them, Frank started partying with them, and they shared with him many of their escapades, and those of their previous choral director. Cecil Stewart, a conductor-turned-piano-tuner, periodically spent the morning tuning Frank and Margo's piano. He shared his disappointment in the turn to 'worldliness' of the choir and the college, since retiring. He told them Mount Union had once enjoyed a very spiritual atmosphere, but then the number of non-Christian professors increased, students were on drugs, some professors were sleeping with students...he told them things had really gotten out of hand with Frank's predecessor. Frank didn't say anything; he didn't want to criticize... he didn't tell Cecil that he himself was 'turning cold' in his own faith journey, pretending to be above-board, but wanting to join the wild partying crowd; the kind that he had witnessed so often at ACDA and other music conferences. After all, wasn't that just the 'price one had to pay'...in order to get the good choral jobs? And he was going to be one of America's finest, so he had to act like all his graduate school friends, right? Cecil and Rachel began to worry about Frank. He was trying to be acceptable to the students—by acting like many of the students...and faculty. Some of the voice students criticized Frank to Rachel, and she and Cecil tried to talk to him about restoring a high moral standard, instead of heading in the direction of his predecessor ...but he didn't listen. As he soon found out, contacts had *not* been maintained with area high school choral programs, and recruiting had dried up. Cecil tried to help Frank reestablish contacts by offering Frank as a clinician to area choirs, but many of the good students were already going away to Ohio State and other fine schools. Frank booked several concerts in area schools, but choral directors were more interested in bringing in established clinicians and choirs. Frank had always been active in American Choral Directors, so he attended the North Central ACDA in Columbus. He didn't know anyone, and much of it was in-grown. No one bothered to include him as a new member of the Region, and Frank went home early, feeling alone, missing graduate school, and his friends.

With Margo not working, and inadequate college and church salaries, they struggled to make the rent every month, and there was never enough money to buy Shelley and Steve clothes...say nothing of toys. Many students spoke against Mr. Couchie, but he was kind, and understanding of Frank's financial position, and waited patiently for the rent...sometimes two or three months. Margi came up from Atlanta and stayed a few days. She took pictures at Shelley's special school program, complete with costumes (Shelley went dressed as a 'Chinese maiden'). There were many good times at the church, and with friends, but the financial burden, and lack of spiritual uplift, kept them feeling down much of the time. Then things at the church began to go sour too. Frank found out Pastor Eby had openly criticized Frank and Margo to Rachel for not being 'Presbyterian' enough. People there were unfriendly and seemed to have an air of 'midwestern judgmentalism,' unlike the Episcopal churches they had served in Bend and Seattle, so Frank decided he should start looking for another church job. With the shortness of funds, they also decided to not travel to the Northwest that summer (but they *did* go on a camping trip at Berlin Lake, which was a lot of fun). Frank found a music job opening at St. Mark's Episcopal Church in Canton, about a half hour drive from Alliance; he was offered the position of choirmaster (only if Margo would accept the organist position). They began making plans for the birth of the baby in August. Margo had asked friends where she should plan on having the baby in Alliance; their friends, Don and Cheryl Shonting, had put it this way: "well...if I knew I had twenty minutes to live, I would take a chance and drive into Canton...instead of going to Alliance General!" Wow! I guess that answered *that* question, especially when Margo found out they still used *ether* in childbirth. Through the Shonting's, and new friends at St. Mark's, they were able to find a team of doctors in Canton, and made plans to have the birth at Mercy Medical Center. The first visits with Dr. Howard were good (but Margo did *not* like the other two...especially Dr. Richards; she was *really* upset when she found out the 'doctor-on-call...when Dr. Howard was on vacation,' with a due date in August, was...Dr. Richards! 'Oh, no,' she said, "I can't do this." (she was determined to have this baby completely natural and she and Frank had been taking Lamaze classes), but Frank convinced her everything would be alright, they would just do what they had learned, and the doctor would go along with it...right? Wrong! The baby was already past due by Monday, August 2, when Margo went for her final check-up. Dr. Richards said everything 'looked fine'...but 'no,' Frank could *not* be allowed in the room at Mercy Medical for the birth... and she would have to have a '*saddleblock.*' When she protested about both, he swore at her, *"listen, lady, I'm the doctor, and you're going to 'damn well' have this baby the way I say, do you understand?"* She was shocked, and dismayed at his attitude, and ran crying from his office to the waiting room; when she explained to Frank what had happened, he said, "that's it, let's get out of here!" Frank told the administrator they would not be back, and to *cancel their account.* Margo was alarmed and didn't think they should do that...where would they have the baby, and who would deliver it? Frank said they 'would go to Alliance General before he would allow *this doctor* to talk to his wife that way.' They sat in the car. Margo cried, and Frank prayed. He decided God was allowing him to wander in order to find his own way (he remembered another time when they were 'in a crack' waiting for their car in North Carolina; whom had God brought to bail them out? *Les Peterson*! (and who was the new wrestling coach at Lewisville High School...by Canton?) Pete and Les Peterson! Frank called Les...let's see? Michael would be about the same age as Shelley, and Brian would be a couple years older than Steve...did they know any pediatricians or obstetricians in the Canton and Lewisville area? Matter of fact, Les said...her own doctor: Dr. Joseph Dakoske! She gave them his number and called him herself. Les introduced them to a new 'lamaze class' in Canton. Margo saw Dr. Dakoske that same day, before returning to Alliance...he assured them that Frank would *definitely* be in the labor and delivery rooms, and then they visited Aultmann Hospital, and attended their first 'new lamaze class' that evening. Wait! How can this be happening again? God was still taking care of them? They both burst into tears. By Saturday, Margo was not feeling well, and they made arrangements with the Mount Union president's daughter, Nicki, to come watch the kids while they were at the hospital. With the birth of both Shelley and Steve, Margo had never 'had her water break,' but by that afternoon it broke, and labor started... then it stopped; Frank called Dr. Dakoske; his office said she *had* to come in to the hospital, even without labor, because infection could set in within twenty-four hours. Frank and Margo assured Shelley everything would be fine, and gave instructions to Nicki for Steve, and then left for the hospital. Labor started up again…then stopped. Dr. Dakoske stayed at the hospital, but asked that he be called when labor progressed;he said they would probably induce, and he went to bed. Frank thought he would be able to finally be able to sleep a night at the hospital. [When Shelley was born in Taiwan, they were up all night because he took her to Country Hospital by 5:00 a.m. and she was born about 5:00 p.m. With Steve, they went to the hospital about midnight, and he was born by 5:00 a.m. Frank, both times, had not been able to sleep those nights of birth. But now, he would *finally* be able to sleep…guess again…Margo slept…Dr. Dakoske slept… but Frank did not!] He tried to sleep on one of the hospital couches but couldn't. About 5:00 a.m., he woke Margo to ask if everything was alright…if anything was happening…nothing; by 6:30 a.m., Frank asked the nurse when Dr. Dakoske wanted to induce. 'Oh, no!' The nurse had forgotten to *wake* him! She called…Dr. Dakoske was very upset that she had not called him earlier, and he ordered them to induce…immediately; they did so at 7:00 a.m. and labor started happening in earnest…huge back labor…that Margo had previously *never* had. The only relief she could get was: Frank pressing extremely hard on her lower back. By 8:30, she was crowning, and Dr. Dakoske teasingly said, "Hey, man, you better 'robe up.' Frank, shooting right back at him, said, 'Why? Am I 'singing a solo?' What about you, doc?" Dr. Dakoske said, 'well, if I don't make it back in time, you surely will do a solo!' They both laughed. Frank 'robed up,' and wheeled Margo into delivery; the mirror was set up, but the nurses were getting nervous, because Dr. Dakoske was still not there and Margo was already 'crowning.' Frank said, 'and I thought he was kidding!' but just then Dr. Dakoske casually walked in, as though he wanted Frank to actually 'sweat it out.' The breathing went very well, no drugs *whatsoever* (as Margo had insisted)…even though the nurses tried to offer them. Frank and Margo could see everything in the mirror, even though she didn't remember the actual moment. Dr. Dakoske simply said, "it's a boy, so what's his name?" Frank was wiping his eyes, but blurted out, 'Robert Channing,' Dr. Dakoske, who was helping Margo because she had torn slightly (because of no episiotomy either)…just grunted, and Margo was beaming from ear to ear, and crying. As he was stitching up, Dr. Dakoske looked up at Frank, and said, "Well, are you just going to stand there, or are you going to pick him up?" Thinking they would lay Robbie on her chest first, Frank said, "can I? Do I get to hold him?" Dr. Dakoske said, "she's kind of 'tied up' right now," and then he laughed at his own joke; he left, and Frank went into the recovery room with Margo (but they kicked him out when he took on the 'three hundred pound Godzilla nurse' about how hard she was working Margo's abdomen, even she cried out in pain). Several visited during the next few days, including Les and Pete, the Shonting's, and others from St. Mark's, and Mount Union.

Even before the Fall Semester started, Frank had already begun planning the next choir tour. Since they had gone south the previous year, he decided they would 'go north,' so he planned a tour to Canada…and was able to arrange several concerts or visits in upstate New York, Toronto, and Montreal; coming back, they would visit and have concerts in Ottowa, Toledo, and Sandusky. Classes began, but since a large class of seniors had graduated, existing underclassmen, who had been essentially depending on the leadership of the graduating seniors, faltered and, with the lack of leadership, and marginal recruit talent, the choral program was deeply affected. Frank talked again to Cecil Stewart; he told Frank the quality had gone down due to a lack of recruiting in the past four years, during the last year he was director, and in the next three years. Cecil had recruited this year's graduating seniors as freshman, but little else had bolstered the program. Frank was determined to make the best of it though, and he launched into a challenging program. The graduating seniors had supported Frank strongly, but many of the choir members that remained were immature, and not willing to 'step up to the plate.' A lackadaisical outlook slowly crept in. They presented quality programs for the fall and Christmas, but by tour time, a critical and negative attitude was setting in. A couple of choir members had been found passed out on drugs. False reports, that Frank had made inappropriate remarks about Rachel, circulated.

[Times were getting hard…but one beautiful fall morning Frank was mowing the lawn after breakfast. The leaves were turning yellow and orange; it was so beautiful, Frank thought, 'How even *more beautiful* it would be now in New England, he suddenly thought: "Hey, let's go to New England; we'll make a quick trip; stay at Juli and Larry's house in Baltimore, and then head back." He ran in the house, and told everyone to grab some clothes and overnight stuff because…we're taking a trip to New England." Margo laughed; she thought he was kidding; but she soon found out he wasn't, they grabbed some things, and before you knew it, they were on their way; they drove across Ohio and Pennsylvania, then turned north in New York. They made Albany by supper, and stopped for the night in Bennington, Vermont. They found a beautiful 'bed & breakfast,' and their hostess, Mrs. Braden, took particular care for Margo and the children; there was a milk-white pitcher and basin, and everything was quaint and comfortable. After the delicious breakfast, which her husband Otto fixed for them, they headed out toward Mt. Snow, then across Vermont and New Hampshire, to Kittery, on the southern coast of Maine…Shelley and Steve rolled up their pant legs and waded in the Atlantic. They found a little cafe where they ate fish and chips for lunch. As it started getting late in the afternoon, they headed south through Boston, then Providence, taking pictures as they went, and stopping for supper near the big Navy port in Groton. [Frank tried to look up Chaplain Steve Jones, with whom they had served in Taiwan; (he had been told Steve might be stationed there …but this was unsuccessful); they drove on through New York City, and realizing that they would never make it to Juli's place that night, finally stopped at a small hotel in Elizabeth, New Jersey. Margo knew better than to ask if Frank had lost his mind–she already *KNEW* he had. She locked the car, and put a blanket over the children, while Frank went in and paid cash for the hotel room, slipping the money under the glass-proof window with bars on it! (you can't reason with the insane, she thought). They got up early, found another McDonald's off the freeway, and then headed to Baltimore. Juli and Larry were overjoyed to see them…they couldn't believe the sudden urge of Frank to make this bizarre trip, but were *so* happy to see them; they fixed some Hungarian cabbage rolls, exchanged family pictures and stories since they had last seen each other, and then went to bed, got up early and had breakfast before they hit the road…they arrived back in Alliance that evening. Margo refused to talk about the trip, but years later Frank caught her bragging on him for the 'twelve-states-in-thirty-six-hours' adventure! She smiled sheepishly and shrugged her shoulders–she knew now they were *BOTH* crazy; he laughed and gave her a hug; it became one of their 'stories.'] So...where was I?

Margo was determined to go on tour with Frank this year since she had not been able to go the previous year. She arranged for her parents to come down from Washington state to stay with the children, while she went on tour with the choir. They had a great tour to Canada and Margo and Frank celebrated their ninth anniversary a little early in Montreal, at the top floor lounge and dance floor of the Hilton. The band found out that Frank and his 'bride' were celebrating a wedding anniversary; they played 'Send In The Clowns,' and 'My Funny Valentine.' One 'very inebriated' older gentleman tried to dance with Margo, but she was not too keen on the idea, and told him she was out of breath, and needed to 'sit the next one out.' They drove on to Toronto for a concert the next night and visited the capitol in Ottawa the next day. It started snowing fairly heavily, so they had to cut the tour short; they ate dinner, stayed the night in a hotel, and the next day proceeded on to Toledo; they sang a concert at First Methodist there, stayed in private homes, and then proceeded on to Sandusky; and they finished the tour with a concert in the home church of one of the choir members, at Sandusky Methodist Church. They arrived back in Alliance the next day; the children were so excited when they arrived home. Wilma and Francis left the next day for Wenatchee, calling a couple days later to say they had returned safely.

The winter of 1976 was the worst Ohio had experienced in many years. There was a energy crisis of major proportions. Governor Rhodes declared an emergency, and ordered all thermostats for everyone, except those with infant children, or very elderly persons, to be set no higher than sixty-five. Frank and Margo closed off the living and dining rooms; they dressed by the oven each morning, and used only cold water...for bathing, cooking, and all other uses, except as absolutely necessary. The children wanted to play outside, but Frank and Margo, made sure they were bundled up... coats, caps, gloves (on strings fed through the sleeves), boots, socks, and long underwear. It was such a funny sight, Frank had to take pictures of these 'little snowmen' rocking side to side. Robbie was a baby, so he stayed inside; school was cancelled so many times, they couldn't even make up all the missed days. It didn't get above freezing for forty days! It was a winter no one every forgot. In the spring, after the choir tour, the chair of the music department, Lewis Phelps, came up to Frank in the hall, and asked him if 'he had a minute;' they went into his office, and he told him…they could not offer him tenure yet, which meant Frank had to go on a one-year contract. It was a blow; and Frank talked to his friend, Don Shonting, and also the organ professor, Otis Morgan, who told Frank there were fierce 'academic politics' going on. Don had, in the past, been put on a one-year contract, and so had Otis. They fought it, and proved that they deserved the tenure more than the others competing with them for it. They had been there for several more years than Frank, however, and didn't know if he should fight it or not. Frank decided to talk to the college president. Dr. Getz was gracious, and said he could speak with the chair of the tenure committee, but in cases like Frank's, with so few years of experience, and this being Frank's first four-year college position, he wouldn't guarantee it could help. Did Frank want him to do that? Frank decided to call his mentor, Rod Eichenberger first. Rod was very supportive but thought it might be wise, under the circumstances, to ask around about other positions. Rod told him Richard Clark was planning to leave his position in Texas after one year at the University of Texas–Permian. Larry Marsh had been there for three years before Dick. Rod said he would talk to both of them. Larry called Frank right away to tell him he had talked to Dr. David Sloan in Texas, and was thrilled at the possibility of filling the position of Director of Choral Activities–and conductor of the Midland-Odessa Symphony Chorale so quickly. He wanted Frank to come for an interview at his earliest convenience. Frank called Dick Clark too, and asked about the job. Dick said Connie had already left to go back to La Grande, Oregon, where her folks lived, and he would join his family later. They had been there one year but decided he really wanted to go back to Eugene and work with Royce Saltzman again. He said his job had been a good one: Director of Choral Activities at University of Texas-Permian in Odessa, the Symphony Chorale, *and* First Presbyterian in Odessa. He said that, with *his* recommendation, plus Rod's, *and* Larry's, he could almost 'guarantee' Frank would get the job. He had already talked to Dave Sloan about flying him down as soon as possible; he laughed, 'if

Frank and Margo wanted, they could even buy their house…and it was close to the University.' It appeared that things were going to work out well for them again. He booked his flight to Midland-Odessa, and told Lewis Phelps he needed a couple days off to fly to Texas for a job interview; Lew looked shocked that Frank would not accept the contract…and take a year to look for another job. Frank told him there were others like Rod Eichenberger, Larry Marsh, and Dick Clark, that seemed to have a higher evaluation of him than 'his tenure committee.' Margo stayed with the children, and Frank flew down for the interview; and it went very well. Frank thought he was 'landing on the face of the moon,' it seemed so barren; and when he got off the plane, David Sloan was the man leaning against a post, dressed in his 'grubbies,' chewing on a toothpick! At first, Frank thought he was probably their driver. Dick said, "Frank, I'd like you to meet Dr. Sloan, head of the music department. They told Frank to take off his coat and tie, and as Frank did, he said, "what is that awful smell?" Dave rolled thumb and finger together, and said, "money!" They introduced him to Dr. Hostadt, and Linda, the Symphony and Chorale administrator. He met some of the faculty and the president of UTPB, and then several of them took Frank to the Colorado Steakhouse for dinner. Frank ended up making a spectacle of himself trying to 'show off' by quickly downing two or three whole 'peppers' with his salad, thinking, of course that they were pepperoncini's like he'd had in Ohio (and like other Sichuan red peppers in Taiwan!). They watched with amusement as Frank turned beet red and excused himself to the restroom… they were the first *raw* jalapeno's Frank had ever eaten; they burned his mouth beyond description. They laughed, and Dave said, "well, Frank, you just passed the test…you're hired!" Everyone clapped, and Dave said, "that's how we do things here in west *Texas*." Frank also interviewed for the First Presbyterian job of Minister of Music, and they also hired him. Dick teased, "well Frank, I gave you my college job, my symphony job, my church job, and my house…but I'm not giving you Connie (his wife), Ha!" Frank flew back to Alliance feeling very satisfied, and grateful to God… again, for how well things always seem to turn out. Frank finished up classes, announced his departure and new position in Texas, conducted the last choir concert and graduation, and then started packing up. They had many visitors and friends stop by to congratulate them (Cecil, and Rachel, came by…they just smiled and hugged them…*they* knew). Frank rented a Ryder truck, and they left Alliance for Odessa the second week in June. Shelley rode with her dad and Steve; Robbie (who now was ten months old), rode with Margo in the Manta. Frank started singing to Shelley, "well we're movin' on up, to the *WEST* side…," a take-off on the popular spin-off "The Jeffersons." Shelley kept herself busy with her favorite thing at the time…her drawings. They tented near Mammoth Caves south of Cincinnati in Kentucky, to save money; they ate at McDonald's and stayed at Motel 6 the rest of the way. They pulled into Odessa just at sunset three days later, and Dick met them at the house. He told them they could stay there…he was staying with a friend. As they unloaded the truck, Margo asked Dick, "are those crickets I hear?" There was a very loud whirring sound, almost like electric wires humming. Dick laughed, "Oh no, those are cicada's!" He grabbed one out of the air, and asked Margo for a string or a thread; he put one of the cicada's on a thread, and it flew all around making the most haunting sound. The children wanted to hold the string; they loved seeing them fly around as Frank and Dick captured one for each of them. It was a strange 'ritual' for their welcome to West Texas. They went to Dairy Queen for ice cream…Dick said every town in Texas had one, and it became the 'watering hole' for the Varro family.

The next day, Dick introduced Frank and Margo to Rev. Joe Brown, pastor of First Presbyterian, and Gene Greenwood, a prominent geologist and active member of the Symphony Chorale and First Presbyterian. Frank had interviewed with a committee from the church during his initial visit, but they had largely hired him on the strength of Larry's, Rod's, and Dick's recommendation. Now they wanted to assist them in getting a mortgage on the house they would buy from Dick and Connie. With no established credit, it took Gene's backing and Rev. Brown's influence to get Permian State Bank to agree to this. Dr. Hohstadt, and the Symphony Administrator, Linda Stanton, as well as the Symphony president, John Denton, who gave verification of Frank's employment. University of Texas-Permian Human Resources Director, Susan Hillis, was also able to give verification of the University's employment of Frank; when it was all said and done, the loan committee gave a quick approval, and Dick called Connie in La Grande to tell her they had sold the house…now the Varro's wouldn't have to "sleep on the street!" They all laughed.

Dave took Frank and Margo everywhere. He introduced them to the rest of the UTPB faculty and staff. He took them to meet more of the Symphony and Chorale personnel. Joe Brown was happy to introduce them to the church choir and staff. Frank held his first rehearsal that week at First Presbyterian, That afternoon the previous organist, Lillian Craft, had 'auditioned' Margo, and was pleased to recommend that she be hired as organist, telling her she would be happy 'to sub for her.' [Margo thought she 'had died and gone to heaven.' She loved West Texas! Being from the Midwest, she was embarrassed that Ohio…next to Michigan, her home state…had been such an 'unfriendly experience.' They moved in to their new home, and the church gave them an old fashioned 'pounding'… everyone in the church brought them a 'pound' of something! They filled their cupboards and refrigerator. Connie and Dick had left a good refrigerator, a washer and dryer; lots of meat and vegetables as well. Some people from the church with children had also given toys, blankets, other household items…even furniture, it was a wonderful welcome to West Texas]. The youth choir began work on a musical, 'Come Together In Jesus' Name,' and Frank and Margo helped them rehearse it, complete with outfits, dance movements, lights, and narration. They had told First Presbyterian, when they were hired, that they had committed to being gone to the Pacific Northwest for a China Evangelism Fellowship annual meeting and family get-together, the last week of July and first two weeks of August; 'no problem,' they said. Frank taught a class at UTPB the first summer semester, but was free the last part of the summer. They spent *every* day at the faculty pool in the hot, dry, sun, and the whole family had the best suntans they'd ever had. Frank auditioned over a hundred singers, ending up with eighty-five in the Symphony Chorale; the first rehearsal was great, and everyone was so excited about the coming year; some came from as far away as Monahans, Andrews, Pecos, even Fort Stockton (over a hundred miles round-trip), and one alto said she thought this was the "best chorale since Lara Hoggard," [the well-known conductor who had been there previously for a number of years, and the first to bring Midland's and

Odessa's symphonies and chorales together]. Dr. Hohstadt stopped in and said he 'liked what he heard.' The First Presbyterian youth choir production, 'Come Together,' *came together* without a hitch, and the church was filled. Frank and Margo packed up the car before the concert, so as soon as it was over, they left in the little Manta (incidentally, *without* air conditioning), about 9:30 in the evening; they drove through the night, since it was 'cooler,' to Phoenix, on their way to the Northwest. Frank drove first, as far as Tucson, but as the sun was coming up, so they stopped for gas and he let Margo drive the rest of the way while he slept for a while. They found a McDonald's and had breakfast, and Margo called her Uncle Al and Aunt Alice…for directions to their house. Margo and the kids visited while Frank slept. [The idea was they would travel at night across the desert, then stay with Uncle Lou and Aunt Isabel in San Fernando, go to Disneyland, then again stay the night with Lou and Isabel, and drive on to Redding, California, where they would stay with Guil and Doris]. After supper at Al and Alice's, they said goodbye, and headed out; they were so hot by the time they got to Blythe, California, Margo became alarmed at the beads of sweat and their little red faces, and she appealed to Frank to stop. They stopped at a Denny's to cool off, but they hadn't gotten more than a mile or two when Frank decided they needed to change the plans. They called Lou and Isabel that they were going to stay in Blythe, and go to straight to Disneyland…then stay the next night with them as planned. Isabel said they 'should absolutely stay in an air-conditioned room and come see them *after* Disneyland.' They found a Motel 6 with air conditioning and slept more soundly than they had in forty-eight hours. After breakfast at McDonald's, they drove straight to Disneyland, they got the 'cheap tickets' and everyone had a great time. Steve and Robbie were too small for most of the rides, so Frank and Margo took turns taking Shelley on several rides while the other watched the boys [Shelley sang 'It's A Small World After All,' all the way to San Fernando!]. Lou and Isabel were thrilled to see them again… it had been a while since the last CEF retreat; they hadn't met Robbie yet, and Jonathan and Stephanie had been very small; they had a great visit, and after breakfast the next morning, they hit the road again, heading toward Redding. It was unusually hot, even in northern California, and when they pulled into Guil and Doris's place, everyone was beet-red. Guil took one look at them and said, "Alright everyone, into the pool…immediately!" Shelley and Steve laughed, and got into swimming suits, and jumped in the pool. Margo took Robbie to the shallow end of the pool and let him paddle;' [He had already learned to do this on his own at the faculty pool in Odessa, so he slipped into the pool with his underpants-swimsuit on. Frank jumped in too, and out of the corner of his eye, he saw Robbie's suit come off… followed by a small, round *discharge* that no one knew he had been carrying with him since getting out of the car; when he lost the pants, everything else came out too! In one quick movement, Frank grabbed the underpants, enclosed the discharge, and got out of the pool, while Margo grabbed Robbie. Frank disposed of it in the a-joining bathroom and shower by the pool, and rinsed out the underpants. Guil saw the whole thing and started to laugh; "good thing I have a good pool cleaner isn't it?"]. Robbie paddled all around the shallow end under Margo's supervision, while Shelley and Steve, none the wiser, played and swam, and then all got out when Doris called them to supper. They had a great visit with them, and seeing the kids too, and catching up with the cousins was important, especially to Shelley. At breakfast the next morning. Guil read from Lamentations 3, before eating. *"The steadfast love of the Lord never ceases, his mercies never come to an end, they are new every morning, great is thy faithfulness,"* and then he offered prayer for traveling mercies, they ate the delicious breakfast Doris had fixed, and then they were on their way again. They ate a quick supper just south of Portland, and made it to Wenatchee late that night; they were going to just slip in unnoticed, but Wilma got up to welcome them. The children were asleep, so Frank tucked them in, and Wilma offered them apple juice and a cookie, since it had been six hours since they had eaten supper. They went straight to bed. In the morning, they had breakfast; Margo greeted her dad, who had been asleep when they arrived. Shelley and Steve ran to him and hugged him. Robbie didn't remember him, but Shelley explained this was 'grandpa,' and since his siblings were fine with him, Robbie was too. He was already beginning to walk a little… pulling himself up to chairs and anything else he could hold on to. He let Grandpa pick him up and hold him. It was almost Robbie's first birthday, so after spending some time swimming at the pool, and shopping with her mom, they celebrated Robbie's birthday…a month early. They went to the Methodist Church with them Sunday, and then left for the CEF retreat at 'Son Village' on Mt. Hood. It was a wonderful retreat…singing, worship (everyone shared, and Guil gave some great Bible teachings). Maxine gave a report from Michael and Beth, now their third year with Elizabeth Evans, and China Evangelism. The 'new board' had taken over from the 'old board,' (they liked saying the 'Evans' board welcomed the 'Varro board,' in their place), in order to serve the Varro's, as they assumed the work from Elizabeth Evans, now retired. They had purchased a van that served as a 'bookmobile,' which went from church to church showing the 'Jesus' film which had been translated into Chinese. After retreat, and a short visit to Seattle, they headed back to Texas; after driving three hard days…this time avoiding the desert and driving through Denver, they headed south…to Odessa; here Frank started his first year at UTPB. Frank and Margo enrolled Shelley in third grade at Gonzales Elementary, and they found a daycare called Desert Garden for the boys. Shelley made good friendships with a couple of girls in their neighborhood, Bonnie and Jaye, and the three of them became inseparable. Margo, who had begun a second BA in Education at Mount Union, toward her teacher certification, began courses at UTPB toward it (everything was so much more casual). Some of Frank's students told him about tryouts, at the Globe Theatre, for Shakespeare's 'Romeo and Juliet.' [Marjorie Morris, who had taught English at Odessa High School and Odessa College from the late 1940's to the 1960's, had it built to the exact specifications as the original Globe Theatre in England…and along with Permian Playhouse, and Theatre Midland, a great deal of theater was performed in the Permian Basin; Frank said that while living in Odessa they did 'every show that came down the pike.' They went from rehearsals to performances, to cast parties, back to rehearsals (Shelley said she "had a hard time recovering from it"); after tryouts, Sherry Elliott, one of Frank's voice students, was cast as 'Juliet,' and Frank was cast as 'Paris.' Several other students, faculty, and members of the theater community, were cast and rehearsals began; it was a big hit, and Frank, who had not done much theater other than musicals, did well in his first attempt at Shakespeare. In their two years there…Frank and Margo, even Shelley, as Marta in 'Sound of Music,' at the Globe, did a lot of music and theater]. Frank formed a 'chamber chorus' that often sang with a 'recorder ensemble' in several Renaissance-era concerts, and several area churches, concert halls, and theaters hosted them. Dave Sloan introduced Frank and Margo to several symphony players, especially Sue Smith, Charles Nail and other 'principals' of the orchestra. It was Thanksgiving time, and Dr. Hohstadt, and his wife Lillian, invited Frank and Margo for Thanksgiving dinner at their house. Margo, feeling like it was not really a family affair, got a babysitter (they had already celebrated a day early with the family), and the two of them joined Tom and Lillian. It was a lovely dinner, and afterwards they were sharing their life stories. Within an hour after dinner, Frank was experiencing such severe lower abdominal pain, he had to excuse himself; nothing helped and the pain got progressively worse. Tom decided to call an ambulance and they took Frank to the emergency room; as he was lying face up in the examination room, Frank saw the kind face of a Chinese doctor; without thinking or any introductions, Frank began to speak to him in Mandarin! The doctor was completely taken aback... here in the desert in West Texas, a white, thirty-something musician, friend of the symphony conductor, was speaking to him in Mandarin! So, he engaged in the conversation. Everyone thought it must be a ruptured appendix, but Dr. Li said no, the white blood count, which had been very high, was now returning to normal. [Three other times in the next forty years Frank experienced the same excruciating pain, elevated white blood count, and then return to normal after four or five hours; they never took out the appendix, and said it didn't appear to be stress-related or anything to be unduly concerned about...only if the white count did not return to normal swiftly. Wow!] The story quickly spread through the music community; some members of the symphony teased that it 'must have been Lillian's cooking!' *THAT* was certainly untrue, since she was such a good cook and gracious hostess.

With only a few music students in those early days at the new 'mesa campus' of UTPB, Frank also formed a vocal jazz ensemble...in which he sang. Jeryl, bass, a student teacher of his (and frequent director of shows at Permian and Globe theaters); Cricket, alto, also a voice student; Sherry and Marsha, sopranos, both voice students; and Frank, who sang tenor with them... and all of them sang in the Chorale. They were known throughout the area for their exciting repertoire, especially for their rendition of 'Dixie,' and toured throughout West Texas. Frank's First Presbyterian choir sang special Christmas and Easter Cantata's. Margo was the church organist, and while they were there, they were also fortunate to raise the money to install a 'Casavant Freres' pipe organ. They also introduced 'Amahl And The Night Visitors, in which Frank sang the role of Kaspar; they performed this at Theatre Midland and Permian Playhouse; they also introduced the first Madrigal Dinners the Permian Basin had ever experienced. They were invited to sing on a local television show, promoting the Madrigal Dinners in Odessa and Midland. Frank and Margo were dressed in full costume, ready to drive to the TV studio, when they discovered that Steve was missing again. [Steve was 'always missing,' even as a two-year-old baby; in Alliance one day, the 'little explorer,' as he was called, had made it out to the street; in a flash, before anyone knew he was gone; some kind truck driver stopped and showed up with him at the door, thank the Lord]. Without thinking about how he was dressed, Frank ran from door to door looking for him. One man, obviously having drunk quite a bit (even before lunch), opened the door, and when Frank desperately inquired of his missing son, said, "no wonder he is missing, with a father like you… dressed up like a woman!" Frank slammed the door and ran on; just then he spotted Steve a block away, ran and grabbed him, and with tears of joy, hauled him home; the baby sitter was told to lock all doors and open them for no one. They drove furiously to the TV studio. A block away, Frank heard police sirens behind him, and saw flashing lights. 'O, No!' Frank got out of the car to talk to the policeman, "I don't care what you have to do, follow me to the TV Studio, I'm *ON* in five minutes!" Fortunately, the officer recognized him, "Dr. Varro, I will, in fact, *escort* you there…I heard the promo for the–'*magical dinners*,' he called them; they walked on the set just as the show was beginning. The Chorale also sang special concerts with the Symphony, including performances of the Bach 'Magnificat,' The '1812 Overture,' and the Faure 'Requiem.' Frank composed a 'Te Deum,' that was premiered, with alto soloist Jane Huddleston, the Chorale, and members of the Symphony, as a gift to the community; and a commissioned work 'Jubilate Deo,' by Hanley Jackson of Kansas State; and the composer came down for the premier.

[The thing that came out of that was the following story: the Chorale was working very hard on this first-ever commissioned work; they often celebrated after rehearsals at their favorite 'watering hole' near the airport where the Symphony and Chorale rehearsed... sometimes until it closed. The week of the dress rehearsals in both Odessa and Midland... Frank came down with something, and he couldn't keep anything down; but, *let's back up a second*: earlier that year, Margo and Frank had taken the children... their second winter there...to Ruidoso, New Mexico, where there were cabins, skiing, tubing, and other activities; when they found out the snow was sparse, they changed their plans and went tubing instead; with Robbie on one side, Steve on the other, and Frank in the middle, holding tight to each of the boys, they headed down the hill, trying to 'dodge' the large boulders in their path; refusing to loosen his grip on the boys' waists while heading down, Frank's elbow suddenly slammed into one of the rocks, shattering the cartilage on his right arm. Margo and Shelley came running, screaming, and fearing the worst; with Frank in severe pain, they drove the five hours back down the mountain to Odessa; at the emergency room, they wrapped his arm and gave him something for the pain; the next day, Dr. Neal Craft, a long-time member of First Presbyterian, gave him 'Percodan' (plus taking the time to quiz him about his history of digestive problems... yes, the Thanksgiving story had circulated!). So, he lectured him about being sure to 'chew his food thirty times,' and discharged him].

Fast forward: Frank was so sick he could hardly get through the rehearsals. Hanley Jackson had arrived and was making suggestions about his 'Jubilate deo,' so Frank said, "Hanley, you will have to conduct the concert." "Oh no," he said, I compose the music, but I never conduct it; period!" They got through the rehearsals in Midland and in Odessa, and Frank slept the whole next day. It wasn't getting any better, and then Frank remembered the 'Percodan' Dr. Craft had given him. He popped a couple into his mouth and fell asleep again. Most of the 'rest of the story' Margo had to tell, because he was... well... 'high!' An hour before they were to perform in Odessa, Margo said she went to wake him up. "Frank, you have to get dressed for the concert!" Frank stood straight up on the bed, and waving his arms, said: "Here comes the parade! And Robbie is leading them in his little red wagon!" Oh, brother…she knew 'they were in trouble.' She dressed Frank in his tux and drove him to the concert hall. Frank managed to warm up the Chorale. John Graham, the Master of Ceremonies, introduced them: "The Midland-Odessa Symphony Chorale, under the direction of Dr. Frank Varro," He took a bow, the Chorale sang the commissioned work 'Jubilate deo,' with its myriad muti-metered complexities…flawlessly. The audience went wild, and Frank took three bows, and introduced the composer of their first commissioned work *ever*, which Frank conducted…'*in his sleep.*' After a few other incidental works, they took an intermission. Frank had fallen asleep on the couch in the makeup room…but the Chorale was already going *back* on stage. The audience clapped again…then again. Finally, someone came back stage. "Dr. Varro, we are ready for you… *NOW.*" Frank came on stage, they sang the rest of the program, including the Britten 'Five Flower Songs,' and the 'Duruflé Requiem,' with organ and chamber orchestra; the audience came to their feet—everything was well received…*but Frank remembered only bits and pieces.* The next night, several of Frank's colleagues from around West Texas and Portales, New Mexico, were there; again, a standing ovation. The reception was glorious and Frank, still in a stupor, went around the room, hugging and kissing all his Chorale members. The next day, Margo woke Frank up and said, "come on; we're going to the doctor right now!" Taking one look at his yellow eyes, Dr. Craft, said, "what in the world is going on with you, my friend, you have *hepatitis.*" They took a blood test, confirming it. When the word got out, the entire Chorale rushed out to get their 'gamma globulin shots!' The Odessa American, Permian Basin's main newspaper, came out, and Ronald Bennett, longtime fine arts critic, wrote, "*The Symphony Chorale reached a 'new high' in their spring performance, especially a commissioned work, a wonderful choral piece by Hanley Jackson, 'Jubilate deo,' also the Duruflé 'Requiem,' and the Britten 'Five Flower Songs.' Dr. Frank Varro, Chorale Conductor, is now being compared with one of MOSC's prior conductors, Lara Hoggard…*" When the Chorale members read '*new high*,' they all laughed, having learned of Frank's conducting the two concerts 'high on 'Percodan!.' Other great experiences during Frank and Margo's time in West Texas were the special appearances of Burt Bacharach, Roger Williams, Dave Brubeck, and others, with the Symphony. They each did a featured concert, and then were guests of the Symphony at a hall or home of prominent persons in the area where they gave autographs and spoke with those that wished to stand in line to meet them while others ate and danced. The concert with Bacharach was disappointing; everyone was expecting him to perform at least some of the tunes that Dione Warwick and others had made so famous…the reason they brought him there–and for a 'pretty penny.' He played totally unknown jazz pieces, some of which he hadn't even named yet. He showed up two hours late for the reception, and was not gracious to Frank and several others that tried to visit with him, most of whom had already left. Roger Williams was just the opposite. He was completely gracious, funny, and entertaining. After playing with the Symphony, he played his famous, 'Autumn Leaves,' and then took requests from the audience. Without referring to his list once, he played every single one, tying the entire medley together with 'Blueberry Hill,' every fifth or sixth song. The crowd burst into thunderous applause; they brought Frank backstage to meet him; they told Roger that, like him, Frank was a 'preacher's kid.' Roger came straight over to Frank, put his arm around him, and said to all assembled, "let me tell you something about preacher's kids; they are wonderful people…if you can keep them out of jail." Everyone laughed heartily, and Frank and Roger embraced. Dave Brubeck brought his family with him; after playing briefly with the Symphony, Dave and members of his family played several of the great hits, including 'Take Five,' and afterward met at the home of a prominent Symphony patron. After several drinks and food, Dave, still so hospitable, had his arm around Frank, and showed him one of his scores. He said, "Frank, you promised me you would perform my 'Feliz Navidad,' so don't forget!" Someone suggested that he should 'slow down a little,' laughingly suggested that he was already 'three sheets to the wind.' Dave protested, saying, "now that's simply not true-I'm only *two sh-sh-eets* to the wind!" Everyone laughed, the party ended, and Frank and Margo left, feeling so honored to have been part of this very memorable occasion.

Their second year there, Dave Sloan announced he was leaving to become the head of the School of Music at the University of Mississippi (Old Miss) and had recommended that Frank become the head of the School of Music at UTPB, using adjunct professors from the Symphony, and section leaders in the Chorale, to cover the private lessons and classes. As it turned out, this worked out quite well. They expanded on the successful program Dave had set up in previous years, and the number of music students increased significantly. Marsha Baird, from the Chorale, and a private voice student of Frank's, became administrator in the music department. Frank sponsored Marsha for the Regional NATS (National Association of Association of Teachers of Singing), and she won that regional competition. Frank supervised several student teachers in the Odessa public schools, who also placed well. Margo finished her coursework toward the BA in Education, and started her student teaching. At Christmas time, she surprised the children and Frank...here, in a little basket, was a little 'mocha-colored' puppy! The children were delighted... but she quickly told them, "Wait, it's only temporary," and looking at Frank, "I know we can't keep her!" Frank stifled a laugh, knowing that could never be the case [they named her Mocha...and they had her for sixteen years... blind, deaf, with rheumatism, she just wandered off one day...to find her final resting place; they looked everywhere for her, but never found her; they never had another dog, or pet, as long as Mocha. Margo finished her student teaching, saying "my husband and children 'persuaded me to keep her. Ha!"]. Margo graduated with a BA in Education; they attended her ceremony, and Frank processed with the faculty...as the Head of Music. The second year they took several trips out of town; as soon as church was over, they'd pile into the car...and head out 'somewhere.' Frank had never lost his Hungarian 'gypsy blood' so they might end up in Lubbock (a hundred forty miles), San Antonio (three hundred forty miles), or Ft. Davis (a hundred fifty miles). They especially liked Indian Lodge at Ft. Davis, and often stayed there. Sometimes they would camp out at Big Bend on the Rio Grande; it was stifling hot in the summer–even till midnight–but by 4:00 a.m., it was so cold that even the sleeping bags were not enough to keep them warm, and keeping the fire going was important. One weekend, before leaving for their annual trip to the Pacific Northwest, they decided to go to El Paso (two hundred eighty-five miles), stay in one of the dorms (UT Faculty could stay there free in the summer), and then go into Mexico—one could go twenty five miles south of the border without a permit...so they did. The dorm room hadn't been cleaned and they had to bring sleeping bags; there was broken glass and some clutter, but who cares! It was free! They cleaned it up, went to the local McDonald's for supper, and slept well after swimming in the UT El Paso pool (no problem). The next day they headed to the border, were processed through in a reasonable period of time; they drove as far as they were allowed, and then headed back through Juarez for some lunch. As they were finding a place to eat, Frank noticed the Manta kind of stuttered and acted like it was running out of gas…but the gas gage was not low; some nice young men helped them get going again, and they found a little place to eat (see, *no problem*). They only knew a few words of Spanish, but these included: *pollo, carnes, taco, fajita, fruta,* and *jugo.*" They ate, drank some *aqua* and *cerveza,* paid their bill, and headed out, intending to return by evening to Odessa, but …the Manta wouldn't start. The same two young men that had helped them earlier, jump started it, and they drove back across the border, picked up their stuff at UTEP, went for a short swim, then grabbed a snack at McDonald's before heading out (maybe a problem). Frank had thought they had just enough gas to get back to Odessa, but since they had had a little problem with starting it, he left it running while they grabbed their stuff, swam, and went through the drive-through at Mickey D's. "See, everything is fine," he said…they spent their last ten dollars in Van Horn for some gas…just enough to get back to Odessa (with no city lights, in one of the darkest parts of the United States…between Van Horn and the McDonald Observatory…also *the* reason UT had originally located the observatory there), the motor started acting up again, the lights started dimming, and they ground to a stop… on the side of the road (alright, *problem!)* It was pitch black, except for the cars, vans, and eighteen-wheelers, all of which went roaring by. Frank tried to wave someone down, but to no avail. The children started to cry. Margo started to pray…and told Frank to "get out of the road, you're going to get killed!" Frank finally gave up; he just stood there hoping, praying someone would finally stop, even a State Patrol…anyone. It must have been a half hour or more. Another eighteen-wheeler went whizzing by…*but,* about two hundred yards ahead, he squealed to a halt. He slowly *BACKED UP,* and *asked if he could help.* Frank explained the situation. The driver said it was the alternator; with no other option available, he got a strap out of his truck, hitched it to their little car,

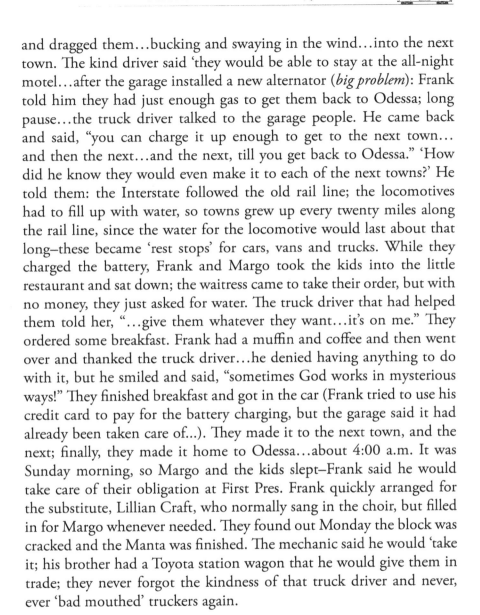

and dragged them…bucking and swaying in the wind…into the next town. The kind driver said 'they would be able to stay at the all-night motel…after the garage installed a new alternator (*big problem*): Frank told him they had just enough gas to get them back to Odessa; long pause…the truck driver talked to the garage people. He came back and said, "you can charge it up enough to get to the next town… and then the next…and the next, till you get back to Odessa." 'How did he know they would even make it to each of the next towns?' He told them: the Interstate followed the old rail line; the locomotives had to fill up with water, so towns grew up every twenty miles along the rail line, since the water for the locomotive would last about that long—these became 'rest stops' for cars, vans and trucks. While they charged the battery, Frank and Margo took the kids into the little restaurant and sat down; the waitress came to take their order, but with no money, they just asked for water. The truck driver that had helped them told her, "…give them whatever they want…it's on me." They ordered some breakfast. Frank had a muffin and coffee and then went over and thanked the truck driver…he denied having anything to do with it, but he smiled and said, "sometimes God works in mysterious ways!" They finished breakfast and got in the car (Frank tried to use his credit card to pay for the battery charging, but the garage said it had already been taken care of…). They made it to the next town, and the next; finally, they made it home to Odessa…about 4:00 a.m. It was Sunday morning, so Margo and the kids slept—Frank said he would take care of their obligation at First Pres. Frank quickly arranged for the substitute, Lillian Craft, who normally sang in the choir, but filled in for Margo whenever needed. They found out Monday the block was cracked and the Manta was finished. The mechanic said he would 'take it; his brother had a Toyota station wagon that he would give them in trade; they never forgot the kindness of that truck driver and never, ever 'bad mouthed' truckers again.

At the end of the year, Marsha Baird announced she and her husband, who worked with Sears, had resigned and had been hired by her father, Doyle Davis, with National Cash Register, and they would be moving back to Beaumont; she would resign as music department administrator. She also told Frank that Dr. John LeBlanc, Director of Choral Activities, at Lamar University in Beaumont, was 'retiring,'…

the position was open; (was he staying on as associate? What was the salary, etc.). The more she told him about the music program at Lamar…three choirs, college and community opera and community theater (and Westminster Presbyterian needed an organist, choir director, hand bells, and youth choir …and all those trees! and *water*!), he said; 'what would it hurt to just apply?' It was about that time that the Chorale had presented their concert and Frank had contracted hepatitis (see previous Chorale story). He had applied for the job and was recuperating when he received a letter from Lamar, asking him to fly to Beaumont for an interview. He graded papers at home in isolation, and Marsha monitored final exams for him, which he then graded. He called his doctor and asked him if he could let him fly to Beaumont for an interview… if you can pass the exam, Dr. Craft said. and he doubted it, but yes, if he passed the exam before graduation, he'd certify it… Frank drank gallons of water every day (his urine each morning was dark, but by drinking water continuously through the day, it became lighter). He did this faithfully, and within a week the color in the morning was continuously lighter. Confident that he would pass the 'wellness test,' Frank wrote Dr. George Parks, the Director of the School of Music at Lamar, that he would be flying in to Beaumont in a few days…but that he had to be back before graduation. The day before his flight to Beaumont, Frank went to Dr. Craft and told him, "Hurry up, I have a flight to catch tomorrow." Dr. Craft growled at him, "who says I'm going to pass you, we at First Pres are not very happy about the possibility of you leaving; well, maybe *you* could leave, but you have to let Margo and the children stay," he joked. Frank told him that even if he were offered the job, he wasn't sure he would take it; they loved it in Odessa. After the exam, he made Frank wait a long time; at first, he said the blood test was 'inconclusive,' but then he smiled and said, "okay, you're good to go," and handed him some lollipops, "these aren't for you, give them to your kids," and walked out of the room. Frank caught his flight to Beaumont. Margo told him to take it easy, not to push himself. She said she would leave if it was what he decided, but truthfully, she wanted to stay in Odessa, get an elementary music teaching job, and just stay there. Frank kissed her goodbye and promised he wouldn't make any decisions before he talked to her. He flew to Beaumont and Dr. George Parks, and some others, met him at the airport and welcomed him to Lamar. They took him on a tour of the campus, where he met several music and fine arts faculty members. After his interview with Dr. Parks and Dr. John LeBlanc, the current Director of Choral Activities, they told him they had one other candidate, they had already interviewed, but based on what they had heard, they planned to offer him the position. Marsha Baird, and Dr. Joe Truncale, with whom she had studied Opera, had pushed Frank's candidacy. Dr. Joe Carlucci, the Orchestra Director and Beaumont Symphony Director, had also voted for Frank to be hired. Frank said he was inclined to accept, but had to talk it over with Margo and his family. They said 'fair enough' and took that as a tentative 'yes' until they could hear back from him. They would give him a week. They put him up at the Cardinal Motel across the street, and the next day he was introduced to more faculty members. One of the piano faculty members heard that Frank was from Seattle. His name was Jerry Berthiaume; his wife was Mary. Jerry asked if they could go have a cup of coffee, he wanted to talk–"about Seattle and the University of Washington" where Jerry was beginning a DMA in Piano Performance. They agreed that it would be a good idea. As soon as they got to the Student Center, Jerry blurted out almost immediately: "don't accept this position! If you do, you'll be sorry." Whoa! Frank didn't even know this guy, but something about him (more than just the fact that they were both from the Seattle), made Frank believe him, and he asked what *that* was all about. Jerry said Lamar was a 'snakepit,' that Dr. Parks was dishonest, the choir hadn't sung anything of college-level repertoire in ten years, and all the high school students went away to the 'good music colleges.' Jerry said he didn't want Frank to get burned, but he also added, "to be fair," there *were* many things that were attractive about the position, and from what he had heard, if anyone could succeed in Lamar's choral activities, he believed Frank could. Frank asked him what he had heard. Jerry just said, "you know what I mean, UW music people…we're all family." They both laughed. Frank was very confused: on the one hand he wanted to advance himself, and the Lamar position, with a well-developed four-year university program, viable church music jobs for both Margo and him, and the advantages of locating to a large metropolitan area near Houston, were very attractive; but on the other hand, he didn't want to give up all the wonderful friends and great position that he had in Odessa: a UT system University, the Symphony, and the theater work they'd done. What bothered him most was what Jerry was telling him about the *choral-vocal music program at Lamar*. He flew home, and Margo and the kids met his plane. He told them the good news…that he had been offered the position. He asked them what they wanted to do to celebrate, and to help him decide if he should take it. Shelley said, "Dad, let's go to the Red Barn again!" They loved going to the Red Barn. Even when they didn't have any money… which seemed like all the time! But they loved the food, the atmosphere… 'and the prices.' You sliced your own cheese from a giant loaf, served right at the table. So, off they went to the Red Barn. Margo was concerned about how tired Frank might be from the trip, given his recent bout with hepatitis. He said he felt fine, and was learning to pace himself. They had a great dinner, and the kids helped themselves to the giant cheese loaf. While the kids were busy helping themselves to the ice cream cones, Frank told Margo about his conversation with Jerry Berthiaume, one of the piano faculty at Lamar. Margo asked if he had accepted already, and Frank admitted he had given Dr. Parks a 'conditional acceptance,' but had agreed to a week's deliberation period, to give him a chance to discuss it with family and colleagues. Before Frank had left for Beaumont, he had discussed his possible resignation with Dr. Brad Ericson, UTPB's Dean…if offered a position at Lamar. Eric said to go ahead and interview, come back for UTPB's graduation, and then they would discuss it. Margo thought they should talk to faculty friends of theirs, and First Presbyterian. She herself wanted to talk to Jerry some more by phone. They asked the kids to get them some ice cream cones too, and then after they all finished, Frank had planned to buy some chocolates, and pay the bill. To his chagrin, he was short ten dollars. He turned to Margo and said in Chinese, "Bu gou qien" ('not enough money'…they often tried to 'tell secrets in Chinese' when they didn't want the children to know what was going on…he knew they would have to forego the chocolates, so he told the kids he would have to buy the chocolates 'next time' and Robbie said, "Daddy, what's wrong? I want chocolates." Frank said, "Daddy doesn't have enough money, Robbie; we'll have to wait." Robbie turned to him and started to cry, "Daddy, can't you just 'write a check'?" Everyone laughed, realizing that Robbie didn't yet understand that money had to be in the bank first…before you could *write* a check. Margo remembered they had some chocolate at home; they paid the bill with cash …the couple bucks for the tip cleaned them out; but they laughed all the way home, and sure enough there were some two month old Hershey bars on the top shelf in the kitchen that Margo had been hiding; Shelley and the boys munched to their delight, and they were off to bed. Frank and Margo stayed up awhile and talked about the 'pros and cons' of Lamar.

The next day was graduation and they all dressed up in their 'Sunday best.' The kids were so excited that 'Mommy was graduating from college (again)' and 'Daddy was marching with the other faculty people in his fancy black robe.' [Frank had talked to Dean Ericson again and asked him if he could 'have his job back if he decided to turn down the Lamar position' but Dr. Ericson told him they had posted the notice of a search for Head of the Music Department position already; but if he was staying, they could probably cancel that. Frank had decided he would turn down the position at Lamar. He was going to call George Parks the next day and tell him, but the phone rang the afternoon after graduation…it was Dr. Parks. He wanted to know when they were going to 'pack up and join them in East Texas.' Frank said he had some questions…and began to tell him bluntly what he had heard; that some of the faculty had 'serious reservations about things there,' and he didn't want to get into a situation that wouldn't be good for him.' Rather than argue with him, Dr. Parks simply told him all the things Dr. Carlucci, Dr. Truncale, and several others, had said about Frank, how excited they were, and the advantages of a more-developed program Lamar would have over UTPB.' He said they had already told the other finalist that the position had been filled. He said he didn't know anyone that was unhappy with him, or the program there, but anything…anyone else (Frank thought he heard him whisper Jerry's name) who might have said anything against him or the program, could easily be refuted by many other faculty members…more than 'someone who might be unhappy.' They talked for another half hour; then Frank asked him if he could call him back in about an hour. Frank and Margo talked about all the reasons *against* accepting the Lamar position, and then they talked about all the reason *for* accepting it… then they prayed. The verse that came to Frank's mind was Isaiah 43:2:

"when you walk through the water…or the fire…fear not, for I will be with you." They didn't realize at that time the full extent of what would become 'one of the most difficult times in their lives,' but despite any fear or hesitation, they knew God was *with* them, and that they need not doubt his care for them. Frank called Dr. Parks back in one hour… and told him they *would accept* the position at Lamar. Frank said they would need help finding a place to live. Yes, they could move to Beaumont in June, but they would need to be gone the last two weeks of July…for their annual CEF retreat to Oregon. They started packing up and contacted a real estate agent that Dr. Brown knew from church. Frank also announced his resignation at the church staff meeting that week. Within a couple days, he had submitted letters of resignation from the Symphony Chorale and UTPB. Dr. Ericson said, "this time… time…it's for sure then?" They laughed, and Dr. Ericson said 'they would miss him, and the family; they had really enjoyed having them; they had acted more like West Texans than most people he knew that were *born* there.' Within days, Frank got a call from Joe Fuller with Permian Real Estate. He came over and did a complete walk through of the house, taking copious notes. The *worst scare of their lives* happened the next day: the inspector came and was up on the roof checking things out. He had parked his car, unlocked, in front of the house. Frank climbed up the ladder to observe the inspection. The boys were playing in the front yard. Something out of the corner of Frank's eye caught his attention in the yard below. What he saw made his blood *FREEZE!* Steve was curiously pointing a handgun directly at the head of Robbie; wanting to scream, Frank forced himself to 'keep his cool.' He spoke in a low reassuring voice, "Stevie, look at Daddy, *put the gun on the ground…slowly,* then waiting for him to do so, 'now step away. Robbie, you go with Steve… both of you step over to the driveway… and wait for Daddy." During all this time, Frank had been coming down the ladder, facing forward, keeping his eyes all the while on Stevie. He slowly crossed the yard, picked up the gun, and then shouted to the inspector, "You get your damn ass down here…right now!! Margo and Shelley heard Frank shouting, and came running out of the house. The inspector sheepishly came down the ladder, as Frank, who looked like he was going to hit him, confronted him: *"you left the car unlocked; a handgun, fully loaded, was found by my boys in the glove*

compartment which was also left unlocked! Margo and Shelley comforted the boys, who were both crying, thinking they were going to get the 'spanking of their lives.' Frank ordered the inspector back to the office (later filing a complaint against him and the company). He bawled out the boys for doing something without permission, but mostly cried for joy that the worst had not happened. Joe Fuller, the real estate agent, apologized profusely, ordered another inspector who came the next day, and they all thanked God for everything turning out so well and without tragedy. The house sold surprisingly quickly (Frank suspected that the bank wanted to take it back, but people at the church and university had insisted that they be given more time). They made sure an interested party took care of everything; but it 'did affect' their credit on their very-first purchased house. They got a rental truck, packed everything up and left for Beaumont before the end of June. Frank had sifted through eight applicants for the Symphony Chorale and UTPB jobs, ending up interviewing two finalists. Stan Engebretzen from Arizona took both jobs with the approval of the Symphony and University. He turned down the First Presbyterian job, but Dr. Brown and the church hired one of the area high school choral directors. They ended their very successful, and in many ways, wonderful, time in Odessa with yet another truck full of their stuff, and a new challenging adventure ahead. [They had committed to going to the CEF retreat, even though they didn't have the money. Maxine suggested that they could ask permission of the CEF Board to take a little money from what had come in, above what was being sent to Rev. Wang Yu-zhung and the mission in Taiwan. Maxine polled the board, telling them it was important that their CEF President attend the Annual meeting, but without assistance, Frank and Margo would be unable to attend that year. All but one wrote back in agreement. Maxine at first wouldn't tell Frank who the one objecting board member was, but finally told him it was his dear cousin Bettye Watson. Frank did not feel hard toward her, though; he knew it wasn't personal; he loved Bettye very much and knew her objection had to do with sending every penny possible to the mission field. Maxine sent them close to six hundred dollars, and they agreed, despite the move from Odessa to Beaumont, and the cost of storing their stuff, that they would make the trip]. They arrived in Beaumont three hours later than planned, but Doyle Davis,

Marsha Baird's father was kind enough to meet them in Winnie, at a truck stop thirty miles southwest of Beaumont, to take Mocha for the three weeks that they would be gone. The Alamo Plaza, where they were to stay would not take pets, so Marsha had persuaded her father to help them out. Frank had contacted a real estate agent before he left to go back to Odessa, and Cheryl Bunning, with Golden Triangle Realty, came by and showed them a small three-bedroom house she thought they would like. Margo and the kids loved it, so they signed the papers, and put down what they could...from the sale of the Odessa house [Permian State Bank would send the rest after the purchase was approved, they said]. The next day, Frank showed up at Lamar, moved into his office while Margo stayed with the kids at the motel. Later, they all went over to Westminster Presbyterian, and Rev. Phineas Washer, the Pastor, showed them around the church. Westminster had a reasonable-sounding Moller pipe organ, and a five octave handbells set. Rev. Washer ('you can call me Phin,' he'd said)...told them there was a pretty good choir of about fifteen to twenty. He also said he had a summer home at Wildwood, about forty miles away, where they could stay while they were waiting to be approved on the house. Frank thanked him, but reminded him they had committed to a CEF Retreat in the Pacific NW, and would be gone their first two Sundays in town; Frank had discussed this possibility when he had interviewed at Lamar, and at Westminster. "O yes, now I remember," he said, "just a thought." Margo said they might have to consider it when they get back...she hated staying at the Alamo Plaza...fixing meals in their room with an electric skillet, crowded, and the children sleeping on the floor in sleeping bags. Frank agreed, but they were leaving in a week, their stuff was in storage, and he didn't want to drive eighty miles roundtrip every day. At least the Plaza had a swimming pool, and "that was all that the kids needed." They made the best of it, and the week went by quickly. They had a chance to go to church at St. Mark's Episcopal that Sunday. It was where Marsha Baird attended, and she introduced them to the Rector, The Rev. Claude Payne, his wife Barbara, and several of the members there. They were invited to transfer their membership from Epiphany in Seattle to St. Mark's (turns out they had never changed it–even after they had moved it from Trinity in Bend, to Epiphany, and even during the time they were at First Pres in Alliance, St. Mark's in

Canton, and First Pres in Odessa). Tom Oliphant, the organist-choirmaster, invited them to sing in the St. Mark's Choir. They said they would, after they got back from Seattle. They quickly deposited the six hundred Maxine had sent, using it as the 'seed money' for the new bank account at Beaumont First Savings and Loan. They carefully planned their itinerary...three days up, plus three days back, including a week to visit family and friends, and two nights at CEF retreat, this time at Molalla Christian Camp in Oregon. The blue Toyota station wagon ran pretty well, as far as Frank was concerned, but he hadn't had a chance to have it checked out thoroughly, thinking how fortunate he was that the Manta, even with a cracked block, could be traded 'straight across' for the Toyota station wagon. Sure, it had a 'few miles on it,' but it ran well in their move to Beaumont. Besides, they were new to the city and didn't know any mechanics he could ask to check it out... before leaving for the Northwest. They left early in the morning the last week in June, going up US287 to I-25 to Colorado Springs. After a light supper, they headed up toward Monarch Pass. They noticed that the transmission was not performing as well as it should, but pressed on anyway. Thinking it might help if he added transmission fluid, they stopped and added some on their way. It was now dark; they slowly climbed up to the Monarch pass summit. Thankfully, the road was dry and they finally made it to the top; they coasted...all the way down to Grand Junction. They found a Motel 6 there, and even though it was 1:00 in the morning, Frank grabbed a snack from the all-night service station for the kids, before falling immediately to sleep. In the morning they headed out. Despite the transmission problems they were able to make it to Salt Lake City, with the added transmission fluid, and then on to Boise. They hadn't arranged for a stay with relatives in Nampa (near Boise), so they found another Motel 6, ate supper and went to bed. Since it was too late to turn around now, Margo decided she should at least call her mother in Wenatchee, to tell her about their transmission ...just in case. So, after supper the kids swam in the pool, and Margo called her mother... while Frank fell asleep watching the kids swim. Margo's mom insisted on wiring them the money to fly from Boise to Wenatchee; she said to leave the car there to be fixed but when Margo told the kids to get out of the pool, she woke Frank up, and when she told him what her mother said... he said 'absolutely not!'

He would never accept such a ridiculous 'solution.' They could "fly there and skip the CEF Retreat if they wanted;." He'd get the transmission fixed and put it on a credit card and attend the CEF retreat by himself, and then drive home… alone; Wilma could fly them back if she wanted to.' Whoa! Margo said, slow down; she hadn't accepted anything, and she never would accept this without Frank's approval, she said. Frank calmed down, and said he was sorry for over-reacting; he took them all to the Dairy Queen across the street, and they downed their ice cream with delight. Frank made everyone go to bed right away. He woke everyone up at 6:00 a.m. and they drove till they got to Ontario, Oregon, had breakfast there, then on to Richland, Washington for lunch; they pulled into Wenatchee by supper time. Wilma had fixed a wonderful meal with corn on the cob, wild asparagus, and barbequed chicken that Francis had cooked on the grill. They had a great visit that evening, and neither Wilma nor Frank mentioned anything about the transmission. Francis said he was ready for bed, but first wanted to tell Frank about a mechanic he used sometimes. Wilma offered to pay for a new transmission, but Frank said he thought a good rebuilt would be alright. They went to bed, and awoke to the wonderful smell of bacon and coffee. Francis had hand-cut the bacon… thick, the way he knew Frank and he both liked. Wilma made blueberry muffins and scrambled eggs. They took the car to the shop after breakfast, examined it, and the mechanic quoted them 'eleven hundred…with a one year warranty. Wilma said she would like to pay for it…since they had spent so much time and money *to come see her*, but Frank was stubborn and independent, so he said she…could *pay half.* There was a long pause. Margo put her arm around her mother, but said nothing. Wilma looked at Francis but he looked away. He'd 'been there before.' Then she slowly said "okay," and they finished the job…before the end of the day. Margo and the kids went shopping with Wilma, and then they all went to China Cafe for Chinese food, at North Valley Mall. They stayed another night; at supper Wilma told them that she and Francis were planning a road trip through 'the south,' and it included Texas. They would be coming through Beaumont in September. What? What a surprise, they could stay with them in their new house! And the kids would be in their new school. Margo said she would love to plan for their visit. After breakfast, they left for Seattle; they stayed with

Irma and boys one night, and then with Al and Les Peterson another night, before going on down to Molalla, to the retreat. It was a wonderful three days of family fun, eating, and laughing together. The worship, tears, and sharing around the campfire, were so uplifting. Frank shared the hopes for the future and the new position at Lamar, but he kept secret the hurt and doubts he still had of the past, and his lukewarm spiritual state. The family noticed it, but thought it was just the adjustments in moving yet again, the pressures of raising the family, and joining another church and social group...which was very different than *theirs*. The kids had a great time, and were sorry when they had to leave to make the long trek home. They packed up the Toyota and headed out from Oregon, along the Columbia River, and then south through Idaho and Utah. They stayed the night at the same place in Boise as on their way up, and left early the next day. Frank started noticing some strange transmission action as they slowed down coming into each town, and the same problem as they left to get back out on the highway. Thinking it would work itself out, they drove on. They had a late lunch in Provo, and headed south, but instead of going through the mountain passes as they had on the way up, they went around...the longer but safer way. By evening the problems were getting worse. They were approaching Moab, Utah, when things were so bad even Frank had to admit they needed to stop for the evening, get a garage to look at the transmission during supper. As they were coming down the hill into Moab, the engine suddenly cut out. They coasted into the town...right into a full-service garage! There was a McDonald's across the street, a small Best Western motel next to it, and the garage was open! Frank explained the problem, and the man said he would look at it while they had supper, and checked into the hotel. 'No,' he said, they had better not count on getting it fixed right away.' Frank stayed with the Toyota while Margo and the kids checked into the Best Western; she got some supper and brought it back to the garage. Frank had been told what the problem was: the transmission had not been set right, so it needed a major adjustment. The garage owner said he could fix it, but they wouldn't get out of Moab before the next day (Frank hoped 'what he had left on his credit card would cover it'). He arranged for the repair, they had supper by the pool at the Best Western, then stayed the night. A couple hours after breakfast the next day, Bob

Sturgeon, the garage guy, had the car fixed already and they headed for the south. They made it to Albuquerque the next day after a short visit at 'Four Corners' where they had lunch. [Of course, the kids had to take pictures of all five of them standing in four states: Utah, Colorado, New Mexico and Arizona. Shelley insisted on leaning over and placing one hand each in Utah and Colorado, with her feet in Arizona and New Mexico…and the boys followed suit]. Driving hard, they made it back to Beaumont late the following day. They stayed at the Alamo Plaza for the night, and in the morning, they went to the 9:00 service… their first Sunday at Westminster Presbyterian. About twelve showed up to sing in the choir, but with no rehearsal, they didn't attempt to sing any anthem. Margo played the organ, Frank led the singing, Rev. Washer introduced Frank and the family, then he preached. They had a small reception to welcome them to their new church job after the service. They went across the street to St. Mark's Episcopal to the 10:30 service there. Many of the parishioners had already heard about Frank and Margo and their family, and his new position at Lamar. They introduced them in the service and they were warmly welcomed. They slept all afternoon, exhausted from the long trip, had supper, swam in the pool, and retired early. Frank called Cheryl Bunning, the realtor, the next morning… [Margo was at a point of refusing to stay another night at Alamo Plaza… and school was supposed to start the next Monday; they had registered Shelley for fifth grade, and Steve for Kindergarten, at Regina Howell Elementary, a few blocks from the house on Dellwood that they were hoping to buy]. Cheryl suggested they meet at the house "to discuss their options." Frank was not sure what that meant, but agreed to meet there. Margo and the kids came along, and while they explored the back yard and neighborhood, Frank and Margo met with Cheryl. She said they *had been turned down*… because they didn't have adequate credit history; they had been late in Odessa for a few mortgage payments, and they had only put down five percent on the earnest contract; but she said 'not to worry,' they could just put down an additional five percent…and get additional references. Their hearts sank; the truth was: they didn't have an additional five percent they could put down, and they were so new to Beaumont, the only references they would be able to get were Dr. Parks, and the music department, which they had already used. Margo started to cry; she wouldn't spend another night at the Alamo Plaza. Cheryl called Dr. Parks. She had sung in the choir at Lamar... way back when he conducted it, and she had graduated as a business major before going into real estate. Dr. Parks said he would have someone call them back in an hour. Cheryl said she would take them to lunch and they could stop by her office and wait for Dr. Parks' call. They visited with her, and Shelley read to the boys. Almost two hours later, Cheryl said she was going to have to leave for another appointment. They said they understood and maybe they could try calling Dr. Parks again the next day. As they were going out the door, the phone rang... but it was not Dr. Parks–it was Jimmy Simmons, the head of bands at Lamar. They talked at some length. Cheryl laughed and said she would "tell them." She called her other client and rescheduled the appointment, and they left the Toyota at her office; she drove them over to McDonald's at College and Major. They met Jimmie Simmons there; he took them across the railroad tracks to a house on Landis...that was just beginning construction. Frank had met Jimmie at his interview, and then again at their orientation just after arrival in Beaumont. He knew he was a well-known band director in Texas, and knew he had a group called the 'Jimmie Simmons Trio;' what he didn't understand was: why was he showing them a 'house under construction in west Beaumont.' Jimmie and Cheryl started to laugh. Jimmie said, "Frank, I have a construction company, that my parents actually own, but I manage on the side; what do you think the name of this company is?" To Frank's blank look, he told him to think of a musical term that means a 'tag on' at the end of a musical composition ... or at the end of one's music career. Margo and Frank just stared... was this some kind of prank? After the difficult news they had just received about being rejected for a mortgage...the children having no school to attend...and no place to live...? Jimmie and Cheryl seemed quite delighted with the moment, and laughed heartily. Finally, Jimmie said, '*Coda*,'–the name of his construction company...was Coda Construction, as in the end of a musical piece, or the tag-on to one's career! Oh! Frank and Margo were beginning to get it. Jimmie would build them a house... and he would take the risk on the mortgage? (Frank thought briefly: *O no, if I don't make the payments, I could lose my job*! But Jimmy was laughing and slapped him on the back). They looked at the house under construction. It was a small three-bedroom house on Landis Street, just off the railroad tracks and US Highway 90 on one side, and three blocks north was another set of railroad tracks, close to Forest Park High School. He showed them drawings of the floor plan. It was a "spec house," (speculative, built while waiting for a prospective buyer–like Frank had done with Percy Dean right after they were married), but they would get to pick all the colors, lighting, etc. They would get a competitive interest rate with one of Jimmie's banks he dealt with. If they stopped by in the morning, his parents would write up the contract–what did they think? Frank's jaw was on the ground. He looked at Margo. She looked happier than she had been since leaving Odessa. God had taken care of them once again. They said they would be there in the morning. One problem: where would they stay? There was *NO WAY* they would continue to stay at the Alamo Plaza. Then suddenly Frank remembered Phin Washer's summer house at Wildwood. A long way to commute, but it would be worth it. He called Phin. By 6:00, they had picked up the keys, driven to Wildwood after checking out of the Alamo Plaza, and were taking a short swim in the lake before fixing a light supper with the groceries they had purchased on the way, and retiring for the night in the Washer's summer getaway. The next day they met Jimmie's parents, James and Wilene, who took them through the contract, and with Cheryl's help, transferred the earnest money, and visited Amelia Elementary, where they enrolled Shelley in fifth grade, and Steve in Kindergarten. School would start Monday, all they needed to show was a letter from Coda Construction, proving to the school and Bank, their residence status. Lamar was starting in two weeks. Jimmie said the house would be done by Thanksgiving. Frank looked at the smile on Margo's face. Shelley said, "Daddy, mommy looks happy again." This was unbelievable! So much had happened in just a few days. They stopped by the grocery store and bought some things on the way back to Wildwood. After supper, they thanked God again for his miraculous provision for them, put the kids to bed, and Margo returned her mom's call; they talked a long time while Frank reviewed music that he had chosen for his first semester at Lamar. Marsha Baird called the next day. She had heard the good news about Jimmie planning to build their house. She said Mocha was doing well (they had visited Mocha several times at the Davises and she seemed to like them, but Marsha wanted to know if Rev. Washer was going to allow Mocha to be with them at the Wildwood house. Frank said unfortunately they wouldn't be able to, because Wildwood management didn't permit it. Marsha said she would be happy to keep her until they moved into their house. She also told them she knew of a church daycare in the Amelia area. They might like to check it out and see if Robbie liked it. So, the next day Margo dropped Frank off at Lamar, took Shelley and Steve to buy supplies for school at Amelia, and enrolled Robbie at a daycare at Wesley United Methodist Church. Frank was involved in meetings and setting up his office, so she and the kids had lunch at a KFC near the church, then stopped by Westminster to practice the organ and plan music for the next few Sundays. She met Miriam, who worked in the church office, and showed them around the church. Margo discovered the five-octave bell set they had talked about; it was in storage on the top floor, so she polished a few of them and played some while the kids played in the nursery. She also straightened up the choir room for their rehearsal that night. Frank called for them to pick him up, they had supper, went to the rehearsal, and then the long trip home. The rest of the week they made the long roundtrip in from Wildwood, held auditions for the Lamar choirs, voice students, explored the Golden Triangle area, ate meals on the run, and then returned to Wildwood…exhausted every day. The church choir went well though, and Margo recruited several to her new bell choir. They visited Mocha often and Mrs. Davis gave the kids cookies and milk each visit.

Margo interviewed for the Lamar Music Department accompanist job, where she met Jerry Berthiaume, and some of the piano faculty. She felt unsure of herself, but Dr. Parks waved off her insecurity, promising she would only accompany the students with whom she felt comfortable. Sunday was routine, and then, suddenly, it was time for school to start. Even though Steve had already met his Kindergarten teacher, and some of the kids, he was terror-stricken the opening day of school. He cried and clung to Frank, and then Margo, but they gently pushed him toward the teacher and his class. Shelley entered fifth with a great deal of confidence. This was her fourth school already …Kirkland, Alliance, Odessa, and now Beaumont. She made some new friends right away, and some of these remained her closest during the entire time she lived in Beaumont. Lamar started the following two weeks and Frank and Margo fell into a routine. The only thing that became increasingly difficult was the eighty-mile roundtrip commute to and from Wildwood. Sometimes Frank had after-school make-up rehearsals or lessons; and Margo sometimes had rehearsals after school too; she picked Shelley and Steve up later…no place for a snack or down-time after classes, then she'd pick Robbie up at the daycare by 6:00. They ate supper on the run most days, and Wednesdays they had to stay for church choir rehearsal. Sometimes they shopped for groceries on the way back to Wildwood, and the kids would be asleep in the car by the time they arrived…sometimes it was as late as 10:00, or 11:00p.m., and then they had to get up early to do the same thing all over again the next day. Rev. Washer decided that, since they were going to be staying there an extended period of time, they would need to pay rent. This added an additional strain on their already-tight budget! The days had turned into weeks, and the weeks into months. Their house wouldn't be ready until Thanksgiving…at the earliest. Margo tried to hide it, but Frank caught her crying in the bathroom almost every night after they put the kids to bed. Frank tried to help with the cooking, cleaning, and the kids, but he knew this wasn't working. They would have to change their plans again. Since they were having to pay rent now anyway, why shouldn't they just rent a short-term apartment in Beaumont? He called Cheryl the next day while Margo was at Lamar. She asked about the house on Landis. Frank said he talked to Jimmie almost every week about it. Jimmie said they couldn't speed things up on spec houses; with less expensive labor and material, meant they couldn't always control the timing. Jimmie had promised Thanksgiving, but that was still almost three months away. Cheryl said getting an apartment for an abbreviated period of time might be a problem…without paying a penalty. She said, "but I'll work on it" 'she'd get back to him right away;' the situation was getting fairly 'intolerable' as Frank put it. Three days later, after rehearsals and voice lessons, Frank got the message that Cheryl had called…she had a place they could rent on a temporary basis. He told Margo what he had been up to with that 'I've got a secret' look she knew so well. She brightened a little and said they should go get the kids, have some supper, and then go meet Cheryl. So, they did; Margo told the kids they were going to find another place to live that wasn't so far away. They all expressed their delight, grabbed some hamburgers at McDonald's, and then met Cheryl at her office. They all got in her van and headed out. She warned them: they might have to be a little 'adaptable' since it was only *temporary* housing...until they moved into their new house. She drove across the I-10 bridge toward Vidor. She kept saying she *had done the best she could* 'under the circumstances.' They were ready for anything. 'Was it a really small apartment', Margo asked? 'Not exactly,' Cheryl said. 'Was it an old house' Shelley asked? 'Not exactly,' Cheryl said. Frank stayed silent. They were headed to Vidor, Texas. [He had learned that the Grand Wizard of the KKK had lived there, and Vidor was known for its strong prejudice toward other-than-white individuals. Cheryl pulled into a trailer court; they walked into a large trailer that had three small bedrooms. The layout was okay; the kitchen and bathroom seemed to be alright. Cheryl kept apologizing. Frank and Margo were shocked and dismayed...what kind of choice was this: caught between 'the devil and the deep blue sea!' They couldn't rent a house or a short-term apartment, the penalty was just too high–but the Wildwood commute was unbearable. It was taking its toll on both Frank and Margo, say nothing of the kids. Frank said they would take it. In fact, they would take it tonight...it was too late to go to Wildwood. Cheryl saw the disappointed look on their faces, but she didn't know what to say or do. She told them to pile back in her van. She had some snacks and Sprite which she offered the kids; Margo and Frank waved off any snacks but accepted the Sprite. They drove south of Vidor, out some lonely road. She had told Frank the trailer was owned by an elderly woman who at one time had lived in it, and now had a little cottage in the woods. They traveled down a rough road...with just two 'ruts' in the grass...no lights; but Cheryl's headlamps. It was silent in the car. The kids munched on their snacks and drinks. Margo grabbed Frank's hand as if to say, "I don't like this, but I'm going to trust you." They arrived, deep in the East Texas woods. An old dog howled his warning. An elderly, very overweight woman appeared on the porch; Cheryl introduced them to Carin Cavineau; she was toting a shotgun, and an elderly man sat rocking in his squeaky rocking chair on the porch, smoking an old corncob pipe, looking them over...not saying a word. Cheryl told her this was the young couple and their kids that were going to rent the trailer. She smiled, they signed the contract...

three months, at eighty dollars a month, mail it to her before the fifth of the month to avoid a late charge. Frank signed for them. Margo and the kids stayed at the bottom of the stairs. When it was completed, Ms. Cavineau turned to Frank and said, "I hear y'all are 'yankees,'" to which Frank replied, "O no, we're from Seattle–by way of Ohio, and West Texas." She paused, as if to not say something rude. "Anybody north of Dallas is a *Yaangkee*, as far as I'm concerned!" Cheryl looked like she was going to apologize for Carin, but Frank waved her off. He laughed and said, "Well, I wasn't born in Texas…but I got here as soon as I could." They laughed, even her husband, Willis, who now got up out of his rocker, and shook Frank's hand. Margo and the kids came up on the porch, and Ms. Cavineau brought some 'Texas Tea' out for them to drink. They drove back into Vidor to the trailer. Cheryl found some blankets that had been left by the last tenants, and Frank told her not to worry, they would 'make do' until after the kids' schooling the next day, and Margo and his classes at Lamar, then they would move all their stuff from Wildwood… 'maybe even get some other stuff out of their storage, and move in.' After Cheryl left, they noticed that there were fleas in the carpet…and all through the trailer. It was a miserable night, but the next day Frank got fumigator spray, and activated it before they returned to Wildwood for their things.

Thus began one of the more 'interesting' chapters in their lives. It was not home, but it would do… until their new house was finished. It also eliminated the long commute; it was much closer to the daycare, school, church job, and Lamar. Shelley and Steve seemed to really enjoy Amelia, and Robbie liked the daycare so much that Margo had a hard time getting him to leave at the end of the day. One day, the kids were playing with some of the neighborhood children in Vidor. Frank had just come home and was helping Margo start some supper, when all three kids burst into the trailer… in tears. They were shouting back at the neighborhood children who came up on the porch after them. "Whoa, whoa, whoa" Frank shouted at them, "what is going on here?!" Shelley cried out, "they said they won't play with us anymore!" Margo followed Frank and the kids out onto the porch. "What seems to be the problem," he said. The older boy and girl scowled and turned on their heels to go. Frank said, "I'm talking to you, did you do or say something to my children that made them so upset?" Skeeter, the older boy looked like he wasn't going to say anything, but Frank persisted. Margo took the boys aside while Shelley stepped forward, as if she were going to say something. Skeeter said, "we cain't play with them... they go to school in Beaumont...they go the school with 'nig---s,' and our daddy say we cain't play with them no mo." Margo grabbed Steve and Robbie...to shield them from the degrading language. When Frank finished recoiling, he took all three kids inside with Margo, and then he returned to talk to the neighbor children. "You go back to your trailers, *and don't let me ever catch you here again*; I don't want my children to be with you; they have plenty of other children to play with at school and church." He knew it wouldn't do any good to tell the parents, management, the police, or community leaders. Vidor might be bad, but he knew Beaumont wasn't much better; at least Judge Parker, and the rest of the Beaumont leaders, were trying to comply with the new discrimination laws. He was glad they were only going to live there about another month or so. He had witnessed unsuspecting black Americans, traveling cross-country, who stopped to eat at the McDonalds, on I-10 in Vidor; they were 'run-out' of there after dusk, like: "sorry we are closed for cleaning" (at 8:30?), and other such examples.

It quickly became clear that the choral program at Lamar was going to be a great challenge. In fact, the Liberal Arts in general were not strong. It had a good business school, and the petrochemical school was given by far the most attention, money...and students. Lamar had started as a community college; it grew to a four-year college; then Lamar Technical University, and finally, Lamar University. Many in the community, and across the state, still called it 'Lamar Tech.' Most Fine Arts students in the Golden Triangle went away to other music schools in the state, and little had been done to recruit strong music faculty or students from the area. The community was in-grown, and cautious of the 'outside' culture. Frank talked with his new friend Jerry often, and they both decided it would be a real challenge for Lamar to have a first-rate choral program. Frank avoided talking to Dr. LeBlanc, the retired previous Director of Choral music, or the music Chair, Dr. Parks, who had started the choir...and the music department. However, Frank did find a previous Director of Choral Music to talk to: Dr. Ray Moore, who had left after ten years, to be the Director of Choral Music at the

University of Houston; he was eager to tell Frank all about his difficult time at Lamar. Instead of easy 'Junior-High' choral literature, Frank selected some of the best, but achievable, classic choral repertoire. He had held auditions for the Concert Choir and the Chamber Choir, and even though there were a number of surprisingly good singers, most of them were 'fillers,' Frank was told that a number of the students had already 'auditioned' and had been promised *choral scholarships...* and 'would he please honor these.' Frank of course complied, but found out that most of the good students who were already juniors and seniors, were already voice majors...and students of Mary French Barrett, who prepared them for Dr. Truncale's Opera Workshop. The others? Oh, they had signed up for voice lessons with... well, Frank. In their first voice lessons, Frank found out many of them couldn't even *match pitch*! But Frank didn't let this get him down; he applied all of his training as a NATS member (National Association of Teachers of Singing), to bring out their best. He *WAS* able to work with some of the best singers though...in his Chamber Choir. He did choral works by Mendelssohn, Brahms, Rachmaninoff, and folk songs and spirituals in his first year's concerts. They went on a short tour in the spring to churches and universities in Louisiana, and northeastern Texas. The second year, they went on tour to Dallas and San Antonio area churches and universities. Two weeks after classes started at Lamar, Frank got a call from David Llewellyn, the choir director at Vidor High School. He said he was the Choral-Vocal Region Chair. They had selected Frank to be the conductor-clinician for the High School Region Choir. Frank was ecstatic– Region Choir! Maybe not everything was so bad after all; he accepted; they met at Port Neches-Groves High School, Frank held a clinic with the choir, and then conducted the final performance; his accompanist was Julie McClellan, the choir director at West Orange-Stark High School, and Frank quickly understood why David had been so blunt when he told Frank that 'their region' had only about three good schools for choral music: Vidor, West Orange-Stark, and Nederland, where Twyla Nau conducted. But despite their support for Frank as the new Director of Choral Music at Lamar, most of their best students went away to college. Fortunately, most of the region choir consisted of those three high schools' singers, so it was a fine performance.

Among the many difficulties in Beaumont and Lamar, was wide-spread promiscuity among faculty, students and the whole arts community; this included members of Frank's church choir, as well as St. Mark's choir, mostly their young adult group. It was also a very difficult time for Frank and Margo. Besides this, it was becoming *intolerable* to live in the trailer in Vidor, and the construction at their house had been delayed several times, due to weather...and getting construction materials as well. Their relationship was also strained to the limit. Margo was watching helplessly as Frank tried to make the best of his decision to take this questionable job. He was trying to fit in, reasoning that compromising his faith, and his own temptations of the world were part of it. By October, this full display of decadence was evident when the St. Mark's Choir attended the annual Diocesan Choral Festival. They had rented a bus to take them into Houston to the cathedral for the afternoon rehearsal and evening performance. Choirs from all over the diocese attended and congregations filled the cathedral. There was so much drinking to and from the festival, that several of the choir were in no shape to be singing...or anything else. By the time Sunday came around the word had already gotten to Claude Paine, the Rector, and the Lay leadership of St. Mark's too, and subsequent trips to diocesan events prohibited alcohol. By Halloween, Jimmie Simmons told Frank that they had made up some time and that he would be able to deliver the new house to them on time by Thanksgiving. Two female students, and one church choir member, had propositioned him, asking for 'good grades' in his music class... for unspecified 'rewards.' Drinking to excess at all of the St. Mark's choir, and Beaumont Little Theatre parties, were commonplace. Trying to belong, even Margo had gotten caught up in it. The first week in November Margo told Frank they had to leave the trailer... 'no matter what.' She couldn't take any more. She said she had called her mother. She planned to quit her job at Lamar and the church, take the children for Thanksgiving and Christmas to Wenatchee, and 'then they would see.' Frank could 'stay and finish' at Lamar, if he wanted;' it hit Frank like a ton of bricks. He didn't want this job any more, it wasn't worth it. It was Saturday afternoon; he called Jimmie at home; he told him they would have to back out of the deal, he told him he would have to quit his job at Lamar. 'Whoa, whoa!' Jimmie told Frank the house would be finished in two weeks; everything was going to be 'okay.' He was so very caring and understanding, that Frank promised he would talk it over with Margo. They decided to leave Shelley with the boys "for just a little while" and went to Westminster where Margo could practice the organ...and they could talk. They talked a long time. Finally, Margo agreed that she had let everything all build up. Frank admitted he too had let things get out of hand...it would be better in their new home. After church the next day, she called her mother and told her they were *not* coming; they were going to 'try again'...they would move into their new home, and enjoy Thanksgiving and Christmas. Wilma was very encouraging, and said times were sometimes hard; she'd pray that God would 'smooth their path.' Sure enough, the week before Thanksgiving, Jimmie told Frank his mom and dad would meet them at the house, give them the walk-through, the keys, and they could make arrangements to end their lease in Vidor, open up their storage unit, and start moving! Their mortgage would be paid to Beaumont Savings and Loan. Their new home was on Landis Drive in west Beaumont. Frank couldn't remember a 'happier day' in a very long time. They went to the storage after renting a small U-haul. Willis Cavineau showed up at the trailer to help move the few things they had there onto the truck, picked up Mocha, and signed off on the month-to-month lease (Carin Cavineau was so mad at losing the income from the lease, she refused to come). Two Lamar students showed up to help move furniture and other things from storage. Sissy, a female music student wore her lowest-cut top...working on 'getting Dr. Varro's attention;' she had said she was the 'girlfriend of the other guy,' Justin, even though he knew she wasn't (since she had just propositioned Frank a few weeks earlier). Margo hadn't witnessed this; she had gone to the store to buy a small turkey and groceries for their dinner on Thanksgiving. Frank was relieved she wasn't there to witness this; it would have upset her all over again. They hung sheets over the windows for privacy, and enjoyed Hungarian goulash Margo made in celebration of their 'house warming.' They slept on mattresses on the floor–they hadn't had a chance to set up the beds; but it was the most enjoyable evening they had had in months.

The fall concert went well, especially the folk songs and spirituals at the end. Thanksgiving and Christmas were especially festive, and

David Llewellyn, Julie McClellan, and Twyla Nau and several of their students were in the audience for the Chamber Singers Christmas concert, which was especially gratifying. Frank and Margo also sang with the St. Mark's choir for their Christmas concert. Margo started the bell choir at Westminster as promised, and Frank conducted the Westminster Christmas concert choir with almost ten singers. Rev. David and Linda McKechnie, pastors at St. Andrew's Presbyterian, were in the audience. [David had asked Frank early in the semester to come sing a solo for their Sunday service; this was well received, and following the service he asked Frank to come to his office; after some chit-chat about his position at Lamar, David abruptly asked Frank if he would accept the position of Director of Music at St. Andrews. Frank stammered, "Uh, uh… your present Director of Music, George Parks, is my boss at Lamar." David said bluntly, "yes, he is, we would hire you, and dismiss him." Frank told him he felt his place at the present was in academia, and he had decided to stick it out at Lamar." Years later, Frank wondered several times 'what things might have been like,' had he accepted that offer]. Linda on the other hand, with a reputation as a master bells teacher, had made a 'deal' with Frank and Margo… if she tutored the Westminster bells choir, 'could she borrow a couple octaves of the five-octave bells at Westminster?' They *made* that deal, and both churches benefitted greatly! Frank and Margo were honored that they came to their Westminster Christmas concert. There was also the usual scurry of activities: getting Christmas letters out, Christmas parties at St. Mark's… the Choir, the young-adults group, and Westminster's choir party too. Shelley and Steve had Christmas concerts at Amelia; even Robbie had a little Christmas program at Wesley Methodist Day School. Frank finished giving exams at Lamar, concerts, and Music Department Christmas Reception…and suddenly their first semester in Beaumont was over. Frank took a volunteer group from the Lamar choir to some nursing homes to do caroling…to the utter delight of those attending. The next day, Frank and Margo took the kids Christmas shopping, and then they piled into the car for a joy-ride to Houston. Their good friends—Les and 'Pete' Peterson, from Taiwan…whom they kept 'running into'—in Virginia, Ohio, and now Texas. Pete got a job with a garage door-opener company; they called and invited Frank and Margo and family, to visit them in Houston.

They had a great visit, but they hadn't prepared to stay the night…they 'made-do' anyway, and stayed over. Incredible, how this friendship had developed; four times now they were in close proximity to each other. Michael Peterson and Shelley were the same age; Steve and Robbie were close in age to Brian. They had a great time reminiscing about Taiwan, Virginia, Ohio, Seattle, and now Texas. It was a good trip, and they returned to Beaumont for a restful and wonderful Christmas celebration. Before coming home for their own family celebration, they sang the 'Midnight Christmas Mass' with the St. Mark's Choir, complete with trumpets, strings, and solos. Growing up, Margo's and Frank's families had always opened presents on Christmas Eve, and on Christmas morning, 'Santa came' and they opened stocking gifts. So, they continued that celebration with the kids. After Christmas, they did some exploring of the Golden Triangle [what they called the three cities of Beaumont, Orange and Port Arthur]. During the Christmas break, they read all their Christmas cards and letters, had a wonderful Christmas dinner, and a 'Twelfth Night' party at St. Stephen's Episcopal. That week, they bought curtains for their new house, and shrubs and flowers to dress up their yard.

The Spring semester was taken up with recitals, classes, and preparing for the Choir tour, which took them to Northwest Louisiana State, East Texas State, and some Methodist churches in Louisiana and northeast Texas. Weekends were taken up with Lamar football games, more exploring of the Golden Triangle, St. Mark's young-adults get-togethers, and more parties. Frank was losing a grip on his spiritual life. Desperate to turn the choral program around, he was going into a depression. Margo tried to talk to him about it, but he became more detached. He made friends with as many choral directors as possible, and he volunteered to conduct clinics in area schools. It seemed to Margo as though 'school music people' partied even more than church music people. Frank was always gone. He went to Orange, Vidor, Liberty, Lake Livingston, Galveston, and Houston, to volunteer as an adjudicator, clinician, and every school music program. He wanted to recruit good music students to Lamar, but most were already committed to other schools with well-known choral programs. The band program at Lamar far exceeded the choral, and received the lion's share of the music department budget already, but Frank wanted to recruit quality choral-vocal students, and so he went to Dr. Parks to talk about scholarships...but with no response.

The children had made friends quickly in Amelia where they lived, and they spent most of their time at friends' houses, school and church functions, and playing in the neighborhood. A Russian couple came to Lamar and both of them taught violin. Frank got to know Eduard Schmieder, since their offices were next to each other. His wife Elena was suggested as a violin teacher for Shelley, so Frank talked to Margo about starting lessons with her. Shelley had been part of the Susuki program in Odessa; she loved it, and had done very well. to put it mildly, Elena was 'old school.' [After the first three lesson, Shelley came home crying. Elena had 'hit her with the bow,' she said, 'whenever she didn't hold the bow right, stand straight, or hold the violin 'correctly' Frank talked to Elena about this, but she denied it. By the fifth lesson, Shelley refused to go to her lesson. Under threat of a spanking, Frank managed to get her to the lesson, but she came out crying and refused to take any more lessons. Frank knew Shelley loved music...and the Suzuki program had been such a great success. When she got in the car, Frank held her tight as she cried, then they drove home in silence. Margo was livid and wanted to confront Elena, but Frank said it wouldn't accomplish anything. Disappointed, and believing Shelley could have gone on to be a great violinist, they decided to wait and see if she might take it up again; she never did, and to this day, she counts it as one of the most painful memories of her life; but she went on to be a superb musician and teacher of music, particularly to elementary school students]. Steve and Robbie, on the other hand, enjoyed collecting crawfish, and after numerous storms, flooding their back yard with water from the many rice fields in the area, they collected piles of them! Margo had to boil them up, and their 'Cajun' neighbors taught them to eat these little delicacies...head and all.

Frank had met Clay Reynolds, Director of Theater at Lamar, at a St. Mark's young adults party; Clay wanted to know more about theater that Frank had done at Permian Playhouse, Theater Midland, and the Globe Theater...in Midland and Odessa. Between snacks and drinks, they talked about all the musicals, Shakespeare, and 'Amahl' productions Frank had done. Clay had done several plays, both at Lamar, and at the Beaumont Little Theater. He said he knew they needed a Director of Music at BLT and he said he would talk to them about the possibility of Frank applying for the position. He also said he was planning on doing the 'rest of the *Texas Trilogy*'. They had already done the first of them the previous year—'The Oldest Living Graduate,' (a role Henry Fonda had made famous). He was now casting for 'The Last Meeting of the Knights of the White Magnolia,' and hoped to do the third, 'Lu Ann Hampton Laverty Oberlander,' the following year. He asked Frank if he was interested in a role in the second. Frank was not familiar with it, so he asked if it was a musical. Clay laughed and said, "no, but I guess you could sing it if you wanted to." Margo was close by…she said she had done *enough* theater and didn't want to have anything to do with it. Frank showed up for auditions though, and read the part of Rufe Phelps. There was only one other person who read the part, but Clay cast Frank as Rufe, and another person, who became a friend of Frank's during the rehearsals and run, Eldon Richards, was cast as Ramsey. Even though Rufe was a fifty-something guy, Frank ended up playing him as a seventy-something old person. Ironically, in Bend, Frank had played a seventeen-year-old character when he was almost thirty, and now he was playing a fifty-something character, but more like a seventy-something character…when he was only in his late thirties. He did his own makeup and sprayed his hair white. Instead of chewing tobacco, Frank managed to make a wad of bubble gum fill his cheek like a 'chaw.' The run went very well and Paula Bothe, the Little Theater Director, asked her board to consider the application of Frank for Director of Music for the Little Theater. He was accepted and did many shows there, including 'My Fair Lady,' 'Annie,' several patrons specials, and others. He mostly conducted the pit orchestra, and sang lead parts in musicals, but he also helped build sets, did makeup, and served on the board, but he also played non-musical parts as well. He was best known for his rendition of 'You are Love' (Showboat) for the 'Patrons' Special' each year for three to four years in a row. It was a time-consuming role, but he never let it take away from his primary employment of Lamar Director of Choral Activities. Margo changed her mind, and played the piano for many shows in addition to her accompanist position at Lamar.

They took a number of trips to Atlanta to see Frank's sister Margi, her husband Alan, and her kids. They had adopted Sean, a Vietnamese boy from Florida, Jamie, a half-Chinese-half Bunung tribal girl from Taiwan, and Jason, a son they birthed. They had great fun spending Thanksgiving, either in Houston, or in Atlanta. One year they met on the lower Alabama coast near Florida. They stayed in a hotel on the beach, and visited all day in the lobby that looked out of huge windows onto the beach where they could watch the children. Sean was close in age to Steve and Robbie, and Jamie had fun with her older 'sister-cousin' Shelley. It was a great hit, and on the way back to Mobile, they toured the battleship, the USS Alabama, before heading back to Atlanta and Houston, respectively. Of course, there were the annual trips to the Pacific Northwest, always a highlight of the year.

As Frank's depression over the dead-end choral situation at Lamar deepened, the influence of the St. Martin's Choir, and Little Theater group as partying escapes heightened. Both he and Margo were not being spiritually fed. They had no real Bible study or worship opportunities, either at Westminster or at St. Mark's. They were growing further and further apart in their relationship. The children were not making healthy friendships, and the neighborhood children were also getting them in trouble. Frank had taken the responsibility of coaching the St. Stephen's Episcopal Church-All Saints School Soccer Team. He had taken the certification courses, but with the cut-throat competition in the league, other coaches looked for ways they could undermine him and his team, The Saints. Frank's team was the only one to ever beat the Rogues, the previous year's championship team. J.J. LeVoy, their coach, swore he would get even, and got the board to require new certifications; he told the other coaches to sign up for them, but 'somehow omitted' notifications to Frank. The Saints showed up for their game with the Rogues, and J.J. walked over to Frank to inform him he 'would not be allowed to coach his team.' Maree Calcote, the wife of The Rev. Dean Calcote, Rector of St. Stephen's Church, and Headmaster of All Saints School, knew immediately what J.J. was up to. She 'hit the ceiling' and had a few choice remarks about J.J. She had dealt with him before, and knew what 'a snake he was.' She called one of the parents at All Saints, Sheila Felder, over to where they were discussing the matter. The Game was to start in five minutes, and J.J. had already informed the referees that the Saints would have to 'forfeit,' without a coach. Sheila had taken all the courses, including the new one, because she had wanted to start another team at All Saints school, but did not know that J.J. had failed to notify Frank. Maree registered Sheila at the table as the 'coach' (for that one game) and Frank as the 'assistant coach,' whereby he could *actually coach* the team as 'assistant' even though Sheila was registered as 'coach.' The ref called for the game to start, and Maree saw J.J. throw down his hat on the ground. A sly grin came across Maree's face knowing she had gotten the last laugh. Even though the Saints lost that game, everyone remembered how Maree Calcote and Frank Varro had gotten the best of the 'cheating, conniving, bad-ass J.J. LeVoy.' Now the irony of the whole thing: Frank had noticed Shelley hanging-out at the soccer games with another girl…on the other side of the field. He didn't think anything of it…until she introduced her to him. She said, "Dad, this is Jennifer LeVoy…my best friend; her dad is the coach of the Rogues." Frank felt himself jumping out of his own skin, but he managed to calm himself, and say, "how nice to meet you, I know your dad very well." Shelley rolled her eyes. She wasn't stupid… she knew some of what was going on. Frank got certified and coached the Saints for the rest of the season. The next year, however, he became so involved with his duties at Lamar, Westminster, and Little Theater, he turned the coaching of the Saints over to Sheila Felder. They went on to beat the Rogues and won the championship. Sheila invited Frank to the area Soccer League banquet to share in the victory. The Rogues came in second, but J.J. 'skipped' the banquet…they said he didn't want to face Sheila and Frank; but Maree was there, she walked around with her head held high…and a smile on her face.

The next Christmas, Frank organized the first 'Madrigal Dinner' Beaumont had ever seen. He decided his Chamber Choir would present it at the Gray Center on the Lamar campus, and it was surprisingly well attended. Many from the Golden Triangle heard about it and were curious as to what it was all about. The choir had a great time dressing in period Renaissance costumes, singing Christmas choral works, serving the dinner, and acting out their parts, with the help of Dr. Truncale, whose many experienced opera workshops students took the lead. The choir was also improving. Frank had attended all TMEA (Texas Music Educators), TCDA (Texas Choral Directors), and ACDA

(American Choral Directors) conventions, and took in all the sight-reading workshops and concerts he could. He was determined to raise the standard for the Lamar choral program. He brought home the John Rutter 'Gloria,' which many college choirs were performing; he decided he would program it for the spring concert. The choir worked hard, and he spent a good amount of time in sections. While his section leaders were working with the sections of the choir, he arranged to have Raul Ornelas, the resident trumpet faculty leader get together an ensemble of brass which the Rutter 'Gloria' required. It was not easy, but Raul promised they would have the three-movement ready by the performance in May. By the dress rehearsal, the choir amazed Frank with their hard work. They had come a long way in two years. Frank had reminded Raul of the dress rehearsal, but only five of the eight brass (four trumpets, three trombones, tuba), and percussion players showed up. Raul said they "would all be there for the performance" despite Frank's protest that the choir, and he, still needed to "rehearse it together!" Word had gotten around...the Lamar choir was now venturing into 'totally unexplored territory!' Area high school choral directors were there: David Llewellyn, Twyla Nau, Julie McClellen, and Kathy Hackett were there...and the Lamar faculty was there. The first half of the concert came off very well. As soon as Frank started the Rutter, however, he sensed this was not going to be good. Not only were the brass unprepared, they were very exposed in their 'unpreparedness.' By the second movement, it was falling apart. Instead of ending the piece then and there, Frank went on and tried to pull it together. Except for a great ending, it was embarrassing. Some tried to applaud 'the effort,' but the final product was not good, and Frank felt humiliated. David, and his fellow choral conductors came up to console Frank, and openly criticized the brass, while complimenting Frank and the choir. Dr. Parks simply dismissed it, and said it was a mistake to program it. Raul and the brass left without taking any of the responsibility for the 'trainwreck.' Jerry and Mary complimented Frank for even trying to bring real college choral music to Lamar, but Frank and Margo went home dejected .... and completely humiliated. Raul Ornelas, at Dr. Park's insistence at least, had apologized for his lack of concern and preparation. Needless to say, the choir tour that Frank had planned did not include the Rutter. They left the next week for the

Dallas and Houston areas. Frank felt discouraged and the concerts were lackluster. Frank went into a depression. Jerry and Mary invited them over for 'beer and barbeque,' when they got back. Jerry and Frank started throwing the 'Frisbee' to see how many times they could throw it without dropping it. Margo and Mary stayed in the house to visit; they heard Jerry and Frank yelling, so they came out to see what was going on, and 'shush' them from yelling so loud they might wake the neighbors. Mary, telling their friends later said, "the more Jerry and Frank drank, the longer they kept the 'Frisbee' going, (ha!)" but they lost count something over a hundred times...so they finally called it a night. Frank's dad came that spring for a visit, similar to his mother coming by herself to visit in Odessa a couple years before. He 'couldn't stay but a couple days,' but long enough to figure out things were terribly wrong...especially the rumors of Frank's depression, drinking, and 'wandering'. He had made some calls while he was there and at dinner that night, he said he had arranged an interview...at Northwest Nazarene College in Idaho...in the Music Department...for Frank. There was a long silence. Frank wouldn't say anything. Margo excused herself and took the children into their bedroom. Frank had always had a hard time talking openly with his dad. He told Michael that he had to see this thing through, he appreciated his concern and 'encouragement' but Frank was really angry, and didn't want to say much...for fear he would explode, even though he knew almost anything would be better than the situation he found himself in. The next day they toured Lamar, and to make matters worse, Frank introduced Michael to Dr. Parks and other faculty, including Jerry. George asked if Michael could talk to him in his office. Jerry took Frank outside and said for him to *stop this immediately*. Frank knocked on the door, and stuck his head in saying, "Sorry to break up this nice visit, but I promised Jerry we would have lunch with him," and whisked his dad out of the office and they went to lunch. At lunch, Jerry blurted out...in front of Michael...that he 'wouldn't blame Frank if he took the NNC job, but would it really be what he wanted?' Michael was polite, but continued to push for the idea of a good 'Christian school' and Jerry quickly finished his lunch and excused himself...he had 'lessons to teach, so nice to meet you,' etc., and left. On the way home, Margo, who was just as miserable with Beaumont as Frank, but not liking this 'control' element from her father-in-law at all; she looked straight at Frank, and said bluntly that *they would decide… together…*what was best for the family.' Michael didn't say much after that, and the next day they put him on the plane to Dallas, where he would eventually connect to other places on his 'deputation trip,' before returning to Taiwan. Frank did end up applying for three other choral positions that spring, though—one on the west coast, the other two in Texas—but none of them were actually acceptable to Frank. Bob Culbertson, a friend of Frank's on the band faculty, had decided to leave Lamar, as well as Wayne Dyess, and some others, but eventually they changed their minds and stayed. A couple weeks later, Bob was having lunch one day at the faculty dining room with Frank, and he told him about a job he had applied for…but it was not a music job. Frank said, "I'm listening," and Bob told him all about his visit with Bob Harris and Gene Koch at Metropolitan Life. "Insurance?" Frank said, "I can't imagine you doing anything but music, Bob." Bob told Frank he ought to look into it anyway. He lowered his voice and said… confidentially, Lamar was becoming a 'dead-end for an increasingly larger numbers of music and non-music faculty alike, who were either: not-yet-tenured or too far from retirement, to stay; and the salaries were near the bottom of college music people in the state.' Frank agreed, acknowledging that Jerry and several other faculty members had their resumes out there all over the country. His own chances of tenure were probably next to nil, given his short stay at the last *three* college music positions. So much for trying to 'climb the ladder' by trying to 'move up quickly.' Frank admitted to Bob that he had already looked into three other jobs—two in Texas, and one in the Pacific Northwest. They ended their lunch. Bob said, "if it were me, I'd at least give Gene Koch at Metropolitan a call." Bob paid for the lunch," save your money, I got this one," he said. Frank laughed and thanked him for the lunch. He said he would think about it. That afternoon, Frank told Margo about the lunch with Bob. To his surprise, Margo said, "Do it Frank! If what Bob says they are reporting—that you'd double your income in even the first year…do it!" Margo had taken a new job in Port Arthur with the Vietnamese Resettlement Program as an ESL teacher, and was also working for Rabbi Levi Rutman at Temple Emmanuel until his sudden death. She said she was as miserable as he was. They could keep the church job at Westminster…along with his work at the Beaumont Little Theater, and his newly formed Southeast Texas Chorale she said… she thought they should pray about it. Frank hesitated, his spiritual life was less than lukewarm, and his disillusionment, and anger at his hard work had not been recognized; this had led to spending too much time with the wrong crowd, more partying and drinking…he was less than close to God, unlike previously. Nevertheless, he awkwardly took her hands and mumbled something like, "we want to find…we've kind of lost our way…help us do what you want … Amen!" He started to break down, but brushed it aside. Margo looked strangely at him. This was not the man she had married. Frank suddenly said, "here's what we'll do." He told her he had already applied for choral jobs at UT-Austin, and TUI in Corpus Christi…and one in Oregon. If none of those three positions he had applied for panned out he'd check out Metropolitan Life.

Frank prepared the choir for graduation. He found himself just going through the motions at Lamar, so he poured himself into the Westminster job, Little Theater, and called each of the choral jobs weekly to check on his application. In the next three weeks, he found out that he was still in the running for two of the three jobs, but not among the top two finalists and interviews. It was mainly because of his lack of Music Education courses at the graduate level…the jobs were two-thirds music education, and one-third choral, conducting one performance ensemble in each position. Rod Eichenberger, and others, had gone to bat for him, including the head of choral music at one, but the requirements were pretty much set. He didn't make the cut on the third position because it was being filled internally. It seemed like a sign. Frank was ready to leave. And, of course, he was not getting tenure…which he already knew since he had 'moved up too quickly,' trying to advance himself. He had also been vocal about his displeasure with his private voice caseload of mediocre students, while other voice instructors, who had tenure, were advancing their students. Dr. Carlucci and Dr. Truncale asked a few students why they had not changed private voice teachers, if they were getting "better voice instruction in choir than in private study." Frank was a NATS (National Association of Teachers of Singing) member and had sponsored a couple of singers for competition. This did not go over well with their private voice teachers…not only because the private teachers were not NATS members and could not sponsor them, but Frank was willing to do so, even at the risk of 'pissing them off badly,' as Jerry put it. He knew they had complained, and he decided the 'dead-end' was fast approaching. He thought about the Northwest Nazarene Choral position his dad had suggested, but decided that taking that route still was not what he wanted…and besides, it had been filled. The St. Andrew's Presbyterian job had also been filled…and David and Linda McKechnie were leaving; they had accepted a great position: senior pastor at Grace Presbyterian in Houston. Frank told Margo that night that he didn't get any of the three positions he applied for, St. Andrew's was out, and NNC was filled. She didn't cry; the next day, Frank handed George Parks his letter: short and sweet: "thank you for the opportunity…I resign my position, effective with graduation, blah, blah, etc."

Family visits Grandparents

Frank leads Vera Voce Singers

New MetLife Manager

Lou/Isabella Varro+Michael/Beth Varro & Frank Varro families

Frank leads music at CFO meeting

'I Still Do' Conference

*It's not what one **does**, that is wrong…*
*but rather what is **not learned** from it*

Chapter Twenty-Two

The Bottom... but 'Guess Who' Was There?

Finally fulfilling the call to 'Ordained Ministry'

HUGE RELIEF CAME OVER HIM. HE HAD LUNCH WITH JERRY AND A GROUP of his closest students, who all congratulated him. That same afternoon, he went straight to Metropolitan Life...he wanted to make an appointment with Gene Koch, and Bob Harris...but both said they would see him immediately...Bob Culbertson had said that, even though he couldn't accept their offer, Bob thought 'Frank Varro would be giving them a call.' By the end of a three-hour interview, Frank had passed their initial exam, filled out papers, and made arrangements to take the state insurance exams. They said they had heard of him, through Little Theater and St. Mark's, and thought he would do very well. Frank got home early, fixed a nice dinner, and waited for Margo and the kids to come home. When they walked in, he jumped out at them and tickled everyone, told them the whole story, and everyone hugged him. This time, Frank prayed sincerely…God was with them; he would take care of them.

Margo kept her job as ESL Teacher with the Vietnamese Project, and also as Westminster organist. She even took on a few piano students… ones that Jerry had referred to her; it was temporary…just to help out, until Frank could get up and running with MetLife. Instead of cutting back on music, Frank actually expanded his work in music… he formed a chamber group at Westminster Presbyterian; he increased the size of the Southeast Texas Chorale that he had founded…from twelve to twenty-four, adding singers through his contacts with Little Theatre, and former students at Lamar. Soon churches and civic clubs were inviting them to sing almost every week. He was invited to be on the faculty at the Beaumont School of Music, where he taught private voice lessons, small ensembles, and even a few brass and woodwind students. They asked him to be director, but he declined, agreeing only to help out as interim director until a permanent director could be found. He did, however, agree to serve on the board. His days were spent in training with Metropolitan, and his evenings with music and theater. He made sure he took time with Margo…to attend the kids' concerts, sports events, and school programs. Margo made new friends with the Vietnamese program, the children also made new friends, went to birthday parties, programs, school events, and slumber parties. Everyone seemed to be busy, too busy in their own world; sure, the whole family went to church…twice every Sunday, both Westminster and St. Mark's, but…the partying continued, especially with the young-adult groups, and the spiritual life just continued to go down. Frank made new friends at MetLife too, especially Tony Abbo, Vic Campbell, and Shiv Bagri…the three 'big hitters,' and all of them were very successful, financially and socially. They loved the fresh approach that Frank brought to the office. Tony even wanted Frank to drive him, in his car, into Houston to visit his Iraqi friends ('what am I now, your chauffeur?' Frank laughed). He took Frank to his Group I License and Property-Casualty exams; after each, they would dine on Arab food and drink, and then Tony would sleep while Frank drove him back to Beaumont. Bob Harris was the Beaumont district manager and Gene Koch was Frank's branch manager ...they both had promised Frank a manager's position...if he made Leader's Conference in his first two years. Frank and Margo wanted to get out of Beaumont in the worst way, it was a '*peyton-place*,' and it was sucking them down into a pit. Met had made Frank a promise: he would double his income in his first year, just like they said; so, make 'Leaders Conference' twice, and then...'*get the hell out of Dodge*'...so to speak. But more theater meant more cast parties, late nights, and babysitters for the children–church parties at Sartin's in Port Arthur (the 'best seafood place on earth'), beach parties, and overnight on Bolivar Peninsula. Ironically, the better Frank did in his new job–the wilder the life-style became. Frank was becoming distant from the family, sometimes sleeping over at friends' houses after theater parties...rather than trying to drive home. By spring, the whole theater scene, late nights at Beaumont School of Music...and appointments every night, it seemed–trying to sell 'everyone and his brother insurance'...was taking its toll. Frank told Margo after a big argument, he thought it might be better if he just lived somewhere else ...for a while. Margo, and the kids, were dismayed; they failed to understand. This wasn't the man she had married. Margo and Mary, Jerry's wife, started going to a women's Bible study, and she tried getting Frank to go with her; and to see a counselor... but he was not himself. He focused on the 'quick sale'–auto and homeowners' insurance; every friend, their families, contacts, business associates; he wanted ten referrals for each sale–and health and life insurance policies where he could. MetLife, the parent company, had given the newly-formed Met Property and Casualty millions of dollars (the plan was to compete with State Farm, Farmers, and Allstate; they hired managers away from 'the big three,' promising mega salaries and benefits; but in a few years, they had blown through millions of dollars, and in the end, many just went back to their former carriers. Frank was going to strike while the iron was hot; he was 'going to set the world on fire,' and leave this *little town* behind! Get out of Beaumont...like he had promised Margo. Tony, Vic, and Shiv were only too happy to help. He made Leader's Conference...and sure enough... he doubled his salary in the first year! He asked Margo if she wanted to go with him on the 'Leaders Conference' trip to Colorado that he had earned. 'She wasn't sure,' she said, and wanted to make some sarcastic remark, like "why don't just take one of your girlfriends," (but she didn't). She went, hoping they could get back together...things were strained between them; so, she was surprised when they had a really great time, and he almost seemed like his 'old self'...at least until they got back. He was often gone to Tulsa–to the MetLife 'Territory Office' for training...and more all-night wild partying. By his second year, Frank was deep into a depression; he would come home for a week or so, then a new show at the 'Little Theater,' or insurance trips, would take him back out again. They did have a few good times though; he took her dancing sometimes. They learned to line dance...the 'cotton-eyed Joe, and other stuff, and several times they went dancing with friends at their favorite place: the Texas Country Corral, just north of Beaumont. Without good supervision, the kids started getting in trouble. [Every time Shelley would hang-out with her next-door neighbor friend, Desiree, or Jennifer LeVoy, she would get in trouble; once she stayed overnight without Desiree's dad's permission (Shelley didn't know Desiree hadn't gotten her dad's approval); she ended up hiding under the bed in the morning till Desiree's dad left for work (it was the last time Shelley ever trusted her). Then Shelley was also bused across town, in accordance with Judge Parker's final ruling [When she drew 'the yellow ping-pong ball...instead of the white one,' she was devastated–she would be bused across town...she came home and threw herself on the bed sobbing... until she found out most of her close friends would *also* be bused–they could all go to Odom Middle School together! It turned out to be a great experience for her though, in the end]. But she got in trouble again...when she and Jennifer started hanging out with an '*underage*' guy Joey, the preacher's kid from Chapel in the Pines...who got drunk– with no license, and drove them into the ditch...("what do you mean you never drank alcohol before"... when Jennifer told Shelley to call her dad 'to drive them home, Joey threw up all over the back seat, and then on Frank, while he was trying to get out of the car...you know, things like that). Frank later looked back on that...so ashamed for not being a better example...like he should have been...too busy trying to please the world...going his own way. Steve and Rob often left the neighborhood without permission; they got in trouble, with friends that were not a good influence on them. Margo pleaded with Frank to come home...please come help her with the children, and accept the father-role he had been ignoring.

After the Colorado trip, Frank began pouring himself into the process of making Leader's Conference again. Met needed Branch Managers, and they had promised him management; it was all he could think about. More late-night rehearsals, more trips with Tony into Houston. Margo started hanging out with people from the Vietnamese Project, and she told them *she would no longer play piano for any shows at the Little Theatre.* The job at Westminster was falling apart; people had been gossiping about Frank and Lois, one of the choir and bells members...ever since Lois invited Margo and Frank for an overnight trip to Bolivar peninsula, as guests of the Breitenberg's...Lois's in-laws. Then out of the blue, Daniel, a former student of Frank's at Lamar, called and asked him if he would take the cantor-choir director position at St. Anne's Catholic; and Daniel also wanted Margo to take the organist position there. Frank laughed, 'let me see if I've got this straight:' Daniel, a Baptist, had served four years at a Catholic church, and now he was asking his former choir director-professor, Frank, a lapsed Nazarene preacher's-kid-turned-Episcopalian, serving in a Presbyterian church music position, to take his Catholic music job? They both laughed. 'Yes,' he said, that was exactly what he had recommended. Frank thought, "what good timing...he could escape the scandal he was facing at Westminster; and Margo wanted out of the Westminster job for the same reason...and it might get them back together. So, they interviewed for the job, and were quickly offered the cantor-choir director-organist positions. Phin Washer had left for a position in Houston, and Westminster had a new pastor, Rev. Denny Watson; Frank and Margo liked him very much; he had come over to their house with some friends, before Frank moved out, to play cards, dinner, and to meet parishioners. When he found out they had lived, and taught music in Taiwan, he suggested a Chinese feast at the church! Margo and Frank, and four other couples (including Lois and her husband, Dale), helped Frank and Margo cook for some hundred people, and it was a great success! This was all before the 'tongues started wagging.' He was very disappointed when Frank and Margo turned in their resignations. Pastor Denny tried to persuade them to reconsider; he'd heard the rumors too, and reluctantly accepted their resignations, on 'one condition,' he said (Margo looked away; Frank had heard rumors about her too, but refused to accept them). Denny took both their hands in his: "I pray to God that you both return to each other, renew your commitment, and use this to strengthen what the 'Evil-One' has dumped on you...to tear you apart." Then he hugged both of them, and prayed a blessing over them...on their future ministry at St. Anne's. The next week, they met the choir at St. Anne's, the Rector, Father Nicholas; Father Jude, and some of the St. Anne School faculty. Denny called and said that the young couple, Dale and Lois Breitenberg, and his parents, longtime members of Westminster, had shown up at the church office demanding that Rev. Watson call Frank in for a 'discussion' about his relationship with Lois. Denny had told them that he had no jurisdiction over them since Frank and Margo had already resigned. He suggested that they drop it, and since it was none of their business, they should let it go. Dale's mother told Denny that Lois and Frank had been 'carrying on' since they stayed at their beach house on Bolivar, but Denny wouldn't budge, he said that was the end of it...and they left (but Lois never hit on Frank again). The new job entailed Wednesday morning chapel for the school, a Thursday night choir rehearsal, and two Masses on Sunday (they were using the new 'Glory And Praise' songbook, and most of the songs were from the 'Second Vatican' reform of Pope John XXIII. John Michael Talbot, John Foley, Bob Dufford, and many other 'contemporary' songs...which actually sounded more Protestant than anything). Frank and Margo thought they 'could really get into this'—anthems that were classical choral works, and worship songs that were familiar, because of their evangelical backgrounds. Then things got a little strange. The Rector, Father Nicholas, called Margo and Frank in...to tell them that Father Jude, the young priest in charge of the chapel program and school chaplain, was suddenly being moved to Orange (they found out later Father Jude was among many Catholic priests that had been accused of molesting young boys). Father Nicholas took over the chapel and school programs, while continuing supervision of the Sunday worship and rehearsal ministry; the choir grew…people 'loved the Varro's.'

The Beaumont School of Music asked Frank to stay on as 'interim director'…he had added more voice students and BSM was making a profit. Little Theater had brought in a guest director to do 'Lil' Abner,' and Frank conducted the pit orchestra, and sang and danced in some scenes. During that difficult time, Little Theater Director, Paula, and Frank became good friends…she knew he was struggling, but she encouraged him and promoted him every chance she got. She informed him that Beaumont Opera Society was bringing in a guest director, and principals, for 'I Pagliacci,' but *secondaries* would be auditioned…and she had recommended Frank. He was excited about this opportunity, and allowed Paula to submit his name. That afternoon, Frank met Jerry Martin, associate director of Houston Opera, who had come with Martin Gilder, was to sing the part of Canio (Pagliaccio), Reece Donnelly, the part of Nedda (Columbina), and Frank found out he was to audition for the part of Harlequin (Arlecchino); two other tenors, and three baritones were there to audition for the other parts. It helped that Paula, now designated the 'tech' director, was promoting Frank for the role, but Frank sang well, even though he did not know the main arias yet. Paula called him the next day to tell him he'd gotten the part. It was Frank's first real opera part; he had only starred in operettas…and sung in the chorus. They began production right away. Frank had never been grilled like he was in this opera. Martin chewed him out so ruthlessly…for not being 'off book,' that Frank thought he was going to have to quit. Paula talked him out of it, and told him he had to work harder–this was not just a Little Theater 'show,' this was a *serious opera*. Frank spent hours on it by himself, and then with Reese in their scene. Many of Frank's former Lamar students were in the chorus; (in fact, all but a handful of other singers already were). One of the chorus members, Skyler Manning, who had been a dance partner with Frank in 'Lil' Abner,' asked him if he was accepting new voice students as Beaumont School of Music. He said yes, and they set up a time for her private voice lesson. The opera was a great hit, and the Beaumont Enterprise gave it a good review. Paula suggested to them that they do a feature article on Frank…since it was a 'local boy *done good'* situation, the paper came out the next week, and it seemed like they were telling his whole life's story…they called it: *All for the love of a song.* Skyler came to her first two lessons at the BSM studio. That's when it all started: she began making excuses for him to come over to her house… her son was: "sick, and I couldn't get a babysitter, but I didn't want to miss my lesson," to whatever–he fell for it. Then one day, her husband came home…right in the middle of her lesson; the lesson ended immediately. She made excuses for the next several weeks to be out together: go dancing, drinking, etc., mostly at the Sabine, where everyone went (she wanted her friends 'to meet her new voice teacher.' She knew Frank was *having trouble* at home, and she had obviously 'set her cap for him' (ever since 'Lil' Abner). Before he knew it, she was planning to 'divorce her husband,' she 'had found an apartment' for them. Frank remembered it later…he was coming up the sidewalk to see the apartment…with her children…and something snapped in his head ['*how far down this road are you actually willing to go?'* God said to him]. He turned to Skyler, "I'm sorry, I can't do this." She burst into tears and begged him to not abandon her, blaming him for 'ruining her marriage.' He drove them back home, then went straight home. He had been living, off and on, with a friend of Tony Abbo. Tony's wife, Shirley, had become good friends with Margo, and she strongly disapproved of Tony promoting Frank's wild struggle for recognition. He fixed supper again and waited for Margo and the kids to arrive. Everyone was quiet this time, and the kids went to their rooms as soon as they saw dad. Margo looked curiously at Frank, when she walked in the door. He had been crying, and was sitting on the old ugly orange couch with a pillow stuffed in it…to block the spring that had come up through the cushions. He quickly wiped his eyes and told her he had made supper, and "tomorrow we are going to go buy a new living room suite." She asked 'what that meant.' He smiled and said he was 'coming back home,' he was 'on-time' to make the Leaders Conference [on-time meant: the monthly sales quota indicated the agent would make the goal]; he'd made enough to buy the furniture he'd promised. Margo made sure the children were in their rooms before she asked: *"what about Skyler?"* Shirley must have been keeping her up to date, Frank thought. He pretended like nothing was going on, so she told him not to come home again…if he wasn't going to make better choices in their lives. Frank looked sheepishly at her and, said, "a *LOT* of things are going to be different." She told him she'd have to see it. They ate… after she called the kids to supper, and everyone hugged dad. She said, "Daddy says we are going to buy the new furniture we talked about." They squealed with delight, and they later piled in his car and went to Dairy Queen. The next day Frank called Skyler to tell her 'he needed to see her.' She didn't want to talk to him right then, but agreed to meet him that night. He told Margo he had to go *see* Skyler…not to be with her. Margo looked away, she said she didn't believe him. Frank spent the next two hours at the park…where he talked to Skyler in her car. She tried everything…sweet talk, pleading, then screaming at him, blaming, threatening. Frank listened, he apologized, waiting for her to finish crying hysterically. Finally, he told her he would always remember her, and her good work in the theater, her voice, and friendship. He had told her earlier on the phone that he and Margo were going to buy the living room suite…now she threw that in his face, saying as soon as he told her that, she *knew* he was going back to his wife. He ended it with a friendly hug, got out of the car…while she was still pleading and crying…and went back home. The next day, they bought the beautiful new furniture set. They rented a small U-Haul rather than pay for the delivery. They set it up…it was beautiful: dark blue with a flowered pattern. The kids wanted to tell all the neighbors to come see it, Margo said she thought that might be 'over doing it.' The next day was Sunday and they were all together at St. Mark's. They had been dropping the kids off there on their way to St. Anne's, but this Sunday they all went to the early service, and then left the children there for Sunday School, while they went to St. Anne's for a rehearsal and the Mass. Frank had chosen the song before the homily, 'Be Not Afraid,' not realizing how healing that song would be for him that week. Margo smiled at him, and a tear rolled down her cheek as they sang it together. It was the first time she had smiled in months [even though things had to get much worse in the next few years, there was a healing that came that week— they believed somehow God would find a way through this].

Walt Ridlon, the new MetLife Region manager, called a special meeting to get new agents acquainted with area managers; it was a very fancy luncheon in Houston at the Wyndam Hotel. MetLife had been busy recruiting Asians all over the country, and Frank had seen several names on the 'big hitters' weekly bulletin, that he knew were Chinese. Even more interesting was the fact that Walt had placed Frank at a table with several other Asians: George Gee, Joe Chen, Abe Chua, and Peter Wu, along with Tai Chiang, a newly-named Korean branch manager–somebody had been 'reading Frank's bio' evidently. He hadn't spoken Chinese in many years now, but when they sat down, Frank just opened his mouth... and out came Chinese! He was amazed; they were even *more* amazed. [In the next couple years, every single Chinese agent at Frank's table that day was named branch managers!]. After lunch, Walt Ridlon, whom Frank had met in Tulsa several times at the MetLife Marketing Office, called out to Frank, "I'm watching you! This is August; if you are still 'on-time' by Christmas, we have a 'special place' for you, so keep it up, man!" Frank's heart skipped a beat. He kept singing, "Well, we're movin' on up...," (like they sang from Ohio to Odessa). He got back to Beaumont, burst into the house, just as Margo and the kids arrived after school: "What's going on, dad...why are you so happy" they said." Margo replied, "I bet daddy is going to be a *new manager* soon." Inspired, Frank had his best three months. Tony, Vic, and Shiv heard about what Walt had said, and each of them 'just happened' to line up some cases that they gave to Frank as referrals. It was the Monday after Thanksgiving, and Frank was doing his paperwork at the kitchen table and the phone rang. It was Walt. "Frank, I just looked at the 'Region Weekly Report;' it says 'Frank Varro–Big Hitter' for the third week in a row." Long pause (Frank held his breath), Walt went on to say that this meant he was 'on-time' for Leader's Conference... he said *he was promoting him to Marketing Specialist*, a 'manager's position' in Houston, while waiting for a branch to come open; he would be salaried as a new manager, expenses paid, and he would come home to Beaumont on week-ends. Walt asked Frank if he would accept this appointment...without hesitation, Frank said **'Yes!'** 'When would he start, and how would he go about it?' Walt went on to tell him he would be working out of the 'Long Branch' in Pasadena, and Jeff Hankla, the former manager who was opening a *new* branch in northwest Houston, would be in charge of his orientation. Walt said he would follow up on this telephone conversation with a letter, outlining the position and how to go about starting; for now, he was just asking if Frank would show up the following Monday. Did Frank know the address and directions to the Long Branch? He gave him the phone number, and asked him to call Jeff, and his administrator, Irene Adame. Frank asked...was it official? Could he announce it? Walt laughed, 'absolutely.' Frank thanked him and they ended the call. Frank was 'over the moon,' and called Margo at the Vietnamese Project immediately; then he called Bob Harris and Gene Koch; they already knew of course, and congratulated him. He drove over to the branch office, and everyone showered him with praise, especially the three he called his 'branch trio,'– Shiv, Vic, and Tony. That evening, Frank took the whole family out to the Carlos' restaurant to celebrate; it was like old times. The following Monday, Frank drove to Pasadena to the Long Branch MetLife office. Irene Adame met Frank and told him Jeff had already left for the new branch, but had left instructions with Irene for his orientation. Frank greeted the agents, some of whom he had already met at the district marketing meetings: Ron Biddle, Paula Larson, and some others. Irene showed Frank the branch manager's office, where he'd be 'hanging out.' [everyone knew it would only be weeks before the office would actually be his]. She said they should go to lunch now at the Hilton near Hobby Airport, and check in, since that was where he would be staying. They had lunch while Irene told Frank all about MetLife and her time there; they checked Frank in to the Hilton, and then returned to the office. He called Margo and the kids after supper to share the good introduction he'd had to his new role as 'marketing specialist' (or 'manager-designate') at the Long Branch. Then he went with some people he had met at the Hilton restaurant to the bar; he felt he deserved to celebrate. Everyone was nice and 'helped him celebrate' his new 'marketing specialist' position. Things got hectic quickly: three and a half days in Pasadena, then on the road again, returning to Beaumont on weekends. Irene said not to worry, she would handle most of it, and that he was just in training, so 'slow down a little;' weekends were hectic too. He needed to leave between 2:00 and 3:00 Fridays, to get back to the family in Beaumont, but it seemed like he always ended up hanging out with some of the agents and managers at TGI Friday's, so he was not really getting back to Beaumont until late. The Christmas and New Year rush of activity kept him busy in Beaumont on weekends, and he dropped out of the last Little Theater show he was supposed to be music director for. Rose Newman, an older Lebanese agent in the branch, had been planning to transfer to Jeff's new branch, but after she met Frank, she said 'maybe I'll just stay in Pasadena...I *do* live here, and I wouldn't have to commute so far away.' She told Jeff and Frank: "You both look like movie stars," and after a couple of drinks at Jeff's 'going away' party, she told Frank she wanted him to be...her 'escort' to the 'Branch of the Year' gala. [Jeff and she both had been agents in Fred Feigley's Houston Branch before Jeff became a manager; then as a 'big hitter' he was promoted to manager of the Long Branch, and promoted again...as the new manager of the start-up office: 'Northwest Houston Branch.' Frank had to remain as a 'marketing specialist,' even though everyone knew when Jeff left, the new Long Branch manager would be Frank]. Houston Branch had been named 'Branch of the Year,' so everyone told Frank it was a big deal; and Irene said it would a good time to be introduced as the *'new manager-designate'* of the Long Branch. Walt Ridlon and Jeff were best friends, so when Walt was appointed as the new Houston Regional Manager, he made sure Jeff would get a new branch, and that Frank would take Jeff's place at the Long Branch. Frank called Margo and told her he would be late arriving back in Beaumont that Friday night...because he was to be introduced as a 'manager' at the 'Branch of the Year' party for Fred Feigley and his staff. Rose had brought along a bottle of chardonnay to the branch in Pasadena, where they had decided to meet, before she would drive them in her car to the Houston Branch for the party; it was a 'congratulatory gift' to Frank, she said. He thanked her, and started heading for the car; but Rose quickly took back the bottle, opened it in the kitchen, poured two glasses, and laughed, "we have plenty of time, let's see if you like my gift." They chatted about what Frank might expect as manager, and who were the 'big hitters.' Frank told her he already knew, from the Regional MetLife Weekly Report, that she and Ron Biddle were the two top agents. After Rose poured two more glasses, Frank washed his glass out in the sink and said they 'needed to get going;' he was anxious to meet all the new Regional MetLife people.' He offered to drive, but she waved him off. They talked all the way from the office to Northwest Freeway about her experiences as a leading agent, and how she had helped 'start the branch' there in Pasadena. Frank was not only concerned about her driving after finishing off her

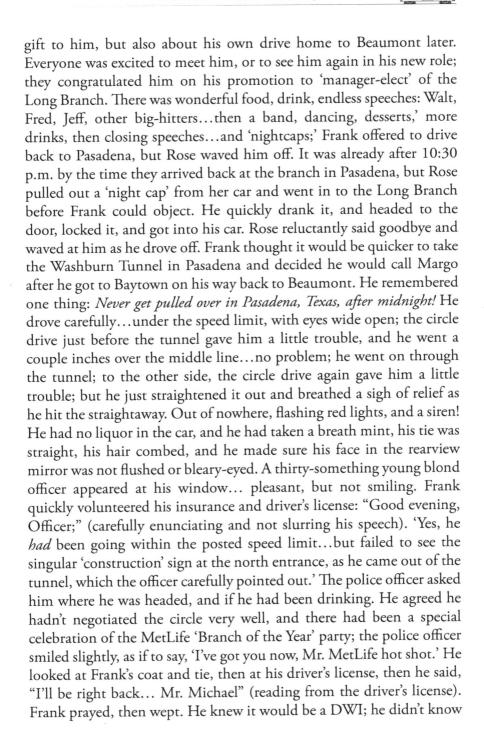

gift to him, but also about his own drive home to Beaumont later. Everyone was excited to meet him, or to see him again in his new role; they congratulated him on his promotion to 'manager-elect' of the Long Branch. There was wonderful food, drink, endless speeches: Walt, Fred, Jeff, other big-hitters…then a band, dancing, desserts,' more drinks, then closing speeches…and 'nightcaps;' Frank offered to drive back to Pasadena, but Rose waved him off. It was already after 10:30 p.m. by the time they arrived back at the branch in Pasadena, but Rose pulled out a 'night cap' from her car and went in to the Long Branch before Frank could object. He quickly drank it, and headed to the door, locked it, and got into his car. Rose reluctantly said goodbye and waved at him as he drove off. Frank thought it would be quicker to take the Washburn Tunnel in Pasadena and decided he would call Margo after he got to Baytown on his way back to Beaumont. He remembered one thing: *Never get pulled over in Pasadena, Texas, after midnight!* He drove carefully…under the speed limit, with eyes wide open; the circle drive just before the tunnel gave him a little trouble, and he went a couple inches over the middle line…no problem; he went on through the tunnel; to the other side, the circle drive again gave him a little trouble; but he just straightened it out and breathed a sigh of relief as he hit the straightaway. Out of nowhere, flashing red lights, and a siren! He had no liquor in the car, and he had taken a breath mint, his tie was straight, his hair combed, and he made sure his face in the rearview mirror was not flushed or bleary-eyed. A thirty-something young blond officer appeared at his window… pleasant, but not smiling. Frank quickly volunteered his insurance and driver's license: "Good evening, Officer;" (carefully enunciating and not slurring his speech). 'Yes, he *had* been going within the posted speed limit…but failed to see the singular 'construction' sign at the north entrance, as he came out of the tunnel, which the officer carefully pointed out.' The police officer asked him where he was headed, and if he had been drinking. He agreed he hadn't negotiated the circle very well, and there had been a special celebration of the MetLife 'Branch of the Year' party; the police officer smiled slightly, as if to say, 'I've got you now, Mr. MetLife hot shot.' He looked at Frank's coat and tie, then at his driver's license, then he said, "I'll be right back… Mr. Michael" (reading from the driver's license). Frank prayed, then wept. He knew it would be a DWI; he didn't know what he would tell Margo, the kids… the church, his friends; he cried out to God to rescue him. In his mind, this was only confirmed when the officer didn't come back for what seemed like 'an eternity;' seriously, it had to have been at least ten to fifteen minutes, even though it seemed like an hour. The officer appeared at his window. He was smiling. He handed Frank his driver's license and insurance card, and said, "I'm sure you'll need these in your work as a new manager with MetLife, we appreciate all you are doing for us." 'Wait! No sobriety test? DWI? Impounded car? What about the ticket: 'speeding, in a construction zone'? What about crossing the middle line? He walked away smiling, waving; no speeding ticket…no warning ticket–but this was Pasadena, Texas, after dark… 'white cops that throw you in jail, and throw away the key;' Frank drove off slowly, he was sobbing; what just happened, God? Why did you just do that *again*? I don't understand you…you bless me, but I don't deserve it!' Frank couldn't see the road for the tears, so he pulled over at the rest stop in Baytown and called Margo; he was 'stone-cold sober' now, but Margo thought he was long-gone, and…half asleep, she said, "I'm glad you didn't get a ticket, hurry home." He arrived about 2:30 a.m.; she rolled over and kissed him goodnight, "glad you are home, goodnight,"

They slept in. It was Saturday, but the kids got up and were playing in the back yard when Frank got up to answer the phone. It was Father Nicholas. One of the St. Anne's choir members had died right after they returned from Dallas, and would Frank and Margo do the music for the funeral?' 'Yes,' Frank said, and reminded him also that after Christmas and Epiphany, he had told him they may be moving to Houston, since he had been promoted to a MetLife management position; he would be assigned to a branch in Pasadena, probably starting in February or March. Father Nicholas said he remembered that conversation, and that the choirmaster-organist from Orange had applied for both St. Anne positions Frank and Margo had held. He said St. Anne's had really enjoyed them and would miss them; Margo had gotten up later, made coffee, washed the dishes, and started a load of laundry, while Frank was busy in the back bedroom. He called Paula to tell her that he would be resigning his position as music director of the Little Theater, effective the first week in February. She said Steve and Marie Schottmiller, associate directors, were getting a divorce, and Steve would be moving to Houston with Subaru…he would be selling cars there, and doing theater there in Houston Heights. She said Marie's cousin, George, from a theater in New Orleans, was applying for Frank's music director position. Frank had already turned the Southeast Texas Chorale director's position over to David Llewellyn. There was only one other thing he had to do: Frank had to call Jenny Ferguson, who sang in his St. Anne's choir, to not call him anymore, that he was leaving, and had never wanted any 'romantic' relationship anyway; he said he was sorry if he had led her to believe otherwise. She hung up on him, and never returned to St. Anne's, but Frank was troubled; he scratched off all of the items on his 'things-to-do' list, ate breakfast with Margo and the kids, and mowed the lawn; he wanted to work things out in his life, but many things still troubled him.

Sunday was a special time of worship for the family at St. Anne's. The kids usually just went to St. Mark's, but today they wanted to go with mom and dad to St. Anne's. They told him they wanted to 'sing in the choir' so Frank just said, "why not?" Then they went to church school at St. Anne's…they were having a special program. They all returned to eat the pot roast Margo had fixed for them at home, and Sunday naps were definitely in order, while the kids went swimming at the Landis area pool.

In the next three months, the weekly commute, the numberless marketing and managers' meetings, weekly branch meetings, orientation, and agents training…was beginning to take its toll. The next Saturday morning the phone rang, and Frank answered it. It was Wilma, so Frank offered to give the phone over to Margo. She said "No, Frank…I'm glad you answered, her father has suffered a heart attack and is not expected to live." Frank protested; he thought she should tell Margo herself, but she refused, thinking it would be "better coming from her husband;" It was a very awkward moment, and Frank was thinking she was treating her like a child, but he said he would, and then she could call her back if she wanted to. Frank took Margo to the bedroom, told her, and then they told the boys. Shelley was on a ski trip with the St. Mark's youth, so they made arrangements for Father Mike to tell her. He did, and then they met the bus when she returned. Francis died after a second attack after they got him home.

Arrangements were made, and they flew to Wenatchee for the funeral, then they went to Coldwater, Michigan, for a memorial service, graveside service, and reception. Frank sang 'We Shall Behold Him' at the funeral. Auntie Ruth met them in Coldwater and assisted with the graveside service; Margo was of course devastated, but held up well, especially seeing how greatly loved he had been. She had hoped all her life for a closer relationship with him, but they were close in their own way. Frank returned to work, but there was a big void in his life. He needed to have Margo and the kids with him in Houston. He needed to fill the musical and spiritual void in his life...and he needed to process some of his 'garbage.' The next couple weeks, he started looking for houses. Irene advised him not to locate too close to the office... 'mixing personal life with business was a bad idea,' she had said, and he agreed with her. He crossed off Pasadena, Deer Park, and LaPorte; instead, he focused on Clear Lake, Friendswood, and Pearland. Irene said she lived in the Friendswood-Pearland area, and she would be happy to ask friends of hers to keep a lookout for houses for sale. He searched about a dozen possibilities, and focused on six or so: a couple in Clear Lake, two or three in Friendswood, and one or two in Pearland. He also asked around about church music positions, as well as a job for Margo. He inquired of the local Episcopal, Catholic, and Presbyterian churches, for choir and organ positions, and found out that St. Andrew's Episcopal, a small parish in Pearland, with a priest commuting weekends from Bastrop, had no choir, and only a volunteer organist; St. Helen Catholic was a mission parish out of St. John in Alvin...they were using only volunteers as well; Pearland First Presbyterian, and other churches in the Clear Lake, Friendswood, and Pasadena areas? The same thing. But two days later, St. Pius V in Pasadena, called back to say they had music and school positions open, and wanted to interview them as soon as possible. Excitedly, they made an appointment with Father Lou for them to interview the following week. Then Frank decided to start looking for a clerical position for Margo as well. Irene, and Bill Paynter, the MetLife region office administrator, asked around, and a contact MetLife had, Charles P. Young Printers, called to say they would like her resume, and an interview with her. Before returning to Beaumont for the weekend, Frank picked three houses he wanted the family to see: one each in Clear Lake, Friendswood, and Pearland. He was excited and called Margo Thursday to tell her the good news, and that he was taking Friday off, and would be there late that evening. There was a long pause. Margo said, 'Wait! They needed to talk.' She would see him later that evening when he got back. Frank felt the blood 'just drain from his body.'

[Someone at St. Anne's had told Margo why Jenny was no longer coming to rehearsal. In the meantime, Robert Harris, son of Frank's former MetLife boss, Bob Harris, told Margo stuff she did not know about Frank... stuff about them, and the St. Mark's young adults, and some of the Little Theater parties, stories, and liaisons. That was it! Margo had had it. She believed all of it...and she didn't want to go on. Frank hung up, but he was a mess; he left the office before 5:00...no carousing with anyone, no quick visit to TGIF's, he drove straight home with his heart in his throat...on his way home, he remembered the tortured truth. Jenny, who sang alto at St. Anne's, had tried to start something...when he sold her husband auto and home owner's insurance policies; she had asked him to come back... when her husband was gone to Dallas, *to buy health and life policies as well.* Frank did, but when he found out she only wanted him to run away with her, to leave her husband who was cheating on her in Dallas... Frank offered to cancel the policies, but she kept them...until her husband left for good...for the woman in Dallas. Frank was also very naive about the St. Mark's young adult group, some were gay—but they were his friends...and the life of the party, and Frank and Margo both enjoyed the fun they all had at church and theater parties. The husband of one of Margo's and Frank's best friends was rumored to have had 'other same sex relationships' outside their marriage. Marty, and Lisha...another dear friend—whose husband also had the same reputation—knew, but 'chose...not to know.' Marty's husband, we'll call him 'Jack,' had even gotten away with giving St. Mark's young people alcohol and, drugs (reportedly marijuana and quaaludes) at church parties. So, when Margo and Marty were out of town at a St. Mark's Women's retreat, 'Jack' invited Frank over for dinner, while 'our better halves are gone.' Frank, who thought there were to be other guys there, offered to help cook, but 'Jack' said no, everything was all set. As a 'good guest,' Frank had brought a bottle of Chardonnay, and after the delicious Italian dinner Jack had fixed, they finished off the wine, and watched some ballgame on the TV. After a few 'shots of something' 'Jack' was 'promoting,' Frank felt unusually strange. He had had shots before…but something was *seriously wrong* here. He asked 'Jack' what he had put in his drink. 'Jack' just laughed…*it was the last thing Frank remembered*…he woke up at home; Margo and Marty were standing over him…Jack could not be found, and *never returned*. Marty filed a missing person's report, but they didn't hear from him, until he called from New Orleans. 'Jack' had decided to leave his 'pretend life' and join a group of his *friends*. Marty couldn't stop crying; she tried to help Frank and Margo process what had just happened, but all she could say was,"…we were both abused by the same person…and me, for years." Margo turned away, she couldn't do this anymore, she didn't want to; she decided to leave with the children, and go to Wenatchee. Frank was totally depressed–he felt like it was all over].

Frank suddenly came back to the present. He got home about 7:00 p.m. He walked in the door, but the kids were not there…Margo had not fixed supper; she had been crying, and he asked what he could do. She said, "nothing." He asked if they should go out…'where were the kids?' She said they were at a friend's house…they *should go out* for supper…they 'needed to talk.' They went to Carlos' and had dinner. Frank let it all pour out after they had had a glass of wine…he had made 'so many mistakes …he offered no excuses for his compulsive-driven need for recognition, or his inexcusable life style. He knew she wanted out of Beaumont as desperately as he did, and the 'primrose path' had turned into the 'road to destruction.' He wanted her to believe he loved her, and had wanted to do this all for the family…just get out of there; but it didn't sound right at all…like he was using her *to justify all his wrong-doing*. She just sat there… finishing her plate in silence. She finally said: "I don't believe you; you've said it all before; you've broken every promise you've ever made to me; what we need… is 'radical change.' We're not where we should be…with God or each other! We only 'do church' because of our music jobs…But, I *am* willing to move to Houston…on three conditions: "first, we get into a good church there, with *good* friends…not just the music; second: I get a job that will fulfill *me*, and, third: you find a way to get back on track in your life, or we're done." She said, "I mean it this time; you can't hide behind your excuse of not being recognized any longer. Frank stared at her; he started to explain how he had felt…since they'd left Odessa, but he realized how stupid that was. He just looked at her… for a very long time…she would not smile, or say a word. Then he said: "I cannot make promises anymore…I just haven't kept them, and there's no reason to trust me." They finished in total silence; Frank paid the bill, and they went home. Lisha called to say she was on her way over with the kids. Margo had gone to bed; Frank thanked Lisha, and left. Shelley wouldn't look at her dad; Lisha had allowed her to invite her friend Jennifer over, so she had had a good time; she and the boys had a snack, and then went to bed…life was 'coming unraveled.'

On Monday, Frank asked Irene, after the branch meeting, if Bill had called from the region Office. She said he had, but she had been in orientation with two of Frank's new recruits, and wasn't sure what he had called about yet. After the new recruits finished meeting with Frank, Irene told him: Bill had heard from Chas P. Young Printers; they had taken the liberty of scheduling an interview with Margo for the following Friday at 9:00 a.m.; and Irene had gotten Bill's okay to engage a realtor for Frank and Margo; his name was Surrinder Aliwallia, with Gulf Realtors, and he would show them houses MetLife had approved for showing, when Margo and the children came on Friday; Walt Ridlon had gotten regional approval for the move, the selling of the Landis street house, and the assistance for relocation from Beaumont to the Houston area. [Good timing, God! Margo had just agreed *not* to leave with the kids for Wenatchee, and told him so; "thank you, God… again! Please take over; I'm in a really *bad* place"]. Frank spent the rest of the week looking for a new location for his office. Walt had suggested something closer to I-45 as a business upgrade, and Frank had found two locations: one closer to Clear Lake Mall, and one close to the Southpoint Area, near Almeda-Genoa, right off of I-45. He took Irene out to lunch to thank her for all her assistance…with "breaking him in," and the transition from Beaumont to Houston; he couldn't believe it had already been almost six months. She said they could live wherever they wish, but she hoped, selfishly, that they would choose something closer to Friendswood, where she and her family lived, rather than in Clear Lake, where Frank was hoping to live, and relocate the new office. Surrinder, had eliminated all but three: one in Clear Lake–the one Frank wanted; one in Friendswood, and a new choice, one that Frank had just found on his own, in Pearland. Surrinder had himself eliminated two in Pearland, and four others in Clear Lake and Friendswood, all out of the price range Frank had given him, or were not available. The plan was to have Margo interview at Chas P. Young at 9:00 Friday morning, have lunch with Surrinder and discuss their options, then visit as many houses as possible. They planned to stay the night with Irene in Friendswood. The kids took an excused absence from school, so they could be in on the choice. Frank finished the MetLife work-week a day early, so he could drive back to Beaumont, stay the night at home with the family, and then leave together at 6:30 a.m. in order to drive in to Houston, have breakfast at McDonald's near Channelview, and make it to Margo's interview by 9:00. It was exciting to be 'on the road again' after so long; Frank and the kids waited in the car while she went inside for the interview. She came out in about thirty to forty-five minutes; she was smiling, but told them all not to get their hopes up–they still had three more to interview that day. Irene had assured them that Walt Ridlon knew someone in their corporate office, and he said he knew one of their directors (who was responsible for their MetLife coverage); they would finish interviewing the last three that same day, and announce the new employee by late Friday. Bill had made a call to Anne Herring, the administrator for their corporate division...the one who had interviewed Margo later that afternoon. Anne didn't want to say anything, but she let it slip that Margo was in the 'final three.' Anne said Margo did not have the most clerical experience, but she had stronger references...the Vietnamese ESL Program, Temple Emmanuel, 'and MetLife in particular.'...but it was really 'up to the agency,' she said...Anne stopped there; she said she was 'speaking on her own here' without authority, but they would have to pay more for the other two, due to the greater amount of experience. Bill, speaking on his own...but with Walt nodding his head in approval, said that MetLife would 'pick up the placement fee.' Anne seemed very confident, and told Bill she would call him in an hour. Frank and Margo were at lunch with Surrinder, but had forgotten they had to fit in another interview; one at St. Pius V in Pasadena. They made some quick arrangements to eat lunch before meeting with Father Lou, and then join Surrinder at his office near I-45 and Sagemont. The children wanted Dairy Queen, so they all wolfed down burgers and ice cream before showing up at St. Pius V at 11:30. Father Lou showed them around the church…and the school. Then he took them to his office, and while the children waited in the school library, Father Lou told them St. Anne's had highly recommended them, and he was offering them the positions of cantor-music director, and organist, for the church and school, a full-time position for them both. Frank looked at Margo, then at Father Lou. Frank said he was so sorry to have to turn it down…his job with MetLife was a 'full-time position.' Could Margo work 'full-time, and he work part time?' No, unfortunately the position had to include the daily Mass at the school…for both of them. Frank looked at Margo in silence; he really wanted to accept, but he knew they could not do so. Father Lou was disappointed, but he said, 'wait, he had just gotten a call from Deacon Darin Marleau and Father Jason Jordaine, the priest at St. Helen's Catholic in Pearland that morning…' they needed an organist-choirmaster. It seemed like it might be another answer to prayer. Would they be able to interview on a Saturday, as in 'tomorrow?' Father Lou picked up the phone and called Deacon Marleau…but Deacon John Householder answered instead; he said he knew all about the position, and 'yes, they would set up something for Saturday, the next day.' Everyone was all smiles and they left very upbeat. Irene had gotten a call from Bill, and she called Frank at Surrinder's office. She wouldn't say what it was about, but it sounded like good news. Frank was told to have Margo call Anne Herring. By now, Surrinder was upset and wanted them to start seeing houses, but Frank insisted on Margo being able to call Anne before seeing houses. Margo called; (Irene had given Bill the Summit Realty number that Bill passed on to Anne). Margo looked serious, then anticipatory, then finally smiling, as she hung up the phone—she had gotten the job! Walt was going to pick up the placement fee…could she start in April? Now Surrinder was smiling; Frank and the kids were all smiling. Frank called Irene, Bill, and Walt, and thanked everyone for their help and concern. They left immediately for Clear Lake. The house which Frank had liked so much…was not liked particularly by either Margo or the kids. Frank frowned. He didn't like the red interior either, but he thought Margo and the kids would like it; they could always repaint it, he'd said. It was close to the new Met office site he liked, 'let's move on then' he said. They liked the Friendswood house better, but it was 'boxy' she said; it was close to Irene's, but not to the office, or the new church music position, if they got it. Frank thought the Pearland house was way too expensive...out of their budget, and the builder had gone out of business; the first owners had only 'lived there' less than a year, had never fully moved in, and then, it was rumored, they had gotten a divorce...but Margo loved it at first sight; the kids loved it, too. Surrinder wanted to show them even more expensive houses (once he found he could make a higher commission). Frank was taken back... his plans were foiled; everything was 'now up in the air' he said—but not so for Margo and the children; they steadfastly stuck by their preference for the Pearland house; and so it was: the next fifteen and a half years they lived in this wonderful house on Heather Lane: home to the Varro family! Saturday, after spending the night at Irene's, and a wonderful breakfast (which she called 'Monterrey egg casserole'), and fruit, sweet rolls, coffee (and juice for the kids); they headed to St. Helen Catholic Church for their interview. Being Saturday, Irene suggested that the children just hang around her home while 'mom and dad did their interview,' which pleased everyone. Deacons Marleau and Householder met them there; Father Jordaine (with the Basilian order), would stop in briefly after his meeting. Father Lou, and Father Nicholas from St. Anne had been very complimentary of them both, they said; Margo played Handel's 'Hornpipe' on the organ; Frank sang the Ave Maria, and then they described the position: one Mass Saturday evening, and three Masses on Sunday; they would pay them for each individual Mass, and for additional Masses on feast days, weddings, funerals; and special times like Easter, Christmas, Pentecost, etc. It was a lot, and it would keep them very busy!! Did they think Margo and Frank could handle it...with their full-time jobs at Chas P. Young, MetLife, family and social commitments? Always the optimists, Frank and Margo nodded their heads, thinking immediately of the extra income—that would pay the mortgage... now greatly increased because of their 'champagne-taste-on-a-beer-budget' *new home*! Father Jason walked in just as Deacons John and Darin were congratulating them. Darin introduced him, and everyone shook hands all around. Father Jason smiled and said he had heard Margo's 'concert' from his office. He saw that Darin and John had obviously just offered the positions to Frank and Margo, and was in full agreement with that. He said he had taken some seminary courses with Father Nicholas, and also knew Father Lou very well, even though they were parish priests; he was a Basilian, a mission priest. They decided that their first Sunday would be the first Sunday in May…giving them a chance to finish well at St. Anne, and have a couple weeks to move; they all agreed. As they were all going out the door together, Father Jason said, "Oh, by the way, your *first* Sunday here will be my *last* Sunday here." 'What?' Frank and Margo were speechless; had they chased the priest away so soon? They all laughed, and then Father Jason explained that the parish had started as a mission at St. John in Alvin, and as a Basilian, he covered both locations. He was being sent to the 'valley' (Harlingen, McAllen, Brownsville) as a missionary, and St. Helen's was becoming a diocesan parish. A new priest, Monsignor Braden, and his associate, Father Haick, would be coming to serve St. Helen's. Thus began a wonderful relationship of six years at St. Helen's. Frank and Margo picked up the kids, thanked Irene again for her invaluable assistance, drove home to Beaumont, and slept the rest of the afternoon. Shelley had made plans to see Jennifer, the boys went swimming, and Frank and Margo crashed in front of the television. Everyone was so kind at St. Anne's that Sunday, and Father Nicholas made some quick arrangement for a going-away reception the following Sunday. The St. Martin's Episcopal young adults also planned a going away reception, and everyone had a chance to say goodbye—dear friends despite some unpleasant experiences.

The next two weeks were a blur. Frank had to leave Monday to return to the MetLife office. After the branch meeting, Irene reminded Frank that Walt Ridlon was taking him to lunch; he wanted to see the two office sites he had selected; he also wanted to see the house in Pearland where they had chosen to live. Sure enough, right at 11:45 Walt showed up, and they went to see the one closest to the Clear Lake Mall; Frank had marked it as his first choice. It was a very good location, but it was further from Pearland where they would live. It was also upstairs, and not as accessible. Walt said he wanted to see the house they had chosen, since it was on their way back, and he wanted to see it before viewing the second office location, close to where they were going to have lunch. Frank called Surrinder, and had him meet them there on Heather Lane in Pearland. Walt liked it very much, and promised they would assist in the sale of the Beaumont house, and in the financing of the Pearland house as well. Surrinder tried to make another proposal on the two houses in Sagemont they had viewed, but Walt assisted Frank in helping him realize their choice had already been made, so Surrinder promised he would expedite the paperwork as soon as possible. They left for Southpoint and Frank showed Walt the second office site. At lunch, Frank admitted the Featherwood office site was more accessible, a very good location right on I-45, less traffic, and actually was a more attractive business building. It was very easy to make the decision, especially since the current lease on the Pasadena office was coming up right away. Since the moving van was already ordered, and Frank could not take any more time off, he had to allow others to do the 'one move without his supervision' he had ever done. Big mistake! Three boxes arrived upside down, broken glass, one with soy sauce, and other bottled condiments leaking all through the box! Margo said to let it go, but Fank was upset. He had packed and driven trucks cross country, packed a crate in Taiwan, shipped it thousands of miles over the ocean, with even a piano in it, and not a single item was broken. Everyone had to laugh, except Frank, but he finally let it go. They hadn't qualified for the less-than-ten-percent down, and thirty-year mortgage; too-short a credit history for Odessa, and Beaumont both. Walt Ridlon came to the rescue. MetLife was able to sell the house in Beaumont, and the region vouched for the reduced down payment…it went through! On April 16, 1984, they closed on the house on Heather Lane in Pearland… they lived there almost sixteen years. It was where the family grew up, and the home they treasured so dearly, but where the struggles were the greatest…before God stepped in. There it was that Frank experienced the greatest defeat, but also his greatest triumph!

Within the next several weeks, Frank did several things to advance his music career: He made contact with several Texas choral musicians about his availability for adjudication, choral workshops, and private voice instruction. His friend, Sally Schott, past-president of Texas Music Educators, called to tell him she had arranged for him to teach a few private voice students, not only at South Houston High School (where she'd been a longtime choral director), but also Dobie High School. She also had booked him for a few weekends of adjudication in the coming months. Frank had talked to David Llewelyn, who had taken over for Frank as director of the Southeast Texas Chorale, about the high school Shelley would be attending, once they knew they would be living in Pearland. (After Odom, Shelley had attended Westbrook High School-freshman campus, and was in choir there; Frank and Margo were naturally concerned about her finding a good music program). David was very excited to tell Frank that his good friend, Nancy Martin, had been choral director at Pearland High School for years, where Shelley would be attending; since Nancy was also a good friend of Sally's, it would work out for Frank to, not only teach several voice students there, but their accompanist, Cynthia DePrang, Nancy's accompanist, joined his new chamber choral group; Frank had placed an ad in the Houston Chronicle for auditions to the new choral group; some graduates from the University of Houston, like Nancy Morton, and a few choral directors in the area showed up, auditioned, and a new community choir was founded: Vera Voce. They were featured in several area concert series, radio and TV appearances, and regular spring and fall concerts. The Sante Fe High School choir director, Howard Holt (who followed Nancy Martin at Pearland after she took a choral job in Dallas) sang in the Vera Voce as well. Frank and Margo were unable, because of their commitments to St. Helen's, and their work schedules at that time, to attend their own Episcopal church, but were invited to join... 'when available,' the St. Martin's Episcopal choir. Father Claude Payne, Rector at St. Mark's in Beaumont, became Rector of St. Martin's in Houston (known as the 'President George HW Bush church'), and Father Payne later became Bishop. Frank and Margo were invited to be 'honorary members of the St. Martin's choir, and performed many concerts, evensongs, and programs there, at the insistence of John Marsh, the choirmaster-organist. They also sang for seasonal music performances. Frank and Margo did many weddings and funerals, not only at St. Helen's, but in other churches all over town. They sang in the Houston Masterworks Chorale for several seasons, as well as the smaller chorus, Masterworks Chamber Chorus. Frank had solos in some of these performances. Their conductor, Bob Brewer, and other guest conductors, made for a great team, and their performances of Bach's B Minor Mass, Bernstein Lark, Chichester Psalms, and other major works, were of the highest quality.

Despite their very busy music schedule, Frank managed to do a fair amount of agent recruiting, and Frank topped the charts there as well. Margo wanted to celebrate his success with a surprise 'fortieth-birthday party.' So, with the help of Irene...and Shelley, Steve, and Rob, secretly planned the celebration of Frank's fortieth birthday. She had sent him to the store for a big shopping, while she engaged several friends from the church, MetLife friends, and family. When he got back home, they all jumped out to surprise him with a Mongolian Barbeque celebration and 'Kegger.' The children had made friends from school already and some of them, and the neighbors, stopped by for the big 'Four-O' celebration.

Frank thought things were going well, so he talked to Margo about buying a new car. The Subaru kept breaking down and they almost had to break the lease several times. No problem she said, if they could get a good financing package...*AND* they bought the grand piano he had always promised her! Whoa! A new mortgage, a new car, which of course he said he '*HAD* to have as a new successful branch manager' and reward...for getting them out of Beaumont and out of debt. It was a lot. The piano would have to wait. She didn't say anything. She just looked at him, then turned on her heel and walked away. Whoops! That probably meant something, Frank thought. After they financed the car with GMAC, the family took a ride in Frank's new 'chariot.' The children squealed with delight and told all their neighbor friends, their dad was *rich* now! When they got back, Margo quietly informed him that her *mother* had arranged to give her an 'early fortieth birthday present' of her own...a full six-foot Young Chang grand piano! Frank hit the ceiling! To him, it was like she had gone behind his back (as she 'often did,' according to him). He told her, "No, every time I am 'not good enough' for you, your mother steps in and gives you 'what I am not able to provide!" She walked away, the children went outside, or to their rooms, like they usually did when things got heated. They were 'right back where they were before' she said. After an hour Frank met her in the kitchen and asked her how he could make things better; she said it seemed only fair that if *he* bought a car, *she* should be able to have a piano. He said the issue was one of necessity in work, over and against a promise about a less-than-absolutely-necessary piano...a promise that he felt he couldn't keep at this time...without continuing a dependence on her mother. In the end, he agreed on buying both, but on the condition that her mother and he would split the down payment, and help with payments 'once in a while... only if they were unable to make them.' They went ahead and turned in the Subaru, but had to pay a big penalty on the 'incomplete' lease agreement, and condition of the car. Frank found out Margo, and Wilma, had *already* made contact with Balcom Vaughn in Houston, and had priced a new six-foot Young Chang piano...but 'with a good discount' for it having been a display model...at a little over four thousand; if they put down a thousand, they could get payments as low as two hundred fifty dollars for fifteen years...car payments, mortgage, piano—it didn't seem feasible...without increasing their monthly. Frank would have to increase his sales, and also his recruiting activities, Margo's and Frank's church job, and Margo's printer's job. He said 'okay,' but he didn't like the pressure, and continuing to let 'Wilma step in' definitely put a crimp in his plans. When they didn't have the thousand dollars by fall... Wilma quietly put the thousand dollars down...on her own, and the arrangement almost fell through. By the end of 1984, his new branch—now renamed 'Southpoint Branch,' came in only eighth, out of sixteen branches, in recruiting and overall production. But... by the close of 1985, he was in the *TOP FIVE* branches in the same categories. Irene came in his office after the year-end closeout...the whole branch was seated, smiles on their faces; Irene stood and announced to him and the rest of the branch, that Frank had won a manager's trip to South Padre Island! The MetLife incentive program, and improvements in the manager's compensation plan, had worked well for them; and the Southeast Territory had the second highest paid managers in the company...three days of fun, seminars...and partying; but Frank was able to meet the obligations of a new mortgage, even at *THIRTEEN* percent...a new car, and a piano for Margo! Frank loved the attention he got as a Top-Five branch manager. He was strutting around like he owned the place, which did not endear him to the family, the branch, or his fellow managers, especially when this was followed by an invitation to the MetLife home office in New York for a week...more of the same: testimonials, marketing seminars ...and partying. Southpoint branch also had the 'worst lapse rate,' though; not a good sign, but Irene had warned him about it; he unwisely brushed it off, though, not wanting to recognize what this might mean later on.

By Christmas, the Vera Voce was able to present three wonderful concerts in Pearland, Pasadena, and Houston. However, voice lessons at South Houston, Dobie, and Pearland high schools eventually became too much for him, and he had to give that up. The same with adjudication, clinics, and workshops. The Fall and Christmas concerts at St. Helen's Catholic and St. Martin's Episcopal went well; and along with all this, he made many friends, got caught up in the sports, drama, and music programs at Pearland High School where Shelley attended... and football every weekend. They had decided to hold Steve and Rob back after they moved from Beaumont to Pearland; the boys were not only summer and fall birthdays, but the schools in Pearland seemed to have a more challenging program; and since they had made few friends in second and fourth grades (after moving to Pearland in late April), it was an easy, and very smooth, transition in repeating second and fourth. They had excellent teachers and excelled with their new social group. Shelley thrived as a soprano in the choir with Nancy Martin, was in several drama productions, and was active in the sports and music programs. Later, Steve and Rob were active in music as well. Steve loved long distance running, and they enrolled Rob in gymnastics at South East Area Gymnastics Association (SEAGA). The children attended the Methodist Church (while Frank and Margo worked their St. Helen's Catholic jobs), and Shelley became part of the youth group there; the boys, after first staying with mom and dad during services at St Helen's, also transitioned to the Pearland Methodist church. They all made friends and participated in the activities there. Mike Baker, who had been an associate rector at St. Mark's in Beaumont, and a graduate of Virginia Seminary, came to Pearland as the newly appointed rector of St. Andrew's Episcopal Church. Margo and Frank had known Father Mike before leaving Beaumont, and were very happy to welcome him. Mike and Kim wanted Frank and Margo to come be a part of the St. Andrew's family in the worst way, but Frank and Margo knew they couldn't...without replacing the income they were receiving from St. Helen's Catholic (even though Mike had suggested it; at less than half what they were receiving from St. Helen's, it was not possible; but Shelley. and the boys started attending some of the youth activities at St. Andrew's, Frank and Margo were invited to some of the social gatherings there, and Father Mike talked about building a new church building. Evening services and choir at St. Martin's Episcopal–fifty miles round trip every week…became too much, so they started singing, occasionally, an evensong or two, with Philip Kluckner, the new organist-choirmaster at St. Andrew's. They made new friends there, and Father Mike started talking about getting them to come… someday, 'just in case Philip ever left, of course,' and they knew they would have to match what St. Helen's was paying. So, Frank and Margo began to be a part of the social life of St. Andrew's at least, and became good friends with the mayor, Tom Reid, and several other community leaders… especially Sherry Gladstone, mother of the Pearland Oilers football quarterback, a real civic leader, and prominent member at St. Helen's. She managed to arrange a 'Pearland Night' at the Astrodome. She told everyone Frank was *going to* sing, the 'Star-Spangled Banner' before the game. The Astros were playing the Montreal Expos, but the man who was scheduled to sing 'O Canada,' became ill that afternoon; without consulting Frank, Sherry told them Frank could sing that as well…rather than just eliminating it (since it wasn't a home game for Montreal anyway); it was a nice gesture, she told them, and she didn't want to change the plan. Frank had heard it many times–(after all, his dad's side of the family were all from Canada)–but…he had never sung it! Sherry stuck the music score in his face. "You have an hour; learn it!" He was fortunately in 'good voice' and sang the American national anthem with gusto…and the Canadian national anthem with equal confidence (after meeting with the organist of course). A number of people came up to him to thank him for his singing, "especially that Canadian song," one lady from Canada said, "I had never heard it before!" They all laughed, realizing that she didn't recognize her own national anthem!

By the end of the year, Walt Ridlon had become the president of Pacific Life, and left the regional office. Tai Chang was the highest producing branch manager in the region, in production and sales, so he became the new regional manager. Unfortunately, the other managers were not ready for an 'Asian,' who had difficulty communicating, and with no real managerial experience, they gave him a 'no-vote-of-confidence.' Fred Feigley became the new regional manager. Unfortunately, MetLife was experiencing a number of problems... a large suit was filed against both MetLife and Prudential, the two top insurance companies in the world at that time. 'Life' and 'Variable-Life' plans were being sold as 'retirement plans.' Everyone had rushed to get their CLU's (Chartered Life Underwriter), 'registered-representative' designations (certified to sell securities)...plus, taking auto and homeowners insurance agents away from Allstate, State Farm, and Farmers...promising better compensation, while rolling clients over to MetLife; but...losing millions of dollars on get-rich-quick schemes. Met Property and Casualty company blew through millions... and then folded; then they decided that branch managers' compensation plans should be changed...compensation based not *primarily* on recruiting and production, but rather on a *combination* of 'personal production ...**plus** branch production.' Agents and managers began leaving in great numbers. Lapse rates, poor training, and too many inexperienced reps, was washing out hundreds of good managers, many of whom went back into personal production, or who just left the company. Frank did what so many other young managers were doing; and most of them came primarily from other insurance companies; they had been successful 'overnight,' largely as 'property and casualty' agents; with little or no experience, they sold 'tons of insurance' the same way 'tangible product' sales-people did. Making the necessary quota, on a pro-rata basis, was what they were *quickly trained* to do; and they did it on the promise of running their own branch office, not worrying about the quality of customer, or the lasting quality of the sale; lapse rates went up, promises were not kept, and branches began closing and managers leaving for other companies...who were also doing the same thing...but there was one caveat for Frank, in this whole experience...the Houston Association of Life Underwriters (HALU). They needed new, young, leadership; many of the older, successful...and frankly, wealthy agents and managers...had been in association leadership positions for decades. Membership was going down...until several of the leaders got together, hired a new administrator, Teddy Chandler, and they started visiting insurance companies all over Houston. To general-agents and managers...they offered incentives, at the corporate level, to become 'one-hundred-percent agencies.' Past presidents of the association were placed in charge of forming a committee, and named the membership chair, Sudie Forman, to form a task force, along with other committee members, Sudie visited several MetLife branches, and the region office in The Woodlands; and that is how Frank met Sudie. On the phone she suggested a visit to his branch. She suggested 'one-hundred-percent agencies for all the MetLife branches...only three out of the sixteen districts or branches in the MetLife region were interested...but Frank's Southpoint branch was one of them. Frank then offered incentives to all his agents to become members of HALU. He 'required it,' but only half joined; one of his agents reported him to the region, and Bill called Frank and told him he could not require it ...but he could have a 'branch fund' (like they did in his Beaumont district), and if his agency voted to give a scholarship to everyone who became a member of HALU, he could do that, which he did. One of his agents, Andy Dorn, became good friends with Frank, and they started spending a lot of time together. He was a 'big hitter' and so Frank placed him in charge of the 'branch fund.' In the next year, the Southpoint branch became a 'one-hundred-percent agency, Frank enrolled in LUTC (Life Underwriters Training Courses), and the first of ten CLU (Chartered Life Underwriter)– eventually taking six of them. He became good friends with Teddy, and several of the officers of HALU, and then, as a manager, began attending also General Agents & Managers Association meetings (GAMA). Joe Scruggs, Jim McCarty, and even some of the Texas state association administrators, and officers, Ken Tooley (TALU), and visiting national officers (NALU). Life Association and Managers Association meetings, the training courses, the association recruiting... *and partying...* became what Frank enjoyed; recognition–more than the branch...more time spent with his new friends than his family, his church job, even his music...again; *then MetLife changed the compensation plan.* They wanted personal production more than recruiting; they wanted him in MetLife meetings...more than in recruiting agents for branch production; his paycheck dropped lower and lower. He tried to keep up with personal production, region meetings, marketing seminars; and personal, family and spiritual life. He began making fewer family sporting events, theater, concerts, and church functions. He started making new friends in other insurance companies, showing up late for MetLife regional managers meetings... he even stayed out all night with Andy and some of his insurance friends and managers. Every time Margo, or their friends, tried to get him to slow down, he brushed it off. Instead, he tried secretly adding 'other insurance companies,' to his sales (MetLife was, at that time, a 'captive agency' meaning agents could not sell for other companies), he signed on to sell children's books as well, rather than tell Margo the truth... that he was going down in the *cesspool*. She became desperate and started seeing a counselor. She suggested that they go together, but he refused. Everything he had worked so hard for seemed to be turning to ashes...but he admitted nothing. He had gone to a wonderful pastoral counselor in Odessa, Ray Brittan, but just when everything seemed better there, they had moved to Beaumont, and, all of what has already been written about, had unfolded...so poorly. The annual trips to the Pacific Northwest were becoming perfunctory, less of the great family get-togethers and spiritual uplift, than they had been in the past, so they just skipped it for a while. Shelley was busy with her friends and youth group at Pearland First Methodist, but now, as a teenager, she was getting into trouble with a less-than-wholesome group of friends; Steve and Rob were also caught up with their friends, schooling, and getting in trouble in the neighborhood without Frank's time and supervision. Frank just couldn't admit anything to the family, his friends, his work associates... and especially Margo; the paychecks kept going down, and the car was repossessed (in the middle of the night... twice), but he was able to make arrangements with GMAC, and got it back. They were late on the mortgage payments, but MetLife again was able to help them refinance at a lower rate (interest rates were finally coming down from thirteen percent to nine, but they were still late, and it was affecting their credit). And, Margo's mother had gone ahead and made the payments on the piano at that time; Frank felt low; he felt humiliated, but he wouldn't talk about it...to anyone...he felt like he was 'going down.' He tried to talk to Father Mike, but they were not close at that time, and Mike was busy trying to build a new church campus...with a lot of opposition, so they never got together. He wasn't Catholic, and didn't feel comfortable discussing anything personal with Monsignor Bradon either. Margo had poured herself into her work, but Chas P. Young 'very suddenly' filed a Chapter 13 bankruptcy.

Margo and all the staff on both the financial side and the corporate side *were let go*. The company was sold to another interest, and a handful of staff on both sides were rehired, salaries were frozen, but fortunately, Margo was one of them that was rehired (some of the company's free-flowing 'receptions and outings,' often including Frank, had been wild and wasteful. Some close friends of Frank suggested bankruptcy, but he flat-out refused to even consider it…as long as they still had income from Margo's job, the church job, and whatever else Frank could 'pick up' along the way. Sometimes Frank stayed out all night with Andy, and some of his other agents (on the pretext, that *it was overnight out-of-town business*). Andy divorced his wife Jenny… after she moved out (to live with her new boyfriend). Some of the other agents—who were 'the only real producers left,' went to other insurance companies…or were fired for 'not making quota'. Andy tried to persuade Frank to follow him to Wisconsin Life, the company where he landed (Andy said he 'would share the referral fee with Frank if he did,' of course). He said Frank could be a 'free man…like me…' *If it wasn't 'the bottom,' you could see it from there.*

One night, Thursday, May 7,1987, after everything had closed up and Frank… *really needed* to go home; Andy, and his friends had gone on to another party…at some girl's house. Frank stood there in a stupor…he couldn't breathe…he couldn't *stand* it; he couldn't stay here any longer. He had to get *home*… and against everyone's advice… Frank refused to take a taxi… He made it to…a block from home, but couldn't remember where he was…

Frank HIT THE BOTTOM.

…with tears streaming down his face, he pulled over into a cul-de-sac near their house; new construction lined the streets; half-built houses were dark and empty…no street lights yet installed, Frank sat there confused; he hadn't listened to Christian radio since his first year in Beaumont, yet somehow there it was—a Christian radio station, playing a song he had never heard before: '*When God Ran*,' by someone named Benny Hester; the song gripped him like nothing ever had before; it was the story of the 'prodigal son,' but it spoke of the 'Father' *who **ran out to welcome** his undeserving son…home again!* Frank found the Bible he had buried in the bottom of his glove compartment; but instead of finding the story in the New Testament parables of Jesus, he flipped open to Psalm 139, "*...where can I flee from your presence, if I ascend to the heavens, you are there, if I make my bed in hell, YOU ARE THERE...*" The song went on...the wayward son, slowly walking, with dread in his heart toward home, just to be a 'lowly servant,' when the Father 'runs out to welcome him back.' The words were hitting him in the face, "*I saw Him run to me, with forgiveness in His voice...he said son, do you know I still love you?...and then I ran to him...*" Frank choked up; he turned to look...someone was in the passenger's seat... he had stirred next to him; he was gently amused at him...not a derisive laugh...a kind, loving, genuinely amused, laugh; the one like his father and mother had, when he took his first steps, and fell down; or ate his first whole food...half of it running down his face...it was Jesus...he embraced Frank as he wept. **Something had happened!** *And Frank knew he could never again be the same.* He sat there an hour or more trying to figure out what had happened to him. He tried to find the song again, but it was gone; it wasn't even a Christian station...but he hadn't *touched* the dial! He drove home...he woke Margo up, 'babbling incoherently,' she had told others... about some *song* he heard on the radio. Finally going to sleep for a few hours, he woke up and tried to find the Christian radio station he had told Margo about. She turned to it right away...it was Dr. James Dobson; he was talking about the role of the *father* in the home...on his program 'Focus on the Family.' Now Margo realized Frank wasn't delirious, and he tried to share what happened the night before. *Just another promise*, she thought; it would pass, just like everything else had. She had grown cold and unfeeling since Beaumont, she was just going through the motions—her job, the church, a few new St. Andrew's friends, the kids and their schooling; no women's Bible study, no musical challenges...just weekly church choir, accompanying, UIL solos or ensembles, no real singing except the occasional Vera Voce 'gig', for which she and the others would rehearse a few weeks, then sing the performance. Life was mundane, and her mind was mostly on work, and a few close friends there. The kids didn't pick up on the radical change that their dad had experienced either— but Frank started reading his Bible daily. He would drop Margo off at work, find a place to park close by... before returning to southeast Houston to his MetLife job, and *there he found God* in an intimate and meaningful way, daily...like he had never experienced before; he prayed, cried out to God, and scoured the scriptures he had ignored for years. He told Irene and his agents something wonderful had happened to him...they smiled, and went on their way; like Margo and all the others, they had heard it all before; but he stopped going with them to party, refused to order any alcohol at meals, and came home after work; he tried to play with the kids, even built a tree house in the backyard...having them help him build it together. He started feeling desperate...all alone, even angry that no one seemed to share his 'new life' with him. He re-read Psalm 139 every day *"...search me O God, know my heart...lead me in the way everlasting."* He felt cold and unmoved. "Thanks a lot, God, I turn back to you, and no one is here to share this with me..." Instead of things 'getting better,' they only got worse. After a MetLife Managers' meeting, Fred called Frank in and told him things had to get better in his branch, or he would have to go back into personal production and lose his manager's position. That's when the car was repossessed a second time, the mortgage was late again, and Margo was busy at work, while the kids were still getting into trouble. Margo and he had started attending St. Andrew's for all the evening and weekend functions, while still covering the services for St. Helen for their paycheck. They got extra for weddings and funerals, even some outlandish ones [like one in Galveston where they put them up for the night in the very reputable historical Tremont Hotel, and others around town, that brought in extra income]. They made some close friendships in the 'Married with Children' group, including the DeVore's, the Yates', and the Ledbetter's, and others; they went on some weekend retreats to Camp Allen. They got to know Randy and Peggy Ferguson, 'senior warden,' and Vestry chair, and through them, Pat and Richard Arneson; she found out Frank had started selling children's books, and invited him to sign up with 'Big Books,' which she currently sold; they took a trip to the 'Valley' to introduce him to her market for children's books. She seemed to know all the 'in's and out's'... and the gossip...especially the gossip, at St. Andrew's. But she knew Father Mike well, and planted the idea of coming up with the money to 'bring the Varro's *home*, from St. Helen's...over to St. Andrew's. Phil, the organist-choirmaster suddenly took a new job in Lake Jackson, so Father Mike talked with Randy, and they came up with an offer that was a match, but the previous senior warden, Bob Reid, and some others, while approving the yearly amount, resisted the monthly match, only approving the annual amount when divided by nine months (meaning no pay in the summer months); Frank said that would not work. Mike didn't say where it came from, but suddenly *someone must have given an anonymous gift* for the summer months. Still, without the extra number of funerals and weddings... since St. Andrew's was a considerably smaller parish... they accepted it anyway, and, sadly for St. Helen's, since they had dearly loved Margo and Frank as cantor-director and Margo as organist, they resigned their positions there, and went over to St. Andrew's. It was early 1990, and Father Mike, having apparently *fulfilled* his quest, informed them, and the rest of St. Andrew's, that he had been chosen to found a new mission church in southwest Houston. 'What? The minute we are hired, the priest leaves again?' No, Mike laughed, as he told them, it was 'already in the works, but he couldn't leave before accomplishing his goal of getting the Varro's to their home church.' Phil's last Sunday was Easter, the same as Frank's and Margo's at St. Helen's. Tears of joy and sadness at both parishes. Frank and Margo, and a group of volunteers, spent three weekends helping stuff envelopes and calling on the telephone to help with the start of the new parish, All Saints Episcopal, in a school on the Brazos River.

It was the first week in June, and Frank got a call from his mother in Taiwan. She wrote often, but *NEVER* called, so he knew something was wrong. She was calling from the hospital; she said. Dad had been taken, on their Golden Wedding Anniversary, June 6, 1990, to the Changhua Hospital, a short drive from where they lived in Xinzhu in Taiwan. She said he had had a persistent cough since the beginning of the year, but ignored it; he had finally given up going up into the mountains to the 'aborigine churches,' but never considered going to the doctor; now he was spitting up blood, and was treated, apparently, for tuberculosis. Frank insisted on speaking with his dad, so he came on the phone. Frank told him that he, and Dave (in Seattle), Margi (in Atlanta), and Juli (in Baltimore) could all, hopefully, come out to Taiwan, and meet him there. Michael said absolutely not, that it was tuberculosis, and he would be back home soon; it would be a completely wasted trip to do so. His doctors were beginning to think it might be cancer, and were able to send some of the lab samples, through Frank's sister Margaret, to Dr. David Tharpe (brother of her husband Alan) in Alabama, where he was a doctor. Sure enough, they came back positive for 'squamous cell carcinoma of the lungs.' How cruelly ironic that someone so opposed to nicotine in any form, and who had never smoked or used it in any form, would be diagnosed with cancer of the lungs [Frank's brother believed it to be the result of dad's numerous trips to the mountain churches, where they slept under mosquito netting, next to highly toxic burning anti-mosquito 'incense coils.']. Other ideas were that the pollution in Taiwan was very toxic, and statistics during that time showed a great spike in lung cancer deaths. The doctors decided he had contracted the lung cancer between the previous January and April, and it had worsened gradually until their wedding anniversary in June. They estimated that it had spread to almost eighty percent of his lungs. They decided to life-flight him immediately to the Mackay Memorial Hospital in northern Taipei. Juli, who had accumulated a great number of air flight credits, shared these with David in Seattle, and he flew to Taipei within the next several days; Frank decided the day before his own wedding anniversary, to travel to Taiwan, and got the approval of the regional office to take emergency family leave. On Sunday, their twenty-third Anniversary, June 24, 1990, Margo had made an anniversary-birthday cake, but told Frank that they would have to wait and see what God had in mind for them...to see if they would even continue to be married by the next anniversary... she just let go, and put it all in God's hands. Frank gathered the family in the living room; he prayed earnestly that God would allow him to see his father one more time...and share the news of God's recent work in his life... The next day was Frank's forty-sixth birthday. Everyone said it would be impossible to get air travel tickets, passport, and visa in the *same day*. Frank called one of his Indian agents, Sameet Patel, who had a friend in the travel business; he was able to secure a round-trip ticket on an 'emergency' basis at a reasonable price; he prayed that the charge on his only credit card would not be rejected. Since the U.S. government had recognized the Peoples Republic of China, and no longer recognized Taiwan (Republic of China), he had to go to an outlet they called the North American Travel Institute in Houston. Even on an emergency basis, they told Frank it was at least a three-day wait to get a travel visa; he had been told at the Mickey Leland Federal building, where he went to renew his passport, that there was also a wait. It seemed impossible to overcome this. He would have to postpone his departure. Frank had assumed that Sameet was Hindu, but when he told him of the situation they faced, Sameet suggested that he call the people in his 'church' and have them pray that God would open a door, so they did...and waited. Frank went back to the Travel Institute, but it was already 2:00 in the afternoon. As he waited, he heard a man and his wife speaking Mandarin, and even after all these years, Frank listened to them and knew they were Christians. He started speaking to them in Chinese...how his father and mother had served God in Jiangxi, Hong Kong, and Taiwan, and how his mother grew up in north China. Frank admitted he was not a pastor like his father and maternal grandfather; he told them how he had run from God, but how he had recently been 'restored.' Frank had not told them that his father was 'Fan, Mu-shi' [Pastor Fan, the Chinese name given him], but now they recognized that the one Frank spoke of was *known* to them, and they became very excited. They wanted to pray with him; he began to weep as the man prayed in Chinese, and then his wife started to sing softly in Chinese, "*only believe, only believe, all things are possible, only believe...;*" then all three of them wept. And the officials came out to see what was going on. One of the assistant managers was a Christian; his name was Wu. He offered to call the passport office. After several minutes, he came out to tell them that: if Frank could be at the passport office by 4:00, and return to them by 5:00, they would get the passport renewal *AND* the visa. Sameet called Frank to say that his aunt Dhirha had called to tell him God had *assured her* that their prayers *were answered*. Frank laughed and said, 'no kidding!' He ran to his car, praying as he went that he would not be stopped or delayed; there were no parking spots at the Mickey Leland, but right around the corner, a car was just pulling out. Frank parked there... with time still on the meter! He ran into the building, upstairs to the passport office...but there was a long line. And it was 3:45. Mr. and Mrs. Liu, the ones Frank had met at the North American Travel Institute had called a Chinese friend of his who 'just happened' to work in the passport office. He came out from the side door, looking all around; he called out: "Fan, Xian-sheng," several times; people were looking at him, and Frank was not paying attention…he was praying, but he finally registered that someone was calling out in Chinese. He answered him: "Wo shi Fan, Xian sheng." ('I am Mr. Fan'). He told him he was Mr. Zhao, friend of Mr. and Mrs. Liu; would Frank please come with him. They went in the side door; he didn't take time to explain anything to Frank; he just handed him the renewed passport, and told him to hurry back to the Institute. It was 4:30. Again, praying that he would get through rush hour traffic, not get a speeding ticket… and still arrive before 5:00. It was several miles, innumerable lights, and rush hour was just beginning…thankfully, it was Monday, not Friday. Now, Frank never considered himself 'lucky' when it came to 'making the lights,' and always assumed they would all be red… but not today; how does that saying go? 'Coincidence is when God chooses to remain anonymous,' was never 'truer' than that day…on Frank's forty sixth birthday! *Every-single-light-was-green!* He arrived at the Travel Institute by 4:55; he parked the car in the garage, he ran up the stairs, he got to the office…but it was locked…it was exactly 5:01. He knocked on the door; then he went to the glass window, and knocked again; someone said in English, "sorry, we are closed." Frank was desperate, and said in Chinese, "Wo shi Fan xian-sheng!" No response, but Frank could hear them speaking Chinese inside. He called out "Mr. Wu," and then finally they opened the window. Mr. Wu smiled… he asked for the passport, which Frank handed him, and gave him the visa…it was 5:04. How did that happen?! God had done *AGAIN* what 'everyone else said was impossible.' Frank's plane was to leave at 7:30pm for San Francisco. Frank drove back home. Margo, the kids, and Irene and some St. Andrew's friends, had gathered to wish them 'Happy Anniversary' (from the previous day), and 'Happy Birthday' to Frank; Margo had packed his suitcase for his trip to Taiwan, and a lunch which he could eat on the plane, she said. They got to Hobby Airport…to the ticket counter to pick up the ticket…but they were told they had the *WRONG* airport…it was to fly out of Houston Intercontinental! They would never make it in time. Fortunately, they called–rebooked the ticket for later, and called San Francisco to tell them Frank would *not* arrive the 'two hours required before departure' for Taiwan, but because of an 'impending death' in the family, he needed to connect with the flight to Taiwan, and would arrive *one* hour before departure. They booked him on a shuttle from Hobby to Houston Intercontinental, in order to catch the cross-country flight. *Just amazing... just amazing.* Margo hugged Frank, then started to cry. 'Everything is going to be alright; God will take care of us,' she said "Happy twenty-third anniversary, and Happy forty-sixth birthday, Frank–I love you." Frank embraced her and ran to catch his plane; he was able to catch the later flight, with almost an hour in between flights in San Francisco...and thirteen hours later, Frank was landing at the new Chiang Kai Shek International Airport, in Taoyuan, in Taiwan. Dave met his plane, and they went directly to the Mackay Memorial Hospital. His dad was still awake when Frank arrived. Beth embraced Frank warmly, then started to cry. Frank cried too as he hugged his mom. She beamed from ear to ear, "God is calling home one of his special **'messengers'** but we do not grieve 'as those with no hope; in her tears, and advancing dementia, she smiled...she still remembered a devotional Frank had given at one of the last CEF retreats they had attended more than two years previously. [Frank, in the middle of his spiritual struggle, had shared a JB Phillips translation of Ephesians 4:11, *"...and some he made his 'messengers."* When he finished, he broke down in tears; his sister Margaret, visiting that time, and other aunts, uncles, and cousins, wondered what was going on in Frank's life; his intentions had been to honor his parents thirty-five years of dedicated ministry in China, Hong Kong, and Taiwan. Now here, amazingly, she still remembered the theme of that devotional, given more than two years before. Frank hugged his mom again warmly]. Dave took Frank and his mom into the room where their dad had fallen asleep again but awoke suddenly when Beth touched his arm and said, "Michael, your son Franklin is here." He smiled and looked up at Frank, "Hello, Franklin, I am so glad to see you, did you have a good flight..." Frank leaned down and hugged his dad, as Frank wiped a tear from his smiling face. "Dad, you sure have a lot of people lifting you up in prayer right now; I know God would lift you right out of this bed if he thought that was the best thing..." His voice trailed off as he fought back the tears. Michael's 'eyebrow alert' was now active. He said nothing for a few minutes as he looked deep into Frank's eyes, then he smiled and told them that he 'would really like to stay longer,' but it looked like maybe God wanted him to have a 'change of address,' even though he wanted to 'finish what God called him to do.' Dave suggested that Frank offer a prayer...it was getting late, and they needed to check in at the Nazarene seminary; they had said they would allow Michael's family to stay in the dormitories, and would provide meals for them... and Margi and Juli after they arrived. Frank felt like he was on the verge of tears, but agreed to pray, then he, Dave, and Beth, hugged dad and said goodnight. Dave had driven Beth and Michael's car up from Xinzhu to the Mackay Memorial Hospital at the beginning of the week so they could get around the Taipei area, and not rely on public transportation. Frank had had little to eat since he left San Francisco, so they stopped for a snack briefly, and then dropped Beth off at the women's dormitory at the Nazarene seminary. It was so hot and humid that Dave and Frank, even wearing nothing but their shorts, and the ceiling fan set on high, got little sleep. The next day after breakfast, they dropped Beth at the hospital and had a brief visit with Michael. Dave and Frank went to the airport and met Juli's plane; since Margi's plane was arriving that same afternoon, the three of them grabbed lunch at a local 'hole in the wall' and then all four of them went to the hospital. The four grown children, Michael, and Beth...all six of them, were together for the first time in twelve years! Amazing how it took the impending death of their father to bring all six, literally from the four corners of the earth... South Carolina, Georgia, Texas, Seattle, and Taiwan...to bring them together. They spent most of the day in and out of the hospital, meeting with doctors and nurses, and catching 'cat naps' from the jet lag, Frank squatted down and leaned against the wall in dad's room. The next day, they were invited to Overseas Radio and TV to see the new building and studios, which had been built since Margo and Frank left the island in 1970. Luis Palau, the well-known Argentinian evangelist was speaking there for their morning devotions; many from other churches and missions had come to share that devotional time, knowing Pastor Palau was going to be there; the staff knew Michael and Beth Varro personally. As a former ORTV staff member himself, Frank was familiar with a lot of the surroundings, but couldn't believe all the changes! They asked him to come speak briefly; and after he spoke, they all extended their hands, lifting up Michael in their prayers, as Pastor Palau led them. It was a very moving time, and Frank was particularly glad to meet, and speak with Luis Palau...such a wonderful man of

God. Dave reminded Frank that their plans included going south to Xinzhu where mom and dad had been living, in order to pick up a suit in which Michael would be dressed for the eventual cremation. Doris Brougham took Frank on a quick tour of the new facilities, and hosted a brief luncheon for them. [Frank had at one time entertained the idea of turning the CEF mission over to ORTV, but Michael was strongly opposed to this, and had chosen one of the pastors he had groomed, Rev. Wang Yu Zhung, to succeed them; Frank had had some strong disagreement with his dad about this, but in the end, Frank relented... along with some pointed advice from his brother Dave, to leave things alone]. Despite Frank's 'better solution' for the future CEF, they headed south to Xinzhu and met some of the Varro's Chinese neighbors, who were all in tears about Michael's condition, but because they were also Christians, they rejoiced in the knowledge that they would see him 'again in glory.' Something *life-changing' happened to Frank when they opened the front door...*Frank saw the walls of their home covered with every picture of Frank's success in sports, music, schooling, friends, relationships; every album on the coffee table, copies of music... and the song, 'Da Shan Kui No Kai' (the 'breakthrough song' Frank and his dad had sung together while building the Kirkland house). Frank's lifelong doubt that his dad had ever been 'proud of him,' was erased *in that moment*, and Frank broke down; Dave understood the significance of it also, and broke down as well. When he recovered his composure, Frank hugged Dave, and said, "see, women may connect by *talking* to each other, but men connect by *doing* things together; they had *'built an house as unto the Lord'* in Kirkland where they both had lived, and the healing was now finally realized in this; Dave had suffered some of the same doubts, so it was a breakthrough moment for him as well. They took the time to go through some of the Morrison yearbooks Michael had saved, not only Frank and Dave's sports and school events, but also Juli's and Margi's years there as well. They selected a nice tan suit of dad's, and collected some of the pictures, to take back to Juli, Margi, and mom. On the way back, it started to get dark, and both were hungry again; at first, they both thought they should wait until the 'girls' could join them for supper, but in the end, they were so hungry, they agreed they should stop and get some 'jiao ze's' and soup. Dave said, "you know they will *never* forgive us for leaving them out, don't you?" Frank laughed and said, "I know, but we won't tell them until we all go out for 'jaio ze's' *again!*" Dave laughed and agreed, and then quoted one of their dad's verses from the Bible…"all things are lawful, but not all things are expedient." (I Corinthians 6:12). They stopped for a wonderful meal of soup and 'jiao ze's.' When they were finished, Dave handed Frank some mint candy; Frank smiled: "yes, they'll smell the 'jio zai' (leeks) on our breath, and we'll be *found-out* for sure! They were still laughing about Taiwan, all the memories of growing up there together… both the joys and the heart aches, now they were here; Dave pulled into Mackay Memorial Hospital parking lot. Upstairs, their mother and sisters were worried about them, but grateful that they had arrived safely back. 'Yes, they had 'eaten something in the hospital dining' but looked strangely at Dave and Frank when they held their sides trying not to laugh out loud about their 'little secret of eating 'jiao ze's' without them. It was Saturday night, and dad had requested one final visit from the head doctor, Dr. Feng, Zhu Wen, the next day. Mother said she wanted to have 'their own worship service' in the room with dad; she wanted the children to sing dad's favorite song, "His Eye Is On The Sparrow," for Frank to 'preach' on a short Bible lesson, from John 11:25, 'I am the resurrection;' both Juli and Margi said they wouldn't be able to make it through the song, so Frank agreed he would try to sing it, and they could join in if they liked, that he would try to teach, or preach, what he could, as long as they knew he might not be up to it either. They talked briefly about some of the things that had happened that day; some of it was very difficult. Juli, as a nurse had a hard time not interfering; Margi and the other three, had many debates about some of the paperwork that needed to be signed–like DNR's (do-not-resuscitate), final treatments, hospital care, final arrangements, insurance, etc. They debated in the hallway…not in front of Beth…but consulted with her periodically. Margi seemed to take a view contrary to the other three, but in the end they all agreed on the proper response. They said goodnight, and Dave drove them all to the seminary dormitories, but not before Dave surprised them with a late-night snack of 'wam-wee's' (traditional Chinese dried-salted-plums), that he had purchased on the side; they all squealed with delight at his surprise, but mother would have nothing to do with 'that street food.' It was another intolerably hot and humid night, but they were able to sleep a little. The next day after seminary dining hall breakfast again, they met at dad's room for the worship service. Dr. Feng was there already when they arrived; the results of his findings were not encouraging. The squamous cell carcinoma had spread so critically, that dad had less than ten percent capacity lung function; Dr. Feng was an outstanding Christian, though, and led everyone there in a marvelous prayer: 'Divine Most Holy Healer, you created us with your own hands, that even with the nail scars through your hands and feet, you could raise up your servant, Fan Mu-shi (Pastor Fan), even now; but as you yourself said in the Garden…not our will, but *Thine be done! Amen!* Michael looked at Dr. Feng for a long time…and then he said very faintly, "I wanted to stay…because I didn't feel my work was done, but now I know the 'One who called me' can finish the harvest with…or without me…in the hands of my brothers and sisters in the Lord"…and then looking straight at Frank, and each of them, "and Lurabeth, Franklin, Margaret, Dave, and Elizabeth." He smiled faintly, and turning to Dr. Feng, he said, "Gan xie wo men qing ai de Tian Fu."('thanks be to our loving God in heaven'). Dr. Feng left, and each of his children and Beth hugged him. He said, "I think I'll catch a nap now…it *IS* my 'Shabat' you know, *my day of rest.*" Frank smiled and started singing a line from 'Elijah' by Mendelssohn, "O rest in the Lord, wait patiently…" Juli joined in with what she could remember. Michael smiled, closing his eyes. They waited; Beth stayed a little longer, wanting to stay the night, but finally agreed to go to the seminary. It was Sunday, July 2, 1990, and the former American military community that had stayed in Taiwan despite the recognition of Communist China, was gathering for a baseball game, hot dogs, and chili, at a park near the previous US military base. So, Frank and Dave, went over to help them celebrate the Fourth of July. Juli and Margi declined, saying they would rather go back to the dorm at the seminary for a nap; they had asked Beth to go with them, but she declined in favor of staying at the hospital with Michael. They hadn't had lunch though, so Dave said, "why not meet later together for something to eat," and looking at Frank, he said, "Frank and I have a confession to make to you." The girls looked strangely at Dave, and then at Frank who was stifling a laugh; "you guys are up to something; what's going on," Juli and Margi said; Dave and Frank feigned innocence, and said, "see you later then," and started for the car. Juli and Margi told them 'this had better be good, or you're both in very *BIG* trouble!' They laughed and jumped in the car, dropping them off at the seminary for a couple hours. In order not to ruin their appetites, Frank and Dave ate lightly, one hot dog each, and a small chili; they enjoyed the baseball game, billed as: 'Americans' (stateside newcomers) against the 'Nationalist' (longtime US citizens that were now Taiwan residents); it was fun and the 'Nationalists' won two to one. Frank met some people that remembered him, from when he and Margo lived there, and taught at TAS (Taipei American School). When Dave and Frank arrived at the seminary, Margi and Juli were already waiting for them…with miniature plastic 'baseball bats,' to bop them on the head for whatever 'surprise' they might have for them. After Dave had ordered four dishes and soup at a local Chinese restaurant [none of them could believe that many restaurants now had air conditioning, and what a respite from the terrible heat they had endured without it], as Dave asked what the price might be; they quoted him something, to which he responded, 'no, they would have an additional two or three dishes, plus a surprise (which he ordered in Taiwanese so none of his siblings would understand); but…he said they would pay only about two thirds of the price they had quoted him. Margi, Juli, and Frank, sat there with their jaws on the floor when they agreed to all of it…including the new price! When the food came, they ate it all, relishing every morsel…*and then they brought out the Jiao ze's!!* Twenty each! What the girls didn't finish, Dave and Frank did. Then Juli said, "I know what your confession is…you brats! You must have had 'jiao ze's' the other night without us! And they commenced to hit Dave and Frank over the head with their plastic baseball bats. Frank and Dave feigned being in great pain, and the proprietor was asking it he should call the police; everyone laughed and always remembered it as one of the only times the four adult Varro children were ever together. They spent the rest of the afternoon in the seminary offices… planning the memorial service. Frank talked to Rev. Wang, Yu Zhung, and called Doris Brougham to arrange for the ORTV choir to sing at the service. They were not hungry after the big late-afternoon Chinese feast, so they decided to just pick up a snack after their evening visit with their dad. They were going to order something from the hospital dining hall for mom and dad, but Beth had already gotten herself, and dad, something to eat. Michael seemed to 'rally' a bit, but he still couldn't talk much above a whisper. They all talked about some of the wonderful adventures they had shared together: High Prairie, Sumner, Jiangxi, China; North Dakota, Ephrata and Quincy; and the years together in Taiwan: Xinsheng near Heping, Mu Shan, Morrison, and then all the years apart. It was a precious time, and dad smiled faintly…one story after another. It was about eight o'clock, and Beth started to doze off, so Frank suggested that they continue the next morning. He said before they go, he wanted to spend just a few minutes alone with his dad, and would they all mind leaving the room… including mother. When they had left, Frank took his dad's hand and said, "Dad, I wanted to spend just a moment with you…just you and me." He leaned over and said, "you were always a good example of a loving father; sure, you and I did not always agree, but like Dave said, 'iron sharpens iron,' and I know I disappointed you sometimes, but I always knew you loved me, and I always loved you; I also broke your heart, and said some things that were wrong…I did things that were wrong…I'm sorry, and I ask you to forgive me…;" with tears brimming in both men's eyes, faces still smiling, Michael said, barely audible, *"I already have…,"* then Frank strained to hear what he said next; he could not detect it at all…what he was saying to him; Frank even laid his head on his chest, with his ear touching his dad's face, but he couldn't make out a single word he was saying. Finally, Frank squeezed his hand, kissed his cheek, and said, "it's alright, dad, *I'll see you in the morning…* "The four kids left; Beth decided to stay at the hospital…to be with Michael.

The next morning, after a quick breakfast at the seminary, they were coming down the hall; they saw mother coming toward them. When she got closer, she said, "he's gone…he's gone." They all burst into tears, but she said, "he wanted to be home, so we had to let him go; now he's home!" They went to the room; he had probably died about 9:30 p.m., Sunday night, July 2, 1990, about an hour after they had left him; the report said just after midnight, but it was later revealed that no one had actually checked in on him, and with Beth asleep in the room, they didn't bother to check; the findings were: death had occurred a couple hours earlier, right after Frank and his dad's final visit. How true were those last words to his dad: ***"I'll see you in the*** *morning*" [Frank started to sing to himself, with tears streaming down his face, the old black spiritual, 'In that great getting' up morning,' and as he hummed it, the others started singing it with him]. The orderlies came and took the body to the basement morgue. There were *NO* openings in the schedule, at *ANY* crematorium in Taipei. Dave had called all of them that he knew of. [They would just have to leave the body in the morgue, conduct a memorial at the Nazarene Seminary; Juli and Frank would leave to go stateside, Margi and Dave would help mom move out of the Xinzhu house, pack the crate for shipping to Seattle; Marlene, Dave's wife, the only spouse not currently working, could care for Beth (who, with advancing dementia, was unable to live by herself), their plans at least. Juli arranged for her departure. Frank, however, did not believe this was the only option, and talked to Dave about still trying to locate a crematorium in the area; maybe find some non-Christian crematorium, mausoleum, or other burial means. [Dave told Frank that 'the former U.S. Embassy, which became the AIT (American Institute in Taiwan) in 1979, and many former U.S. State Department personnel had stayed in Taiwan, and were associated with it – hadn't Frank said he had a friend with the U.S. State Department, way back in the 1970's?' Dave said that some U.S. citizens used them for a number of different services]. Frank's jaw dropped to the floor. That's right! Jack and Ellie Kingston, who had worked for the U.S. Embassy, and Dr. Steve Beckman (who had delivered Shelley at Country Hospital in 1969, and then retired in Michigan). 'Yes, Jack and Ellie had gone to work at the American Institute;' Dave agreed, and when Dave and Marlene worked for dad at CEF, he had known someone who knew Jack and Ellie (Frank and Dave both wondered if they still worked there). Dave called AIT immediately...and asked if Jack Kingston still worked there; there was a long pause, and a woman said, "this is Ellie Kingston, Jack is my husband, but he's out on an assignment, may I ask who's calling? Dave quickly handed the phone to Frank, "Ellie, you may not remember me, this is Frank Varro; Margo and I knew you and Jack back in 1969 before we left for the States, we taught at TAS, and you sang in my Navy Chapel choir; Dr. Beckman delivered our daughter Shelley...it's been over twenty years...and Shelley is getting married next year!" Ellie almost dropped the phone. They went on to talk about Frank's dad dying the day before, and AIT had helped other U.S. citizens…maybe they even had connections with a crematorium, or other services? Ellie told them Jack would be back in an hour; he did know some Chinese pastors that might have those contacts. She wanted to be sure they would see Frank–and so sorry Margo wasn't able to be with him. Dave got a call three hours later… from a Chinese pastor, Pastor Yip, Sum Guei (from Hong Kong, but now in Taiwan), he was with a Canadian Presbyterian mission, and had contacts with both funeral homes and crematoriums. Jack had come back, and Ellie told him about Frank's dad dying. Unfortunately, because he was on assignment, and with Ellie tied up at the AIT, they would not be able to get together if Frank was leaving in a couple days; they really wanted to see him, could he give them his 'stateside' address and phone number? They would be in Houston in 1991 on their way to Michigan, where they would be reassigned…and would also be seeing Steve Beckman! Unbelievable! By 6:00 that evening, Pastor Yip had found a crematorium… on the other side of Taipei; it had just that afternoon had a cancellation; Pastor Yip laughed and said they even had the flowered van, and the paid 'mourners,' left over from a Chinese traditional funeral that afternoon [Frank smiled, recalling as a twelve-year-old in Hong Kong, the traditional Chinese funeral procession, complete with flowered truck, paid mourners in gunny-sack 'cloth and ashes,' crying and carrying on, and a band playing a very slow mournful tune, which he had recognized as 'It's Howdy Doodie Time;' so when Dave and he recalled the story Frank had told so many times, they both burst out laughing; how wonderful that 'Christians don't grieve as those who have no hope,' Dave said]. Dave made arrangements for the morgue (to take the body 'out of freezing'); he also located a beautiful cobalt-colored urn in downtown Taipei…they were to show up the next day before going to the morgue, crematorium, and memorial service…in order to etch the 'English version' of ['Michael F. Varro, Sr., February 14, 1913 – July 2, 1990, *Some he made his messengers*']. The shop proprietor had already carved the beautiful Chinese characters on the other side; Dave and Frank were to carve the English. They did their best, but it seemed a little 'crude' compared to the masterful calligraphy on the other side (even though many raved about it anyway). Dave had taken a portrait of dad to a photo shop he knew of; they enlarged and framed it nicely…to be put on the table with the urn. The seminary, and dear Nazarene missionaries, the Reider's, and Kellerman's, had notified the missionary and Chinese Christian community that the memorial was back on; they also prepared a lovely reception following the memorial, as well as printed programs; the ORTV choir sang ('Whispering Hope' a favorite duet of Beth and Michael; and led all in Blessed Assurance and Amazing Grace); Pastor Wang Yu Zhung, spoke, and led in the obituary, eulogies, music, and other parts of the program; Marlene's father, Rev. Dale Wine (Dave's father-in-law, who was visiting Taiwan), and Frank, assisted in the program. Frank spoke: 'Gifts My Father Gave Me' and sang 'His Eye Is On *Michael Varro*, rhymes with *Sparrow*; Mackay Hospital sent a number of their staff who had cared for Pastor Varro (Fan Mushi), including Dr. Feng, nurses; some of the Peniel (CEF) pastors were also in attendance.

[But first, going back to before the memorial service, with everything prepared, they had slept fitfully, woke early, and ate a light breakfast at the seminary dining hall; the memorial was to be at 4:00 p.m., so by the time they loaded the casket ('loaned' by the morgue for the cremation), picked up the urn, and rode in the flowered truck across town, it was almost 10:00 a.m. The crematorium staff, though non-Christian, were very kind, and ceremonially unloaded the casket, waited for the family to view his remains, in his nice tan suit and tie... for as long as they wanted; they asked Frank to pray; he didn't know if he could, but decided he would try: *"Lord, you gave us this 'house' to live in while we are here, to enjoy each other, and be the family you made; (you even loved your own human body so much, that you took it, in its glorified form, with you back to heaven, and will return with it, when we see you again) – bless this earthy 'tent' of your servant, Michael; and as we say 'ashes to ashes, dust to dust,' we commit it now to your care, even as his spirit is already dwelling with you. Amen."* And then Frank teared up with the rest of them. They watched it go down the ramp slowly into the giant oven. A while later, Dave came to Frank to ask him, awkwardly, if it was "alright if they put it through the oven again"–due to the long-frozen nature of the body in the morgue, and their oven not being up to United States standards; it needed to go through again. Frank and Dave informed the rest of the family, then after the second time, the staff very ceremoniously fitted all of the ashes–from the toes up to the head—into the urn, and then closed it. Dave tried to 'settle up' with them, but they said it had 'already been taken care of' (Pastor Yip said that his church and the Kingston's had paid for it as a memorial)].

After the beautiful memorial service, they took pictures together of so many friends and family, and enjoyed the nice reception that the Nazarene seminary had graciously prepared. Juli had to leave right after the memorial, so Dave and Frank saw her off on the plane later that day with love, and promises that it wouldn't be 'another thirty years before they got together again, Ha!' Since Dave wanted to give Frank one more chance to experience a real culinary treat, they stopped for lunch at Wan Sui Tang, some famous Taiwanese Beef Noodles... before returning to the seminary. Frank left the next day; but Margi and Dave stayed the night at the seminary dorm; and the Nazarenes provided dinner. The next day the three of them left for Xinzhu; they spent two weeks sorting and throwing out things from *thirty-three years* in Taiwan, then loaded the crate that would be sent by ship to Seattle. Margi caught her plane back to Atlanta. Dave and mother left shortly thereafter for Seattle. [Beth lived with them, and went on two business ventures to Xiamen in south China, Qingdao in north China, and then in Belize for seven years; then she lived with Margi in Atlanta another six years until her death in 2003]. Frank flew back to Houston, and Margo and the boys met his plane; he had flown into San Francisco, then to Houston Intercontinental, and taken the same shuttle back to Hobby Airport; where he had departed. Shelley had a late afternoon class at the University of Houston, where she was a music major. The boys had come from gymnastics and basketball workouts to join their mom in welcoming their dad back. MetLife was not too happy about extending his personal leave, but *did* allow him one more week. Margo had covered for the two of them at St. Andrew's, and they were informed that St. Helen's had designated a special Mass for the 'soul of The Rev. Michael Varro,' a kind and loving gesture. Frank tried to get back into the business of insurance, the continuingly vigorous schedule of music and worship at St. Andrew's, family and school life, concerts, sporting events and relationships. He could not shake the grief, the sense of loss, not only with his dad, but also the spiritual 'uneasiness' in his relationships...with Margo, the children, his work...everything

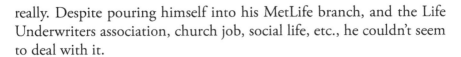

really. Despite pouring himself into his MetLife branch, and the Life Underwriters association, church job, social life, etc., he couldn't seem to deal with it.

[They started making plans for Shelley's and Tom's wedding; she had dated some in high school, but she was mostly focused on her studies, and was nearly a straight-A student; she was very involved in music, and popular with a large group of friends, both male and female, ever since grade school; she had been involved in the Susuzki strings group in Odessa, but had had a bad experience in Beaumont with private violin lessons (which has been written about earlier); she even sang in Frank's chamber group, Vera Voce, for a short time; she made regional soloist and sang in the high school pop group; she had done theatre in Odessa, and later in high school, and was in the school plays; she was very spiritual, and very active in junior high school, eventually taking a leadership role at Pearland Methodist, and later at St. Andrew's; but it was through her involvement in the University of Houston choir that she met Tom Harrington, master trumpet player, and music education major like herself; this brought her real focus on her future; he was four years older, and she was not sure if that was right for her or not...they broke up briefly, because she 'wanted to finish college, but soon they decided they *were* right for each other, and were engaged the same year that Frank's dad got ill with cancer and died. Shelley introduced Tom Harrington to them, and later the two families met. Things were good all around, and everyone pitched in to make the 'glorious event' happen. It was June 15, of 1991...but things couldn't have been worse financially for Frank and Margo. With all of Frank's bravura, and spiritual struggle, things finally came to a head. The Harrington's were gracious and offered to help financially, but because Frank was proud, he downplayed everything ('why can't we just make it a smaller inexpensive wedding, blah, blah, blah'). Margo and he were also going through their worst time; she wanted the wedding that is every girl's dream, and she would 'beg-borrow-and-steal' to have that for Shelley. Frank already felt he could never be 'good enough' for Wilma-and-Margo...now for Shelley, too. He had just 'preached' at his father's funeral: 'gifts-my-father-gave-me,' but he didn't feel like he had anything to offer his own family; and he obviously wasn't helping them understand what he was going through (in one bad fight after supper one night, they felt so hard at him, they 'voted him out of the family' for his hurtful words, not knowing he overheard them when he stormed out of the dining room, but was actually listening in while sitting on the staircase). His life had been radically changed inside, but the 'old wineskins' were still not worked-through; he had buried his father, but he still needed to go through the 'discipling process' long enough to *bury* some of his own stuff, and work through what he had *become already*…in Christ Jesus, he *had* become *good enough* for his own family…and *himself* (what Frank now calls what happened '5-7-87' (May 5, 1987). They met with the young adults' group that Frank and Margo had helped found, at St. Andrew's, *Koinonia* (Greek for 'Fellowship'), in particular: the Devore's, Yates,' Thomas's, McKeel's, Robertson's, Terry Brown, and Father Mike and Kim Baker. When they found out, through the 'prayer and share' time they always had Sunday evenings… of the plight Margo and Frank were in, they pitched in and provided, or donated to, much of the reception, flowers, candles, and rental of the church and community center. Frank and Margo finally did accept the gracious assistance of Bob and Fran Harrington's with the drinks, photography, dancing and disc jockey. Tom and Shelley's college music friends provided a stunning musical performance, cousins and friends sang and played. Frank sang to Shelley and walked her down the aisle. Father Mike officiated…it was a spectacular event. Frank still had put some on credit, or post-dated checks, but God was certainly 'making a way, where there is no way'. Grandmothers—now both widows—Beth Varro, Wilma Moore; Shelley's 'Auntie-Grandma Irma'; Uncle Lou and Aunt Isabelle Varro, Frank's sisters Margi, Juli, and their families were there, and also in the wedding party. It was a beautiful joyous milestone-event].

Fred Feigley called Frank in after a managers' meeting…he said he was putting Frank back into personal production (ala 'stripping him of his management position'), but Fred did not know that, through Frank's contacts with HALU and GAMA, Frank was already being recruited by several other insurance companies for management positions, including Massachusetts Mutual, Prudential, Connecticut Mutual, and American General. Frank had been elected to serve on the governing boards of both associations. He eventually 'went through the chairs', and was a speaker, insurance courses instructor, and in demand locally, regionally, and nation-wide...he became president of both the HALU, and GAMA. [He had been the local, and then Texas state, insurance PAC (political action committee) chair; he 'hob-nobbed' with national insurance presidents...as area, state, and regional guest, at state, regional, and national conferences, such as Boston, and Washington DC...where he stayed at the Ritz-Carlton, attended a dinner-conference on a yacht on the Delaware River (and attended church the next day at the National Cathedral)]. When Fred Feigley... not a member of HALU, GAMA, or any other insurance associations, failed to see Frank as 'management quality' Frank decided to accept Derby Wilson's offer to become a manager with Massachusetts Mutual. After ten...some bad, but mostly good...years with MetLife, Frank resigned, and started a MassMutual branch from scratch. They trained him locally, set him up in an office lease, in a building near Hobby Airport, leased him office equipment and electronics, and MassMutual office furniture...then said he was on his own. It all happened so fast... Derby was probably the most 'overly-optimistic person' Frank had ever met, certainly in the entire HALU family (but Derby was also a millionaire), and Frank was overwhelmed! He recruited some of his agents that had left Met, who were not happy where they 'landed' so Frank hired them on. They had to produce a quota that would cover the pro-rata office expenses, Frank's income, and an agent that Frank would pay as a part-time administrator along with office expenses. "Good plan...upward and onward!" Derby always said. Sheth Seneca, and Paul Sherman, former agents of his at Met, who left Met for better contracts, but big contracts-big promises from A-minus-level companies, had them running back to Frank at MassMutual. They became his first two big hitters; three others only lasted through training, and two other MetLife agents that couldn't make the quota there...thought they might make it with Frank at MassMutual; they lasted an additional month or two...these are the ones that made up his team... then there was Wanda Richards. She was recruited as an agent from another B-level company; she had a clerical background, so when she didn't work out at the first insurance company, Frank hired her to do half-time clerical and half-time insurance with him. Frank had been doing the clerical himself before she arrived, but with his involvement in the associations, and his church and music jobs, there was little time to do personal production, say nothing about clerical responsibilities. She still had to meet quota which was only half of what Paul and Sheth had to meet; she happily agreed to this arrangement. In six months, the overrides from these three, plus whatever Frank could produce, and two others Frank was still training, was still not meeting the branch minimums–rent, the lease on the electronic equipment, or even enough overrides for Frank to live on; least of all–for Wanda (enough to pay for the other office expenses, or paying her. Paul and Sheth tried to 'crank it up,' but Wanda took no responsibility for the quota, rent, overrides, or anything; she just wanted to be paid, but spent little time on personal production…or clerical duties. Frank ended up going back to doing most of the clerical stuff himself, Paul and Sheth barely produced enough to pay the rent, lease on office equipment, or manager compensation; Wanda got paid little for administration…and she got angry; Frank felt bad, and so he paid her a little out of his own pocket (Paul and Sheth ignored her plea for help, despite her reasoning that she had done clerical for them too, because she still hadn't produced up to her own quota anyway), so she complained to Derby, but he wouldn't touch it, saying it was according to their mutual agreement. Then Wanda, who was a member of HALU…at the time Frank was president… filed a complaint with the HALU ethics committee; Mark Jones, was chair; he had been passed over already for a position on the HALU board, and had an 'ax to grind;' he interviewed Wanda while Frank was gone; he filed a report of 'ethics violation' against Frank… with no documentation, no copy of any written agreement (because there was none) …nothing! When Teddy Chandler, found out, she gave a copy of the report to past president, Mac Brockman, also the chair of the nominations committee. With no corroborating evidence, and Mark's own history of ethics problems, Mac called him in for a conference. It would serve two purposes, Mac said; he would hear the 'report' of the Ethics Committee chair; he would also interview Mark for the Nominations Committee (Mark had nominated himself… without the minimum of two other HALU board members; after the interview, Mac told Mark he would never be considered for the HALU board, or the Ethics Committee chair, because he had two violations of ethics himself: one cannot nominate themselves, especially without two other board members supporting him, and also, he had filed a

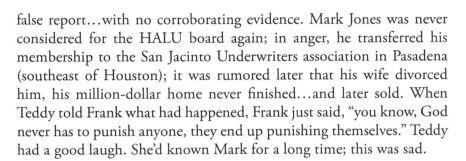

false report…with no corroborating evidence. Mark Jones was never considered for the HALU board again; in anger, he transferred his membership to the San Jacinto Underwriters association in Pasadena (southeast of Houston); it was rumored later that his wife divorced him, his million-dollar home never finished…and later sold. When Teddy told Frank what had happened, Frank just said, "you know, God never has to punish anyone, they end up punishing themselves." Teddy had a good laugh. She'd known Mark for a long time; this was sad.

Things were getting so 'tight,' Frank didn't know what to do: default on the house? Get another job? (he certainly wasn't making anything on children's books). He prayed for God to show him what to do; he was late paying back money he owed on Shelley's wedding; they were behind in the mortgage, cars, and other bills; Paul and Sheth were now talking about leaving too. Frank told his family that there couldn't possibly be much of a Christmas.

[Shelley and Tom were living up in Spring, north of Houston; Tom had gotten his first middle school band job the year before they were married, Shelley had lived on campus for a while until they were married, and she finished up the last year, and her student teaching, so she needed to pay her back-rent on her on-campus apartment, so before she could check out, Frank had to let go of his last fifteen hundred dollars (which he was saving for a desk-top computer), to pay her rent so she could check out; he tried to replace it, but was never able to do so; they had no savings whatsoever. Margo had asked for a raise. She had left Chas P Young printers, and followed her friend, Liz Medley to American Capitol, but her boss, Norris Woodley, was very temperamental and hard to get along with. When she asked him, he hit the ceiling and belittled her, she left in tears, so she herself was looking for another job. Things looked pretty bleak. Robbie and Steve looked down; they didn't know what to say. They were getting in trouble often now; with Frank and Margo working long hours during the week, and long hours at church on weekends, neighbors began to complain. [Robbie had made friends with Herbie down the street, and when he handed Robbie his BB gun (since Robbie had never shot any kind of gun, pistol, or rifle, he didn't know how to handle it); he ended up *shooting out the neighbor's plate glass window*. Herbie's father blamed

Frank, but after Frank pointed out that Robbie knew nothing about guns, and Herbie and Robbie were equally at fault, Herbie's dad agreed to 'going halves' on replacing the window; (Steve also had hearing and development problems going all the way back to his ear infections; he was often getting beat up or was defending himself from getting beat up). The two of them found some tennis balls one day, soaked them in some kerosene, and set them on fire; they threw under some parked cars; neighbors, while thinking it was funny, still, thankfully, put a stop to it before any disaster. Another time, Frank came home to the pronounced smell of a cigar in the house, as well as a distinct smell of burning plastic. No matter what Frank threatened them with, they denied any wrong doing–Frank decided to teach them a lesson *one that they both tell others to this day, was THE lesson of their life about lying.* Frank said he was going to spank them within an inch of their lives, ground them, and not let them participate in any sports after school, because he knew they were lying, *BUT…*if they told him the truth, he would not punish them at all (retribution maybe, but not punishment). They went round and round; Robbie and Steve said they didn't believe him; Frank said, to test him: Lie= punishment, Truth=no punishment. Steve finally said 'okay;' Robbie wasn't so sure, but maybe he'd just go along with Steve. They slowly took Frank upstairs; there was a cigar smoldering in the bathroom waste basket…one of their friends had found their dad's cigar, and they were trying to smoke it, when they heard Frank arriving in the driveway; they ran upstairs and threw it in the waste basket. Even though they were now teenagers, they almost started crying and said they were sorry…for lying to their dad. Frank had to stifle his laughter. He said, "alright, thank you for telling me the truth…but you *owe me one plastic wastebasket!* And your absolute obedience! He smiled, "I've done worse, God forgives when we are sorry and confess;" they came over to hug him, and Frank opened his arms…they never forgot that moment…ever!]

Now Frank had to break the news to Margo and the boys…that there wouldn't be much, if any Christmas; they might even lose the car and house–he might have to declare bankruptcy…Margo looked down, the boys looked at each other, and then asked to be excused, and went up to their rooms. Margo didn't know what to say…hmmm, if Frank was at a better level, it sure didn't seem like it; he prayed, but it seemed hollow, and empty; he finally went to bed; Margo was asleep. The next morning the boys went off to school; he took Margo to work, and then he just sat in the parking lot at his job, and just listened to Christian radio, but he was in a trance. He had begun reading the Psalms through again; he had gotten through the first sixty or so, but he couldn't remember where he was, so he just started over; he read Psalm 1-5, and then he tried to pray, but he felt numb, so he decided to read just a little further, and began to read Psalm 6; tears rolled down his face at verse 3: "…my soul is in anguish…who praises you from the grave (on and on through to Psalm 9:9…the Lord is the *refuge* for the oppressed!" That did it! Frank jumped out of the car, and went in to the office and sat at his desk. He could not do this anymore–he would just have to trust God. He started singing 'When God ran'…*"and then he ran to me, held me in his arms, said 'my son' do you know I still love you…"* Paul didn't knock, just walked in, and looked at Frank, "I knew you had lost it," he said, then he walked out. The phone rang, and Frank just let it ring a few times; 'probably bill collectors' he thought. Finally, he answered it. A man with a New York accent said in a very tired tone: "is this Michael Varro?" Frank thought he sounded like the FBI…that he was going to tell him he was under investigation, but he said, "this is Frank Varro; my first name is Michael, is there something wrong?" Frank heard the man give a huge sigh of relief, and then laughed, "I've been looking for you for three years!" Now Frank was *really* frightened, 'they have a contract out on me,' he thought; but the man went on to tell him he was with TIAA-CREF (Teachers Insurance Annuity Association-College Retirement Equities Fund), and he had 'a check for him for ten thousand dollars!'. Then Frank really thought it was a 'scam,' but the man went on to explain: Frank started teaching at Kent Junior High, on staff at the University of Washington, then in Oregon, Ohio, and Texas…they had lost track, and the annuity money kept building up…but now they'd found him. Frank cried out, and almost dropped the phone; *was this for real?* "If this is really Michael Franklin Varro, Jr., we will need you to verify the Social Security number, address we have; and verify that you *are* really he; if so, we will be sending you three thousand dollars now, and two other payments of thirty-five hundred in the next several weeks. Frank shouted out again so loud that both Paul and Sheth opened the door and asked if he was alright. Frank waved them off, finished giving the address, social security number, and home phone. Frank called Margo… he said he was taking her to lunch at the Galleria (across from her American Capitol building), he would be there to tell her some incredible news! They had lunch, he told her everything, how God had promised that "the Lord is the refuge for the oppressed," and listened, but then she cried…she had to find another job; this time he said, confidently, he knew *God would find one right away*…for her! He picked her up after work, they picked up the boys from their gymnastics and basketball practice, and went out to celebrate the "wonders of God's power at Gringo's, a now famous and favorite restaurant all over Houston, that had just started up in Pearland at that time. Margo called Shelley and Tom with the good news. God was truly 'their refuge.' They shared the news with their Koinonia group who praised God with them for his 'unspeakable kindness.' There'd be rough roads ahead, but they'd rest in him. Frank arrived at the office Monday early…Sheth and Paul were sitting in his office. They said they were leaving, and Wanda had already left. The building management had put a demand letter on his desk; Sheth said it was none of his business, but 'George upstairs' (George Bixly with Perry Homes, owners of the building) had told him they were evicting Frank and 'Gulf Freeway branch' (the name Frank had given to his MassMutual startup) for non-payment; they would give them a few days to pay, leave, or 'lock them out.' (George had said they don't normally warn them, just lock them out). Frank panicked; he didn't know what to do. Sheth said, "we can't talk here, let's go for coffee, I've been in your shoes before, I'll tell you what you have to do." They went for coffee, and made their plans; Frank didn't like it, but Sheth and Paul said he really had no choice; otherwise, he'd be bankrupt; after 10:00 p.m. that night, Frank, Sheth, and Paul arrived at the office, with a U-Haul truck, moved all of the MassMutual furniture, electronic equipment, and everything else into the truck, and drove to Frank's house, and locked it. In the morning, Frank called his friend, George's wife, Sherry, who was the administrator for Perry Homes upstairs; she was always so kind, and he felt he could talk to her; he said he was so sorry…they'd had to leave the way they did, but he was shutting down his office; Sherry said she didn't even know they had left…she hadn't been downstairs yet that day. [The previous month, the office next to Frank's, 'Olympic Textiles' had approached him about getting a 'right-of-first-refusal' on each other's lease, 'just in case' either of them left and wanted to expand into the other's space; Frank was naïve and said 'no' at first, but now he was so glad that they had done it anyway. He told Sherry he had talked to Fred at 'Olympic Textiles' and he still wanted to take over his lease...if that was alright; she said 'no, it's not done that way' but she said they could probably work it out]. Frank called and told Derby the bad news. Derby asked if they were 'locked out' and Frank said 'no,' that the borrowed furniture and electronic equipment could be returned to Mass Mutual...long pause, (no 'upward and onward' this time). Derby said he would call him back in an hour. Frank prayed; he knew he could end up bankrupt, but was pleading with God to spare him. Derby called back in an hour; he said, "well, Frank you really did it this time; then he laughed, and said the warehouse people would pick up the furniture; he'd had to lean on the owners of the electronic equipment people...because all of it was leased in Frank's name...but because it hadn't been a full year yet, he was able to break the lease, as the 'guarantor,' but only if they put it in his (Derby's) name; he would sublease it to another startup branch. Derby said, "that only leaves the money *you owe me... and MassMutual.*" There was a long pause; finally, Frank said, "and how much would that be?" Derby said, *"a mere fifty-six hundred dollars!*" Then there was a *really* long pause; Frank would be bankrupt after all, he thought. Finally, Derby started laughing, "you don't know about the *account* you have with me at MassMutual? You can pay me out of it... on a monthly basis. Frank knew nothing of this 'account.' But, as it turned out, Derby had renewals from thousands of accounts he owned over the years...by putting all of these accounts in Frank's name, *Frank would be 'paying Derby back' monthly...with money that was ALREADY Derby's!!* Frank didn't know if Derby was a 'believer' or not, but he thought that was probably the kindest thing ever, and he thanked him profusely; he thanked God for him, and you know what Derby said? Yep... 'upward and onward.' There really are some loving millionaires!

George Reynolds and Frank had become good friends, by working together in HALU. They would go for coffee, and sometimes lunch, with Teddy Chandler, and also through GAMA. George was very active on the HALU and GAMA board, so when George and Teddy went to lunch with Frank, George had questioned his move from MetLife to MassMutual. He teased Frank when he made the move, saying "so you like jumping from the frying pan into the fire," as Teddy tried kicking George under the table. Now, George offered condolences and asked Frank point-blank, "why not come over to American General as my associate general agent?" Frank was so naïve; he hadn't realized that George *had* any such position open. Frank asked about the compensation and the requirements for a monthly quota. George talked about not needing to do any recruiting, and George said some personal production would be required; but he would pay him directly out of the Houston Agency, instead of American General; it would be a management contract so a monthly income would be assured. Frank was overjoyed, and told George what a fine friend he was. So, plans were made, and Frank would start immediately. Frank said he was so grateful, but... dare he ask him for one more favor? Margo was at American Capitol...and very miserable; she needed to leave right away; did George know of any clerical or human resource positions... anywhere? George smiled. Frank didn't know that American Capitol had previously been part of American General, and George knew all of the personnel in all the subsidiaries of American General. 'Yes,' he told Frank, he would be glad to explore that.

Frank and George worked well together for three years; they went to Austin together to help rewrite the Texas state insurance code; they worked together in GAMA to bring great speakers and special workshops to HALU and GAMA both. George helped Frank take a leadership role in GAMA and he was the main reason Frank eventually became president of that association board as well as HALU. Frank covered some of the agency meetings for him, subbed for his LUTC classes occasionally (Life Underwriters Training Course); consequently, he had little time for personal production; George still considered him an asset to the Houston City agency, and Frank's financial picture improved. George didn't forget his promise to help Margo get a position in the family of AG companies either; Frank had only been there a few months; George asked Frank if Margo was interested in applying for a human resource position that had 'just come open' at AG-owned Variable Annuity Life Insurance Company (VALIC).

He was good friends with Betsy Jorgenson, and Steve Miller. It was a good fit, and Margo really enjoyed working there several years, even after Frank left.

Frank was appointed to serve on the search committee at St. Andrew's for a new rector. After Father Mike left, they had a couple months of guest priests, sent out by the diocese; then for the next several months, The Reverend Gerard Gamble, a retired priest from Wisconsin, was an interim priest there. The Vestry appointed Frank, two men and two women, to visit candidates applying to be priest at St. Andrew's. Margo covered for Frank in his absence. They looked at eight applications (already screened by the bishop's office), considered six of these, and then visited four in a two-month period. It came down to two candidates; they presented these two to the Vestry. The one chosen was Phil Webb. He was a young, sandal-wearing, guitar-playing, impulsive, but warm and friendly, new priest. [He was connected in the new wave of church growth, music, youth, and outreach, in what some called the charismatic 'second wave,' begun by the Jesuits in Spain, which spread across the Anglo-Catholic and Evangelical-Conservative mainline churches—The 'Convergence Movement;' many at St. Andrew's became active in it; and Steve and Rob enjoyed the new youth activities and Bible study; they attended a youth version of the week-end retreats program—called 'Happening,' and experienced the saving grace of Christ in their own lives at that time. [Shelley, while leading the youth at St. Andrew's, had already made her own profession of faith in Christ, and had married Tom, with the understanding that *he had* as well]. Soon, a group of young adults, including the 'Koinonia' group, started meeting in small groups. Frank and Margo became active in this. Phil called them in for a meeting soon after his arrival; he not only wanted contemporary songs included, along with the tradition 'hymns, anthems, and spiritual songs;' but he enlisted all the guitar players in the church to play in all services; he shed his 'priestly vestments' whenever he could. He signed Margo and Frank up for 'Cursillo' [meaning 'Basic Christian Walk,' a weekend-retreat ministry]. So, Frank and Margo attended Texas Cursillo #142; it began life-changing dynamics in their relationship with God...and their relationship with each other; Phil called them in again, right after they got back—he said they were scheduled to go to Evergreen, Colorado, for an ERM (Episcopal Renewal Ministries), a music conference. Fourteen 'high-brow,' classically trained musicians from all over country, met there 'kicking and screaming' so to speak–they didn't want to have anything to do with those 'camp songs and guitars;' some of them were organist-choirmasters in very 'high church' cathedrals; and were very reluctant participants. 'Long story short,' as they say, the closing night of their music conference, they were praying and singing the most glorious harmonies together, when all of a sudden, the 'spirit of God' descended on them in a powerful way; Margo described it as: those that were not 'speaking in a 'prayer language,' were certainly *singing* it. [Frank realized for the first time that he had experienced several *visitations* of God's spirit, going all the way back to the first, in North Dakota when God spoke to him through the song, 'I Need Thee Every Hour," to Quincy, after church one Sunday just weeks before Stevie's death, to his call to ministry at Morrison, and now again at Evergreen in 'prayers too great for words.' God was working in their lives in mysterious ways. Frank decided that what happened was, music for him was not the 'end,' but rather the 'means,' the 'vehicle' of his worship of God. They came 'down from the mountain;' there was training for the Kairos prison ministry–with Frank speaking at Ferguson maximum prison unit; the experience for Frank, which few had, in attending as adults involved in youth ministry–Rob's next 'Happening,' but as a staff person; when, as part of the program, Rob washed his dad's feet, Frank lost it; it was indescribable! –such precious moments. Steve, Rob, and Shelley all experienced moments such as Cursillo, Evergreen, and Happening]. But Frank still had to work through so many things–like his father's death, and then what he called 'the years in the desert' with Jesus (just like Paul). Yet, another great moment was about to occur in Frank's life. Though he had been called to ordained ministry, like his dad, and his medical missionary grandfather, Dr. RG Fitz (this call had come the last week of his senior year at Morrison–but as Frank always told people, "like Jonah, I just said "no"); he went his own way, and ended up miserable…until he surrendered to that call. As he told it, his life had been dedicated to the 'worship *of* music' rather than 'worship *through* music.' He had wanted to go 'his own way,' and become the best musician and conductor possible, and he thought this meant turning his back on God…God's plans for Frank's life, ministry, and all the joys and rewards of a life dedicated to God. Though he had *Hit Bottom* in May of 1987, that was only the beginning of his *Re-call,* as Frank called it. That happened at the Faith Alive Conference in May of 1992. Frank finally found himself at this conference...when he said 'yes' to the call to ordained ministry that God had laid on his heart... in the spring of 1962 at Morrison Academy]. Jeremiah 29:13 became a key verse in his life...the key to unlocking the main problem in his life: *"...and you shall seek me and find me, when you search for me with all your heart...and I WILL BE FOUND OF YOU, says the Lord, and I will turn away your captivity, and I will gather you from all the nations..."* At the invitation of Father Phil, and several other charismatic Episcopal leaders, including Bishop William Bastrop from Oklahoma and Bishop Oong Chor-Ku, a gifted Chinese musician and organist, the conference was also a life-changing event for many others at St. Andrew's. Bud Garrett, Buddy and Patty Thomas, Marilyn Horn, and several others, along with Father Phil Webb, were the local organizers, but the Faith Alive team led the service, the music, and the Eucharist. The week-end conference included many of the songs Frank and Margo had learned in Colorado at the Episcopal Renewal Ministries conference...many of them were songs from Vineyard Ministries, previously unknown to many; there was a healing service; there was Holy Spirit-inspired Bible teaching and homilies; the Sunday-night final service was about 'Full Surrender'...and Frank joined others in letting go of the reins of his life...in his *Re-call* to full time ordained ministry! [he thought at that time the call was to be an Episcopal priest]. They sang 'Spirit Song,' after Bishop Bastrop spoke, and then he invited everyone who was still holding on to things in their lives...that belonged to God, to come forward and lay it all 'on the altar.' Then, when they shared the Eucharist together, everything broke wide open! As they sang, Frank felt the voice of God so gently pulling him forward...*"O let him have the things that **hold** you, and His Spirit like a dove, will descend upon your life and make you **whole!**"*He *ran* down the aisle...like the Father *had run* out to meet him...in the song, 'When God Ran,' May 7, 1987. He surrendered it all that night...in his *Re-call!* After they had all prayed at the altar rail, they returned to their seats...as everyone was singing 'You Are Awesome In This Place'...*'past the gates of praise, into* *your sanctuary, till we're standing face to face... you are awesome in this place, Mighty God...Abba Father.'* Margo and the boys were there too, and shared this wonderful moment.

Within the next two weeks, after much prayer and soul searching, Frank made an appointment with Father Phil to talk about his call to ministry at age seventeen, his years running from that call, his hitting the bottom, and the recovery, and now a renewed sense of call at Faith Alive. Phil agreed to sponsor him, and assisted him in applying for the priesthood in the Texas Diocese of the Episcopal Church. He met with other clergy in the Diocese; but some were honest with Frank, and revealed their own doubts about staying in the Episcopal church; as 'charismatics' they were coming under attack, as part of the 'Convergence movement;' John Wimber, and others sought unity with in the Anglo-Catholic, and Evangelical-Conservative communities, but others saw this as a threat to the traditional 'church.' John Hall, Rector at St. John Episcopal, an 'evangelical-conservative' himself, as well as Frank's former pastor, Father Claude Paine, were willing to accept Frank's application, but they themselves were unsure of the 'future face' of the church they served; some had many doubts about the very future of the 'charismatic and evangelical' nature of things there. Ultimately, Frank's application was put 'on hold' and deferred. After Claude Paine became Bishop, it was reviewed again, but them placed on 'permanent hold,' *at this time.* Frank had joined a pastors' fellowship group in Pearland, and his 'charismatic and evangelical; friend, Winfred "Casey" Jones, agreed to form a prayer cell; they met nightly for a few days; he brought in another Presbyterian charismatic friend, Jim McGill, who was planning to retire and start a new charismatic ministry in Pearland; the three of them met nightly for a few days, 'spread-eagle on the platform of Pearland First Presbyterian (a 'charismatic Presbyterian pastor?! Frank laughed; he said they *got that reaction all the time*). In the end, Casey and Frank agreed, in their prayers, that it was time to leave St. Andrew's. God was leading him to come to First Presbyterian in Pearland; in six months Frank would become a candidate for ordained ministry in the PCUSA (Presbyterian Church of the USA). Margo and Frank prayed, then decided she would stay as choirmaster-organist at St. Andrew's; Frank and she would stay in the evangelical charismatic group at St. Andrew's, as well as Koinonia, but Frank would become

Bible teacher, and part-time Choir Director at First Presbyterian. Many things in their relationship still needed to be worked out [she confessed that since Colorado (and ERM) she didn't know who she was, and was needing to work through some poor self-image issues, relationship with God, her marriage, relationships, family and friends].

Meanwhile, Shelley graduated from University of Houston, after giving a wonderful Senior Recital, commuting from Spring, north of Houston, where Tom and she had moved into an apartment, and was beginning teaching music at Clark Elementary. Steve graduated from Pearland High School in 1993, and Rob in 1995. Steve and Rob eventually became roommates with two other friends; they began college at Sam Houston University, both on track and field scholarships–Steve, as a long distance and cross-country runner, placing well in many high school meets...and Rob, as a pole-vaulter (he had 'graduated' from gymnastics to pole-vaulting his senior year in high school (even though many said he was a possible US Olympics contender, yet unwilling to give up his devotion to trumpet, marching band, and spiritual leadership in the Episcopal Youth, in order to get there). Frank had finished his term as HALU president, and had been offered other contracts by two other companies for manager positions, and foolishly (in retrospect) left his good friend George Reynolds at American General for something he thought would be even more lucrative, but his heart was not in it, and he began to search for a seminary to attend, in pursuit of his *new* call to ministry. Margo stayed on at VALIC. [Despite the transforming events of ERM in Colorado, Cursillo, and Faith Alive, their lives continued to move further apart...as Margo, in her own search for resolution of her sheltered past, her own identity, and her new sense of independence, to human resources, the job at St. Andrew's, also her depression, and with the children 'leaving the nest.'] Frank decided, after his first meeting with his Presbytery Ordination Committee, that the PCUSA was definitely not where God was leading him to be.

Frank had been chosen to lead an American General Independence Day Choir, and Margo, as a VALIC (and therefore American General) employee, was chosen to accompany the choir on piano. Frank made friends with Bob Merton, one of the baritones, an American General actuary, and told him he was planning to go to seminary...and possibly become an ordained Presbyterian minister, that he was now 'under care' with First Presbyterian Pearland. Frank suggested they go for coffee, and as soon as they sat down, Bob smiled and told Frank he was also a Presbyterian, and his minister, Buck Oliphant was a wonderful pastor. Frank asked him 'which' Presbyterian; Bob said Cornerstone Presbyterian in Katy; Bob said Frank reminded him of Buck: funny, intelligent, and resourceful – their church was not 'PCUSA' but rather 'EPC' (Evangelical Presbyterian); 'and what is that,' Frank said. Bob told him all about the 'orthodox-conservatives' leaving First Presbyterian, Houston (PCUSA), where Buck Oliphant had been Director of Education; Buck served with Christ EPC in leased school space in the Galleria area for a couple years before getting ordained and becoming the Cornerstone EPC pastor. Frank was immediately interested, and Bob said he would arrange for Buck and Frank to have lunch. That afternoon, Frank met with Dr. Jerry DeSobe at the Samaritan Counseling Center, to talk about becoming a Licensed Professional Counselor. In discussing classes in counseling, Jerry told Frank about the Houston Graduate School of Theology, and Frank immediately called them to make an appointment to discuss enrolling there in an M.Div. (Master of Divinity) program. Through Casey, he also found out about the International Christian Institute in west Houston. Frank wanted to be a Texas state-licensed counselor, but he also wanted to be a 'Certified Christian Counselor, and at International Christian Institute he was able to take his first courses in Christian Counseling. Samaritan Center wanted him to start first as a Chaplain intern at St. Luke's Hospital, and then do an internship at Samaritan Center. Lunch with Buck the next week was wonderful, [and they became life-long friends]. Frank told him he was not happy with him his PCUSA ordination committee, and Buck arranged for Frank to meet Bob Peterson, the pastor of Christ Evangelical Presbyterian (Christ EPC), the first of several Presbyterian churches that left the PCUSA during that period of time…some went to the PCA (Presbyterian Church in America), EPC, or independent Presbyterian affiliations. Buck wanted Frank to eventually become a minister in the EPC, he said. In his last three years as insurance manager, Frank served briefly at Businessmen's Insurance, Sunset, and Acacia. He needed a way to at least finance seminary, living expenses, and the rest. But he didn't have to keep his security license, or renew his insurance association and managers memberships, having served his time as President and Past President of both HALU and GAMA, so he just walked away from it all…just keeping enough agents and personal production to pay the bills. He told Casey he was looking at the possibility of being ordained in the EPC…Casey was silent for a few minutes; then he said, "yes, Frank, I think that is the voice of God to your heart, and, though I hate to say it, they are more orthodox and biblical." With Casey's blessing, Frank attended church the next Sunday, and met 'Dr. Bob,' as they called him. They had lunch the next week; Bob said he would welcome Frank's membership, and sponsor him after six months in becoming a candidate for ordained ministry in the EPC. Margo and he had supper alone that week… they both agreed they needed individual counseling… as well as marriage counseling. Through Dr. Bob, as a first step in preparation for ordination, Frank was referred to Gary Nettleton at the Raffa Counseling Center in Spring—not far from where Shelley and Tom lived. Margo began seeing a counselor at the Diocesan Bishop' office. Frank had always said he had several counselors…some with Margo, and others on his own… but only two stood out in his mind– as 'effective…and biblical' – those were: Ray Brittan in Odessa, and Gary Nettleton in Houston, both fine Christian counselors. As Margo finally confronted some of these issues, she decided to live for a while on her own… similar to Frank decision for separation while they were in Beaumont. Both of their counselors were in agreement with this arrangement–this would be a 'constructive separation,' with the goal of 'rebuilding,' rather than 'deconstructing' the marriage. During that time, God was so 'in it,' and much of it had to do with both of them rebuilding 'self-image.' Frank was enjoying the counseling classes he had at Christian Counseling with Dr. Russell Finton, the instructor…a Baptist minister and a recovering alcoholic himself. Frank met three students at International Christian Institute on a break their first week; they each had their own stories of how God had rescued each of them from a broken past, but now were sharing what God was doing in their lives, to be restored and becoming Christian counselors; they were of immense help; they invited him to a weekly Bible study they had formed, where Frank experienced for the first time, besides ERM in Colorado, a powerful 'language beyond words,' as the Apostle Paul had called it. Frank was sharing his concerns of counseling classes, seminary, ordination, his marriage to Margo, his past issues with his father, and what he had learned about himself, etc....it was his turn to *'sit on the hassock and share;'* with his hands extended and his face lifted up, a beautiful wave of the Holy Spirit 'came over him' and he fell from the hassock; Brenda, Sherri, Susan (they used only first names there), and the others...about eight all together, continued praying in tongues, as Frank began just as naturally as before, but as 'God gave him utterance.' They also introduced him to a black pastor in west Houston, Pastor Wilson from Kenya, where Frank began attending Freedom Chapel Tuesday evenings (Wednesday evenings were Choir practice at Christ EPC); one evening...*the Holy Spirit was so strong in that place,* Frank went forward for prayer, and was 'peacefully resting' on the floor, when Pastor Wilson came over and started to tell Frank, and the others gathered there by him, what he saw: 'a dry cracked desert floor with nothing for miles...but in the distance was a 'lone tree;' it was green, and producing the most beautiful fruit...'that tree' is Frank, he said! Everyone there began to weep, and lift their hands in praise...Pastor Wilson said it was a prophecy of Frank's ministry to come, and they all began rejoicing in prayer, as they sang, 'I Love You, Lord.' Frank continued to meet with Brenda, Sherri and Susan weekly. Brenda called him every day to check on him, and she always had a verse...she said it was from the Lord, but in closing with prayer, she always left him with a verse...the same verse...Proverbs 5:18: "...*rejoice in the wife of thy youth,*" and she always promised that Frank's and Margo's marriage would be restored...she said he was on a journey down the mountain road, *boulders* would keep falling onto the road, which would delay the trip; but after God was finished ministering to Frank during this 'special time' in his life...all the *boulders* would be gone, and restoration would take place...and that is exactly what happened! After seminary, he tried to find Brenda, and Sherri...but no one had any record of them having even been at International Christian Institute at all! At one point, he had thought God was telling him that he and Susan might date (if Margo was indeed ending the relationship), and get married; Susan had surprised him, and came over to his house once, but she quickly told him she was only his 'sister in the Lord,' and romance was *not* any aim of hers; she later remarried, and introduced Frank to her new husband Stan, when they ran into each other at his favorite Chinese restaurant, Pagoda, near where he was writing his dissertation.

Sometimes his panic attacks during seminary...which Frank believed were personal attacks from Satan, were so strong, Frank thought he would pass out; he found healing in Psalm 73 (the whole chapter... which he would read over and over (once it was five times!) during the instructor's lecture, until it passed...but particularly verse 25-28, *"whom have I in heaven but thee?...my flesh and my heart fail, but God is the strength of my heart...it is good for me to draw near to God...";* He had also joined another prayer group at Living Stones Church in Alvin, just south of Pearland, where Susan was a member. She introduced Frank to Lillian Martin, the leader of the *Isaiah Fifty-Four* group. Over the next few years, Lillian had a tremendous impact on Frank's life. Her husband had abandoned her for another woman, she had descended into such a deep depression that she was suicidal... but 'the Lord found her,' she said, at the *Living Stones Church*, and through a divorced-and-separated group...which expanded into this *Isaiah Fifty-Four* group, she became a dynamic leader for this Bible and Prayer group. She had remarried...it was one of the pastors at the church. Frank thought the scripture, from which they derived their name, was so significant to his own life [Isaiah 54:10 says: *"though the mountains may depart, and the hills be removed, yet my steadfast loved will never depart from you..."* were the very words of the song in Chinese that was the breakthrough time when Frank and his dad built the Kirkland house together]. He told Lillian the story and she wept with him. Her own verse, and the reason for the group's name, was Isaiah 54:5-6 *"For your Maker is your husband...and the Lord has called you like a wife forsaken and grieved in spirit."* There were nights when Frank called a national Charisma prayer line; he called several times and got the same sweet black women who prayed with him, assuring him God was going to do 'a wondrous thing'...and would restore his marriage; she never said her name, and Frank must have called a dozen times; when several months later he received the answer to his prayer and Margo and he were back together, he called again to rejoice and thank her...someone else answered, but they didn't know anything about a young black prayer partner. Frank insisted on talking to her, but the person who answered said there had never been anyone there of that description!! God had sent this 'mystery person' for that season only, and Frank was convinced it was an angel sent by God himself! One other significant blessing that God sent Frank during this time was *Joshua's Men*. Lillian and Susan both had suggested that Frank visit a men's ministry group at a church in The Heights called *The Ark*, which was headed up by her friend, John Fox. Frank had met John after their first meeting there, and he became completely committed to this year-long discipleship program that John had started: *Joshua's Men*. They met monthly, just twelve men...no wives, for sharing, study, and prayer; each man had a prayer partner and they prayed together weekly —in person (or over the phone mostly). Halfway through the year, they joined together, with wives (or as singles, engaged, or with girlfriends), for a Friday night get-together of sharing what they had learned, and then at the end of the year, they met for a full weekend retreat with spouses or significant others.

God blessed this year of discipleship, and many of these men remain friends and prayer warriors to this day.

Frank's studies at the seminary were going well, but he kept having to defer payment, because he simply didn't have the money. The Dean, Jack Richards, approached him with a proposition: since Frank already had a doctorate in music...and they needed a post-doctoral person to be the Head of Music there, in order to receive their accreditation from ATS (Association of Theological Schools), besides, they told him, he should be seeking a second doctorate in their new D.Min. Program (Doctor of Ministry) in counseling anyway...if he was to continue on to be a Pastoral Counselor. That is how Frank became the M.Div. student, concurrently enrolled in a D.Min. Pastoral Counseling program...who just happened to be the Head of Music! [HGST was successful in receiving their accreditation with the ATS, thanks in part to Frank's 'student-faculty' status! It helped tremendously with financing Frank's seminary studies [in five years, Frank completed an M.Div in Church Music; an M.A.in Counseling; and a D.Min.in Pastoral Counseling. At his Commencement program in 1997, Frank remarked that the Houston Graduate School of Theology had given him 'the Third Degree' (first: M.Div., second: M.A., and then 'the third degree: D.Min.! to uproarious laughter]. *But*...there is a miraculous story that must be told in connection with this: despite his student-faculty status, there remained an outstanding bill; Frank was compensated for part-time adjunct professor status, and Head of Music, but the great number of courses necessary to complete these programs was great; a new Dean had come, and after a required audit of the seminary, Frank still owed sixty-five hundred dollars; they had allowed him time to pay a little at a time, but now 'doomsday' had finally come – the HGST Board of Directors had determined that Frank would not be allowed to graduate, and 'walk' for his D.Min., unless it was paid (no more delays; the bill had not been taken care of completely...in over three years!). Frank tried to get a faculty 'advance,' he tried to borrow the money from the board, his credit had been marred by their mortgage and high interest problems (many people had just walked away from houses with over eighteen percent interest in those days). The Board held firm – no more allowances or delays. Frank and Margo had applied for many credit cards, and were turned down; Frank had finally resorted to a pay-in-credit-allowance type of credit card, but it had only a thousand dollar 'credit' limit. Frank and Margo still had supper or lunch together almost every week, and they began to pray. He would periodically apply for credit card offers almost weekly, but they all came back 'denied.' It looked dark. Frank didn't know what he was going to do. The new president of the seminary, David Robinson (and a D.Min. classmate for his first three years), and his wife, Becky–the registrar, joined him in prayer. The week before commencement, and the *last day* to get one's name in the program, Frank had lunch with Margo; she handed him the old mail; Frank opened it, tossing the junk in the waste basket as they talked; he started to toss an envelope in the trash, when something caught his eye–it was a credit card; just another denial...but it wasn't!...it was actually a new credit card; yes, but it was probably just one of those 'credit on your own money' type of thing...it wasn't! "Welcome to Integrity Bank's credit card, your credit limit is... 'sixty-five hundred dollars!' To the cent. Margo burst out crying. Frank hugged her, and began to weep himself. He immediately called Becky to see if the proof had already been sent back to the printers. He told her what had happened, and then said: "I know Dave Ramsey wouldn't approve of this, but God works in mysterious ways. Becky began to cry over the phone. Dave was there and she told him the news. She told Frank they had already sent the proof – without his name in it – but they had left one of the faculty members names off the proof, so they hadn't returned it for printing yet. The news spread quickly to the faculty, board, and student body. Alumni still talk about the 'HGST miracle of 1997.' They topped out the credit limit with one payment…Frank's seminary bill…but paid off in a year! The year previous to his graduation, Frank had finished the course work for his D.Min. dissertation; he began writing his dissertation on pastoral counseling, and for this he did research in Christian counseling in the area of married relationships; he was assisted in this by Dr. Terry Curtis, Dean of the D.Min. program. He selected three couples from his Koininia group, at St. Andrew's to do the relationship study; he completed the study (but each couple was unaware of the identity of the other two couples); he asked them the same questions and then wrote up his findings. It was very successful and his committee, headed by Dr. Curtis, approved it following his defense. After the amazing miracle in God providing the funds for the payment of his seminary debt, Frank made plans for the commencement; he invited his family and friends. [following his coursework at International Christian Institute, he had been invited to come be the English pastor at Houston's Taiwanese Presbyterian Chinese, and he served there for one year during his time at HGST]. He invited Brenda, Sherri, Susan, and also Lillian Martin from Living Stones Church, He invited pastors and members of Christ Evangelical Presbyterian, St. Andrew's Episcopal, and some from the musical community. It was a great time, and God's presence was in the commencement. Frank had finally been obedient to God's call, and his training to become a Pastoral Counselor. Two of the Ruling Elders at Christ EPC, Charlie Haden and Lil Gough had an important impact on Frank's life. As a prominent Attorney and leader at CEPC, Charlie had a strong influence on Frank and helped him found the Chinese ministry there as well as promoting him for ordination. Lillian Gough, who was a good personal friend of Buck Oliphant before the move away from First Presbyterian to CEPC, was particularly fond of Frank and attended the Chinese fellowship that was founded later. Wanda Fuller, an administrator there, sang in the choir, and always dropped everything to talk or pray with Frank.

These were great warriors of the faith for him. Margo continued as Choirmaster-Organist at St. Andrew's, and Frank joined the choir at Christ Evangelical Presbyterian. Michael Shust, the worship leader at CEPC was working on his doctorate in music, and appreciated Frank's friendship and willingness to sing in the choir there. They later decided to bring Rev. Max Shiller, pastor of an EPC church in Birmingham, Alabama, to found a new EPC church, City of Refuge, in the Medical Center. So, Michael recommended Frank to be the new Director of Music at Christ EPC, another miracle of God! Almost penniless, and in debt when, he graduated from Houston Graduate School, here again God provided–a new music director job for him. Frank had attended Presbytery meetings in Mississippi, Tennessee, and Illinois (EPC Southeast Presbytery included parts of seven states) as a candidate for ministry, but now, also as a church staff member! When the mortgage company had returned his partial payments (they had told Margo and Frank that they were planning to foreclose on them on the house), Koininia, met and decided to pitch in anonymously to match the returned partial payments …another blessing from God… and they were able to keep the house! Now that Frank had passed the exams in 'doctrine/theology, Bible, and polity (but it did take Frank twice on the doctrine exam…he was not quite *up* on Reformed doctrine, but got a tutor and passed the second time, ha!); through the combined efforts of Pastor Franklin Li, Chinese Bible church, Dr. and Mrs. Bruce McFarland of Christ EPC, and Frank, they founded the American-Chinese Fellowship, Frank now had completed all the requirements for ordination. The Presbytery met in Rowlett, Texas, near Dallas. There was an 'open-mic' public examination by the clergy delegates, and Frank 'knocked 'em dead,' as his mentor, Buck Oliphant, put it;' then Frank was required to preach his ordination sermon. He chose Philippians 3:10 'That I May Know Him' [he used three words in Chinese: 'zhi dao' (know-'to have knowledge of'); 'ren shi' (know-'be acquainted with'), and 'ming bai' (know-'have inner understanding'); all were pleased to hear something unique rather than mundane, and Frank was unanimously voted in by the clergy. He had also started his sermon time by singing, 'O The Wonder Of It All,' and Buck, who was the 'candidate-sermon moderator,' said to those assembled, that they now had 'a new level of ordination requirement' for candidates; they all laughed. Margo, Steve and Rob, were in attendance, and Margo played the piano for Frank's 'surprise musical addition to the event.' After a few months...the EPC requires 'placement in the setting *where called*,' so Christ EPC officially set up the *'American-Chinese Ministry'* as the *called entity*. Prior to his ordination, Frank had been granted internships at St. Luke Episcopal hospital... for chaplain training, and at Samaritan Center...as Pastoral-Care Intern. One last, and to Frank the most important piece in the puzzle, was...Margo and Frank getting back together. He had begun listening to Dennis Raney, and 'Family Life Today,' and learned of a conference to be held in Houston. It was called 'I Still Do.' He prayed earnestly about it, and then asked Margo to meet him at their house that evening. He cooked supper (she had always loved his cooking, she said), and they shared what each had been learning...Margo, in her counseling at the Diocesan counseling center, and Frank, with Gary, at Raffa.[One quick note: Ray, in Odessa, had done a wonderful exercise with Frank–he had him sit in a chair and *confront* his father ...in the other chair facing him,' which was easy; but then, Ray had him switch places–Frank had to be 'Michael' his dad...and talk to his 'son *Franklin*.' Frank burst into tears, a barrier had come crashing down, and he saw life, for the first time, from his father's perspective. Gary, at Raffa, had done something similar: he asked Frank to shut off the lights, and lean back on the couch...he placed him 'at the end of a cul-de-sac... desperately trying to get his dad's attention, as he played in the street, 'Michael' sat in his rocking chair motionless, in the porch at the house on the left... oblivious of his son; then Frank saw Jesus, his 'heavenly father,' in a chair on the porch of the house on the right, quietly rocking; he called Frank to come and sit in his lap...when Frank did, 'Michael' came and sat in Jesus' lap *with him*... it was the beginning of some great healing inside of Frank... and in his relationship with Margo as well].

Margo also shared some things that she had learned from her counselor, the bishop's wife. Then Frank suggested they attend the 'I Still Do' conference together. She began to cry; Frank was curious, what was she getting at? She continued, "I knew when I saw you at your ordination exam, and heard you sing, as I played for you, that God wanted us to be back together again [she had told Frank two years previously, after all her hurt and anger at him, "I don't love you,

I don't think I ever did …and I don't know how I ever could again]. But…she prayed every day after seeing the bishop's wife, *"Holy Spirit, give me the love for Frank you gave me when we knelt at the altar at our wedding."* She told Frank that God had 'given it *back* to her…that's when she realized God had called her too…to be a *Pastor's Wife!* They went to the conference. God touched them, and healed them there! At the conclusion of the conference, they were all given a plaque… to hang above their bed: It says: 'I said '*I do*' on our wedding day…and after all these years, and all we've been through…*I STILL do!*' They both signed it. And after fifty-six years, it still hangs there. Plans were made for Frank's ordination. Family came from all over…Frank's sister, Margi, and his mother, Beth, now deep in dementia, attended…it was her last real public outing of this sort. Frank, and Joyce Petterson, wife of Dr. Bob, Christ EPC, sang 'Be Strong and Take Courage.' Dr. Bob preached the sermon: 'Called Into The World,' and then, Buck, and other Presbyters spoke, and finally Frank was introduced; after speaking briefly about his excitement of being able to pastor this new Chinese ministry, he closed the meeting with prayer; then they gathered at the altar rail, Frank knelt…and God came down and blessed that moment! All the Elders and Presbyters laid their hands on him…Frank was ordained: *'after the order of Melchizedek'*–The Reverend Doctor Michael Franklin Varro, Jr.–an 'ordained elder' in the Evangelical Presbyterian Church! Then pictures were taken at the altar rail with Frank's family, friends, and new congregation–the American-Chinese Fellowship. Also, Rev. Franklin Li, and many from Christ Evangelical Presbyterian Church. Margo, Steve, Rob, Shelley and her son Robert, and many of Frank's other family and friends, took pictures together; this was followed by a wonderful reception, where his mother, despite advanced dementia, sat sweetly between him and some of his Chinese parishioners from the Chinese Fellowship, as she chatted away with them…in perfect Mandarin, to the delight of all those present. Her prayers for thirty years, for her son Franklin, had been answered. It was a great evening…dad would be *proud,* Frank thought…as he looked up, he saw Jesus, next to the Father, his 'audience of one,'-just one more of the many great…

'Stories from the Boxcar'

Renaissance Madrigal Dinners : Midland-Odessa & Beaumont

Kids cutting up in Wenatchee

Frank and Doctor of Ministry degree

Frank—top right

Frank – as Student and Faculty

Margo and Frank-Ordination

Four-Generation Picture at Ordination

Varro family–three children, with spouses, and five grandchildren

Son Steve, and wife Christie in Montana

EPILOGUE

The long journey…from God's call on Frank's life in 1962, to ordained ministry, the detours, the lessons learned, the emotional and spiritual growth…culminated on June 22, 1997, just three days before his fifty-third birthday. He went on to finish Internships at St. Luke's Episcopal Hospital, and Samaritan Counseling Center; then Resident, Advanced Resident, and Staff Therapist, at Samaritan Center. He became President of China Evangelism Fellowship, aka Evangelism Fellowship International, and pastored three churches: Christ EPC, as Associate Pastor for Chinese Ministry; then four years later, his orders were recognized by the Methodist Church, and he pastored two churches – Splendora First Methodist, and on Houston's west side, Westchase Methodist; in these two assignments, new church buildings were constructed. He founded Varro Counseling, after being on staff at Samaritan Counseling Center for five years. He continued his hospice ministry as chaplain with three different hospice companies; he had been an attendee ('pilgrim') with St. Andrew's Episcopal, but he was later a speaker, twice, and Spiritual Director at 'Walk to Emmaus'. (Methodist), what others called 'Cursillo;' he also continued the prison ministry of Kairos, as a speaker, clergy, board Member, and 'runner' (he liked to say he brought them the 'bread' (food brought in), and then he brought them the 'Bread of Life'). Vera Voce Singers continued singing for many years. Later in retirement, he and Margo sang in The Woodlands Methodist Church Chancel Choir, Goldenaires, Men's Chorus, and Bells Choir, as he freelanced preached, did Bible studies (and attended The Woodlands Methodist Men's Quest), and as clergy for special times like Ash Wednesday, Advent, and other times. He and Margo are grandparents, and his three children, their spouses, children, five grandchildren and one great grandchild are all Christians and active in their churches!

Thankfully, the clay is always in the Potter's hand… not mine

The Chinese character for 'Righteous' consists of a top part 'Yang' (Lamb) and the bottom part 'Wo' (I, myself); put them together, and you have:

'[I] am under the [Lamb] (of God)' ... And it is He who makes me Righteous!'

'Like Ruth Graham, fellow China 'missionary Kid,' this character is to be on Frank's memorial urn 'Yi' – Righteous

The next book he plans to write is about his continuing ministry.

The Epilogue is but a foretaste of that wonderful story to come

THE RES MOZAR

Like gold in the fire…

the Res Mozar grinds the spice… until it is pure…

Zechariah 13:9 (adapted)

Printed in the USA
CPSIA information can be obtained
at www.ICGtesting.com
LVHW070048091123
763325LV00026B/174/J